*Germany after the First World War*

# GERMANY AFTER THE
# FIRST WORLD WAR

RICHARD BESSEL

CLARENDON PRESS · OXFORD

*Oxford University Press, Walton Street, Oxford* OX2 6DP
*Oxford New York Toronto*
*Delhi Bombay Calcutta Madras Karachi*
*Kuala Lumpur Singapore Hong Kong Tokyo*
*Nairobi Dar es Salaam Cape Town*
*Melbourne Auckland Madrid*
*and associated companies in*
*Berlin Ibadan*

*Oxford is a trade mark of Oxford University Press*

*Published in the United States*
*by Oxford University Press Inc., New York*

*British Library Cataloguing in Publication Data*
*Data available*

*Library of Congress Cataloging in Publication Data*
*Bessel, Richard.*
*Germay after the First World War/Richard Bessel.*
*p. cm.*
*Includes bibliographical references and index.*
*1. Germany—Social conditions—1918–1933. 2. Germany-History—1918–1933.*
*I. Title. HN445.B47 1993*
*306'.0943'09042—dc20 92–40025*
*ISBN 0–19–821938–5*

3 5 7 9 10 8 6 4

*Printed in Great Britain*
*on acid-free paper by*
*Bookcraft Ltd, Midsomer Norton, Bath*

# Preface

From the Heidelberger Platz onward, the streets were black with people. A great excitement lay upon them. The tension grew. People thought they heard distant drum-beats. A wave of shouts rolled along the streets. The stewards formed a chain to hold back the mass of people. And now the trumpets were indeed approaching.

And then came the sight that caused many in the crowd to weep. Men as well as women, moved by a feeling of humanity's common fate, remembering the long war and all the dead.

Did the people see the troops? They were looking at the long war, at victories and at the defeats. Before them a piece of their own life was marching past, with wagons and horses, machine-guns and cannons.[1]

MORE than seventy years separate us from that grey day in December 1918 when the first German front-line troops arrived back in Berlin. Almost all those who fought in the First World War are now dead. The soldiers' graveyards in northern France have become tourist attractions rather than places of pilgrimage. The heated passions which once accompanied discussion of the First World War have been replaced by measured academic debate. Yet the world in which we live is still shaped by the Great War and its aftermath. The First World War was a watershed, marking the destruction of an old world in an orgy of senseless violence and the beginnings of the uncertain modern age in which we live. Today, after the collapse of Marxist-Leninist socialism and the re-emergence of bitter national conflict in eastern Europe, the First World War seems in some ways closer to us than it did ten or twenty years ago. As we face the possibility that Europe is no longer quite the stable place we had assumed it to be, the First World War and its aftermath may assume an immediacy which was unimaginable just a few years ago, when my work on this book began.

An author owes it to his readers to explain what his book is about and why it was written. As with so many monographs, the origins of this book are both professional and personal. The professional origins are perhaps obvious. Much of my research over the past decade has involved an attempt to explain the failure of German democracy in the 1920s and 1930s—to examine the social and political roots of that failure and to probe the effects of violence in politics.[2] Again and again, the experience of

---

[1] Alfred Döblin, *November 1918*, iii, *Heimkehr der Fronttruppen* (Munich, 1978), 152–3.

[2] Richard Bessel, *Political Violence and the Rise of Nazism: The Storm Troopers in Eastern Germany, 1925–1934* (New Haven and London, 1984); id., 'Politische Gewalt und die Krise der Weimarer Republik', in Lutz Niethammer *et al. Bürgerliche Gesellschaft in Deutschland: Historische Einblicke,*

(and defeat in) the First World War appeared to be of fundamental importance. In particular, the First World War loomed large in any attempt to
explain the origins and effects of the political violence which afflicted the
Weimar Republic to an extent and in a manner quite unknown in Germany before 1914 and which contributed significantly to undermining democratic government. However, to ascribe political radicalism and political
violence to the brutalizing effects of the War seemed to me unsatisfactory
and altogether too simple. The ways in which the War affected Germany's
social and political history, it seemed to me, needed to be examined more
carefully.

The personal origins are no less important. In a sense, this book is a
search for a grandfather I never knew. My mother's father served in the
Württemberg army during the First World War, winning battlefield promo-
tion to the rank of lieutenant. I was told only the bare outlines of what
happened to him: that he spent the War fighting in northern France; that
after the Armistice he marched his troops in good order over the Rhine (an
achievement of which he was apparently very proud); that he was demobilized in Schweinfurt; that his first wife died in the influenza epidemic in
1918 and that he subsequently married my grandmother in 1920; that he
returned to the Swabian village where he had lived before the War, built a
house and small dry-goods business together with one of his brothers; and
that he felt an abiding animosity towards France. After the War he settled,
apparently without great difficulties, into normal family life. I suspected that
his story might have been far more typical of members of the 'front
generation' of the First World War than were the activities of those who
joined the Freikorps rather than face life in civil society. After all, whatever
psychological damage had been inflicted on the men in the trenches, most
of the surviving soldiers of the Great War, like my grandfather, managed
somehow to pick up the pieces of their civilian lives.

The history of the ill-fated Weimar Republic's early years has been framed
by three broad themes: the political revolution of 1918–19 and its reversal,
the great inflation and the subsequent stabilization, and the 'inner liquidation
of the War'.[3] In the literature on Weimar Germany, the revolutionary
politics of 1918–19 and their suppression have figured prominently, with
the publication over the past few decades of a vast number of studies
covering just about every conceivable aspect of the revolution, the coun-

---

*Fragen, Perspektiven* (Frankfurt/Main, 1990), 383–95; Richard Bessel, 'Why Did the Weimar
Republic Collapse?', in Ian Kershaw (ed.), *Weimar: Why Did German Democracy Fail?* (London,
1990), 120–52; Richard Bessel, '1933: A Failed Counter-Revolution', in E. E. Rice (ed.), *Revolution
and Counter-Revolution* (Oxford, 1991), 109–28.

[3] This is the phrase used by Detlev Peukert in his superb study of the Weimar Republic:
Detlev J. K. Peukert, *Die Weimarer Republik: Krisenjahre der klassischen Moderne* (Frankfurt/Main,
1987), 57.

cil movement, and its suppression;[4] in recent years, the inflation too has finally been examined in the detail it requires, thanks in large measure to the work of Carl-Ludwig Holtfrerich and Gerald Feldman.[5] However, the third major theme framing the history of the failed gamble of Weimar democracy, the 'inner liquidation of the War', has attracted rather less attention.

This book is an attempt to examine some of the consequences of the First World War for Germany. It forms part of an attempt to understand why and how democracy failed in Germany after 1918, and is based upon a belief that the consequences of the First World War formed a crucial element of that failure. It is intended to be what its title promises: a social history of Germany in the aftermath of defeat in the first global conflict. It concentrates on the demobilization after the First World War, with demobilization taken in its broad sense as a social and psychological as well as an economic and military process. As such, its main focus is neither the revolutionary politics of 1918–19 and their suppression nor the economics and politics of the inflation. Rather, its focus is Germany as a *post-war* society. It forms an attempt to examine the contribution of the War, the defeat, and the post-war transition to the political culture of Weimar Germany—an attempt not only to delineate the terrible social and economic damage caused by the War but also to probe the significance of how the First World War was remembered during the Weimar period. Implicit in such a project is the assumption that Germany's social, economic, and political problems after the First World War stemmed as much from the extraordinary upheavals after 1914 as from long-term economic and political structures fixed during the nineteenth century. This is not to assert that underlying structures had no role in framing the tragic course of German history during the first half of the twentieth century, but it is to suggest that we need to concentrate on the contingent as well as the structural determinants of historical phenomena.

References to the enormous literature which the First World War has generated will be found as appropriate through this book, and so it is not necessary to parade bulky footnotes here. However, some studies deserve

---

[4] Although it is now somewhat dated, a measure of this huge literature can be gained from the bibliography prepared by Georg P. Meyer, *Bibliographie zur deutschen Revolution 1918/19* (Göttingen, 1977).

[5] Carl-Ludwig Holtfrerich, *The German Inflation 1914–1923: Causes and Effects in International Perspective* (Berlin and New York, 1986); Gerald D. Feldman, Carl-Ludwig Holtfrerich, Gerhard A. Ritter, and Peter-Christian Witt (eds.), *Die deutsche Inflation: Eine Zwischenbilanz* (Berlin and New York, 1982); (eds.), *Die Erfahrung der Inflation im internationalen Zusammenhang und Vergleich* (Berlin and New York, 1984); eid. (eds.), *Die Anpassung an die Inflation* (Berlin and New York, 1986); Gerald D. Feldman (ed.), *Die Nachwirkungen der Inflation auf die deutsche Geschichte 1924–1933* (Munich, 1985); id., *The Great Disorder: Politics, Economics and Society in the German Inflation, 1914–1924* (Oxford, 1993).

particular mention. Among these are the pioneering work of Gerald Feld-man,[6] Jürgen Kocka,[7] and Wilhelm Deist,[8] the imaginative recent studies of Robert Whalen,[9] Ute Daniel,[10] Modris Eksteins[11] and George Mosse,[12] and the important studies of other major combatant countries by Jean-Jacques Becker,[13] Antoine Prost,[14] Arthur Marwick,[15] and Jay Winter.[16] Like others who have studied the First World War and its aftermath, I have profited greatly from their work—more so than any formal references can testify.

The gestation of this book has taken an inexcusably long time, during which I have accumulated enormous debts of gratitude. My first debt is to the staffs in all those archives in Germany and Poland who made materials available to me and helped me find a way through mountains of documents. No less important was the funding necessary to undertake numerous and extended research-trips. It therefore gives me great pleasure to express my profound gratitude to those institutions which provided the support which enabled me to carry out my research: to the Open University, which repeatedly provided travel grants over the years; to the Wolfson Foundation, which provided a grant for an extended period of study based in Hamburg; and especially to the Alexander von Humboldt Foundation, which generously provided the funding for my study leave based at the Technische Universität in Berlin in 1985, during which time the bulk of my archive research was carried out. I also owe a tremendous debt to those scholars whose works are mentioned above and who charted the historical territory through which I have wandered. More specifically, I want to thank friends and colleagues who have read and commented on my attempts to make some sense of the aftermath of the First World War in Germany—in particular David Black-bourn, David Crew, Ute Daniel, Wilhelm Deist, Laura de Sherbinin, Richard Evans, Gerald Feldman, Dick Geary, Reinhard Rürup, Cornelie Usborne, and Gerhard Wilke. Finally, I want to declare my debt to two

---

[6] Gerald D. Feldman, *Army, Industry, and Labor in Germany 1914–1918* (Princeton, NJ, 1966).

[7] Jürgen Kocka, *Facing Total War: German Society 1914–1918* (Leamington Spa, 1984).

[8] Wilhelm Deist (ed.), *Militär und Innenpolitik im Weltkrieg 1914–1918* (2 vols.; Düsseldorf, 1970); id., 'Der militärische Zusammenbruch des Kaiserreichs: Zur Realität der "Dolchstoßlegende" ', in Ursula Büttner (ed.), *Das Unrechtsregime: Internationale Forschung über den Nationalsozialismus*, i: *Ideologie, Herrschaftssystem, Wirkung in Europa* (Hamburg, 1986), 101–29.

[9] Robert Weldon Whalen, *Bitter Wounds: German Victims of the Great War, 1914–1939* (Ithaca, NY and London, 1984).

[10] Ute Daniel, *Arbeiterfrauen in der Kriegsgesellschaft: Beruf, Familie und Politik im Ersten Weltkrieg* (Göttingen, 1989).

[11] Modris Eksteins, *Rites of Spring: The Great War and the Birth of the Modern Age* (New York, 1989).

[12] George L. Mosse, *Fallen Soldiers: Reshaping the Memory of the World Wars* (New York and Oxford, 1990).

[13] Jean-Jacques Becker, *The Great War and the French People* (Leamington Spa, 1985).

[14] Antoine Prost, *Les anciens combattants et la société française 1914–1939* (3 vol.; Paris, 1977).

[15] Arthur Marwick, *The Deluge: British Society and the First World War* (London, 1965).

[16] J. M. Winter, *The Great War and the British People* (London, 1986).

friends who, sadly, died before this book was completed: to Tim Mason, without whose help and encouragement I would never have begun historical research and who long ago suggested many of the themes which surface in this study; and to Detlev Peukert, with whom I discussed much of what is presented here and who was an amazing source of stimulating and challenging ideas. Those who knew these fine historians will understand how much I owe them and how much we have lost through their untimely deaths.

Historical research is a collective enterprise not only in its production but also in its consumption. Accordingly, I hope that this book will be read with interest and profit by others who, while perhaps neither sharing my assumptions nor agreeing with my conclusions, agree that ours is a common effort to understand this fateful chapter in modern European history.

R.B.

*Stony Stratford*
*28 May 1992*

# Contents

# List of Tables

# *Abbreviations*

## Political Parties and Other Organizations

| | |
|---|---|
| DDP | Deutsche Demokratische Partei |
| DHV | Deutschnationaler Handlungsgehilfen-Verband |
| DLV | Deutscher Landarbeiterverband |
| DNVP | Deutschnationale Volkspartei |
| DVP | Deutsche Volkspartei |
| NSDAP | Nationalsozialdemokratische Deutsche Arbeiterpartei |
| SPD | Sozialdemokratische Partei Deutschlands |
| USPD | Unabhängige Sozialdemokratische Partei Deutschlands |
| ZAG | Zentralarbeitsgemeinschaft |

## Archive and Document Collections

| | |
|---|---|
| APP | Archiwum Panstwowe w Poznaniu |
| APS | Archiwum Panstwowe w Szczecinie |
| APW | Archiwum Panstwowe w Wrocławiu |
| BAK | Bundesarchiv Koblenz |
| BA/MA | Bundesarchiv-Militärarchiv Freiburg i.B. |
| BAP | Bundesarchiv Potsdam |
| BBA | Bergbau-Archiv Bochum |
| BHStA | Bayerisches Hauptstaatsarchiv |
| BLHA | Brandenburgisches Landeshauptarchiv Potsdam |
| GStAB | Geheimes Staatsarchiv preußischer Kulturbesitz Berlin-Dahlem |
| GStAM | Geheimes Staatsarchiv preußischer Kulturbesitz Merseburg |
| GLAK | Generallandesarchiv Karlsruhe |
| HHStA | Hessisches Hauptstaatsarchiv Wiesbaden |
| HStAD | Hauptstaatsarchiv Düsseldorf |
| LHSA | Landeshauptarchiv Sachsen-Anhalt Magdeburg |
| MLHA | Mecklenburgisches Landeshauptarchiv Schwerin |
| NHStA | Niedersächsisches Hauptstaatsarchiv Hannover |
| PLA | Pommersches Landesarchiv Greifswald |
| StAB | Staatsarchiv Bremen |
| SHAD | Sächsisches Hauptstaatsarchiv Dresden |
| SSAL | Sächsisches Staatsarchiv Leipzig |
| StAH | Staatsarchiv Hamburg |
| StAM | Staatsarchiv Münster |

StAO        Staatsarchiv Osnabrück
StAW        Staatsarchiv Weimar
StdABo      Stadtarchiv Bochum
StdABr      Stadtarchiv Bremerhaven
StdADo      Stadtarchiv Dortmund
StdADu      Stadtarchiv Duisburg
StdAHd      Stadtarchiv Heidelberg
StdAKi      Stadtarchiv Kiel
StdALu      Stadtarchiv Ludwigshafen
StdALü      Stadtarchiv Lübeck
StdAM       Stadtarchiv Münster
WWA         Westfälisches Wirtschaftsarchiv Dortmund

## Other

IHK         Industrie-und Handelskammer
KAKI        Kriegsausschuß für Konsumenteninteressen
RMdI        Reichsministerium des Innern
RWM         Reichswirtschaftsministerium
RMwD        Reichsministerium für wirtschaftliche Demobilmachung

# I

# German Society During the First World War

*Es ist alles Schwindel:*
Der Krieg ist für die Reichen,
Der Mittelstand mu weichen,
Das Volk, das stellt die Leichen.[1]

(*It is all a swindle:*
The War is for the wealthy,
The *Mittelstand* must give way,
The people provide the corpses.)

WHEN the First World War began, on 4 August 1914, the German people had experienced over a quarter of a century of peace and increasing prosperity. The population of the German Empire had grown rapidly, from 49.2 million in 1890 to 67 million in 1913, and its cities had mushroomed. National income, and income per capita, had risen steadily.[2] Germans had become healthier; life expectancy had increased,[3] as mortality (and infant mortality specifically) declined steeply.[4] Germany, which had displaced Britain as Europe's premier industrial power, appeared to offer its population

---

[1] This little poem was left in a train compartment by German soldiers in early 1918. See GLAK, 456/E.V.8, Bund 86: stellv. Gen.kdo XIV. A. K. to Ministerium des Innern in Karlsruhe, Karlsruhe, 1 Feb. 1918.

[2] In nominal terms national income had grown from 24.6 thousand million Marks in 1891 to 49.8 thousand million Marks in 1913, national income per capita from 494 Marks to 746. In real terms the rise was less steep but none the less impressive: in terms of purchasing-power in 1913, national income rose from 33.4 thousand million Marks in 1891 to 49.8 thousand million in 1913 (during which period it rose *every single year*) and income per capita from 671 to 746 Marks (and, except in 1893, when it remained steady, this figure too rose every year during the period). See Statistisches Reichsamt, *Das deutsche Volkseinkommen vor und nach dem Kriege* (Einzelschriften zur Statistik des Deutschen Reichs, no. 24; Berlin, 1932), 68. This rise in income was reflected in real improvements in living-standards, as real wages grew fairly steadily from the beginning of the 1880s until the outbreak of the War. See the table in Ashok V. Desai, *Real Wages in Germany 1871–1913* (Oxford, 1968), 125. At the same time, the length of the average working-week fell substantially (from 72 hours in 1872 to 57 in 1914), as did the frequency of fatal accidents at work. See Hans-Ulrich Wehler, *Das Deutsche Kaiserreich 1871–1918* (Göttingen, 1973), 49; Jürgen Kocka, *Facing Total War: German Society 1914–1918* (Leamington Spa, 1984), 13.

[3] Life expectancy increased from 37.17 years for men and 40.25 for women in 1881–90 to 47.41 years for men and 50.68 for women in 1910–11. See *Statistisches Jahrbuch für das Deutsche Reich 1921/22* (Berlin, 1922), 47.

[4] General mortality fell from 226 per thousand in 1880 to 15 in 1913, and infant mortality fell from 226 per thousand live births in 1881–85 to 174 in 1906–10. See Statistisches Bundesamt Wiesbaden (ed.), *Bevölkerung und Wirtschaft 1872–1972* (Stuttgart, 1972), 101–2; John E. Knodel, *The Decline of Fertility in Germany, 1871–1939* (Princeton, NJ, 1974), 156. The sharp decline in infant mortality set in around the turn of the century.

steadily widening horizons on the eve of the First World War. Of course, life in Imperial Germany had been characterized by glaring inequalities and serious political tensions; its economy had not remained immune from fluctuations, and a large portion of its people had lived in considerable poverty and insecurity.[5] Yet when the First World War broke upon them, most inhabitants of the German Empire could look back upon decades of peace and material improvement. This shared perspective framed both how Germans reacted to hardships they were to face in wartime and how they would conceive of the transition to come when the War ended. For the ways in which people approached the post-war transition were shaped by what they imagined to be the normal, natural conditions of 'peace'.

The outbreak of war brought a sudden end to the pre-1914 world. As Gerhard Ritter and Klaus Tenfelde observe in the introduction to their mammoth account of the condition of workers in the German Empire, 'seldom do social-historical caesura allow themselves to be fixed so clearly as for the year 1914'.[6] The declaration of war was greeted with a bewildering mixture of patriotic euphoria and anxiety about day-to-day concerns. August 1914 saw an outpouring of patriotic enthusiasm which has fascinated historians ever since and which gave Germans 'the intoxicating illusion that the social rifts of the past had disappeared'.[7] This illusion was fostered by the fact that the enthusiasm for war did not just permeate the upper and middle reaches of German society but extended to the suspected 'enemies of the Reich', whose loyalty had long been doubted by Germany's rulers. Few expressed this more clearly than the Berlin Polizeipräsident von Jagow, who—no doubt in sharp contrast with what he might have predicted a few months earlier—rapturously described the 'elated spirits' in the Reich capital in late August: 'Even in the north and east of Berlin [Berlin's working-class districts], which were formerly hardly responsive to patriotic emotion, masses of black-white-red flags are displayed.'[8] (No less pleasing for the Berlin Police President and long-time scourge of the Left was the fact that party-political activity in Berlin had come to a standstill and that 'Social Democracy is no longer capable of action, as almost half of its functionaries have been called to the colours and those left behind display little interest'.) Not even Germany's Polish population remained indifferent: in the Upper Silesian mining town of Beuthen the Landrat reported gleefully on 11 August that,

---

[5] This can be seen clearly with regard to working-class households, particularly where people suffered illness or accidents. On working-class incomes and living-standards, see Gerhard A. Ritter and Klaus Tenfelde, *Arbeiter im Deutschen Kaiserreich 1871 bis 1914* (Bonn, 1992), 467–528.

[6] Ibid. 3.

[7] The phrase comes from Robert Wohl, *The Generation of 1914* (London, 1980), 48. See also Eric J. Leed, *No Man's Land: Combat and Identity in World War I* (Cambridge, 1979), 40–72.

[8] GStAM, Rep. 77, tit. 332r, no. 126, fos. 4–5: Polizeipräsident, 'Zweiter Stimmungsbericht', Berlin, 26 Aug. 1914.

'just as among the German population, the declaration of war aroused unanimous enthusiasm among the local Poles', and in nearby Pleß (with its overwhelmingly Polish population) his counterpart praised the 'splendid attitude' of the local population after the declaration of war.[9] The way in which the events of August 1914 were frozen in memory is encapsulated well by the entry of a miner in the Ruhr community of Recklinghausen-Hochlarmark in his war diary: 'High went the waves of enthusiasm in the days of the mobilization. Never have I heard the song "Deutschland über alles" sung more passionately than at this time.'[10]

A less prominent place in the popular memory of August 1914 was occupied by the expressions of anxiety, bordering on panic, about everyday concerns. When war was declared Germans did not devote themselves exclusively to signing up for a quick trip to Paris, hoisting the black-white-red flag from working-class tenements, singing 'Deutschland über alles', and cheering the soldiers. They also spent a lot of time and energy queueing to withdraw their savings from banks, buying up and hoarding food and other goods thought likely to be in short supply in the months ahead, and—if they owned shops—raising the prices of products suddenly in great demand and refusing to accept paper money in payment.[11] In addition, not everyone liable for military service was keen to be in uniform. Already during the early weeks of the War there were, perhaps predictably, petitions to get or keep men needed at home (for example, on family farms) excused from military service.[12] Even during those glorious weeks when the Kaiser saw before him no political parties but only Germans, the conflicting economic interests which so divided German society—and which were soon to tear it apart—had not been suppressed entirely.

In trying to assess popular opinion during the early weeks of the War, two points should be considered. First, the outpourings of enthusiasm in 1914 did not take place against a background of unanimous adulation of

[9] APW, Rejencja Opolska Pr. B., no. 141, fo. 195: Landrat des Kreises Beuthen O-S to Regierungspräsident, Beuthen, 11 Aug. 1914; ibid., fos. 223–5: Landrat to Regierungspräsident, Pleß, 12 Aug. 1914.

[10] Quoted in Michael Zimmermann, ' "Alle sollen auf dem Altar des Vaterlandes ein Opfer bringen": Die Bergarbeiterschaft in Kreis Recklinghausen während des Ersten Weltkrieges', in *Vestische Zeitschrift: Zeitschrift der Vereine für Orts- und Heimatkunde im Vest Recklinghausen*, 81 (1982), 68.

[11] See G. A. Baumgärtner, *Deutsches Kriegsbuch. Tagesberichte und Stimmungsbilder von Daheim und Draußen. Die ersten Monate des Weltkrieges. Erinnerungsgabe der Bayerischen Kriegsinvalidenfürsorge* (Munich, 1916), 13, 20–1; LHSA, Rep. C 50 Querfurt A/B, no. 2799, fo. 89: Regierungspräsident, 'Bekanntmachung', Merseburg, 3 Aug. 1914; Lothar Burchardt, 'Konstanz im Ersten Weltkrieg', *Politik und Unterricht*, 7: 3 (1981), 12; Carl-Ludwig Holtfrerich, *The German Inflation 1914–1923: Causes and Effects in International Perspective* (Berlin and New York, 1986), 64; Robert G. Moeller, *German Peasants and Agrarian Politics 1914–1924: The Rhineland and Westphalia* (Chapel Hill, NC, and London, 1986), 44.

[12] LHSA, Rep. C 50 Querfurt A/B, no. 2799. See also Moeller, *German Peasants and Agrarian Politics*, 47, for later examples.

things military in German society. Not only had the largest and most popular political party, the Social Democratic Party of Germany, campaigned long and hard against militarism before 1914;[13] antipathy towards the military had also been prevalent among the peasant population, which was loath to see its young men called away at harvest time or to pay higher taxes for military expenditure.[14] It is also unlikely that all the men conscripted into the peacetime Imperial Army developed wholly positive feelings towards the values and institutions with which they were confronted.[15] Second, we need to remember just what people were enthusiastic about in the summer of 1914. The popular outpourings of August 1914 were not enthusiasm for war in general but for a specific war: for rapid victories in the west and a defensive struggle against Tsarist Russia. The fact that the Russian Empire had mobilized against Germany was a key factor in damping opposition to the war effort among the two groups which held the most obvious potential for anti-war sentiment, Social Democrats and Poles. The former rallied to an apparently defensive struggle against the bastion of European reaction; and the latter were not ill-disposed to the prospect of killing Russians. These points suggest that the apparent popular enthusiasm for war in 1914 was not necessarily the culmination of a long process of integration of outsider groups into Imperial German society, but something of an aberration—conditional support for a particular (illusory) cause—and soon to be replaced by doubts and finally by extreme hostility to the War and those who pursued it.

Also important in shaping popular attitudes towards the German state in wartime was the fact that with the declaration of war, the military took over the internal civil administration, in accordance with the Prussian Law of Siege of 4 June 1851.[16] This placed the civilian administration under the command of the Deputy Commanding Generals in the Army Corps Regions and the Governors of the larger military fortresses (and, in Bavaria, of the Regional Commanders, who were subject to the Bavarian War Ministry). The Deputy Commanding Generals were given wide-ranging powers: to organize army recruitment and labour distribution, to intervene in the organization of the food-supply and in the conduct of the press, and to

[13] See Alex Hall, *Scandal, Sensation and Social Democracy: The SPD Press and Wilhelmine Germany 1890–1914* (Cambridge, 1977), 116–42.

[14] See Ian Farr, 'Populism in the Countryside: The Peasant Leagues in Bavaria in the 1890s', in Richard J. Evans (ed.), *Society and Politics in Wilhelmine Germany* (London, 1978), 150, 155; also David Blackbourn, 'Peasants and Politics in Germany, 1871–1914', *European History Quarterly*, 14:1 (1984), 54, 62–3.

[15] The popular experience of military life in Imperial Germany is a subject which still needs to be explored.

[16] See Gerald D. Feldman, *Army, Industry and Labor in Germany, 1914–1918* (Princeton, NJ, 1966), 31–3; Wilhelm Deist (ed.), *Militär und Innenpolitik im Weltkrieg 1914–1918* (2 vols.; Düsseldorf, 1970), i, pp. xxxi–li; Ute Daniel, *Arbeiterfrauen in der Kriegsgesellschaft: Beruf, Familie und Politik im Ersten Weltkrieg* (Göttingen, 1989), 53–4.

oversee social policy and ensure domestic order. This military take-over of civilian government—what Gerald Feldman has described as the reduction of the Bismarckian state to its 'ideal form'—proved a recipe for disaster. The administrative boundaries of the Army Corps did not coincide with civilian administrative boundaries; except in Bavaria, there was no provision for co-ordinating policy among the Deputy Commanding Generals; and the problems which these regional military dictatorships faced grew more difficult as the war dragged on. The result was not the smooth running of the civilian administration by an efficient military, but, ultimately, the discrediting of the military in civilian eyes amidst mounting chaos.

Prior to the First World War the strength of the German army had been fixed at roughly 1 per cent of the total population of the Reich. Thus in 1910 the army numbered 622,483 men altogether, of whom 25,718 were officers and 85,226 were non-commissioned officers.[17] By the eve of the War, however, its size had been increased to 800,646 men (1.18 per cent of the population of the Reich), as a result of the military build-up of 1913. With the declaration of war, that size grew tremendously, as hundreds of thousands of young men rushed to volunteer in an orgy of patriotism and in the hope of a glorious—and short—conflict. In August 1914 the strength of the army jumped to 2,931,756, of whom 1,527,919 were sent into the field; by January 1915—despite the huge losses suffered in the offensives of summer and autumn 1914—the figure had increased to 4,357,934, of whom 2,618,158 were in the field; by mid-1917 it was well over 7 million, of whom 5 million were in the field, and the size of the army remained at roughly these levels until after the spring offensives of 1918, when it fell fairly substantially.[18] During the four years of war there were on average roughly 6,372,000 men in the army, of whom about 4,183,000 were in the Feldheer (field army) and about 2,189,000 in the Besatzungsheer (army behind the lines and within the Reich). The total number of men who served in the German army between August 1914 and July 1918 was 13,123,011, 19.7 per cent of Germany's population in 1914.[19] In other words, roughly one-fifth of the German population experienced wartime military service,[20] of whom

[17] Gerd Hohorst, Jürgen Kocka, and Gerhard A. Ritter, *Sozialgeschichtliches Arbeitsbuch: Materialien zur Statistik des Kaiserreichs 1870–1914* (Munich, 1975), 171. See also Michael Geyer, *Deutsche Rüstungspolitik 1860–1980* (Frankfurt/Main, 1984), 83–96. The navy numbered 57,374 men at that time.

[18] The size of the 'field army' fell from 5,265,801 in January 1918 to 4,227,201 in July, while the number behind the lines increased somewhat, from 2,093,529 to 2,232,750. See Reichswehrministerium, *Sanitätsbericht über das deutsche Heer (Deutsches Feld- und Besatzungsheer) im Weltkriege, 1914–1918*, iii: *Die Krankenbewegung bei dem Deutschen Feld- und Besatzungsheer* (Berlin, 1934), 8.

[19] Ibid. 12, 31.

[20] Similar estimates—in this case for Württemberg—may be found in Hermann Koetzle, *Das Sanitätswesen im Weltkrieg 1914–1918* (Stuttgart, 1924), 10. In the case of Württemberg the 508,482 men who were mobilized up to the end of July 1918 comprised more than one-fifth of the total population.

on average not quite half were in the army and about one-third were at the front at any one time.

Turnover among the soldiers was enormous. Death, injury, illness, capture, call-back to work in the hard-pressed war-economy, and periodic leave took a tremendous toll. Altogether 4,814,557 German soldiers were reported wounded during the War, and there were 14,673,940 registered cases of illness among servicemen.[21] Roughly 2 million German soldiers were killed: according to the Central Record Office for War Casualties and War Cemeteries, as of the end of 1933 the number of confirmed war-dead stood at 1,900,876 men from the army, 34,836 from the navy, and another 1,185 who had died in Germany's former colonies; over and above this, there were an estimated 100,000 men recorded as missing in action whose fate remained unknown and who were presumed dead.[22] In other words, deaths of German soldiers averaged 465,600 per year—about 3.5 per cent of the total who served.[23] The greatest casualty-rates occurred in the early months of the War, when heavy losses were suffered on both the eastern and western fronts and more than half the Feldheer was killed or wounded. For most of the time, trench warfare was more monotonous than dangerous; it was when offensives were ordered that the First World War assumed its murderous character and men were slaughtered in their tens of thousands.[24]

Altogether 10,573,242 German soldiers served in the field between August 1914 and July 1918. Of these, 6,346,041 (60 per cent) had to be removed at one time or another from the front as a consequence of wounds or illness and had to be replaced—which meant an average monthly turnover of about 130,000 men in and out of the Feldheer during the War.[25] On average, the army lost roughly one-third of its men (due to death, injury, or illness) each year.[26] About half the replacements were new recruits; the other half were casualties (sick and wounded) who recovered and were returned to the front as fit for duty. Indeed, three-quarters of the

[21] Reichswehrministerium, *Sanitätsbericht*, iii. 31. Army doctors treated nearly as many cases of stomach and intestinal disorders as of combat wounds. See Robert Weldon Whalen, *Bitter Wounds: German Victims of the Great War, 1914–1939* (Ithaca, NY, and London, 1984), 52–3.

[22] Reichswehrministerium, *Sanitätsbericht*, iii. 12.

[23] Ibid. 63; Whalen, *Bitter Wounds*, 40–1.

[24] This can be seen clearly, for example, from German losses recorded on the western front in early 1918. Of the 3,762,717 German soldiers on the western front in Feb. 1918, 1,705 were reported as having been killed in action, 1,147 as missing, and 30,381 as wounded; in Mar. when the spring offensives began, out of a total strength of 3,882,655 the comparable figures were 31,429, 19,680, and 180,898; in Apr., out of a total strength of 3,795,581 the comparable figures were 36,218, 17,734, and 190,380. See Wilhelm Deist, 'Verdeckter Militärstreik im Kriegsjahr 1918?', in Wolfram Wette (ed.), *Der Krieg des kleinen Mannes: Eine Militärgeschichte von unten* (Munich, 1992), 149–50.

[25] Reichswehrministerium, *Sanitätsbericht*, iii. 32.

[26] See Whalen, *Bitter Wounds*, 39.

soldiers (or 4,173,463 men) who were wounded recovered and were reclassified as fit for active duty.[27]

Willingly or not, millions of soldiers had been uprooted from civilian
existence and, after a relatively short training-period, sent to war. From a
world which had been characterized by peace and stability they were
catapulted into a world characterized by death and destruction. Furthermore,
after the failure of the initial German offensives in the west and abandonment of hopes for a victorious return home by Christmas, it appeared that
death and destruction might continue indefinitely in the stalemate of trench
warfare. Very quickly the desire to be a hero was replaced by the desire
just to survive. At the same time the nature of the trench warfare gave rise
to new divisions between men at the front and men behind the lines, out
of range of enemy artillery; alongside the *Frontgemeinschaft* (front-community)
which linked together men sharing a common fate and about which so much
has been written, there also arose deep animosities behind the lines and
tremendous gulfs between officers and men.[28] It was there, behind the front
lines, that military drill and preferential treatment for officers stirred up most
resentment.

It would be mistaken to assume that the German armed forces constituted
a world unto themselves cut off from the home front. Most soldiers did not
spend the war years constantly in battle, at or near the front. Many spent
long periods recovering from wounds or illness in military hospitals or in
medical institutions and convalescent homes in Germany, and the most
severely wounded and disabled were discharged; many were moved from
front to front as the course of the War altered; many were called back to
Germany during the second half of the War to provide badly needed labour
in war industries; others were drafted and sent to the front only during the
later stages of the War, bringing with them fresh news of conditions back
home;[29] some were called to the colours, released, then called up again; and
throughout the conflict there was constant rotation to relieve units at the

---

[27] Reichswehrministerium, *Sanitätsbericht*, iii. 62. Whalen, using the figures from the *Sanitätsbericht*, incorrectly states that 74.7% of the wounded who recovered returned to active duty. See
Whalen, *Bitter Wounds*, 40. The 74.7% in fact refers to the proportion of the *total* wounded (of
whom more than one million died of their wounds) who were subsequently reclassified as fit
for duty or who remained in the army. Only 344,576 (or 7.6%) of the total who survived their
wounds were reclassified as unfit for service.

[28] See Wilhelm Deist, 'Der militärische Zusammenbruch des Kaiserreichs: Zur Realität der
"Dolchstoßlegende"', in Ursula Büttner (ed.), *Das Unrechtsregime: Internationale Forschung über den
Nationalsozialismus. Ideologie, Herrschaftssystem, Wirkung in Europa* (Hamburg, 1986), 107–8.

[29] e.g. in the city of Osnabrück (which had a population of 71,384 on 31 Aug. 1918), between
1 June and 31 Aug. 1918 290 men were discharged from the army and another 509 were
drafted. There were 385 prisoners of war in the city and 700 people in its military hospitals;
and on any given day there were an average of 94 soldiers on leave in the city. See StAO,
Rep. 430, Dez. 905, Zug no. 16/25, no. 15, fo. 158: 'Nachweisung über die Fortschreibung
der versorgungsberechtigten Bevölkerung für die Zeit vom 1. Juni 1918 bis zum 31. August
1918. Regierungsbezirk Osnabrück. Kreis Osnabrück Stadt.'

front.[30] There was no 'typical' experience of the conflict, no uniform experience of the 'front generation'. The War meant many different things to the people who fought in it, and a picture of millions of men gladly going off to battle in 1914 to return to the Fatherland four years later would not be an accurate representation of how the conflict was experienced by most of the Germans who fought in it.

Who were the soldiers who fought for Germany during the First World War? Altogether roughly 13.2 million (or about 85 per cent) of the 15.6 million males eligible for military service were mobilized at some stage during the War.[31] From the beginning of 1915, between about one-quarter and one-half of the men in this age-range were serving in the armed forces at any one time. Young men who saw no service—usually as a consequence of physical weaknesses or the fact that they had been retained in key sectors of the war economy at home—were the exception. Obviously, with a mobilization on such a scale, it was also inevitable that the soldiers would come from all walks of life. The composition of the army differed greatly from that of the German population, not with regard to their occupational background but with regard to their age and sex.

That said, it appears that the age-structure of the men serving in the German armed forces altered fairly substantially during the course of the War. In the early months of the War probably the majority 'of men in uniform were in their mid-twenties. However, as casualties mounted and new recruits were conscripted to replace the men destroyed at the front, the proportion of older and—particularly—younger soldiers increased.[32] The changing age-structure of the German army can be seen in a statistical breakdown of German soldiers who died during the War (see Table 1). These figures suggest that in one respect at least the German army was becoming less homogeneous as the War progressed. Whereas during the early months of the conflict less than one-tenth of the soldiers were aged 20 or under, during the last two years of the War this proportion approached one-quarter. Not only does this reveal the rather gloomy prospects of adolescents in wartime Germany, who could look forward to a high probability of being killed or wounded shortly after their eighteenth birthday;

[30] Some indication of how soldiers were moved about during the War may be gained from the records of men who later became patients in the psychiatric hospital of Eichberg, near Wiesbaden, in HHStA, 430/1.

[31] Whalen, *Bitter Wounds*, 39. See also Rudolf Meerwarth, 'Die Entwicklung der Bevölkerung in Deutschland während der Kriegs- und Nachkriegszeit', in Rudolf Meerwarth, Adolf Günther, and Waldemar Zimmermann, *Die Einwirkung des Krieges auf die Bevölkerungsbewegung, Einkommen und Lebenshaltung in Deutschland* (Stuttgart, 1932), 57–64.

[32] It should be noted as well that in 1915, after the failure of the German military to bring a speedy end to the War, the War Ministry reversed its policy of sending the older men off to battle first. See Feldman, *Army, Industry and Labor*, 68.

Table 1. *Deaths among German soldiers by Age, 1914–1918*
(cases recorded as of 1919)

| Age | 1914 No. | 1914 % | 1915 No. | 1915 % | 1916 No. | 1916 % | 1917 No. | 1917 % | 1918 No. | 1918 % | 1919 No. | 1919 % | Total No. | Total % |
|---|---|---|---|---|---|---|---|---|---|---|---|---|---|---|
| 15–17 | 2,069 | 0.85 | 4,200 | 0.97 | 954 | 0.28 | 406 | 0.14 | 1,042 | 0.27 | 113 | 0.79 | 8,784 | 0.52 |
| 18–20 | 18,429 | 7.64 | 51,577 | 14.19 | 62,628 | 18.39 | 68,753 | 24.39 | 91,286 | 24.04 | 2,761 | 19.29 | 305,434 | 18.05 |
| 21–24 | 90,150 | 37.35 | 144,750 | 33.35 | 102,407 | 30.08 | 73,705 | 26.15 | 101,850 | 26.82 | 3,204 | 22.38 | 516,066 | 30.50 |
| 25–29 | 74,617 | 30.92 | 108,927 | 25.10 | 74,903 | 22.00 | 53,392 | 18.94 | 75,491 | 19.88 | 2,574 | 17.98 | 389,904 | 23.05 |
| 30–34 | 36,953 | 15.31 | 68,018 | 15.67 | 50,712 | 14.89 | 37,348 | 13.25 | 52,748 | 13.89 | 1,981 | 13.84 | 247,760 | 14.64 |
| 35–39 | 14,965 | 6.20 | 34,359 | 7.92 | 35,887 | 10.54 | 27,220 | 9.66 | 33,579 | 8.84 | 1,557 | 10.88 | 147,567 | 8.72 |
| 40–44 | 2,702 | 1.12 | 9,700 | 2.23 | 10,891 | 3.20 | 16,287 | 5.78 | 17,744 | 4.67 | 1,276 | 8.91 | 58,600 | 3.46 |
| 45 + | 1,109 | 0.46 | 2,385 | 0.55 | 2,044 | 0.60 | 4,739 | 1.68 | 5,920 | 1.56 | 839 | 5.86 | 17,036 | 1.01 |
| unknown | 349 | 0.14 | 118 | 0.03 | 42 | 0.01 | 55 | 0.02 | 117 | 0.03 | 9 | 0.06 | 690 | 0.04 |
| Total | 241,343 | 100.00 | 434,034 | 100.00 | 340,468 | 100.00 | 281,905 | 100.00 | 379,777 | 100.00 | 14,314 | 100.00 | 1,691,841 | 100.00 |

*Source*: Statistisches Reichsamt (ed.), *Statistik des Deutschen Reichs*, vol. cclxxvi: *Bewegung der Bevölkerung in den Jahren 1914 bis 1919*; (Berlin, 1922), pp. xlix–lvii.

it also suggests that generational differences were growing within the German armed forces. Viewed against this background, it should hardly be surprising that within the Reich, adolescents so often seemed to be living just for the moment, or that within the army, conflicts between officers and enlisted men became so sharp as the War neared its end.

It also appears that a disproportionate number of the casualties among German soldiers—and therefore probably of their number as a whole—came from rural regions.[33] Among the regions which suffered a particularly high number of military casualties relative to their total populations were Mecklenburg-Schwerin, Schleswig-Holstein, Pomerania, and Württemberg. The regions which registered the lowest proportions included the Rhineland, Westphalia, and Saxony—where large numbers of men were held back from military service in order to work in war industries. Finally, casualty statistics suggest that most of the soldiers were single. Of the German soldiers who were killed during the Great War, 68.75 per cent were single and 30.64 per cent were married; by contrast, in 1910, 59.6 per cent of the men in the Reich between the ages of 15 and 45 were single and 39.6 per cent were married.[34] (The small remainder were widowed or divorced.) What is more, it appears that the proportion of single men in the army increased somewhat during the last two years of the War, as the proportion of men in the ranks aged between 18 and 20 rose steeply.[35]

The First World War saw the development of two quite different but interdependent societies: the one a male society structured within the military; the other a civil society which consisted disproportionately of women. In the former, new bonds and new frictions were created against a backdrop of fear and the horrors of modern warfare; a new social framework was created for and by millions of men, a framework which most, understandably, were keen to leave behind. In the latter, few households were left

---

[33] See Statistisches Reichsamt, *Statistik des Deutschen Reichs*, Vol. cclxxvi: *Bewegung der Bevölkerung in den Jahren 1914 bis 1919* (Berlin, 1922), p. xlix; Meerwarth, 'Die Entwicklung der Bevölkerung', 69–70.

[34] Meerwarth, 'Die Entwicklung der Bevölkerung', 72. See also Statistisches Reichsamt, *Statistik des Deutschen Reichs*, vol. cclxxvi, p. lviii. There were considerable regional differences. For example, in Saxony 59.96% were single, while in Württemberg the figure was 76.32%.

[35] In 1910, 99.8% of men aged 18–20, 85.2% of men aged 21–5, 41.7% of men aged 26–30, and 19.3% of men aged 31–5 were single. See *Statistisches Jahrbuch für das Deutsche Reich 1919*, 6. How the composition of the army altered is shown by the following breakdown (%) of fallen soldiers from the Thuringian states:

|         | 1914 | 1915 | 1916 | 1917 | 1918 |
|---------|------|------|------|------|------|
| Single  | 60.9 | 63.1 | 59.0 | 63.0 | 64.7 |
| Married | 38.7 | 36.4 | 40.3 | 36.2 | 34.5 |

See Thüringisches Statistisches Landesamt (ed.), *Statistisches Handbuch für das Land Thüringen, 1922* (Weimar, 1922), 73.

untouched by the War, by the loss of a son, a husband, a father, a brother. Hundreds of thousands of families were robbed of their male breadwinners. Employment patterns changed abruptly; new stresses entered family life; old structures of authority were weakened, both within the household and within society generally.

On the home front, the most noticeable changes were those registered on the job market. Although they are open to some question,[36] unemployment levels recorded among trade-union members give a rough indication of how the German labour-market altered during the War (See Table 2).

Table 2. *Unemployment among Members of Trade Unions in Germany, 1913– 1918* (%)

|           | 1913 | 1914 | 1915 | 1916 | 1917 | 1918 |
|-----------|------|------|------|------|------|------|
| January   | 3.2  | 4.7  | 6.5  | 2.6  | 1.7  | 0.9  |
| February  | 2.9  | 3.7  | 5.1  | 2.8  | 1.6  | 0.8  |
| March     | 2.3  | 2.8  | 3.3  | 2.2  | 1.3  | 0.9  |
| April     | 2.3  | 2.8  | 2.9  | 2.3  | 1.0  | 0.8  |
| May       | 2.5  | 2.8  | 2.9  | 2.5  | 1.0  | 0.8  |
| June      | 2.7  | 2.5  | 2.5  | 2.5  | 0.9  | 0.8  |
| July      | 2.9  | 2.9  | 2.7  | 2.4  | 0.8  | 0.7  |
| August    | 2.8  | 22.4 | 2.6  | 2.2  | 0.8  | 0.7  |
| September | 2.7  | 15.7 | 2.6  | 2.1  | 0.8  | 0.8  |
| October   | 2.8  | 10.9 | 2.5  | 2.0  | 0.7  | 0.7  |
| November  | 3.1  | 8.2  | 2.5  | 1.7  | 0.7  | 1.8  |
| December  | 4.8  | 7.2  | 2.6  | 1.6  | 0.9  | 5.1  |

*Source: Statistisches Jahrbuch für das Deutsche Reich 1921/22* (Berlin, 1922), suppl. *Internationale Übersichten*, 78.

Immediately after war was declared, unemployment soared to heights never seen before. This was a consequence partly of the disruption caused by the sudden shift to a war economy (and the concomitant abrupt cessation of export trade, which, for example, seriously affected employment in the chemical, electro-chemical, and steel industries)[37] and partly of the lack of planning and co-ordination with which this shift was carried out. In the initial rush to enlist and recruit for the conflict, scant consideration was given to the economic effects of this sudden flow of men into the armed forces, or to planning the distribution of manpower between the military

[36] See Wladimir Woytinsky, *Der deutsche Arbeitsmarkt: Ergebnisse der gewerkschaftlichen Arbeitslosenstatistik 1919 bis 1929* (Berlin, 1930), i. 11.

[37] See LHSA, Rep. C 48 I.e., no. 918/I, fos. 263–4: Magistrat zu Bitterfeld to Regierungspräsident, Bitterfeld, 21 Sept. 1914; Anneliese Seidel, *Frauenarbeit im Ersten Weltkrieg als Problem der staatlichen Sozialpolitik. Dargestellt am Beispiel Bayerns* (Frankfurt/Main, 1979), 36–43.

and the domestic economy.[38] It was expected that the war would be over quickly, and little thought was given to what might happen if it were not.

Not only did the lack of planning soon lead to a crisis of munitions production; in many cases it also had immediate catastrophic consequences for employers and their remaining work-forces. One good example of what this meant in a sector particularly important to the war economy is provided by the Gewerkschaft Leonhardt, a lignite mine and briquette-factory near Merseburg.[39] Before the mobilization its work-force had numbered 397; by 10 August, 162 had been called up and a further 70 were due for duty in the Landsturm, and of the remainder 20 were loaders (*Verlader*) under 17 years of age who could not be employed in the factory proper. According to the management (which was seeking to get its workers excused from duty in the Landsturm), this sudden loss of so large a proportion of the work-force endangered the continued employment of those left behind, as well as fuel shipments to state and private-sector armaments factories, military garrisons, and electricity works. The management of the Gewerkschaft Leonhardt was not alone in its concerns. Many large firms of key importance to war production lost one-third or even half their workers in August 1914, and production slumped.[40] In some factories production ceased entirely because the disruption of rail transport left them without coal or other necessary raw materials.[41] While rural regions managed largely to escape the worst effects of the unemployment during the first weeks of war,[42] joblessness in other areas was catastrophic—as, for example, in the shoe-making town of Weißenfels, where nearly two-thirds of the industrial work-force were said to be without work in August 1914.[43]

This soon changed, however. Very quickly labour became scarce and, once their hopes for a quick victory evaporated, the German authorities had

---

[38] See Feldman, *Army, Industry and Labor*, 64–5.

[39] LHSA, Rep. C 50 Querfurt A/B, no. 2799, fos. 224–6: Gewerkschaft Leonhardt, Braunkohlengrube und Brikettfabrik Neumark to Landrat in Querfurt, Frankleben, 10 Aug. 1914.

[40] e.g. the firm of Bosch in Stuttgart lost 52% of its work-force at the beginning of the War, and by the beginning of Sept. the Bayer chemicals works had lost 3,800 of its 8,000 workers and 450 of its 1,550 white-collar staff to the armed forces, while production fell by half. See Ute Stolle, *Arbeiterpolitik im Betrieb: Frauen und Männer, Reformisten und Radikale, Fach- und Massenarbeiter bei Bayer, BASF, Bosch und in Solingen (1900–1933)* (Frankfurt/Main, 1980), 169; Gottfried Plumpe, 'Chemische Industrie und Hilfsdienstgesetz am Beispiel der Farbenfabriken, vorm. Bayer & Co.', in Gunther Mai (ed.), *Arbeiterschaft in Deutschland 1914–1918: Studien zu Arbeitskampf und Arbeitsmarkt im Ersten Weltkrieg* (Düsseldorf, 1985), 181. Not even the mining industry was spared; e.g. by Dec. 1914 the Hibernia mining company in Herne had lost 5,951 (or 29.7%) of the 20,043 workers it had employed in July. See BBA, Bestand 32/4310: 'Höhe der Gesamt-Belegschaft (ohne Beamter)'.

[41] See LHSA, Rep. C 48 I.e., no. 918/I, fos. 263–4; ibid., fos. 275–6: Polizeiverwaltung to Vorsitzender des Kreisausschusses zu Liebenwerda, Elsterwerda, 18 Sept. 1914; ibid., fos. 370–6: Magistrat der Stadt Weißenfels to Regierungspräsident, Weißenfels, 23 Sept. 1914.

[42] Ibid., fo. 312: Magistrat to the Regierungspräsident, Bad-Kösen, 1 Oct. 1914; ibid., fos. 379–80: Magistrat der Stadt Wittenberg to Regierungspräsident, Wittenberg, 22 Sept. 1914.

[43] Ibid., fos. 370–6.

to consider how to manage the competition among employers for workers—in particular, skilled workers.[44] The problem was how to reconcile the military's insatiable manpower-requirements with industry's desperate need for skilled labour—a problem whose seriousness was demonstrated by the fact that, at the beginning of June 1915, of the roughly 56,000 employees of the arms manufacturer Krupp, roughly 22,000 were men being withheld from military service.[45] During the spring of 1915—after War Ministry policy changed from sending older, trained men to the front first to sending younger ones, and the need to organize the distribution of labour was more widely recognized—'guide-lines' for the granting of exemptions from military service were formulated by the War Ministry's newly formed Office for Exemptions (Abteilung für Zurückstellungswesen = AZS). These 'guide-lines'—sent in mid-June 1915 as recommendations to the Deputy Commanding Generals—set out a hierarchy of those to be exempted from the military according to their physical fitness: from men considered to be 'a.v.'—*arbeitsverwendungsfähig*, or fit for work—through those who were 'g.v.'—*garnisonsverwendungsfähig*, or fit for garrison duty—to those classified as 'k.v.'—*kriegsverwendungsfähig*, fit for field duty—who were the last to be granted exemptions. However, the problem defied solution. By early 1916, 740,000 men classified as 'k.v.' and a total of 1.2 million exempted workers (i.e. including those classified 'a.v.' and 'g.v.') were working in industry. At the beginning of 1918 there were in Germany 2,154,387 exempted workers, of whom 1,097,108 were *kriegsverwendungsfähig*; by June–July 1918 the number of exempted workers had risen to 2.5 million, of whom 1.3 million were classified 'k.v.'.[46]

In the wake of the Battle of the Somme (July–November 1916), with its huge losses of men and *matériel*, and the introduction of the Hindenburg Programme to increase armaments production in 1916–17, with its disregard for the limitations imposed by the material and human resources Germany had at her disposal, the German economy was stretched to, and ultimately beyond, the limit. The Auxiliary Service Law, with which the military had hoped to lay the basis for a total mobilization of Germany's labour reserves, failed to solve the insoluble problem.[47] Skilled workers were in particularly short supply, and it became necessary to call many soldiers back from the

---

[44] See Feldman, *Army, Industry and Labor*, 64–73; Daniel, *Arbeiterfrauen in der Kriegsgesellschaft*, 54–7.

[45] Daniel, *Arbeiterfrauen in der Kriegsgesellschaft*, 55.

[46] Deist, *Militär und Innenpolitik*, i. 640 n. 6. See also Daniel, *Arbeiterfrauen in der Kriegsgesellschaft*, 94.

[47] It did, however, signify a major change in the relation of organized labour to the German state. On the Auxiliary Service Law, see esp. Feldman, *Army Industry and Labor*, 197–249, and Daniel, *Arbeiterfrauen in der Kriegswirtschaft*, 74–97. For two extremely good studies of the effects of the Auxiliary Service Law upon particular industries, see Plumpe, 'Chemische Industrie und Hilfsdienstgesetz', and Hans-Joachim Bieber, 'Die Entwicklung der Arbeitsbeziehungen auf den Hamburger Großwerften zwischen Hilfsdienstgesetz und Betriebsrätegesetz (1916–1920), in Mai (ed.), *Arbeiterschaft in Deutschland*.

front to man essential war-industries. A striking example is provided by figures compiled by the management of the Hibernia mining company in Herne of its work-force in October 1918, a month before the Armistice.[48] Of the slightly more than 20,000 people employed by Hibernia in July 1914, 12,114 had been conscripted into military service since the beginning of the War. Of these, 1,140 had been recorded by October 1918 as having fallen in combat. (This number rose to 1,297 by May 1920, as cases of men missing in action were cleared up.) Of the surviving remainder, 5,477—or about half—*had already returned* and were working for Hibernia once again. Of course, the fate of Hibernia employees was not typical of the entire German male adult population, as mining had a particularly strong call upon scarce labour-resources. However, it was not unique either. It was estimated by the authorities in Berlin that during the second half of the War those called back from military service comprised more than one-third of the work-forces of many factories.[49]

Nothing could have put into sharper relief the essential problem of the German war-effort: that the only way adequately to supply the soldiers needed at the front was to call them back to Germany! The requirements of fighting industrial world war were, for a country with limited reserves of men and *matériel*, mutually contradictory. In addition, the ill-fated attempts to square the circle had important consequences for the home front. The severe labour-shortages, exacerbated by the Hindenburg Programme, brought the world of the front and the world of the home front into closer contact, helping to make each more aware of the injustices and privations of the other. They also make attempts to speak of a 'front generation' as a real thing, forged by the shared, uniform experience of men for whom combat in the First World War meant four years of uninterrupted fighting in the trenches, rather questionable.[50]

Labour shortages did not arise just in war industries. Indeed, in some respects it was easier for employers in war industries to deal with the problem. They could offer significantly higher wages than their counterparts whose factories produced for civilian needs, and they could lay claim to skilled men sent back from the front—an option not available to those producing for the domestic market. The labour shortages had particularly serious consequences for agriculture—which also suffered from a lack of planning in 1914 due to the expectation of a short, victorious

---

[48] Reports in BBA, Bestand 32/4324 and 4325.
[49] BLHA, Rep. 30 Berlin C, Polizeipräsidium Berlin, Tit. 47, no. 1958, fos. 229–338: Regierungs- und Gewerberat zu Berlin, 'Jahresbericht für die Kriegsjahre 1914–1918'.
[50] For discussion of the 'front generation' as an imaginary construct, and its impact upon the politics of post-war Germany, see Richard Bessel, 'The "Front Generation" and the Politics of the Weimar Republic', in Mark Roseman (ed.), *Generation Formation and Conflict in Modern Germany* (forthcoming).

war.[51] The mobilization not only of millions of men but also hundreds of thousands of horses left German agriculture in a bad way,[52] all the more so since it was the sector of the economy which offered the lowest remuneration. Although some relief was gained initially from the fact that about 300,000 agricultural workers from Congress Poland who found themselves in Germany when war had been declared and were forced to remain,[53] as Martin Schumacher has noted, the relatively high wages available in the armaments factories 'almost completely dried up the rural labour-market'.[54] The only new source of agricultural labour was prisoners of war, largely Russians, who often displayed little enthusiasm for hard work on German farms. Furthermore, the worst shortages were of skilled labour—of supervisory staff, of skilled workers who could operate and repair farm machinery, of wheelwrights, etc.—while the prisoners of war essentially made good the loss of day labourers.[55] Small farms were often affected even more severely than large ones. They were less able to afford the guards required when using war prisoners, and military service often claimed at one stroke both the labourer and the manager of the small farm.[56] This left the vast majority of German farms run by women, who lacked sufficient help to accomplish all the necessary work; according to one estimate from Baden in 1917, 80 per cent of farms there were being run by women.[57] In the eastern Prussian provinces the labour shortages were made still worse by the efforts of agents recruiting seasonal workers (for example, women who worked to bring in the sugar-beet harvest) for farms in central and western Germany.[58] By the middle of the War the labour shortage on the land had approached crisis proportions, as food shortages undermined morale and threatened the war effort. Once again, the needs of the German military for manpower to fight a world war undermined the ability of the German economy to supply the goods necessary to the fight that war.

---

[51] See Feldman, *Army, Industry and Labor*, 97–9; Martin Schumacher, *Land und Politik: Eine Untersuchung über politische Parteien und agrarische Interessen 1914–1923* (Düsseldorf, 1978), 33–5.

[52] The number of horses in the German army reached 1.5 million during the War. See Horst Rhode, 'Faktoren der deutschen Logistik im Ersten Weltkrieg' in Gerard Canini (ed.), *Les fronts invisibles: nourrir—fournir—soinger* (Nancy, 1984), 109.

[53] Ulrich Herbert, *Geschichte der Ausländerbeschäftigung in Deutschland 1880 bis 1980: Saisonarbeiter, Zwangsarbeiter, Gastarbeiter* (Berlin and Bonn, 1986), 82.

[54] Schumacher, *Land und Politik*, 35.

[55] MLHA, Ministerium des Innern, no. 16200, fos. 371–2: Großh. Statistisches Amt to Großh. Ministerium des Innern, 'Bericht über die Lage des Arbeitsmarktes im Großherzogtum Mecklenburg-Schwerin im Monat Mai 1916', Schwerin, 9 June 1916.

[56] See Robert G. Moeller, 'Dimensions of Social Conflict in the Great War: The View from the German Countryside', *Central European History*, 14: 2 (June 1981), 161–2.

[57] GLAK, 456/E.V.8., Bund 101: stellv. Gen. Kdo. XIV. A.K., Kriegsamtstelle, to Kriegsamtstelle XIV A.K., Vorstandsabteilung, Karlsruhe, 3 Feb. 1917.

[58] See APW, Rejencja Opoloska I, no. 2173, f. 339: Graf Matuschka to Kriegswirtschaftsamt des stellv. Gen.Kdo VI. A.K., Rittmeister Kraker v. Schwarzenfels, Leobschutz, 19 Jan. 1918.

During the War there were tremendous changes in the sectors of the German economy where people found work. Most striking was the enormous expansion of armaments production: on the eve of the Armistice it was estimated that between 2.5 and 3 million people were employed directly in Germany's munitions industries.[59] The labour shortages increased the opportunities to switch jobs, as workers took advantage of being a scarce commodity to move from employer to employer in search of higher pay.[60] War-related industries—to which scarce raw materials were channelled, in which the demand for labour was greatest, and where wages were the highest—attracted employees. Industries producing for civilian needs lost on all counts: their male employees were more likely to be conscripted; their wages were lower; they had greater difficulty getting the raw materials they needed.

Comparison of the numbers of employees in German factories employing ten or more people in 1913 and 1918 reveals the scope of the changes. In 1918, the German textile-industry employed fewer than one-quarter the number of men that it had employed in 1913 (down from 400,275 to 98,487) and less than three-fifths the number of women (down from 461,607 to 266,537), and the numbers of people employed in the building industry more than halved between 1913 and 1918. At the same time, the numbers employed in mining remained more or less constant, in metalworking they rose somewhat (with a decline of roughly 100,000 men more than compensated by a rise of roughly 200,000 women workers), in the chemical industry the numbers of men employed rose from 145,944 in 1913 to 256,353 in 1918 and of women from 26,749 to 208,877, and in the machine industry the number of adult male employees rose from 1,007,753 to 1,097,020 while the number of adult women employees shot up from 74,642 to 493,374. Altogether, the number of adult males employed in factories with ten or more employees fell from 5,409,546 to 3,875,676 between 1913 and 1918 (while the number of males under 17 rose from 384,489 to 421,293), and the number of adult women thus employed increased from 1,405,621 to 2,138,910 (while the number of females under 17 thus employed declined slightly, from 186,517 to 180,764).[61]

These changes had profound effects upon regional employment-structures, particularly in regions where war industries were concentrated. In the

---

[59] SHAD, Ministerium der Auswärtigen Angelegenheiten, no. 2494, Band I, fos. 46–9: Kgl. Gesandtschaft Berlin to Kgl. Ministerium der Auswärtigen Angelegenheiten, Berlin, 29 Oct. 1918.

[60] See e.g. MLHA, Ministerium des Innern, no. 16200, fos. 274–5: Großh. Statistisches Amt to Großh. Ministerium des Innern, 'Bericht der Zentralauskunftstelle für den Arbeitsmarkt im Großherzogtum Mecklenburg-Schwerin über die Lage des Arbeitsmarktes im Juni 1917', Schwerin, 10 July 1917.

[61] Figures from Waldemar Zimmermann, 'Die Veränderungen der Einkommens- und Lebensverhältnisse der deutschen Arbeiter durch den Krieg', in Meerwarth, Günther, and Zimmermann, Die Einwirkung des Krieges, 350–1.

Regierungsbezirk Danzig, for example, the number of factory workers rose from 49,000 in 1913 to 60,000 in 1917, and in the Regierungsbezirk Potsdam (which included Spandau) the number employed in factories rose from 220,000 to 343,000 in the same period.[62] Not all industrial centres gained, however: Saxony lost nearly 10 per cent of its population between 1910 and 1917 (while Prussia as a whole lost less than 2 per cent), a fact which the Saxon Interior Ministry attributed both to the poor food-supply and to 'the reduction in employment possibilities'.[63] In many rural and eastern regions, where war industries were thin on the ground, the number of factory workers declined particularly sharply: between 1913 and 1917 their number fell in the Regierungsbezirk Gumbinnen in East Prussia from 26,000 to 16,000, in the Regierungsbezirk Posen from 32,160 to 21,400, in the Regierungsbezirk Breslau from 159,986 to 111,670, in the Regierungsbezirk Liegnitz from 127,696 to 82,029, and in the Regierungsbezirk Frankfurt/Oder from 114,500 to 78,160.[64] Thus the needs of the war economy gave a new twist to the east-to-west migration patterns which had been established as Germany's industrial economy grew during the second half of the nineteenth century.

Many who abandoned work in agriculture, as well as employment in such industries as textiles, moved into cities where major armaments factories were located, such as Spandau and Essen, or where there were large navy-yards, such as Danzig.[65] However, this is not to say that all, or even most, German cities gained population during the War. Some gained while others lost. Among the winners were Essen (which—including Altenessen and Borbeck—had 406,403 inhabitants in December 1910 and contained a civilian population of 454,792 in 1917), Danzig (where comparable figures were 170,337 for 1910 and 177,840 for 1917), and Spandau (which had 85,855 inhabitants in 1910 and a civilian population of 93,659 in 1917).[66] Other notable cities which gained population were Dortmund, Kiel, and Mannheim. However, most urban centres lost population once the men went off to the front. Among the biggest losers were Berlin (where the population dropped from 2,071,257 in December 1910 to 1,681,916 in December 1917), Hamburg (931,035 in 1910 to 811,908 in 1917), Elberfeld and Barmen (from 170,195 to 136,703 and 169,214 to 138,362 respectively), Strasburg (from

[62] SHAD, Ministerium der Auswärtigen Angelegenheiten, no. 2494, Band I, fos. 19–21: Kgl. Gesandtschaft Berlin to Kgl. Ministerium der Auswärtigen Angelegenheiten, Berlin, 12 Oct. 1918.

[63] Ibid. fo. 118: Kgl. Sächsisches Ministerium des Innern to Ministerium der Auswärtigen Angelegenheiten, Dresden, 16 Nov. 1918.

[64] Ibid.

[65] In Danzig, of the women who took up work in the city for the first time during the War the largest number came from the land. See GStAB, Rep. 180, no. 15913: 'Bericht über den Arbeitsmarkt in Danzig während des Krieges', Danzig, 17 Feb. 1919.

[66] *Statistisches Jahrbuch für das Deutsche Reich* 1919, 18.

178,891 to 138,824), and Plauen (where the population fell from 121,272 in 1910 to 87,602 in 1917).[67] This meant not only that many German cities held significantly fewer people during wartime than before 1914, but also that the demobilization would result in a huge and sudden increase in their population.

The population left behind in wartime Germany was, in greater proportion than ever before, female, and with the recruitment of millions of men into the armed forces the position of women in the labour market altered considerably. The rapid rise in unemployment which followed the outbreak of war in August and September 1914 hit working women hard—for example, in the clothing and textile industries, which employed large numbers of women and which suffered from being cut off from sources of raw materials (particularly of imported cotton).[68] But things soon changed. The enormous fluctuations in women's employment outside the home were reflected in changes in the number of female members of compulsory health-insurance schemes, which registered a sudden drop immediately after the outbreak of war and then a sharp rise in 1915 and 1916:[69]

| | |
|---|---|
| July 1914 | 3,705,577 |
| October 1914 | 2,300,000 |
| July 1915 | 3,636,371 |
| July 1916 | 4,200,720 |
| July 1917 | 4,269,656 |
| February 1918 | 3,782,425 |

As noted above, the number of women employed in factories with ten or more employees increased by more than 50 per cent during the War, with particularly steep rises in mining, metalworking, machine-building, and chemicals. The number of women working on the railways increased tenfold during the War; thousands found jobs with municipal tram-companies and with the military authorities; women were trained in skilled factory-work previously reserved for men; and many occupations were opened up to women for the first time.[70] In the AEG factories in the Brunnenstraße in

[67] *Statistisches Jahrbuch für das Deutsche Reich* 1919, 18.

[68] The unemployment among women textile-workers lasted well into the War, and the women were not really mobilized effectively for the labour-short economy. See Ute Daniel, 'Fiktionen, Friktionen und Fakten: Frauenlohnarbeit im Ersten Weltkrieg', in Mai (ed.), *Arbeiterschaft in Deutschland*, 299–304; Daniel, *Arbeiterfrauen in der Kriegsgesellschaft*, 67–71.

[69] Figures given in Michael Schneider, *Die Christlichen Gewerkschaften 1894–1933* (Bonn, 1982), 365. These figures do not reflect the absolute numbers of women employed during the War, but they do indicate trends. They probably understate by a considerable margin the numbers of women earning wages, as some insurance organizations did not report their figures regularly and as home workers were not included in these figures at all during the War. See Daniel, 'Fiktionen, Friktionen und Fakten', 279–80. The reasons for the drop of nearly 500,000 between July 1917 and Feb. 1918 are unclear.

[70] The key text now is the superb study by Ute Daniel, *Arbeiterfrauen in der Kriegsgesellschaft*. See also Hilde Oppenheimer and Hilde Radomski, *Die Probleme der Frauenarbeit in der Übergangs-wirtschaft* (Mannheim, Berlin, and Leipzig, 1918), 26, 127; Marie-Elisabeth Lüders, *Die Entwick-*

Berlin (Wedding) the number of women rose from about 3,000 before the War to 11,000 in 1917;[71] the firm of Thyssen, which before the War had a work-force of only about 1,800, employed 24,000 by November 1918, of whom about one-third were women; and in the Krupp works, where no women had been employed before the War, the total number of employees rose from 41,000 when the conflict began to 110,000 on 1 November 1918, of whom 30,000 were women.[72]

The recruitment of women into munitions works and other war-related employment left large gaps elsewhere. The problems this created for agriculture were particularly serious for a country facing mounting food-shortages. Further cause for complaint was the increasing difficulty during the second half of the War in finding anyone willing to carry out many menial tasks usually reserved for women—'domestic work and other simple activities such as peeling potatoes in public kitchens'.[73] In particular, it became extremely difficult to find 'strong young individuals' willing to take up positions in domestic service; they could earn much more in the armaments factories.[74] While their working conditions in industry were often far from ideal, the new employment opportunities which wartime labour-shortages opened up for working women offered many a temporary escape from the severe limitations which had circumscribed their choice of jobs hitherto.

Who were the women who streamed into munitions works and other industries during the War? A portion were drawn into paid employment by the loss of household income when husbands, fathers, or brothers were called to the colours, or by the steep wartime rises in the cost of living.[75] Very few

*lung der gewerblichen Frauenarbeit im Kriege* (Munich and Leipzig, 1920), 30–54; Harry Oppenborn, *Die Tätigkeit der Frau in der deutschen Kriegswirtschaft* (Hamburg, 1928), 41–3; Stephan Bajohr, *Die Hälfte der Fabrik: Geschichte der Frauenarbeit in Deutschland 1914 bis 1945* (Marburg, 1979), 121; Seidel, *Frauenarbeit im Ersten Weltkrieg*, 51–4; Richard Bessel, ' "Eine nicht allzu große Beunruhigung des Arbeitsmarktes": Frauenarbeit und Demobilmachung in Deutschland nach dem Ersten Weltkrieg', *Geschichte und Gesellschaft*, 9 (1983), 214–15. For evidence of women working as office assistants with the military authorities, see BAP, RMwD, no. 18/1, fo. 53: Vorstand der Kriegsamtstelle Posen, Posen, 21 Dec. 1917 (*sic!* This should read 1918); for evidence of women having worked as nurses behind the lines, see the files concerning their dismissal in PLA, Rep. 60, no. 3106, 3107, 3109, and 3110.

[71] BLHA, Rep. 30 Berlin C, Polizeipräsidium Berlin, Tit. 47, no. 1958, fos. 210–15: Kgl. Gewerbeinspektion to Regierungs- und Gewerberat, 'Die Entwicklung der Lohnverhältnisse', Berlin, 28 Sept. 1918.

[72] See Martin Sogemeier, *Die Entwicklung und Regelung des Arbeitsmarktes im rheinisch-westfälischen Industriegebiet im Kriege und in der Nachkriegszeit* (Jena, 1922), 10–55; Renate Bridenthal, 'Beyond Kinder, Küche, Kirche: Weimar Women at Work', *Central European History*, 6 (1973), 155.

[73] MLHA, Ministerium des Innern, no. 16200, fo. 253: Großh. Statistisches Amt, Zentralauskunftstelle für den Arbeitsmarkt, to Großh. Ministerium des Innern, 'Bericht der Zentralauskunftstelle über die Lage des Arbeitsmarktes im Großherzogtum Mecklenburg-Schwerin im September 1917'.

[74] GLAK, 456/E.V.8., Bund 86: stellv. Gen.Kdo. XIV A.K., Kriegsamtstelle, to stellv. Gen.Kdo., Aufklärungsstelle, Karlsruhe, 19 Nov. 1919.

[75] See Sogemeier, *Die Entwicklung des Arbeitsmarktes*, 50.

of the women who came to work in war-related industries had worked in these branches before 1914, although large numbers had had previous experience of factory work. Many had previously found employment in industries producing for civilian needs (such as the textile industry), in domestic service, or on the land; others—especially teenagers entering the job market—had had no experience of paid employment at all.[76] Generally the women who took advantage of the new employment possibilities created by the War came from among the working class; the majority were in their thirties and forties; most had worked previously; and often women took up the places that their men had vacated. For example, according to statistics compiled by the transport-workers' union (Deutscher Transportarbeiter-Verband) in October 1915, roughly 20 per cent (2,800) of the 14,000 women employees of the 70 major tram-operators in Germany were the wives of tram workers who had been called up;[77] and from Berlin it was reported that the wives or older children of soldiers often found work in the factories which had employed their husbands or fathers.[78] According to a comprehensive statistical investigation of female labour in Bavarian war-industries as of December 1916, of the married women workers, 70 per cent were the wives of soldiers. The great majority, however, were single: over 65 per cent in the case of the Bavarian statistics. (Nearly 5.4 per cent were widows.)[79]

[76] For details of former occupations of women drawn into war work, see Bessel, ' "Eine nicht allzu große Beunruhigung des Arbeitsmarktes" ', 215–16; Daniel, 'Fiktionen, Friktionen und Fakten', 284–8; Ute Daniel, 'Women's Work in Industry and Family: Germany, 1914–1918', in Richard Wall and Jay Winter (eds.), *The Upheaval of War: Family, Work and Welfare in Europe, 1914–1918* (Cambridge, 1988), 268–78; Daniel, *Arbeiterfrauen in der Kriegsgesellschaft*, 42–50. The most detailed statistical breakdown of women working in war industries was assembled for Bavaria in Dec. 1916, when information on 90,865 women was tabulated. The main difficulty with the Bavarian figures is that they underestimate the numbers who came from agriculture, as moving out of agricultural employment was forbidden and thus women were not likely to admit to having done it. See Bayerisches Statistisches Landesamt (ed.), *Die Frau in der bayerischen Kriegsindustrie nach einer amtlichen Erhebung aus dem Jahre 1917* (Beiträge zur Statistik Bayerns, 92; Munich, 1920), 12–13.

[77] Oppenborn, *Die Tätigkeit der Frau*, 42; Daniel, *Arbeiterfrauen in der Kriegsgesellschaft*, 65.

[78] BLHA, Rep. 30 Berlin C, Polizeipräsidium Berlin, Tit. 47, no. 1958, fo. 327.

[79] 28.88% of the 90,865 female employees recorded as working in 771 Bavarian factories engaged in war production were married, 65.22% were single, 5.41% were widowed and 0.49% divorced. These figures differed only marginally from pre-war percentages:

|                | Single | Married | Widowed or Divorced |
| -------------- | ------ | ------- | ------------------- |
| Germany, 1907  | 67.1   | 21.3    | 11.6                |
| Bavaria, 1907  | 57.8   | 33.3    | 8.9                 |
| Bavaria, 1917  | 66.22  | 28.88   | 5.90                |

See Bayerisches Statistisches Landesamt (ed.), *Die Frau in der bayerischen Kriegsindustrie*, 12–13. Evidence from Upper Silesia also indicates that single women predominated in heavy industrial work, in particular in mining. See APW, Rejencja Opolska I, no. 9880, fos. 343–4: Kgl. Gewerbeinspektor to Regierungspräsident in Oppeln, 'Regelung und Besserung der Arbeits- und Lohnverhältnisse der Arbeiterinnen Oberschlesiens', Beuthen, 23 Oct. 1918.

Generally such employment was regarded, both by the employers and by the women involved, as an emergency response to an emergency situation. Typically, as the district administration noted in a report about the wartime economy in Berlin, the use of female labour during the War was viewed among employers 'predominantly only as a temporary replacement for the missing men'.[80] Long hours (with many women having to endure twelve-hour shifts doing heavy work),[81] bad working-conditions (for example, poor sanitary conditions, where employers failed to provide sufficient toilet and washroom facilities for their new female labour-force), and, in some cases, hostility from male colleagues gave women added reason to regard their wartime employment as temporary and something to be jettisoned at the first opportunity.[82] Yet the women who took up war-related factory-work do not comprise the whole story. Many others found employment not in factories but in the form of home work.[83] The war economy gave many women an opportunity to work at home as seamstresses, producing uniforms, gas masks, shoes, containers for grenades and shells. For many women, who otherwise might have felt compelled to take up work in factories (as the authorities hoped), such work allowed them to stay in the home, perhaps looking after children, while earning enough to subsist. After the surge in unemployment in 1914, the war economy presented German women with temporary but unprecedented opportunities—as well as unprecedented pressures—to engage in paid employment.

The same was true of adolescents. They too were faced with new possibilities of employment in an economy characterized by a desperate shortage of labour, and they too faced pressure to contribute to household incomes constantly being eroded by inflation. Compared with 1913, by 1918 the number of males under 17 employed in factories with ten or more employees had increased by nearly 10 per cent, and this increase was concentrated in particular branches of industry: in machine-building, for example, it grew from 86,095 to 136,967 (an increase of 59 per cent).[84] (Among girls under 17 the total fell slightly, as noted above. This was due perhaps to a need to remain at home to care for younger siblings while

---

[80] BLHA, Rep. 30 Berlin C, Polizeipräsidium Berlin, Tit. 47, no. 1958, fo. 275.

[81] See e.g. APW, Rejencja Opolska I, no. 9880, fos. 143–4: Kgl. Gewerbeinspektor, Kattowitz, 31 Mar. 1917.

[82] Ibid., fos. 302–9: 'Eingabe der Bezirksorganisation der Gruben- und Hüttenarbeiterinnen Oberschlesiens im Verbande katholischer Vereine erwerbstätiger Frauen und Mädchen Deutschlands betreffend Regelung und Besserung der Arbeits- und Lohnverhältnisse' to Oberschlesischer Berg- und Hüttenmännischer Verein, Berlin-Kattowitz, 27 May 1918; ibid. fos. 322–6: Kgl. Gewerbe-Inspektor to Regierungs-und Gewerberat in Oppeln, Kattowitz, 10 Aug. 1918; ibid., fos. 349–64: Kgl. Gewerbeinspektion to Regierungspräsident, Geliwitz, 28 Sept. 1918. The failure of employers to build women's washrooms was not simply a product of miserliness or insensitivity; during wartime it was extremely difficult to get the necessary building-materials or building-permits.

[83] Daniel, 'Women's Work in Industry and Family', 276–8; Daniel, *Arbeiterfrauen in der Kriegsgesellschaft*, 65–7.

[84] See Zimmermann, 'Die Veränderungen der Einkommens- und Lebensverhältnisse', 350–1.

mothers were working; nevertheless, certain war-related industries—such as metalworking, machine-building, and chemicals—registered fairly substantial increases in the employment of adolescent females.) Although the wages they received remained far below those of adult men—and even below those of adult women—many were able to earn amounts which appeared rather substantial and which were considerably higher than what they might have earned in peacetime.[85]

The War changed the composition of Germany's labour force in other ways as well, in particular with regard to the employment of foreign labour.[86] At the time war broke out there had been roughly 1.2 million foreign labourers working in Germany, about 700,000 in industry and 500,000 in agriculture. During the early stages of the War the number of foreigners employed in Germany dropped sharply. Many—in particular, those from Austria-Hungary—were called back home to serve in the armed forces of their own countries; others—in particular, from neutral states—lost their jobs in the unemployment which accompanied the outbreak of war; and the main source of foreign labour—Congress Poland—became enemy territory.[87] By the second half of the War, however, the Germans had pushed the Tsarist armies out of Poland, and the growing need for labour meant that the numbers of foreigners working in Germany rose again. In September 1917 it was estimated that the total number of foreign Polish workers in Germany stood at roughly 600,000,[88] and in 1918 the 700,000 foreign agricultural workers exceeded the numbers employed in Germany before 1914.[89]

Large though these numbers were, they came to be overshadowed by the numbers of prisoners of war put to work in Germany. Prisoner-of-war labour was used both by many larger industrial concerns, which found it easier to provide the required living-quarters for the prisoners than did smaller employers,[90] and, particularly, in agriculture. Altogether more than 2.5 million enemy soldiers were taken prisoner by the Germans during the First World

---

[85] Eve Rosenhaft, 'A World Upside Down: Delinquency, Family and Work in the Lives of German Working-Class Youth 1914–1918', (paper delivered to the conference on 'The European Family and the Great War: Stability and Instability 1900–1930' at Pembroke College, Cambridge, 11–14 Sept. 1983), 20.

[86] On foreign labour see Friedrich Zunkel, 'Die ausländischen Arbeiter in der deutschen Kriegswirtschaftspolitik des Ersten Weltkrieges', in Gerhard A. Ritter (ed.), Entstehung und Wandel der modernen Gesellschaft. Festschrift für Hans Rosenberg zum 65. Geburtstag (Berlin, 1970), 280–311; Ulrich Herbert, 'Zwangsarbeit als Lernprozeß: Die Beschäftigung ausländischer Arbeiter in der westdeutschen Industrie im Ersten Weltkrieg', in Archiv für Sozialgeschichte, 24 (1984), 285–304; id., Geschichte der Ausländerbeschäftigung, 82–113; Daniel, Arbeiterfrauen in der Kriegsgesellschaft, 57–61.

[87] See Herbert, Geschichte der Ausländerbeschäftigung, 87.

[88] APW, Rejencja Opolska I, no. 12410, fo. 217: 'Aufzeichnung über die Sitzung am 22.9.17 in Breslau', comments by Hauptmann Krüger, stellv. Gen. kdo. Breslau. See also Herbert, Geschichte der Ausländerbeschäftigung, 91.

[89] Schumacher, Land und Politik, 35.

[90] See APW, Akta Miasta Wroclawia, no. 30999, fo. 278: Breslauer Kriegsausschuß der Industrie to Magistrat, Breslau, 21 Oct. 1915.

War, of whom 535,411 had been in the French army and 1,434,529 in the Russian. In August 1916, of the 1,625,000 soldiers in German captivity, 735,000 had been put to work in agriculture and 331,000 in industry; in coal mining they comprised 14 per cent of the work-force in December 1916.[91] By September 1917 the total number reached nearly 2 million (about 800,000 of whom were employed in agriculture and nearly 400,000 in industry).[92] However, the use of prisoner-of-war and other foreign labour was not without its problems. The productivity of prisoners, whose motivation to aid the German war-effort was not particularly great, remained comparatively low; guards were needed to oversee the prisoners; and towards the end of the War increasing numbers of foreign workers fled from their place of work.[93]

With millions of men called away to war, those who remained behind— often women and youths who lacked the skills and training of the men they had replaced at the work-bench—had to adapt quickly and develop new skills. However, apprenticeship and industrial training systems were among the domestic casualties of the War. Young people abandoned apprenticeships for better-paying jobs for which intensive training was not necessary; the numbers of apprenticeships were reduced to a fraction of pre-war totals;[94] and the authorities jettisoned apprenticeship and training requirements in a desperate attempt to bring people into production as quickly as possible. What is more, the demand for their labour lent adolescents an independence which their seniors often found difficult to accept. They now had money in their pockets and allegedly felt they could do as they pleased—which in early 1916 provided sufficient cause for the district authorities in Pirna, in Saxony, to ban 'the pointless gadding-about of young people after nine in the evening'.[95] As pay differentials narrowed due to the wartime inflation, as hundreds of thousands of people took on new jobs with little or no training, and as lines of age and sex demarcation were breached due to the demands of an overstretched war-economy, structures of status and authority in and around the workplace faced radical challenges.

The same occurred within the home. With the men away, women became the head in millions of households, while young people often commanded higher earnings than previously and made substantial contributions to the family budget. Old structures of authority no longer appeared to function. To many contemporary observers the changes heralded a moral crisis, as

[91] Herbert, *Geschichte der Ausländerbeschäftigung*, 84–5.

[92] In Oct. 1918 it was still estimated that German agriculture had come to employ roughly 800,000 prisoners of war. See SHAD, Ministerium der Auswärtigen Angelegenheiten, no. 2494, Band I, fos. 46–9.

[93] Herbert, *Geschichte der Ausländerbeschäftigung*, 86, 94.

[94] In Berlin in 1916 the number of apprenticeships stood at one-third of the pre-war figure. See Rosenhaft, 'A World Upside Down', 20.

[95] SHAD, Amtshauptmannschaft Pirna, no. 495, fos. 73–7: Amtshauptmannschaft to Kgl. Ministerium des Innern, Pirna, 30 Jan. 1916.

values of thrift and respect seemed to have been thrown overboard and the social fabric seemed to be disintegrating. Without the 'strong hand' of the father, children appeared out of the control of their elders; theft seemed to reach epidemic proportions; moral standards no longer seemed to be upheld. Worries about the disappearance of an allegedly healthy social order, combined with fears of moral decay and ruin, surfaced in anxious reports by the government about conditions within Germany. For example, in 1917 in Berlin, it was claimed, only 8 per cent of adolescents working in industry were under the supervision of both a father and a mother, while 18 per cent had neither parent present; this, it was alleged, was a prime cause for the 'frightening increase in the tendency to theft' among youths during the second half of the War.[96] Even in tight-knit mining-communities the social cement began to loosen, as people stole bread-ration cards from one another and took food from other people's allotments.[97] Even what had been the most stable social networks seemed vulnerable to the corrosive effects of the War.

Further concern arose from the disruption of the state education system. During the War teachers became in short supply, as many were called up for the armed forces; by the beginning of 1916, more than half the primary school teachers (*Volksschullehrer*) in Prussia, for example, had been conscripted.[98] Remaining teachers often had to teach more than one class (in rural areas in more than one school), lessons were cut, and teaching was frequently carried out on a shift system. Many school buildings were requisitioned by the army for military purposes: in Breslau, for example, more than half the city's school buildings were being used by the military at any given point during the War, and between August 1914 and March 1915 only eight of the city's seventy-two school buildings were available for teaching.[99] During the winter of 1916–17 schools were shut because of the cold resulting from inadequate coal-supplies; children frequently stayed away from school in order to queue for rationed food and fuel or to help working mothers by caring for younger siblings; and in the autumn of 1918 the influenza epidemic kept large numbers of children from school.[100] Thus the schooling of many children was interrupted for long periods, and as a consequence yet more young people were left to their own devices, beyond the control of adults. Yet another institution which served to enforce social discipline among young people had been severely disrupted.

---

[96] BLHA, Rep. 30 Berlin C, Polizeipräsidium Berlin, Tit. 47, no. 1958, fo. 285.

[97] Zimmermann, ' "Alle sollen auf dem Altar des Vaterlandes ein Opfer bringen" ', 74.

[98] Klaus Saul, 'Jugend im Schatten des Krieges: Vormilitärische Ausbildung, Kriegswirtshaftlicher Einsatz, Schulalltag in Deutschland 1914–1918', *Militärgeschichtliche Mitteilungen* (1983), no. 2, 112.

[99] See the report of the Breslau city administration about the wartime crisis of the city's school system, in APW, Akta Miasta Wroclawia, no. 31021, fos. 309–11: Magistrat to 'sämtliche Zeitungen', Breslau, 17 Feb. 1919.

[100] Saul, 'Jugend im Schatten des Krieges', 113–14.

With schools often closed and children often lacking parental supervision at home, fears multiplied about youth running out of control. According to a report for 1917 on youth in care in Pomerania: 'The children are mostly left to their own devices, they no longer obey their mothers, and all too often the inadequate diet induces them to misappropriate other people's property.'[101] From Köslin came the claim in October 1916 that growing 'licentiousness' during wartime among female pupils made increased resort to 'correctional education' necessary.[102] In the rural Pomeranian district of Grimmen the Landrat reported in August 1918 that 'school-age children are falling into neglect (*Verwahrlosung*) and as a consequence of inadequate supervision are committing thefts':

In most of the cases the fathers are in the field and the mothers must go off to work daily in order to provide for the family, so that parental supervision at home is lacking. The children are left to their own devices, stay away from school and rove about.[103]

Again, the appropriate response was said to be 'corrective education' for those children 'where any supervision is lacking and when the parents themselves are guilty of moral offences'.

Parallel to fears about the alleged moral decline of German youth were fears that the War had led to a loosening of moral standards among German women. The spectre of an uncontrollable increase in prostitution surfaced repeatedly in the reports of agitated state bureaucrats, and seemed to require special attention. In July 1918 the Prussian Minister of the Interior recommended the adoption of the 'Bielefeld System' of assigning specific social workers to look after women judged to be in moral danger; as a consequence of the long war, it was feared, 'a large number of young girls and women' were on the way to 'moral decline' and a considerable increase was expected after the War in the number 'of women who enter into prostitution or are on the way to doing so'.[104] Few things so symbolized loss of control as the alleged spread of sexual promiscuity among women.

Of course the reports of alarmed and frightened officials did not necessarily reflect reality. One may question, for example, whether the War really did cause a massive increase in the number of girls who turned to prostitution (especially at a time when on average roughly 4 million of their potential

---

[101] APS, Oberpräsidium von Pommern, no. 2915: Landeshauptmann der Provinz Pommern to Oberpräsident, 'Bericht über die Ausführung der Fürsorgeerziehung Minderjähriger im Rechnungsjahr 1917', Stettin, 3 Oct. 1918. See also ibid.: Regierungspräsident to Oberpräsident in Stettin, Stralsund, 14 Nov. 1916.

[102] Ibid.: Regierungspräsident to Oberpräsident in Stettin, Köslin, 26 Oct. 1916.

[103] PLA, Rep. 65c, no. 1186, fo. 40: Landrat to Regierungspräsident in Stralsund, Grimmen, 21 Aug. 1918. See also the report about youth in care in Stralsund, ibid., fo. 37: Bürgermeister und Rat to Regierungspräsident, Stralsund, 26 Aug. 1918.

[104] BAP, RMwD, no. 21, fos. 13–15: the Minister des Innern, Berlin, 15 July 1918.

customers were on the battlefield), or whether women really did, as one report had it, demand that their husbands be conscripted because they had adopted a 'dissolute' life-style due to high wartime wages.[105] Such utterances probably reveal less about what actually was happening than what people *believed* was happening and *ought* to be happening. Germans looked forward to the post-war transition as a transition from social chaos to social order—to a world in which people knew and accepted their place.

Wartime changes in social relations were bound up closely with changes in people's economic circumstances. Incomes and prices represented not just material values; they were also expressions of social relationships and values, which were profoundly shaken in a wartime Germany characterized by inflation, shortages, and a thriving black market. Wages and, to a lesser extent, salaries rose steeply during the War. However, real incomes generally declined fairly considerably, as increases in earnings failed to keep pace with increases in prices. (See Tables 3 and 4).

Table 3. *Average Daily Wages of Male Workers in 350 Factories, 1914–1918*
(Marks, last two weeks of month)

| Industry | 1914 | | 1915 | | 1916 | | 1917 | | 1918 | | Sept. 1918 as % of Mar. 1914 |
|---|---|---|---|---|---|---|---|---|---|---|---|
| | Mar. | Sept. | Mar. | Sept. | Mar. | Sept. | Mar. | Sept. | Mar. | Sept. | |
| Quarrying | 4.48 | 4.00 | 4.13 | 4.66 | 4.98 | 5.41 | 6.12 | 7.07 | 7.78 | 8.79 | 196.2 |
| Metal industry | 5.54 | 5.67 | 6.29 | 6.93 | 7.47 | 8.02 | 9.88 | 11.81 | 12.01 | 12.94 | 233.6 |
| Machine building | 5.32 | 5.22 | 6.41 | 7.01 | 7.39 | 7.91 | 9.19 | 10.79 | 12.93 | 13.04 | 245.1 |
| Electrical industry | 4.52 | 4.02 | 4.99 | 5.31 | 5.76 | 7.44 | 9.25 | 10.93 | 12.06 | 13.46 | 297.8 |
| Chemical industry | 5.16 | 4.97 | 5.37 | 6.07 | 6.43 | 6.93 | 8.09 | 10.01 | 10.50 | 11.95 | 231.6 |
| Textiles | 3.64 | 3.19 | 3.67 | 4.05 | 4.00 | 4.17 | 4.45 | 5.18 | 5.79 | 6.47 | 177.7 |
| Paper | 3.93 | 4.17 | 4.49 | 4.88 | 5.08 | 5.56 | 6.29 | 7.37 | 8.27 | 9.43 | 239.9 |
| Leather and rubber | 5.07 | 4.95 | 4.94 | 5.78 | 5.85 | 6.37 | 7.30 | 7.81 | 8.21 | 8.78 | 173.2 |
| Wood | 4.22 | 4.30 | 4.56 | 4.60 | 5.20 | 5.61 | 6.22 | 7.80 | 7.77 | 9.96 | 236.0 |
| Food processing | 5.69 | 5.78 | 5.94 | 5.96 | 5.88 | 6.14 | 6.47 | 7.51 | 7.81 | 8.52 | 149.7 |
| Clothing | 3.79 | 2.72 | 3.58 | 3.70 | 4.00 | 3.68 | 4.94 | 5.98 | 6.82 | 8.17 | 215.6 |
| Printing trades | 6.65 | 5.95 | 6.74 | 7.24 | 7.51 | 7.69 | 9.23 | 9.10 | 9.59 | 11.68 | 175.6 |

*Source: Reichsarbeitsblatt, 17:8 (1919), 622.*

[105] This allegation may be found in the 'Jahresbericht für die Kriegsjahre' for Berlin written by Regierungs- und Gewerberat Hartmann, in BLHA, Rep. 30 Berlin C, Polizeipräsidium Berlin, Tit. 47, no. 1958, fo. 232.

Table 4. *Average Daily Wages of Female Workers in 350 Factories, 1914–1918*
(Marks, last two weeks of month)

| Industry | 1914 | | 1915 | | 1916 | | 1917 | | 1918 | | Sept. 1918 as % of Mar. 1914 |
|---|---|---|---|---|---|---|---|---|---|---|---|
| | Mar. | Sept. | Mar. | Sept. | Mar. | Sept. | Mar. | Sept. | Mar. | Sept. | |
| Quarrying | 1.67 | 1.49 | 1.62 | 1.87 | 1.96 | 2.19 | 2.57 | 2.87 | 3.10 | 3.87 | 231.7 |
| Metal industry | 2.05 | 1.66 | 2.22 | 3.02 | 3.46 | 4.11 | 4.68 | 5.67 | 5.88 | 6.65 | 324.4 |
| Machine building | 2.28 | 1.96 | 2.87 | 3.20 | 3.63 | 3.88 | 4.31 | 4.88 | 6.01 | 6.26 | 274.6 |
| Electrical industry | 2.75 | 2.09 | 3.01 | 3.40 | 3.91 | 4.80 | 5.24 | 6.18 | 6.58 | 7.35 | 267.3 |
| Chemical industry | 2.36 | 1.92 | 2.35 | 2.62 | 3.08 | 3.55 | 4.11 | 5.21 | 5.93 | 6.60 | 279.7 |
| Textiles | 2.30 | 2.05 | 2.22 | 2.32 | 2.41 | 2.33 | 2.57 | 3.31 | 3.92 | 4.29 | 186.5 |
| Paper | 2.15 | 2.23 | 2.29 | 2.53 | 2.64 | 2.85 | 3.65 | 4.09 | 4.57 | 5.37 | 249.8 |
| Leather and rubber | 2.82 | 2.37 | 2.49 | 2.77 | 3.05 | 3.18 | 3.79 | 4.15 | 4.18 | 4.82 | 170.9 |
| Wood | 1.99 | 1.78 | 2.31 | 1.95 | 2.21 | 2.59 | 3.17 | 3.81 | 4.36 | 5.45 | 273.9 |
| Food processing | 2.10 | 1.89 | 2.09 | 2.31 | 2.40 | 2.89 | 2.84 | 3.72 | 4.04 | 4.24 | 201.9 |
| Clothing | 2.25 | 1.50 | 2.14 | 1.79 | 2.24 | 2.13 | 2.81 | 3.50 | 3.94 | 4.92 | 218.7 |
| Printing trades | 2.56 | 2.30 | 2.29 | 2.64 | 2.82 | 2.93 | 3.22 | 3.77 | 4.27 | 5.10 | 199.2 |

*Source*: as Table 3.

In many cases, the outbreak of war was followed by cuts in wages, and the substantial rise in money wages did not come until the second half of the War. Not surprisingly, wages rose most swiftly in war-related industries, while workers in industries meeting primarily civilian needs tended to fall behind in the earnings league. Thus it was in the metal, machine, electrical, and chemical industries that wages rose the most, while textiles and food processing were among the sectors where wages rose least.[106] As a percentage of nominal wages in 1914, women's wages tended to rise more than those of men—a reflection of the narrowing of pay differentials which accompanied wartime inflation. Nevertheless, by the end of the War women still received on average only about half the wages of men working in the same industries.[107]

[106] See also Gerhard Bry, *Wages in Germany 1871–1945* (Princeton, NJ, 1960), 200, 434–5; Kocka, *Facing Total War*, 20. The discrepancies between the figures given here (taken directly from the *Reichsarbeitsblatt*) and those in Bry and Kocka (who takes his figures from Bry) are due to errors in Bry. Thus, for example, the number of factories involved was 350, not 370; the average male worker's wage in quarrying in Mar. 1914 was 4.48 Marks, not the 4.68 Marks given in Bry, and so forth.

[107] Detailed statistical investigations of different groups of industries in Bavaria during the War suggest similar patterns. See Bry, *Wages in Germany*, 199, 433: figures taken from Karl

Changes in earnings were a consequence not only of wage rates but also of hours worked. In this regard as well considerable changes took place during the War. Table 5 shows the number of days worked in the 350 factories which provided the wages figures discussed above.

Table 5. *Days Worked by Adult Workers, 350 Factories, 1914–1918,*
(Last two weeks of month)

| Month | Days Worked | | | Index (Mar. 1914 = 100) | | |
|---|---|---|---|---|---|---|
| | Men | Women | Total | Men | Women | Total |
| March 1914 | 1,997,052 | 315,822 | 2,312,874 | 100.0 | 100.0 | 100.0 |
| September 1914 | 1,452,297 | 249,620 | 1,701,917 | 72.7 | 79.0 | 73.6 |
| March 1915 | 1,693,173 | 312,921 | 2,006,094 | 84.8 | 99.1 | 86.7 |
| September 1915 | 1,650,540 | 382,808 | 2,033,258 | 82.6 | 121.2 | 87.9 |
| March 1916 | 1,664,224 | 468,168 | 2,132,392 | 83.3 | 148.2 | 92.2 |
| September 1916 | 1,698,786 | 566,160 | 2,264,946 | 85.1 | 179.3 | 97.9 |
| March 1917 | 1,897,134 | 704,499 | 2,601,633 | 95.0 | 223.1 | 112.5 |
| September 1917 | 2,024,464 | 739,209 | 2,763,673 | 101.4 | 234.1 | 119.5 |
| March 1918 | 2,069,792 | 771,478 | 2,841,270 | 103.6 | 244.3 | 122.8 |
| September 1918 | 2,115,936 | 754,414 | 2,870,350 | 106.0 | 238.9 | 124.1 |

*Source*: *Reichsarbeitsblatt*, 17:8 (1919), 619.

These figures reflect clearly the economic disruption, huge military call-up, and high levels of unemployment which followed the declaration of war, as well as the increased working hours later in the War and—from late 1916—the effects of bringing men back from the front to supply badly needed labour at home. The number of shifts worked by women increased much more swiftly from 1915 onwards than did the number worked by men; yet, despite the fact that millions of men were away in uniform, by late 1917 more shifts were being worked by men than before the War—an indication of the long hours which people had to work. The total numbers of days worked rose in industries which produced directly for the war effort and generally offered higher wages, while they fell in industries focused largely on the civilian market.[108] Since workers in war industries tended both to put in longer hours and to receive higher wages, the increases in the hours worked widened the earnings differentials between those employed in

Kreiner, 'Die Arbeits-, Lohn- und Produktionsverhältnisse der bayrischen Industrie im Juni 1914, Oktober 1918 und Mai 1919, auf Grund der Wirtschaftserhebung des Staatskommissars für Demobilmachung', *Zeitschrift des bayerischen Statistischen Landesamts* (1921), 33.

[108] The number of days worked by adult workers in Mar. 1918, as a percentage of days worked in Mar. 1914, was as follows: quarrying 43.0; metal industry 177.0; machine industry 162.7; electrical industry 137.5; chemical industry 114.0; textiles 48.4; paper 65.5; leather and rubber 39.4; wood 59.3; food processing 83.5; clothing 46.9; printing trades 60.1. See the table in *Reichsarbeitsblatt*, 17:8 (1919), 619, as well as the commentary on 620.

industries producing for military needs and those in industries producing primarily for civilian needs.

Perhaps even more striking than what happened to working-class incomes during the War was the fate of incomes of middle-class groups, in particular the salaried 'new *Mittelstand*'. Indeed, in his study of 'class society' in the First World War Jürgen Kocka has spoken of a 'proletarianisation of the "new *Mittelstand*"'.[109] Between 1914 and 1915 nominal average earnings among white-collar workers fell, while price levels rose.[110] White-collar staff benefited from increases in the supplements to their salaries for children and compensation for inflation (the *Teuerungszulagen*), but rises in their earnings nevertheless fell far behind the increases in workers' wages. For example, in Württemberg the salary of a typical primary-school teacher (30 years old, married, two children) increased by only 23 per cent between 1914 and 1917 (by 1918 it had slightly more than doubled).[111] According to a poll of its members by the right-wing German National Union of Commercial Employees (Deutschnationaler Handlungsgehilfen-Verband), between 1 August 1914 and 31 December 1917 average yearly earnings among the membership rose from 2,393 to 2,829 Marks—a mere 18.2 per cent.[112] During the same period the nominal wages of shop-floor workers in war industries had roughly doubled, and even the wage rates of workers in industries producing largely for civilian needs had increased by two-fifths.

Civil servants also suffered from low salary-increases during the War, and those who worked in the higher reaches of government service saw their pay fall furthest behind inflation. Some indication of their predicament may be found in Table 6, which shows the nominal and real monthly salaries of three different civil-service grades (married, with two children). White-collar workers and civil servants were at a considerable disadvantage compared with industrial wage-earners. They lacked the leverage of workers whose labour and skills were in desperately short supply, especially those in war industries. What is more, the workers on the shop floor were paid extra for overtime. The consequent squeezing of income differentials, which were an inescapable effect of the inflation and the war economy, played an important role in shaping the perception that the established social order was under threat, as income hierarchies (and with them status differentials) between salaried and waged employees were eroded.

[109] Kocka, *Facing Total War*, 84.
[110] Ibid. 84–5. See also Adolf Günther, *Die gesunkene Kaufkraft des Lohnes und ihre Wiederherstellung,* ii: *Kriegslöhne und -preise und ihr Einfluß auf Kaufkraft und Lebenskosten* (Jena, 1919), 44, for following years.
[111] Gunther Mai, *Kriegswirtschaft und Arbeiterbewegung in Württemberg 1914–1918* (Stuttgart, 1983), 397.
[112] Kocka, *Facing Total War*, 85. The figures for average yearly earnings (taken from *Deutsche Handels-Wacht*, 35 (1918), 40) were: 1.8.1914, 2393 Marks; 31.12.1914, 2266 Marks; 31.12.1915, 2632 Marks; 31.12.1917, 2829 Marks.

Table 6. *Nominal and Real Monthly Salaries of Three Civil-Service Grades, 1913–1919* (Marks)

| | Grade XI: Reich Office of the Interior | | Grade VIII: Senior Postal Official | | Grade III: Railway Guard | |
|---|---|---|---|---|---|---|
| | Nominal | Real | Nominal | Real | Nominal | Real |
| 1913 | 608 | 608 | 342 | 342 | 157 | 157 |
| 1914 | 608 | 590.86 | 342 | 332.36 | 157 | 152.58 |
| 1915 | 608 | 469.86 | 342 | 264.30 | 157 | 121.33 |
| 1916 | 608 | 358.28 | 342 | 201.53 | 157 | 92.52 |
| 1917 | 660 | 260.97 | 420 | 166.07 | 213 | 84.22 |
| 1918 | 891 | 284.48 | 589 | 188.06 | 342 | 109.20 |
| 1919 | 1015 | 244.58 | 778 | 187.47 | 582 | 140.24 |

*Note*: It should be noted that the index upon which the figures for real incomes are based is open to some criticism
*Source*: Statistisches Reichsamt, *Zahlen zur Geldentwertung in Deutschland 1914 bis 1923* (*Wirtschaft und Statistik*, 5, Sonderheft 1; Berlin, 1925), 43.

Those materially worst off as a consequence of wartime changes were neither workers nor civil servants, however. They were people dependent upon state relief: the aged, and the dependants of men who had been called up into the armed forces. When war broke out, on 4 August 1914, the minimum levels of family support available to women and children whose husbands or fathers were serving in the armed forces were increased: for soldiers' wives, 9 Marks per month from May to October and 12 Marks per month from November to April; and for children under 15 years of age, 6 Marks per month.[113] This provided a woman with three dependent children, for example, 30 Marks monthly during the winter months and 27 during the summer. This sum was below what it had cost to feed a worker's family of four before the War, and by October 1915 comprised only about 60 per cent of what it cost just to provide food for the family. The rates were raised in January 1916 (to 15 Marks per month for wives and 7.50 Marks for children) and again in December 1916 (to 20 Marks and 10 Marks). By the end of the War, the rates had risen to 25 Marks for wives and 15 Marks for children (the differentiation between summer and winter months was dropped), but the increases never matched the increases in prices.

The numbers of people involved were huge: by the end of 1915 the number of families receiving war-related family-support was estimated at 4 million—or more than a quarter of the 14.8 million households in

---

[113] See Seidel, *Frauenarbeit im Ersten Weltkrieg*, 109–12; Lothar Burchardt, 'The Impact of the War Economy on the Civilian Population during the First and Second World Wars', in Wilhelm Deist (ed.), *The German Military in the Age of Total War* (Leamington Spa, 1985), 56; Burchardt, 'Konstanz im Ersten Weltkrieg', 12; Daniel, *Arbeiterfrauen in der Kriegsgesellschaft*, 169–83.

Germany—and the number of individuals at 11 million—or more than one-sixth of the entire German population; by early 1918 between one-quarter and one-third of the population of many cities were receiving family support.[114] To be sure, benefits fixed by the Reich government were often not the sole source of support for such people; local authorities and employers (particularly the larger employers) also made additional sums available. Yet for those dependent upon fixed state benefits and private charity, the constant shortages and rampant inflation were especially hard to bear, and gave cause for widespread bitterness about their treatment by the German state.

The wartime inflation, which undermined the living-standards of all Germans, whether or not they were dependent upon state support, posed a threat in both a material and a symbolic sense. It destroyed savings and eroded real incomes, and it demonstrated in countless everyday transactions that the fixed relationships of the pre-war world had been destroyed. When attempting to assess the importance of the wartime inflation, two preliminary points should be noted: first, the wartime inflation followed a long period of relative price-stability in Germany. In 1900 the cost of living in the Reich was roughly the same as it had been in 1871, and between 1900 and 1913 it rose altogether by only 23.4 per cent—an average of less than 2 per cent per year during the thirteen years prior to the outbreak of the War.[115] This meant that Germans had come to regard the pre-war price-levels (and relationships between the prices of different goods and services) as normal and natural; most Germans in 1914 had never known anything else. Thus when prices began to rise steeply—in 1915 alone by more than in the previous forty-five years together—this was seen as a shocking aberration. Second, although the wartime price-rises were relatively modest when compared with 1922 and 1923, by the end of 1918 the pre-war Mark (and thus pre-war savings) had already lost roughly three-quarters of its 1913 value. In other words, most of the deterioration of pre-war money savings had already occurred by the Armistice, well before billions of Marks were needed to post a letter or to buy an egg.

Although it is probably impossible to describe the movement of prices in Germany during the War perfectly accurately, there are a number of indices which, taken together, provide some idea of how the cost of living rose between 1914 and 1919. One of those most commonly cited is the index of food prices compiled monthly by Richard Calwer (see Table 7).There are problems with the Calwer index: it was compiled on the basis of the official price-ceilings for various foods and therefore disregarded the effects of the black market—which was extremely important in 1917, when Calwer

[114] Daniel, *Arbeiterfrauen in der Kriegsgesellschaft*, 173–4.
[115] Desai, *Real Wages in Germany*, 117.

indicated almost stable food-prices; furthermore, it assumed an unrealistically high per capita calorific intake.[116] Nevertheless, it gives a rough indication of rises in the price of food, at a time when food comprised half the expenditure of most working-class households. Another frequently cited index of price levels is the cost-of-living index, averaged yearly, by Gerhard Bry (See Table 8).[117]

Table 7. *Index of Average Food Prices in 200 Cities, 1913–1919* (1913 = 1)

|           | 1913 | 1914 | 1915 | 1916 | 1917 | 1918 | 1919 |
|-----------|------|------|------|------|------|------|------|
| January   | 1.01 | 0.99 | 1.15 | 1.61 | 2.09 | 2.20 | 2.48 |
| February  | 1.01 | 0.98 | 1.23 | 1.69 | 2.11 | 2.20 | 2.53 |
| March     | 1.01 | 0.98 | 1.28 | 1.88 | 2.13 | 2.22 | 2.62 |
| April     | 1.00 | 0.96 | 1.34 | 2.02 | 2.13 | 2.22 | 2.71 |
| May       | 0.99 | 0.96 | 1.42 | 2.03 | 2.12 | 2.23 | 2.87 |
| June      | 0.99 | 0.96 | 1.45 | 2.05 | 2.14 | 2.24 | 3.06 |
| July      | 1.01 | 0.98 | 1.48 | 2.08 | 2.15 | 2.26 | 3.20 |
| August    | 1.01 | 1.03 | 1.52 | 2.08 | 2.13 | 2.31 | 3.32 |
| September | 1.00 | 1.02 | 1.55 | 2.08 | 2.12 | 2.37 | 3.72 |
| October   | 1.00 | 1.05 | 1.63 | 2.08 | 2.13 | 2.40 | 3.92 |
| November  | 1.00 | 1.08 | 1.51 | 2.06 | 2.16 | 2.43 | 4.23 |
| December  | 0.93 | 1.12 | 1.53 | 2.07 | 2.18 | 2.45 | 4.46 |

*Source*: Gerhard Bry, *Wages in Germany, 1871–1945* (Princeton, NJ, 1960).

Table 8. *Cost-of-Living Index*, 1913–1919

| 1913 | 1.00 |
|------|------|
| 1914 | 1.03 |
| 1915 | 1.29 |
| 1916 | 1.70 |
| 1917 | 2.53 |
| 1918 | 3.13 |
| 1919 | 4.15 |

[116] For a discussion of the problems with Calwer's index, see Holtfrerich, *The German Inflation*, 43–4.

[117] Bry, *Wages in Germany*, 440–5. It is unclear just where these figures come from. Bry claims that they were prepared by the Statistisches Reichsamt and taken from Statistisches Reichsamt, *Zahlen zur Geldentwertung in Deutschland 1914 bis 1923* (*Wirtschaft und Statistik*, 5 Sonderheft 1; Berlin, 1925) 5, but this cost-of-living index is not to be found there for the period before Feb. 1920. Other indices, which show a similar pattern, may be found in Mai, *Kriegswirtschaft in Württemberg*, 394. The most widely used cost-of-living index for this period is the one interpolated by Bry from the Statistisches Reichsamt and Calwer indices; this provides the basis for Bry's computations of real wage-levels and is used in most of the subsequent literature, including Jürgen Kocka's *Facing Total War*. However, Bry's index not only reproduces the problems with Calwer's figures but also was, by Bry's admission, 'done graphically' and leads only to a rough approximation of monthly living-costs. See Bry, *Wages in Germany*, 445.

Such indices are necessarily crude, and give only a rough picture of how price levels rose during the War, when shortages were acute, inferior goods were substituted for better products, and the black market (with its exorbitant but unrecorded prices) assumed growing importance in people's everyday lives. Yet, however the cost of living is measured, it is clear that prices rose sharply and ate deeply into living-standards.

What mattered, of course, was not indices, but the prices Germans actually paid, particularly for food. In Hanover, where local authorities resisted imposing price controls (with the result that food prices were among the highest in Germany), food prices in the shops rose between the end of July 1914 and the beginning of January 1916 as shown in Table 9.

Table 9. *Increases in Food Prices in Hanover, July 1914 to January 1916*

|  | 31.7.1914 | 1.1.1916 | Increase |
| --- | --- | --- | --- |
|  | (Marks) | (Marks) | (%) |
| Rye flour (kg.) | 0.28 | 0.42 | 50 |
| Wheat flour (kg.) | 0.34 | 0.48 | 41 |
| Potatoes (kg.) | 0.10 | 0.13 | 30 |
| Butter (kg.) | 2.62 | 5.10 | 95 |
| Beans (kg.) | 0.25 | 1.10 | 300 |
| Eggs (unit) | 0.08 | 0.23 | 188 |
| Chickens (unit) | 2.00 | 5.50 | 175 |

*Source*: Friedhelm Boll, *Massenbewegungen in Niedersachsen 1906–1920: Eine sozialgeschichtliche Untersuchung zu den unterschiedlichen Entwicklungstypen Braunschweig und Hannover* (Bonn-Bad Godesberg, 1981), 195.

This meant that by the beginning of 1916 few working women in Hanover could earn enough daily to buy more than about a dozen eggs, and half a chicken cost about twice as much as most women could hope to earn in a day—if they could find a chicken! In Ingolstadt, in Bavaria, 500 g. of fat cost between 2.30 and 2.40 Marks in March 1916, and between 3 and 5 Marks in November; butter, whose price in a number of Bavarian cities was fixed in 1917 at 2.30 Marks for 500 g , was being sold by farmers for between 6 and 7 Marks in January 1917, and between 10 and 15 Marks in August 1918.[118] In other words, in the summer of 1918, 2 kg. of butter could cost as much as many women might earn in a week.

Almost all Germans were materially worse off during the First World War than they had been before 1914. With the possible exception of some women employed in metalworking factories, no group of workers had

[118] See Seidel, *Frauenarbeit im Ersten Weltkrieg*, 91–3.

incomes which kept pace with inflation; many people—civil servants, white-collar employees, and workers in industries producing for civilian needs—saw their real incomes halve during the War. Yet the question remains: How did the sharp deterioration in real incomes affect consumption? Some indication is offered by data on the spending-patterns of sample households before and during the War. Pre-war statistics, compiled by the Reich Statistical Office and showing expenditure patterns of workers' households in 1907, are given in simplified form in Table 10.

Table 10. *Structure of Expenditure in Worker Households, 1907* (%)

| Expenditure category | Total Annual Expenditure (Marks) | | |
|---|---|---|---|
| | 1200–1600[a] | 1600–2000[b] | 2000–2500[c] |
| Food and drink | 54.9 | 51.7 | 50.2 |
| Heating and lighting | 4.9 | 4.3 | 3.9 |
| Housing and housekeeping | 16.8 | 17.7 | 17.0 |
| (of this: rent) | (14.3) | (14.9) | (14.1) |
| Clothing and linen | 9.4 | 11.0 | 12.0 |
| (of this: clothing) | (7.3) | (8.7) | (9.3) |
| Miscellaneous[d] | 14.0 | 15.3 | 16.9 |

[a] 154 families.
[b] 196 families.
[c] 127 families.
[d] Includes health, education, amusements, insurance, transport, gifts, savings.

*Sources*: Kaiserliches Statistisches Amt, Abt. für Arbeiterstatistik (ed.), *Erhebung von Wirtschafts-rechnungen minderbemittelter Familien im Deutschen Reiche* (*Reichsarbeitsblatt*, Sonderheft 2; Berlin, 1909), 61–4.
See also Waldemar Zimmermann, 'Die Veränderungen der Einkommens- und Lebensverhältnisse der deutschen Arbeiter durch den Krieg', in R. Meerwarth, A. Günther, W. Zimmermann, *Die Einwirkungen des Krieges auf die Bevölkerungsbewegung, Einkommen und Lebenshaltung in Deutschland* (Stuttgart, 1932).

Rough comparison with these pre-war expenditure-patterns is offered by the analyses of spending by sample households during the War prepared by the War Committee for Consumers' Interests (Kriegsausschuß für Konsumenten-interessen = KAKI) (See Table 11). Probably the most important change in expenditure patterns during the War was that the proportion of income devoted to housing diminished. As a consequence of rent controls and inflation, money spent on rent (as well as on repaying mortgages) fell considerably in real terms. Spending on clothing appears to have risen fairly sharply, a reflection of the particularly steep increases in clothes prices. Other changes—the slight increase in the proportion of workers'·incomes spent on food, a larger proportion of incomes spent on fuel and lighting in 1917 and 1918—may have been due more to the statistical consequences of the decline in real housing-costs than to significant changes in consumption patterns with regard to food and fuel.[119] Yet perhaps the most striking aspect of these statistics is that consumption patterns did not alter more during the War than in fact was the case. Once allowance is made for the effects of rent controls, wartime consumption-patterns do not appear vastly different from what they had been before 1914.

Table 11. *Structure of Household Expenditure, 1916–1918*
(April of each year, %)

| Expenditure category | Average of all income groups | | | Worker households | |
|---|---|---|---|---|---|
| | 1916 | 1917 | 1918 | 1917 | 1918 |
| Food and drink | 52.1 | 51.0 | 48.0 | 59.8 | 53.5 |
| Fuel and lighting | 3.6 | 5.4 | 5.4 | 5.5 | 5.5 |
| Rent | 10.7 | 11.3 | 8.3 | 8.1 | 6.8 |
| Clothing, Shoes, repairs | 7.6 | 9.9 | 16.8 | 10.1 | 14.1 |
| Taxes | 3.1 | 2.4 | 2.6 | 1.7 | 2.2 |
| Miscellaneous[a] | 22.9 | 20.0 | 19.0 | 14.8 | 17.8 |

[a] Includes linen, soap, books and newspapers, transport, medical expenses, insurance, organizational dues, amusements and sports, presents, household appliances.
*Sources*: *Reichsarbeitsblatt*, 15:2 (1917), 147. *Beiträge zur Kenntnis der Lebenshaltung im dritten Kriegsjahre auf Grund einer Erhebung des Kriegsausschusses für Konsumenteninteressen* (*Reichsarbeitsblatt*, Sonderheft 17; Berlin, 1917), 14, 26; *Beiträge zur Kenntnis der Lebenshaltung im vierten Kriegsjahre auf Grund einer Erhebung des Kriegsausschusses für Konsumenteninteressen* (*Reichsarbeitsblatt*, Sonderhaft 21; Berlin, 1919), 28, 51. See also Waldemar Zimmermann, 'Die Veränderungen der Einkummens- und Lebensverhältnisse der deutschen Arbeiter durch den Krieg', in R. Meerwarth, A. Günther, W. Zimmermann, *Die Einwirkungen des Krieges auf die Bevölkerungsbewegung, Einkommen und Lebenshaltung in Deutschland* (Stuttgart, 1932).

What seems to have changed was not consumption *patterns* so much as consumption itself. Germans continued to spend their money in patterns broadly similar to those evident before 1914, but in poorer, shabbier circumstances, characterized by widespread shortages. They consumed the same sorts of things but less of them, particularly of food. The reasons for the crisis of food supply have been examined by historians at length: poor planning; the Allied blockade; the cessation of food imports, which before the War had accounted for one-fifth of the grain needed for bread and half the fodder in Germany; and poor harvests.[120] In 1915 rationing was intro-

---

[119] For further discussion, see Holtfrerich, *The German Inflation*, 252–4.

[120] In 1917 and 1918 German grain and potato harvests stood at roughly two-thirds of their pre-war levels. For discussion of the declines in agricultural production, fertilizer and feed inputs, labour available for farm work, and food consumption, see Jens Flemming, *Landwirtschaftliche Interessen und Demokratie: Ländliche Gesellschaft, Agrarverbände und Staat 1890–1925* (Bonn, 1978), 80–9. See also C. Paul Vincent, *The Politics of Hunger: The Allied Blockade of Germany, 1915–1919* (Athens, Oh., and London, 1985); Anne Roerkohl, *Hungerblockade und Heimatfront: Die Kommunale Lebensmittelversorgung in Westfalen während des Ersten Weltkrieges* (Stuttgart, 1991); Burchardt, 'The Impact of the War Economy', 41–3; Avner Offer, *The First World War: An Agrarian Interpretation* (Oxford, 1989), 45–78.

duced, beginning with bread early in the year, and the ration amounts were cut repeatedly in the following years (See Table 12).

Table 12.  *Wartime Rations of Basic Foods as a % of Peacetime Consumption*

|                | 1.7.16–<br>30.6.17 | 1.7.17–<br>30.6.18 | 1.7.18–<br>28.12.18 |
|----------------|--------|-----------|---------|
| Meat           | 31.2   | 19.8      | 11.8    |
| Fish           | 51.0   | —         | 4.7     |
| Eggs           | 18.3   | 12.5      | 13.3    |
| Butter         | 22.0   | 21.3      | 28.1    |
| Cheese         | 2.5    | 3.8       | 14.8    |
| Pulses         | 14.2   | 0.9       | 6.6     |
| Sugar          | 48.5   | 55.5–66.7 | 82.1    |
| Potatoes       | 70.8   | 94.2      | 94.2    |
| Vegetable fats | 39.0   | 40.5      | 16.6    |
| Flour          | 52.5   | 47.1      | 48.1    |

*Source*: Waldemar Zimmermann, 'Die Veränderungen der Einkommens- und Lebensverhältnisse der deutschen Arbeiter durch den Krieg', in R. Meerwarth, A. Günther, W. Zimmermann, *Die Einwirkungen des Krieges auf die Bevölkerungsbewegung, Einkommen und Lebenshaltung in Deutschland* (Stuttgart, 1932).

When drawing conclusions from these figures one should remember that Germans found additional food on the black market—the inevitable consequence of rationing, requisitioning from farmers, and price controls; however, it should also be remembered that possessing ration coupons did not guarantee the receipt of food, which was not always available everywhere. An indication of the quantities of food actually consumed is provided by data collected by the KAKI of the food consumption of a number of families during the second half of the War, which have been compared with the results of pre-war investigations.[121] This makes clear that the consumption of protein-rich foods (in particular, fresh meat), bread, and, especially, fresh fruit and vegetables declined substantially. To some extent the decline was compensated for by an increase in potato consumption, although in 1917 this also fell sharply as a result of the 1916 harvest failure—with the result that Germans faced the terrible 'turnip winter' of 1916–17. Furthermore, such data may present too positive a picture of the wartime nutrition of Germans, since not only the quantity but also the quality of food declined. Substitute foods were provided for a hungry population (the best-known

[121] See Zimmermann, 'Die Veränderungen der Einkommens- und Lebensverhältnisse', 448–51; Holtfrerich, *The German Inflation*, 252–4. As the KAKI families were primarily lower-income, their food consumption is best compared with the pre-war figures for working-class families rather than with national averages.

being 'K-bread'—bread mixed with potatoes to make the flour go further),
and people tended to buy the less expensive, lower-quality items.[122]

The severe food-shortages and the clumsy manner in which the Berlin
government reacted to the problem added to tensions between urban and
rural interests.[123] Policies which, for example, in 1915 had led first to the
slaughter of 35 per cent of the country's pigs (because farmers lacked fodder)
and then to the fixing of maximum price-levels for pork, and which resulted
in its disappearance from the shops and appearance on the black market at
vastly inflated prices,[124] could hardly be expected to promote harmony
between rural and urban dwellers. Tensions between consumers and producers of food were heightened not simply by the inevitable conflicts over
prices but also over whether food would be available at any price. Town
and country were divided more bitterly than ever before. On the one hand,
the food shortages gave rise to understandable resentment and anger among
undernourished urban dwellers who looked at their better-fed rural cousins
with envy. On the other hand, the rural population also had reason to feel
resentful, for the wartime food-supply system was, as Gerald Feldman has
put it, 'organized in defiance of the farmers and the peasantry'.[125]

The imposition of state controls also gave rural anger a clear focus, in a
way that the 'invisible hand' of the market had not done. As Robert Moeller
has observed, 'once the government took over the regulation of the war
economy, the villain seemed more easily identified and far less remote'.[126]
Agrarian interests complained forcefully about the 'restrictions on the freedom of movement of farmers, the restraints and formal abolition of their
independence in economic management'.[127] From a rural perspective, the
imposition of the 'controlled economy' (*Zwangswirtschaft*)—of price controls,
requisitioning, and, during 1917 and 1918, even searches of farms (by the
military if need be) for hidden reserves of food[128]—spelled unfair interference
on behalf of urban food-consumers against the interests of food producers.
Farm producers, after all, already faced severe shortages of labour, fertilizers,
fodder, and draught animals; they had to pay high prices for manufactured
goods; and they were angered by thefts of food by city dwellers from fields
near the larger towns. Many who remained on the land—including women
who were left to manage both family and farm—felt tremendous resentment

---

[122] The KAKI figures indicate that one-eighth of the average family food-budget in 1916 was
spent on what Waldemar Zimmermann described as 'problematical, artificially prepared foodstuffs'. See Zimmermann, 'Die Veränderungen der Einkommens- und Lebensverhältnisse', 454–5.
[123] See Feldman, *Army, Industry and Labor*, 463–5; Kocka, *Facing Total War*, 119–23; Schumacher,
*Land und Politik*, 73–4; Moeller, 'Dimensions of Social Conflict'; id., *German Peasants and Agrarian
Politics*, 44–67.
[124] See Burchardt, 'The Impact of the War Economy', 41.
[125] Feldman, *Army, Industry and Labor*, 463.
[126] Moeller, 'Dimensions of Social Conflict', 151.
[127] Quoted in Kocka, *Facing Total War*, 120.
[128] Moeller, 'Dimensions of Social Conflict', 156–8.

towards an urban population which drew relatively high wages and were ignorant of the demands which farming involved. One Pomeranian farm-woman (whose husband was a soldier and who ran her farm alone with the help of a prisoner) probably spoke for many when she was reported to have said in the autumn of 1916: 'I am not going to flog myself for the people of Berlin; they are not going to come and clean out my stables.'[129] Of course, the resentment cut both ways. Ill feeling towards their rural cousins was common among the hungry urban population, which 'looks with envy at conditions in the countryside where the products the townspeople particularly miss, such as butter, milk, eggs and pork, are still said to be available in quantities which are perhaps exaggeratedly large, and where living standards are not supposed to have changed much since before the War'.[130] Food had become the subject of bitter conflict in wartime Germany.

Table 13. *Deaths among the German Civilian Population, 1914–1923*

| Year | Men | Women |
| --- | --- | --- |
| 1914 | 536,720 | 502,982 |
| 1915 | 510,826 | 495,466 |
| 1916 | 455,709 | 467,686 |
| 1917 | 516,140 | 523,285 |
| 1918 | 566,077 | 644,163 |
| 1919 | 475,252 | 491,681 |
| 1920 | 451,204 | 458,216 |
| 1921 | 431,127 | 426,716 |
| 1922 | 441,335 | 436,979 |
| 1923 | 429,741 | 426,263 |

Note: The 1914 and 1915 figures do not include the two Mecklenburgs; 1916–18 do not include Alsace, Lorraine, or the two Mecklenburgs; 1919 does not include those parts of the Province of Posen which fell to Poland, or Alsace, Lorraine, or the two Mecklenburgs; 1920 does not include any of the territories lost by Germany after the First World War, with the exception of Upper Silesia; 1921–23 do not include any territories lost by Germany after the War or those parts of Upper Silesia which fell to Poland.
Source: *Statistisches Jahrbuch für das Deutsche Reich 1924/25* (Berlin, 1925), 44–9.

The deterioration in German civilians' diet damaged both the health and the morale of the German population during the War. To begin with health: although other factors were also involved—in particular the fuel

[129] Quoted in Kocka, *Facing Total War*, 121.
[130] Thus the Deputy General Commander in Kassel, quoted in Kocka, *Facing Total War*, 121–2.

shortages, which left Germans cold as well as hungry—poor diet clearly affected morbidity and mortality, especially during the second half of the War. This is perhaps best illustrated by the fact that in 1918 the number of *civilian* male deaths was higher than it had been in 1914 (and over 130,000 higher than in 1921), despite the fact that millions of men were in uniform (See Table 13). The number of deaths among women due to tuberculosis—a key indicator of social conditions—rose from 40,043 (11.7 per 10,000) in 1914 to 58,614 (17.6 per 10,000) in 1917 and 66,608 (20.1 per 10,000) in 1918, a rise of two-thirds compared with 1914.[131] Deaths among women due to pneumonia rose from 35,700 (10.5 per 10,000) in 1914 to 42,399 (12.7 per 10,000) in 1917 and 74,468 (22.5 per 10,000) in 1918. Dietary deficiencies also probably contributed to the severity of the influenza epidemic of 1918, which claimed the lives of 72,721 men and 102,130 women within Germany and which was at its height just as the military situation and political system collapsed, in October and November 1918.[132] In contrast, deaths due to diseases not linked so immediately with living-standards, such as heart disease and cancer, remained fairly steady during the war years.

The effects of poor wartime nutrition were not limited to higher mortality from particular diseases. The food shortages also caused general lethargy, increased susceptibility to illness, and undermined labour productivity.[133] In

---

[131] For these and the figures below, see *Statistisches Jahrbuch für das Deutsche Reich 1924/25*, 44–9; *Statistisches Jahrbuch für das Deutsche Reich 1927* (Berlin, 1927), 38–41. See also Statistisches Reichsamt (ed.), *Statistik des Deutschen Reichs*, cccxvi: *Die Bewegung der Bevölkerung in den Jahren 1922 und 1923 und die Ursachen der Sterbefälle in den Jahren 1920 bis 1923* (Berlin, 1926), 60–3. For discussion of wartime mortality among women, see Daniel, *Arbeiterfrauen in der Kriegsgesellschaft*, 221–3. For statistics of mortality due to these diseases in Württemberg, see Mai, *Kriegswirtschaft in Württemberg*, 38–9; in Wuppertal, see Jürgen Reulecke, 'Der Erste Weltkrieg und die Arbeiterbewegung im rheinisch-westfälischen Industriegebiet', in Jürgen Reulecke (ed.), *Arbeiterbewegung an Rhein und Ruhr: Beiträge zur Geschichte der Arbeiterbewegung in Rheinland-Westfalen* (Wuppertal, 1974), 222. In Wuppertal the death rate among civilians rose from 10.7 per thousand in 1914 to 15.9 per thousand in the influenza year of 1918.

[132] e.g. in the city of Leipzig, of the 1,286 people who were killed by influenza in 1918, 651 died in Oct. and 377 in Nov. See Statistisches Amt, *Statistisches Jahrbuch der Stadt Leipzig*, V, 1915–1918 (Leipzig, 1921), 50–1. Civilian deaths roughly doubled as a result of the influenza epidemic; e.g. in Osnabrück 605 civilians died during Sept., Oct., and Nov. 1918, whereas during the previous three months the total had been 285. See StAO, Rep. 430, Dez. 905, Zug no. 16/25, no. 15, fo. 158: 'Nachweisung über die Fortschreibung der versorgungsberechtigten Bevölkerung für die Zeit vom 1. Juni bis zum 31. August 1918. Regierungsbezirk Osnabrück, Kreis Osnabrück Stadt'; ibid., fo. 207: 'Nachweisung über die Fortschreibung der versorgungsberechtigten Bevölkerung für die Zeit vom 1. September bis zum 30. November 1918. Regierungsbezirk Osnabrück, Kreis Osnabrück Stadt'.

[133] On the effects of undernourishment upon labour productivity, particularly among prisoners of war working in Upper Silesian industry, see APW, Rejencja Opolska I, no. 10051, fos. 90–105: 'Aktenvermerk über die Verhandlungen in der Vorstandssitzung des Oberschlesischen Berg- und Hüttenmännischen Vereins vom 2. Juni 1917', (Kattowitz) 3 June 1917. Here it was asserted that prisoners of war had actually collapsed at work due to undernourishment. See also Feldman, *Army, Industry and Labor*, 107–8.

April 1917, as Germany was emerging from the 'turnip winter', the area medical officer in Wiesbaden assessed the effects of the food shortage upon public health, noting that although schoolchildren generally had escaped its detrimental consequences to their health, as one went up the age scale and down the social scale the negative effects of inadequate food-supply increased:[134] among those aged between 14 and 30 it was among the poorer classes and 'especially the female sex' that the problems of inadequate food-supply made themselves felt; many adolescents were reported to be 'pale and flaccid' and did not gain weight as they gained height. Members of the 30–60 age group frequently registered substantial weight-loss, which averaged around 20–50 lb. per person (while losses of 60 lb. were 'no rarity') and while their general health usually remained satisfactory, there were frequent complaints of susceptibility to fatigue. However, it was among older people that the unsatisfactory nutrition had the most serious consequences, as their resistance to disease plummeted and acute illness affected them more quickly and severely. Urban dwellers were affected more than their country cousins, and those who were plagued by chronic illness—especially tuberculosis—also suffered disproportionately.

So, Germany did not starve as a consequence of the severe wartime problems associataed with food, but the shortages made the lives of Germans inside the Reich quite miserable.[135] The most fateful consequences of the food shortages, therefore, were probably upon morale. The problems of getting food in sufficient quantity and of sufficient quality dominated the way in which a tired and hungry population went about its everyday affairs, and from 1915 food became *the* issue around which popular discontent coalesced. As one local official in Saxony put it in January 1916, 'the most burning question is the adequate provision of the population with foodstuffs at affordable prices'.[136] Beginning in 1915 and with increasing frequency during 1916, the food shortages led to angry demonstrations, to hunger riots and the plundering of food shops.[137] During 1915 and 1916 protests against food shortages and high prices were often sparked by price increases and poor organization at food-distribution points. They tended to be urban phenomena, since food distribution was essentially an urban problem. The winter months were the worst, when food was most scarce

---

[134] HHStA, 405/6358, fos. 135–8: Regierungs- und Geheimer Medizinrat Dr. v. Hake to Regierungspräsident, Wiesbaden, 18 Apr. 1917. Dr. von Hake also noted that, by contrast, the situation with regard to the spread of infectious diseases such as smallpox, scarlet fever, diptheria, and typhus was satisfactory. See also Mai, *Kriegswirtschaft in Württemberg*, 39.

[135] This conclusion matches the assessment put forward by Avner Offer in his recent book, *The First World War: An Agrarian Interpretation*, 45 53.

[136] SHAD, Amtshauptmannschaft Pirna, no. 495, fos. 73–7.

[137] See Feldman, *Army, Industry and Labor*, 108, 362, 375; Kocka, *Facing Total War*, 48–50; Friedhelm Boll, *Massenbewegungen in Niedersachsen 1906–1920: Eine sozialgeschichtliche Untersuchung zu den unterschiedlichen Entwicklungstypen Braunschweig und Hannover* (Bonn-Bad Godesberg, 1981), 201–6; Schumacher *Land und Politik*, 39–40; Burchardt, 'The Impact of the War Economy', 46.

and tempers shortest. Trouble frequently arose at queues at food-distribution points and shops, where people often had to wait together for hours to receive inadequate quantities of poor-quality food at high prices, and the spontaneous disturbances over food tended to involve women and young people, who often took matters into their own hands and simply grabbed the food they needed or else paid for it without producing their ration cards.[138]

After the harvest failure of 1916 and the 'turnip winter' which followed, morale slumped to new depths and the discontent over the food situation took a new turn. The protests began to assume a more organized character, to involve men (including the better-paid skilled workers in the armaments industries), and to develop into strike action. Food (or, more precisely, the lack of it) was the spark. As Jürgen Reulecke has shown in his discussion of conditions in the Ruhr area during the War, overtly political demands played no role in the first wildcat strikes which erupted in 1916, when the issue was the 'stomach question'; and in April 1917 striking Krupp workers were demanding wages which would allow them 'to buy foodstuffs at the prices which the well-off population pay'.[139] The strike wave of April 1917, which in Berlin involved roughly 200,000 workers in about 300 factories (many of them armaments factories), had its origins in a reduction in bread rations for people doing heavy work.[140] At a meeting in the War Office in Berlin, called in late April 1917 to discuss the strike wave, the representative of the regional administration in Münster, who reported that the recent unrest in the Ruhr had been due to cuts in the bread ration and that popular feeling was such that the most trifling incident could provoke a strike, put his finger on the underlying problem: 'The people are of the opinion that the government has not kept to what it has promised the workers.'[141] A government which presided over a grossly unfair and obviously inefficient distribution-system—which could not provide the population with bread, potatoes, or soap—had broken faith with its subjects. The expectations which had been raised about what the German state could and should provide to the civilian population, about what the 'controlled economy' and the wartime 'state socialism' was supposed to deliver, could not be met. In failing to provide the basic necessities to the working population, Germany's wartime rulers had broken the unspoken contract they had made with the German people at the outbreak of the War.

[138] See reports from late 1916 and early 1917 in NHStA, Hann. 122a/XXXIV, no. 365.
[139] Quoted in Reulecke, 'Der Erste Weltkrieg und die Arbeiterbewegung', 221.
[140] See Kocka, *Facing Total War*, 49; Burchardt, 'The Impact of the War Economy', 46.
[141] Deist (ed.), *Militär und Innenpolitik*, ii. 724–35: 'Aufzeichnung des Chefs der Fabrikenabteilung des Reichsmarineamts über eine Besprechung im Kriegsamt aus Anlaß der Streikbewegung', 26 Apr. 1917.

Germans reacted angrily not simply because of the material shortages but also because of perceived betrayal and injustice.[142] The flourishing black market undermined more than simply the 'controlled economy'; the decomposition of 'normal' pre-war economic relationships also spelled the destruction of a perceived moral order, whereby for a hard day's work one could receive a wage sufficient to cover basic needs, and whereby goods were available to buy with the money earned. During the War the ground rules of consumption in a capitalist society appeared to have been altered. For the first time in living memory, money did not necessarily command goods. Money progressively lost its function as a medium of exchange, and was increasingly replaced by barter arrangements, hoarding, and the black market; it was no longer hard work that was the key to survival, but rather 'connections' and the ability to hoard goods. According to some estimates, up to 50 per cent of food supplies was reaching consumers illegally,[143] while farmers were compelled to resort to barter and illegal trading in order to acquire badly needed fertilizer.[144] As the secretary of the Christian textile workers' trade union in Wuppertal said to government representatives present at a public meeting, 'We all live from the black market, because otherwise we would starve.'[145]

However patriotic they might have been (or thought they were), almost all Germans had to participate in the uncontrolled economy. Mutually resentful and suspicious producers and consumers were united in the corruption of the black market.[146] Corruption formed the common bond in an increasingly divided society. People felt themselves entitled to evade the ration controls—a view which in effect was shared by officials who administered a system which allocated less food to people living in smaller towns because of their proximity to the countryside (and therefore to illegal food-supplies). The need to deal on the black market, to break the law, to depend on connections rather than 'honest work', aroused tremendous anger, anger increasingly focused upon those pursuing the War: upon the government and the Kaiser. This, more than almost anything else, undermined the legitimacy of the German government in the eyes of the German people. It also framed expectations of the coming demobilization and post-war transition, which many assumed would bring the return of a properly functioning state apparatus, the reassertion of natural justice, and the reconstitution of a moral society where hard work was rewarded.

[142] On this theme, see Barrington Moore, jun., *Injustice: The Social Bases of Obedience and Revolt* (London, 1978).

[143] Ute Daniel, 'The Politics of Rationing versus the Politics of Subsistence: Working-Class Women in Germany, 1914–1918', in Roger Fletcher (ed.), *Bernstein to Brandt: A Short History of German Social Democracy* (London, 1987), 91–2; Daniel, *Arbeiterfrauen in der Kriegsgesellschaft*, 224–6.

[144] Moeller, 'Dimensions of Social Conflict', 155.

[145] Quoted in Reulecke, 'Der Erste Weltkrieg und die Arbeiterbewegung', 221.

[146] Moeller, 'Dimensions of Social Conflict', 153–4.

The problems of food supply within Germany eroded not only civilian morale. Soldiers too were affected by what they heard, read, and, when home on leave, saw of the deteriorating living-standards within the Reich. Complaints surfaced in letters to soldiers from their families and friends, and the dangers this posed were spelled out clearly in a secret report of the Bavarian War Ministry in early 1916, which pointed out that soldiers' morale rested upon the assumption that 'their families were spared want and privations'.[147] Conditions back home were seen by the soldiers too as a betrayal by the state, a failure of the government to keep its side of the wartime social contract. Particularly in 1917, many soldiers brought back to work in war industries were dismayed by the meagre civilian food-rations—a problem made worse by the fact that the period when most soldiers were returned to the civilian economy, 1916–17, was when the food shortages were at their worst.[148] When cataloguing the reasons for the strikes in the Upper Silesian mining and metal working industries in early 1917, Ewald Hilger, the hard-line General Director of the Oberschlesischer Berg- und Hüttenmännischen Verein, singled out the 'especially unfavourable' influence of workers who had been called back from the front:

These people have naturally been much better provided with food at the front or wherever else they come from than is possible here inside the country, where they have also to make ends meet with their families. They have completely lost the habit of regular work and they—namely those who have become corporals or non-commissioned officers or have the Iron Cross—prove demanding, presumptuous, and refractory in every respect, which gives us a foretaste of how things will look after the peace when the soldiers come back in hordes (*in hellen Scharen*).[149]

Troops who had been stationed behind the lines before being sent back to work in the Reich caused particular difficulties. These former soldiers, as was pointed out in a 'morale report' from the Regierungsbezirk Stade in April 1917, often contributed to the 'deterioration of morale' since 'having been spoilt by the good and plentiful food behind the front, they are

---

[147] Deist (ed.), *Militär und Innenpolitik*, i. 295–6: Bayer. Kriegsministerium to bayer. Staatsminister, 'Stimmung in der Armee und in der Heimat', Munich, 1 Feb. 1916.

[148] German soldiers may not have been terribly well fed, but their rations were far better than those of their civilian compatriots. By 1918 the daily meat-consumption of the latter (28 g.) was less than a quarter that of the former (127 g.). See Flemming, *Landwirtschaftliche Interessen*, 87.

[149] APW, Rejencja Opolska I, no. 10051, fos. 129–36: 'Ausführungen des Herrn Geheimrats Hilger in der Vorstandssitzung des Oberschlesischen Berg- und Hüttenmännischen Vereins in Kattowitz am 2.6.1917'. Among the other reasons for the trouble, Hilger noted the—in his opinion—detrimental effects of the Auxiliary Service Law in increasing trade-union power and the 'cancerous' effects of the 'huge wages' being paid at the Reich Explosives Factory in Chorzow. Hilger had been one of the most hard-line, anti-union of German heavy industrialists during the War. See Feldman, *Army, Industry and Labor*, 91, 360–1, 374, 376–7.

dissatisfied with the diet in the homeland'.[150] Such observations suggest that it may be mistaken to assume that the difficulties soldiers had when readjusting to civilian life stemmed simply from their terrible experiences at the front. The difficulties often also arose from the shock and anger which many felt when confronted with the dreadful conditions which had come to prevail back home.

While the food supply contributed mightily to the collapse of morale, so did the course of the War itself. As we have seen, the War had been greeted initially with considerable popular enthusiasm. But that did not last long. The troops did not return victorious by Christmas and, as casualties rose and the hardships of the civilian population mounted, patriotic euphoria was replaced by war weariness, and wishes for peace became increasingly vocal.[151] Civilian morale began really to plummet during the winter of 1915–16, by which time German military casualties had reached roughly 2.5 million. Reports of street demonstrations in the large cities, with demands for 'peace and bread', and the general deterioration of morale caused grave concern in official circles.[152] In February 1916 the local authorities in the industrial city of Plauen sent the following description of morale to the Saxon Interior Ministry:

The morale of the population is best characterized by the frequently heard wish that the War would soon come to an end. The burdens and sacrifices which the War has brought are becoming ever greater and more noticeable, and the endurance needed to bear the burdens and make the sacrifices is beginning to slacken in many circles. The rising cost of all foods and consumer goods is causing depression, and as a consequence of the long duration of the War and the uncertainty about how things will turn out, a certain despondency and faint-heartedness is gaining ground here and there. Discord is also not infrequently sown by the troops on leave and their accounts of life and activities at, and especially behind, the front. These descriptions in many cases present an unwelcome picture and are well-suited to shaking confidence in the officers.[153]

Clearly soldiers' reactions to their lot did as much to undermine civilian morale as vice versa, and the soldiers themselves contributed greatly to the decomposition of morale within Germany during the second half of the War. Soldiers on leave often described conditions at the front in terms very different from those conveyed in the official propaganda.[154] Far from entertaining friends and relatives with stories of heroism and adventure, soldiers

---

[150] NHStA, Hann. 122a/XXXIV, no. 365, fos. 243–5: Regierungspräsident, Stade, 23 Apr. 1917.

[151] See Kocka, *Facing Total War*, 48–52.

[152] Deist (ed.), *Militär und Innenpolitik*, i. 244–95.

[153] SHAD, Ministerium des Innern, no. 17721, fo. 131/13: Amtshauptmannschaft to Ministerium des Innern in Dresden, Plauen, 21 Feb. 1916.

[154] SHAD, Ministerium des Innern, no. 9574, fos. 237–9: report to Ministerium des Innern, Oschatz, 28 Jan. 1916. See also Feldman, *Army, Industry and Labor*, 506–7.

were far more likely, as the Bavarian War Ministry noted in February 1916, to offer accounts of 'real and imaginary injustices, grievances, etc.' which 'poison the morale of entire villages'.[155]

As the War dragged on, German soldiers found it increasingly difficult to justify risking their lives to preserve a system which denied the majority of the population meaningful access to the political process and which had proved itself incapable of managing the war economy fairly or efficiently. The military authorities busily read the letters soldiers sent back home, were often deeply disturbed by what they found, and prophesied that when new elections were held 'certain statesmen', especially those who opposed change, 'would get the shock of their lives' (*würden ihr blaues Wunder erleben*).[156] In their letters from the front and in conversations while on leave soldiers described the War as a 'swindle'. They complained bitterly about bad treatment by officers; they urged their relatives not to subscribe to war loans; they claimed that the conflict was being continued for the profit of the capitalists: 'The War is being waged only for the money-bags, and only the money-bags are getting any benefit from the War.'[157] The disintegration of morale was increasingly expressed in actions as well as words; in late 1917 up to 10 per cent of troops being transported from the eastern front to the western front used the journey as an opportunity to desert.[158] Soldiers were showing less and less enthusiasm to die for God, Kaiser, and Fatherland.

The decisive turning-point, however, came with the failure of the spring offensives in 1918. Despite the yawning material inferiority of the German forces *vis-à-vis* the Allies on the western front, the offensives achieved impressive initial successes and aroused high expectations.[159] But the hopes were soon disappointed. The peace treaty signed at Brest-Litovsk 'brought no bread' to undernourished German workers;[160] and once the spring offensives stalled, and with more American troops landing in France every week, it became apparent that the German armed forces were incapable of bringing the War to a victorious conclusion. In the early months of the War enormous casualties had been sustained in the hope of victory. Now any

[155] Deist (ed.), *Militär und Innenpolitik*, i. 300: Bayer. Kriegsministerium to höhere Kommandeure des bayer. Kontingents, 'Maßnahmen zur Aufrechterhaltung der Stimmung in der Heimat', Munich, 1 Feb. 1916.
[156] GLAK, 456/E.V.8, Bund 86: stellv. Gen.kdo. XIV. A.K. to Kriegsamt, Abteilung für Volksernährungsfragen, in Berlin, Karlsruhe, 1 July 1917.
[157] HHStA, 405/6360, fo. 86: Landrat to Regierungspräsident, Rüdesheim, 16 Nov. 1917; GLAK, 456/E.V.8, Bund 86: stellv. Gen.kdo. XIV. A.K. to Ministerium des Innern in Karlsruhe, Karlsruhe, 1 Feb. 1918.
[158] Deist, 'Der militärische Zusammenbruch des Kaiserreichs', 109; Deist, 'Verdeckter Militärstreik', 157.
[159] See id., 'Der militärische Zusammenbruch des Kaiserreichs', (on the relative strengths of the forces on the western front) 105–6, (on the course of the offensives) 110–11; id., 'Verdeckter Militärstreik', 152–6.
[160] Schumacher, *Land und Politik*, 57.

action which promised high casualties was seen only as prolonging the conflict. The numbers of deserters increased considerably after the 1918 spring offensives. On the eastern front the war-weariness led to widespread insubordination; in one case 5,000 soldiers refused to be transported to fight in the west, and in another there were bloody confrontations between officers and men.[161] Within Germany mutinies occurred where men were ordered to the front. Soldiers tried to avoid being sent into combat and plundered shops; rowdy scenes and shooting-incidents at railway stations where soldiers were passing through became alarmingly frequent.[162]

The spring offensives in the west and the subsequent counter-offensives, as well as the influenza outbreaks among the troops in June and July 1918, left very great numbers of sick and wounded in their wake: of the 1.4 million German soldiers who participated in the offensives, over 300,000 became casualties between 21 March and 10 April, and the influenza epidemic in June and July alone affected more than a half a million men; altogether between March and July 1918 about 1.75 million German soldiers fell ill at some point and roughly 750,000 were wounded.[163] The medical service was overstretched, and many of the less seriously ill and the lightly wounded used the opportunity not only to keep away from the front but also find transport back home.[164] The number of disciplinary offences sky-rocketed, and Ludendorff himself spoke in July 1918 of an 'increasing incidence of unauthorized leave, acts of cowardice, and refusal to follow orders in the face of the enemy on the western front' while the Army Supreme Command tried (without success) to stem the decline of the 'fighting spirit' with stiffer punishments.[165] As Erich Otto Volkmann, a former Major then working for the Reichsarchiv, wrote in 1925: 'The army stood in the midst of a moral crisis.'[166] Many soldiers simply disembarked *en route* from trains carrying them to replace troops at the front. More and more soldiers took unauthorized leave, and the numbers of so-called *Drückeberger*—'shirkers' who, while not deserting outright, did everything possible (such as deliberately getting sentenced to prison for being absent without leave, or deliberately 'losing' equipment to avoid being readmitted to old units after

---

[161] Ulrich Kluge, *Soldatenräte und Revolution: Studien zur Militärpolitik in Deutschland 1918/19* (Göttingen, 1975), 94–5.

[162] See e.g. Klaus-Dieter Schwarz, *Weltkrieg und Revolution in Nürnberg: Ein Beitrag zur Geschichte der deutschen Arbeiterbewegung* (Stuttgart, 1971), 203; LHSA, Rep. C 48 I.e., no. 937/IV, fo. 42: Polizeiverwaltung Sangerhausen to Regierungspräsident in Merseburg, Sangerhausen, 21 Oct. 1918.

[163] Reichswehrministerium, *Sanitätsbericht*, iii, sect. 2, 142–3; Deist, 'Bemerkungen zur militärischen Demobilmachung', 5; id., 'Der militärische Zusammenbruch des Kaiserreichs', 111–12, 116; id., 'Verdeckter Militärstreik', 149–51.

[164] Deist, 'Der militärische Zusammenbruch des Kaiserreichs', 116; id., 'Verdeckter Militärstreik', 157.

[165] Erich Otto Volkmann, *Der Marxismus und das deutsche Heer im Weltkriege* (Berlin, 1925), 195, 313.

[166] Ibid. 192.

medical treatment) to avoid combat[167]—increased considerably; Volkmann estimated the number of the *Drückeberger* during the final months of the War at between 750,000 and one million.[168] The German army was quite literally falling apart.

In the weeks which immediately preceded the Armistice, war-weariness gave way to outright defeatism. As Wilhelm Deist has noted, the growing realization of the hopelessness of the military situation after the spring offensives and the horrific losses had led to a 'covert military strike', the aim of which was to bring the war to an end.[169] Soldiers on leave were, according to apoplectic authorities, spreading 'the most unbelievable, horrible tales',[170] and urging those at home to ignore the latest war-loan because the military situation was so bad.[171] By the end of October 1918 all faith in the military had evaporated:

Among the working masses the belief is widely held that large-scale desertions are daily occurrences and that one can no longer reckon with a serious capability of military resistance. The masses are supported in this belief by numerous soldiers on leave who, perhaps in order to boast, report about the lack of discipline. The desire for peace is, especially in the big cities, so enormous that the working masses generally are neither angry nor dismayed about the ostensible situation at the front, but rather feel at best a sorry, often malicious satisfaction that the War *must* end, even if it ends with Germany's defeat. Every hopeful word about the military situation is met with mistrust.[172]

Finally it had become obvious to just about everyone that Germany's war was finished. The only thing left to do was to stop the fighting as quickly as possible. Many military units—especially those behind the lines—refused to fight, mutinied, or simply disbanded themselves; officers reported that the soldiers wanted 'peace at any price', 'that the men will no longer continue to fight if we do not get peace right away'.[173] A large number of soldiers on leave did not return to the front but instead remained in large cities within Germany; on 1 November 1918 Captain Gustav Böhm, an adjutant in the Prussian War Ministry, asserted that the number of 'deserters and

---

[167] See Deist, 'Der militärische Zusammenbruch des Kaiserreichs', 115–16.
[168] Volkmann, *Der Marxismus und das deutsche Heer*, 193; Deist, 'Der militärische Zusammenbruch des Kaiserreichs', 117.
[169] Deist, 'Der militärische Zusammenbruch des Kaiserreichs', 119; id., 'Verdeckter Militärstreik'.
[170] HHStA, 405/6360, fo. 117: Landrat to Regierungspräsident, St. Goarshausen, 16 Sept. 1918.
[171] GLAK, 456/E.V.8, Bund 86: stellv. Gen.Kdo. XIV. Armeekorps to Großh. Ministerium des Innern, Karlsruhe, 1 Oct. 1918.
[172] SHAD, Gesandtschaft Berlin, no. 349, fo. 96: Sächsische Gesandtschaft to Staatsminister für die Auswärtigen Angelegenheiten, Berlin, 29 Oct. 1918.
[173] See Hans-Joachim Bieber, *Gewerkschaften in Krieg und Revolution: Arbeiterbewegung, Industrie, Staat und Militär in Deutschland 1914–1920* (2 vols.; Hamburg, 1981), ii. 568; Deist (ed.), *Militär und Innenpolitik*, ii. 1356 n. 4.

similar riff-raff' had reached 20,000 in Berlin alone.[174] At the beginning of November there were mutinies behind the lines, and many men left their units to await the end of the War at a safe distance from the front; Ludendorff later spoke of 'a few hundred thousand', and other estimates put the number at about 200,000.[175] Units in the rear refused to go to the front, and the army proved itself almost completely incapable either of continuing the war or of taking action to suppress unrest within Germany. Like the illusory 'spirit of 1914' on the home front, the German armed forces, which had been the ultimate guarantor of the Imperial system, had disintegrated.

The processes of disintegration which overwhelmed the German army and state were not simply the product of a polarization of economic and class tensions brought about by the War, important as such polarization was in undermining the Imperial political system. At stake were neither just economic and class interests nor simply the power of the military and state bureaucracy, but also social values—conceptions of a just society and of 'normal' social relations which the War had allegedly disrupted. The Imperial system, which had once symbolized order, had degenerated into chaos. This, as much as the economic and political tensions which resulted from Germany's disastrous conduct of the War, set the agenda for the demobilization which was to follow. The War had bankrupted the old regime in every sense: militarily, politically, financially, and morally. The time to try to pick up the pieces had arrived.

---

[174] Heinz Hürten and Georg Meyer (eds.), *Adjutant im preußischen Kriegsministerium Juni 1918 bis Oktober 1919: Aufzeichnungen des Hauptmanns Gustav Böhm* (Stuttgart, 1977), 52.

[175] Erich Ludendorff, *Kriegsführung und Politik* (Berlin, 1922), 154; Deutsche Akademie der Wissenschaften, Zentralinstitut für Geschichte, *Deutschland im Ersten Weltkrieg*, iii: *November 1917 bis November 1918* (2nd edn., Berlin, 1970), 520–1.

# 2

# Wartime Planning for Post-war Demobilization

> It is probably the greatest error of the Reich government that in drawing up the demobilization plans there was no allowance for the possibility that Germany might lose the War. It was always reckoned that the demobilization would proceed slowly, and the new planning for the economy was constructed on that basis. As a result of the course of events the whole demobilization planning has been thrown out the window, and we face the fact that as soon as the War is over the troops will have to be discharged. We will probably be forced to disarm completely and to discharge the veterans back into Germany. That will mean that a huge number of workers will come back home and face destitution.[1]

THUS a trade-union functionary in Bamberg described the prospects for an orderly demobilization in October 1918, as it suddenly dawned on Germans that they had lost the First World War. The fears which he expressed appeared well-founded. Never before had an industrial society been faced with the challenges which confronted Germany in the autumn of 1918: the sudden demobilization of millions of soldiers; the forced dismantling of the armed forces; the compulsory redirection of the economy from war production to meeting civilian needs. The victorious Allies would have time to put plans for an orderly demobilization into practice; the Germans would not: they had to bring about an unprecedented transformation of social and economic relationships almost overnight, after having lost the most destructive war yet fought. The prospects for success seemed slender indeed.

States do not plan during wartime for their own defeat, and Germany during the First World War was no exception. To have developed detailed plans for military and economic demobilization which took into account the possibility that Germany might lose the conflict would probably have been impossible. Such an exercise would have smacked of defeatism in a country where for years government propaganda had been stressing the need to 'see it through' and where in official circles a nationalist, patriotic spirit formed a common denominator, expected of all public figures. In any event no one could have predicted the precise conditions of defeat, conditions which would be dictated largely by the enemy and

---

[1] BHStA, Abt. IV, MKr 14412: comments of Gemeindebevollmächtigter Johannes Steitz (Gewerkschaftssekretär), 'Aufzeichnung über die von der Kriegsamtstelle Würzburg einberufene Besprechung am 18. Oktober 1918 im Sitzungssaale des Rathauses zu Bamberg'.

which would fix the parameters within which the demobilization would have to be carried out.

Nevertheless, the German authorities—like their counterparts in other belligerent countries—devoted considerable time and effort, particularly during 1917 and 1918, to planning for the demobilization which would follow the War.[2] According to the Prussian War Ministry in March 1917, when it requested comments from regional authorities on draft plans for the military demobilization:

> The moment when the demobilization will begin cannot be predicted at the present time, nor can the situation which will have developed by then. A demobilization plan can therefore only draw up general principles and give guide-lines for the preparation. Without timely preparations, however, the smooth implementation of a demobilization is impossible. Consideration of our economy requires early arrangements for the return, accommodation, and allocation of the labour force, as well as the collection and handing-over of the horses and army *matériel* which will become available to agriculture, industry, tradespeople, etc. The authorities responsible for the preparation and implementation of the demobilization must concern themselves in a manner similar to that with which they prepared for mobilization during peacetime. Considering the extent of the tasks, we must not wait until the moment of the demobilization is upon us.[3]

At stake was not only how to return workers to factories and horses to farms, but also broader questions of how the post-war economy was to be organized and what should be the nature of the 'transition economy' (*Übergangswirtschaft*). The vast extension of state intervention in economic affairs—in the allocation of raw materials, the fixing of prices, the direction of labour, and so forth—marked a sharp break from the way the German economy had functioned before 1914 and presented questions of far-reaching significance to those who would have to manage the demobilization. In grappling with the immediate problems which would be created by the return of millions of soldiers and the termination of war contracts, they would inevitably be taking decisions about how the economy was to be managed and structured. To what extent should state controls be dismantled, and what should be put in their place? To what extent was it either possible or desirable to return to pre-1914 conditions and practice?

Already in 1915 it had become obvious that the post-war transition would create tremendous problems and raise important issues that required advance

---

[2] See e.g. the detailed preparations outlined in BAP, RMdI, no. 12400; GStAM, Rep. 77, tit. 332d, no. 1, Bd. 2; GStAM, Rep. 120, BB VII 1, no. 3o, Bd. 1; BA/MA, RM 3, v. 4673–6; StAM, Regierung Münster, no. 3053. See also Martin Sogemeier, *Die Entwicklung und Regelung des Arbeitsmarktes im rheinisch-westfälischen Industriegebiet im Kriege und in der Nachkriegszeit* (Jena, 1922), 82–7. The Reich government also kept careful watch on the British planning for demobilization. See the 'Englische Berichte' in BAP, RWM, no. 7290.

[3] GStAM, Rep. 77, tit. 332d, no. 1, Bd. 2, fos. 5–6: Kriegsministerium, Berlin, 5 Mar. 1917.

planning, but disagreement about who should oversee the process, and about what should be the aims of the planning, delayed action. Proposals were put forward in 1915 and 1916, by Walther Rathenau and Wichard von Moellendorf, for a central Reich organization which would oversee economic affairs, for an 'economic general staff'; but it was not until October 1917 that a rather more modestly conceived Reich Economics Office was established officially.[4]

The first attempt to create an institution whose task was to co-ordinate planning for the economic demobilization and the transition had actually come in 1916, and had not proved a resounding success. The Reich Commissariat for the Transition Economy, (which Moellendorf had proposed in the Interior Office and in whose setting-up he played a major role) was formed in August 1916. Formally subordinate to the head of the Reich Interior Office, it was a characteristic compromise and illustrative of the failure of the German wartime administration to plan the economy effectively. In the absence of clear agreement about what to aim for after the War was over, the Reich Commissariat was allotted essentially an advisory role—rather different from the conception of Moellendorf, who was offered the post of a Deputy Reich Commissar.

Unlike Moellendorf, neither the Reich Commissar, the Hamburg senator Dr Friedrich Sthamer, nor Karl Helfferich, the former head of the Reich Treasury Office and newly appointed State Secretary of the Reich Interior Office, were enamoured of the wartime state economic controls. Both looked forward to the abolition of controls and a speedy return to 'the old peacetime conditions'. The organization Sthammer headed consisted of a small Commissariat (comprising a Reich Commissar and nine members drawn from industry, agriculture, and trade, to head sections of the new organization) and an advisory board of nearly 400 members (which never met), and proved ill-suited to reaching clear conclusions or making clear recommendations. It possessed no real authority to determine the shape of the 'transition economy', and its main work was limited to gathering statistical information—the refuge of the powerless bureaucrat.[5] While it is true that the Reich Com-

---

[4] See Hans Gotthard Ehlert, *Die wirtschaftliche Zentralbehörde des Deutschen Reiches 1914 bis 1919* (Wiesbaden, 1982), 54–72; Dieter Baudis and Helga Nussbaum, *Wirtschaft und Staat in Deutschland vom Ende des 19. Jahrhunderts bis 1918/19* (Berlin, 1978), 326–9. There had been some suggestion before the War that responsibility for economic policy be removed from the Reich Interior Office (which had become a huge ministry with a vast array of functions, and which devoted more attention to social policy than to the formulation of economic policy in the modern sense), but the War gave this idea new life. Karl Helfferich, who headed the Interior Office and who was a steadfast opponent of state intervention in the economy, energetically opposed the setting-up of the Reich Economics Office.

[5] Ehlert, *Die wirtschaftliche Zentralbehörde*, 58–9. For a contemporary description of the work of the Reich Commissariat to the end of 1917, see BHStA, MKr 14411: 'Aktenvormerkung über die am Mittwoch, den 19. Dezember 1917 vormittags 10 Uhr im K. Staatsministerium des K. Hauses und des Äussern stattgehabte Besprechung Übergangswirtschaft', report by Staatsrat

missariat was a 'half-hearted interim solution' to the problem of how to plan for the post-war transition,[6] and one with which its own leadership was dissatisfied, its failure was due not only to the lack of clear powers but also to the wartime situation: no one was quite sure when or how the War might end, and in the absence of clear parameters for making decisions, there was little to do but amass statistical information about the probable need for raw materials, about transport, storage problems, and foreign exchange. When the Reich Interior Office was broken up in October 1917 and the newly created Reich Economics Office given responsibility to prepare for the demobilization and post-war transition, these fundamental uncertainties and obstacles to effective planning remained.

It was assumed by wartime planners for the demobilization and the post-war transition that Germany would emerge from the conflict victorious, although they were concerned to decouple planning for the economic demobilization from the actual course of the War, lest people get the wrong idea about when the conflict might be over.[7] Indeed, the Prussian War Ministry was concerned generally to keep discussion of the demobilization secret from the public.[8] The planning revolved around two interrelated concerns: bringing back the millions of men in uniform; and managing the economy in order to provide a smooth transition from military to civilian production and to provide employment, particularly for the returning soldiers and the workers in armaments factories. Specifically, the planning for the military demobilization and the return of the soldiers was outlined in the Demobilization Plan for the German Navy (first released in 1916) and the Demobilization Plan for the German Army (published in early 1918).[9] These plans outlined fairly comprehensively the order and procedures for the military demobilization to take place at the end of the War, although it was admitted that they remained general guide-lines and would have to be 'adapted to circumstances' when the time came. Attention was also paid to what should be done with the massive amounts of military hardware accumulated during the conflict. However, the principal focus was

von Meinel. On Helfferich, see John G. Williamson, *Karl Helfferich 1872–1924: Economist, Financier, Politician* (Princeton, NJ, 1971), 111–50.

[6] The phrase is from Ehlert, *Die wirtschaftliche Zentralbehörde*, 61.

[7] LHSA, Rep. C 3o Salzwedel, A, no. 1940/I, fo. 147: printed circular about 'Wirtschaftliche Demobilmachung' from the Kriegsamtstelle Magdeburg, Feb. 1918.

[8] See the introductory comments by Major von Gall at a conference called to discuss the economic demobilization in the Prussian War Ministry, in GStAM, Rep. 120 BB, Abt. VII, Fach I, no. 30, Band I, fos. 52–84: Kriegsministerium, 'Bericht über die Sitzung vom 9. Februar 1917, betreffend wirtschaftliche Demobilmachung, im Preußischen Kriegsministerium', Berlin, 19 Feb. 1917. The comment by Major von Gall may be found on p. 2 of the report, fo. 55.

[9] See GStAM, Rep. 77, tit. 332d, no. 1, Bd. 2, fos. 55–66: 'Demobilmachungsplan für das Deutsche Heer'; Wolfram Wette, 'Die militärische Demobilmachung in Deutschland 1918/19 unter besonderer Berücksichtigung der revolutionären Ostseestadt Kiel', *Geschichte und Gesellschaft*, 12 (1986), 66–7.

the men in uniform: the main concern of the military and civilian authorities was that the soldiers be discharged in a planned, gradual manner—with the older men demobilized first—in tune with the capacity of the German economy to absorb the returning labour-power.

Such planning necessitated a detailed picture of local conditions throughout Germany, and at the beginning of 1918 the War Office in Berlin instructed the regional War Office Boards (Kriegsamtstellen, set up in November 1916 in the districts of the Deputy Commanding Generals to inform the War Office about local developments and to implement its orders)[10] 'to gain a general overview as soon as possible of which and in what quantity workers will be required on the labour market'.[11] The Kriegsamtstellen in turn urged private firms to 'prepare information now concerning the extent to which they want to increase their hitherto existing work-force of male and female labourers in the course of the demobilization, and in what way they will probably make a change in their present work-forces': 'In this regard', as the Kriegsamtstelle in Magdeburg made clear in February 1918, 'we must consider in good time how of course first of all to make their jobs available for the returning soldiers, but on the other hand how to deal with the war invalids, women, youths etc. among the present labour-force without creating hardship.' The emphasis, however, was on private initiative, not direct state intervention. The Magdeburg Kriegsamtstelle (echoing the assessment in the Demobilization Plan for the German Army) went on to note:

Probably a large proportion of the labour force will already have made contact with their former employers on their own initiative, in order to be certain of a job after their discharge. Equally the employers will certainly attach great importance to getting their old tried and tested workers back. Establishing this mutual contact as soon as possible cannot be recommended emphatically enough.[12]

Of course not all the returning soldiers would be in such a happy position: some had been self-employed or would be unable to find work with their old employers—for example, where employers had gone out of business. According to the army's Demobilization Plan, 'these people should be

---

[10] See Gerald D. Feldman, *Army, Industry und Labor in Germany 1914–1918* (Princeton, NJ, 1966), 194.

[11] LHSA, Rep. C 30 Salzwedel, A, no. 1940/I, fo. 144: Kriegsministerium, Berlin 3 Jan. 1918. See also APS, Oberpräsidium von Pommern, no. 3951: Minister für öffentliche Arbeiten to Oberpräsidenten, Regierungspräsidenten, and Polizeipräsidenten in Berlin, Berlin, 7 Feb. 1918; APP, Landratsamt Grätz, no. 732: Kriegsamtstelle Posen to Landratsämter im Bereiche des V. Korpsbezirkes, Posen 12 Jan. 1918.

[12] LHSA, Rep. C 30 Salzwedel, A, no. 1940/I, fo. 147: printed circular about 'Wirtschaftliche Demobilmachung' from Kriegsamtstelle Magdeburg, Feb. 1918. For the relevant excerpt of the 'Demobilization Plan', see APP, Landratsamt Grätz, no. 732: 'Anhang C zum Demobilmachungsplan für das deutsche Heer', 19–20 ('Anleitung für die Truppenteile über die Arbeits- und Stellenvermittlung bei der Demobilmachung').

supported by word and deed, in order that they get appropriate opportunities for work as soon as possible', which required co-operation between the troop formations and the labour exchanges.[13]

These recommendations presupposed that the army Command would retain a strong role in organizing and supervising economic life during the demobilization period, and should be seen against the background of earlier attempts by the army to put the War Office in charge of managing the demobilization and post-war economic transition.[14] They also obviously presupposed that sufficient time would be available to allow for the gradual, orderly putting into practice of the plans so carefully being drawn up, discussed, and revised at various levels of the government bureaucracy. This, in turn, presupposed victory—which shaped both the assumptions about conditions within which the demobilization would take place and the ways in which the planners themselves legitimated their activities.[15]

There were, however, fundamental contradictions in the wartime planning for an orderly demobilization of the armed forces. On the one hand, the authorities had to plan for a demobilization which would simultaneously satisfy military requirements and appear just in the eyes of the soldiers. This meant both that the strength of certain units needed to be maintained and that the men who had served the longest should be allowed to return home first. On the other hand, a smooth transition from a wartime economy to production for civilian needs involved a rather different set of priorities. The capacity of the German economy, as perceived by the planners, to absorb the returning soldiers did not necessarily fit with the military criteria for a smooth demobilization. Therefore much of the planning effort involved trying to ascertain the capacity of various sectors of the economy and of individual employers to take on labour once peace arrived, and somehow co-ordinating the planned military demobilization with the planned economic demobilization. The officials concerned were convinced not only that the time and effort they devoted to this exercise was necessary, but also that the demobilization itself, because of its complexity and the difficulties it involved, would require considerable time to be carried out properly. People whose job it was to draft detailed plans, naturally assumed that major social and economic challenges could be met successfully only if there was time to carry out their detailed plans.

It was not just logistical questions which exercised official minds. The severe problem of wartime morale within Germany, and particularly the

[13] APP, Landratsamt Grätz, no. 732: 'Anhang C zum Demobilmachungsplan für das deutsche Heer', 20.
[14] See Feldman, *Army, Industry and Labor*, 298–300.
[15] See e.g. Jürgen Reulecke, *Die wirtschaftliche Entwicklung der Stadt Barmen von 1910 bis 1925* (Neustadt/Aisch, 1973), 111–12.

upsurge of strike activity in early 1918, indicated to many that the economic and social problems which the demobilization would generate required time to sort out. Thus, for example, the Factory Inspector in Elberfeld expressed grave concern after being informed by the representative of the regional War Office Board at a meeting in Düsseldorf on 15 May 1918 that the demobilization should be completed within the space of four months; in his view, so speedy a demobilization would be impossible both militarily and politically:

In Elberfeld roughly 35,000 people have been conscripted, one-tenth of whom have fallen. Therefore if over 30,000 people return in quite a short space of time to Elberfeld, with its total population of 170,000, a sudden collapse of wage levels would be inevitable; for the level of wages is always determined by supply and demand. But food prices and the costs of other necessities (housing, clothing) will not sink to the same extent. Therefore one must strive to harmonize the discharging (of the soldiers) at least to some extent with the reduction of prices, if one is not to produce considerable dissatisfaction and unrest.[16]

Widespread expectations of reductions in prices and wages once the War ended combined with widespread (and rather more realistic) fears of civil unrest to make a successful rapid demobilization appear impossible. After the food riots and strikes which had taken place as living-conditions within Germany deteriorated during the War, there was understandable worry about the possible social and political consequences of letting millions of soldiers loose on civil society and the labour market immediately, once the War was over.

State bureaucrats were not alone in making preparations for the demobilization. Both employers and trade unions were anxious about the post-war transition. Employers were understandably concerned that their requirements for labour and raw materials should receive proper attention. Particularly during the later stages of the War, employers actively set about planning to re-employ former workers then in uniform.[17] Many employers kept careful records of workers who had gone off to war, in order to facilitate rehiring them once hostilities ended.[18] The Herne mining firm Hibernia, for example, kept month-by-month records of those of its workers—more than 12,000— who had been called up between August 1914 and October 1918.[19] The

---

[16] HStAD, Regierung Düsseldorf, no. 33557: Kgl. Gewerbeinspektor to Regierungspräsident, Elberfeld, 30 July 1918.

[17] BAP, RMdI, no. 13088, fos. 45–8: 'Denkschrift der Vereinigung der Deutschen Arbeitgeberverbände. Forderung der Übergangszeit und Friedenswirtschaft', Mar. 1918. See also the letters of various firms to the Chamber of Industry and Trade in Dortmund concerning the re-employment of soldiers, in WWA, K1/172.

[18] See e.g. WWA, K1/172: Westfälisches Verbands-Elektrizitätswerk to Handelskammer Dortmund, Dortmund, 29 July 1918; ibid., Schüchtermann & Kremer Maschinenfabrik to Handelskammer Dortmund, Dortmund, 31 July 1918.

[19] Reports of the BBA, Bestand 32, no. 4324 and 4325.

trade unions, fearing that post-war unemployment would undermine their bargaining-strength,[20] were also concerned that their interests be safeguarded. Increasingly the government, the army leadership, and major employers became convinced that the help of trade-union leaders would be necessary when the demobilization arrived.[21] Indeed, employers looked to collaboration with the trade unions in order to avoid the 'bureaucratic' management of the demobilization by the War Office. They felt that they probably had less to fear from trade-union leaders than from government agencies determined to extend state economic controls well into the post-war period. Trade-union leaders, for their part, were keen to extend their influence and to build upon the official recognition granted them through the implementation of the Auxiliary Service Law;[22] and, as Carl Legien, SPD Reichstag deputy and Chairman of the General Commission of Trade Unions, noted at a conference about the economic demobilization held in the Prussian War Ministry in February 1917, they wanted to avoid unpleasant surprises of the sort which had occurred on the labour market after the war was declared in 1914.[23] In this way the need to plan for the post-war transition drew employers and trade-union leaders together during the second half of the War, and helped pave the way for the corporatist settlement between industry and labour in the form of the Stinnes–Legien Agreement of November 1918.[24]

Planning for the post-war transition was driven by two great fears. On the one hand, there was the fear that public order would break down when the troops came home. This lent urgency to plans to ensure that the veterans of the trenches be brought home as quickly, efficiently, and in as orderly a manner as possible; few things seemed more threatening than the prospect of millions of soldiers eager to return home at the War's end being frustrated because the demobilization machinery was not functioning properly. On the other hand, there was anxiety that a poorly organized demobilization would lead to a collapse of the post-war German economy and to massive unemployment. In particular, there was the frightening spectre of hundreds of thousands of demobilized soldiers gathering in Germany's cities with little

[20] See Feldman, *Army, Industry and Labor*, p. 118.

[21] Ibid. 435–9; Hans-Joachim Bieber, *Gewerkschaften in Krieg und Revolution: Arbeiterbewegung, Industrie, Staat und Militär in Deutschland 1914–1920* (2 vols.: Hamburg, 1981), 595.

[22] See esp. Feldman, *Army, Industry and Labor*, 197–249.

[23] GStAM, Rep. 120 BB, Abt. VII, Fach I, no. 3o, Band I, fos. 52–84: Kriegsministerium, 'Bericht über die Sitzung vom 9. Februar 1917, betreffend wirtschaftliche Demobilmachung, im Preußischen Kriegsministerium', Berlin, 19 Feb. 1917. The comment by Legien may be found on p. 26 of the report, fo. 67.

[24] See Gerald D. Feldman, 'German Big Business between War and Revolution: The Origins of the Stinnes–Legien Agreement', in Gerhard A. Ritter (ed.), *Entstehung und Wandel der modernen Gesellschaft. Festschrift für Hans Rosenberg zum 65. Geburtstag* (Berlin, 1970); Gerald D. Feldman, 'The Origins of the Stinnes–Legien Agreement: A Documentation', *Internationale wissenschaftliche Korrespondenz zur Geschichte der deutschen Arbeiterbewegung*, 19/20 (Dec. 1972).

to do but cause trouble. One set of fears pointed towards planning for a rapid demobilization, the other towards planning for a more gradual return of the soldiers, a return dictated less by the soldiers' immediate desires than by the perceived requirements of the economy. Behind both sets of fears lay a deep, almost desperate anxiety about the maintenance and/or re-establishment of *order*.

Of these two fears, it was the second which had the greater impact upon demobilization planning. As the War entered its final year, and as discussions about the post-war transition gathered momentum, planners focused increasingly upon the soldiers in terms of their role in the economy, noting that 'the entire reconstruction of the German economy depends mainly on the proper allocation of the labour at our disposal'.[25] Fears of unemployment arising from a post-war depression, believed to be inevitable,[26] existed alongside fears of economic dislocation caused by sectoral labour-shortages, also regarded as inevitable. In the eastern Prussian provinces worry was rife that if a large proportion of the troops who came from that part of the world were discharged in the western parts of the country, 'with the great attraction which the West has for workers from the East, they would remain there and be lost to the eastern German labour market'.[27] Everything seemed to depend upon discharging soldiers so that they would return in an orderly fashion to their proper, pre-war places of employment. Strenuous efforts were made to assess the capacity of various industries to absorb labour once the armed forces were demobilized.[28] General guide-lines were prepared for restructuring the labour market and setting priorities to determine who would receive jobs and who would not.[29] Behind all this planning stood the assumption that the purpose of demobilization was somehow to return the German economy and German society to the *status quo ante*, to the allegedly normal conditions which had prevailed in peacetime, before August 1914.

This assumption was reflected most clearly in the approach towards women and adolescents in the labour market. As early as April 1915 Clemens von Delbrück, State Secretary in the Reich Office of the Interior, declared (at a conference in Berlin about providing employment for the returning soldiers) that women would have to vacate their jobs as soon as

---

[25] Thus the War Office Board in Leipzig in Jan. 1918. See SSAL, Gewerbekammer Leipzig, no. 545, fos. 42–3: Kriegsamtstelle Leipzig to sämtl. Hilfsdienstmeldestellen im Bereich des XIX. A.K., Leipzig, 26 Jan. 1918.

[26] HStAD, Regierung Düsseldorf, no. 33557: Kgl. Gewerbeinspektion Düsseldorf-Land to Regierungspräsident, Düsseldorf, 22 Aug. 1918.

[27] GStAM, Rep. 77, tit. 332d, no. 1, Bd. 2, fos. 106–7: Oberpräsident der Provinz Schlesien to Minister des Innern, Breslau, 12 Feb. 1918.

[28] See e.g. SSAL, Gewerbekammer Leipzig, no. 545, fos. 44–9: correspondence of various Innungen to Gewerbekammer in Leipzig, Feb. 1918.

[29] See e.g. HStAD, Regierung Düsseldorf, 33557: Kgl. Gewerbeinspektor to Regierungspräsident, Duisburg, 23 Aug. 1918.

possible after the War—comments which won warm approval from organizations representing (male) office workers.[30] Almost no one questioned the assumption that women would have to vacate positions they had come to occupy during the War, in order to make way for the returning soldiers; planners assumed that, whatever disruption this might entail for the people concerned, it would involve 'not all too great a disturbance of the labour market'.[31] Women working in war industries would simply return to their kitchens. The Prussian Factory Inspector for the region around Düsseldorf, writing in late August 1918, put the case with admirable bluntness when he surveyed the probable course of the 'personal and economic demobilization'. Noting that roughly the same numbers were employed in the district as had been the case before the War, although their composition was different, he wrote:

It is assumed that of the workers who are presently in the armed forces the great majority, especially all those who had been employed in large-scale industry, will be able to find work again in their former trades, indeed in their former positions. . . . There can be no doubt that, if we seriously do everything possible to find jobs for all the retuning veterans and the German prisoners of war, a not inconsiderable proportion of the female workers and youths employed hitherto will simply have to be disposed of (*glatt abgestoßen werden muß*). In so far as married women are concerned whose husbands are fighting and who will again be able to devote themselves to their former duties of taking care of the home and raising children after their men return and are reintegrated into economic life, this exchange will take place without a hitch.[32]

While he did foresee difficulties, especially for the unmarried, who would 'face a quite extraordinarily unfavourable employment situation for some time', he regarded these problems as the unavoidable consequences of a necessary campaign to give the returning soldiers 'their' jobs back.

Such assumptions provided grounds for optimism about the job prospects at least for the men in uniform. In Dortmund the Factory Inspectorate noted with satisfaction that all those local employers questioned about the job prospects of the returning soldiers 'responded that they will re-employ their former employees'. The dismissal of women workers

[30] MLHA, Mecklenburg-Strelitzer Ministerium, Abteilung des Innern, no. 4553, fos. 2–3: Soziale Arbeitsgemeinschaft der kaufmännischen Verbände und Deutschnationaler Handlungsgehilfen-Verband to the Großh. Mecklenburgisches Staatsministerium für das Innere, Hamburg/Leipzig/Frankfurt a. M., 8 Oct. 1915.

[31] See Richard Bessel, ' "Eine nicht allzu große Beunruhigung des Arbeitsmarktes": Frauenarbeit und Demobilmachung in Deutschland nach dem Ersten Weltkrieg', in *Geschichte und Gesellschaft*, 9 (1983), 211–29. The quotation comes from a discussion about planning for demobilization in Berlin in Jan. 1918. See BHStA. Abt. IV, MKr 14111: 'Bericht über die Sitzung am 14. und 15.1.18 in Berlin'.

[32] HStAD, Regierung Düsseldorf, no. 33557: Kgl. Gewerbeinspektion Düsseldorf-Land to Regierungspräsident, Düsseldorf, 22 Aug. 1918.

would, it was believed, cause little difficulty, especially in Dortmund's steel works, where 'a large voluntary exodus of the women workers' was expected 'so that a dismissal of the youths and above all of war invalids will hardly come into question'. Confidence was also expressed that the men who would eventually return from Allied prisoner-of-war camps 'will all find work again'.[33] The personal hardship which might result from the reabsorption of millions of soldiers into the civilian economy was expected to fall on groups either which would accept them or whose concerns were of secondary importance: foreign workers, prisoners-of-war, and women.

Planning for demobilization was, in large measure, a projection of expectations and of ideas about how society was and/or should be ordered. Employers expected that they would re-employ the returning soldiers, and the soldiers expected that they would be re-employed after the War ended. These assumptions were hardly ever questioned, and rested upon the belief that it was both possible and desirable to return social and economic relations to what they had supposedly been before 1914. This belief, together with the universal wish to express gratitude to the heroes of the trenches, underpinned basic tenets which guided the wartime planning for the demobilization: that the re-employment of the returning soldiers was, as the Association of German Employer Organizations (Vereinigung der Deutschen Arbeitgeberverbände) put it in March 1918, a 'moral duty', and that the dismissal of women workers to bring this about was necessary not only for the management of the labour market but also for the 'health of the nation' (*Volksgesundheit*).[34]

With economic stability and the *Volksgesundheit* at stake, public officials planning for the post-war transition did not just passively accept the changes in the labour market likely to result from an end to the War; they actively welcomed them. It was all part of the process of putting society back on a healthy, orderly footing. If some people—women—suffered temporary hardship, that was a small price to pay for returning German society to moral health. Anyway, it was good for them. The assessment of the Factory Inspector in Elberfeld, when discussing demobilization planning in July 1918, is revealing. After expressing optimism that 'the discharged soldiers will find work again in Elberfeld', partly because many employers 'regard themselves honour-bound to rehire their former employees, even if they do not have any work for them', he went on to claim:

When the (male) workers are rehired to fill their former positions the dismissal of the many women workers presently employed will be unavoidable; generally,

---

[33] Ibid.: Kgl. Gewerbeinspektor to Regierungspräsident, Duisburg, 23 Aug. 1918.
[34] BAP, RMdI, no. 13088, fos. 45–8.

however, it is to be welcomed if the women workers are removed from the types of jobs that they have taken on but to which they cannot permanently measure up, and are channelled back into their proper vocation.[35]

This willingness to accept, even welcome, disruption for some rested upon a pervasive vision of the sorts of 'vocation' appropriate and 'proper' for different groups of people. Clearly the need to reconstitute (a particular vision of) peacetime conditions and 'proper' social and economic relationships was of greater importance than the hardships to which particular, subordinate groups might be subjected in the process.

Of course not all the planning for the post-war transition was inspired by such lofty motives. When ringing appeals were made to uphold or reconstitute a morally sound social order, economic and political interests were rarely far beneath the surface. Employers may not have been completely insincere when they proclaimed their moral duty to re-employ the soldiers; but they also preferred the reintegration of the soldiers into the labour market to take place on a voluntary basis rather than see the state step in with yet more regulations.[36] Factory owners and trade associations frequently responded to enquiries about their capacity to take on labour after the War by pressing for privileged consideration when it came to the distribution of raw materials in short supply.[37] Organizations representing employees—in particular the conservative German National Union of Commercial Employees (Deutschnationaler Handlungsgehilfen-Verband), which was almost hysterically concerned to prevent women from encroaching on male preserves in office work—took the opportunity to urge that the interests of their members be given special attention.[38]

The desire to recast social and economic relationships in a conventional mould was not confined to government bureaucrats and interest groups which had their own reasons for wanting a return to 'normal'. Many, if not most, of the new recruits who took the places, in factories, in offices, and on farms, of the men in uniform, also regarded their wartime employment as a temporary, abnormal affair. They too assumed that things would return to 'normal' once the War came to an end and that they would have to vacate their jobs when the nation's heroes returned. There was no question

[35] HStAD, Regierung Düsseldorf, no. 33557: Kgl. Gewerbeinspektor to Regierungspräsident, Elberfeld, 30 July 1918.

[36] See Reulecke, *Die wirtschaftliche Entwicklung der Stadt Barmen*, 118.

[37] See e.g. SSAL, Gewerbekammer Leipzig, no. 545, fo. 44: Maler- u. Lackierer Innung für Leipzig und Umgegend to the Gewerbekammer Leipzig, Leipzig, 6 Feb. 1918.

[38] See e.g. the pamphlet prepared by the DHV in 1916 outlining its 'socio-political and economic demands' for the transition to the peacetime economy: 'Wenn der Friede kommt. Sozialpolitische und wirtschaftliche Forderungen der deutschen Handlungsgehilfen für die Überleitung der Kriegs- in die Friedenswirtschaft. Eine Denkschrift an die deutschen Gesetzgeber' (Hamburg, 1916). Copy in MLHA, Mecklenburg-Strelitzer Ministerium, Abteilung des Innern, no. 4455, fos. 11–42.

about this for the large number of war prisoners working in Germany (largely in agriculture), and the hundreds of thousands of foreign labourers who found employment in the overstretched German wartime economy probably also expected to return home after the War. The same appears to have been true for many, if not most, of the women drawn by wartime conditions into full-time employment outside the home—employment which, it should be remembered, was often characterized by long hours, poor working-conditions, and hostility from male colleagues. It should hardly be surprising that such people looked forward to the return of 'normal' peacetime conditions—in which they could return to their native lands or hope to find relative comfort and security in the socially acceptable roles of wife, mother, housekeeper. A normalization of employment patterns was thus widely regarded as the key to a necessary return to proper and ordered social relationships.

Although the labour question dominated the thoughts of the authorities, other aspects of the coming post-war transition were not ignored entirely. The needs of the many young couples who would be setting up households once the conflict was over also aroused official concern. Wartime marriages were monitored, with an eye to providing financial help (usually loans) for those setting up independent households after the War;[39] well-meaning schemes were put forward to help newly married couples acquire household effects after the War, as wartime shortages had made getting such things as cooking utensils and furniture very difficult.[40] However, where such plans were put into practice, not much came of them. After the Armistice other problems were more pressing, and there appears to have been relatively little take-up of the loans on offer.[41] Such measures are more important as expressions of a particular conception of how society should be ordered than as actions which materially changed the circumstances of those they were supposed to help.

Housing, which was regarded—rightly—as a major problem facing the returning soldiers and their families, also generated official concern, but little

[39] See StdALü, Neues Senatsarchiv, XVII, Gruppe 2, no. 11a: Stadt- und Landamt, Dar-lehnskasse für Kriegsbeschädigte, to Senat der Freien und Hansastadt Lübeck, Lübeck, 6 Feb. 1918. This was a proposal to make 100,000 Marks available for such loans. The proposal was rejected by the Lübeck Treasury, which did not agree that it was up to the state to provide such aid.

[40] MLHA, Ministerium des Innern, no. 16345, fos. 2–3: Großh. Ministerium des Innern to Großh. Ämter, Schwerin, 28 Oct. 1918. Here the proposal was to concentrate on providing loans for young couples to enable them to buy the necessary domestic equipment.

[41] Thus in Mecklenburg-Schwerin 300,000 Marks were earmarked in Aug. 1918 for such interest-free loans, but only about half was used (much of it during the later stages of the inflation, so that the total Gold Mark value of the loans was a mere 8,318.15 Marks). Altogether only 82 loans were made between 1919 and 1923, 25 of which were made in 1919. Ibid., fos. 479–82: Mecklenburg-Schwerinisches Landeswohlfahrtsamt (Landesfürsorgeverband) to Mecklenburg-Schwerinisches Ministerium des Innern, Abteilung für Sozialpolitik, Schwerin, 19 Dec. 1925.

action. Although many flats in German towns became empty during the
early stages of the War—as families were forced to give up their own
dwellings once the men had been conscripted and women and children
moved in with parents or in-laws—during the second half of the War housing
became extremely scarce.[42] In some industrial areas, such as the coal-mining centres of the Ruhr, housing shortages formed a major obstacle to
attracting much-needed labour to industries vital to the war effort.[43]
However, the main worry of officials concerned with housing was what
might happen when millions of soldiers suddenly returned and hundreds
of thousands of them married and established new households, at a time
when little or no supply would be available to meet the additional demand.
When faced with an essentially insoluble problem, German civil servants
reached for their pens and gathered more statistics. Much time and effort
were devoted to cataloguing the existing housing-stock and calculating the
probable demand for dwellings after the War.[44] Fears were expressed that
small, and cheap, flats would be in desperately short supply, and recommendations were therefore made 'not to discharge anyone for whom no
housing is available'.[45] Yet again, official planning presupposed a leisurely
demobilization.

Measures which might have helped to avert the coming acute housing-
shortage, in particular the building of more low-cost flats, were impossible
to implement in wartime. The conviction grew—not only among Social
Democratic town councillors but also among their 'bourgeois' counterparts—
that after the conflict substantial state involvement would be necessary,
particularly to provide subsidies for co-operative house-building and to plan
new housing-projects.[46] But that was for the future. During the War the
more immediate tasks of providing the population with food, and the
day-to-day problems of social-welfare work, took precedence within local
government. Then once the demobilization became imminent, in the autumn
of 1918, the German authorities had little time to develop and implement
long-term plans for the post-war housing-stock; they then had no choice but
to focus their activity almost completely upon the need to transport men

[42] See Georg Bieber, 'Der Wohnungsmarkt und die Bekämpfung der Wohnungsnot' (Univ.
of Erlangen, Phil. diss., 1925). See also below, Ch. 6.
[43] See e.g. BBA, Bestand 32, no. 4327: Kgl. Berginspektion 4 to Kgl. Bergwerksdirektion in
Recklinghausen, Waltrop, 24 Jan. 1917.
[44] See e.g. the report of June 1918 about the housing market in Neubrandenburg, in MLHA,
Mecklenburg-Strelitzer Ministerium, Abteilung des Innen, no. 5071, fo. 16: Magistrat to Großh.
Ministerium, Abteilung des Innern, in Neustrelitz, Neubrandenburg, 20 June 1918.
[45] BHStA, MKr 14411: (Bay.) Kriegsministerium to Preuß. Kriegsministerium, 'Betreff: Demobilmachung, hier Sicherung von Erwerb und Unterkunft für die Entlassenen', Munich, 26 July
1917; StdABr, 011/37/1, fos. 1–2: Minister der öffentlichen Arbeiten to sämtl. Regierungspräsidenten and Oberpräsident in Potsdam, Berlin, 6 Oct. 1917. See also below, Ch. 6.
[46] See e.g. Dieter Rebentisch, *Ludwig Landmann: Frankfurter Oberbürgermeister der Weimarer Republik*
(Wiesbaden, 1975), 77, 79.

and material back to Germany quickly and to secure employment for the millions of soldiers returning to civilian life in the coming weeks.

While understandable, viewing the demobilization in this manner necessarily left many aspects of the post-war transition out of the planning process—and largely out of the field of vision of the German state. Typically, as Jürgen Reulecke noted in his study of Barmen during this period, the planning for demobilization 'involved above all considerations about the expected need for labour and raw materials during the period of the "transition economy" '.[47] The concern was with organizing *things*: raw materials, work-forces. Where attention was paid to the reintegration of the soldiers into civil society, this meant essentially their reintegration into the labour market. That these men also were returning to families, to neighbourhoods, to communities attracted little attention. They, and the women who had taken their places both in the factories and at the head of households, were seen in terms essentially of their labour power, not of their relationships with other human beings.

Probably this was the only manner in which the state could actually plan for the lives of its subjects, but it is none the less revealing of the ways in which the German population was regarded by those planning for its future. Concern was voiced during the War, for example, about the detrimental effects upon young people of growing up without the supposedly beneficial influence of their fathers; yet nowhere in discussion of the coming demobilization does one find that soldiers are regarded primarily as fathers, or that their return should be organized primarily so as to reunite them with their children. They were referred to either as members of military units—objects to be shipped back to Germany in an orderly manner—or as members of work-forces—objects to be slotted back into the civilian labour-market. Thus while the demobilization was widely regarded as a moral problem, in that its underlying purpose was to reconstruct a social and moral order which had allegedly been torn apart by the strains of war, it was planned as a logistical and economic one. Moral values may have shaped the assumptions about what the post-war transition meant and how its success could be judged, but practical planning involved more tangible matters. The reintegration of the soldiers into families, households, and communities, it was silently assumed, would follow naturally from their reintegration into the economy.

It is also revealing that the soldiers, as well as the people working within Germany during the War, were regarded by the planners essentially as producers rather than consumers. This was a logical consequence of an approach whereby people were viewed in terms of economic functions rather than social relationships. Problems of consumption, it was assumed, would

---

[47] Reulecke, *Die wirtschaftliche Entwicklung der Stadt Barmen*, 111 fo.

pose relatively little problem if production were organized successfully: take care of production, and consumption would more or less take care of itself; organize people properly in terms of their productive functions, and then their social and personal needs would be met. Despite the widespread concern about an alleged decline in morals and a weakening of the social fabric during the War, this approach remained characteristic of the ways in which the German state in practice regarded the German people.

The view of the post-war transition changed rapidly in the autumn of 1918, as the German authorities feverishly prepared for imminent and rapid demobilization in conditions largely beyond their control and obviously quite different from those which they had assumed only a few weeks before. Once it had become clear that the War was lost, anxious assessments of the new situation came thick and fast. At the end of October 1918 the Reich Economics Office, introducing a series of instructions about 'strengthening the labour market through public works and contracts', reported that the demobilization

will not be able to be initiated and carried out according to the plans which provided for a gradual solution that met the requirements of our economic life. Calm and order will depend upon whether, even in the most adverse conditions, we are successful in providing work and income for the men discharged from the armed forces, as well as for the workers who can no longer be employed in the armaments industry.[48]

Plans which had taken months or years to develop were swept aside. Considerations about how a controlled, leisurely demobilization should be organized suddenly became irrelevant. Now, as the Association of Prussian Rural Districts warned in a confidential memorandum on 1 November, the 'entire future depends upon whether we succeed in carrying out the discharging of the troops without economic and political catastrophe'—upon preventing a disorganized military demobilization and a rise in industrial unemployment which 'can bring about the imminent outbreak of Bolshevism'.[49] Orderly bureaucratic planning was replaced by urgent pleas for action and money in order to prevent disaster. The task now was to forestall the collapse of the political and economic order.

The imminent prospect of defeat led many to fear, not without justification, that discipline and order would break down among the troops, who would then stream home on their own. Cassandras appeared from every corner, predicting that refusal to follow plans laid down for the demobilization could 'sweep the entire army away like a landslide'.[50] As final defeat

---

[48] SHAD, Ministerium der Auswärtigen Angelegenheiten, no. 2494, Band I, fos. 44–5: Reichskanzler (Reichswirtschaftsamt), Berlin, 29 Oct. 1918.

[49] StdABo, KrA 706: Verband der Preuß. Landkreise to Vorsitzender der Kreisausschüsse, Berlin, 1 Nov. 1918.

[50] Thus Gustav Ickler, a National Liberal Reichstag deputy and chairman of a railway workers' union, in a letter to the Reich Chancellor in late Oct. See BAP, RWM, no. 7288, fo. 21: G. Ickler to the Reichskanzler, Berlin-Friedenau, 28 Oct. 1918.

rapidly approached, the military authorities, no less than their civil counter-parts, became alarmed about how to discharge the soldiers without com-pletely losing control of the situation. Conflicting concerns came into play. Should the soldiers be dismissed from their military units at the locations where these units had been based in the Reich (as the military authorities wanted), or should more effort be made to ensure that the demobilized men returned to their homes and jobs and did not congregate in the smaller garrison-towns (as the municipal authorities wanted)?[51] Despite the worries of local authorities and despite the rapidly eroding discipline in the armed forces, the War Ministry stuck until the bitter end to its view that the soldiers should be discharged via their units based in the Reich, 'as only then will the maintenance of discipline and of calm be ensured'.[52] Yet this policy was not entirely compatible with the aim of reintegrating the soldiers into the civilian labour-market quickly and smoothly. The military feared a break-down of order unless the demobilization was carried out in a manner suited to its own organizational structures; the civil authorities feared a breakdown of order unless the demobilization was carried out so as to facilitate the return of the soldiers to 'their' civilian jobs and to minimize the disruption to the domestic economy.[53] However, the collapse of the German war-effort, and of discipline within the German army, had made such concerns super-fluous; at the end of October 1918, those who had hoped for an orderly transition could only pray and hope for the best.

While the condition of the army was quite beyond their control, govern-ment officials concentrated their attention on the German labour-market. As the military situation deteriorated during October 1918, discussion re-volved largely around the fear that unemployment, particularly among veterans, would reach enormous proportions in the months ahead. The main task of the demobilization was managing the labour market, but who would organize this? The regional War Office Boards were already playing an active role, passing on to the labour exchanges lists of workers (arranged by occupation) whom employers especially wanted back.[54] But the question was a broader one. By the beginning of October 1918 the men running the Reich Economics Office, in particular Under-Secretaries Dr Heinrich Göp-pert and Hans Karl Freiherr von Stein, who were convinced that the state

---

[51] See the reports of discussions of the ways in which soldiers were to be released from the army, which took place in Berlin on 25 Oct. 1918, in SHAD, Ministerium der Auswärtigen Angelegenheiten, no. 2494, Band I, fos. 38–9: Kgl. Gesandtschaft Berlin to Kgl. Ministerium der Auswärtigen Angelegenheiten, Berlin, 25 Oct. 1918.

[52] Ibid., fos. 96–7: 'Niederschrift über die Besprechung im Reichswirtschaftsamt am 4. November 1918 4 Uhr Nachmittags'.

[53] Almost until the moment of the Armistice, planners urged that skilled workers needed in key sectors of the economy—for example, miners, skilled agricultural workers—be given pref-erential treatment when it came to being demobilized, as had been foreseen in wartime schemes. Ibid.

[54] Ibid., fo. 34: 'Vertrauliche Besprechung im (sächs.) Kriegsministerium am 16.10.1918'.

needed to retain a guiding role in the post-war transition economy,[55] realized that the demobilization would arrive sooner than many had thought and that specific practical steps needed to be taken. To them this meant that the process should be organized by the Economics Office; and a committee was formed in mid-October of some fifty representatives of state departments, trade unions, and industry—under the chairmanship of the Social Democratic Under-Secretary at the Economics Office, August Müller—to set things in motion.

The Economics Office favoured the continuation of state controls and collaboration with the War Office Boards, and envisaged that the demobilization would be overseen by a working committee of nine members[56] chaired by the Economics Office. This approach was challenged by the head of the War Office's Raw Materials Section, Colonel Joseph Koeth. Koeth, who had succeeded Walther Rathenau at the head of the Raw Materials Section in 1915, called for the appointment of a 'dictator' to oversee the demobilization, and was keen to assign a greater role to the employers and trade unions.[57] Together with trade unionists and the industrialist Ernst von Borsig, Koeth attacked the idea that the War Office Boards should be allowed to run the demobilization, 'as they have no knowledge of the peacetime economy'.[58] In Koeth's opinion, 'one should better leave the proper allocation and distribution of manpower to the organizations of the trade unions and the employers associations, in association with the labour exchanges'— sentiments with which employers and trade-union representatives found it easy to agree.

October 1918 marked the beginning of major shifts in the organization of the German economy which occurred after the First World War: from military to civilian control; from economic controls to deregulation; from economic management by a state bureaucracy to management by economic interests. In this process the military were not the only ones to be effectively squeezed out of practical planning for the demobilization; so was the Reich Economics Office—which had been created in 1917 to prepare for and oversee the economic demobilization to follow the conflict.[59] In the economic

[55] On Göppert and von Stein and their appointment to the Reich Economics Office in Nov. 1917, see Ehlert, *Die wirtschaftliche Zentralbehörde*, 66–8.

[56] One each from the Reich Economics Office, the Prussian War Ministry, the Reich Navy Office, and the War Food Office; two representatives of industry; one representative of agricultural interests; and two trade-union representatives—one each from the Socialist and Christian trade-unions.

[57] For the outlines of the discussion, and of the two competing models, see SHAD, Ministerium der Auswärtigen Angelegenheiten, no. 2492, Band I, fos. 26–8: Kgl. Gesandschaft Berlin to (sächs.) Kgl. Ministerium der Auswärtigen Angelegenheiten, Berlin, 17 Oct. 1918. For general discussion, see Friedrich Zunkel, *Industrie und Staatssozialismus: Der Kampf um die Wirtschaftsordnung in Deutschland 1914–1918* (Düsseldorf, 1974), 184–6.

[58] SHAD, Ministerium der Auswärtigen Angelegenheiten, no. 2492, Band I, fos. 26–8.

[59] See Feldman, *Army, Industry and Labor*, 408.

uncertainty and political vacuum which developed in October 1918, comprehensive planning for the post-war transition was swept aside and the views of Joseph Koeth found resonance, and in the political vacuum created by military collapse and revolution Koeth was placed at the head of the demobilization machinery. Economic uncertainty, political bankruptcy, military collapse, and fear of disorder combined to consign most of the detailed planning for the demobilization to the dustbin.

What remained was the desperate concern to avoid catastrophic unemployment once the troops came home. This involved not just organizing workers. It also involved ensuring that sufficient raw materials were available for factories to keep operating, and for this reason much of the feverish planning during the last weeks before the Armistice concerned the distribution of raw materials. Employers, naturally, took a keen interest in this, for not only the fabric of German society but also their profits depended on it. Another interest of the employers was that subsidies should be granted so that they could keep their work-forces employed during the transition period, and calls were raised for emergency works-projects to be financed, in order to provide employment for men who might otherwise run loose on Germany's streets. According to the Saxon representative at a meeting called in Berlin on 15 October to discuss demobilization plans, it was 'better to employ the workers on unnecessary tasks than to maintain them with unemployment benefit and thereby promote idleness'.[60] Government contracts were not to expire immediately upon declaration of an armistice; state armaments factories and private firms working to fulfil war contracts were to be kept going.[61] The Reich Economics Office, in terms little different from those which would characterize Koeth's directives in the weeks ahead, specified that money should be made available, over and above that already budgeted, for emergency works, in order to prevent unemployment from reaching dangerous proportions and 'to help surmount the crisis of the demobilization'. It urged that budgetary considerations be set aside and that local authorities initiate projects to make up for wartime deterioration in infrastructure (road improvements, building work, repairs to water, sewerage, gas, and electricity works) and soak up labour in the process. 'No expenditure', it was claimed, 'is uneconomical which reduces the danger of a shock which destroys far greater assets.'[62]

Thus during the last weeks of the War planning for demobilization remained focused almost exclusively on the labour market—on measures to provide employment during a period of severe shortages and of sudden shifts

[60] SHAD, Ministerium der Auswärtigen Angelegenheiten, no. 2494, Band I, fos. 22–4: Kgl. Gesandtschaft Berlin to Kgl. Ministerium der Auswärtigen Angelegenheiten, Berlin, 15 Oct. 1918.
[61] Ibid., fo. 34.
[62] Ibid., fos. 44–5: Reichskanzler (Reichswirtschaftsamt), Berlin, 29 Oct. 1918.

in industrial production, and during the return of millions of men who expected to get their old jobs back. In a sense, the real planning for the demobilization was that which took place under extreme pressure in the weeks just before the Armistice. The elaborate plans which had occupied so many bureaucrats during the previous two years were cast aside almost entirely in the panicked atmosphere of October and November 1918. The hallmarks of the feverish last-minute planning—the concentration upon men in the labour market, the concern to act quickly regardless of cost, the willingness to allow industry and organized labour to manage much of the post-war transition—were those which would characterize the actual demobilization.

Nevertheless, the panic which overwhelmed German officials in October 1918 did not radically change their basic ideas about how the returning soldiers should be reintegrated and how civil society should be reconstituted. The return to normal, 'healthy' conditions depended, in their eyes, upon successfully getting the soldiers back home and back to work, and sorting out the supply of raw materials and the finance to keep the economy moving and people employed. The rest would fall into place once the main problem—the re-employment of the soldiers—was solved. Indeed, the panic of the weeks preceding the Armistice seems to have reinforced this approach. There simply was not time to consider problems which required more careful planning or longer-term measures (such as housing) or which looked upon people other than as objects in the labour market. This was one of the main reasons why the chief organizer of the economic demobilization, Joseph Koeth, was able to put all other considerations—including plans for restructuring the German economy—on to the back burner. Sorting out the transport arrangements for the soldiers coming back home, distributing scarce raw materials in such a way that the German economy would not come to a grinding halt, and ensuring that the veterans found employment as quickly as possible—these were the urgent demands of the days ahead. Considering anything else, to say nothing of examining critically the assumptions which underpinned plans for the demobilization, seemed a luxury that the German authorities, faced with military and political collapse, could ill afford.

# 3

## The Return of the Soldiers

All Deputy Commanding Generals have been cabled on 12 November 1918... that Appendix C of the Demobilization Plan for the German Army is invalid and that the discharging of the troops will be governed by special orders.[1]

WHEN the German delegation led by Matthias Erzberger signed the Armistice agreement at Compiègne on 11 November 1918, there remained roughly 6 million men in the German army.[2] They were defeated, tired, hungry, ill. For months they had known that the only sure way they would survive the slaughter of the First World War was to end the conflict as soon as possible; morale had plummeted as hundreds of thousands avoided combat during the last months of the War by engaging in what Wilhelm Deist has justly described as a 'covert military strike'.[3] They had lost the War and they knew it, and more than anything else they wanted to return home.

After the military collapse, and in the midst of a political revolution and economic dislocation of staggering proportions, Germany faced a prospect which no developed industrial country had faced before: the sudden and largely uncontrolled demobilization of millions of soldiers. All the careful planning for the military demobilization, delineating who would be discharged from the armed forces when and where, became superfluous. The

[1] GStAM, Rep. 77, tit. 332d, no. 1, Bd. 2, fo. 329: Kriegsministerium to sämtl. Kgl. preuß. stellv. Gen.Kdos., Berlin, 10 Nov. 1918.

[2] Precise statistics, compiled in the *Sanitätsbericht*, give the month-by-month strength of the army until 31 July 1918, at which time there were 4,227,201 men in the Feldheer and 2,232, 750 in the Besatzungsheer. See Reichswehrministerium, *Sanitätsbericht über das deutsche Heer (Deutsches Feld- und Besatzungsheer) im Weltkriege, 1914–1918*, iii: *Die Krankenbewegung bei dem Deutschen Feld- und Besatzungsheer* (Berlin, 1934), 8. According to testimony subsequently presented to the Committee of Inquiry of the German Reichstag on the causes of the military collapse, between 18 July and 11 November 1918 German losses totalled roughly 420,000 dead and wounded and roughly 340,000 missing and taken prisoner. See Wilhelm Deist, 'Verdeckter Militärstreik im Jahre 1918?', in Wolfram Wette (ed.), *Der Krieg des kleinen Mannes: Eine Militärgeschichte von unten* (Munich, 1992), 150. As the Germans were unable to make good their losses during the final months of the War, it is certain that the army contained fewer men in Nov. 1918 than the 6,459,951 recorded at the end of July.

[3] Wilhelm Deist, 'Der militärische Zusammenbruch des Kaiserreichs': Zur Realität der "Dolchstoßlegende" ', in Ursula Büttner (ed.), *Das Unrechtsregime: Internationale Forschung über den Nationalsozialismus*, i: *Ideologie, Herrschaftssystem, Wirkung in Europa* (Hamburg, 1986); Deist, 'Verdeckter Militärstreik'; above, Ch. 1. See also Richard Bessel, 'The Great War in German Memory: The Soldiers of the First World War, Demobilization, and Weimar Political Culture', *German History*, 6: 1 (1988).

German authorities suddenly became aware that 'a planned step-by-step discharging of the soldiers, in the sense that it was intended and would be urgently necessary for the widest variety of reasons, has become impossible'; instead of being able to prepare a smooth post-war economic transition and maintain a military capability while keeping order among the troops, 'it now is a question solely of carrying out the demobilization without a complete collapse'.[4] In the wake of defeat and the fall of the old regime in November 1918, German officials could hope only that public order would not break down altogether and that they would not completely lose control over the demobilization process. Suddenly they were confronted with problems which had figured only in their worst nightmares: the demands of the victorious Allies that Germany's armed forces be dismantled immediately and the desire of increasingly ill-disciplined soldiers that they be brought home without delay. If the German authorities could not manage the military demobilization within the coming weeks, the matter would be taken out of their hands—either by the Allies or by the soldiers themselves!

The prospect of a sudden military demobilization in these new circumstances filled the authorities with dread, and their initial pronouncements often had an air of desperation about them. Faced with a rapidly disintegrating army, the only hope of maintaining order appeared to lie in convincing soldiers—as Field Marshal von Hindenburg stressed in his order of 9 November to the troops in the west about the political upheaval within the Reich—that they still had to obey orders and that 'only then can an orderly return home take place'.[5] On 12 November the new Reich government, the Council of People's Deputies, adopted a similar tone, simultaneously imploratory and alarmist, in the decree it addressed to the field army:

The People's Government is inspired by the wish that every one of our soldiers, after the untold suffering and the unheard-of privations, should return home in the shortest possible time. This goal, however, can be achieved only if the demobilization proceeds according to an orderly plan. *If individual troops were arbitrarily to flood back, they would most gravely endanger themselves, their comrades, and their* Heimat. *Chaos, hunger and misery would necessarily be the consequence.*[6]

---

[4] LHSA, Rep. C 50 Querfurt A/B, no. 2808, fo. 5: (printed circular) Verband der Preuß. Landkreise, Berlin, 23. Nov. 1918.

[5] Wilhelm Deist (ed.), *Militär und Innenpolitik im Weltkrieg 1914–1918* (2 vols.; Düsseldorf, 1970), ii. 1400–1: 'Befehl des Chefs des Generalstabes des Feldheeres an des Westheer betr. den politischen Umsturz in der Heimat'.

[6] 'Erlaß des Rats der Volksbeauftragten an das Feldheer vom 12. November 1918', printed in Gerhard A. Ritter and Susanne Miller (eds.), *Die deutsche Revolution 1918–1919: Dokumente* (2nd edn., Hamburg, 1981), 101–2. Also clear from this decree, which was distributed in leaflet form, was the concern of the new government that 'discipline and order' be preserved. Revolutionary rhetoric was deployed to this end, as the preservation of order in the army was to be based on

In a Cabinet meeting on 16 November Emil Barth, USPD member of the Council of People's Deputies and Chairman of the Berlin Provisional Workers' and Soldiers' Council, and Prussian War Minister Heinrich Scheüch estimated that 6 million soldiers would stream back to Germany to be demobilized in the coming weeks.[7] Barth warned of a probable 'collapse of our food supply' when millions of hungry soldiers came flooding back, and claimed that 4,000 reliable men would be needed just to guard Berlin's railway stations when the soldiers returned: 'if we do not gain firm control of the completely demoralized troops who are flooding back and who may mutiny at the slightest provocation,' claimed Barth, 'everything will go to the devil.'

In fact, however, the immediate prospects for the demobilization were not quite so dismal as Barth believed. The newly appointed head of the Reich Office for Economic Demobilization, Joseph Koeth, was altogether more hopeful. According to Koeth the Demobilization Office had matters well in hand; 'one should not overestimate the demoralization of our troops', he claimed, and supplies of raw materials, he said, were sufficient to keep people employed for six months provided they were managed properly.[8] Indeed, during November and December 1918, after the initial shock of the defeat, Koeth remained generally optimistic about the progress of the demobilization. This was partly a reaction to the dire expectations of complete collapse which had accompanied defeat and which were not realized, partly a reflection of the fact that during this period the primary task was getting the troops back home—which was the aspect of the demobilization that worked best. It was not until the new year, with the mounting economic and political problems facing the new government, that pessimism once more gained the upper hand in the Demobilization Office.[9]

In their attempts to manage the sudden return of the soldiers, Germany's military and civil authorities were aided by the fact that only a minority of the soldiers who served in the German army during the First World War actually returned to their homes during the military demobilization which immediately followed the Armistice.[10] Soldiers had been returning to civilian life almost from the moment the War began, and continued to do so well

---

a fairness and justice which until that time had been conspicuous by its absence: e.g. officers and enlisted men were to receive the same rations, and 'the relations between officers and men are to be based on mutual trust'.

[7] Susanne Miller and Heinrich Potthoff (eds.), *Die Regierung der Volksbeauftragten 1918/19* (2 vols.; Düsseldorf, 1969), i. 62–4: Cabinet meeting, 16 Nov. 1919.

[8] Ibid. 65–6.

[9] See Koeth's deeply pessimistic concluding comments to the meeting at the Demobilization Office on 4 Jan. 1919, in BHStA, Abt. IV, MKr. 14413: Beauftragter des bayer. Ministerium für milit. Angelegenheiten to Staatskommissar für die Demobilmachung, Berlin, 6 Jan. 1919.

[10] Bessel, 'The Great War in German Memory', 22–4.

into 1920. The statistics compiled by the Ruhr mining firm Hibernia, referred to in Chapter 1, illustrate this point well.[11] Of the Hibernia workers who had been called to do military service and who survived the War, about half were back in Germany, working at Hibernia once again, before the Armistice, in October 1918. Of the 12,114 workers who had been called up, 5,497 were recorded as still being in the armed forces at the War's end; of these, about 2,800 (or about half) were demobilized between November 1918 and March 1919 and returned to the firm. (The vast majority of the soldiers who returned to work at Hibernia did so between the beginning of November 1918 and early February 1919.) Of the remainder, nearly 700 had been taken prisoner and did not return until late 1919 or early 1920, and about 1,000 were, as of mid-1920, unaccounted for—presumably because they had decided to look for work elsewhere. Only about one-quarter of the Hibernia workers who had been called away to war came back in the military demobilization of 1918–19.

While the proportion of men held or called back from military service to work in coal-mining had been especially high, the phenomenon highlighted by the Hibernia figures was a general one. Particularly with the introduction of the Hindenburg Programme, large numbers of skilled workers had been recalled from the armed forces during wartime.[12] At the beginning of 1918 a total of 2,154,387 men liable for military service were being held back in Germany, and between June and July 1918 this figure had risen to about 2,500,000.[13] In addition there had been a growing clamour during the War for temporary leave, as military and civilian authorities were inundated with requests by employers and relatives that soldiers be allowed to return home for reasons of economic or family hardship.[14] In short, a large proportion of the veterans of the First World War were already in Germany by October 1918, and therefore posed no particular problem for the authorities once the War ended. They had effectively been demobilized quite differently from their comrades still at the front in November 1918, and did not figure in the concerns and logistics of the demobilization immediately after the Armistice.

The same may be said about the many German soldiers who had been taken into Allied captivity, large numbers of whom fell into Allied hands during the final months of the War as the western front crumbled. Al-

---

[11]  Reports in BBA, Bestand 32/4324 and 4325. See also above, Ch. 1.

[12]  For an account of this development in Berlin, see BLHA, Rep. 30 Berlin C, Polizeipräsidium Berlin, Tit. 47, no. 1958, fos. 229–338: Regierungs- und Gewerberat zu Berlin, 'Jahresbericht für die Kriegsjahre 1914–1918'.

[13]  Deist (ed.) *Militär und Innenpolitik*, (Düsseldorf, 1970), i. 640, n. 6.

[14]  For a good sample of such requests, see APP, Polizei-Präsidium Posen, no. 9095 and 9096. From the evidence in these files, it appears that the authorities were fairly strict about allowing soldiers to take leave.

together, it was estimated that roughly 800,000 Germans were prisoners of the Allies in early 1919.[15] Most of them returned to Germany during late 1919 and early 1920. The speed with which they returned depended largely upon the nationality of their captors. The luckiest were those in British and American hands, for they were handed back in September and October 1919; most of those in French hands were returned between January and March 1920; while the return of the prisoners from Russia did not get under way until mid-May 1920.[16]

In trying to assess the military demobilization in late 1918 and early 1919, it is therefore important to remember that millions of Germany's 'front generation' returned at other times. Their experiences were quite different from those of their comrades who came back immediately after the Armistice. The soldiers who had returned to Germany during the War came back to a country desperately short of labour; even those who had been seriously wounded and disabled had little difficulty at first in finding work, at least until their healthier comrades returned when the War was over. The hundreds of thousands of German prisoners of war also had a different experience of the return to a civilian existence. They missed both the welcome and general political and economic dislocation which greeted those who returned from military service just after the defeat; and they had to worry whether their belated return disadvantaged them relative to those who had come back earlier and for whom the demobilization authorities had worked energetically to provide jobs.

The shape and success of the military demobilization also reflected two important changes which had occurred in the German army during the months immediately preceding the Armistice. The first was that the proportion of the army stationed behind the lines as opposed to at the front rose considerably: in May 1918 there had been roughly 7 million men in the German armed forces, of whom just over 4 million were at the western front, 950,000 at the eastern front and just under 2 million in the Besatzungsheer; by October 1918 the number of German soldiers on active duty had shrunk to roughly 6 million, of whom about 2.5 million were at the western front and 2.9 million in the Besatzungsheer.[17] The second was the widespread breakdown of discipline, particularly behind the lines, after

[15] Hagen Schulze (ed.), *Akten der Reichskanzlei. Weimarer Republik. Das Kabinett Scheidemann 13. Februar bis 20. Juni 1919* (Boppard/Rhein, 1971), 25: 'Vortrag des Generals v. Hammerstein vor dem Reichskabinett über die Arbeit der Waffenstillstandskommission in Spa, 4. März 1919, 10 Uhr in Weimar, Schloß'.

[16] See StAB, 3–M.2.h.2, no. 130: Reichsminister der Finanzen, Dr. Wirth, to Präsident des Reichstags, 'Denkschrift über die Abwicklung des Krieges', Berlin, 26 Oct. 1920.

[17] *Sanitätsbericht*, iii, Sect. 2, 5; Wilhelm Deist, 'Bemerkungen zur militärischen Demobilmachung 1918' (paper delivered to the German Historical Institute and Open University Conference on 'Social Processes of Demobilization after the First World War in Germany, France, and Great Britain', London, 1981), 4.

the failure of the 1918 spring offensives.[18] As the War approached its end, morale among German soldiers plummeted; the ability of the military leadership to exert control over the enlisted men disintegrated; soldiers increasingly took off on their own in attempts to avoid the fighting and, if possible, return home.

The disintegration of the army had contradictory consequences for the demobilization. On the one hand, it became more difficult for so massive a logistical exercise to be carried out effectively, because lines of command no longer functioned as they should[19] and because so many soldiers were unaccounted for. On the other hand, by November 1918 just about the only thing of which the German armed forces were still capable was their own demobilization. At the War's end the strongest desire among the soldiers was to get back home, immediately.[20] In the words of the naval authorities at Kiel on 13 November, soon after the mutinies which sparked the German revolution, 'people can no longer be held back'.[21] The result was a 'spontaneous demobilization' characterized, as the Kiel military command reported, by the 'precipitate, unordered' discharging of soldiers.[22] Those in charge of the demobilization often had only a hazy idea of what was going on, and matters were not made any better by the large numbers of soldiers who were ill and consequently left their units.[23] At the beginning of December 1918, the Western Army reported to the Reich Demobilization Office that perhaps one million of its remaining 3.2 million soldiers had set out on their own.[24] While many units returned to Germany in reasonably good order, once they arrived in the Reich or crossed the Rhine, soldiers

---

[18] See above, Ch. 1. Also, Deist, 'Der militärische Zusammenbruch des Kaiserreichs'; Bessel, 'The Great War in German Memory', 24–6.

[19] This was true up to the highest level. During late 1918 the Army High Command had 'only scanty contact with the individual army groups'. See SHAD, Mininsterium der Auswärtigen Angelegenheiten, no. 2494, fos. 128–9: stellv. Bevollmächtigte zum Bundesrate, Graf von Holzendorff, to Ministerium der Auswärtigen Angelegenheiten in Dresden, Berlin, 23 Nov. 1918. See also the comments of Wolfram Wette in 'Die militärische Demobilmachung in Deutschland 1918/19 unter besonderer Berücksichtigung der revolutionären Ostseestadt Kiel', *Geschichte und Gesellschaft*, 12 (1986), 67.

[20] Lothar Berthold and Helmut Neef, *Militarismus und Opportunismus gegen die Novemberrevolution. Das Bündnis der rechten SPD-Führung mit der obersten Heeresleitung November und Dezember 1918. Eine Dokumentation* (Berlin, 1958), 58–9.

[21] BA/MA, RM 31/v. 1800: Telegramm, admiralstab rma—ostseestation, Festungs Telegraf der Kieler Hafen-Befestigungen, 13 Nov. (1918). In particular it was those who had come from the occupied Rhineland who 'clamoured to be sent home in order to protect their households'.

[22] Wette, 'Die militärische Demobilmachung', 74–5.

[23] See the comments of Col. Reinhardt as reported at the meeting in the Demobilization Office on 23 Nov. 1918, in SHAD, Gesandtschaft Berlin, no. 690, fos. 25–6: Gesandtschaft Berlin, stellv. Bevollmächtigter Graf von Holtzendorff, to Ministerium der Auswärtigen Angelegenheiten in Dresden, Berlin, 23 Nov. 1918. This account may also be found in SHAD, Ministerium der Auswärtigen Angelegenheiten, no. 2494, Band I, fos. 128–9.

[24] BHStA, Abt. IV, MKr. 14413: Beauftragter des bayer. Ministeriums für milit. Angelegenheiten to Staatskommissar für die Demobilmachung, Berlin, 7 Dec. 1918.

often set out on their own.[25] According to Colonel Walther Reinhardt, speaking in a meeting in the Reich Office for Economic Demobilization in mid-December, shortly before he was named Prussian War Minister, 'the breakdown of discipline which resulted from the domestic upheaval meant that the desire to return home could no longer be contained'; while 'the return march of the nucleus of the formations has generally taken place in good order . . . upon reaching the Reich they too are influenced by the raw urge to return home'.[26] Army units which had remained intact while returning from the western front, simply melted away once they crossed the Rhine.[27]

Once inside the Reich, the soldiers were often well nigh uncontrollable. Behind the lines and within Germany, an estimated half a million men abandoned their units in the weeks immediately following the Armistice.[28] The soldiers who remained with their units and in their garrisons did so, in the words of one officer, 'almost without exception solely in order to receive pay and provisions, *not* to fight—under any circumstances'.[29] In Kiel, according to Wolfram Wette's estimates, roughly one-third of the 50,000 military personnel stationed in the city left 'spontaneously' during the weeks following the naval mutinies.[30] On 18 December Ludendorff's successor as Quartermaster-General, Wilhelm Groener, wrote to the Council of People's Deputies that 'everyone wants to return home; all regard for the enemy, horses, and *matériel*, and for the maintenance of the peacetime army is of secondary importance'.[31] A similar picture emerges from the report submitted by the Reich Finance Minister to the President of the Reichstag in October 1920, describing the return of Germany's heroes:

The unfortunate end of the War, the upheavals back home, the demoralization and lack of discipline which set in meant that the carefully worked-out demobilization plans were thrown out of the window even before they came into force. The soldiers took off from their units on their own, some at the front, some during the trip home. . . . The troop formations wound themselves up, each as it thought suitable, in places

---

[25] StAH, Demobilmachung 7, fo. 11: Oberst Reinhardt, 'Rücktransport und Demobilmachung des Heeres (Sitzung mit dem Demobilmachungskommissar am 18.12.18)'. See also Wette, 'Die militärische Demobilmachung', 67, 69–70.

[26] GLAK, 236/22281: 'Niederschrift über die Besprechung beim Reichsamt für wirtschaftliche Demobilmachung in Berlin am 18. und 19. Dezember 1918', Pforzheim, 23 Dec. 1918. Reinhardt succeeded Heinrich Scheüch as Prussian War Minister on 3 Jan. 1919.

[27] See Erich Ludendorff, *Meine Kriegserinnerungen 1914–1918* (Berlin, 1919), 619.

[28] StAH, Demobilmachung, no. 7, fo. 11: Oberst Reinhardt, 'Rücktransport und Demobilmachung des Heeres (Sitzung mit den Demobilmachungskommissaren am 18.12.18)'.

[29] Albrecht von Thaer, *Generalstabsdienst an der Front und in der O.H.L: Aus Briefen und Tagebuchaufzeichnungen 1915–1919*, ed. Siegfried A. Kaehler (Göttingen, 1958), 289.

[30] Wette, 'Die militärische Demobilmachung', 78.

[31] Quoted ibid. 70.

which for a long time remained unknown to the central authorities. Enquiries remained unanswered.[32]

As the Reich War Ministry later admitted, in an account of the return of German soldiers from the eastern front published in 1936, 'a mood developed among the troops which allowed only one single thought: to return home at any price!'[33]

The precipitate and chaotic nature of the military demobilization was not necessarily a bad thing. Rather than make more difficult the task of getting the soldiers back home, it may have done just the opposite. The fact 'that the carefully worked-out demobilization plans were thrown out of the window even before they came into force' was probably one of the main reasons why the process unfolded surprisingly successfully and with less unrest than expected among soldiers impatient to get home.[34] During November and December 1918, when the transport of the troops was 'proceeding more smoothly than one had hoped',[35] the Demobilization Office in Berlin could be rather optimistic about the way things were moving. It was in the new year, once the great mass of the soldiers had been brought home and the Demobilization Office focused its attentions on the more contentious and intractable structural problems of the German economy, that Joseph Koeth really ran into difficulties. Bringing the soldiers home quickly was one of the few things about which there had been general agreement in the immediate aftermath of the First World War. Gerald Feldman has noted how the initial purpose of both the Stinnes–Legien Agreement and the Ebert–Groener alliance 'was to secure an orderly demobilisation',[36] and the soldiers councils regarded it as an important task to aid the smooth return home of the soldiers.[37] Everyone, it seemed, was keen to bring the boys back home.

[32] StAB, 3–M.2.h.2/no. 130: Reichsminister der Finanzen, Dr. Wirth, to Präsident des Reichstages, 'Denkschrift über die Abwicklung des Krieges', Berlin, 26 Oct. 1920.

[33] Reichskriegsministerium, Forschungsamt für Kriegs- und Heeresgeschichte (ed.), *Die Rückführung des Ostheeres: Darstellung aus den Nachkriegskämpfen deutscher Truppen und Freikorps*) (Berlin, 1936), 22.

[34] The military authorities were not unaware of this. In Kiel, where the mutinies which eventually toppled the Kaiser began, instructions were given 'as soon as possible to blow off as much steam as possible from the overheated, bubbling cauldron, i.e. to undertake wholesale discharging of soldiers'. See Wette, 'Die militärische Demobilmachung', 77.

[35] SHAD, Mininsterium der Auswärtigen Angelegenheiten, no. 2494, fo. 151: stellv. Bevollmächtigter zum Bundesrate, Graf von Holzendorff, to Staatsminister der Auswärtigen Angelegenheiten, Herr (Richard) Lipinski, in Dresden, Berlin, 2 Dec. 1918.

[36] Gerald D. Feldman, *Army, Industry and Labor in Germany, 1914–1918* (Princeton, NJ, 1966), 531.

[37] This was recognized by Koeth, who at the Cabinet meeting of 16 Nov. noted that 'those who are returning on their own should be put in order at the barrier of the Rhine with the help of the local soldiers' councils and the trade unions'. See Miller and Potthoff (eds.), *Die Regierung der Volksbeauftragten*, i. 65. More generally, see Ulrich Kluge, *Die deutsche Revolution 1918/1919: Staat, Gesellschaft und Politik zwischen Weltkrieg und Kapp-Putsch* (Frankfurt/Main, 1985), 140–1.

The responsibility for bringing the soldiers back to the Reich and discharging them, however, remained with the Prussian War Ministry and the military. The Supreme Army Command was responsible for the transport of the troops back to Germany, and within the Reich this responsibility fell to the Deputy Regional Commands.[38] Feeding and lodging the soldiers as they passed through was also the responsibility of the military authorities although the Deputy Regional Commands had to rely on the help of local civilian administrations, economic organizations, local Demobilization Committees, the trade unions, and voluntary associations. These tasks provided the main focus of activity for the German military during the weeks immediately after the Armistice; they comprised probably the only function that the defeated and disintegrating German army could still perform.

The Allied pressure to evacuate occupied territories in northern France and Belgium immediately, and the chaos which overwhelmed the German army at the end of the War, meant that it became impossible to keep the soldiers in uniform until a general demobilization order could be put into practice. As Colonel Reinhardt explained at the meeting in the Demobilization Office in Berlin in mid-December, one of the reasons for not issuing a general demobilization order after the Armistice was the 'avoidance of greater disorder'.[39] Instead, soldiers were to be demobilized as soon as their units had returned to their home garrisons within the Reich, except where they were specially required for border defence or internal security; and all those men in uniform born before 1896 (i.e. all those 24 years old or older) were to be discharged without further ado.[40] The idea was to demobilize as quickly as possible, while preserving an army roughly equivalent in size to that which had existed in the summer of 1914.[41] But this plan soon proved ill-founded. By the time the Reich government issued its general demobilization order on 31 December, it had become obvious that there was little hope of reconstituting the pre-1914 army through an orderly demobilization.[42] The Prussian War Ministry ordered that men born in 1896, 1897, and 1898 be demobilized by the end of January, leaving only the professional soldiers and those born in 1899—men whose normal period of conscription

[38] See the report of the plans for the military demobilization, as outlined by the Demobilization Office in mid-November, in LHSA, Rep. C 50 Querfurt A/B, no. 2808, fo. 2: Regierungspräsident to Landräte and Erste Bürgermeister im Regierungsbezirk Merseburg, Merseburg, 17 Nov. 1918.
[39] Reinhardt's comments in GLAK, 236/22281: 'Niederschrift über die Besprechung beim Reichsamt für wirtschaftliche Demobilmachung in Berlin am 18. und 19. Dezember 1918', Pforzheim, 23 Dec. 1918.
[40] See Wette, 'Die militärische Demobilmachung', 67–8.
[41] 'In the present circumstances the demobilization will signify not disbandment of the army, but the return for the time being to peacetime parameters.' See APS, Regierung Stettin, no. 1713, fos. 31–3: Kriegsministerium, 'Richtlinien für die Demobilmachung', Berlin, 28 Nov. 1918.
[42] For the text of the Demobilization Order, see *Reichsgesetzblatt*, 1919, 1.

would have begun in 1919 anyway.[43] By January the German military leadership had recognized that they could preserve virtually nothing of the old army.[44] The old Imperial German Army had ceased to exist.

The Prussian War Ministry and the Reich Navy Office also recognized that the sudden cessation of war production and the simultaneous return of millions of soldiers would spell tremendous economic dislocation. Accordingly, soldiers 'who despite energetic efforts have not found work in civilian life' were permitted to remain in the army 'in so far as they are dependent upon it for their subsistence'—with the proviso that 'the barracks are not intended for the work-shy'.[45] Military units were instructed to liaise with labour exchanges, and the right to remain in garrisons was withdrawn from those who did not accept jobs offered by the labour exchanges. Garrisons within Germany were not to become gathering-places for unemployed and disaffected soldiers unprepared to make the effort to integrate themselves into the civilian labour-market, and the military authorities looked to collaboration with the expanded network of civilian labour-exchanges to ensure that these intentions became reality.

Such instructions were often irrelevant, however. With so many soldiers in effect demobilizing themselves, and with both military and civilian authority in a shambles, this could hardly have been surprising. Not only had uncounted tens of thousands of soldiers set out on their own, but local authorities often went ahead with the demobilization in advance of instructions from Berlin. Thus Gustav Noske, as Governor of Kiel, ordered the demobilization of categories of skilled workers needed for the civilian economy without waiting for instructions from the Reich Navy Office; by the time the Navy Office issued the relevant guide-lines, Noske had already set in motion much of the demobilization of the sailors in Kiel.[46] Considering conditions in the port at that time, he probably had little alternative.

The most noteworthy aspect of the return of the soldiers after the Armistice was the speed with which it took place. Faced with millions of men whose respect for military discipline was dissolving rapidly and who wanted to return home at all costs, the German authorities saw their task as getting as many men back home as quickly as possible: better a sudden return of the veterans of the First World War carried out within a framework at least loosely determined by the military command than having *all* the men take off on their own. Enlisted men were discharged before officers, and men who had been serving in the west were—in large measure because of the better transport facilities—discharged before those still serving in the

---

[43] See Wette, 'Die militärische Demobilmachung', 68.

[44] See GLAK, 233/12401: XIV. Armeekorps Gen.Kdo., Chef des Generalstabs, to Badisches Ministerium des Innern, Durlach, 7 Feb. 1919.

[45] Wette, 'Die militärische Demobilmachung', 72.        [46] Ibid. 75.

east in late 1918. Already by the middle of December, just a month after the guns had been silenced, the size of the German army had been reduced considerably. In a meeting called in the Demobilization Office on 17 December 1918 to take stock of progress, the representative of the War Ministry reported that the size of the Western Army had already been reduced by 300,000–400,000 men and the Eastern Army by 50,000–100,000; the field army still totalled between 1.75 and 2 million men, but 'the mass of the Western Army will return in December, the Eastern Army in January, and the Group Kiev in February'.[47] On 4 January 1919 the War Ministry was able to report that the entire strength of the once-mighty Western Army was only 300,000 men and 200,000 horses, and that it consisted 'essentially only of a large horse- and wagon-depot'.[48] By 18 January the soldiers from the western front were already within the borders of the Reich,[49] and on 24 January the last troop transport from the west rolled into the East Prussian capital of Königsberg; with that, all the millions of men who just a few months previously had been with the German army in northern France had returned home.[50] On 15 February the Reich Finance Minister, Eugen Schiffer, was able to report to the National Assembly that by the end of 1918 the number of men in German uniform had already been reduced to 3 million, and by the end of January to 'perhaps only one million', and that by mid-February the demobilization had largely been completed—'an achievement which is technically nothing short of remarkable'.[51]

The return of the soldiers from the east took rather longer and involved greater difficulties than did the return from the west. The main problem was transport. Not only was the political situation in Poland and Russia much less certain and stable than in France and Belgium, but the German forces were scattered over a much wider area in the east than they had been in the west, and the rail network was much poorer. The irregularity of trains crossing the eastern German border, and the lack of locomotives needed to bring the trains from the border into the Reich, formed serious obstacles to getting the men back quickly from the east.[52] These problems

[47] BAP, RWM, no. 7250, fos. 21–6: Demobilmachungsamt, 'Vermerk über die Sitzung vom 17.12.18 9 Uhr vorm. über Allgemeine Verkehrslage'.

[48] BHStA, Abt. IV, MKr. 14413: Beauftragter des bayer. Ministeriums für milit. Angelegenheiten to Staatskommissar für die Demobilmachung, Berlin, 6 Jan. 1919.

[49] Ibid.: Beauftragter des bayer. Kriegsministeriums für milit. Angelegenheiten beim preuß. Kriegsamt und Vertreter des bayer. Staatskommissars für Demobilmachung beim Demobilmachungsamt to Staatskommissar für die Demobilmachung, Berlin, 21 Jan. 1919.

[50] GStAB, Rep. 30/732: Demobilmachungsamt, 'Niederschrift über die Sitzung am Mittwoch, den 29. Januar vormittags 10 Uhr im Demobilmachungsamt über Allgemeine Lage', Berlin, 29 Jan. 1919.

[51] *Die Deutsche Nationalversammlung im Jahre 1919 in ihrer Arbeit für den Aufbau des neuen deutschen Volkstaates*, ed. E. Heilfron i. (Berlin, 1919), 216.

[52] See GStAB, Rep. 30/732: Demobilmachungsamt, 'Niederschrift über die Sitzung am Mittwoch, den 29. Januar vormittags 10 Uhr im Demobilmachungsamt über Allgemeine Lage', Berlin, 29 Jan. 1919.

in turn gave rise to additional anxieties among the soldiers, in particular
that they might arrive back in the Reich too late to get work, after the
troops coming from the west had been able to settle back into civilian life.[53]
Nevertheless, considering the problems, the speed with which even the
armies of the east were brought back to Germany was remarkable: by March
1919 their return had been completed.[54]

The speed and scale of the operation meant that many basic concerns
about how best to organize and order the demobilization had to be ignored.
For example, insufficient trained personnel sometimes remained to ensure
that soldiers were demobilized properly, with their papers in order.[55] Instructions by the Supreme Army Command for employers to give preference
when hiring to 'properly discharged' ex-soldiers, in order to keep troops
from simply abandoning their units, were often more expressions of hope
than reflections of reality.[56] However desirable the priorities about who
should be discharged before whom, in the conditions of late 1918 they were
often quite impractical.[57] Yet, much to the surprise of those responsible for
the demobilization process, this sudden and chaotic discharge of millions of
soldiers proved remarkably successful. Although they could hardly have been
expected to appreciate it, the German authorities were probably fortunate
to have been spared the difficulties faced by their British and French
counterparts, who had the time to arrange a more orderly demobilization
according to plan. French and British soldiers, having won the War, had to
wait much longer before being discharged; this in turn caused considerable
discontent and disturbances among the ranks, in some instances leading to
'soldiers' strikes'.[58] Most German soldiers, by contrast, were able to go
straight home.

Despite the fears about the maintenance of discipline and control, the
overwhelming desire to get home proved an asset to the War Ministry in
its efforts to demobilize the army. For most soldiers in the field, the quickest
way home was to remain with one's unit and thus get a place on a troop

[53] See Reichskriegsministerium (ed.), *Die Rückführung des Ostheeres*, 22.

[54] See Jürgen Tampke, *The Ruhr and Revolution: The Revolutionary Movement in the Rhenish-Westphalian Industrial Region 1912–1919* (London, 1979), 146.

[55] See Wette, 'Die militärische Demobilmachung', 76.

[56] MLHA, Mecklenburg–Strelitzer Ministerium, Abteilung des Innern, no. 4445. fo. 70:
Reichsamt für die wirtschaftliche Demobilmachung to sämtl. Demobilmachungskommissare,
Ministerium für öffentliche Arbeiten, Reichs-Marine-Amt and Reichs-Postamt, Berlin, 1 Dec.
1918.

[57] See the comments of Col. Reinhardt in GLAK, 236/22281: 'Niederschrift über die
Besprechung beim Reichsamt für wirtschaftliche Demobilmachung in Berlin am 18. und 19.
Dezember 1918', Pforzheim, 23 Dec. 1918.

[58] For the experience of the French soldiers, see Antoine Prost, 'Die Demobilmachung, der
Staat und die Kriegsteilnehmer in Frankreich', in *Geschichte und Gesellschaft*, 9 (1983), 178–82; for
discontent among British soldiers about delays in demobilization, see Andrew Rothstein, *The
Soldiers' Strikes of 1919* (London, 1980), 37–75.

train back to the Reich. Against the background of a general breakdown in authority and the soldiers' demands for a rapid return home, the demobilization became a dangerous balancing-act: an attempt to salvage what could be salvaged of Germany's military institutions while simultaneously moving sufficiently quickly that the soldiers did not simply all strike out on their own. The general maintenance of 'good order' as German military formations marched back from the front was in large measure a consequence of the fact that, until a soldier reached the borders of the Reich, following orders usually offered the best way to get home.

Although the speed of Germany's military demobilization obviated the problem of restraining unruly soldiers eager to get home, discipline among the troops remained a serious problem. Soldiers returning from the front often sold army property to the civilian population—offering horses or even motor vehicles for a few Marks, a loaf of bread, or some cigarettes.[59] Among troops within Germany discipline problems were, if anything, worse, and caused local authorities considerable worry. In Oppeln, for example, the Landrat reported of an infantry regiment stationed in his district that 'the men do not create a trustworthy impression', that 'complete lack of discipline prevails', and that soldiers had allowed weapons and other equipment to land in 'unauthorized hands'.[60] The soldiers stole equipment and food from their units and sold it to the civilian population, refused to follow orders, and behaved in a 'threatening manner'.[61] Altogether many thousands of weapons disappeared during the weeks which followed the Armistice: according to the Reich government in 1920, 1,895,052 rifles, 8,452 machine guns, and 400 mine-throwers were being held illegally in Germany.[62] The problems of public order were by no means limited to men still in uniform. Soldiers on leave at the War's end caused problems—for example in the villages around Ratibor in Upper Silesia, where they removed local officials from their posts and announced to the rural population that they no longer needed to pay taxes or deliver food.[63] The Armistice was followed by a general upsurge in rowdy behaviour and petty crime as civil authority broke down during the revolutionary upheavals, and ex-soldiers played a prominent part in the crime wave.[64]

[59] See Gerhard Kaller, 'Die Revolution des Jahres 1918 in Baden und die Tätigkeit de 'Arbeiter- und Soldatenräte in Karlsruhe', in *Zeitschrift für die Geschichte des Oberrheins*, 75 (1966), 309.
[60] APW, Rejencja Opolska Pr. B., no. 259, fo. 1037: Landrat to Regierungspräsident, Oppeln, 10 Dec. 1918.
[61] Ibid. fo. 1019: Landrat des Kreises Tost-Gleiwitz to Regierungspräsident, Gleiwitz, 26 Nov. 1918; ibid., fos. 1027–8: Landrat to Regierungspräsident, Leobschütz, 25 Nov. 1918.
[62] Moritz Liepmann, *Krieg und Kriminalität in Deutschland* (Stuttgart, 1930), 38.
[63] APW, Rejencja Opolska Pr. B., no. 259, fo. 117: Landrat to Regierungspräsident, Ratibor, 15 Nov. 1918.
[64] Files of local and regional authorities abound with reports of how people, including ex-soldiers, were ignoring the law. See e.g. SHAD, Ministerium des Innern, no. 11094/1,

Certain things were particularly likely to provoke exasperation among the soldiers. With hundreds of thousands of men urgently demanding passage home, large numbers of special trains had to be brought in at short notice, and there were, inevitably, complaints about overcrowded and poorly provisioned troop-trains.[65] Another point of friction was the checking of papers of soldiers passing through Germany by members of the new security-forces, who were frequently younger than the soldiers themselves.[66] Yet another was the distribution of civilian clothing to soldiers upon their discharge. According to the regulations governing the demobilization, soldiers were to receive 50 Marks 'discharge money' plus 15 Marks 'marching money' and a suit of clothes when they left the armed forces.[67] Not only were these disbursements dependent upon soldiers' papers being in order and upon the delivery of their weapons, thus inhibiting the soldiers from setting out on their own and ensuring the collection of the millions of weapons which had been issued during the War; they also presupposed that enough civilian clothing was available. Unfortunately, this was often not the case. The suits were frequently ill-fitting or else the styles found little favour,[68] or there were not enough suits to go round at the distribution points. In some cases the soldiers were simply given cloth, which they then had to have made into clothing, and rumours spread that the suits were given only on loan, to be returned later. The result was understandable anger and often violent incidents at the points where clothing was distributed.[69] The desire of soldiers to get out

fos. 1–2: Kreishauptmann to Ministerialdirektor Schmitt in Dresden, Leipzig, 18. Jan. 1919; ibid., Amtshauptmannschaft Annaberg, no. 3303, fo. 14: Bürgermeister to Amtshauptmannschaft Annaberg, Jöhstadt, 22 Nov. 1918.

[65] See BHStA, Abt. IV, MKr 1760: Bayer. Militärbevollmächtigter in Berlin to Ministerium für milit. Angelegenheiten, Berlin, 11 Dec. 1918; ibid. 14412: 'Referentenbesprechung über Demobilmachung am 13.XI.(1918) nachmittags 5–8 Uhr im (bayer.) Ministerium f. mil. Angelenheiten'; ibid. 14412: Beauftragter des bayer. Kriegsministeriums beim Preuß. Kriegsamt to Staatskommissar für die Demobilmachung, Berlin, 16 Nov. 1918. For details of the transport of men from Kiel during Nov. 1918, when roughly 2,000 were leaving the city daily, see Wette, 'Die militärische Demobilmachung', 76. The demands made on the railways to transport the troops back home also exacerbated difficulties with raw-materials supplies. See Jürgen Reulecke, *Die wirtschaftliche Entwicklung der Stadt Barmen von 1910 bis 1925* (Neustadt/Aisch, 1973), 115.

[66] See e.g. Kaller, 'Die Revolution in Baden', 311.

[67] Ritter and Miller (eds.), *Die deutsche Revolution*, 121–2: 'Erlaß des Kriegsministers Scheüch und des Unterstaatssekretärs Göhre über Entlassungen beim Heimatheer', 16. Nov. 1918; APS, Landratsamt Randow, no. 1713, fo. 23: Kriegsministerium, 'Entlassungen beim Heimatheer', Berlin, 15 Nov. 1918; ibid., fo. 24: Kriegsministerium, 'Merkblatt über Entlassungen unmittelbar vom Feldtruppenteil', Berlin, 16 Nov. 1918; Berthold and Neef, *Militarismus und Opportunismus*, 40. Often the money for these disbursements was advanced by municipalities, which actively worked together with the military authorities to help discharge the masses of impatient soldiers. See Adalbert Oehler, *Düsseldorf im Weltkriege Schicksal und Arbeit einer deutschen Großstadt* (Düsseldorf, 1927), 642.

[68] e.g. see HStAD, Reg. Düsseldorf, no. 15108, fos. 332–3: 'Sitzung des "Dema" am 30. November 1918' (in Rheydt).

[69] See Kaller, 'Die Revolution in Baden', 310; StdADo, 5–569, fo. 6: K.W.A., Altbekleidungsstelle, to Stadtrat Dr. Tschackert, Dortmund, 28 Dec. 1918. On the problems with the

of uniform, and the difficulties which the authorities had in finding and distributing clothing for millions of men within a few weeks, sometimes led to the plunder of distribution points and retail clothes-shops.[70]

Conflict also occurred between returning soldiers and those who had remained behind in the Reich. Trouble occasionally developed between the returning soldiers and local workers,[71] and in some places disagreement arose among the soldiers themselves, between units which had returned from the field and those stationed within Germany at the time of the military collapse. Some of the differences had political origins; it was generally men 'who did not come from the battlefield, but who had been within the country during the last weeks', who had become 'infected by the revolutionary movement'.[72] At its worst, open and bloody conflict erupted between the two groups, as in the Upper Silesian town of Neiße. There a number of people were wounded when fighting broke out between members of an infantry regiment stationed locally and men who had just returned from the front, after the former had raised the red flag on the town's railway station.[73] Generally the soldiers returning from the front were less fractious and better disciplined than those who had been behind the lines; those coming from the front tended to be less concerned with politics than with getting back home.[74]

Apart from having to face the problems of public order during the demobilization and political upheaval, the civilian authorities also had their hands full arranging the reception of soldiers who remained with their units and returned *en masse* to the Reich. The heroes of the trenches had to be given an appropriately enthusiastic welcome home, and the logistical problems involved in feeding and housing hundreds of thousands of men as they passed through Germany were enormous. The first task, however, was to dampen unrealistic expectations of what the *Heimat* might be able to provide for the veterans of the trenches and to encourage soldiers to remain with their units. In mid-November 1918 Joseph Koeth, at the head of the Reich Office for Economic Demobilization, framed a message for the Supreme Army Command to distribute to the returning soldiers:

distribution of clothing, see BHStA, Abt. IV, MKr 14412: Beauftragter des Kriegsministeriums beim Preuß. Kriegsamt to Staatskommissar für die Demobilmachung, Berlin, 16 Nov. 1918.

[70] In some cases the soldiers were joined by civilians, including women and children, for whom shortages and and extremely high prices had put new clothing out of reach during wartime. See, for example, APW, Rejencja Opolska Pr. B., no. 259, fos. 83–4: Magistrat to Regierungspräsident, Königshütte O.-S., 14 Nov. 1918; ibid., fos. 213–14: Polizei-Verwaltung to Regierungspräsident, Königshütte O.-S., 15 Nov. 1918.

[71] See Tampke, *The Ruhr and Revolution*, 75.

[72] APW, Rejencja Opolska Pr. B., no. 259, fo. 1019: Landrat des Kreises Tost-Gleiwitz to Regierungspräsident, Gleiwitz, 26 Nov. 1918.

[73] Ibid., fos. 645–6: Polizei-Verwaltung to Regierungspräsident, Neiße, 2 Dec. 1918.

[74] In addition, in the aftermath of the demobilization there was a disturbing increase in thefts committed by bands of armed men in military uniform, presumably deserters. See StAM, Oberpräsidium, no. 6523: Regierungspräsident to Minister des Innern in Berlin, Arnsberg, 14 Sept. 1919.

Comrades! You know that food, coal, and other necessities are in short supply at home and are distributed to individual residents only in small, specified amounts. If you are billeted on the march home, the people with whom you are billeted will be unable to feed you. You will therefore be dependent on army rations.

A special distribution of coal to the people with whom you are billeted is not possible either. Therefore in most cases food and heating can only be provided for you if you are billeted in mass quarters. Do not regard these measures as unfriendliness towards you on the part of those at home; they only arise due to the constraints imposed by present conditions. . . . Be assured that the *Heimat* will do everything to ease your march home and to accommodate you as well as possible.[75]

In the event, the *Heimat* did try to do everything possible to help the soldiers upon their return home. The military and civilian authorities, as well as the Workers' Councils and employers, made great efforts to ensure that the returning soldiers came home to a festive welcome. In mid-November 1918 the Prussian War Ministry instructed the Deputy Regional Commands to work together with the Workers' and Soldiers' Councils and the municipal authorities to ensure that the returning veterans be greeted appropriately: with 'streets richly decked out with flags and speeches by representatives of the population', in order 'to make the day of their return to the *Heimat* a lasting memory for the soldiers'.[76] The Executive Council of the Workers' and Soldiers' Council in Berlin echoed these sentiments when it outlined to Germany's mayors how the returning soldiers were to be welcomed: 'Everything depends upon arousing the feeling among them that they, who have years of hardship behind them, are heartily welcome.' Railway stations were to be 'perfectly' cleaned, rid of 'all old posters that stir up memories of the War', and decorated throughout; streets leading from the stations were to be decorated with 'triumphal arches and garlands, appropriate decorations and inscriptions such as "Welcome" or "Welcome to the *Heimat*" or "The grateful *Heimat* greets you" '; streets and houses throughout the city were to display festive decorations, and there was to be 'festive music' everywhere.[77]

Judging from contemporary reports, it appears that such instructions were followed.[78] According to a memorandum issued by the Bavarian Ministry of Military Affairs in mid-December 1918 and published in the newspapers, Bavarian troops returning from the western front were 'received in an exemplary manner by the population as they have marched through German

---

[75] GStAB, Rep. 30/733: Joseph Koeth, Demobilmachungsamt, to Oberste Heeresleitung, Berlin, 19 Nov. 1918.

[76] StdAHd, 212a, 7: Kriegsministerium to Oberkommando in den Marken, sämtl. stellv. Gen. kdos., and sämtl. Garnisonkommandos (außer Elsaß-Lothringen), Berlin, 16 Nov. 1918.

[77] Ibid.: Nachrichtendienst des Vollzugrats des Arbeiter- und Soldatenrates Berlin to Mayor, Berlin, 18 Nov. 1918.

[78] See Berthold and Neef, *Militarismus und Opportunismus*, 47–8; Adolf Wermuth, *Ein Beamtenleben: Erinnerungen* (Berlin, 1922), 427–9; Oehler, *Düsseldorf im Weltkrieg*, 639–42.

territory'.[79] Indeed, the returning soldiers were greeted by a civilian population doing its utmost to express thanks and appreciation. The streets of German towns and villages were indeed decorated with flags and flowers as the soldiers made their way home;[80] and many firms went out of their way ceremoniously to welcome back former employees who returned from military service, and often handed out money and cigars.[81] During late 1919 and 1920 similar receptions were prepared for the prisoners of war when they were finally able to return to Germany.[82]

It was with the ostentatious welcome home that the legend that the German army had not been vanquished on the battlefield began to take shape. Prefacing its instructions for preparing a 'festive welcome' for the returning soldiers in mid-November, the Prussian War Ministry asserted: 'Our field-grey heroes return to the *Heimat* undefeated, having protected the native soil from the horrors of war for four years.'[83] Similarly, when instructing that 'everywhere a festive reception be prepared for the returning troops, in order to give expression to the affection and gratitude of the *Heimat*', the Reich Government and the Supreme Army Command spoke of soldiers who had 'stood their ground undefeated up to the last minute'.[84] Representatives of the Workers' and Soldiers' Councils also spoke in effusive terms of the bravery of the returning soldiers whom they welcomed home,[85] and one should not forget Friedrich Ebert's welcome of soldiers in Berlin in early December, when he greeted the troops by asserting that they were returning undefeated.[86] Perhaps it would have been impossible to greet the soldiers in any way other than with banners reading 'the *Heimat* greets the undefeated heroes'.[87] However, the inability to confront the fact that Germany's soldiers *had* been defeated on the battlefield left a damaging political

---

[79] GLAK, 236/22716: Ministerium für milit. Angelenheiten to Staatsregierungen von Preußen, Württemberg, Baden und Hessen, Munich, 12 Dec. 1918. This notice was also printed in the *Karlsruher Zeitung* on 25 Dec. 1918.

[80] See e.g. the reports of the efforts of local and regional authorities in Baden to prepare a warm welcome for the soldiers returning from France, in GLAK, 236/22716. See also Tampke, *The Ruhr and Revolution*, 75–6.

[81] e.g. the Leipzig iron and steel works of Meier and Weichelt. See SSAL, Meier und Weichelt Eisen- und Stahlwerke, no. 226: 'Jahresbericht 1918/19. Bericht über unsere Arbeiter-Kriegs fürsorge im Geschäftsjahr 1918/1919'.

[82] See e.g. GStAM, Rep. 120, BB VII 1, no. 30, Bd. 4, fo. 336: Kriegsministerium, Unterkunfts-Departement, to Minister für Handel und Gewerbe, Berlin, 6 Aug. 1919; WWA, K2/677, fos. 28–34: 'Bericht über die Tätigkeit des Demobilmachungsausschusses für den Landkreis Bochum für die Zeit vom 16. März 1919 bis 31. Oktober 1919'.

[83] StdAHd, 212a, 7.

[84] See LHSA, Rep. C 50 Querfurt A/B, no. 2808, fo. 5: printed circular of the Verband der Preußischen Landkreise, Berlin, 23 Nov. 1918.

[85] See e.g. Tampke, *The Ruhr and Revolution*, 75–6.

[86] Heinrich August Winkler, *Von der Revolution zur Stabilisierung: Arbeiter und Arbeiterbewegung in der Weimarer Republik 1918 bis 1924* (Berlin and Bonn, 1984), 100.

[87] Oehler, *Düsseldorf im Weltkrieg*, 640.

legacy for Germany's first democracy. For if the soldiers had returned undefeated, who then was to blame for the tribulations of the post-war years?

The other major aspect of welcoming the soldiers back home, providing adequate food and shelter for the troops, was much more difficult than greeting them with hymns of praise for their heroic exploits. It was one thing to decorate streets with flags and make laudatory speeches; it was quite another to ensure that ten or twenty thousand soldiers suddenly descending upon a city were cleaned up, deloused, housed, and fed.[88] To take the example of the Silesian capital, Breslau: in June 1918 the army command in Breslau had foreseen little difficulty in coping with the roughly 80,000 men and 20,000 horses which would need to be demobilized in the city and the region immediately surrounding it; but this view had been based upon the assumption that the troops would return home gradually, that they would not all have to be cared for at the same time.[89] However, in November 1918 the Breslau city administration discovered to its alarm that in the coming weeks 100,000 soldiers would be arriving for whom room and board would have to be provided, while the number of Breslau natives soon expected to return from military service to live in the city again was estimated at 70,000; against this it was reckoned that the military barracks in Breslau had space for only 13,350 men, and that mass quarters set up in schools and public halls could accommodate another 33,981.[90]

The difficulties involved in feeding and housing so vast a number of men suddenly descending upon German cities and towns were compounded by extreme shortages of food and fuel, which made providing even for a town's normal population a major problem. Guide-lines were issued in mid-November outlining priorities for securing space for the returning soldiers: first (as in Breslau) all the available buildings suitable as mass quarters—schools, public halls, and the like—were to be used; then empty flats were to be filled; and then, if all else failed, soldiers would be billeted compulsorily in people's homes.[91] Particular concern was expressed that soldiers should return to their native towns. Understandably, the prospect of hundreds of thousands of demobilized men congregating in German cities was quite

[88] In Mannheim, in late Nov. and early Dec. 1918 between 10,000 and 15,000 soldiers were marching through the city *daily*. See Peter Brandt and Reinhard Rürup, *Volksbewegung und demokratische Neuordnung in Baden 1918/19: Zur Vorgeschichte und Geschichte der Revolution* (Sigmaringen, 1991), 87.

[89] APW, Akta Miasta Wroclawia, no. 31201, fos. 414–15: VI. Armeekorps, stellv. Gen.kdo., to Magistrat, Breslau, 19 June 1918.

[90] Ibid., fo. 164: Magistrat, Abteilung für Militärangelenheiten, Breslau, 23 Nov. 1918; ibid., fos. 213–14: Magistrat, Abteilung für Militärangelenheiten, to Kommandantur, Breslau, 9 Dec. 1918; ibid., fos. 961–3: Magistrat, Abteilung für Militärangelenheiten, to Kommandantur, Breslau, 16 Feb. 1920.

[91] StdALu, Akten des Bürgermeisteramtes, Nr. 3542: Deutscher Städtetag, Der Geschäftsführer, 'Rundschreiben Nr. XI 1336/18D to Mitgliedsstädte des Deutschen Städtetages betr. Unterbringung der Heeresangehörigen während der Demobilmachung', Berlin, 16 Nov. 1918.

unwelcome. This was particularly true of Berlin, and conditions in the Reich capital were the subject of special attention by Joseph Koeth, who in mid-November expressed concern that not enough had been done to prepare either for the housing of the soldiers in the major cities or for their sanitary needs.[92] The Mayor of Berlin, Adolf Wermuth, also expressed grave concern and urged that soldiers be housed with individual families rather than gathered in mass quarters, 'because the danger of unrest among the soldiers will be reduced if their lodgings are more dispersed and the soldiers thereby come into contact as soon as possible with ordered family conditions again'.[93]

Despite the anxiety, the most basic needs of the returning soldiers were, in fact, met, if not entirely by the state then by charitable organizations such as the Patriotic Women's Association (Vaterländischer Frauenverein), which helped to provide meals for soldiers in transit or just discharged.[94] There were, inevitably, complaints. Soldiers complained, for example, about inadequate heating in the mass sleeping-quarters—a consequence of the severe coal-shortage in Germany after the War.[95] And civilians complained about the soldiers. Not only did the conduct of those men still in military barracks provoke criticism,[96] but soldiers' unruly behaviour was also cited as a reason why 'billeting was perceived as an onerous burden everywhere'.[97] Generally, however, the process of receiving soldiers at collection points inside the Reich, delousing them, sorting out their papers, and providing them with a suit of civilian clothing and some pocket money appears to have gone fairly smoothly. This may perhaps have been due in no small measure to the fact that so many of the soldiers had in effect deserted and, in one way or another, sorted their problems out on their own. Whatever the reason, the process of returning the soldiers to their homes in Germany turned out on the whole to be surprisingly successful.

---

[92] A particular problem was the setting-up of delousing facilities. SHAD, Gesandtschaft Berlin, Nr. 690, fos. 25–6: stellv. Bevollmächtigter zum Bundesrate, Graf von Holtzendorff, to Ministerium der Auswärtigen Angelegenheiten in Dresden, Berlin, 23 Nov. 1918. The same document may be found in SHAD, Ministerium der Auswärtigen Angelegenheiten, Nr. 2494, Band I, fos. 128–9. For comments about the housing arrangements in Berlin, and the difficulties of making progress with the severe housing-problems in post-war Berlin, see Frauke Bey-Heard, *Hauptstadt und Staatsumwälzung. Berlin 1919. Problematik und Scheitern der Rätebewegung in der Berliner Kommunalverwaltung* (Berlin, 1969), 121–2.

[93] SHAD, Ministerium der Auswärtigen Angelegenheiten, Nr. 2494, Band I, fo. 98: Gesandtschaft Berlin to Ministerium der Auswärtigen Angelegenheiten in Dresden, Berlin, 9 Nov. 1918.

[94] e.g. see the report of the Demobilization Committee in Kiel of its activity from Nov. 1918 to Mar. 1920, in GStAM, Rep. 120, BB VII 1, no. 30/20, fos. 214–46: 'Die wirtschaftliche Demobilmachung im Demobilmachungsbezirk Kiel', 10 (fo. 218).

[95] See e.g. APW, Akta Miasta Wrocławia, no. 31021, fos. 298–9: Kommandantur Breslau to Magistrat, Abteilung für Militärangelegenheiten, Breslau, 18 Feb. 1919.

[96] See e.g. BLHA, Rep. 2A, Reg. Potsdam I SW, no. 793, fo. 142: Vorsitzender der Demobilmachungsausschusses des Kreises Teltow to Regierungspräsident, Berlin, 27 Feb. 1919.

[97] GLAK, 233/12401: XIV. Armeekorps Gen.kdo., Chef des Generalstabs, to Badisches Ministerium des Innern, Durlach, 7 Feb. 1919.

The ways in which the soldiers came back to Germany and were greeted by the civilian population differed radically from the picture of the demobilization which entered into the public vocabulary of Weimar Germany: of war heroes who marched back to Germany after November 1918 to be either ignored or scorned by an ungrateful civilian population; of what a war invalid who had lost a leg and who later turned to the Nazi Party described as 'the shame and humiliation inflicted in the streets upon wounded comrades'.[98] The commentary printed in the organ of the German officers' organization, the *Deutscher Offiziersbund*, in November 1925, upon the return of the remains of Manfred von Richthofen to Germany, is illustrative:

The German army returned home in 1918 after doing its duty for four and a half years, and was shamefully received. There were no laurel leaves; hate-filled words were hurled at the soldiers. Military decorations were torn from the soldiers' field-grey uniforms.[99]

No doubt there was an element of truth in this picture, and it is noteworthy that the quote above comes from an *officers'* organization. Certainly many officers found the defeat and return to the Fatherland humiliating and traumatic; officers were frequently subjected to indignities—in particular, having their insignia torn from their uniforms—during the weeks which followed the Armistice.[100] Yet this picture is generally quite inaccurate. For one thing, it is difficult to see the hostility towards the officers as evidence of a general hostility towards the war veterans, if only because soldiers were often the source of the indignities that the officers suffered. For another, as we have seen, the civilian population, together with all the organizations which were involved in the demobilization process, did their utmost to make the immediate return of the heroes of the trenches as positive and memorable as possible.

What then are we to make of these discrepancies? Certainly they reflect as much the political culture of the middle and later Weimar years as they do the actual processes of the military demobilization of 1918 and 1919.[101] However, they also raise questions about what was happening when all the ceremonies were staged for the benefit of the heroes returning from the trenches. Clearly the disintegration of the German armed forces which had set in with the spring offensives of 1918, and which accelerated with the military collapse and political revolution in the autumn, greatly affected the shape of the return. Indeed, if the German armed forces were in an advanced

---

[98] Quoted in Peter H. Merkl, *The Making of a Stormtrooper* (Princeton, NJ, 1980), 118. This veteran did not experience at first hand what happened 'in the streets' after Nov. 1918, as he was in hospital in Trier at the time of the Armistice.

[99] *Deutscher Offiziersbund* of 25 Nov. 1925, quoted in Robert Weldon Whalen, *Bitter Wounds: German Victims of the Great War, 1914–1919* (Ithaca, NY, and London, 1984), 34.

[100] See e.g. SHAD, Ministerium des Innern, no. 11094/1, fo. 3: Kreishauptmann to Ministerialdirektor Dr. Schmitt in Dresden, Leipzig, 19 Jan. 1919.

[101] See below, Ch. 9. Also, Bessel, 'The Great War in German Memory'.

state of decomposition in 1918 and 1919, then the picture of soldiers returning to an ungrateful Fatherland may have to be stood on its head: it was not those on the home front who had neglected their duty, by failing to welcome returning heroes during the dark days of late 1918 and early 1919; it was the soldiers who had abandoned their units in their hundreds of thousands who were guilty of neglect, missing the festive ceremonies laid on in their honour.

This observation highlights probably the most important characteristic of Germany's military demobilization during 1918 and 1919: it was the demobilization of an army which had largely disintegrated. The German army was an organization in which discipline had broken down, in which hundreds of thousands of men left their units to find their own way back home, and in which the main reason still to obey orders was that doing so offered the speediest exit from military service.[102] As Matthias Erzberger stated in a speech on 15 January 1919, 'the German army has disappeared'.[103] In early February 1919 the Army Command in Baden reported to that state's Interior Ministry:

The Army Command is only too well aware that the lack of the necessary discipline in the army has led to a regrettable state of affairs. This state of affairs is the result of the revolution. With the onslaught against the authority of all superiors, with the partial lifting or alteration of the disciplinary and military power of legal sentencing, with the amnesty decree, the lifting of the obligation to salute, the toleration of unruly outrages against commissioned and non-commissioned officers, with the establishment of soldiers' councils, the throttling of the notion of compulsory military service through the introduction of service for pay, all the foundations of the former army have been shattered.[104]

The fact that 'all the foundations of the former army have been shattered' provides both the framework within which the demobilization needs to be understood and a starting-point for the history of the military in the Weimar period. The disintegration of the German army meant that the state's organizations of armed force had to be recreated in 1919—with the mercenaries in the Freikorps units which the new government employed to suppress revolutionary unrest, and with an army which had to be re-established on a new basis, largely from among younger men who had not been poisoned by the experience of military life during the First World War.[105] Hopes that

---

[102] One reason why discipline problems were more serious among troops stationed within Germany may have been that they had no pressing need to continue to maintain discipline, since they were already home!

[103] Quoted in Wette, 'Die militärische Demobilmachung', 71.

[104] GLAK, 233/12401: XIV. Armeekorps Gen.kdo., Chef des Generalstabs, to Badisches Ministerium des Innern, Durlach, 7 Feb. 1919.

[105] For some perceptive comments about the changes in the army during late 1918 and early 1919, see Michael Geyer, 'Professionals and Junkers: German Rearmament and Politics in the Weimar Republic', in Richard Bessel and E. J. Feuchtwanger (eds.), *Social Change and Political Development in Weimar Germany* (London, 1981), 92–5.

a new mass republican army, loyal to the Left and to Weimar democracy, might be formed somehow in the aftermath of the War had no chance of being realized. Those who might have been expected to join such a force had had their fill of the military and were busy reintegrating themselves into civilian life. The fact that the great mass of soldiers, who wanted nothing more than to get out of uniform and return to civilian life, were demobilized so quickly meant that subsidizing the Freikorps on the one hand and forming a new Reichswehr on the other were the only realistic means left for the German state of placing armed force at its disposal.[106]

The fact that the German army disintegrated in 1918 was a key reason why the military demobilization unfolded as smoothly as it did. The disintegration of the German armed forces in effect removed many of the sources of potential conflict. It left the army with one function and one function only: to expedite the return home of the men who had served during the War. (As this was a major goal of the Soldiers' Councils, it meant that the army leadership and the council movement shared an important aim in the autumn and winter of 1918/19.) The function of the German army as an instrument of force internationally had been nullified by defeat; its function as an instrument of force domestically had been nullified by the collapse of discipline and authority, and here its place was taken temporarily by mercenaries—the Freikorps—who were hired by the government to enforce internal security, with disastrous results. This left the German army in late 1918 capable only of doing precisely what the overwhelming mass of the soldiers wanted it to do: to help them get home. Creating obstacles to a speedy demobilization—as the French and British military did after the War and which led to unrest—was beyond the power of the German military. The fact that when the time came the German military was powerless to implement its carefully laid plans for the demobilization or to prevent its own disintegration was thus one of the main reasons why the return of more than 6 million soldiers within the space of about four months occurred—much to the surprise of people at the time—without major difficulties.

[106] See Wette, 'Die militärische Demobilmachung', 72.

# 4

# The Demobilization of the Economy

> Of course everything really happened differently from what one could
> have predicted.[1]

INTRODUCING his study of the German recession of 1925 and 1926,
Dieter Hertz-Eichenrode observed that 'the economic difficulties during the
demobilization and the inflation were experienced as a state of emergency
which the World War ushered in and which one had to pass through in
order to arrive at normal conditions again'.[2] The post-war economic transition was regarded as an unpleasant and abnormal, but unavoidable,
necessity after more than four years of war. The aim of the demobilization
of the economy, like that of the demobilization of the armed forces, was a
return to 'normality'. This meant a return to what Germans imagined
economic relationships to have been before the enormous and disruptive
changes brought about by war, inflation, and state intervention on a
massive scale.

During the First World War economic activity had been focused largely
on meeting the requirements of the military. Indeed, most of German
industry—one estimate puts the figure as high as 95 per cent[3]—had been
geared to war production. This had meant a fundamental shift from sectors
producing essentially for civilian needs towards those producing for the
military. This shift in turn resulted in changes in the areas where workers
were employed, in a restructuring of wage differentials, and in terrible
shortages of food, fuel, and raw materials—shortages which, as we have
seen, were instrumental in provoking the popular disaffection which led
to the collapse of the Imperial regime in November 1918. When defeat
arrived, the German economy had a shape very different from that it
had possessed in early 1914 and was profoundly skewed away from the
needs of a civilian population exhausted by wartime privations. Not only
had industrial production slumped by 1918 to roughly 57 per cent of the

---

[1] *Kriegsbericht der Handwerkskammer zu Gumbinnen für 1913–1919* (Insterburg, 1920), 77.

[2] Dieter Hertz-Eichenrode, *Wirtschaftskrise und Arbeitsbeschaffung: Konjunkturpolitik 1925/26 und die Grundlagen der Krisenpolitik Brünings* (Frankfurt/Main, 1982), 19.

[3] Wolfgang Elben, *Das Problem der Kontinuität in der deutschen Revolution: Die Politik der Staatssekretäre und der militärischen Führung von November 1918 bis Februar 1919* (Düsseldorf, 1965), 77. For Bavaria a figure of 90% was given for the proportion of industrial production going either directly or indirectly to armaments. See Kurt Königsberger, 'Die wirtschaftliche Demobilmachung in Bayern während der Zeit vom November 1918 bis Mai 1919', in *Zeitschrift des bayerischen statistischen Landesamts*, 52 (1920), 196.

1913 figure, but the relative positions of various sectors had altered profoundly (See Table 14).

Table 14. *Production of Important Industrial Sectors,*
*1918* (1913 = 100)

| | |
|---|---|
| Mining | 83 |
| Iron and steel | 53 |
| Non-ferrous metals | 234 |
| Housing construction | 4 |
| Building materials | 35 |
| Textiles | 17 |
| Alcohol, tobacco | 63 |

Sources: Rolf Wagenfuhr, *Die Industriewirtschaft: Entwicklungstendenzen der deutschen und Internationalen Industrieproduction 1860 bis 1932* (*Vierteljahreshefte zur Konjunkturforschung*, Sonderheft 31; Berlin, 1933), 22–3. See also the discussion in Manfred Nussbaum, *Wirtschaft und Staat in Deutschland während der Weimarer Republik* (Berlin, 1978), 11–17, and Carl-Ludwig Holtfrerich, *The German Inflation 1914–1923: Causes and Effects in International Perspective* (Berlin and New York, 1986), 200–2.

Output had declined in most industrial sectors. Those producing exclusively for civilian needs (such as housing construction) fell most precipitously, but even sectors vital to the war effort (such as mining) saw declines in absolute terms. Plant and machinery had been allowed to fall into disrepair; raw materials were often desperately scarce; Germany was cut off from overseas supplies and international markets. In 1919, German hard-coal production stood at 61.4 per cent of the 1913 total, steel at 39.9 per cent, and cement at a mere 30.2 per cent.[4] The German economy had been deformed and exhausted by four years of war, and redirecting it towards the satisfaction of civilian needs appeared a daunting task.

The problem of ensuring a smooth post-war transition was complicated further by the effects of the inflation which had begun during the War. Despite widespread expectations among industrialists that the Mark would rise on the foreign exchanges once the War ended,[5] the Armistice did not magically remove the pressures which had undermined the German currency and driven up prices. The inflation, which had its origins in the manner in which Germany's War had been financed, accelerated after the defeat and

[4] Manfred Nussbaum, *Wirtschaft und Staat in Deutschland während der Weimaier Republik* (Berlin, 1978), 14.

[5] See the comments of representatives of heavy industry at a meeting to discuss the forthcoming demobilization in the Reich Economics Office on 29 Oct. 1918, in BHStA, Abt. IV, MKr 14413: Beauftragter des bayer. Kriegsministeriums beim Preuß. Kriegsamt to Kriegsministerium in Munich, Berlin, 7 Nov. 1918. See also Gerald D. Feldman, *Iron and Steel in the German Inflation 1916–1923* (Princeton, NJ, 1977), 55.

provided much of the disorderly economic and social framework within which the post-war transition would take place.[6] Although the general cost-of-living index based on a 'basket of goods' calculated by the Reich Statistical Office was published on a regular basis only from February 1920, other indices (Richard Calwer's index of foodstuff prices and the Reich Statistical Office's index of wholesale prices) offer a rough indication of the rise in prices during the months following the Armistice (see Table 15).[7]

As can be seen from these indices, the immediate post-war period coincided with a fairly substantial acceleration of wartime inflation, until prices stabilized temporarily during mid-1920. Not only do they demonstrate that the demobilization took place within a context of rising prices which were a constant source of social tensions; they also suggest that the demobilization itself was inflationary. One important, and probably inevitable, aspect of the post-war economic transition was the dismantling of the controls on prices and the distribution of goods which had characterized the war economy. This inevitably meant price increases, as black-market prices in effect came out into the open. Furthermore, the measures taken by government to smooth the demobilization were enormously expensive. Not only was it necessary to fund public-works projects to soak up labour during the post-war transition; the demobilization was also accompanied by a substantial increase in the size of the civil service and in the number of people employed generally in the public sector. The policies of the demobilization themselves stimulated increased use of contractual employers by public authorities, as the problems thrown up by the War and the 'transition economy' led to the establishment of a range of new administrative departments—in particular welfare offices for war victims. For example, in Hamburg, where the number of civil servants had risen substantially and the number of contractual white-collar employees in public service in May 1920 was more than double what it had been six years earlier, 'roughly half' the new posts were described as 'due to the consequences of the War'.[8] This obviously added

---

[6] See Holtfrerich, *The German Inflation 1914–1923: Causes and Effects in International Perspective* (Berlin and New York, 1986), esp. 102–19, 197–278.

[7] As the Calwer index was based upon official price-ceilings rather than the (higher) black-market prices which Germans had to pay for their food during and after the First World War, it would tend to underestimate price rises. The index of wholesale prices, on the other hand, functions as something of a lead indicator, in that wholesale prices tend to rise earlier than retail prices. Ibid. 43–4.

[8] The new posts were created primarily in welfare offices for the war-disabled and war-widows and orphans, youth care, the labour office, the housing office, penal institutions, and in financial administration. See Jürgen Brandt, *Hamburgs Finanzen von 1914 bis 1924* (Hamburg, 1924), 32–3. Brandt also lists (on pp. 38–9) the new administrative departments established in the Hamburg city-state in the wake of the War: 'the Labour Office, the Welfare Office, the Welfare Centre for War Disabled and War Widows and Orphans, the administrative offices of the Demobilization Commissar and of the District Housing Commissar, the Rent Review Office, the Arbitration Commission, the University Administration, the Administrative and Superior Courts, the Trade Supervision Office, the Public Memorial Preservation Office and the State Press Office'.

to the government pay-bill at all levels, and, as Andreas Kunz has shown, the pay demands of civil servants acted in their turn as a motor for inflation.[9]

Table 15. *Indices of Price Levels in Germany, 1918–1920* (1913 = 1)

|  | Calwer Food Index | Wholesale Price Index | Cost-of-Living Index |
|---|---|---|---|
| **1918** | | | |
| January | 2.20 | 2.04 | — |
| February | 2.20 | 1.98 | — |
| March | 2.22 | 1.98 | — |
| April | 2.22 | 2.04 | — |
| May | 2.23 | 2.03 | — |
| June | 2.24 | 2.09 | — |
| July | 2.26 | 2.08 | — |
| August | 2.31 | 2.35 | — |
| September | 2.37 | 2.30 | — |
| October | 2.40 | 2.34 | — |
| November | 2.43 | 2.34 | — |
| December | 2.45 | 2.45 | — |
| **1919** | | | |
| January | 2.48 | 2.62 | — |
| February | 2.53 | 2.70 | — |
| March | 2.62 | 2.74 | — |
| April | 2.71 | 2.86 | — |
| May | 2.87 | 2.97 | — |
| June | 3.06 | 3.06 | — |
| July | 3.20 | 3.39 | — |
| August | 3.32 | 4.22 | — |
| September | 3.72 | 4.93 | — |
| October | 3.92 | 5.62 | — |
| November | 4.23 | 6.78 | — |
| December | 4.46 | 8.03 | — |
| **1920** | | | |
| January | 5.08 | 12.56 | — |
| February | 5.75 | 16.85 | 8.47 |
| March | 6.52 | 17.09 | 9.56 |
| April | 7.38 | 15.67 | 10.42 |
| May | 8.74 | 15.08 | 11.02 |
| June | 9.03 | 13.82 | 10.83 |
| July | 9.82 | 13.67 | 10.65 |
| August | 10.17 | 14.50 | 10.23 |

[9] Andreas Kunz, *Civil Servants and the Politics of Inflation in Germany, 1914–1924* (Berlin and New York, 1986), 32–53 (on the size and composition of the civil service), 74–5 (for the suggestion that civil-service pay acted as a motor for inflation).

Table 15. *Continued*

|           | Calwer Food Index | Wholesale Price Index | Cost-of-Living Index |
|-----------|-------------------|-----------------------|----------------------|
| September | 10.66             | 14.98                 | 10.15                |
| October   | 12.93             | 14.66                 | 10.71                |
| November  | 13.89             | 15.09                 | 11.18                |
| December  | 14.39             | 14.40                 | 11.58                |

*Sources*: For the Calwer Index, Richard Calwer, *Monatliche Übersichten über Lebensmittelpreise* (Berlin, 1918–20), as cited in Carl-Ludwig Holtfrerich, *The German Inflation 1914–1923: Causes and Effects in International Perspective* (Berlin and New York, 1986), 41; for the wholesale-price index, Statistisches Reichsamt (ed.), *Zahlen zur Geldentwertung in Deutschland 1914 bis 1923* (*Wirtschaft und Statistik*, 5, Sonderheft 1; Berlin, 1925), 16–17; for the cost-of-living index, ibid. 33.

These enormous additional demands on the public purse, after the impoverishment of war and the upheaval of revolution, led to massive, and inflationary, deficit spending. Despite the ending of the War and of most military spending, public expenditure in real terms in 1919 was more than double what it had been in 1913.[10] In the absence of an effective system of taxation, the financial demands of the demobilization contributed significantly to the yawning budget-deficits which were a feature of the post-war German economy (and which could no longer be financed by war loans). Although the proportion of government expenditure covered by tax revenues increased from the 20 per cent to which it had sunk during the War, in 1919 tax revenues still covered only about half of expenditure; in subsequent years the proportion again declined sharply, falling to a mere 10 per cent in 1923.[11] Altogether, the real and perceived requirements of the demobilization formed powerful (and probably unavoidable) inflationary pressures; in turn, continued inflation ensured that, whatever people's hopes and expectations for a return to the conditions of 1913, economic conditions after the War would be very different from those which had existed before the guns had begun firing.

The same could be said of the economic damage inflicted by the Allies after the Armistice. In order to maintain pressure upon the German government until it accepted a peace treaty, the Allies maintained their blockade of Germany until the Versailles Treaty was signed in July 1919. Although the blockade was eased slightly in April 1919, the fact that it remained in force after the Armistice meant that crippling shortages of coal and raw

[10] Peter-Christian Witt, 'Finanzpolitik und sozialer Wandel in Krieg und Inflation 1918–1924', in Hans Mommsen, Dietmar Petzina, and Bernd Weisbrod (eds.), *Industrielles System und politische Entwicklung in der Weimarer Republik* (Düsseldorf, 1974), 424.

[11] Ibid. 420. See also Holtfrerich, *The German Inflation*, 129; Nussbaum, *Wirtschaft und Staat in Deutschland*, 20–1.

materials continued to plague the German economy during the demobilization period.[12] Its effects were all the greater since defeat meant that Germany
had to surrender substantial economic resources. The return of Alsace-
Lorraine to France meant the loss of three-quarters of Germany's iron-ore
production and substantial coal-reserves.[13] In the east, Polish uprisings led
to the loss to the Reich of territories around Posen, which had accounted
for an important part of Germany's pre-war agricultural production. Allied
military occupation of the Rhineland, and consequent temporary closure of
bridge links with unoccupied Germany (e.g. in Cologne and Mainz) added
to difficulties.

Enormous difficulties also arose from the disruption which defeat and
demobilization brought to Germany's railway network. As in other industrial
economies at the outset of the twentieth century, in Germany the backbone
of the transport system was the railways. The Armistice terms which
Germany had been forced to accept stipulated that Germany had to deliver
5,000 railway locomotives and 150,000 railway cars—one-sixth and one-fifth
of Germany's rolling stock respectively—to the Allies within thirty-one days;
2,400 railway cars had to be delivered daily, and the Entente threatened
that any failure to meet this requirement within forty-eight hours would
result in a doubling of the number.[14] (Over and above these figures, the
return to France of Alsace-Lorraine brought a further loss of 3,036 locomo-

---

[12] See Nussbaum, *Wirtschaft und Staat in Deutschland*, 12; C. Paul Vincent, *The Politics of Hunger:
The Allied Blockade of Germany, 1915–1919* (Athens, Oh., and London, 1985). Vincent is particularly
concerned to discuss the machinations of the Allies and the effects of the blockade upon
Germany's civilian population.

[13] The loss of foreign iron-supplies was potentially a worse problem for the German iron and
steel industry than was the loss of Lorraine; in 1914 less than a quarter of the iron ore used
in the Ruhr came from Lorraine. However, despite the problems created by the loss of Lorraine
and the disruption of foreign supplies, the German iron and steel industry had adequate stockpiles
of ore in 1919—due in large measure to supplies which had been acquired during 1918 by
Joseph Koeth's War Raw Materials Section in the War Ministry. See Feldman, *Iron and Steel in
the German Inflation*, 15, 92. Nevertheless, the French decision to stop railway traffic between
Alsace-Lorraine and Germany in November caused disruption for factories hitherto dependent
upon supplies from the other side of the Rhine. See the record of the discussions in the
Demobilization Office on 23 Nov. in BHStA, Abt. IV, MKr 14413: Beauftragter des bayer.
Ministeriums für milit. Angelegenheiten beim preuß. Kriegsamt to Staatskommissar für die
Demobilmachung in Munich, Berlin, 23 Nov. 1918.

[14] See Nussbaum, *Wirtschaft und Staat in Deutschland*, 13. In fact the delivery took a bit longer.
As of 23 Feb. the Germans had delivered 4,670 locomotives and 145,420 railway cars to the
Allies. See Königsberger, 'Die wirtschaftliche Demobilmachung in Bayern', 207. Further difficulties were created by the Allies' demand that the rolling stock be in good condition; accordingly
they rejected many of the cars delivered by Germany, which clogged up the railways yet more.
See the record of discussions in the Demobilization Office on 17 Dec. 1918 in BAP, RWM,
no. 7250, fos. 21–3: Demobilmachungsamt, 'Vermerk über die Sitzung vom 17.12.18. 9 Uhr
vorm. über Allgemeine Verkehrslage'; and on 4 Jan. 1919 in BHStA, Abt. IV, MKr 14413:
Beauftragter des bayer. Ministeriums für milit. Angelegenheiten beim preuß. Kriegsamt to
Staatskommissar für die Demobilmachung in Munich, Berlin, 6 Jan. 1919; SHAD, Ministerium
der Auswärtigen Angelegenheiten, no. 2494 Band I, fos. 219–22: Demobilmachungsamt, 'Vermerk über die Sitzung am 24. Dezember 1918'.

tives, 4,613 passenger cars, and 77,087 freight cars.)[15] The problems this caused were complicated by the fact that from mid-November 1918 to mid-January 1919 the military demobilization greatly reduced the capacity available to handle other railway traffic; according to one estimate, the returning soldiers comprised more than two-thirds of railway passengers during that period.[16] In mid-December 1918, 800 trains daily were being used to transport the troops home, passenger travel on Germany's railways had been cut by half, and for travel to Berlin a special certificate of urgent need was required.[17] At a time when shortages were already acute and when the railways keenly felt the lack of proper maintenance during the War, the loss of so much of their rolling stock was a major blow.

In the midst of the return of the soldiers, the Allied blockade, crippling shortages, and extreme difficulties on the overstretched transport-system, government purchases of war *matériel*, which had provided the lion's share of orders for much of German industry, had to cease. During the War German military procurement offices gave out war contracts worth an estimated annual average of roughly 25 thousand million Marks.[18] This created enormous problems when the War ended. Not only did the flow of war-related orders, upon which industry had come to depend, have to cease abruptly. In addition, at the time of Germany's military collapse, there was a huge backlog of war contracts outstanding. On paper, the Reich Demobilization Office acted decisively to liquidate this backlog. On 21 November it nullified all war orders still current; only in exceptional cases, where firms found themselves quite unable to make the shift and would have had to dismiss their labour forces, was a continuation of war work permitted for a short period.[19] To some extent, the Reich government (in the form of the Reichsverwertungsamt) could convert war contracts into orders for 'peace-time' goods; for example a contract which had originally been for baskets for shells might be completed to provide baskets to carry coal. However, as Koeth noted at a Cabinet meeting on 21 November, 'one cannot for instance simply convert a grenade factory to the building of railway carriages'.[20] For cases where relatively easy conversion was impossible, there was provision for limited financial help; the Reich Demobilization Office had at its disposal an aid fund which allowed it to grant modest low-interest or interest-free loans, and in some cases grants, to firms whose survival was endangered by the sudden cessation of war contracts.[21] However, legal entitlement to

---

[15] Holtfrerich, *The German Inflation*, 141.

[16] See Königsberger, 'Die wirtschaftliche Demobilmachung in Bayern', 208.

[17] BAP, RWM, no. 7250, fo. 22.

[18] Königsberger, 'Die wirtschaftliche Demobilmachung in Bayern', 196.

[19] Ibid. 196–8; Hermann Schäfer, *Regionale Wirtschaftspolitik in der Kriegswirtschaft: Staat, Industrie und Verbände während des Ersten Weltkrieges in Baden* (Stuttgart, 1983), 342.

[20] Minutes of Cabinet meeting on 21 Nov. 1918, in Susanne Miller and Heinrich Potthoff (eds.), *Die Regierung der Volksbeauftragten 1918/19* (Düsseldorf, 1969), i. 116.

[21] See Königsberger, 'Die wirtschaftliche Demobilmachung in Bayern', 197.

compensation for lost profits due to the cessation of war orders was expressly withdrawn.[22]

In practice, the Demobilization Office acted decisively to subsidize the continued operations of many factories and the continued employment of many workers. Although there was a sudden reduction in government orders to industry, a great deal in fact was done to cushion the blow. According to information presented at the Demobilization Office at the end of February 1919, on 10 November 1918 there had been 10,312,000,000 Marks' worth of war contracts outstanding.[23] Just under a quarter of these contracts were actually delivered: 996 million Marks' worth in November; 761 million in January; and 655 million in February. 2,300 million Marks' worth were cancelled; 1,387 million were converted into 'peace contracts'; and 2,787 million were terminated after compensation was paid.[24] Although this spelled substantial losses in business for German industry, it meant that only about a quarter of the war contracts outstanding at the time of the Armistice were in fact nullified completely.

The speed with which production shifted away from war work was impressive. By mid-January the number of workers still dependent upon armaments orders for their jobs was minimal.[25] Nevertheless, for firms which had been dependent on war orders, and for their employees, the sudden shift to a civil production often meant massive dislocation. In some cases, where military contracts had been for such items as clothing, furniture, or cooking utensils, the change-over could be relatively easy; in others, where factories were producing items with no conceivable civilian use (especially in firms which had been founded during the War and had no 'normal' civilian production to which to return), the change-over involved enormous problems. Although there was considerable pent-up demand for consumer goods denied to a hungry population during the War, switching over to civil production during a period of shortages, transport difficulties, inflation, and political upheaval was no easy task. As Carl-Ludwig Holtfrerich has observed, 'the economy now faced a restructuring process as drastic as that faced in 1914; only in the reverse direction'.[26] No major industrial economy

---

[22] *Reichsgesetzblatt*, 1918, 1323: 'Verordnung über die Festsetzung neuer Preise für die Weiterarbeit in Kriegsmaterial', 21 Nov. 1918.

[23] SHAD, Gesandtschaft Berlin, no. 691, fo. 78: Reichsministerium für wirtschaftliche Demobilmachung, 'Vermerk über die Sitzung am 28. Februar 1919 nachm. 3 Uhr, betreffend militärische Beschaffungsstellen', Berlin, 28 Feb. 1919. See also Gerald D. Feldman, *The Great Disorder: Politics, Economics and Society in the German Inflation, 1914–1924* (Oxford, 1993), ch. 3.

[24] The remaining 1,420 million Marks' worth of contracts were still the subject of negotiation at the end of Feb. 1919, to determine whether they would be settled through financial compensation or be maintained as emergency works-projects.

[25] e.g. for Bavaria, see Königsberger, 'Die wirtschaftliche Demobilmachung in Bayern', 200.

[26] Holtfrerich, *The German Inflation*, 201.

had ever been compelled to undergo such a restructuring process in so short a period and in such adverse circumstances.

The economic demobilization which followed the Armistice had two main characteristics: its improvised nature as a series of emergency measures, and its overarching aim of re-establishing order by returning the German economy somehow to the *status quo ante*. In Germany, as in other former combatant countries, the keynote of the economic demobilization was de-control—the dismantling of economic controls which had been put into place during the War. Gerald Feldman, who pioneered research in this area, has pointed out:

In every case (Germany, France, Britain and the United States), the demobiliza-tion was primarily a process of decontrol, of sometimes rapid and sometimes more protracted dismantling of the institutional and legal machinery through which the state had exercised unprecedented control over the economy during the war. The period 1918–1921 was marked by the defeat throughout the Western world of those governmental, technocratic and popular forces which had expected that the wartime machinery and regulations governing economic and social policy would be adapted to the needs of reconstruction and postwar management of economy and society.[27]

Of course there were significant differences in the contexts within which economic demobilization and decontrol were attempted in Germany and in other major combatant countries. In the first place, as Feldman noted, 'state interference in the economy had always been more acceptable in Germany than in either Great Britain or the United States, and, much more important, collective action in the private sector had always been more acceptable in Germany'.[28] Thus the wisdom of dismantling economic controls was not quite so self-evident in post-war Germany as in Britain or America. In the second place, Germany had lost the War. This meant that her economic planners had much less time to refine and implement plans for the demo-bilization than did their counterparts in France, Britain, or America. They could not delay the return of German soldiers for the sake of a smooth management of the labour market, and there was no question of a gradual halt to war production. Germany's economic planners had to face the prospect of territorial losses, the occupation of parts of the Reich by foreign troops, massive reparations demands, and Allied-imposed restrictions upon German trade. Thirdly, Germany was experiencing a political revolution. This generated great popular expectations (and fears) about what the post-war political and economic order would deliver, and meant that questions

---

[27] Gerald D. Feldman, 'Economic and Social Problems of the German Demobilization 1918–19', *Journal of Modern History*, 47 (1975), 2.

[28] Ibid. 4.

about the future structure of the economy occupied an especially prominent and contentious place in political debate.

In the aftermath of the War there were many obstacles to a fundamental restructuring of the German economic order. Government authorities with responsibility for economic affairs believed that the problems facing them were serious enough without their having simultaneously to cope with the disruption arising from a comprehensive programme of socialization—sentiments with which owners and managers in trade and industry could agree wholeheartedly. Another, serious obstacle was lack of information. In the wake of wartime economic mismanagement and against the background of a thriving black market, loss of territory, political upheaval, and a sudden and often uncontrolled demobilization, the Reich government was unable to gain precise information about stocks of raw materials and food, the development of wages and prices, or even the size and location of its armed forces.[29] Against such a background, even the proponents of socialist change often felt compelled to allow the pragmatic tackling of immediate problems to take precedence, and to postpone the building of 'socialism'. Thus Wilhelm Dittmann, USPD member of the Council of People's Deputies, explained to the General Congress of Workers' and Soldiers' Councils on 16 December 1918 that the decrees emanating from the newly created Reich Demobilization Office were 'direct consequences of the War' and had 'resulted from the present emergency'. 'Only once this period of transition is mastered,' he asserted, 'only then will socialism develop and unfold completely and be able to bring culture and prosperity to the working people.'[30] Although Dittman's confidence in the socialist future brought cheers from his comrades, the time when socialism would bring culture and prosperity to the working population was not exactly around the corner. Instead, the measures which resulted 'from the present emergency', the temporary expedients of the 'period of transition', were to form the parameters for subsequent economic and social policy.

This was naturally to the liking of industrial interests, who looked forward to the dismantling of the restrictions under which they had operated during the War.[31] For them economic demobilization promised the lifting of price controls and the 'granting of freedom of movement through the release of

---

[29] See Peter-Christian Witt, 'Bemerkungen zur Wirtschaftspolitik in der "Übergangswirtschaft" 1918/19: Zur Entwicklung von Konjunkturbeobachtung und Konjunktursteuerung in Deutschland; in Dirk Stegmann, Bernd-Jürgen Wendt, and Peter-Christian Witt (eds.), *Industrielle Gesellschaft und politisches System: Beiträge zur politischen Sozialgeschichte* (Bonn, 1978), 86–93. Witt observes that this period saw a concerted effort to improve the compilation of economic data in Germany, particularly with regard to the labour market.

[30] *Allgemeiner Kongress der Arbeiter- und Soldatenräte Deutschlands vom 16. bis 21. Dezember 1918 im Abgeordnetenhaus in Berlin. Stenographisches Bericht*, ed. Zentralrat der sozialistischen Republik Deutschlands (Berlin, 1919), 21–2.

[31] See esp. Feldman, *Iron and Steel in the German Inflation*, 79–90.

raw materials for export and through the lifting of exchange control, as only without these shackles could they [the industrial interests] participate again in foreign trade'.[32] From their perspective the economic demobilization promised to be as much an opportunity to advance their interests as a threat to their position, despite the political unrest which toppled the Imperial regime under which they had prospered. They were not to be disappointed.

It was not only powerful economic interests which looked to the demobilization for an abolition of controls. There was great popular desire for decontrol as well. This was due in part to a widespread belief that when controls were dismantled the economy would quickly return to 'normal' and the extraordinary economic problems created by the War would evaporate. But there was another, insistent source of pressure for decontrol: the powerful urge among people from various walks of life to get the state off their backs. The desire to reduce state control and interference in economic matters was felt in almost all quarters. Farmers wanted an end to the *Zwangswirtschaft*; consumers wanted an end to rationing and state controls over what they could purchase; employers wanted an end to state controls over hiring practices; workers wanted an end to restrictions on where they might work and live; soldiers wanted to get out of uniform and no longer take orders. This widespread desire to remove state control had curiously contradictory consequences. On the one hand, it proved a powerful force for revolutionary upheaval in 1918 and 1919, when state authority was shattered temporarily; on the other, it underpinned pressures for a restoration of pre-war economic relationships, which appeared quite positive in comparison with conditions after 1914 and in which the state played a much less prominent role economically.[33] In this way the widespread antipathy towards state control and state interference in everyday life which resulted from the wartime experience simultaneously propelled 'revolutionary' agitation and capitalist restoration.

The agenda for the economic demobilization embraced both short-term and long-term problems. Inevitably the immediate problems of unemployment, transport bottle-necks, shortages of raw materials, and the like received the most attention. However, underlying the economic problems of the moment was the fact that Germany had been made significantly poorer by the First World War. As we have seen, by the end of the War German industrial production stood at less than three-fifths of the 1913 figure, and

---

[32] Comments by representatives of industry at a meeting to discuss demobilization in the Reich Economics Office on 29 Oct. 1918, in BHStA, Abt. IV, MKr 14413: Beauftragter des bayer. Kriegsministeriums beim Preuß. Kriegsamt to Kriegsministerium in Munich, Berlin, 7 Nov. 1918.

[33] For a development of this argument, see Richard Bessel, 'State and Society in Germany in the Aftermath of the First World War', in W. R. Lee and Eve Rosenhaft (eds.), *The State and Social Change in Germany 1880–1980* (Oxford, Munich, and New York, 1990).

in 1919 it slumped to less than two-fifths;[34] and in 1919 real national income ('net social product') was only about two-thirds of the 1913 figure, which meant that real national income per capita at the end of the War was less than three-quarters of what it had been before the conflict began.[35] This in turn meant that there was significantly less economic cake to share out during the post-war years and consequently that the ability of the German government to satisfy the expectations of the German people was severely circumscribed. Post-war German governments, whatever their political complexion, faced the task not of how 'to bring culture and prosperity to the working people' but of how, in effect, to distribute poverty.

The uncomfortable fact of the matter was that one way or another Germany had to pay for the War. This problem was not faced squarely, although it framed not only the economic demobilization but also the economic and political history of Weimar Germany as a whole. While few politicians could accept the fact, much less base policy decisions upon it, the enormous costs of the War had impoverished the country, limited the possibilities for building a prosperous peacetime economy, and made a return to 'normality' or the *status quo ante* impossible. Instead of constituting an attempt to face this fundamental long-term problem, the economic demobilization consisted essentially of short-term emergency-measures to deal with immediate difficulties. The longer-term problems and consideration of the ramifications of policy decisions were left for another day.

The economic problems which had to be solved immediately were massive. Jobs were needed by roughly 6 million rapidly demobilized German soldiers and roughly 3 million German workers who until that time had been employed making armaments. Industrial production had to be redirected swiftly to civil needs, while desperate shortages of fuel and raw materials and transport bottle-necks threatened to bring what was left of the German economy to a halt. Those responsible for managing the economy had to tackle these problems, at once. There was simply no time to test options, to put detailed plans drawn up during wartime into operation, or to develop carefully crafted proposals for dealing with the underlying long-term problems. With the benefit of hindsight one might claim that the need to act without delay and in the absence of detailed plans actually proved an advantage, as many problems were resolved largely because they had to be resolved so quickly, without time for much debate. However, so sanguine a view would have seemed quite out of place at the time of the Armistice.

[34] See Holtfrerich, *The German Inflation*, 200–4; Rolf Wagenfuhr, *Die Industriewirtschaft: Entwick-lungstendenzen der deutschen und internationalen Industrieproduktion 1860 bis 1932* (*Vierteljahresheft zur Konjunkturforschung*, Sonderheft 31; Berlin, 1933), 23, 64.

[35] Witt, 'Finanzpolitik und sozialer Wandel', 424. The precise figures are 67.1% and 73.6%. For other estimates, see also Holtfrerich, *The German Inflation*, 224.

This, in rough outline, was the situation facing Joseph Koeth when he was appointed State Secretary of the newly created Reich Office for Economic Demobilization in November 1918. Koeth was in a remarkably good position to assess the problems involved in dismantling Germany's war economy. Born in Lower Franconia in 1870, Koeth had begun his career in the Bavarian army, was called to work in the Prussian War Ministry in 1909, and succeeded Walther Rathenau as head of the Raw Materials Section of the War Office in 1915. Koeth had thus been intimately involved in the management of the wartime economy and the distribution of scarce raw materials, and had become one of those in the army bureaucracy most acutely aware of the limitations imposed upon the war effort by shortages and insufficient economic capacity. As head of the organization which controlled the wartime allocation and pricing of raw materials, Koeth was regarded as sympathetic to industry, and he opposed plans to base a new post-war economic order upon the extension of state controls which had occurred during the War.[36] Koeth arrived at his new desk in November 1918 with a conviction that the state should not and could not exert direct control over the whole of the post-war economic transition. Instead, he felt, its role should consist essentially in specific interventions (massive though they may have to be, due to the massive scale of the problems) to assist private industry and the capitalist economy to get over a difficult, painful, and dangerous period of adjustment. At the same time, however, he was well aware of the need to accompany this limited interventionism with an emphasis upon social policy. This view gained him the approval of representatives of organized labour, but was far removed from the state-centric or socialist visions of economic organization put forward elsewhere.

The Reich Office for Economic Demobilization which Koeth headed was given extremely wide jurisdiction. It was authorized to intervene in virtually all social and economic questions and became, for a few short months, a sort of super-ministry with extraordinary powers. According to the Decree of 12 November 1918, on the creation of the Demobilization Office, Koeth was empowered

to take charge immediately of the entire operation of the economic demobilization, to establish contact for this purpose with all the relevant central, provincial, and local authorities of the Reich and federal states, to agree the necessary measures with them, or if need be to take action independently.

The Decree went on:

All civil and military authorities are called upon to comply with Herr Koeth's instructions in matters of economic demobilization without fail and with the greatest

---

[36] See Feldman, 'Economic and Social Problems', 4–7.

alacrity, and to assist him in every respect in carrying out his most important tasks for the welfare of our people.[37]

Two weeks later, on 27 November, Koeth was given powers to prosecute those who opposed his orders.[38]

The new State Secretary for Economic Demobilization set to work immediately. His first major piece of legislation, a decree issued on 13 November outlining the administration of unemployment relief,[39] was followed by an avalanche of decrees from the Demobilization Office during the next few weeks. Initially things went rather more smoothly than had been hoped; the utter disaster predicted at the time of the military collapse did not materialize. There seemed grounds for cautious optimism in the Demobilization Office, as the problems of food-supply, transport, and raw materials, serious though these were, remained more or less under control.[40] The need to get the troops home, something about which everyone involved could agree, pushed other problems into the background. But this changed, as Koeth had believed it would, once the return of the soldiers was largely completed. By the beginning of January 1919—with political unrest mounting, the railway system jammed, acute coal-shortages affecting the whole of the economy, and workers showing deep unwillingness to work—the head of the Demobilization Office despaired that 'the situation is so strained that I do not believe it can be sustained over a matter of weeks'.[41] During the first two months of the demobilization, Koeth had essentially been swimming with the tide. With the new year, however, a second and much more difficult

[37] *Reichsgesetzblatt*, 1918, 1304–5.

[38] The penalties were terms of imprisonment of up to five years and fines of up to 10,000 Marks. See *Reichsgesetzblatt*, 1918, 1339. It remains unclear whether these powers were ever used. In his study of the economic demobilization in Bavaria, Kurt Königsberger noted that despite his 'extraordinary power to impose legal penalties', the Bavarian State Commissar for the demobilization 'never used the full discretionary power given to him without obtaining the agreement of the appropriate minister'. See Königsberger, 'Die wirtschaftliche Demobilmachung in Bayern', 194.

[39] *Reichsgesetzblatt*, 1918, 1305–8. For discussion of demobilization and the German labour-market, see below, Ch. 5, and Richard Bessel, 'Unemployment and Demobilisation in Germany after the First World War', in Richard J. Evans and Dick Geary (eds.), *The German Unemployed: Experiences and Consequences of Mass Unemployment from the Weimar Republic to the Third Reich* (London and Sydney, 1987), 23–43.

[40] See the reports of discussions in the Demobilization Office in BHStA, Abt. IV, MKr 14413, and SHAD, Ministerium der Auswärtigen Angelegenheiten, no. 2494, Band I. See also Feldman, 'Economic and Social Problems', 15–16.

[41] Koeth's concluding remarks at a meeting in the Demobilization Office on 4 January 1919, in BHStA, Abt. IV, MKr 14413: Beauftragter des bayer. Ministeriums für milit. Angelegenheiten beim preuß. Kriegsamt to Staatskommissar für die Demobilmachung in Munich, Berlin, 6 Jan. 1919. Koeth remained pessimistic for the remainder of his tenure as demobilization supremo. At the last meeting he chaired at the Demobilization Office, on 26 Apr. 1919 and under the shadow of strikes in the Ruhr, Koeth opened with the observation that in his opinion 'at the moment we find ourselves on a further march downhill'. See BHStA, Abt. IV, MKr 14413: Beauftragter des bayer. Ministeriums für milit. Angelegenheiten beim preuß. Kriegsamt to Staatsministerium für Handel und Industrie in Munich, Berlin, 26 Apr. 1919.

phase of the demobilization had begun; after the soldiers had returned, Koeth had to concentrate on urging workers to work hard, channelling them towards sectors of the economy where they were needed, and overseeing industry's transition from war production to a post-war economy. In the midst of shortages, chaos on the railways, political unrest, and massive strike-movements, these goals were terribly hard to achieve. Here Koeth's labours proved largely in vain, and he proceeded to antagonize many of the interests which had been so pleased to see him installed in the Demobilization Office during the previous November.[42]

Although the powers concentrated in Koeth's hands were extensive, he was determined not to use them to create the foundations of a new economic system. His aim was to solve urgent problems immediately: as Gerald Feldman has put it, to 'make one ad hoc decision after another without regard for their long-range implications'.[43] The demands he made were hardly modest, however. At a meeting in the Demobilization Office on 15 November, Koeth observed that '90 per cent of industry would shortly have no orders' unless 'significant resources' were made available; 'under these circumstances', he claimed, 'one must make grants from the Reich available immediately—one will not get by with under two to three thousand million Marks monthly'.[44] Yet seeking to distribute government grants was rather different from seeking to reshape the German economy. Koeth put his case in particularly dramatic language at a Cabinet meeting on 12 December 1918, when he argued for, and received, money to provide orders and financial guarantees in order to ensure that factory owners were willing and able to keep their factories—and workers—working. Whereas Under-Secretary of State Wichard von Moellendorff pressed for the more far-reaching (and more costly) proposals of the Reich Economics Office for organizing the post-war economy, and demanded that, despite the 'provisional' nature of the Demobilization Office's tasks, 'the more distant goal must not be lost sight of and the future economic system must already be prepared for now', Koeth responded:

In my office I can have no grand and visionary ideas. I must only see how I get over the coming weeks. . . . I am crying out for help, I have only the small idea: how do I get from one day to the next.[45]

[42] See Feldman, 'Economic and Social Problems', 17–21.
[43] Ibid. 21.
[44] BHStA, Abt. IV, MKr 14412: Beauftragter des bayer. Kriegsministeriums beim preuß. Kriegsamt to Staatskommissar für die Demobilmachung, Berlin, 16 Nov. 1918.
[45] Miller and Potthoff (eds.), *Die Regierung der Volksbeauftragten*, i. 325–6. On Moellendorff and his aims in the Reich Economics Office/Ministry, see Feldman, *Iron and Steel in the German Inflation*, 100–8; Witt, 'Bemerkungen zur Wirtschaftspolitik', 93–6; Feldman, *The Great Disorder*, ch. 3. One important reason for the failure of Moellendorff to gain acceptance for his more far-reaching proposals was resistance on the part of the Treasury. His plans would clearly have involved even greater deficit-spending. The head of the Treasury, State Secretary Eugen Schiffer (an outspoken liberal proponent of a market economy), was determined to resist not only a

This sentiment was very much in keeping with the approach of Friedrich Ebert, who regarded the government he headed not as a revolutionary vanguard but as a provisional administration that would remain in power until elections could be held for a National Assembly. The major decisions would be taken later. In the meantime the task was how to get 'from one day to the next'.

The enormous economic problems facing Germany provided Koeth with ample justification for regarding the task of the Demobilization Office as holding things together and warding off socialist experimentation rather than mapping out a new economic order. Speaking at the Reich Conference held in Berlin on 25 November 1918 and attended by more than 100 leading government figures, Koeth expressed his belief that in order to complete the demobilization successfully one had to jettison the idea of putting new economic principles into practice, and he bluntly stated that 'it would be a fundamental error to assume that political change and economic change must go hand in hand'.[46] A few weeks later, in mid-December 1918 he explained:

The main goal of the new Reich Office is the attempt to accommodate the workers within the economy of the old system for the time being and to prevent the teetering economy from collapsing completely. The new Reich Office therefore could also be labelled as the Office for the Avoidance of Damage from the Revolution. At the present time it is necessary to refrain from socialization experiments. Nevertheless one must jettison the idea of the transitional economy, as this transition must remain for the future. The first requirement is the provision of jobs.[47]

In a retrospective analysis, he put the following innocent gloss on his aims while at the Demobilization Office:

The preservation of the economy meant simultaneously the preservation of the existing economic system; not due to fundamental misgivings about the socialist economic programme—these did not enter into consideration here—but solely out of the conviction that a change, regardless of what the new system might be, would necessarily accelerate the collapse of the economy during such a crisis.[48]

Koeth essentially regarded the Demobilization Office as something of a caretaker organization, albeit an extremely interventionist one, and ex-

---

continuation of inflationary wartime financial policies but also the schemes which meant substantial state intervention and which blocked a return to the 'individualistic economic order'. See Schiffer's response to Moellendorff at the Cabinet meeting of 12 Dec. 1918, in Miller and Potthoff (eds.), *Die Regierung der Volksbeauftragten*, i. 326–30.

[46] Miller and Potthoff (eds.), *Die Regierung der Volksbeauftragten*, i. 206–7.

[47] GLAK, 236/22281: 'Niederschrift über die Besprechung beim Reichsamt für wirtschaftliche Demobilmachung in Berlin am 18. und 19. Dezember 1918'.

[48] Joseph Koeth, 'Die wirtschaftliche Demobilmachung: Ihre Aufgaben und ihre Organe', in *Handbuch der Politik* (3rd edn.), iv: *Der wirtschaftliche Wiederaufbau* (Berlin and Leipzig, 1921), 164. See also Feldman, 'Economic and Social Problems', 7.

plained subsequently that 'the policy that the Demobilization Office pursued was one of wriggling through'.[49] It was in keeping with this conception that the Demobilization Ministry (its title was changed from 'Office' to 'Ministry' in March 1919) was wound up in April 1919, after Koeth's failure to manage the 'second act' of the demobilization. It was also consistent with this idea that Koeth should have criticized the continued existence of local and regional demobilization machinery in early 1921.[50] After all, by that time the German economy had already 'wriggled through'.

The reluctance to maintain or extend state direction of the economy owed much to wartime experience. Massive state intervention had failed to provide the needs of the military, secure adequate living-standards for the German population, or win the War. State intervention had not brought order; it had brought chaos. Confidence in the wisdom of state direction of economic life was shaken deeply and trust in the German state itself was shattered, something which contributed mightily to the political revolution of November 1918. Koeth himself characterized the upheaval of 1918 not as a 'collapse of the old system' but more properly as a 'collapse of the people, of its sense of duty towards the state'.[51] The disintegration of faith in the desirability and legitimacy of state intervention found resonance among industrialists, who had little taste for state direction of their economic affairs. (State subsidies, of course, were a different matter.) Organized labour, too, had little enthusiasm for restrictive state controls during a period in which labour's bargaining-power seemed to have increased considerably. It is thus hardly surprising that industrialists and trade-union leaders joined together in November 1918 to form their 'working association', the Zentralarbeitsgemeinschaft (ZAG), in order to manage industrial relations while trying to escape government regulation.[52] The economic demobilization and the policies of the Demobilization Office were framed very much in this spirit, in contrast to the hazy ideas of a government-organized technocratic rationalization of the German economy which lay behind Moellendorff's initiatives at the Reich Economics Office. As Gerald Feldman has noted, Koeth's demobilization tactics, and the general aim of decontrol which underlay them, 'had the effect of retransferring policy control in economic matters to industry's trade associations'.[53] Small wonder then that Dr Jakob Reichert, the Executive Director of the Association of German Iron and Steel Industrialists and member of the ZAG, could write that with Koeth's

---

[49] Koeth, 'Die wirtschaftliche Demobilmachung', 167.
[50] Ibid. 168.    [51] Ibid. 164.
[52] On the ZAG, see above all Gerald D. Feldman and Irmgard Steinisch, *Industrie und Gewerkschaften 1918–1924: Die überforderte Zentralarbeitsgemeinschaft* (Stuttgart, 1985); Gerald D. Feldman, 'The Origins of the Stinnes–Legien Agreement: A Documentation', *Internationale wissenschaftliche Korrespondenz zur Geschichte der deutschen Arbeiterbewegung*, 19/20 (Dec. 1972), 45–102.
[53] Feldman, 'Economic and Social Problems', 15.

appointment as head of the new Demobilization Office in early November 'the leadership of the demobilization has come into the best of hands'.[54]

The demobilization machinery put into place in November 1918 was thus a product of temporary collaboration between industrialists and trade-union leaders 'in alliance against the Reich Economics Office',[55] in order to prevent an extension of wartime 'state socialism' into the post-war period. Indeed, the initiative for setting up the Demobilization Office, and for placing Koeth at its head, had come from leading representatives of industry and labour acting jointly at the beginning of November 1918.[56] Then pressure had been applied successfully on the government of Prince Max of Baden to remove responsibility for the demobilization from the Reich Economics Office, which had overseen the planning hitherto, and to place it in the more trustworthy hands of Koeth and a new Demobilization Office. After 9 November the new revolutionary government, which was inclined neither to oppose initiatives supported by the trade unions nor to favour revolutionary plans for restructuring the German economy, allowed these arrangements to remain. Accordingly the decree of the Bundesrat of 7 November 1918, which had called for setting up an 'agency' (*Stelle*) to oversee economic demobilization, was translated into the Decree of the Council of People's Commissars of 12 November, which called the Reich Office for Economic Demobilization into being.[57] In this way the collapse of confidence in, and legitimacy of, state power which had paved the way for political revolution in 1918 also, perhaps paradoxically, paved the way for a management of the post-war transition which helped to forestall a revolutionary restructuring of the German economy.

Nevertheless, and Koeth's concern to steer clear of structural economic change notwithstanding, the creation of the Demobilization Office was something of a victory in terms of the centralization of economic decision-making. The federal states had been excluded from the discussions which

---

[54] Quoted in Feldman, *Iron and Steel in the German Inflation*, 83. For another hymn of praise by Reichert for Koeth and expressions of satisfaction that responsibility for the demobilization did not end up in the untrustworthy hands of the Reich Economics Ministry, see his speech in Essen on 30 Dec. 1918 before the Association of Chambers of Commerce of the Rhine-Westphalian Industrial Region, printed in Feldman and Steinisch, *Industrie und Gewerkschaften*, 154.

[55] Feldman, 'Economic and Social Problems', 6.

[56] On the discussions which led to the creation of the Demobilization Office and the appointment of Koeth at its head, with the approval of industrial and trade-union leaders, see Elben, *Das Problem der Kontinuität*, 71–3; Gerard D. Feldman, *Army, Industry and Labor in Germany, 1914–1918* (Princeton, NJ, 1966), 524–5; Hans-Joachim Bieber, *Gewerkschaften in Krieg und Revolution: Arbeiterbewegung Industrie, Staat und Militär in Deutschland 1914–1920* (2 vols.; Hamburg, 1981), ii. 601–4; Arnim Knoop, 'Wirtschaftliche Demobilisierung nach dem Ersten Weltkrieg: Zur Tätigkeit des Demobilisierungskommissariats in Hamburg 1918–1920' (Univ. of Hamburg thesis, 1981; copy in Staatsarchiv Hamburg, Maschinenschriftsammlung 1134), 9.

[57] For discussion of differences in the wording of the two decrees, see Koeth, 'Die wirtschaftliche Demobilmachung', 163.

had paved the way for establishing the Office,[58] and the way the nationwide demobilization machinery was organized meant that the bureaucracies of the federal states were essentially to carry out the policy of the Reich government. Yet this was a far cry from central dictatorial control of economic policy. Not only was the authority of the Reich government rather shaky in 1918 and 1919, but the ways in which decisions made in Berlin actually affected people depended upon how they were implemented by regional and local authorities. Accordingly, the Reich Demobilization Office in Berlin restricted itself largely to general policy issues and left their application to the regional and local authorities dealing with demobilization. The Berlin Office did not have the inclination, the information, or the personnel to control the specifics of the economic demobilization, and thus the regional authorities in particular were allowed a considerable degree of autonomy.[59] While the formulation of policy guide-lines was centralized, the ways in which those guide-lines were put into practice remained decentralized.

The demobilization machinery hastily put into place in November 1918 was essentially three-tier. At the top were the central authorities under Koeth's direction in Berlin, with Koeth also acting as State Commissar for Demobilization in Prussia. The next tier consisted of the regional Demobilization Commissars. In the case of Prussia, these were the regional Regierungspräsidenten (with the provincial Oberpräsidenten expected to act in their customary supervisory, rather than executive, role and to ensure that the demobilization was carried out in a uniform manner in their areas);[60] the smaller states, such as Hamburg and the Thuringian States, had a single State Commissar for the Demobilization at this regional level. Finally, at the district (*Kreis*) level there were local Demobilization Committees, consisting of local employers and labour representatives in equal number and chaired by the mayor in urban districts or by the Landrat in rural districts.[61] This regional and local demobilization machinery long outlasted the ministry which it had been created to serve. Whereas the Reich Ministry for Economic Demobilization was wound up in April 1919, the local Demobilization

[58] Feldman, *Army, Industry and Labor*, 524.
[59] See Koeth's comments to the Reich Conference held in Berlin on 25 Nov. 1918, in Miller and Potthoff (eds.), *Die Regierung der Volksbeauftragten*, i. 205–7; and Schäfer, *Regionale Wirtschaftspolitik in der Kriegswirtschaft*, 354–5.
[60] See e.g. PLA, Rep. 60, no. 3113, fo. 48: Oberpräsident, Stettin, 18 Nov. 1918.
[61] For details of the organization of the demobilization machinery, see *Nachrichtenblatt des Reichsamtes für wirtschaftliche Demobilmachung*, 1 (9 Dec. 1918), 2–3; Koeth, 'Die wirtschaftliche Demobilmachung', 166–7; Martin Sogemeier, *Die Entwicklung und Regelung des Arbeitsmarktes im rheinisch-westfälischen Industriegebiet im Kriege und in der Nachkriegszeit* (Jena, 1922), 88–9. Local committees 'for the transitional economy' sometimes pre-dated the central directives which called for them to be set up. See e.g. StAO, Dep. 3b, III, no. 694: 'Niederschrift über die Verhandlung der Kommission für Übergangswirtschaft'.

Committees were not dissolved until March 1921[62] and the post of regional Demobilization Commissar—which had initially been created to provide regional organization and assistance for Koeth—was not abolished formally until April 1924, a full five years after the abolition of the Berlin Ministry.[63]

The main focus of the demobilization machinery was the regulation of the labour market—'to keep the economy going, to place workers, in so far as they can no longer be employed in the armaments factories, as well as discharged soldiers, back in work and in their old regions'.[64] The day-to-day work this involved fell largely to the local Demobilization Committees, while the regional Demobilization Commissars served essentially to oversee and co-ordinate the work of various authorities.[65] The Demobilization Committees were called upon to set up emergency works-projects where necessary, to intervene to secure jobs—guaranteed by law—for the returning soldiers, to supervise the dismissal of categories of workers (such as women) whose needs were regarded as less important than those of men leaving military service,[66] to press employers to adhere to the demobilization regulations in their hiring and dismissal practices, and to settle the many conflicts which arose in these areas. The Demobilization Committees often worked in parallel with city labour-exchanges and local chambers of commerce and industry. It was in the work of these local committees that the decrees issued by Koeth affected people's everyday lives and that the collaboration of employers and trade unionists found practical expression. In this connection it is revealing that at the point where the demobilization actually affected people's lives, the committees charged with this work were comprised not of paid government officials but of representatives of economic interests acting in a voluntary capacity. The Demobilization Committees were, in effect, an expression of corporatism at the local level. Locally, as well as nationally, the administration of the demobilization comprised an important

---

[62] *Reichsgesetzblatt*, 1921, 189: 'Reichsverordnung über die Beendigung der wirtschaftlichen Demobilmachung vom 18. Februar 1921'.

[63] Ibid. 1924, 375: 'Reichsverordnung über die Aufhebung des Amtes des Demobilmachungskommissars vom 25.3.1924'.

[64] *Nachrichtenblatt des Reichsamtes für wirtschaftliche Demobilmachung*, 1 (9 Dec. 1918), 3.

[65] See the guide-lines issued by the State Commissar for the Demobilization in the Thuringian States in StAW, Thüringisches Wirtschaftsministerium, no. 130, fos. 3–4: Staatskommissar für die Demobilmachung in den Thüringischen Staaten to Demobilmachungsausschüsse der Thüringischen Staaten, Weimar, 20 Nov. 1918. See also Königsberger, 'Die wirtschaftliche Demobilmachung in Bayern', 194.

[66] For examples of cases dealt with by local Demobilization Committees, see descriptions of cases of women facing dismissal dealt with by the Demobilization Committee in Bochum in June and July 1919, in Richard Bessel, ' "Eine nicht allzu große Beunruhigung des Arbeitsmarktes": Frauenarbeit und Demobilmachung in Deutschland nach dem Ersten Weltkrieg', in *Geschichte und Gesellschaft*, 9 (1983), 224–5. The correspondence generated by these cases may be found in StdABo, B 265.

step in the penetration of government in Weimar Germany by economic interests.

The Demobilization Committees and industrial employers were desperately concerned about supplies of raw materials and the availability of transport facilities. Without sufficient rail-transport, the required raw materials, and in particular vital coal-supplies, could not get through. Without raw materials, orders could not be filled. Without orders, employers could not continue to pay their work-forces. An artisan representative at a meeting of the Demobilization Committee in Osnabrück no doubt spoke for many employers when he observed in mid-November that 'there is a lack not of orders but of the necessary raw materials'.[67] There seemed good reason to suppose that preventing mass unemployment and averting a collapse of the German economy depended upon the supply of raw materials. Thus despite Koeth's eagerness to remove controls—for example, on the compulsory purchase and sale of metal collected from the population—the various 'war societies' (*Kriegsgesellschaften*) which had overseen the collection and distribution of key raw materials during wartime were not dismantled until the summer of 1919.[68]

The most important of the raw materials in short supply was coal. The German economy was dependent on coal to satisfy almost all its energy needs. Railways needed coal for the locomotives; electricity works needed coal to supply power; the population, particularly in the cities, needed coal to heat their homes; coal shortages seriously reduced the supply of gas; and without adequate coal-supplies few of Germany's factories could operate properly. In his 1920 analysis of the economic demobilization in Bavaria, Kurt Königsberger claimed, with ample justification, that 'whoever had the opportunity to study the papers of the demobilization authorities would be struck again and again in all letters and reports, telegrams and notices, by the words: coal shortage!'.[69] This was the problem which preoccupied factory owners more than any other. They lost rather little sleep over the demand for their goods; in a Germany starved for years of articles for consumption, selling what was produced caused comparatively little worry. The problem was how to get production moving, and that meant in large measure how to acquire scarce supplies of coal.

The coal shortage was the consequence of a crippling combination of the loss of the coalfields of Lorraine and the Saar, the cutting-off of supplies

[67] StAO, Dep. 3b, III, no. 694: 'Niederschrift über die Verhandlung der Kommission für Übergangswirtschaft am 18. November 1918'. See also ibid., no. 695: Verein Osnabrücker Metall-Industrieller to Oberbürgermeister Dr. Rissmüller, Osnabrück, 26 Nov. 1918; *Die wirtschaftliche Demobilmachung*, 2: 16 (21 Jan. 1919), 127, 129; Hans Drüner, *Im Schatten des Weltkrieges: Zehn Jahre Frankfurter Geschichte von 1914–1924* (Frankfurt/Main, 1934), 353; Schäfer, *Regionale Wirtschaftspolitik in der Kriegswirtschaft*, 343–4.

[68] See Schäfer, *Regionale Wirtschaftspolitik in der Kriegswirtschaft*, 344–5.

[69] Königsberger, 'Die wirtschaftliche Demobilmachung in Bayern', 201.

from abroad (for example, from Bohemia), bottle-necks on the railways, and steep drops in coal production within Germany. The introduction of the eight-hour day (and of correspondingly shorter shifts in the mines), an upsurge in labour unrest, the effects of undernourishment, and a general disinclination to work, combined to drive productivity down to record low levels in 1919.[70] In the Ruhr, coal output per man per shift had declined from 0.97 tonnes in 1913 to 0.66 in November 1918 and subsequently declined still further; in Upper Silesia, the decline was from 1.18 tonnes output per man per shift in 1913 to only 0.57 tonnes in December 1918.[71] The sharp drops in productivity were made worse in early 1919 by strikes and political conflict: the labour unrest and nationality disputes in Upper Silesia and the repeated strikes in the Ruhr.[72] Between October and November 1918 coal production of both hard coal and lignite declined by roughly one-third; during January 1919 in Upper Silesia the average production per man per shift stood at less than two-fifths the 1913 average, and in the Ruhr daily production during mid-February was less than half the 1913 figure.[73] Altogether, as a result of territorial losses, declining productivity, labour unrest, lower-quality seams, and shorter shifts, Germany's hard-coal production in 1919 was only about three-fifths that of 1913;[74] in the Ruhr, production stood at a mere 71 per cent of the pre-war figure, even though the numbers of miners had increased from 390,647 in 1913 to 447,359 in December 1919.[75]

The problem was compounded by poor discipline among labour on the railways, which were already crippled by shortages of rolling stock.[76] In late

---

[70] Holtfrerich, *The German Inflation*, 183. On the reduction of the lengths of shifts and of productivity in the Ruhr mining industry, see Gerald D. Feldman, 'Arbeitskonflikte im Ruhrberg-bau 1919–1922', *Vierteljahreshefte für Zeitgeschichte*, 27: 2 (Apr. 1980), esp. 169–74. For figures of coal production, size of the mining work-force, wage costs, and turnover of the industry from 1913 to 1919, see *Statistisches Jahrbuch für das Deutsche Reich 1921/22* (Berlin, 1922), 85. See also Königsberger, 'Die wirtschaftliche Demobilmachung in Bayern', 220–3.

[71] See also SHAD, Gesandtschaft Berlin, no. 690, fos. 199–206: Demobilmachungsamt, 'Auszug aus der Niederschrift der Besprechung am 20. I. 1919 über die Allgemeine Lage', Berlin, 20 Jan. 1919.

[72] In the Ruhr more than 20,000 miners struck between 14 and 17 Dec. 1918; between 2 and 25 Jan. 1919 the unrest meant an average daily loss of 19,470 shifts worked; a general strike call was heeded by 353,000 miners on 20 Feb. 1919; and a second general strike call led to a daily average of 225,300 miners missing work between 1 and 26 Apr. 1919. See Peter Borscheid, 'Vom Ersten zum Zweiten Weltkrieg (1914–1945)', in Wilhelm Kohl (ed.), *Westfälische Geschichte*, iii: *Das 19. und das 20. Jahrhundert: Wirtschaft und Gesellschaft* (Düsseldorf, 1984), 347; a graphic illustration of the size and productivity of the work-force in Ruhr mining is reproduced on 354.

[73] Figures from Königsberger, 'Die wirtschaftliche Demobilmachung in Bayern', 204.

[74] Lignite production increased marginally, but this was due to the fact that the number employed in the industry in 1919 was nearly double that in 1913. For the figures, see *Statistisches Jahrbuch für das Deutsche Reich 1921/22*, 85.

[75] Feldman, 'Arbeitskonflikte im Ruhrbergbau', 172.

[76] In Nov. 1918 Koeth complained bitterly that workers throughout the Reich displayed 'no enthusiasm for work' and that labour productivity had declined 'in all areas', 'especially in the

April, after an extended strike in the Ruhr coal-field, low levels of production and severe cutbacks in the transport of goods on the railways combined to ensure that 'industry could get virtually no coal whatsoever'.[77] What was more, due to shortages and labour problems the production of railway locomotives and carriages slumped.[78] In early 1919, as Königsberger noted, the German economy was falling victim to a vicious circle: 'We have no coal because we have no locomotives, and we have no locomotives because we have no coal.'[79] He was also not without justification when he described as the central problem of the demobilization economy 'that we are working less than ever although we have to produce more than at any other time!'.[80]

Coal was not the only item in short supply. Railway bottle-necks also affected supplies of wood (which was needed for props in coal mines, especially since the mines were in a poor state of repair after the War). Coal shortages led to shortages in other materials—such as iron and steel, bricks and cement, and chemicals—which required coal for their production.[81] Shortages in these areas had further effects, as they then prevented many finishing industries from working near capacity. In this way, the effects of the widespread shortages multiplied, threatening to paralyse the German economy and to throw millions of people out of work. In the circumstances, it may seem remarkable that the economy did not seize up entirely. The fact that it did not points to another aspect of the shortages: that they were in part the consequence of hoarding and of the reluctance of many businesses

unloading of railway goods wagons'. See SHAD, Ministerium der Auswärtigen Angelegenheiten, no. 2494, Band I, fos. 128–9: Der stellv. Bevollmächtigte zum Bundesrate to Ministerium der Auswärtigen Angelegenheiten (in Dresden), Berlin, 23 Nov. 1918. For a description of the difficulties facing the railways in Baden—which included the results of deferred maintenance during the War, massive troop-transports, disruptions caused by new borders in east and west, and loss of rolling stock—see Schäfer, *Regionale Wirtschaftspolitik in der Kriegswirtschaft*, 345. The workings of the railways in late 1918 were also adversely affected by the influenza; see BHStA, Abt. IV, MKr 14412: Beauftragter des bayer. Kriegsministeriums beim Preuß. Kriegsamt to the Staatskommissar für die Demobilmachung, Berlin, 16 Nov. 1918.

[77] Report of the last meeting in the Berlin Demobilization Office, on 26 Apr. 1919, in BHStA, Abt. IV, MKr 14413: Beauftragter des bayer. Ministeriums für milit. Angelegenheiten beim preuß. Kriegsamt. Kriegsamt to Staatsministerium für Handel und Industrie in Munich, Berlin, 26 Apr. 1919.

[78] Königsberger, 'Die wirtschaftliche Demobilmachung in Bayern', 207.

[79] Ibid. 204.      [80] Ibid. 221.

[81] Apparently, however, electricity supplies generally were maintained, since electricity generating stations were able to draw on coal reserves, as were supplies of lignite for home heating. See Schäfer, *Regionale Wirtschaftspolitik in der Kriegswirtschaft*, 346. See also the report of the discussions on 24 Dec. 1919 in the Demobilization Office, in SHAD, Ministerium der Auswärtigen Angelegenheiten, no. 2494, Band I, fos. 198–200: Der stellv. Bevollmächtigte zum Bundesrate to Staatsminister für die Auswärtigen Angelegenheiten in Dresden, Berlin, 24 Dec. 1918; report of the meeting on 17 Dec., SHAD, Ministerium der Auswärtigen Angelegenheiten, no. 2494, Band I, fos. 249–50: Der stellv. Bevollmächtigte zum Bundesrate to Staatsminister für die Auswärtigen Angelegenheiten in Dresden, Berlin, 17 Dec. 1918; and SHAD, Gesandtschaft Berlin, no. 690, fos. 199–206: Demobilmachungsamt, 'Auszug aus der Niederschrift der Besprechung am 20. I. 1919 über die Allgemeine Lage', Berlin, 20 Jan. 1919.

to part with valuable raw materials in advance of scheduled price-rises.[82] But whatever their cause, alleviating the shortages, and especially the coal shortage, with its many ripple effects, formed a key to the reconstruction of the German economy and to the satisfactory stabilization of the labour market.

Thus there is reason to believe that the swift rise in unemployment in Germany during late 1918 and early 1919 was due as much if not more to shortages of raw materials than simply to the sudden return of millions of soldiers. It appears more than just coincidental that the unemployment figures peaked in January and February 1919, precisely when industry was experiencing the most severe difficulties of supply.[83] Not just a surplus of labour but also a scarcity of raw materials determined the levels of joblessness during the demobilization period. The shortages of raw materials, especially of coal, had led to widespread temporary closures of factories.[84] The removal of women workers, foreign labourers, and prisoners of war from factory employment, as well as the reduction of the working day, had done much to free the necessary jobs for the returning soldiers, and the huge pent-up demand for consumer goods virtually ensured that employment would be available provided factories could acquire the raw materials needed to produce these goods.[85] The key, therefore, was gaining access to scare raw materials—something of which industrialists were acutely aware, as they used the fears about unemployment to press their case.[86]

Why then, if the shortages were so serious, did unemployment not rise significantly higher than the figure of 1.45 million registered at labour exchanges as looking for work in January 1919?[87] In part, the answer lies in the fact that large numbers of people were shunted out of the German labour-market after the War and are not to be found in unemployment statistics—prisoners of war, foreign labourers, women. Another reason is the sharp drop in the number of hours worked. For example, at the Daimler works in Unterürkheim, where a working week in excess of 60 hours had

---

[82] For the iron and steel industry, where this problem was acute, see Feldman, *Iron and Steel in the German Inflation*, 95–6. In Dec. 1918 the Bavarian Ministry for Military Affairs noted that it was impossible to get a 'complete picture of the raw-materials situation' because 'industry may not have reported its entire stocks'. See BHStA, Abt, IV, MKr 14413: Ministerium für milit. Angelegenheiten to all Regierungspräsidenten, Munich, 4 Dec. 1918.

[83] For the unemployment figures, see Bessel, 'Unemployment and Demobilisation', esp. 24–6; see also below, Ch. 5.

[84] See e.g. the report of the Thuringian Commissar for Economic Demobilization, complaining about the causes and effects of labour shortages in the lignite fields, in StAW, Thüringisches Wirtschaftsministerium, no. 130, fo. 57: Staatskommissar für wirtschaftliche Demobilmachung in den Thüringischen Staaten to sämtl. Demobilmachungausschüsse, Weimar, 31 Dec. 1918. According to this report, 'many industrial factories' had shut as a result.

[85] On this theme, see the suggestive description of developments in the Frankfurt/Main region in Drüner, *Im Schatten des Weltkrieges*, 413–14.

[86] See below, Ch. 5.

[87] Bessel, 'Unemployment and Demobilisation', 24, 26.

been common during the War, the work-week was reduced to 44 hours on 12 November and to 30 hours on 3 December; 'normal working hours' of 44 per week were not restored until mid-April 1919.[88] Furthermore, the efforts of the demobilization authorities, and the emergency public-works projects they sponsored, were partly responsible for keeping the unemployment figures within bounds during the crucial months after the Armistice. However, one major reason why post-war unemployment did not rise more was that a large proportion of the costs of demobilization were, in effect, borne by employers, who continued to employ and pay their workers even when their revenues had dried up.

One good example of what happened is provided by the case of the chemicals giant BASF, whose production facilities in Ludwigshafen and Oppau were shut down between November 1918 and June 1919.[89] The shut-down was due to a number of factors: the ending of armaments orders, the need for technical re-equipment, uncertainty over the status of the Palatinate (where the factories were located) in advance of the Versailles Treaty, and the lack of coal supplies from the Ruhr. Despite the shut-down, however, the BASF work-force was kept employed 'without noteworthy reductions' during this seven-month period. Unable to produce anything which the firm could sell, the workers were kept busy with clearing-up operations, tasks connected with the change-over in production, and with building-work.

The pressures upon employers to keep workers on the payroll were considerable. Government decrees stipulated that employers had to re-employ their old work-forces; the political instability generated fears of far worse things happening to employers than having to pay wages to unnecessary workers; and many employers believed it was good policy to retain workers in anticipation of a rise in post-war demand. Of course, not all the costs were borne by the employers. Regional and local governments on occasion could be induced to provide money to cover the gap between the wages workers continued to receive despite a reduced working week and those they would have received had their pay been cut in line with their reduced hours.[90] Yet the costs to employers of keeping on substantial work-forces who produced very little in the chaotic conditions of late 1918 and early 1919 were considerable. According to Kurt Königsberger:

The main burden of the losses due to the (post-war) readjustment were borne by trade and industry. The relatively favourable condition of the labour market was maintained only by the fiction that manufacturing could keep the greatest part of

[88] Bernard P. Bellon, *Mercedes in Peace and War: German Automobile Workers, 1903–1945* (New York, 1990), 147.

[89] See Dieter Schiffmann, *Von der Revolution zum Neunstundentag: Arbeit und Konflikt bei BASF 1918–1924* (Frankfurt/Main and New York, 1983), 50–1.

[90] Bernard Bellon details how Daimler and other firms in Stuttgart were able to get financial assistance to pay the additional labour costs, first from Württemberg's provisional government and then from Stuttgart's unemployment funds. See Bellon, *Mercedes in Peace and War*, 148.

the work-force busy. In fact this was impossible due to the absence of half our coal needs, the shortage of raw materials, the continuation of the blockade, the general insecurity. The costs of the transition therefore had to be covered in large measure by the reserves of industry. Presumably after the boom during the War the reserves of very many factories were not insubstantial.[91]

Threatened by political revolution and labour militancy, often resting on substantial profits made during wartime, private industry was in effect compelled to pay its share for the costly demobilization—in many cases a fitting penalty for the profiteering during the War. Declines in productivity and shortages of raw materials, together with the need to maintain a sizeable labour-force, drove employers into unprofitable operations, which could be financed only out of reserves, borrowing, or government aid.[92]

The spending of reserves and government aid to finance temporarily unprofitable operations helped to tide the German economy over the worst in the months immediately after the Armistice, until the blockade was lifted and shortages of raw materials eased somewhat. Then, during the second half of 1919, strong domestic demand for consumer goods and an upsurge in foreign demand for relatively cheap German products created boom conditions and 'an orgy of exports',[93] which in effect delivered the German economy from the immediate problems of the demobilization and eliminated the threat of mass unemployment.[94] In these new and favourable trading-conditions, private industry began to lose its concern about holding down prices and to see the advantages of a 'pro-inflationary course'.[95] The sacrifices made by private industry, in the economic sphere no less than in the political sphere, were of rather short duration.

The financial pressures varied tremendously from industry to industry, however, and it would be mistaken to assume that all were forced to operate

---

[91] Königsberger, 'Die wirtschaftliche Demobilmachung in Bayern', 211.

[92] Königsberger gives a long list of examples of firms in Bavaria which in May 1919 were producing a fraction of what they had done in 1914 but with work-forces of comparable—and sometimes greater—size. See Königsberger, 'Die wirtschaftliche Demobilmachung in Bayern', 212–13. Other evidence that company profits were sacrificed to finance the demobilization is provided by the sharp drop in undivided profits at the Bayer chemicals firm; these profits, which had held up well during the War, fell in 1919 to less than one-fifth the 1913 figure in real terms. See Gottfried Plumpe, 'Chemische Industrie und Hilfsdienstgesetz am Beispiel der Farbenfabriken, vorm. Bayer & Co.', in Gunther Mai (ed.), *Arbeiterschaft in Deutschland 1914–1918: Studien zu Arbeitskampf und Arbeitsmarkt im Ersten Weltkrieg* (Düsseldorf, 1985), 184.

[93] The phrase is from Charles S. Maier, *Recasting Bourgeois Europe: Stabilization in France, Germany, and Italy in the Decade after World War I* (Princeton, NJ, 1975), 70.

[94] e.g. during the period from the summer of 1919 until the autumn of 1920 BASF was (according to its own annual reports) able sell its products for 'lucrative prices' and 'with good profit'. Quoted in Schiffmann, *Von der Revolution zum Neunstundentag*, 51. The numbers of people employed by BASF in Ludwigshafen and Oppau, which had been 12,072 in 1913, grew from 10,038 in 1917 to 13,286 in 1918, 13,775 in 1919, and 18,031 in 1920 (yearly averages). Ibid. 459.

[95] See Witt, 'Finanzpolitik und sozialer Wandel', 416–17.

at a loss during the first few months after the Armistice. Whether they did or not depended to a great extent upon whether they required imported goods or large supplies of coal. Those which did not could take full advantage of the huge demand and rising consumer purchasing-power to profit handsomely. Those which did, or which had to replace scarce materials requisitioned during the War, were in a far more difficult position—as for example the brewing industry, which needed coal and had to acquire new vats, wagons, and horses to replace those lost in the War.[96]

Although many employers had to keep people on their payroll with no productive work for them to do, private industry did not emerge from the demobilization empty-handed. Among the main aims of the demobilization regime was the abolition of the *Zwangswirtschaft*, the controlled economy. Here a most cherished demand of private industry was to be met; while many firms operated at a loss during the months immediately following the War, the abolition of controls promised substantial profit in the near future. No sooner was the Demobilization Office established than it began the process of dismantling controls over the distribution and prices of goods, ending compulsory state purchases and returning to a market economy.[97] This process was a rather drawn-out affair, and was far from complete when the Demobilization Ministry was wound up in the spring of 1919, but the direction which post-war policy was to take had been fixed. The policy was not without its problems: it stimulated further inflation as controls were lifted in a country where many items were in short supply, and exacerbated shortages since there was incentive to hoard goods in anticipation of the abolition of government controls. However, it was very much to the liking of industry.

Of course, not all the responsibility for combating unemployment was left to private enterprise. Where the private sector was unable to provide adequate opportunities for employment, emergency works-projects were to be undertaken at public expense. The Demobilization Office urged local authorities to implement such projects where necessary, and large amounts of money were made available.[98] However, subsidies from the Reich government were not intended to cover the entire costs, but only the *additional* costs which resulted from the inflation; local authorities were to bear the expense of what the works would have cost in 'normal' peacetime conditions. That is to say, the Reich was willing to cover only the increases in costs since 1914 ('the overcharge caused by the war conditions'), and then not

[96] See Borscheid, 'Vom Ersten zum Zweiten Weltkrieg', 387.

[97] e.g. this process began for the textile industry in Dec. 1918, when state requisitions and maximum prices were abolished for a number of types of cloth. See Schäfer, *Regionale Wirtschaftspolitik in der Kriegswirtschaft*, 347.

[98] In Bavaria alone the sum exceeded 500 million Marks. See Königsberger, 'Die wirtschaftliche Demobilmachung in Bayern', 218.

the entire amount but rather five-sixths of the additional costs.[99] Thus any local authority which applied for such money—and only public authorities, not private firms, could receive this money directly—had to provide a rather substantial amount of the funding itself, a measure no doubt aimed at preventing profligacy with Reich funds by local government.

Throughout the country a vast number of works were planned: drainage and sewerage projects, road improvements, forestry work, planting trees along streets, cleaning up cemeteries, and the like.[100] The aim was, as the Bavarian State Commissar for Demobilization made clear, to promote emergency works 'which while using the fewest possible and least valuable materials employ the greatest number of workers'.[101] Yet plans did not always get translated into action. In many places, as Frauke Bey-Heard has noted for Berlin at this time, 'more was spoken and written about the emergency works-projects of the local authorities than could actually be undertaken, because they were held within narrow limits by the lack of coal, materials, and money'.[102] Furthermore, there appears to have been a widespread disinclination among the unemployed to accept jobs on emergency works-projects.[103] This, together with the crucial importance of raw-materials shortages in fuelling unemployment, suggests that it may be mistaken to overemphasize the role played by public contracts in the reduction of unemployment in 1919.[104]

As noted above, it was the local Demobilization Committees which were responsible for the everyday application of government policy. The Reich Demobilization Office in Berlin provided the overall guide-lines and money; the regional Demobilization Commissars delegated and co-ordinated the

[99] 'Grundsätze über die Bewilligung von Zuschüssen zu öffentlichen Notstandsarbeiten' in *Nachrichtenblatt des Reichsamtes für wirtschaftliche Demobilmachung*, 1: 2 (10 Dec. 1918), 12.

[100] See e.g. the descriptions of emergency works-projects in the Regierungsbezirk Potsdam in BLHA, Rep. 2A Reg. Potsdam I SW/795; in the Regierungsbezirk Bromberg in APP, Rejencja w Pile, no. 1486; and for the town of Delitzsch in SSAL, Stadt Delitzsch, no. 1002, fo. 20: Magistrat zu Delitzsch to Landrat, Delitzsch, 21 Nov. 1918. See also Königsberger, 'Die wirtschaftliche Demobilmachung in Bayern', 218–19.

[101] Quoted in Königsberger, 'Die wirtschaftliche Demobilmachung in Bayern', 218.

[102] Frauke Bey-Heard, *Hauptstadt und Staatsumwälzung. Berlin 1919. Problematik und Scheitern der Rätebewegung in der Berliner Kommunalverwaltung* (Stuttgart, 1969), 117–18.

[103] e.g. in Jan. 1919 the Association of Bavarian Labour Offices reported to Berlin that although the labour market in Munich had 'become considerably worse' than in Dec., 'the emergency works which have been provided are taken up only reluctantly by the urban work-force'. See BAP, RMwD, no. 3, fos. 231–7: Verband bayer. Arbeitsämter to Reichsamt für wirtschaftliche Demobilmachung, 'Die Lage des Arbeitsmarktes in Bayern im Monat Januar 1919', Munich, 11 Feb. 1919. During the same month in the Reich capital, which was also the capital of German unemployment, works projects designed to employ 2,000 people in the Berlin forests could attract only 400 'people eager to work'; apparently, it was claimed, 'there is no inclination among the majority of the unemployed to accept this work'. See BAP, RMwD, no. 20, fo. 187: Verbandsdirektor des Verbandes Groß-Berlin to Staatssekretär des Demobilmachungsausschusses, Berlin, 30 Jan. 1919.

[104] For a different view, see Witt, 'Bemerkungen zur Wirtschaftspolitik', esp. 95–6.

work in their regions; and the local Demobilization Committees were left the often complicated task of ensuring that the regulations emanating from Berlin were applied in rapidly changing circumstances. This involved the Demobilization Committees in a vast number of disputes about how regulations were to be interpreted. The Committees were called upon to decide such questions as whether an employer had the right to retain female workers in the face of challenges from trade unions; whether an employer should be compelled to hire labour; whether claims were justified that economic difficulties made the shedding of labour necessary; whether people who had moved into a locality to work during the War had the right to remain and work there during the demobilization. Was it right to dismiss a young woman supporting an invalid father, when returning soldiers claimed her job? Should hotel and restaurant owners be allowed to hire employees of their own choice while unemployed waiters were available, or should they be compelled to dismiss female staff and replace them with men newly returned from military service?[105] Should an employer have to hire additional war-invalids when he insisted that he had no work that was safe for invalids to do? In attempting to judge in such cases, the Demobilization Committees were responsible not only for the smooth functioning of the local labour-market but also for the fate of countless thousands of people.

To their credit, the local Demobilization Committees often went to considerable lengths to avoid the severe social hardships that would have resulted from too rigorous an application of the regulations. This may be seen in their resistance to extreme pressure to remove women from paid employment during 1919. Trade-union leaders were vocal in their demands that women be removed from their jobs in favour of men, with the most bitter attacks on continued female employment coming from organizations of office staff.[106] The defenders of working women tended to come from the ranks of the employers, some of whom went so far as to offer 'to hire the unemployed if they were allowed to keep the women'.[107] The Demobilization Committees—on which both employers and trade unions were represented— had to steer a middle course, fending off the most callous calls for the wholesale dismissal of women regardless of their circumstances while simultaneously ensuring that women not deemed dependent upon continued employment for their survival vacated their jobs in favour of men.[108]

---

[105] See e.g. the protests of waiters' organizations in Osnabrück in StAO, Dep. 3b, III, no. 697: Arbeitsgemeinschaft freier Angestellten-Verbände im Gastwirtsgewerbe to the Demobilmachungsausschuß der Stadt Osnabrück; and ibid., no. 695: Ausschuß der vereinigten Kellner in Osnabrück to Demobilmachungskommissar, the Regierungspräsident, Osnabrück, 31 Jan. 1919.

[106] See Bessel, ' "Eine nicht allzu große Beunruhigung des Arbeitsmarktes" ', 224–5.

[107] BLHA, Rep. 30 Berlin C, Polizeipräsidium Berlin, Tit. 47, no. 1959, fos. 235–311: 'Jahresbericht des Oberregierungs- und Gewerberats für die Stadt Berlin für das Jahr 1921'.

[108] For a description of how this problem was dealt with by the demobilization machinery in Lippe, see MHLA, Mecklenburg-Strelitzer Ministerium, Abteilung des Innern, no. 4453, fo. 10:

For a short period after the First World War, the Demobilization Committees attempted to act as local representatives of the public good. In the
thousands of disputes over how the demobilization regulations affected
individuals, about who had the right to a particular job and who did not,
the Committees consciously served as guardians of the common interest
as they perceived it. This approach was also evident in the ways in which
they discussed general issues such as strikes and labour productivity.[109]
However, their members remained representatives of economic interest-
groups, and it is illustrative of the way in which the economic demobilization was carried out that the thousands of disputes which arose over
employment and related topics were handled by committees composed of
representatives of economic interest-groups. The resulting combination of
interest-group representation, *ad hoc* state interventionism, and a general
policy of 'wriggling through' became characteristic of the politics of the
Weimar Republic.

However, one can perhaps take the argument that the economic demobilization signified a major innovatory step on the road to an emerging
corporatist state—to an 'organized capitalism'—too far. Such an argument
may describe how the demobilization machinery operated in theory, but it
is worth asking how the Demobilization Committees actually carried out
their tasks. Exactly how much did the Demobilization Committees, and in
particular the members representing employer and employee interests, actually do? Some Committees certainly did appear to be the temporary
nerve-centres of the local corporatist state. In Baden, for example, they
appear to have been essentially the extension of regional chambers of
commerce, whose geographical boundaries, staffs, and offices they shared
and who came to take the leading role in carrying out demobilization tasks
at local level.[110] Certainly many local Demobilization Committees took their
duties extremely seriously, and actively intervened in the affairs of local
businesses to ensure that demobilization decrees were implemented.[111] In
other cases, however, they were far less energetic. Particularly in more rural
communities, Committees rarely met, their unpaid members—the representatives of local businesses and labour organizations—had little involvement
with their working; and it tended to be the chairmen (the mayors or
Landräte) who effectively carried out the tasks which fell to local demobil-

Demobilmachungs-Kommissar Geh. Regierungs- und Baurat Kellner, 'Die Wirtschaftliche
Demobilmachung in Lippe vom 9. November 1919 bis 15. Oktober 1919', Detmold (1919), 18.

[109] e.g. HStAD, Reg, Düsseldorf, no. 15108, fos. 316–18: Protokoll von Demobilmachungsausschuß, Duisburg, 24 Jan. 1919.

[110] The employees' representatives on the Demobilization Committees seem to have been
content to go along with these arrangements. See Schäfer, *Regionale Wirtschaftspolitik in der Kriegswirtschaft*, 337–8.

[111] A well-documented example is the Demobilization Committee in the city of Osnabrück.
See StAO, Dep. 3b, III, no. 695.

ization organizations.[112] In any event, local Demobilization Committees were really active only during 1919;[113] many, if not most, were dissolved in 1920, and all were wound up in 1921. What is more, the demobilization machinery did not displace municipal employment-offices and chambers of commerce and industry, which continued to concern themselves with the regulation of the labour market.[114] In other words, at the level where it actually intervened in the local economy and directly affected individuals, this extremely influential demobilization machinery was often little more than the conventional state bureaucracy by another name.

Parallel observations may be made about the enforcement of that key piece of demobilization legislation, the Decree on the Release of Jobs during the Period of the Economic Demobilization.[115] Many local authorities had little or no cause to invoke this decree, 'as even without the decree the local employers, as far as conditions permitted, employed their old people without any urging being necessary'.[116] Similarly, employers willingly complied with requirements that they hire war invalids without being prodded by the Demobilization Committees. In Lippe, for example, the Demobilization Commissar reported that both public and private employers displayed 'complete sympathy' with the legislation and 'voluntarily far exceeded the requirement to hire war invalids introduced by the decree of 9 January'.[117] This was no doubt due partly to patriotic sentiment and feelings of debt to the ex-soldiers and partly to a preference to co-operate semi-voluntarily with the demobilization authorities rather than provoke further state controls. But whatever the reason, the extent to which local Demobilization Committees had to intervene actively in order to ensure that instructions issued in Berlin were being carried out remained limited.

This is not to argue that the entire demobilization machinery at regional and local level counted for nothing, or that there were no conflicts over the

[112] In Mar. 1921, when the Demobilization Committees were scheduled to be dissolved by the government, the Regierungspräsident in Stralsund wrote to the chairmen of all the Committees in his region to ask what they had been doing and what administrative arrangements were needed in their place. In response he was informed that in most cases they had met only once or twice over the previous two years, and their tasks had been carried out by the normal state bureaucracy (the Landratsämter etc.). See the responses to the Regierungspräsident in PLA, Rep 65c, no. 2903.

[113] See Schäfer, *Regionale Wirtschaftspolitik in der Kriegswirtschaft*, 357.

[114] See Jürgen Tampke, *The Ruhr and Revolution: The Revolutionary Movement in the Rhenish-Westphalian Industrial Region 1912–1919* (London, 1979), 76.

[115] *Reichsgesetzblatt*, 1919, 355–9.

[116] See reports to the Regierungspräsident in Schneidemühl in early 1920, in APP, Rejencja w Pile, no. 1484. The quotation is from a report of the Vorsitzender des Kreisausschusses to the Regierungspräsident, Schönlanke, 5 Feb. 1920.

[117] MLHA, Mecklenburg-Strelitzer Ministerium, Abteilung des Innern, no. 4453, fo. 10. According to the 'Verordnung über Beschäftigung Schwerbeschädigter' of 9 Jan. 1919, all public and private employers were required to hire one severely disabled person per 100 employees. See *Reichsgesetzblatt*, 1919, 28–30.

application of decrees affecting hiring practices. The demobilization authorities could, and in many cases (particularly in the industrial cities of the
Ruhr) did, get involved deeply in the management of local job-markets;[118]
and their activities often provoked complaints from employers, particularly
after the initial post-war crisis had passed.[119] But in the main this involved
the existing bureaucracy and owed its success not to compulsion by a vast
new state machinery but to widespread general compliance with measures
monitored by the established bureaucratic structure.[120] It succeeded in large
measure because it was regarded as temporary, as a necessary step towards
inevitable decontrol, and because in practical terms it did not really signify
a massive new expansion of the state. It signified perhaps less a victory for
a new local corporatism than a fairly smooth continued functioning of a state
bureaucracy which, in a new political framework and administering new
regulations, carried on much as before, legitimized through the widespread
belief that its activity was aimed at a normalization of social and economic
relations. Here, on the ground, Charles Maier's observation, that 'while
Europeans sought stability in the image of prewar bourgeois society, they
were creating new institutional arrangements and distributions of power',[121]
was only partially accurate. The image of pre-war bourgeois society remained
the unattainable goal, but the post-war institutional arrangements and distributions of power actually may not have been so new after all.

Altogether, the economic demobilization and post-war transition turned
out to be less of a disaster than had been expected. Despite its periodic
panics and frustrations, particularly in early 1919, and despite its costs, which
ran into thousands of millions of Marks, Joseph Koeth's crisis management
worked rather well. Perhaps not all his colleagues would have agreed with
the upbeat retrospective assessment of the Demobilization Commissar for
Lippe, that 'the entire dismantling of the war industry and the allocation of
peacetime work was by and large carried out almost without a hitch'.[122]
However, compared with the dire predictions of total collapse which had
been rife in early November 1918, and compared with Koeth's expressions
of despair in January 1919, the economic demobilization actually proved
rather successful in the short term. The problem of outstanding war-contracts

[118] One example of an active Demobilization Committee may be found in Bochum. See
StdABo, B 265 and 266.

[119] See e.g. GStAM, Rep. 120, BB VII 1, no. 30, Bd. 8, fos. 15–16: Vereinigung Erfurter
Arbeitgeberverbände to Minister des Innern, Erfurt, 5 Jan. 1921; PLA, Rep 65c, no. 2903, fo.
72: Arbeitgeber-Hauptverband für Industrie, Handel und Gewerbe Vorpommerns to Demobilmachungskommissar, Stralsund, 17 Dec. 1920.

[120] This was also true for the regional/state level, where, as Kurt Königsberger observed in
Bavaria, 'it was not conceived that the State Commissar should replace the permanent authorities
or force his will upon their heads'. See Königsberger, 'Die wirtschaftliche Demobilmachung in
Bayern', 194.

[121] Maier, *Recasting Bourgeois Europe*, 9.

[122] MLHA, Mecklenburg-Strelitzer Ministerium, Abteilung des Innern, no. 4453, fo. 10.

was resolved within a few months; the mass unemployment which many feared would accompany the return of the soldiers did not really materialize; economic activity soon recovered from the depths plumbed in late 1918 and early 1919, as Germany experienced an inflationary boom in the early 1920s. By the late spring of 1919, the demobilization had essentially run its course and the transition from a wartime to a peacetime economy had largely been completed.

Nevertheless, the apparent and surprising success of the economic demobilization was soon followed by new difficulties and reflected broader failure. Within a few weeks of Koeth's Demobilization Ministry being wound up, the Allies announced the harsh peace-terms which they intended to dictate to Germany. Neither the German government nor the German people were prepared for the harsh treatment they received; substantial losses of territory and economic resources and substantial demands for reparation placed huge new burdens on the German economy and on Reich government finances. The inflationary financing of the War and the demobilization, combined with the demands imposed in the Versailles Treaty, meant that the difficulties of the transition in 1918–19 were soon replaced with the massive disorder and resulting political bitterness brought about by post-war inflation and hyperinflation.[123] The economic demobilization did not lay the foundations for a solid recovery and stable economic growth. Instead it was a highly inflationary emergency response to an emergency situation, in which the economic difficulties facing the war-weakened German economy were evaded. 'Wriggling through' may have worked in the short term, and there may have been no practical alternative, but in the longer term Germany was left with enormous economic problems. The success of the demobilization consisted essentially in the postponement, through an inflationary set of emergency measures, of the hard economic choices and bitter social conflicts arising from the fact that Germany had fought and lost a world war.

The way in which the economic demobilization was handled proved of profound importance for the subsequent history of the Weimar Republic. Not only did it prefigure the combination of interest-group politics and the *ad hoc* state interventionism which characterized the fragile Weimar welfare state erected during the 1920s; it was also, in essence, an expression of the classic dilemma of the Weimar Republic: that measures which were probably economically necessary for the long-term health of the country were politically impossible in the short term. The extreme political pressures created by defeat in the First World War and the subsequent revolutionary upheaval made Koeth's inflationary, *ad hoc* crisis-management of the economic

[123] On this theme, reference will have to be made to what promises to be the definitive text, Gerald Feldman's *The Great Disorder*.

demobilization the appropriate approach. An alternative policy—whether the comprehensive corporatist organization of the German economy favoured by Wichard von Moellendorff and SPD Economics Minister Rudolf Wissell, or the fiscal stringency and honesty favoured by the liberal Finance Minister Eugen Schiffer—might have enabled Germany to avoid some of the economic and political disasters of the coming years. However, in the crisis created by the abrupt ending of the war economy, these were not really realistic alternatives. The interests ranged against those who favoured economic planning and corporatist organization were too powerful, and the political dangers inherent in facing up to the costs of the War and the demobilization rather than resorting to the printing presses were too great. The way in which the economic demobilization was managed was both temporarily successful and politically necessary, but it essentially put off the evil day when the economic and political bill for the War would have to be paid. Unfortunately for Germany, and for Europe, the evil day was to prove very evil indeed.

# 5

## Demobilization and Labour

> Most people, especially the young, have a completely false picture of
> the possibilities of peacetime employment.[1]

SPEAKING at a conference called on 29 October 1918 to discuss the
imminent demobilization, August Müller (the right-wing Social Democrat
who in 1916 had been appointed to represent the labour movement in the
War Food Office, and in October 1918 Unterstaatssekretär at the Reich
Economics Office) concluded his report with two assertions: that 'the main
issue of the entire demobilization is the provision of work' and that 'a certain
optimism' was warranted with regard to how this would be achieved.[2] He
was right on both counts. With the exception of the physical return of the
soldiers, more than anything else demobilization after the First World
War meant the demobilization of labour. The labour market had been the
main preoccupation of demobilization planners during the War; it formed
the principal focus of governmental activity during the demobilization
period; it was the issue which took up most of the time of the regional
and local demobilization machinery; and it formed the principal focus of
popular attitudes and responses to the demobilization processes. The
tendency of Germans to identify themselves publicly in terms of their
occupation—of their position in the labour market—meant that the objects
as well as the planners of the demobilization process regarded employment
as the key problem of the post-war transition. Policy makers and the objects
of policy alike viewed solutions to problems of housing, family life, the
reintegration of former soldiers into civilian life as essentially dependent
upon the degree to which a buoyant peacetime labour-market could be
re-established.

In the autumn of 1918, however, the immediate challenge was a daunting
one. As we have seen, on the eve of the Armistice, the German labour-
market was profoundly distorted. The numbers of people employed in
war industries had mushroomed; according to August Müller, in October
1918 between 2.5 and 3 million workers were employed in the armaments
industry.[3] Other sectors, such as housing construction, which had previously

---

[1] BHStA, Abt. IV, MKr 14413: Arbeitsamt Ingolstadt to Kriegsamt Nürnberg, Oberhaunstadt, 2 Jan. 1919.
[2] SHAD, Gesandschaft Berlin, no. 695, fos. 50–2: Kgl. Gesandschaft Berlin to Kgl. Ministerium der Auswärtigen Angelegenheiten, Berlin, 29 Oct. 1918.
[3] Ibid., 50.

employed large numbers, had run down almost completely.[4] In the summer
of 1918 over 6 million Germans were still in uniform, the size of the labour
force in Germany was approximately 20 per cent below what it had been in
July 1914,[5] and the overstretched German economy was dependent upon the
labour of nearly one million foreign workers and another million prisoners
of war.[6] Hundreds of thousands of people had moved into regions where war
industries and military installations (such as shipyards) required labour, while
in many cities dependent upon industries such as textiles, and in agricultural
regions—particularly in eastern Germany—the population declined. No less
important than the physical distribution of Germany's working population on
the eve of the demobilization was their physical condition. After years of
inadequate supplies of food and fuel and long working hours, German workers
were tired, underweight, and prone to illness.[7] To these chronic problems
had been added the influenza epidemic, which coincided with the defeat and
revolution and which attacked millions of Germans in late 1918. Furthermore,
because of the severe coal-shortages which followed the Armistice many
employees found that they had to work in unheated factories.[8] The widely
reported decline in labour productivity during the post-war months was a
consequence not only of political revolution and economic disruption, but
also of cold, hunger, and physical exhaustion.

Further difficulties arose from the suddenness of the military collapse.
Germany's defeat had nullified most wartime planning for an orderly
post-war transition; millions of soldiers returned home in a matter of
weeks and expected that their old jobs would be waiting for them; and
millions of civilians had been employed in factories where war production
came to a halt; hundreds of thousands of war prisoners, upon whom the

---

[4] Housing construction in 1918 stood at roughly 4 per cent of the 1913 figure. See Jürgen
Kocka, *Facing Total War: German Society 1914–1918* (Leamington Spa, 1984), 27.

[5] See the calculations, based on health-insurance statistics, in Joseph Müller, 'Die Regelung
des Arbeitsmarktes in der Zeit der wirtschaftlichen Demobilmachung' (Univ. of Erlangen, Phil.
diss., 1922), 2.

[6] Estimates in Ulrich Herbert, *Geschichte der Ausländerbeschäftigung in Deutschland 1880 bis 1980:
Saisonarbeiter, Zwangsarbeiter, Gastarbeiter* (Berlin and Bonn, 1986), 114. To take one specific
example: at the BASF chemical-works, of the 10,490 male BASF workers recorded at the
beginning of Dec. 1918, 581 were Belgians, 922 were prisoners of war of various nationalities,
879 were German soldiers assigned to work for BASF, and 42 were German military prisoners.
See BHStA, Abt. IV, MKr 14413: Ministerium für milit. Angelegenheiten to all Regierungspräsidenten, Munich, 4 Dec. 1918.

[7] See, C. Paul Vincent, *The Politics of Hunger: The Allied Blockade of Germany, 1915–1919* (Athens,
Oh., and London, 1985), 124–56; Avner Offer, *The First World War: An Agrarian Interpretation*
(Oxford, 1989), 24–78.

[8] This happened in the BASF factories, where management imposed a 'heating embargo',
which meant that workers had to work in the cold and were unable to warm up the food they
had brought with them and which led to a short 'cold strike'. See Dieter Schiffmann, *Von der
Revolution zum Neunstundentag: Arbeit und Konflikt bei BASF 1918–1924* (Frankfurt/Main and New
York, 1983), 175.

German economy had come to depend, had to be returned to their homelands; and acute shortages of raw materials, especially of coal, put millions of jobs at risk. Added to these problems were the longer-term effects upon the labour market of the abolition of compulsory military service and the reduction of the army to 100,000 men once the terms of the Versailles Treaty came fully into effect, of the laying-up of the German merchant navy (which had employed about 77,000 men in 1913), and of the return of roughly 800,000 Germans from abroad and from territories lost to Germany after the War.[9] Moreover, not all the German veterans of the First World War flooded on to the labour market in the chaotic months after the Armistice. The return of the soldiers to the civilian labour-market occurred in stages. As we have seen, many men had returned to civilian life already during the War; millions then streamed home in late 1918 and early 1919, after the military collapse; in May 1919 the old army was dissolved and those soldiers who were not taken into the new Reichs-wehr had to leave the garrisons for a civilian existence;[10] and in late 1919 and early 1920 hundreds of thousands of prisoners of war returned from Allied camps to Germany. Thus not only were the problems of recreating an orderly labour-market in Germany enormous, but they also rumbled on well into 1920.

Even in the best of circumstances, safeguarding the employment of the German work-force during the post-war transition would not have appeared easy. However, Germany was in the midst of a political revolution fuelled by labour unrest and the consequence of the privations, government bung-ling, and injustices of the War. Thus when peace broke out in November 1918, resurrecting a well-functioning peacetime labour-market appeared virtually impossible. Yet, in the event, the re-employment of the veterans of the First World War comprised the great success story of the economic demobilization.[11] By the beginning of December 1918 a fair amount of optimism about the transitional labour-market was being expressed in government circles,[12] and after some considerable difficulties in early 1919

[9] See Frieda Wunderlich, *Die Bekämpfung der Arbeitslosigkeit in Deutschland seit Beendigung des Krieges* (Jena, 1925), 2.

[10] GStAM, Rep. 120, BB, Abt. VII, Fach 1, no. 30, Band 4, fos. 400–3: Reichsarbeitsmin-isterium to (Preuß.) Ministerium für Handel und Gewerbe, Berlin, 5 June 1919. As of 10 May, however, there were 118,000 ill and wounded soldiers still in military hospitals. See GStAM, Rep. 120, BB, Abt. VII, Fach 1, no. 30, Band 4, fo. 404: Kriegsministerium and Reichsarbeits-ministerium, Berlin, 2 Aug. 1919.

[11] For a general discussion of the post-war labour-market and unemployment problem, see also Richard Bessel, 'Unemployment and Demobilisation in Germany after the First World War', in Richard J. Evans and Dick Geary (eds.), *The German Unemployed: Experiences and Consequences of Mass Unemployment from the Weimar Republic to the Third Reich* (London and Sydney, 1987), 23–43.

[12] A good example of this is a report circulated in early Dec. by the Bavarian Ministry of Military Affairs, which summarized information gathered at the end of Oct. from factories with

were past, that optimism generally proved justified. This is to assert neither that unemployment presented no problem in 1918–1919 nor that the labour market had not been profoundly disrupted by the post-war transition. The transition was far from smooth, conditions were chaotic, and the changes massive and sudden. Yet the problem was largely solved, at least for the short term.

Why did this remarkable and unexpected success come about? There were a number of reasons. First, the re-employment of Germany's ex-soldiers was made possible by the shunting of many hundreds of thousands of other people—in the main, women and foreign labourers—out of their wartime jobs and, in many cases, out of the German labour-market entirely. Second, the widespread assumption that the soldiers would get 'their' old jobs back after the conflict acted as a self-fulfilling prophecy, since few employers contemplated anything other than welcoming back their former workers. Third, government policy—in general the acceptance that in a revolutionary situation political considerations took precedence over economic consider- ations, and in particular the financing of public-works projects[13] and main- taining contracts with private firms in order to preserve jobs—kept positions open. Fourth, there was a substantial increase in employment in the public sector: the administrative staff in Reich ministries was roughly 45 per cent greater in 1920 than it had been in 1914, and the number of civil servants in the Prussian administration nearly doubled; the personnel of the German postal administration was more than one-quarter greater in 1919 than it had been before the War, and the number employed on the railways was two-thirds higher (with an increase of over 200,000 between 1918 and 1919).[14] Fifth, the reduction of the working day, at a time of continuing inflation which allowed employers to raise   prices to cover for increased labour-costs, increased the need for workers. Sixth, many employers were willing to take on ex-soldiers even where there was no immediate economic

200 or more employees. In the report the Ministry concluded that 'one can expect with some certainty' that male workers already in Bavaria during the War would find employment, as would most of the workers returning from military service. The problem of finding work, so it was felt, would be limited essentially to women who had taken up jobs during the War. See BHStA, Abt. IV, MKr 14413: Ministerium für milit. Angelegenheiten to all Regierungspräsiden- ten, Munich, 4 Dec. 1918.

[13] Emergency works-projects designed to soak up unemployment during the demobiliza- tion period probably employed between 300,000 and 400,000 people altogether. See Müller, 'Die Regelung des Arbeitsmarktes', 79. It should also be noted that deferred maintenance during the War had left local government with a great deal of work to be done repairing the infrastructure.

[14] See Andreas Kunz, *Civil Servants and the Politics of Inflation in Germany, 1914–1924* (Berlin and New York, 1986), 36–44. Part of the reason for the increase in public-sector employment, particularly among contractual employees, was the demobilization itself. According to Kunz (pp. 48–9), 'demobilisation *tasks* as well as demobilisation *policy* favored the increased use of contractual employees in the German public sector after the First World War'.

justification, because they wanted a reliable labour-force at their disposal in order to meet an expected post-war upsurge in consumer demand. Seventh, in so far as they were not severely crippled, ex-soldiers formed the most desirable group of potential employees—male, in the prime of life—and the section of the labour force which normally experiences the lowest unemployment. Finally, it needs to be remembered that, although German unemployment was far below that in other industrial countries after the War, it remained generally above pre-war levels for most of the 1919–24 period (with the exception of the period from the autumn of 1921 until the winter of 1922), and it was pre-war conditions rather than joblessness elsewhere in Europe which formed the basis of comparison. Furthermore, during 1919–21 periods of unemployment lasted on average one and a half times as long as they had before the War.[15]

Table 16. *Unemployment among Members of Trade Unions in Germany, 1918–1924* (%)

|           | 1918 | 1919 | 1920 | 1921 | 1922 | 1923 | 1924 |
|-----------|------|------|------|------|------|------|------|
| January   | 0.9  | 6.6  | 3.4  | 4.5  | 3.3  | 4.2  | 26.5 |
| February  | 0.8  | 6.0  | 2.9  | 4.7  | 2.7  | 5.2  | 25.1 |
| March     | 0.9  | 3.9  | 1.9  | 3.7  | 1.1  | 5.6  | 16.6 |
| April     | 0.8  | 5.2  | 1.9  | 3.9  | 0.9  | 7.0  | 10.4 |
| May       | 0.8  | 3.8  | 2.7  | 3.7  | 0.7  | 6.2  | 8.6  |
| June      | 0.8  | 2.5  | 4.0  | 3.0  | 0.6  | 4.1  | 10.5 |
| July      | 0.7  | 3.1  | 6.0  | 2.6  | 0.6  | 3.5  | 12.5 |
| August    | 0.7  | 3.1  | 5.9  | 2.2  | 0.7  | 6.3  | 12.4 |
| September | 0.8  | 2.2  | 4.5  | 1.4  | 0.8  | 9.9  | 10.9 |
| October   | 0.7  | 2.6  | 4.2  | 1.2  | 1.4  | 19.1 | 8.4  |
| November  | 1.8  | 2.9  | 3.9  | 1.4  | 2.0  | 23.4 | 7.3  |
| December  | 5.1  | 2.9  | 4.1  | 1.6  | 2.8  | 28.2 | 8.1  |

Source: *Statistisches Jahrbuch für das Deutsche Reich 1921/22* (Berlin, 1922), Suppl., *Internationale Übersichten*, 78; *Statistisches Jahrbuch für das Deutsche Reich 1924/25* (Berlin, 1925), 296.

After the severe labour-shortages of the final war-years, unemployment in Germany rose sharply during late 1918 and early 1919 (see Table 16) This was hardly surprising, as roughly 6 million soldiers were discharged (or discharged themselves) from the armed forces during the last two months of 1918 and the first four months of 1919 and (as Joseph Koeth later put it) 'the armaments industry—and that was more or less the whole of German industry—was paralysed by the sudden end of the

[15] On this point, see Robert Scholz, 'Lohn und Beschäftigung als Indikatoren für die soziale Lage der Arbeiterschaft in der Inflation', in Gerald D. Feldman, Carl-Ludwig Holtfrerich, Gerhard A. Ritter, and Peter-Christian Witt (eds.), *Die Anpassung an die Inflation*, (Berlin and New York, 1986), 288–90.

War'.[16] Recorded unemployment peaked at between 6 and 7 per cent of the labour force in early 1919, and in February 1919 about 1.1 million unemployed people were receiving relief in Germany.[17] In the second half of 1919 this number approximately halved;[18] unemployment rose again during the summer of 1920, but by late 1921 only about 150,000 people in the entire Reich were receiving unemployment benefit; and in the summer of 1922, at the peak of the inflationary boom, the number receiving unemployment benefit was a mere 12,000.[19] In 1923 things changed, however, and the number of people receiving unemployment relief jumped from about 150,000 in the summer to roughly 1.5 million at the year's end.[20]

The shock delivered by the military demobilization to unemployment levels therefore appears to have been fairly sharp, but it was also short. What happened during the crucial weeks and months following the Armistice to reduce the threat of mass unemployment? Some clues are offered by aggregate figures of people who registered at Germany's labour exchanges (See Table 17).These figures show clearly that the demobilization had its greatest effect upon the labour market between December 1918 and March 1919. However, no less striking than the rise in unemployment in early 1919 was the speed with which the unemployed appear to have found work. In January 1919 there were 775,588 new registrations of men looking for work, yet one month later the *total* number of men so registered was less than a million despite the addition of more than half a million new male registrations in February. During the second half of 1919 the German labour-market was apparently absorbing roughly 400,000 additional men

[16] Joseph Koeth, 'Die wirtschaftliche Demobilmachung: Ihre Aufgaben und ihre Organe', in *Handbuch der Politik* iv: *Der wirtschaftliche Wiederaufbau* (Berlin and Leipzig, 1921), 165.

[17] Ludwig Preller, *Sozialpolitik in der Weimarer Republik* (Stuttgart, 1949), 236. The number of people receiving unemployment relief was considerably below that of people looking for work, which may have been nearly twice as high; e.g. in Breslau in mid-May 1919 the labour exchange recorded 6,280 people (3,566 men and 2,714 women) looking for work, of whom 3,856 (2,274 men and 1,582 women) were receiving unemployment relief. See GStAM, Rep. 120, BB, Abt. VII, Fach 1, no. 30, Band 3, fos. 286–92: Zentralauskunftstelle für den Arbeitsmarkt in der Provinz Schlesien, 'Wochenbericht', Breslau, 24 May 1919. In Bavaria (including the Palatinate), which held slightly more than 10% of the German population, registered unemployment peaked at about 113,000 in early 1919; this was the equivalent of between 8% and 11% of the population employed in trade and industry (depending on whether figures for the labour force from 1910 or 1917 are used). See Kurt Königsberger, 'Die wirtschaftliche Demobilmachung in Bayern während der Zeit vom November 1918 bis Mai 1919', *Zeitschrift des bayerischen statistischen Landesamts*, 52 (1920), 210. Königsberger stressed how low this unemployment was, considering the problems arising during the demobilization.

[18] Georg Gradnauer and Robert Schmidt, *Die deutsche Volkswirtschaft: Eine Einführung* (Berlin, 1921), 193.

[19] Preller, *Sozialpolitik in der Weimarer Republik*, 164. Robert Scholz, however, has presented a convincing case that true unemployment was considerably higher, as many 'long-term unemployed' (such as elderly and disabled workers), were not registered as such and received no unemployment relief. He suggests that perhaps 500,000 Germans were unemployed in the summer of 1922. See Scholz, 'Zur sozialen Lage der Arbeiter in der Inflation', 311–14.

[20] Preller, *Sozialpolitik in der Weimarer Republik*, 164.

and 175,000 additional women registering for work every month.[21] What is more, many positions were filled without reference to the labour exchanges, much to the chagrin of the officials in charge.[22] Altogether, few of the men looking for work in early 1919 seem to have remained unemployed for very long. Furthermore, when compared with the effects upon the German labour-market of the mobilization in 1914 or of the currency stabilization of late 1923 and early 1924, the military demobilization does not appear to have caused terribly high unemployment. Small wonder then that, when reflecting on the efforts of his Demobilization Office to put people to work, Joseph Koeth regarded the figure of approximately one million Germans receiving unemployment relief in early 1919 as 'not too disturbing'.[23]

Table 17. *People Registered at Labour Exchanges as Looking for Work in Germany, December 1918–November 1919*

|  | Total | | New registrations | |
|---|---|---|---|---|
|  | Men | Women | Men | Women |
| December 1918 | 650,446 | 196,621 | 596,443 | 169,501 |
| January 1919 | 1,068,923 | 381,735 | 775,588 | 291,226 |
| February 1919 | 978,774 | 387,714 | 557,673 | 224,083 |
| March 1919 | 840,395 | 353,657 | 458,378 | 173,910 |
| April 1919 | 695,325 | 321,761 | 368,714 | 166,823 |
| May 1919 | 756,869 | 346,558 | 380,929 | 178,098 |
| June 1919 | 740,739 | 329,499 | 391,202 | 168,583 |
| July 1919 | 708,948 | 305,142 | 417,578 | 168,873 |
| August 1919 | 738,144 | 311,990 | 432,277 | 172,316 |
| September 1919 | 731,023 | 299,800 | 455,076 | 178,946 |
| October 1919 | 734,616 | 284,311 | 477,142 | 179,225 |
| November 1919 | 721,363 | 243,404 | 457,004 | 148,758 |

*Note*: Month-by-month figures are not absolutely comparable, since in some months statistics from certain labour-exchanges were unavailable. Thus the Dec. 1918 figures omit the unemployed in Württemberg and Hamburg; the Jan. 1919 figures omit the unemployed in Württemberg; the Feb. figures omit Bremen; the Mar., May, and Nov. figures omit Württemberg; and figures from the Prussian province of Posen are either completely or partially lacking from June 1919.
*Sources*: *Reichsarbeitsblatt*, 17:1 (1919), 36–7; no. 2, 166–7; no. 3, 246–7; no. 4, 334–5; no. 5, 410–11; no.6, 476–7; no.7, 560–1; no.8, 632–3; no.9, 714–15; no.10, 788–9; no.11, 788–9; no.12, 962–3.

These impressions find an echo in Wladimir Woytinsky's examination of the German labour-market between 1919 and 1929:

---

[21] See also Gradnauer and Schmidt, *Die deutsche Volkswirtschaft*, 193.
[22] e.g., see the complaints of the Stettin labour exchange in APS, Regierung Stettin, no. 13266, fos. 156–7: Arbeitsamt to Oberbürgermeister Dr. Ackermann, Stettin, 2 Jan. 1920.
[23] Koeth, 'Die wirtschaftliche Demobilmachung', 167.

During the period 1919 to 1922 the considerable economic disturbances had almost no effect upon the labour market. The destruction of hundreds of thousands of men on the battlefields made itself felt in the inadequate supply of human labour. With cheap money and starvation wages, the employers had no need to be especially thrifty with regard to labour. There was a rush to repair the damage of the war period and to replace the factories which had been lost in the territories taken from Germany with new factories with even greater capacity. . . . The demand for labour was also stimulated by the shortening of the working day. Of course this situation was not 'normal', but for the labour market (more precisely: for the development of unemployment) the abnormality of the situation consisted solely in the fact that a very high demand for labour was met by an inadequate supply and that as a result almost all those looking for work could find employment. . . . The first really severe disruption of the labour market came at the end of 1923: the stabilization crisis![24]

As Gerald Feldman has observed (while noting, in contrast to Woytinsky's comment about 'starvation wages', that there was a considerable rise in real wages in 1919–20), immediately after the War 'unemployment remained at remarkably low levels given the difficulties of the period'.[25]

Given what was, under these circumstances, rather low unemployment, it should not be surprising that the post-war period witnessed high levels of labour turnover. The return to work after the War did not necessarily involve people coming back to their old jobs and then staying put. For example, Dieter Schiffmann has shown in his study of BASF that between 1918 and 1923 (as the work-force of the chemicals works expanded to an inter-war peak) roughly 35,000 new workers were hired and at the same time about 30,000 workers left the company (mostly on their own initiative); of these, 17,000 arrived and 13,000 left during 1920 alone.[26] Younger workers were particularly likely to leave their employer, and usually during their first two years in the factory. It was not until the stabilization crisis of 1923–4 that a long-term reduction in labour turnover set in.

Although the post-war surge in unemployment proved temporary, the demobilization crisis had lasting consequences for the regulation of the German labour-market.[27] The post-war emergency was met with initiatives of far-reaching significance. First and foremost there was the question of what to do with the unemployed themselves. The problems which fol-

---

[24] Woytinsky, *Der deutsche Arbeitsmarkt: Ergebnisse der gewerkschaftlichen Arbeitslosenstatistik 1919 bis 1929* (Berlin, 1930), i. 19–20.

[25] Gerald D. Feldman, 'Socio-economic Structures in the Industrial Sector and Revolutionary Potentialities, 1917–22', in Charles L. Bertrand (ed.), *Revolutionary Situations in Europe, 1917–1922: Germany, Italy, Austria-Hungary* (Montreal, 1977), 163.

[26] Schiffmann, *Von der Revolution zum Neunstundentag*, 77–9. During the War, over 11,000 BASF workers had been conscripted into the military.

[27] See Preller, *Sozialpolitik in der Weimarer Republik*, 226–37, 290–1; Müller, 'Die Regelung des Arbeitsmarktes', 21–35.

lowed in the wake of the Armistice appeared to demand government action. The prospect of millions of embittered soldiers coming home to unemployment caused the German state hastily to put into place a system of support for those without work. No sooner had the new Reich Office for Economic Demobilization come into being than it issued a decree requiring local authorities to provide unemployment relief (for which the Reich bore half the cost, the federal states one-third, and local councils one-sixth).[28] While this was not a fully-fledged system of unemployment insurance—something which did not come into being until 1927 and collapsed soon after under the financial pressures of the Depression—it marked a major turning-point.

Providing payments to the unemployed in order to prevent a further radicalization of German workers was not enough, however. More direct intervention was deemed necessary, and during January 1919 the government published a series of decrees governing the hiring and dismissal of employees.[29] The terms of these decrees reflected generally accepted notions of how the labour market should be ordered—for example, that women not dependent upon their incomes should be dismissed in order to make way for men, and that people from outside a community should make way for local residents. Nevertheless, during early 1919 the regulations governing dismissals were often evaded.[30] These were followed at the end of March by a new decree governing 'the release of employment positions during the period of the economic demobilization', which was the most important piece of legislation delineating the powers and responsibilities of the local Demobilization Committees.[31] This marked a major new incursion of the state into the workings of the labour market. No longer was hiring and firing the sole prerogative of the employer; the state determined the order in which

---

[28] *Reichsgesetzblatt*, 1918, no. 153, 1305–8: 'Verordnung über Erwerbslosenfürsorge. Vom 13. November 1918'. See also Anselm Faust, 'Von der Fürsorge zur Arbeitsmarktpolitik: Die Errichtung der Arbeitslosenversicherung', in Werner Abelshauser (ed.), *Die Weimarer Republik als Wohlfahrtsstaat: Zum Verhältnis von Wirtschafts- und Sozialpolitik in der Industriegesellschaft* (Stuttgart, 1987), 263; Merith Niehuss, 'From Welfare Provision to Social Insurance: The Unemployed in Augsburg 1918–27', in Evans and Geary (eds.), *The German Unemployed*, esp. 44–5.

[29] For workers, *Reichsgesetzblatt*, 1919, no. 3, 8–13: 'Verordnung über die Einstellung, Entlassung und Entlohnung gewerblicher Arbeiter während der Zeit der wirtschaftlichen Demobilmachung. Vom 4. Januar 1919'; for invalids, ibid., no. 6, 28–30: 'Verordnung über Beschäftigung Schwerbeschädigter. Vom 9. Januar 1919'; for white-collar employees, ibid., no. 18, 100–6: 'Verordnung über die Einstellung, Entlassung und Entlohnung der Angestellten während der Zeit der wirtschaftlichen Demobilmachung. Vom 24. Januar 1919'.

[30] This lay behind the tightening of enforcement provisions in the Decree on the Release of Employment Positions during the Period of the Economic Demobilization of 28 Mar. 1919. See Gunther Mai, 'Arbeitsmarktregulierung oder Sozialpolitik? Die personelle Demobilmachung in Deutschland 1918 bis 1920/24', in Gerald D. Feldman, Carl-Ludwig Holtfrerich, Gerhard A. Ritter, and Peter-Christian Witt (eds.), *Die Anpassung an die Inflation*, (Berlin and New York, 1986), 218.

[31] *Reichsgesetzblatt*, 1919, no. 71, 355–9: 'Verordnung über die Freimachung von Arbeitsstellen während der Zeit der wirtschaftlichen Demobilmachung. Vom 28. März 1919'.

groups of employees were to be dismissed; and Demobilization Committees (which included representatives of employee interests, i.e. trade-union functionaries) were enabled to intervene extensively in matters of employment. Now the local Demobilization Committees were empowered, for example, to stop employers from laying off workers 'if this measure proves necessary for the combating of considerable unemployment' (§1), to forbid the hiring of workers if it contravened the terms of the March decree (e.g. to forbid the hiring of someone who came from outside the local district) (§14), to determine whether an employer had to hire someone in the place of a person who had been dismissed (§15), and to fine employers up to 3,000 Marks each time they failed without good reason to hire someone referred to them by the labour exchanges for a vacant position (§16). Although these measures sometimes proved difficult to enforce, they provided the framework for the intervention of Demobilization Committees in the dismissal and replacement of thousands of employees during 1919.[32]

Extensive state intervention in the labour market presupposed the effective monitoring of that market, and this pointed to a transformation of the system of labour exchanges. Despite the massive disruption of the labour market which had accompanied the mobilization of 1914, and despite the tremendous labour-shortages during the second half of the War, in 1918 Germany still lacked a centralized, comprehensive system of labour exchanges which effectively monitored and regulated the labour market. Workers seeking help had to look to the trade unions, which were the main source of German unemployment statistics before the Weimar Republic was established. The demobilization crisis changed this. With the end of the War, the labour exchanges set up during the conflict fell under the control of the Demobilization Office, and the new government rapidly set about centralizing, co-ordinating, and expanding the network of exchanges and employment counselling.[33] Desperate to overcome the simultaneous growth of unemployment in some areas and crippling labour-shortages in others, Koeth demanded that all jobs on offer be registered with the labour exchanges and that all employers (including those in the public sector) use the labour exchanges to fill vacant posts.[34] But appeals were not sufficient. Legal compulsion was deemed necessary. In February 1919 Koeth published a decree which placed a legal requirement upon employers with five or more

---

[32] On the ways in which the March decree was employed by local authorities, in particular the numbers of people dismissed from their jobs in a number of cities (Frankfurt/Main, Nürnberg, Kiel), see Müller, 'Die Regelung des Arbeitsmarktes', 66–8.

[33] See *Reichsgesetzblatt*, 1918, no. 180, 1421–2: 'Anordnung über Arbeitsnachweise. Vom 9. Dezember 1918'; BHStA, Abt. IV, MKr 14414: Ministerium für milit. Angelegenheiten, 'Arbeitsnachweiswesen', Munich, 31 Jan. 1919.

[34] BHStA, Abt. IV, MKr 14413: Reichsamt für wirtschaftliche Demobilmachung, Berlin, 27 Nov. 1918.

employees to use the labour exchanges;[35] and in March Koeth decreed that labour exchanges be prohibited from placing former agricultural workers in jobs other than on the land.[36] During the chaotic post-war months it proved relatively easy for employers and workers to evade the new state controls.[37] However, the initiative was important. Although Koeth's Demobilization Ministry was dissolved in April 1919, the machinery regulating the German labour-market continued to be developed, and in May 1920 the Reich Labour Exchange (Reichsamt für Arbeitsvermittlung) was established under the Reich Labour Ministry. This office became responsible for the centralized monitoring of the German labour-market, as well as of the programmes of unemployment relief and employment counselling.[38] Thus while the demobilization machinery was conceived of as temporary, it left behind a permanent legacy: the regulation by the state of the German labour-market.

These developments took place against the background of a tremendous increase in trade-union membership. Such an increase occurred in all major industrial countries after the First World War, and was lent extra force in Germany by industrialists' recognition of trade unions as collective-bargaining partners in the Stinnes–Legien Agreement of November 1918. During the War, the number of trade unionists in Germany had fallen precipitously, as male workers were called to the colours and many of those who replaced them (in particular, women) viewed their industrial employment as a temporary affair and did not bother to join unions. The socialist Free Trade Union Federation, which could count over 2.5 million members in 1913, saw the combined membership of its affiliated unions sink to less than one million in 1915 and 1916; the Catholic trade-unions and the liberal Hirsch–Duncker Associations also experienced steep declines in membership.[39] Although membership recovered somewhat in 1917 and 1918, at the

---

[35] *Reichsgesetzblatt*, 1919, no. 42, 201–2: 'Verordnung über die Pflicht der Arbeitgeber zur Anmeldung eines Bedarfs an Arbeitskräften. Vom 17. Februar 1919.'

[36] Ibid., no. 60, 310–11: 'Verordnung zur Behebung des Arbeitermangels in der Landwirtschaft. Vom 16. März 1919.'

[37] Müller, 'Die Regelung des Arbeitsmarktes', 24–5.

[38] See Preller, *Sozialpolitik in der Weimarer Republik*, 290–1. For a discussion of the expansion of vocational counselling and vocational training during the demobilization period, see Müller, 'Die Regelung des Arbeitsmarktes', 80–91. Once the old army was dissolved, at the beginning of May 1919, employment counselling offices (*Arbeitsbeschaffungsstellen*) in the rump army units were used to help discharged soldiers find work as the size of the army was reduced. These offices were managed by trade-union functionaries, and also helped the returning prisoners of war find work in late 1919 and early 1920. For the guide-lines for these offices, see BHStA, Abt. IV, MKr 14414: Reichsministerium für wirtschaftliche Demobilmachung, Berlin, 12 Apr. 1919; ibid.: Reicharbeitsministerium, Berlin, 2 May 1919. See also GStAM, Rep. 120, BB, Abt. VII, Fach 1, no. 30, Band 4, 400–3: Reichsarbeitsministerium to (Prussian) Ministerium für Handel und Gewerbe, Berlin, 5 June 1919.

[39] See Dietmar Petzina, Werner Abelshauser, and Anselm Faust, *Sozialgeschichtliches Arbeitsbuch*, iii: *Materialien zur Statistik des Deutschen Reiches 1914–1945* (Munich, 1978), 111.

War's end it still lay substantially below the pre-war figures (in the case of the socialist trade-unions, more than 40 per cent below). This changed suddenly after November 1918, as the trade unions were flooded with new members. By the end of 1918, the Free Trade Unions registered a total membership nearly twice that recorded three months previously and already in excess of the pre-war figure; by the end of March 1919 membership stood at nearly twice the pre-war total (See Table 18).

Table 18. *Growth in Membership of the German Free Trade Unions,*
*1918–1919*

|  | Total membership | Increase over previous quarter | |
|---|---|---|---|
|  |  | Absolute | % |
| End September 1918 | 1,468,132 |  |  |
| End December 1918 | 2,866,012 | 1,397,880 | 95.2 |
| End March 1919 | 4,677,877 | 1,811,865 | 63.2 |
| End June 1919 | 5,779,291 | 1,101,414 | 23.5 |
| End September 1919 | 6,562,359 | 783,068 | 13.5 |
| End December 1919 | 7,338,132 | 775,773 | 11.8 |

*Source*: Heinrich Potthoff, *Gewerkschaften und Politik zwischen Revolution und Inflation* (Düsseldorf, 1979), 41.

The largest increase in trade-union membership, both in absolute and percentage terms, coincided precisely with the military demobilization, and the great majority of workers who streamed into the unions during late 1918 and 1919 had not been organized in the labour movement previously. Altogether about 1.4 million trade-union members had been conscripted into the armed forces during the War, of whom at least 200,000 were killed and many others could no longer work, as a result of war injuries.[40] While the number of trade-unionists who had served in the military and who at the end of 1918 had not yet renewed their membership stood at a little over one million, the number of new members joining during 1919 totalled nearly 4.5 million.[41] Indeed, the greatest increases were among young workers: nearly 27 per cent of the increase in socialist trade-unionists in 1919 as compared with 1913 (from 79,961 to 364,235) was among people aged 20 years or less.[42]

Not surprisingly, the increases in trade-union membership were particularly large in sectors where, for various reasons, the reserves of unorganized

---

[40] Peter von Oertzen, *Betriebsräte in der Novemberrevolution: Eine politisch-wissenschaftliche Untersuchung über Ideengehalt und Struktur der betrieblichen und wirtschaftlichen Arbeiterräte in der deutschen Revolution 1918/19* (Düsseldorf, 1963), 274.

[41] Figures in Heinrich Potthoff, *Gewerkschaften und Politik zwischen Revolution und Inflation* (Düsseldorf, 1979), 41.

[42] Ibid. 58.

workers had been the largest: in the public sector, agriculture, the railways, and the mines, where workers had previously faced legal restrictions or extreme pressure from employers against trade-union activity; and in the textile industry, where large numbers of women joined trade unions for the first time.[43] Extremely large gains in trade-union membership were also registered among white-collar workers, who were far more willing after the War to advance their collective interests in a manner parallel to workers on the shop floor.[44] These developments were reflected in the changed geographic distribution of trade-union membership; in areas such as the Ruhr, the Saar, and in eastern Germany, where the labour movement had been relatively weak before the War, trade unions registered greater gains than in the old labour strongholds of Berlin, Hamburg, Saxony, Nürnberg, and Bremen.[45] The upsurge in unionization on the land and in industrial areas where labour organizations had previously made relatively little headway meant that the demobilization period saw not only a vast increase in trade-union membership but also a move towards a somewhat more even geographical distribution across Germany. No longer were there industries or regions which remained immune from labour organization.

The wartime fall and post-war rise in trade-union membership was paralleled by a wartime reduction and post-war expansion of union bureaucracies. During the War the decline in membership and the conscripting of many union activists into the army had led to a substantial dismantling of trade-union bureaucracies and a sharp reduction in the number of functionaries on trade-union payrolls. After the Armistice, however, not only were these processes reversed, but also the political and legal changes caused by the revolution and demobilization created a host of new tasks for union officials. Not only did they now have to represent the interests of many times more members and involve themselves in many more wage negotiations; they also had to sit on local Demobilisation Committees, committees to oversee the distribution of food, industrial tribunals, job-counselling centres and the like, and were far more likely to hold elected positions in local and regional legislatures.[46] Their representative duties in the public sphere expanded enormously as the interest-group politics which characterized the Weimar Republic took shape in the aftermath of the War.

[43] Ibid. 50–1; Hans-Joachim Bieber, *Gewerkschaften in Krieg und Revolution: Arbeiterbewegung, Industrie, Staat und Militär in Deutschland 1914–1920* (2 vols.; Hamburg, 1981), ii. 582–5. For a breakdown of increases in the Christian Trade Unions, which also saw massive gains among agricultural labourers and textile workers (as well as among metalworkers), see Michael Schneider, *Die Christlichen Gewerkschaften 1894–1933* (Bonn, 1982), 448–9, 768–71.

[44] Potthoff, *Gewerkschaften und Politik*, 50; Hans Speier, *German White-Collar Workers and the Rise of Hitler* (New Haven, Conn., and London, 1986), 128–31. On the development of employee associations among civil servants, see Kunz, *Civil Servants and the Politics of Inflation*, 132–45.

[45] See the table in Potthoff, *Gewerkschaften und Politik*, 48.

[46] For a good description of this on a local level, in Ludwigshafen, see Schiffmann, *Von der Revolution zum Neunstundentag*, 141–3.

However, growth in membership and an enhanced public role did not guarantee increased influence or power. It was a great paradox of the revolution and demobilization period that while the trade unions grew explosively they were nevertheless, as the General Commission of the Free Trade Union Federation admitted in a retrospective survey of 1918, 'pushed somewhat into the background'.[47] During the War, labour leaders in effect had traded influence on the shop floor for influence in government, specifically in helping to shape and apply the Auxiliary Service Law. The trade unions had played no significant role in the strikes of January 1918, and after the political upheaval in November trade-union leaders were able to exert rather little influence on workers' demands and were left behind by the council movement.[48] Rather than regarding themselves as the representatives of a radicalized working class, trade-union leaders saw their main task during the economic and political upheavals of 1918 and 1919 as helping to re-establish order amongst the workers. In November 1918 they urged an end to 'wildcat strikes', particularly in the coal mines, since it was 'in the interests of the entire population that interruptions of production are stopped',[49] and in early January 1919 their language became quite extreme: 'Wildcat miners' strikes' were now described as 'suicide and lunacy' and anyone taking part in them denounced as aiding 'the worst enemies of the workers and the people'.[50] It is not terribly surprising that workers' representatives who expressed such sharp reservations about what many workers were doing, and who urged 'more steadfastness on the part of the employers *vis-à-vis* the strike movement and the excessive demands of some workers',[51] felt 'pushed somewhat into the background' during late 1918 and early 1919.

In view of their earnest concern to see order reimposed, it was appropriate that the Reich Demobilization Office allotted trade-union officials the task of 'enlightening' workers about their patriotic duty—in particular, encouraging them to accept undesirable but economically necessary work in agri-

[47] 'Rückblick auf das Jahr 1918', *Correspondenzblatt der Generalkommission der Gewerkschaften Deutschlands*, 29: 1 1 (4 Jan. 1919), 3.

[48] See e.g. Hans-Joachim Bieber's description of these processes in the Hamburg shipyards, 'Die Entwicklung der Arbeitsbeziehungen auf den Hamburger Großwerften zwischen Hilfsdienstgesetz und Betriebsrätegesetz (1916–1920)', in Gunther Mai (ed.), *Arbeiterschaft in Deutschland 1914–1918: Studien zu Arbeitskampf und Arbeitsmarkt im Ersten Weltkrieg* (Düsseldorf, 1985), esp. 132, 141–2. In late Nov. 1918 the General Commission expressed concern that workers' councils ('with dictatorial power within the revolution') were making uncalled for 'incursions' (*Eingriffe*) in factory matters which were rightly the responsibility of the trade-union bureaucracy; this was attributed to the fact that many of the workers had not yet been organized in trade unions and were not accustomed to bringing problems to union officials. See 'Die wirtschaftliche Interessenvertretung der Arbeiter in der Revolution', *Correspondenzblatt* 28: 48 (30 Nov. 1918), 439.

[49] 'Die wirtschaftliche Interessenvertretung der Arbeiter in der Revolution', 440.

[50] 'Warum wilde Bergarbeiterstreiks?', *Correspondenzblatt*, 29: 2/3 (18 Jan. 1919), 23.

[51] Thus a trade-union functionary at a meeting of the Demobilization Committee in Duisburg in late Jan. 1924. See HStAD, Regierung Düsseldorf, no. 15108, fos. 316–18: minutes of a meeting of the Demobilmachungsausschuß in Duisburg, 24 Jan. 1919.

culture and mining.[52] The 'enlightenment work' involved both acting as a 'liaison' between employers and workers and preaching to workers who did not come into contact with the labour exchanges (e.g. to men who had been discharged from the army but continued to be fed and housed in army camps).[53] Although it offered union leaders further opportunity to press for better wages, improved working-conditions and employee housing in regions which desperately needed labour, such 'enlightenment work' was a thankless task. It does not appear to have been terribly successful in changing workers' attitudes about accepting farm work, and it is indicative of the ambiguous and compromised position of the trade unions in the new political framework. As Ludwig Preller pointed out in his classic study of social policy in the Weimar Republic, the trade unions were caught between their awareness of the needs of an undernourished and exhausted labour-force and their realization that increased production was economically absolutely necessary.[54]

The huge upsurge in trade-union organization which accompanied the demobilization was a reflection of the relaxation of the old authoritarian system and the patterns of discipline and deference which it had sustained. When that system collapsed and Germans from all social groups rushed to join interest organizations, millions of people with only a tenuous commitment to the labour movement flocked to the trade unions. However, when the political and economic climate changed in the early and mid-1920s, millions of these new members left again. The hyperinflation (during which prices rose so quickly that the idea of negotiating and maintaining incomes through collective bargaining became absurd)[55], mass unemployment, and the reimposition of longer shifts and a longer working-day in many industries, combined to cut the ground from under the trade unions.[56] The end

[52] SHAD, Gesandschaft Berlin, no. 691, fos. 93–6: Reichsministerium für wirtschaftliche Demobilmachung, 'Vermerk über die Sitzung am 8. März 1919 nachmittags 2 Uhr über die Tätigkeit der Gewerkschaftsfunktionäre', Berlin, 10 Mar. 1919; ibid., fos. 97–8: Reichsministerium für wirtschaftliche Demobilmachung, 'Richtlinien für die Tätigkeit der Gewerkschaftsfunktionäre', Berlin, 1 Feb. 1919. See also Mai, 'Arbeitsmarktregulierung oder Sozialpolitik?', 211.

[53] Discharged soldiers had the right to remain in the garrisons for four months after leaving military service. This was granted in order to stagger the movement on to the civilian labour-market, but it was felt in government circles that this provision was taken up by many men who did not really need it. BHStA, Abt. IV, MKr 14413: Beauftragter des bayer. Ministeriums für milit. Angelegenheiten beim preuß. Kriegsamt und Vertreter des bayer. Staatskommissars für Demobilmachung beim Demobilmachungsamt to Staatskommissar für die Demobilmachung, Berlin, 12 Dec. 1918; SHAD, Gesandtschaft Berlin, no. 690, fo. 48a: Der stellv. Bevollmächtigte zum Bundesrate to Staatsminister für die Auswärtigen Angelegenheiten in Dresden, Berlin, 11 Dec. 1919.

[54] Preller, *Sozialpolitik in der Weimarer Republik*, 248.

[55] Michael Schneider also makes this point, in *Die Christlichen Gewerkschaften*, 449–50. For an excellent description of the collapse of collective bargaining during the hyperinflation, see Kunz, *Civil Servants and the Politics of Inflation*, 362.

[56] For a good, concise discussion of this undermining of the trade unions in 1923–4, see William L. Patch, *Christian Trade Unions in the Weimar Republic 1918–1933: The Failure of 'Corporate Pluralism'* (New Haven, Conn., and London, 1985), 87–90.

of the demobilization period coincided with the end of the extraordinary period of explosive trade-union growth.

When one examines the changes in the post-war German labour-market, three things stand out: the differences in the ways the demobilization process affected different segments of the labour force, the concern to remove women from paid employment, and the readiness of employers to rehire the ex-soldiers. Fairly typical is the picture which emerges from the report of the Prussian Factory Inspectorate for the old industrial districts of Lennep and Remscheid, to the south of the Wuppertal cities, for the year 1919. According to this report, while the total number of workers remained roughly the same in 1919 as during the previous year, there had been 'significant shifts among the categories of workers': the number of adult male workers had risen by 3,968, as the numbers of female and adolescent workers fell by 4,150 and 766 respectively—'an expression of the fact that the workers discharged from military service have come back into their old positions, and that the female and adolescent substitute labour (*Ersatz-Arbeitskräfte*) have had to make way'. The report's author went on to note that the re-employment of the war veterans had 'taken place smoothly in the entire district'. 'Without exception, he said, 'the employers have been very pleased to rehire their old workers. Many firms have stated to me that administrative compulsion to do this would not have been needed at all.'[57] Whether all employers really would have been so welcoming of their former workers returning from military service in difficult times without the threat of state compulsion looming in the background is perhaps doubtful; certainly most would have preferred to see less state interference in the workings of the labour market.[58] The point, however, is that they did rehire their former employees, despite the tremendous political and economic uncertainties during the months which followed the Armistice.

One major reason why this proved possible was the rapid removal of women from new jobs which they had taken up during the War.[59] The lion's share of the wartime influx of women into factories seems to have been reversed by February 1919. In Danzig, for example, at the beginning of February, factories were operating with only about 10 per cent of the female employees that they had had in October 1918; and in Spandau the great

---

[57] HStAD, Regierung Düsseldorf, no. 34345: Gewerbeinspektor zu Lennep für die Kreise Lennep und Remscheid, 'Jahresbericht 1919', Lennep, 29 Jan. 1920.

[58] e.g. the Association of Erfurt Employers' Organizations wrote to the Prussian Interior Minister in Jan. 1921, urging the annulment of the demobilization regulations and arguing that on the one hand 'the (demobilization) decree imposes extraordinary burdens and restrictions on German employers and the permanent labour-force, while on the other hand it benefits only a small portion of the labour force'. See GStAM, Rep. 120, BB VII 1, no. 30, Bd. 8, fos. 15–16: Vereinigung Erfurter Arbeitgeberverbände to Minister des Innern, Erfurt, 5 Jan. 1921.

[59] Richard Bessel, ' "Eine nicht allzu große Beunruhigung des Arbeitsmarktes": Frauenarbeit und Demobilmachung in Deutschland nach dem Ersten Weltkrieg', in *Geschichte und Gesellschaft*, 9 (1983), esp. 219–20.

majority of the women living outside the city (meaning essentially those living in Berlin) who had been employed in the armaments works lost their positions in mid-January.[60] In Stuttgart the firm of Bosch, which had employed 580 women workers when the War broke out and 5,245 when it ended, employed 1,578 at the beginning of March 1919; in order to cope with the ending of war contracts and simultaneously to rehire 1,714 returning soldiers, Bosch dismissed 3,500 women at the end of November 1918.[61] Demobilization decrees stipulating who could and should be dismissed in order to make way for the returning soldiers were most consistently and effectively employed against women.[62] Largely regarded by the state, by their employers, and often by themselves as 'substitute labour', women were shunted with relatively little difficulty out of wartime jobs.

During the post-war months employers attempted in effect to recreate the *status quo ante*—to undo the wartime changes in their work-forces and, as far as possible, to employ the sorts of people who had worked for them before the summer of 1914. Firms which found themselves in considerable difficulties nevertheless made great efforts to provide jobs for their former employees as they left military service. Where orders or supplies of raw materials were insufficient to keep people working a full week, employers reduced the length of shifts and kept their workers busy with maintenance work rather than show them the door. One such was a Heidelberg grain-milling firm which reported to the local chamber of commerce in January 1919 that, due to inadequate supplies of grain, shifts had had to be reduced and the mill itself shut down periodically:

We then have had our workers occupied with relief work, so that they are protected from unemployment. With regard to the labour question, we are hiring all the people who were employed by us at the outbreak of the War, and have also taken on yet other workers who were not employed by us previously although there was not an absolute need for them.[63]

Not only did employers take on labour which they did not require immediately, but it seems that they did so willingly; at least that was the impression which they tried to give to the local demobilization authorities. These Demobilization Committees made surprisingly little use of their legal power to compel employers to take on former employees returning from military service. For example, when the district Demobilization Committees in the

---

[60] GStAB, Rep. 180, no. 14430, fo. 129: Kriegsamtstelle Danzig to Reichsamt für wirtschaftliche Demobilmachung, Danzig, 1 Feb. 1919; BLHA, Rep. 2A, Reg. Postdam I SW, no. 795, fo. 458: Demobilmachungsausschuß to Regierungspräsident, Spandau, 20 Jan. 1919. See also Bessel, ' "Eine nicht allzu große Beunruhigung des Arbeitsmarktes" ', 219.

[61] Mai, 'Arbeitsmarktregiulierung oder Sozialpolitik?' 214–15.

[62] Ibid. 218–19; Karin Hagemann, *Frauenalltag und Männerpolitik: Alltagsleben und gesellschaftliches Handeln von Arbeiterfrauen in der Weimarer Republik* (Bonn, 1990), 434–6.

[63] GLAK, 236/22273: Handelskammer für die Kreise Heidelberg und Mosbach to Ministerium für soziale Fürsorge, Heidelberg, 16 Jan. 1919.

Regierungsbezirk Schneidemühl were asked in January 1920 what use they had had to make of the provisions in the Decree on the Release of Jobs during the Period of the Economic Demobilization', one reported that it had been invoked only twice, another that in 'only a few cases' was it necessary to remind employers of the legislation, and the remaining seven had not used it at all.[64] From Stettin it was reported that, already before the legislation on the hiring and dismissal of workers was published, 'the employers in the district re-employed their former workers and white-collar employees who had been discharged from military service, although in many cases there is no work or only limited work for them to do as a result of depressed economic activity due to workers' excessive wage-demands and the shortage of raw materials'.[65]

How can one explain the apparent and uncharacteristic masochism of German employers, who seem to have been willing to pay wages to workers they did not require? No doubt many employers were genuinely motivated by feelings of patriotism and a belief that Germany in general, and they in particular, owed a debt to those who had risked life and limb for the Fatherland. However, noble motives were seasoned with self-interest. Employers' testimonials to state authorities of their concern for their former employees and of their patriotic conduct were also used to frame cases for preferential treatment when it came to the handing-out of state contracts or the distribution of scarce raw materials. A fairly typical example was that of the Hirsch Copper and Brass Factory near Eberswalde, north-east of Berlin. The factory had employed roughly 1,800 workers before the War, and during the conflict this figure had risen to about 3,000. In February 1919, however, the number was back down to 1,845, while production had slumped to two-fifths of what it had been in August and September 1918 due to the ending of war contracts. Writing to the Regierungspräsident in Potsdam in his capacity as Demobilization Commissar, the firms' directors pointed out that 'immediately after the outbreak of the revolution we gave work to all the soldiers returning from the battlefield and the garrisons who presented themselves to us' and that even after having had to increase wages in January 'we would always attempt to keep the number of workers in future at the same level as we had had before the War'. However, 'unfortunately' they now had to contemplate the partial closure of the factory if new orders were not forthcoming 'immediately'. The letter closed with a plea that, 'in the interest of the maintenance of our factory and in the interest of avoiding the dismissal of workers, which with the current condition of the factory could number many hundreds, we ask you to recognize

---

[64] See the correspondence in APP, Rejencja w Pile, no. 1484.
[65] BAP, RMwD, no. 43/1, fo. 168: Regierungspräsident, von Schmeling, to Reichswirtschafts-amt (*sic*) für wirtschaftliche Demobilmachung, Stettin, 26 Jan. 1919.

our present emergency' and help with securing contracts.[66] Desperate factory directors presented desperate state officials with the spectre of yet greater unemployment if sufficient contracts were not pushed their way during the transition from war to peace.

This was not the only element of self-interest which induced employers to take on workers they did not really need. Another was the threat of state intervention: the explicit threat embedded in the demobilization legislation, in particular the decree of 4 January 1919, which stipulated that factories with twenty or more workers were required 'to hire those workers who at the outbreak of the War had been employed in the factory as industrial workers';[67] and the implicit threat that state controls might be extended further if existing measures proved insufficient to deal with the emergency.[68] In addition, not too far in the background lurked the spectre of something even worse: a revolution which might do away altogether with private ownership. On 13 November 1918 the Association of German Employer Organizations (Vereinigung der Deutschen Arbeitgeberverbände) urged its members 'to employ people in the coming weeks, even if it is necessary to introduce double shifts of four hours each'. The Association went on to recommend that people be put to work doing something, even if 'they must tear it down again tomorrow; but they must be employed'.[69] As Ewald Hilger, speaking for Germany's iron and steel industrialists on 14 November 1918, declared: 'It is not a question of money now . . . right now we must see that we survive the chaos.'[70]

These worries enabled employers to swallow temporarily the introduction of the eight-hour day, agreed by representatives of German industry and trade-union leaders and written into the Stinnes–Legien Agreement of 15 November 1918.[71] Although the reduction in the working day without a corresponding reduction in wages raised industry's costs considerably, it was a price worth paying, if only to strengthen the hand of moderate trade-unionists and deflect the new government or a more radical working-class movement from taking direct control of factories. It also greatly increased the need for labour. With the shorter working day (often leading to the

---

[66] BLHA, Rep. 2A, Reg, Potsdam I SW, no. 796, fo. 150: Hirsch-, Kupfer- und Messingwerke to Regierungspräsident als Demobilmachungskommissar, Messingwerk, 15 Feb. 1919.

[67] *Reichsgesetzblatt*, 1919, 8–13: 'Verordnung über die Einstellung, Entlassung und Entlohnung gewerblicher Arbeiter während der Zeit der Demobilmachung. Vom 4. Januar 1919.'

[68] Richard Bessel, 'State and Society in Germany in the Aftermath of the First World War', in W. R. Lee and Eve Rosenhaft (eds.), *The State and Social Change in Germany, 1880–1980* (Oxford, Munich and New York, 1990), 209–10.

[69] Quoted in H.-J. Bieber, *Gewerkschaften in Krieg und Revolution*, 610.

[70] Quoted ibid.

[71] For discussion of the negotiations culminating in, and the significance of, the Stinnes–Legien Agreement, see Gerald D. Feldman, 'The Origins of the Stinnes–Legien Agreement: A Documentation', *Internationale wissenschaftliche Korrespondenz zur Geschichte der deutschen Arbeiterbewegung*, 19/20 (Dec. 1972), 45–103; H.-J. Bieber, *Gewerkschaften in Krieg und Revolution*, 595–619.

introduction of an additional, shorter shift), employers needed to maintain the size of their work-forces even as output slumped and many had to take on additional workers to maintain production.[72] Thus many employers, like the city electricity works in Dortmund, were able to rehire returning soldiers without having to dismiss all those people taken on during the War.[73] In other cases, where coal shortages forced employers to occupy workers with maintenance tasks and emergency works, acceptance of the eight-hour day proved a convenient way to link a necessary concession to labour to temporary economic imperatives.[74] Thus the most significant achievement of the labour movement in 1918, and the main concession of the employers in the face of the revolutionary threat, greatly facilitated the reabsorption into the civilian labour-market of the millions of men leaving military service.

Worried employers had many of their fears confirmed by the waves of industrial unrest which accompanied the political upheaval of 1918 and 1919.[75] With the collapse of the old order and the advent of democratic government, and with employers much more vulnerable than before to pressure, strike action became widespread. In 1919 more than seven times as many strikes took place as in 1918 and, perhaps more important, affected more than thirty times as many factories. Only a small proportion of these strikes ended with a victory for the employers.[76] This meant not only that strikes were more frequent and their outcomes more likely to reflect the new muscle of the workers, but also that they affected large numbers of smaller firms which hitherto had avoided industrial conflict.

Serious though they were, strikes and other overt expressions of worker militancy formed but the tip of the iceberg. After being compelled to make sacrifice upon sacrifice during the War, few Germans remained keen to exert themselves at the work-bench after the old order had been swept away. In the immediate aftermath of the military collapse and during the revolutionary upheaval, virtually the whole of the German economy was affected by an unwillingness of people to work hard. Employers and government officials complained of a widespread 'disinclination to work' (*Arbeitsunlust*). Many

---

[72] See e.g. WWA, K1, no. 171: Westfälisches Verbands-Elektrizitätswerk to Handelskammer zu Dortmund, Dortmund, 13 Dec. 1918.

[73] Ibid.: Städtisches Elektrizitätswerk to Handelskammer, Dortmund, 20 Dec. 1918.

[74] This was true of the giant BASF chemicals works. Although the French occupying authorities in the Palatinate (where the BASF factories were located) initially refused to enforce the demobilization decrees, the management of BASF introduced the eight-hour day at the beginning of Dec. 1918—largely because coal shortages meant that longer shifts were unnecessary. Other industrial employers in the Palatinate, however, used the French attitude as an excuse not to accept the eight-hour day until the spring of 1919. See Schiffmann, *Von der Revolution zum Neunstundentag*, 100–1, 164–5.

[75] For accounts of the major strike-waves, in the Upper Silesian industrial region and among Ruhr miners, see esp. H.-J. Bieber, *Gewerkschaften in Krieg und Revolution*, 637–84.

[76] In 1919 only 584 of the 3,682 recorded strikes ended in clear victory for the employers. See *Statistisches Jahrbuch für das Deutsche Reich 1934* (Berlin, 1934), 321.

prisoners of war simply walked out of their jobs after the Armistice, leaving German employers to cast about for German workers to replace them.[77] Demobilized men were often unwilling to take up jobs in agriculture and mining, even when the post-war unemployment was at its peak in January and February 1919, despite the desperate shortages of labour in Germany's farms and mines, and despite the country's desperate need for food and fuel.[78] Former soldiers were often in no hurry to return to work. Many of the men demobilized before Christmas 1918 did not bother to go to work until after the holiday, preferring to live off their savings for a while and to wait for better offers of employment, and many refused to accept work at pay which they regarded as too low.[79] Others preferred to remain with the army, where they allegedly could earn between 3 and 5 Marks a day 'for very little effort', and therefore refused other employment.[80]

The unemployed were no more accommodating than the newly returned soldiers. Complaints abounded about the 'disinclination of the unemployed to accept work on the land or in forestry',[81] and about 'the so-called unemployed' in the cities who preferred drawing unemployment benefit to working in agriculture.[82] During 1919 attempts were made to resettle some of the urban unemployed on the land,[83] but such efforts often met with resistance from the unemployed, in some cases resulting in 'stormy demonstrations'.[84] Understandably, few city dwellers—even if they were without

[77] See e.g. APS, Oberpräsidium von Pommern, no. 3951, and PLA, Rep. 38 b, Jarmen, no. 23, fo. 14: Zentralauskunftstelle Stettin, 'Wochenbericht über den Arbeitsmarkt der Provinz Pommern', Stettin, 21 Dec. 1918.

[78] See Joseph Koeth's observations of the labour market at the beginning of Feb. 1919, in BLHA, Rep. 2A Reg. Potsdam I SW, no. 793, fo. 114: Reichsamt für wirtschaftliche Demobilmachung, Berlin, 1 Feb. 1919. Immediately after the War the labour shortages on the land were exacerbated by the effects of the influenza epidemic. See GStAM, Rep. 120, BB, Abt. VII, Fach 1, no. 3o, Band 2, fos. 121–2: Oberpräsident der Provinz Schlesien to (Preuß.) Ministerium für Handel und Gewerbe, Breslau, 22 Dec. 1918. Attitudes among German prisoners of war returning in late 1919 were no different from those of soldiers returning immediately after the Armistice. See PLA, Rep. 65c, no. 2891, fos. 3–4: Reichszentrale für Kriegs- und Zivilgefangene to Kriegsgefangenenheimkehrstellen in Königsberg, Berlin, 30 Oct. 1919.

[79] BAP, RMwD, no. 18/1, fos. 6–8: Kriegsamtstelle to Reichsamt für wirtschaftliche Demobilmachung, Stettin, 14 Dec. 1918; GStAB, Rep. 30, no. 733: Zuckerfabrik Nakel to Regierungspräsident in Bromberg, Rudtke, 7 Dec. 1918; BHStA, Abt. IV, MKr 14413: Arbeitsamt Ingolstadt to Kriegsamt Nürnberg, Oberhaunstadt, 2 Jan. 1919. See also Königsberger, 'Die wirtschaftliche Demobilmachung in Bayern', 209.

[80] BHStA, Abt. IV, MKr 14413: Arbeitsamt Ingolstadt to Kriegsamt Nürnberg, Oberhaunstadt, 2 Jan. 1919.

[81] StAH, Demobilmachungskommissar, no. 50, 41: stellv. Gen.kdo. IX. A.K. to Demobilmachungskommissar bei der Stadt Hamburg, Altona, 19 Dec. 1918.

[82] e.g. BAP, RMwD, no. 2, fos. 371–2: Arbeitsnachweis der Landwirtschaftskammer für die Provinz Schlesien to Kriegswirtschaftsamt Breslau, Breslau, 4 Jan. 1919; GStAM, Rep 120, BB, Abt. VII, Fach 1, no. 3o, Band 2, fos. 121–2.

[83] This was done e.g. by the authorities in Spandau. See BLHA, Rep. 2A Reg. Potsdam I SW, no. 796, fos. 131–2: Magistrat to Regierungspräsident in Potsdam, Spandau, 4 Feb. 1920.

[84] See e.g. NHStA, Hann. 80 Hann. II, no. 1981: Vorsitzender des Kreisausschusses to Regierungspräsident in Hannover, Neustadt a/Rbg., 5 Feb. 1919; NHStA, Hann. 122a/XXXIV,

jobs and especially if they were married—had much desire to uproot themselves in order to perform strenuous work on the land for low wages.[85] It made more sense to remain in the cities, and draw unemployment relief if possible, in the hope of finding a better-paid job in industry. Emergency works-projects, which the state subsidized in order to soak up extra labour during the demobilization, also met with responses which were less than enthusiastic. From Hamburg, for example, came complaints about the 'disinclination of skilled workers to take part in emergency works-projects'.[86] In Spandau, which had a particularly serious unemployment problem because the local economy had been so dominated by the huge armaments works, the Demobilization Committee reported in February 1919 that, while the emergency works-projects planned by the city had been started, 'at present there is still a lack of workers'; the problem was that 'most of the unemployed have little desire or inclination to accept emergency work, despite the relatively high wages', and there was 'a particular disinclination towards forestry work'.[87]

No less worrying were the attitudes of the people who actually took the jobs available. A few weeks after being named head of the Demobilization Office, Joseph Koeth observed 'that throughout the Reich the labour force is showing no enthusiasm for work and as a result work performance has diminished significantly in all areas, now at the very moment when everything depends upon doing one's utmost'.[88] What to many employers and government officials seemed a shocking aversion towards hard work formed

no. 368, fos. 440–1: Kriegsamtstelle to Reichsamt für wirtschaftliche Demobilmachung, Hannover, 15 Mar. 1919. This latter report describes a demonstration in Hanover of young women protesting against being sent to work on the land. It should also be noted that the authorities were wary in early 1919 of sending out to the countryside urban unemployed who were 'unsuited' to agricultural labour or were contaminated with 'Bolshevism'. See, PLA, Rep. 38b Loitz, no. 1010, fos. 32–4: Kriegsamtstelle Stettin and Zentralauskunftstelle Stettin to Landräte, Vorsitzenden der landwirtschaftlichen Vereine, Magistrate and Arbeitsnachweise, Stettin, Feb. 1919.

[85] APS, Oberpräsidium von Pommern, no. 3952: Zentralauskunftstelle Stettin, 'Wochenbericht über den Arbeitsmarkt der Provinz Pommern', Stettin, 25 Jan. 1919. According to a report about the labour market in Danzig in July 1920, where unemployment had reached 13,000 shortly before, and at that time stood at 9,000, it was chiefly among the *unmarried* unemployed that the authorities had success in inducing people to accept work outside the city. Danzig had special problems: it had become a 'Free City', independent of Germany under the terms of the Versailles Treaty, and also had to deal with the 18,736 people who lost their wartime jobs in state institutions (including 4,507 from the Reich dockyards, 3,470 from the rifle factory, and 6,003 from the artillery depot) between Dec. 1918 and Dec. 1919. See GStAM, Rep. 120, BB, Abt. VII, Fach 1, no. 3o, Band 5, fos. 12–13: Magistrat der Stadt Danzig to Auswärtiges Amt in Berlin, Danzig, 19 July 1920.

[86] StAH, Demobilmachungskommissar, no. 50, fo. 41.

[87] BLHA, Rep. 2A Reg. Potsdam I SW, no. 796, fos. 104–8: Demobilmachungsausschuß to Reichsamt für wirtschaftliche Demobilmachung, Spandau, 11 Feb. 1919.

[88] SHAD, Ministerium der Auswärtigen Angelegenheiten, no. 2494, Band I, fos. 128–9: Der stellv. Bevollmächtigte zum Bundesrate to (Saxon) Ministerium der Auswärtigen Angelegenheiten, Berlin, 23 Nov. 1918. Koeth was particularly concerned that no one was unloading goods trains in Berlin.

a *leitmotiv* of post-war reports of conditions in German industry. Complaints about the effects of the eight-hour day and workers' demands for higher wages and shorter working hours were voiced alongside concern that *Arbeits-unlust* prevented manufacturers from meeting buoyant demand because it kept productivity low.[89] Employers frequently claimed that state unemployment relief undermined the work ethic and drove up wages. However, while relief payments to the unemployed may have allowed some men to postpone a return to work, particularly in the cities, sponging off the nascent German welfare state in fact was not easy. Local labour-exchanges were used to keep a close watch on the labour force and emergency works-projects were used to keep down the numbers receiving unemployment relief.[90] But that did not prevent complaints from surfacing about the effects of allegedly high levels of unemployment relief. From Heidelberg one firm reported in January 1919 that 'it has occurred repeatedly that people who were employed with us previously and whose families we supported with monthly payments throughout the War have downed tools and claimed that it is possible to earn more by not working';[91] and in February the chamber of commerce for the Wupper industrial region claimed that the long war 'has caused the work-force in many cases to become alienated from working'.[92] Officials in the Franconian city of Hof no doubt expressed the feelings of many when they asserted in mid-January 1919 that, 'if we do not consider the

[89] See e.g. SSAL, Braunkohlenabbau-Verein 'Zum Fortschritt' no. 2, fos. 130–1: Braunkohlen-abbau-Verein 'Zum Fortschritt' to the Allgemeine Deutsche Credit-Anstalt, Zweigstelle Meuselwitz, Meuselwitz, 18 July 1919.

[90] Thus the State Commissar for the Demobilization in the Thuringian States stipulated at the end of 1918: 'We absolutely must keep a careful watch that only truly unemployed people, only those who cannot find appropriate work, benefit from unemployment support. . . . Only with proper surveillance can unemployment relief exhibit its beneficial effect. Without sufficient surveillance it tempts those able to work into letting themselves be paid support instead of working.' See StAW, Thüringisches Wirtschaftsministerium, no. 130, fo. 32: Staatskommissar für wirtschaftliche Demobilmachung in den Thüringischen Staaten to alle Ministerien, Weimar, 30 Dec. 1918. On the use of emergency works-projects to weed out the work-shy, see ibid., fo. 13: Staatskommissar für wirtschaftliche Demobilmachung in den Thüringischen Staaten to Demobilmachungsausschüsse, Weimar, 27 Nov. 1918. For an example of a particularly ill-fated attempt by state officials to compel the unemployed to accept the work on offer in late Jan. 1919, see Gerald D. Feldman, 'Saxony, the Reich, and the Problem of Unemployment in the German Inflation', *Archiv für Sozialgeschichte*, 27 (1987), 111. In this case an attempt by officials in Leipzig to seize the control cards of the work-shy unemployed ended in violence, and workers took the (relatively well-paid) jobs on offer only after being urged to do so by a representative of the Workers' and Soldiers' Council, a trade-union official. Emergency works-projects were also supposed to be closed to workers who had previously worked in agriculture and mining, although former agricultural labourers and miners were found working on emergency projects. See Müller, 'Die Regelung des Arbeitsmarktes', 78.

[91] GLAK, 236/22273: Handelskammer für die Kreise Heidelberg und Mosbach to Ministerium für soziale Fürsorge, Heidelberg, 16 Jan. 1919. Essentially this letter was a protest against the payment by the city of Heidelberg of allegedly high rates of unemployment benefit which had just been introduced.

[92] HStAD, Reg. Düsseldorf, no. 15107, fos. 107–8: Handelskammer für den Wuppertaler Industriebezirk to Deutscher Industrie- u. Handelstag, Barmen/Elberfeld, 18 Feb. 1919.

dismantling of the whole system of unemployment relief soon, all desire to work will expire'.[93]

Trade-union officials too felt compelled to admit that the attitudes of German workers towards their work had changed. Although they contested employers' assertions that this was due to a move from piece-rates to hourly wages,[94] and although they tended to see the reasons for 'the present-day disinclination to work' in the effects of a long war and the poor conditions which the labour force had had to endure—particularly the inadequate nutrition[95]—they did agree with the employers on basics. Echoing the employers, trade-union leaders viewed the lack of enthusiasm for hard work and the consequent decline in labour productivity as 'a cancer which is eating away at our existence',[96] and they too urged that workers resume orderly and disciplined behaviour. In some cases, when responsibility for administering the new regulations governing the labour market landed in their laps, labour leaders went even further. Thus Johannes Sassenbach, who was a member of the General Commission of the Free Trade Unions and who had been given responsibility in November 1918 for administering unemployment relief in Berlin, launched a tirade at a conference of union executives in February 1919. He sharply criticized levels of relief which in his eyes attracted the unemployed to the cities, in particular to Berlin, claimed that 'the pressure to accept work is considerably reduced by the high levels of support', and alleged that in Berlin 'there is fraud in at least 25 per cent of the cases'.[97] Concern about the allegedly detrimental effects of generous support for the unemployed was also voiced in the Cabinet: on 21 January August Müller (by that time head of the Reich Economics Office) complained to the Council of People's Deputies that relief payments had been raised to such an extent that 'a large family obtains the top salary of a salaried government administrative officer (Regierungsrat) as unemployment relief'.[98]

The changes in workers' attitudes towards work in the immediate aftermath of the First World War suggest that the demobilization of labour involved a lot more than simply shifting people in and out of employment.

---

[93] For this and similar comments from throughout Bavaria, see Königsberger, 'Die wirtschaftliche Demobilmachung in Bayern', 215–6.

[94] 'Die Zerrüttung des deutschen Wirtschaftslebens', *Correspondenzblatt*, 29: 13 (29 Mar. 1919), 113.

[95] HStAD, Reg. Düsseldorf, no. 15108, fos. 316–18: minutes of meeting of Demobilmachungsausschuß, Duisburg, 24 Jan. 1919.

[96] 'Die Zerrüttung des deutschen Wirtschaftslebens', 113.

[97] 'Konferenz der Verbandsvorstände' of 1–2 Feb. 1919, in Klaus Schönhoven (ed.), *Die Gewerkschaften in Weltkrieg und Revolution 1914–1919* (Cologne, 1985), 630–8.

[98] Müller went on to say that he 'would favour the forced removal of the unemployed on to the land if we could carry it out, but we do not have the power to do it'. See Susanne Miller and Heinrich Potthoff (eds.), *Die Regierung der Volksbeauftragten 1918/19*, (2 vols.; Düsseldorf, 1969), i. 285–6.

To the quantitative problems were added qualitative ones, which were no less worrying to state authorities concerned to regulate the labour market and return economic and social relations to 'normal'. The demobilization of labour was also a psychological demobilization—a relaxation after the rigours and exertions of the War while the power of government and employers to impose work discipline was crumbling. Here the demobilization and the political revolution essentially overlapped; as Kurt Königsberger observed, 'the revolution is nothing else but the demobilization of the nerves'.[99] The post-war malaise and erosion of work discipline propelled the revolutionary unrest, and the revolutionary upheavals led to further erosion of work discipline.

Not surprisingly, the erosion of work discipline, together with the introduction of the eight-hour day and against the background of political revolution and massive strike-waves, led to sharp declines in labour productivity. This, in turn, exacerbated the economic difficulties confronting the new regime. In no sector of the economy was this more apparent—or alarming—than in coal mining. As we have seen, the severe coal-shortages which Germany experienced in 1918 and 1919 posed a fundamental threat to hopes for the reconstruction of a stable economy. The problem was to get the coal out of the ground. The obstacles to maintaining urgently needed production were outlined succinctly by the management of a lignite mine in Rositz (near Altenburg, to the south of Leipzig) in its annual report for the stormy period between the summer of 1918 and the summer of 1919: sickness among the work-force (due especially to the influenza epidemic of autumn 1918), the effects of the political upheaval in November and 'its devastating economic consequences', the collapse of work discipline (beginning with a refusal by prisoners of war to continue working), and the introduction of a shorter working day, meant that by December 1918 production had slumped to a mere 68 per cent of the levels of the previous July. During 1919 production at the mine was maintained only through a sizeable increase in the work-force, from 1,491 (including women and prisoners of war) in July 1918 to 2,123 in June 1919.[100]

The effects of the decline in labour productivity were many and varied. On the one hand, low productivity meant that industries whose products were in great demand, such as coal mining, needed to hire additional workers in order to maintain production. On the other hand, the decline in labour productivity in the pits led to unemployment elsewhere, and during early 1919 state authorities cited the coal shortage as one of the main reasons

---

[99] Königsberger, 'Die wirtschaftliche Demobilmachung in Bayern', 196.

[100] SSAL, Grube Rositz der Deutschen Erdöl AG (DEA), Berlin, no. 123/38: 'Geschäftsbericht der Rositzer Braunkohlenwerke Actiengesellschaft Rositz S.-A. über das Geschäftsjahr vom 1. Juli 1918 bis 30. Juni 1919'. For aggregate figures which reveal the decline in labour productivity in coal mining, see Bessel, 'Unemployment and Demobilisation', 34, and above, Ch. 4.

for the rapid rise in unemployment in other industries.[101] Numerous calls were made for the demobilization authorities to place unemployed workers in coal mines. For example, the Commissar for Economic Demobilization in the Thuringian States noted at the end of December 1918 that 'numerous industrial factories have been shut down due to the present coal-shortage', that (as a result of the loss of prisoner-of-war labour and the reduction of the working day) coal production had declined, and that in the lignite field of Zeiss-Weissenfels there existed 'a shortage of 30,000 workers'; to meet the challenge, he called on the Demobilization Committees throughout Thuringia to 'use their influence so that those without jobs accept work in the Zeiss-Weissenfels lignite field'.[102] But shifting people to suit the needs of an economy in crisis was no easy matter, not least because of the severe housing-shortages in coal-mining areas and an understandable reluctance of men, especially after wartime military service, to be separated from their families for the sake of what someone else defined as the common good.

This general problem was one of the main reasons why Joseph Koeth, who had been fairly upbeat in the weeks after the Armistice, became extremely pessimistic about the prospects for a successful post-war transition in the new year. In a conference called at the Demobilization Office in mid-January to discuss 'putting people to work', Koeth cast about for ways to induce unemployed workers to accept employment where they were needed so desperately. Although he admitted that the Auxiliary Service Law (which had been abrogated by the Council of People's Deputies on 12 November 1918) had been a failure, Koeth noted the problem might be solved only with new legislation 'like the Auxiliary Service Law, through which all people or certain birth-cohorts who do not have particular jobs are encouraged to perform work in agriculture and in coal mining'.[103] Koeth also noted that while the Decree on Unemployment Relief required the unemployed to accept the work offered even if it was located away from where they lived, the state did not possess the means to make them willing to work.[104] 'The simplest means of pressure', according to Koeth, would have been the removal of ration cards for food and coal from workers who refused 'to perform the necessary work'—a measure which the French had applied successfully in occupied Saarland. However, the conference partici-

[101] See e.g. SHAD, Amtshauptmannschaft Pirna, no. 496, fos. 9–10: Amtshauptmannschaft Pirna to (Sächs.) Ministerium des Innern, 'Stimmungsbericht', Pirna, 16 May 1919.

[102] StAW, Thüringisches Wirtschaftsministerium, no. 130, fo. 57: Staatskommissar für wirtschaftliche Demobilmachung in den Thüringischen Staaten to sämtl. Demobilmachungsausschüße, Weimar, 31 Dec. 1918.

[103] BHStA, Abt IV, MKr 14413: Beauftragter des bayer. Ministeriums für milit. Angelenheiten beim preuß. Kriegsamt und Vertreter des bayer. Staatskommissars für Demobilmachung beim Demobilmachungsamt to Staatskommissar für die Demobilmachung, Berlin, 16 Jan. 1919.

[104] For the text of the decree, see *Reichsgesetzblatt*, 1919, 1305–8: 'Verordnung über Erwerbslosenfürsorge. Vom 13. November 1918'. On the failure effectively to enforce the decree, see e.g. GStAM, Rep. 120, BB, Abt. VII, Fach 1, no. 3o, Band 2: fos. 121–2.

pants recognized that such a move would involve enormous practical difficulties. The German government could not treat Germans in Berlin as the French military authorities treated Germans in Saarbrücken. After years of war and in the wake of a political revolution, German workers were ill-disposed to follow orders, and a weak German state was unable to force them to do so.

Women proved no easier than men to channel into jobs deemed necessary and suitable by the state authorities. In his discussion of the demobilization in Bavaria, Kurt Königsberger described the attempt 'to channel the weaker sex on to paths which are beneficial to the economy'—particularly the attempt to induce women who had worked in the armaments industry to accept positions in domestic service once again—as 'a labour of Hercules'.[105] During the demobilization period, unemployment among women was significantly higher than amongst men.[106] What is more, levels of female unemployment were probably understated in the available data, because the authorities tended not to consider home workers, mostly women, eligible for support and were more restrictive about granting women unemployment relief.[107] Nevertheless, the expectations of the demobilization authorities that unemployed women could easily be placed in agricultural work or in domestic service were frequently disappointed. Despite the high unemployment during 1919, positions for women in domestic service, in cleaning, and on the land often remained unfilled.[108] For example, from Danzig, where thousands of women had been drawn to the city for wartime work and were dismissed soon after the Armistice, it was reported in February 1919 that 'many were alienated from their former occupations by high wages usually

---

[105] Königsberger, 'Die wirtschaftliche Demobilmachung in Bayern', 213.

[106] See the tables of male and female unemployment between 1919 and 1924 in Bessel, 'Unemployment and Demobilisation', 35.

[107] GStAM, Rep. 120, BB, Abt. VII, Fach 1, no. 3o, Band 5, fos. 197–203: 'Eingabe des Berufsverbandes der Katholischen Metallarbeiterinnen (Abteilung Grubenarbeiterinnen) und der Berufsorganisation der Textilarbeiterinnen (Heimarbeiterinnen) im Verbande Katholischer Vereine erwerbstätiger Frauen und Mädchen Deutschlands', Kattowitz, 22 July 1920; Helgard Kramer, 'Frankfurt's Working Women: Scapegoats or Winners of the Great Depression?', in Evans and Geary (eds.), *The German Unemployed*, 115; Hagemann, *Frauenalltag und Männerpolitik*, 435. This had, in fact, been codified in the Decree on Unemployment Relief of 13 Nov. 1918, which stipulated that 'female persons are to be supported only if they depend upon employment for their livelihood', and that 'persons whose previous breadwinners return and are capable of working are to receive no unemployment relief'. See *Reichsgesetzblatt*, 1918, no. 153, 1305–8. These clauses were retained in the Reich Decree on Unemployment Relief of 16 Apr. 1919. See *Reichsgesetzblatt*, 1919, no. 89, 418.

[108] BAP, RMwD, no. 18/1, fos. 154–5: Landwirtschaftsamt to Reichsamt für wirtschaftliche Demobilmachung, Karlsruhe, 11 Jan. 1919; ibid., fos. 195–8: Kriegsamtstelle to Demobilmachungs-amt, Münster, 18 Jan. 1919; ibid. fos. 276–7: Kriegsamtstelle to Reichsamt für wirtschaftliche Demobilmachung, Magdeburg, 1 Feb. 1919; ibid. fos. 297–301: Kriegsamtstelle to the Reichsamt für wirtschaftliche Demobilmachung, Breslau, 8 Feb. 1919; GStAM, Rep. 120, BB VII 1, 17, Bd. 13, 424–5: Reichsministerium für wirtschaftliche Demobilmachung, 'Vermittlung von Haus-angestellten', Berlin, 22 Mar. 1919. See also Bessel, 'Unemployment and Demobilisation', 33.

for a short working day, and when the dismissals began at the end of 1918 many showed little inclination to return to their homes (*Heimat*) and to accept positions in service either on the land or in the towns, even though there is a great shortage of domestic servants'. The report concluded that 'the consequences of [women's] factory work will make themselves felt in this regard for a long time yet'.[109]

This last prediction seems to have come true. Many women remained quite resistant to being shunted into service after their experiences during the War. In June 1919 the Danzig labour exchange reported that 1,730 women were unemployed in the city, and in August the number had risen to 2,155, despite the continuing demand for female domestic servants and agricultural labour in the surrounding region.[110] Attempts to retrain women factory-workers, with day and evening vocational courses which concentrated on 'domestic subjects' and were designed to channel women into domestic employment, failed to induce large numbers of women to seek positions in service.[111] The wartime experience of relatively better-paid employment—and, no doubt for many, the prospect of marriage at the War's end—had changed the ideas of many women about the sorts of work they were willing to accept.

It would be mistaken, however, to assume that all the post-war unemployed were without work because they refused the jobs on offer. Some groups found it quite difficult to find employment. The labour exchange in Ludwigshafen, for example, reported at the end of 1919 (when unemployment was a fraction of its February peak and when women had largely been removed from the relief rolls) that there had been little success in placing some categories of workers: 'mainly clerical staff, commercial employees, artisans, war-wounded, disabled and older people for whom in any case it is difficult to find positions'.[112] The most serious unemployment problems and the most bitter competition over the jobs which were available arose among clerical staff. Providing appropriate work for ex-soldiers who had previously had white-collar jobs, and expected to occupy similar positions after leaving military service, often proved difficult.[113] In Bavaria, Kurt

<hr>

[109] GStAB, Rep. 180, no. 15913: 'Bericht über den Arbeitsmarkt in Danzig während des Krieges', Danzig, 17 Feb. 1919. See also Bessel, ' "Eine nicht allzu große Beunruhigung des Arbeitsmarktes" ', 223.

[110] GStAB, Rep. 180, no. 14430, fo. 245: Zentralauskunftstelle für Arbeitsnachweis to Regierungspräsident, Danzig, 7 June 1919; ibid., fo. 384: Zentralauskunftstelle für Arbeitsnachweis to Regierungspräsident, Danzig, 23 Aug. 1919.

[111] See Müller, 'Die Regelung des Arbeitsmarktes', 82–4.

[112] StdALu, no. 6670: Städtisches Arbeitsamt, report for 1919. For more discussion of this report, see Bessel, 'Unemployment and Demobilisation', 36–7.

[113] See e.g. GLAK, 456/E.V. 6, Bund 112: Ministerium für soziale Fürsorge, 'Arbeitsbeschaffung für kaufmännische und technische Angestellten', Karlsruhe, 8 Jan. 1919. In late Jan. labour exchanges in Pomerania reported 634 men and 245 women applying for office work, while not a single post was on offer. See APS, Oberpräsidium von Pommern, no. 3952: Zentralauskunftstelle Stettin, 'Wochenbericht über den Arbeitsmarkt der Provinz Pommern', Stettin, 25 Jan. 1919. See also Mai, 'Arbeitsmarktregulierung oder Sozialpolitik?' 223–4.

Königsberger described the employment prospects of commercial employees of both sexes as 'quite bleak';[114] and in his dissertation on the regulation of the post-war labour-market Joseph Müller observed that, while the re-employment of workers returning from military service caused few difficulties, cases involving white-collar staff frequently required arbitration by the demobilization authorities.[115] Thus office work, which had been a largely male preserve before the War, formed the area where continued working by women stirred the greatest resentment;[116] and the Deutschnationaler Handlungsgehilfen-Verband (DHV) in particular made strident demands that women be removed from their jobs to make way for men.[117] Although the militantly anti-feminist and conservative ideology of the DHV made its campaign against the employment of women in offices predictable, the intensity of the protests also stemmed from the fact that the job prospects for white-collar staff generally were much less rosy than for workers seeking jobs on the factory floor.

The difficulties faced by white-collar workers after the War underscore the fact that the post-war labour-market in Germany was characterized by tremendous variations: from industry to industry, region to region, according to type of work and according to the skill and the sex of the employee. Skill level formed a fundamental divide. Skilled workers were in demand; the unskilled were not. As the War was coming to a close and during the first few weeks after the Armistice many employers had made strenuous and even desperate efforts to get *skilled* labour released from the military especially quickly.[118] According to the 1919 report of the Ludwigshafen labour exchange, for example, two-thirds of the unemployed in that city were

---

[114] Königsberger, 'Die wirtschaftliche Demobilmachung in Bayern', 213.

[115] Müller, 'Die Regelung des Arbeitsmarktes', 53.

[116] In Dresden, one meeting held by a women's white-collar union to protest against proposals to sack female employees was broken up by male clerks in early 1919. See Feldman, 'Saxony, the Reich, and the Problem of Unemployment', 112. In Cologne, a local 'committee for the representation of the interests of unemployed commercial employees' demanded that women be removed from white-collar jobs, arguing that this was 'not just a purely economic but also a moral demand, because the man is first of all the founder and provider of the family and the women should take care of domestic affairs and educate the children'; 'eminent physicians and hospital statistics demonstrate sufficiently that—with few exceptions—women's employment in trade and industry, as in all male occupations, is associated with serious health-risks and leads to demoralization and deterioration of the race'. See GStAM, Rep. 120, BB, Abt. VII, Fach 1, no. 3o, Band 5, fos. 73–5: Ausschuß zur Vertretung der Interessen der stellenlosen Handlungs-gehilfen to Demobilmachungs-Kommissar, Cologne, 10 Aug. 1919.

[117] e.g. APP, Rejencja w Pile, no. 1485: Deutschnationaler Handlungsgehilfen-Verband to Demobilmachungskommissar zu Marienwerder, Hamburg, 12 Nov. 1919. See also Stefan Bajohr, *Die Hälfte der Fabrik: Geschichte der Frauenarbeit in Deutschland 1914 bis 1945* (Marburg, 1979), 163; Bessel, ' "Eine nicht allzu große Beunruhigung des Arbeitsmarktes" ', 220–1.

[118] See e.g. the pleas of employers to the navy for the release of skilled workers in BA/MA, RM 31, v. 1801, 1802, 1803, and 1804. Also quite common were requests by artisans for their sons to be released speedily to return to the family business. See also GLAK, 456/E.V.8, Bund 112: Mez Seiden-Zwirnei und Färberei to stellv. Gen.kdo. 14. A.K., Freiburg i.B., 2 Nov. 1918.

unskilled.[119] In Aachen the regional labour-exchange reported in March 1919 that, despite relatively high unemployment, the demand for skilled labour exceeded supply.[120] This problem was compounded by the fact that many young people who had worked in munitions factories during the War frequently had not received proper training and, although they felt entitled to the higher wages of skilled labourers, joined the ranks of the unskilled unemployed in early 1919.[121] It also appears that the great majority of the unemployed were single—hardly surprising since married people tended to be older, and more often skilled, than the unmarried, and since the de-mobilization decrees were designed especially to return *married* men to their old jobs so that they could provide for their families. In Ludwigshafen, for example, 63 per cent of the men reported unemployed in the city in 1919 and fully 80 per cent of the women were single.[122] During the demobilization period, therefore, the German labour-market was deeply fragmented: rela-tively high unemployment among some groups (single women, the unskilled, low-grade clerical staff) existed alongside considerable demand for skilled labour in specific industries.

Regional variations in unemployment levels were also conspicuous, and unemployment after the First World War was very largely an urban problem (see Table 19). Most of the unemployed were to be found in cities; relief provision was more developed in cities and the levels of support were higher, which meant that people without work were more likely to register there if they could;[123] and to many men who had returned from military service it made better sense to look for work in the cities than to accept low-paid farm-work during the harsh winter months, especially when they lacked the necessary clothing, and the wages on offer were insufficient to support a family.[124]

Altogether in January 1919 over 38 per cent of the male unemployed and 47 per cent of the female unemployed were registered in Greater Berlin, the Rhineland and Hohenzollern and Saxony—regions which together ac-counted for a little over a quarter of Germany's population.[125] Thus female

[119] StdALu, no. 6670: Städtisches Arbeitsamt, report for 1919.

[120] HStAD, Reg. Aachen, Handel und Gewerbe, no. 7760, fo. 159: Bezirksstelle für Arbeits-nachweis für den Regierungsbezirk Aachen to Regierungspräsident, Aachen, 25 Mar. 1919.

[121] See the revealing report from the labour exchange in the Bavarian city of Ingolstadt, in BHStA, Abt. IV, MKr 14413: Arbeitsamt Ingolstadt to Kriegsamt Nürnberg, Oberhaunstadt, 2 Jan. 1919. Another revealing facet of the problem was that few young workers were willing to accept positions as apprentices.

[122] StdALu, no. 6670: Städtisches Arbeitsamt, report for 1919.

[123] See Feldman, 'Saxony, the Reich, and the Problem of Unemployment', 110.

[124] See Bessel, 'Unemployment and Demobilisation', 32; Feldman, 'Saxony, the Reich and the Problem of Unemployment', 111–12.

[125] The high figures for the Rhineland were due partly to the effects of Allied occupation. In neighbouring Westphalia relatively few people were registered as looking for work: in Jan. 1919 43,787 men (4.1% of the total) and 10,211 women (2.7%).

unemployment was even more geographically concentrated than male. However, a much smaller proportion of the female population registered as unemployed than of the male, since unemployed women rarely encountered sympathy in labour exchanges and since so many women worked in the home or as 'helping family members' on farms; indeed, in predominantly agricultural regions (such as Mecklenburg or Pomerania outside Stettin) almost no women registered as unemployed. In general, cities dependent upon heavy industry (for example, in the Ruhr) had lower unemployment levels than those with a more mixed economy and which attracted large numbers of people from other areas (such as Berlin or Hamburg) or those more dependent on the textile industry (such as Elberfeld, Barmen, or Plauen). A particularly clear illustration of this is the pattern of unemployment in Silesia, where three-fifths of the registered unemployed were to be found in Breslau while the centres of heavy industry in Upper Silesia (Gleiwitz, Beuthen, Hindenburg) had relatively few people looking for work. Similarly, in western Germany there was considerable unemployment in Düsseldorf, Elberfeld, and Barmen, while mining firms nearby were searching desperately for labour.[126]

While the figures in the table below (Table 19) highlight the concentration of unemployment in the Reich capital and in the Saxon textile-towns, other estimates put unemployment in Berlin and Saxony even higher. For example, in March 1919 the demobilization authorities asserted that Greater Berlin accounted for roughly 275,000 of Germany's registered jobless.[127] (The fact that the figures produced by the Berlin labour exchange for January included only 3,153 people who had come into the city from elsewhere—at a time when by all accounts Berlin was attracting large numbers from outside its boundaries, most of whom could expect no help from the labour exchanges in finding work—also suggests there were more unemployed people in the capital than indicated by official statistics.) One reason for this was that Berlin proved a magnet for demobilized soliders. According to the records of the Food Administration, which was responsible for the distribution of food-ration cards in Greater Berlin, between September 1918 and March 1919 about 305,000 former soldiers received bread-ration cards in the Reich capital.[128] No doubt many more ex-soliders without a legal residence in

---

[126] See also APS, Regierung Stettin, no. 13266, fo. 149–52: Regierungspräsident to Oberbürgermeister in Düsseldorf, Elberfeld, and Barmen and the Zentralauskunftstelle in Düsseldorf, Düsseldorf, 7 July 1919.

[127] BLHA, Rep. 2A Reg. Potsdam I SW, no. 798, fo. 78: Vorsitzender des Demobilmachungsausschusses des Kreises Teltow to Regierungspräsident in Potsdam, Berlin, 14 Feb. 1920. See also GStAM, Rep. 120, BB, Abt. VII, Fach 1, no. 3o, Band 4, fo. 413: Demobilmachungsausschuß Groß-Berlin to Minister für Handel und Gewerbe, Berlin, 16 July 1919; Frauke Bey-Heard, *Hauptstadt und Staatsumwälzung. Berlin 1919. Problematik und Scheitern der Rätebewegung in der Berliner Kommunalverwaltung* (Stuttgart, 1969), 114.

[128] Susanne Rouette, 'Die Erwerbslosenfürsorge für Frauen in Berlin nach 1918' (unpubl. MS, Apr. 1985), 5.

Berlin—people from other areas of Germany who would not surface in the official statistics—decided to try their luck in the capital, despite attempts to restrict movement into the cities.[129]

Table 19. *People Registered at Labour Exchanges as Looking for Work in Germany, January 1919*

| Region (City) | Number | | As % of total unemployed | | Population of region (city) as % of Reich |
|---|---|---|---|---|---|
| | Men | Women | Men | Women | Population[a] |
| Prussia: | | | | | |
| East Prussia | 19,084 | 3,786 | 1.79 | 0.99 | 3.72 |
| (Königsberg | 11,015 | 2,055 | 1.03 | 0.54 | 0.44) |
| West Prussia | 17,096 | 4,927 | 1.60 | 1.29 | 2.62[b] |
| Greater Berlin | 125,468 | 65,631 | 11.74 | 17.19 | 6.35 |
| Brandenburg | 19,038 | 5,843 | 1.78 | 1.53 | 4.09 |
| Pomerania | 20,116 | 3,002 | 1.88 | 0.79 | 2.99 |
| (Stettin | 11,640 | 2,270 | 1.09 | 0.59 | 0.39) |
| Posen | 13,940 | 2,450 | 1.30 | 0.64 | 3.23[b] |
| Silesia | 55,081 | 12,516 | 5.15 | 3.28 | 7.17 |
| (Breslau | 31,911 | 7,665 | 2.99 | 2.01 | 0.88) |
| Province of Saxony | 41,780 | 16,849 | 3.91 | 4.41 | 5.23 |
| Schleswig-Holstein | 27,587 | 9,715 | 2.58 | 2.54 | 2.44 |
| (Altona | 7,721 | 4,308 | 0.72 | 1.13 | 0.28) |
| (Kiel | 7,569 | 2,845 | 0.71 | 0.75 | 0.34) |
| Hanover | 30,305 | 9,765 | 2.84 | 2.56 | 5.06 |
| (Hanover | 15,837 | 6,076 | 1.48 | 1.59 | 0.66) |
| Westphalia | 43,787 | 10,211 | 4.10 | 2.67 | 7.50 |
| Hessen-Nassau | 41,144 | 19,013 | 3.85 | 4.98 | 3.80 |
| (Kassel | 12,325 | 6,521 | 1.15 | 1.71 | 0.27) |
| (Frankfurt/Main | 18,194 | 10,243 | 1.70 | 2.68 | 0.72) |
| Rhineland[c] and Hohenzollern | 157,909 | 52,216 | 14.77 | 13.68 | 11.43 |
| (Barmen | 10,143 | 3,877 | 0.95 | 1.02 | 0.26) |
| (Cologne | 44,503 | 14,706 | 4.16 | 3.85 | 1.06) |
| (Düsseldorf | 18,513 | 7,375 | 1.73 | 1.93 | 0.68) |

[129] e.g. workers who had come into a city from elsewhere during the War were not to be placed in jobs by the labour exchanges without an official certificate allowing them to work in that particular city. See the Decree on the Hiring, Dismissal and Remuneration of Industrial Workers during the Period of the Economic Demobilization of 4 Jan. 1919, in *Reichsgesetzblatt*, 1919, 8–13, esp. 10. See also the comments of the State Commissar for Economic Demobilization in the Thuringian States at the end of 1918, in which he urged that the unemployed from rural regions be sent back from the industrial cities to whence they had come, in StAW, Thüringisches Wirtschaftsministerium, no. 130, fo. 32: Staatskommissar für wirtschaftliche Demobilmachung in den Thüringischen Staaten to alle Ministerien, Weimar, 30 Dec. 1918.

Table 19. *Continued*

| Region (City) | Number | | As % of total unemployed | | Population of region (city) as % of Reich |
|---|---|---|---|---|---|
| | Men | Women | Men | Women | Population[a] |
| (Elberfeld | 15,360 | 4,254 | 1.44 | 1.11 | 0.26) |
| (Essen | 13,661 | 4,619 | 1.28 | 1.21 | 0.73) |
| Bavaria: | 104,063 | 43,191 | 9.74 | 11.31 | 11.80 |
| (Augsburg | 7,994 | 5,367 | 0.75 | 1.41 | 0.26) |
| (Munich | 40,308 | 12,807 | 3.77 | 3.35 | 1.05) |
| (Nürnberg | 18,104 | 10,639 | 1.69 | 2.79 | 0.59) |
| Saxony: | 125,681 | 62,541 | 11.76 | 16.38 | 7.79 |
| (Chemnitz | 22,501 | 12,707 | 2.11 | 3.33 | 0.51) |
| (Dresden | 27,719 | 12,382 | 2.59 | 3.24 | 0.98) |
| (Leipzig | 34,266 | 12,781 | 3.21 | 3.35 | 1.01) |
| (Plauen | 5,719 | 3,931 | 0.54 | 1.03 | 0.18) |
| Württemberg | (No figures available for Jan. 1919)[d] | | | | 4.21 |
| Baden | 31,399 | 12,738 | 2.94 | 3.34 | 3.69 |
| Hessen | 15,844 | 5,930 | 1.48 | 1.55 | 2.16 |
| Mecklenburg | 5,357 | 615 | 0.50 | 0.16 | 1.28 |
| Thuringian States | 31,438 | 11,795 | 2.94 | 3.09 | 2.64 |
| Oldenburg | 8,683 | 2,710 | 0.81 | 0.71 | 0.86 |
| Braunschweig Anhalt[c] | 9,887 | 2,654 | 0.92 | 0.70 | 1.36 |
| Lübeck | 4,612 | 1,809 | 0.43 | 0.47 | 0.20 |
| Bremen | 16,280 | 5,949 | 1.52 | 1.56 | 0.52 |
| Hamburg | 103,344 | 15,879 | 9.67 | 4.16 | 1.75 |
| Reich | 1,068,923 | 381,735 | 100.00 | 100.00 | 100.00 |

[a] Population on 8 Oct. 1919.
[b] Population figures used for 1 Dec. 1910.
[c] Figures from Duisburg were incomplete.
[d] In Feb. 1919 the registered unemployed in Württemberg accounted for 3.68 per cent of the registered unemployed men in Germany and 3.88 per cent of the women.
[e] Includes both Lippe states and Waldeck.
*Sources: Reichsarbeitsblatt*, 17:2 (1919), 166–7. Population figures taken from *Statistisches Jahrbuch für das Deutsche Reich 1921/22* (Berlin, 1922), 1–11.

The massing of Germany's unemployed in Berlin terrified the authorities. In late November 1918 the Berlin Oberbürgermeister (and Demobilization Commissar) Adolf Wermuth wrote to all the Prussian Oberpräsidenten and the Interior Ministries of the other Länder, warning of the dangers that the mass influx into Berlin might create and urging that 'all means' be used to dissuade people from flooding into the city:

The difficulties of providing work, food, and housing in Greater Berlin make it necessary for us to issue an urgent warning about the immigration of people into Greater Berlin who have neither a flat nor a job here. If we do not succeed in preventing this influx of unemployed and homeless people into Greater Berlin, we will be faced with a general collapse which could have the gravest consequences for the whole of Germany.[130]

The Berlin city government also pressed for high levels of unemployment benefit nationwide ('nowhere less than 3 Marks per head for male adult workers'), in order to discourage men from congregating in the Athens on the Spree.[131] The political dangers of unemployed, homeless men congregating in the Reich capital were obvious, and those discussing the political upheavals of 1918–20 should note that many areas in which the post-war unrest was most pronounced (such as Berlin and Saxony) contained disproportionately large numbers of Germany's unemployed.[132] Scarcely less obvious were the economic dangers, in particular the concentration of the unemployed in places like Berlin while acute labour-shortages existed elsewhere. Consequently, a concerted campaign was mounted to convince people to leave the city, and during the months after the Armistice, posters were put up throughout Berlin about the need for labour in the mines and on farms.[133] Yet for all their propaganda urging that people take on work elsewhere, the authorities registered little success in shifting large numbers of the Berlin unemployed to places where their labour was desperately needed.

In Saxony and Hamburg as well the numbers of unemployed were probably higher than the numbers of registered job-seekers would indicate. In Saxony high unemployment in centres of the textile industry (such as Plauen) constituted a particular problem, and estimates by the Saxon government of unemployment levels were far in excess of the labour-exchange figures. In a speech to the Volkskammer in Dresden, Saxon Labour Minister Max Heldt gave the number of unemployed at about 220,000 at the end of February 1919,[134] and according to another estimate over 230,000 people in Saxony were without work in April 1919.[135] In Hamburg, according to the figures provided by the city-state's labour exchange, almost 21

---

[130] HStA, Hann. 122a/XXXIV, no. 368, fo. 120: Magistrat to sämtl. preuß. Oberpräsidenten and Minister des Innern von Bayern, Sachsen, Württemberg, and Baden, Berlin, 25 Nov. 1918.

[131] APP, Rejencja w Pila, no. 1486: (printed leaflet) 'Erwerbslosenfürsorge und Notstandsarbeiten (Sitzung mit den Demobilmachungskommissaren am 18.12.18)'. Comments by Geheimer Oberregierungsrat Fischer—Berlin.

[132] See Dick Geary, 'Radicalism and the Worker: Metalworkers and Revolution 1914–23', in Richard J. Evans (ed.), *Society and Politics in Wilhelmine Germany* (London, 1978), 274.

[133] Bey-Heard, *Hauptstadt und Staatsumwälzung*, 119 fo. The problem, while most serious in Berlin, was not restricted to the Reich capital. Gunther Mai has discussed the similar problems in the Württemberg capital of Stuttgart, where the government thought that 40,000 had migrated into the city between Oct. 1918 and the spring of 1919 and where a variety of measures were taken to stem the tide (including an embargo on migration into the city in Mar. 1919). See Mai, 'Arbeitsmarktregulierung oder Sozialpolitik?', 225–7. In Stuttgart, as elsewhere, such measures appear to have been rather ineffectual.

[134] Feldman, 'Saxony, the Reich, and the Problem of Unemployment', 109.

[135] SHAD, Gesandschaft Berlin, no. 681, fos. 179–80: Gesandschaft Berlin to Reichspostministerium, Berlin, 19 May 1919. For the special problems of Plauen, see ibid., Kriegsarchiv/Kriegs-

per cent of the *entire* male population (including children) were registered as unemployed in January 1919.[136] During the early 1920s, Berlin and Saxony continued to account for a major proportion of Germany's jobless; according to the Reich Labour Ministry, of the 404,000 people in Germany unemployed in September 1920, 150,000 were to be found in Greater Berlin and 160,000 in Saxony, with 50,000 of the remainder in Greater Hamburg.[137] Thus Berlin, Hamburg, and Saxony shared the 'dubious distinction' of continuing to be plagued by fairly substantial unemployment even when it had subsided in Germany as a whole.[138]

Finally, it is worth noting that many areas with high post-war unemployment had experienced especially sharp declines in their resident population during the conflict. Between 1910 and 1917 the population of Berlin fell by 15.8 per cent, that of Saxony as a whole by 9.6 per cent, and that of Plauen by 24.3 per cent.[139] In many places, therefore, it would appear that high unemployment in 1919 resulted partly from the sudden return of a disproportionately large section of the pre-war working population.

What did all this mean for the returning soldiers? First and foremost, it seems clear that most ex-soldiers found work during the demobilization period and found it fairly quickly. The assumption which had underpinned wartime planning for the post-war labour-market—that the men would return to their old jobs after the conflict was over—was largely realized after the Armistice, even though the demobilization occurred much more quickly and in much less orderly circumstances than could have been imagined before the autumn of 1918. Employers generally played the part expected of them, welcoming their old workers back and dismissing many of those who had taken their places during the War.[140] Altogether, judging from the

---

ministerium, no. 25012, fo. 564: Beauftragter des Min. fo. Mil. Wesen, Garn. Kdo. Plauen, Plauen, 13 Aug. 1919.

[136] *Reichsarbeitsblatt*, 17: 2 (1919), 166–7. Population figures taken from *Statistisches Jahrbuch für das Deutsche Reich 1921/22* (Berlin, 1922), 1. For further comparisons of unemployment in various regions, see Königsberger, 'Die wirtschaftliche Demobilmachung in Bayern', 214.

[137] Potthoff, *Gewerkschaften und Politik*, 191–2 fo.

[138] Feldman, 'Saxony, the Reich, and the Problem of Unemployment', 106.

[139] SHAD, Ministerium der Auswärtigen Angelegenheiten, no. 2494, Band I, fos. 118–20: Sächsisches Ministerium des Innern to Ministerium der Auswärtigen Angelegenheiten, Dresden, 16 Nov. 1918.

[140] See e.g. the letters of local industrial employers to the Demobilization Committee in Bochum in early 1919, outlining how they had dismissed women employees and rehired the men, in StdABo, B 307. Subsequently, however, some employers resisted further pressure (particularly from the DHV) to dismiss yet more women workers; they noted that many women still employed were in difficult circumstances, were trained and worked well, and were often performing tasks regarded as appropriate for women. See StdABo, B 265 and B 307. From Berlin it was reported that some employers even offered to take on unemployed men if their women workers were allowed to stay at their jobs. See BLHA, Rep. 30 Berlin C, Polizeipräsidium Berlin, Tit. 47, no. 1959, fos. 235–311: 'Jahresbericht des Oberregierungs- und Gewerberats für die Stadt Berlin für das Jahr 1921'. See also Bessel, ' "Eine nicht allzu große Beunruhigung des Arbeitsmarktes" ', 224.

numbers of men who made their own way home in 1918 and 1919 and the speed with which the ex-soliders were re-employed, it does not appear that the disorganized nature of the demobilization greatly hindered the rapid reconstitution of a peacetime labour-market.

This rather unexpected success was due in large measure to a powerful desire to return to 'normal' conditions and a widespread expectation that this would occur. Expectations became self-fulfilling, as ex-soliders returned to their old jobs and women and other 'dependants' moved (or were moved) out of wartime employment to accommodate the men. The underlying assumption was, of course, that the needs of the man as head of household and primary breadwinner were paramount; if these needs were met most other pieces of the post-war social order were expected to fall into place. Although in many families the men had *not* been 'head of household' during the war years, the conventional vision of natural, normal relationships framed the transformation of the post-war labour-market because virtually everyone involved in the demobilization process expected that it would. The reconstitution of a 'normal' labour-market, based upon 'normal' social and economic relationships, matched widespread expectations of what should and would be done.

One of the main reasons why a reconstitution of traditional roles at work and within households could occur was that the demobilization was accompanied by a short-lived but substantial rise in real wages. Of course, for a period characterized by shortages, black-marketeering, and tremendous upheavals on the labour market it is extremely difficult to calculate real wages with any degree of precision. Nevertheless, it has been suggested that, as a result of substantial wage-increases granted against the backdrop of the revolutionary threat, during 1919 and 1920 real wages in Germany rose to within 10 per cent of their pre-war levels—a process which Gerald Feldman has described as 'bribery through wage concessions'.[141] Although they complained bitterly about it, employers preferred to concede higher wages to a militant work-force than to close down their businesses or lose their property altogether. The spectre of left-wing uprisings in Germany's cities, the rapid spread of the Workers' and Soldiers' Councils (which supported workers' wage-demands),[142] and the mushrooming of trade-union membership led employers to accept reductions in the working day and wage rises as the lesser of evils. This meant that for a short time, during the demobilization period, it was possible for the man to function economically as 'head of household'—to provide for a family on his income alone. Thus, paradoxic-

[141] Feldman, 'Socio-Economic Structures', 163. See also the tables of real weekly wages for railway workers, printers, and Ruhr coal miners in Carl-Ludwig Holtfrerich, *The German Inflation 1914–1923: Causes and Effects in International Perspective* (Berlin and New York, 1986), 233.
[142] See e.g. GStAM, Rep. 120, BB, Abt. VII, Fach 1, no. 3o, Band 2, fos. 35–6: Regierungspräsident to Minister für Handel und Gewerbe, Marienwerder, 18 Nov. 1918.

ally, the pressures of labour militancy and political revolution helped bring about a reconstitution of traditional roles in the labour market and within the family, by allowing men to reoccupy the position of economic head of household and thus allowing many women (who in any case were being pressured to leave paid employment) to return to the home.

The general reduction in the numbers of unemployed during the early 1920s reflected the continuation of a process which became apparent during 1919: a return to 'normal' conditions made possible in large measure by the abnormality of galloping inflation. Nevertheless, the reduction of unemployment was not uninterrupted, and this posed problems for one particular group of war veterans: prisoners of war. After having fallen fairly steadily from early 1919, unemployment rose again during 1920 due to a short-lived appreciation of the Mark on foreign exchanges (and to the detrimental effects this had upon German exports), and then due to a renewed coal-shortage towards the end of the year.[143] This rise in unemployment occurred not long after the bulk of the German prisoners of war had returned from Allied captivity, and at a time when the Germans had to reduce the Reichswehr to 100,000 men as stipulated in the Versailles Treaty. During 1919 there had been understandable worry in government circles about what would happen, as Wilhelm Groener put it in mid-August, 'if we were to receive 800,000 men thrown on to the labour market at a single stroke'.[144] Although in fact the number of prisoners who arrived by mid-1920 was closer to 600,000,[145] their return contributed to the increase in unemployment during 1920.[146] The former prisoners themselves expressed concern that their delayed homecoming put them at a disadvantage on the labour market.[147]

The short-term upturn in unemployment in 1920, together with the return of the prisoners and the reduction in the size of the Reichswehr, led to renewed pressure for the removal of women and young people from jobs

[143] See Wunderlich, *Die Bekämpfung der Arbeitslosigkeit*, 2–3.

[144] BA/MA, RW1/W 01-2/5, fos. 1–2: 'Besprechung am 18. August 1919 in Kolberg'.

[145] 800,000 was the figure used in government discussions of the prisoners of war during 1919. See Hagen Schulze (ed.), *Akten der Reichskanzlei. Weimarer Republik. Das Kabinett Scheidemann. 13. Februar bis 20. Juni 1919* (Boppard/Rhein, 1971), 25: 'Vortrag des Generals v. Hammerstein vor dem Reichskabinett über die Arbeit der Waffenstillstandskommission in Spa, 4. März 1919, 10 Uhr in Weimar, Schloß'. In fact, by Aug. 1920 about 600,000 prisoners had returned to Germany. The first to come home were those in British and American hands, in Sept. and Oct. 1919; those in French captivity followed between late Jan. and late Mar. 1920; and the return from Russia began in May 1920. See StAB, 3-M.2.h.2/N, 130: 'Denkschrift über die Abwicklung des Krieges', Berlin, 26 Oct. 1920.

[146] See BLHA, Rep. 30 Berlin C, Polizeipräsidium Berlin/Tit. 47, no. 1959, fos. 121–81: Oberregierungs- und Gewerberat Hartmann, 'Jahresbericht für das Jahr 1920. Aufsichtsbezirk Berlin'.

[147] See e.g. the outline of demands presented by the 'Reichsvereinigung ehemaliger Kriegsgefangener' in BAP, RMdI, no. 13090/9, fos. 24–5: Reichszentrale für Kriegs- u. Zivilgefangene to Reichsministerium des Innern, Berlin, 14 Oct. 1920.

which were regarded as rightly belonging to the men.[148] Indeed, 1920 saw something of a repetition, on a smaller scale, of the developments which had accompanied the military demobilization of 1918 and 1919. The re-employment of the prisoners of war was guided by much the same considerations as had framed the reabsorption of the men who had left military service immediately after the War: agreement by employers that it was their patriotic duty to re-employ the returning men, legislation stipulating that these men had a right to their old jobs, general willingness to comply voluntarily with these guide-lines rather than provoke additional state intervention in the labour market, and a conviction that the solution to the problem involved a 'normalization' of the German labour-market, in the sense that priority for jobs was given to male breadwinners. Despite some initial difficulty, many returned prisoners were able to go back to their pre-war jobs (as the ex-soldiers had done after the Armistice) and most appear to have found work fairly quickly.[149]

The return of German prisoners of war was followed soon afterwards by an inflationary boom in which joblessness was replaced by labour shortages. Against this background, the activity and responsibility of local Demobilization Committees to intervene in the labour market was reduced in 1920, and at the end of March 1921 they were disbanded altogether.[150] With the coming of full employment, therefore, most of the remaining demobilization machinery was dismantled. Skilled workers were in particularly short supply; overtime working became commonplace; women and young people, who had been chased out of the factories and offices with such vigour in 1919 and 1920, were recruited once again; renewed employment opportunities allowed people who had previously emigrated into the mining areas to return to their home regions; and, even in former centres of high unemployment such as Saxony, by September 1921 people were 'working double shifts and overtime'.[151] As the Pomeranian Labour Office in Stettin noted when

[148] e.g. on the labour market in Berlin: BLHA, Rep. 30 Berlin C, Polizeipräsidium Berlin/Tit. 47, no. 1959, fos. 121–81: Oberregierungs- und Gewerberat Hartmann, 'Jahresbericht für das Jahr 1920. Aufsichtsbezirk Berlin'.

[149] e.g. see the list of former prisoners of war in Wunstdorf, in the Regierungsbezirk Hanover, showing the dates of their release from captivity and of their return to work (which generally occurred a few weeks later, in later 1919 or early 1920), in NHStA, Hann. 174, Neustadt/Rbg., no. 3011. See also the reports from the first half of 1920 of the trade-union functionary who headed the army's job-counselling centre in Nürnberg, in BHStA, Abt. IV, MKr 14414. Although he reported difficulty in finding work for returned prisoners in Jan. and Feb., in mid-May he was able to conclude that 'the task of bringing men dismissed from the army, occupants of the garrisons and returned prisoners of war back into economic activity' was completed. Ibid., Arbeitsbeschaffungsstelle, Gewerkschaftsfunktionär Baierlein to Abwicklungs-amt fr. III.b.A.K. Nürnberg, Nürnberg, 19 May 1920.

[150] See Mai, 'Arbeitsmarktregulierung oder Sozialpolitik?' 228–30. The remaining functions of the local Demobilization Committees were handed over to the labour exchanges or to the regional Demobilization Commissars.

[151] SHAD, Gesandtschaft Berlin, no. 692: Reichswirtschaftsminister to Reichspräsident, Berlin, 21 Oct. 1921.

surveying developments during 1921, 'the well-known conditions on the foreign exchanges, the collapse of the Mark and resulting foreign attempts to buy things up' in Germany had led to a 'powerful increase in production' and 'created the appearance of an economic boom'.[152] Low unemployment, labour shortages, and the return of women to employment continued to characterize the German economy through most of 1922, until the accelerating depreciation of the German currency began to undermine rather than stimulate economic activity.[153] As long as the cracks in the German economy and the huge costs resulting from the War could be papered over with billions of Marks, the appearance of an economic boom could be maintained and the threat of mass unemployment pushed into the background.

Although a combination of the easy availability of jobs and the reduction in real wages due to inflation[154] drew many women back to paid employment in the early 1920s, they did not necessarily return to the sorts of work which they had taken up during the War—in heavy industry, for example. Instead they tended to return to what had traditionally been considered work suitable for women: in the textile and clothing industries, in food processing, cleaning, and laundry work. Some, however, were unable to take up their former types of work because their health was no longer up to it—often seen as a result of wartime work in the munitions factories. Many married women remained at home and worked from there, 'in order to devote themselves to family and domesticity'; this, so it was reported from Berlin for the year 1921, was 'true as well for the recently married, who had initially worked for a short time but then, either at the request of their husbands or compelled by the demobilization decrees, had to give up their jobs'.[155]

The changing position of women in the German labour-market after the War illustrates particularly clearly the underlying drive for a 'normalization' of economic and social relationships. First, the relatively high unemployment led to the removal of women from jobs not generally considered to be appropriate for them. Then, the full employment of the inflationary boom years of 1921 and 1922 saw the return of many women to paid employment, but largely to sectors which were regarded as suitable for them and which paralleled the types of work they were expected to do in the home: cooking, cleaning, sewing. The gender-specific organization of the labour market, which to a considerable extent had been eroded during the second half of

---

[152] PLA, Rep. 38 Loitz, no. 1382, fos. 166–9: 'Verwaltungsbericht des Pommerschen Landesarbeitsamt und des Provinzialberufsamts für das Jahr 1921'.

[153] See BLHA, Rep. 30 Berlin C, Polizeipräsidium Berlin/Tit. 47, no. 1959, fos. 361–401: Regierungs- und Gewerberat Wenzel, 'Jahresbericht für das Jahr 1922'. The most direct effect of the inflation upon women's employment came with the recruitment in 1922 of an additional 1,500 women to work in printing factories producing banknotes.

[154] See the tables showing the changes in real wages in Holtfrerich, *The German Inflation*, 233–4. For a yet more negative view of wage levels during the inflation, see Scholz, 'Zur sozialen Lage der Arbeiterschaft in der Inflation'.

[155] BLHA, Rep. 30 Berlin C, Polizeipräsidium Berlin/Tit. 47, no. 1959, fos. 235–311.

the War, was quickly reinstituted; and the fact that women were drawn back into paid employment during the early 1920s not only did not counteract this process but actually reinforced it.[156] Indeed, with the increased demand for labour in the early 1920s the *patterns* of women's employment came to resemble more closely those of the pre-war period, although the *number* of women working outside the home once again reached that of spring and summer 1918.[157]

The reversal of wartime changes and reassertion of conventional values emerges as a major theme permeating the history of labour during the demobilization. Employment was the central concern in the post-war tran-sition, and not just in a quantitative sense. The concern was not just to provide jobs for all those thrown on to the German labour-market after the War, but also to ensure that people were in the kinds of jobs considered appropriate to them. The reconstitution of a peacetime labour-market involved not just economic but also social engineering. In both regards the Germans were, in the short term at least, surprisingly successful—far more successful than most people had thought possible in November 1918.

While the qualitative restructuring of the German labour-market between 1918 and 1922 may be characterized, at least in part, as a process of normalization and the reassertion of conventional social values, it did not coincide with economic normalization. Indeed, it proved possible to return so many social relationships to 'normal' after the First World War because of a highly *abnormal* economic situation: an inflationary boom which ended in a hyperinflation that brought hardship and mass unemployment in its wake. In the summer of 1923, as inflation galloped ahead, joblessness began to rise steeply, and after the German currency was stabilized in late 1923 unemployment reached a level far higher than that which had caused such alarm in early 1919. By the end of 1923 more than a quarter of German trade-unionists were without jobs, and the numbers of jobless remained high throughout 1924. The advent of high, structural, and long-term unemploy-ment facilitated the rolling-back of revolutionary gains. This economic shock was delayed (in comparison, for example, with events in Britain and the United States)[158] by the inflation of the early 1920s, and its coming during the stabilization crisis of 1923–4 marked the final and real transition of the German labour-market to 'normal' peacetime conditions. Employers were pleased to see the final dismantling of demobilization legislation which had often functioned to protect workers from arbitrary dismissal, [159] as hundreds

---

[156] Rouette, 'Die Erwerbslosenfürsorge für Frauen in Berlin', 9.

[157] Friedrich Hesse, *Die deutsche Wirtschaftslage von 1914 bis 1923: Krieg, Geldblähe und Wechsellagen* (Jena, 1938), 480.

[158] On points of international comparison, see Bessel, 'Unemployment and Demobilisation', 28.

[159] Mai, 'Arbeitsmarktregulierung oder Sozialpolitik?', esp. 231–3.

of thousands of workers were sacrificed on the altar of economic necessity and lost their jobs, and the strength of the trade unions was dealt a major blow.[160] The stabilization, which constituted the belated triumph of economic considerations over political ones, marked the end of the demobilization; with the arrival of high unemployment, labour was finally put back firmly in its place.

On one level, the demobilization of the German labour-market after the First World War had been amazingly successful. The millions of returning soldiers were reintegrated swiftly into the post-war economy, and unemployment, although a serious problem in early 1919, remained within bounds and rapidly diminished thereafter. Emergency works-projects and legislation regulating the labour market functioned reasonably well, given the chaotic circumstances prevailing in Germany during the months after the Armistice; women were shunted back into occupations regarded as fitting; and gradually the widespread disinclination to work and erosion of work discipline were reversed. However, the successful demobilization of labour in Germany rested upon an inflationary economy, which itself could not be sustained indefinitely and which in effect postponed the inevitable post-war depression until 1923–4. Indeed, the demobilization of labour—particularly the need to stimulate the economy so as to provide employment for the millions of returning soldiers and former employees of war industries—contributed greatly to the German post-war inflation. The political and economic dangers inherent in the demobilization probably left Germany's new rulers no other option in 1919, but the solution they found was necessarily temporary. Seen from a longer-term perspective, the attempt to reconstitute a stable peacetime economy which could provide work for all Germans was a failure. When the demobilization period formally came to an end on 31 March 1924, the labour movement was in retreat, real wages were substantially below pre-war levels, and unemployment was at dizzying heights. The 'normalization' of the German labour-market, when it finally arrived in 1923–4, was to prove extremely painful.

---

[160] See Gerald D. Feldman and Irmgard Steinisch, 'Die Weimarer Republik zwischen Sozial- und Wirtschaftsstaat: Die Entscheidung gegen den Achtstundentag', in *Archiv für Sozialgeschichte*, 18 (1978). See also Mai, 'Arbeitsmarktregulierung oder Sozialpolitik?', 233 4.

# 6

## Demobilization and Housing

> The housing question does not arise simply from the fact that there is
> still a great deal of housing misery, that in all states a portion of the
> population—and not only in the large cities—lives in conditions that
> appear objectionable from the standpoint of hygiene and of morality.
> The existence of a certain degree of housing misery in this sense is only
> another expression of the fact that generally there is destitution and
> poverty in human society.[1]

AFTER the First World War, Germany's 'housing question' was more
pressing than ever before. Dwellings were in desperately short supply,
hundreds of thousands of new households were being established, and
inflation distorted the financial framework within which housing was built
and let. Compared with the urgent problems associated with the labour
market in the aftermath of the War, the 'housing question' proved more
resistant to short-term solution. Whereas the development of unemployment
relief, the surprisingly rapid reduction in post-war unemployment, and a
significant, if temporary, rise in real wages at the end of the War[2] masked
the extent to which Germany had been impoverished by four years of war,
the post-war housing situation gave no grounds, however illusory, for
optimism. Housing was an area where the impoverishment brought about
by the War was most disturbingly apparent. Lower standards of housing
reflected lower national wealth,[3] and this could be masked neither by
inflationary social-welfare programmes nor the short-term upsurge in economic activity which helped revivify the job market. The housing shortage
defied quick solution, and exposed the human upheaval involved in Germany's post-war transition.

The First World War and the subsequent demobilization fundamentally
transformed the German housing-market. Before 1914, housing in Germany

---

[1] L. Pohle, 'Die Wohnungsfrage: Mieterschutz', in *Handbuch der Politik iv: Der wirtschaftliche
Wiederaufbau* (3rd. edn., Berlin and Leipzig, 1921), 230.

[2] See Dietmar Petzina, Werner Abelshauser, and Anselm Faust, *Sozialgeschichtliches Arbeitsbuch, iii:
Materialien zur Statistik des Deutschen Reiches 1914–1945* (Munich, 1978), 83. The figures given here
indicate that real wages for unskilled workers were higher in 1919 than in 1914. Those of skilled
workers remained lower than the pre-war figures, but in all cases were far higher than in 1917.

[3] There is an interesting parallel with the effects of the War in Britain, as analysed by Jay
Winter. According to Winter, the health of the British civilian population (unlike the German)
actually improved during the War; the one area where the War did claim its toll on civilian
living-standards in Britain was housing. See J. M. Winter, *The Great War and the British People*
(London, 1986), esp. 242–3.

had essentially been left to the free market. Although building regulations and health codes restricted what could and could not be built, and although municipalities sold land to developers, provided utilities and streets in order to encourage housing construction, and occasionally offered credit for house-building co-operatives or built housing for city employees, the German state only rarely involved itself directly in the building of housing. The disposition of private property was a private affair, and the state did not intervene in the contract between landlord and tenant.[4] As Germany rapidly industrialized and her population—especially her urban population—grew during the late nineteenth and early twentieth centuries, the private building-industry provided vast numbers of flats in German cities. The scale of the undertaking was enormous: between 1850 and 1913 roughly 30 per cent of all investment in Germany went into non-agricultural housing construction, and an average of 250,000 dwellings were built yearly between 1900 and 1913. However, the vast building-programmes undertaken during the Empire were initiated with little reference to the needs of the people who came to live in the new urban environment.[5] The motive for the building was financial: to take advantage of lucrative investment opportunities rather than to provide for human need. As such, it rested upon a persistent underlying housing-shortage, and a massive and growing demand for economical living-space—a demand which could not be satisfied.

Although enormous numbers of dwellings were built in Germany during the decades before the First World War, and the condition of working-class housing generally improved, many people lived in cramped, unsanitary, and costly accommodation. This was rental accommodation: by the late nineteenth century roughly 90 per cent of the population of most German cities lived in rented housing; in Berlin during the 1890s only 0.5 per cent of households were owner-occupiers.[6] For millions of working-class Germans 'home' had been a succession of small, overcrowded, poorly heated flats periodically abandoned when the rent could not be found or a room or bed (in some instances, a part of a bed for part of a

---

[4] Herbert Anker, 'Die Wohnungszwangswirtschaft und ihre volkswirtschaftliche Bedeutung' (Univ. of Freiburg i. B., phil. diss., 1927), 9–10; Dan P. Silverman, 'A Pledge Unredeemed: The Housing Crisis in Weimar Germany', *Central European History*, 3:3 (1970), 116; Martin H. Geyer, 'Wohnungsnot und Wohnungszwangswirtschaft in München 1917 bis 1924', in Gerald D. Feldman, Carl-Ludwig Holtfrerich, Gerhard A. Ritter, and Peter-Christian Witt (eds.), *Die Anpassung an die Inflation* (Berlin and New York, 1986), 127–8.

[5] See Peter-Christian Witt, 'Inflation, Wohnungszwangswirtschaft und Hauszinssteuer: Zur Regelung von Wohnungsbau und Wohnungsmarkt in der Weimarer Republik', in Lutz Niethammer (ed.), *Wohnen im Wandel: Beiträge zur Geschichte des Alltags in der bürgerlichen Gesellschaft* (Wuppertal, 1979), 387–91.

[6] See Clemens Wischermann, ' "Familiengerechtes Wohnen" ': Anspruch und Wirklichkeit in Deutschland vor dem Ersten Weltkrieg', in Hans Jürgen Teuteberg (ed.), *Homo habitans: Zur Sozialgeschichte des ländlichen und städtischen Wohnens in der Neuzeit* (Münster, 1985), 172–3.

day) in someone else's flat; for hundreds of thousands of urban workers, living five people to a room was the norm, and in many towns during the late nineteenth century a large proportion of workers lived in unheated rooms.[7] While conditions in the 'rental barracks' of Berlin were bad enough, they were worse in many of the fast-growing industrial towns of the Ruhr and Upper Silesia; in cities from one end of Imperial Germany to another there were shortages of decent housing which working people could afford.[8] Housing conditions in the countryside, particularly the housing which was available for agricultural labourers and their families, were generally even worse.

Within the framework of a liberal, private market for housing, the possibilities for greater improvements were limited. Working-class incomes were neither sufficiently high nor sufficiently regular to underpin the investment which could provide adequate housing within a market framework. Furthermore, the 'boom and bust' cycles of industrializing Germany's economy posed problems with regard to the production of housing. Because of the long lead-times involved in construction, the speculation which fuelled housing construction in Imperial Germany was frequently out of phase with demand; projects financed and begun during buoyant periods were often not completed until the beginning of a new recession which saw workers losing their jobs and temporarily abandoning urban housing-markets.[9] During the final decades of the Empire social reformers and state authorities paid increased attention to the problems of housing, in part because of concern that housing problems might provide a good platform for Social Democratic agitation and in part due to the growing appreciation of links between poor, damp, and overcrowded housing on the one hand, and the spread of disease (especially tuberculosis) on the other.[10] However, until the First World War, the German housing-market remained characterized by

[7] See Lutz Niethammer and Franz-Josef Brüggemeier, 'Wie wohnten die Arbeiter im Kaiserreich?', in *Archiv für Sozialgeschichte*, 16 (1976), 61–134; Adelheid von Saldern, 'Kommunalpolitik und Arbeiterwohungsbau im deutschen Kaiserreich', in Niethammer (ed.), *Wohnen im Wandel*, 344–5; Wischermann, ' "Familiengerechtes Wohnen" ', 169–98. Wischermann, however, stresses that it would be wrong to regard the urbanization period in Germany simply as 'a time of quasi-permanent acute housing shortage': urban housing in Germany during the second half of the nineteenth century generally marked a great improvement over earlier conditions, although it was also characterized by 'extraordinarily high social disparities' (p. 197).

[8] See e.g. S. H. F. Hickey, *Workers in Imperial Germany: The Miners of the Ruhr* (Oxford, 1985), 36–69; Clemens Wischermann, 'Wohnquartier und Lebensverhältnisse in der Urbanisierung', in Arno Herzig, Dieter Langewiesche, and Arnold Sywottek (eds.), *Arbeiter in Hamburg: Unterschichten, Arbeiter und Arbeiterbewegung seit dem ausgehenden 18. Jahrhundert* (Hamburg, 1983), 339–58; Willi Breunig, *Soziale Verhältnisse der Arbeiterschaft und sozialistische Arbeiterbewegung in Ludwigshafen am Rhein 1869–1919* (Ludwigshafen/Rhein, 1976), 68–71.

[9] See Lutz Niethammer, 'Ein langer Marsch durch die Institutionen: Zur Vorgeschichte des preußischen Wohnungsgesetzes von 1918', in Niethammer (ed.), *Wohnen im Wandel*, 368–9, 374.

[10] On this last point, see Paul Weindling, *Health, Race and German Politics between National Unification and Nazism, 1870–1945* (Cambridge, 1989), 164–5.

minimal state intervention and was shaped by private finances rather than a coherent perception of housing need.

The massive upheavals caused by the First World War destroyed the basis for a fundamentally free-market approach to the housing market, and pushed the 'housing question' towards the top of the public agenda. The preoccupations of social reformers—worried about the detrimental effects of bad housing upon health, social and sexual behaviour, and political life—found resonance far beyond academic circles. Desperate concern about healthy family life and the need for a buoyant birth-rate—at a time when families were being torn apart, the social and political order appeared to be breaking down, hundreds of thousands of Germans were being killed at the front, and the birth rate was plummeting—focused attention on the 'housing question'. The 'housing question' became a housing crisis. Not only were there the obvious and enormous difficulties which had arisen during the War; even more alarming was the spectre of what would probably happen when hordes of soldiers returned to Germany intending to establish new households in a country desperately short of domestic living-space. The crisis was symbolic as well as real: the upheaval of War, the extraordinary and harrowing existence forced upon millions of soldiers at the front, made more important the need to preserve a warm and comforting mythology of hearth and home and more threatening those forces which appeared to be breaking up 'healthy' family life. This presupposed not merely that the men had somewhere to which to return, but also that human needs, and not just the dictates of a free-market economy, had to be met. As a result, the First World War marked a transition in the manner in which housing was discussed and provided in Germany—a transition which led to Article 155 of the Weimar Constitution, in which a commitment was embedded for the state 'to secure a healthy dwelling for every German and a place of residence and work for every German family, especially those with many children, appropriate to their needs'.[11] Housing became irrevocably a *public* concern.

The outbreak of the First World War changed the shape of the German housing-market almost overnight. Initially, however, it did not exacerbate the chronic housing-shortage which had plagued Imperial Germany for decades. In fact, just the opposite occurred. The tumultuous changes in August 1914 substantially, if temporarily, reduced the demand for housing as thousands of families were compelled to abandon their own, separate

---

[11] See Witt, 'Inflation, Wohnungszwangswirtschaft und Hauszinssteuer', 385; Michael Ruck, 'Der Wohnungsbau. Schnittpunkt von Sozial- und Wirtschaftspolitik. Probleme der öffentlichen Wohnungspolitik in der Hauszinssteuerära (1924/25–1930/31)', in Werner Abelshauser (ed.), *Die Weimarer Republik als Wohlfahrtsstaat: Zum Verhältnis von Wirtschafts- und Sozialpolitik in der Industriegesellschaft* (Stuttgart, 1987), 95–6; M. H. Geyer, 'Wohnungsnot und Wohnungszwangswirtschaft', 128–9.

dwellings. The main reason was the sudden loss of the regular incomes of male breadwinners. On the one hand, the mobilization of hundreds of thousands of men during the first weeks of the War removed a large proportion of the male population from the local community.[12] On the other, the precipitate switch to war production led to sudden and steep increases in unemployment; in some cases the economic disruptions of August and September 1914 threw half a town's work-force out of a job.[13] Many families, having suddenly lost their main economic support, left their own homes to move in with parents or in-laws; in some cases families were compelled by economic circumstances to leave the cities and return to the countryside.[14] Furthermore, the mobilization and economic uncertainty accompanying the outbreak of war sharply curtailed the formation of new households. After the rush of 'war betrothals' immediately following the declaration of war in August (when 80,226 couples were married in Germany, as compared with 38,407 in July and 32,978 in August 1913), the number of marriages in Germany plummeted: in September 1914 there were only 18,744 and in October 25,322. Altogether the number of marriages in Germany declined from 513,283 in 1913 to 460,608 in 1914 and 278,208 in 1915.[15] Fewer marriages meant fewer new couples seeking their own dwellings.

The economic difficulties created by the outbreak of war, particularly the sudden loss to millions of households of their main breadwinners, prompted the state to intervene in the housing market. The Law for the Protection of Servicemen of 4 August 1914 granted dependants of soldiers protection against eviction, and legislation enacted on 14 January 1915 prevented landlords from obtaining eviction orders against fighting men.[16] In August 1914 legislation was also passed which allowed the courts to grant three-month deferments on debt payments, legislation designed to provide general protection for tenants in arrears (allowing the courts to postpone evictions).[17] And in December 1914 a decree was issued which provided for the setting-up of local 'rent settlement offices'

---

[12] e.g. by mid-September 1914 the small town of Belgern, near Torgau, had lost 220 men to the army out of a total population of 2,800. See LHSA, Rep. C 48 I.e., no. 918/I, fo. 226: Magistrat der Stadt Belgern to Regierungspräsident in Merseburg, Belgern, 23 Sept. 1914.

[13] Thus in Weißenfels, where shoemaking was a major source of employment, it was estimated that by mid-August 1914 between 5,000 and 6,000 of the city's approximately 9,000 industrial workers were without work. See ibid., fos. 370–6: Magistrat der Stadt Weißenfels a.S. to Regierungspräsident in Merseburg, Weißenfels, 23 Sept. 1914.

[14] See Georg Bieber, 'Der Wohnungsmarkt und die Bekämpfung der Wohnungsnot' (Univ. of Erlangen, Phil. diss. 1925), 15–16.

[15] Statistisches Reichsamt, *Statistik des Deutschen Reichs*, Vol. cclxxvi: *Bewegung der Bevölkerung in den Jahren 1914 bis 1919* (Berlin, 1922), pp. xvii, xxii.

[16] For discussion of this legislation, and of the fears aroused over what awaited men when they left military service and lost this protection, see GStAB, Rep. 84a. no. 1764, fos. 165–6: (Preuß. Justizminister) to Staatssekretär des Reichsjustizamts, Berlin, 4 Dec. 1918.

[17] Ludwig Preller, *Sozialpolitik in der Weimarer Republik* (Stuttgart, 1949), 67.

(*Mieteinigungsämter*).[18] These measures marked the beginnings of state intervention in the German housing-market and protection of tenants which
continued and expanded during the War and the post-war period.

While demand for housing was affected immediately by the upheavals of
mobilization, it took slightly longer before the hostilities affected housing
supply, since construction did not cease abruptly the moment war was
declared. Altogether roughly 180,000 dwellings were built between August
1914 and December 1918, fewer than during 1913 alone and leaving a
deficit of some 800,000 dwellings not built between 1914 and 1918 but
which would probably have been constructed had there not been a war.[19]
Buildings still under construction when war broke out were generally completed in late 1914 and 1915, and it was not until the second or third year
of fighting that housing construction came to a virtual stop due to shortages
of labour and building materials.[20] In Ludwigshafen, for example, 510
dwellings were completed in 1913, 317 in 1914, 275 in 1915, and 24 in
1916; it was not until 1917 that house-building in the city stopped altogether.[21] In Munich, where the net annual increase in flats had been over
5,000 per annum between 1911 and 1913, the number fell to 1,824 in 1914,
665 in 1915, 129 in 1916, and 99 in 1917.[22] Because demand for housing
dropped sharply during the first months of war, while the supply of new
dwellings fell back more gradually, in many cities considerable numbers of
flats were standing empty during late 1914 and 1915.[23] Thus while demand
for housing was dwindling in wartime Germany, dwellings continued to be
completed, but later, as large numbers of people were drawn into cities with
important war-industries (such as Ludwigshafen, with the BASF chemicals
works), the supply of new housing dried up completely.

These changes were reflected in the changing proportion of dwellings left
vacant. In Mannheim, for example, the number of empty flats 'suddenly
went sky high' following the outbreak of war, but conditions changed
thereafter: in November 1913, 1.27 per cent of the city's flats had been

[18] Anker, 'Die Wohnungszwangswirtschaft', 17.

[19] Witt, 'Inflation, Wohnungszwangswirtschaft und Hauszinssteuer', 391; Ruck, 'Der
Wohnungsbau', 94.

[20] Not only were building materials in short supply; their distribution was also restricted by
government authorities, who were concerned to channel these as far as possible to war industries;
e.g. in Bavaria the Deputy Commanding Generals ordered a complete stop to new residential
building in 1917. See G. Bieber, 'Der Wohnungsmarkt', 21.

[21] *Die Maßnahmen der Stadt Ludwigshafen am Rhein auf dem Gebiet der Wohnungsfürsorge seit dem Jahre
1914* (Ludwigshafen/Rhein, n. d.) (copy in Stadtarchiv Ludwigshafen), 5. In Augsburg the
numbers of flats completed fell from 796 in 1914 to 187 in 1915, 50 in 1916, and a mere 8
in 1917, before rising to 145 in 1918. See Merith Niehuss, *Arbeiterschaft in Krieg und Revolution:
Soziale Schichtung und Lage der Arbeiter in Augsburg und Linz 1910 bis 1924* (Berlin and New York,
1985), 158. See also Pohle, 'Die Wohnungsfrage', 233.

[22] M. H. Geyer, 'Wohnungsnot und Wohnungszwangswirtschaft', 157. G. Bieber, 'Der
Wohnungsmarkt', 19, gives slightly different figures.

[23] G. Bieber, 'Der Wohnungsmarkt', 16–17.

empty, and two years later this figure stood at 3.14 per cent; thereafter the proportion of empty flats fell—to 2.28 per cent in 1916, 1.11 per cent in 1917, and only 0.82 per cent in 1918.[24] In nearby Ludwigshafen, the municipal administration reported that from 1917 there were no longer any empty flats in the city.[25] In Munich the proportion of empty flats peaked at 4.53 per cent of the total in November 1915, before falling to less than 1 per cent in 1917 and roughly 0.5 per cent in 1918.[26] Shortly before the end of the War, in September 1918, it was estimated that 3,600 new flats would have to be built in the Bavarian capital during the first year of peace in order to meet demand. By the third year of the War, not only had housing again become extremely difficult to find but its scarcity posed problems for managing the wartime labour-market. In some areas, most notably in the coal-mining cities of the Ruhr, the shortage of housing proved a major obstacle to attracting the labour urgently required for the war effort. Shortages, combined with the return of large numbers of soldiers called back during 1916 and 1917 to work in key industries, made it impossible to provide housing for additional workers in those areas where they were needed most.[27]

Concern about the housing crisis during the conflict was not focused only on the wartime imbalances between supply and demand or on difficulties in finding temporary accommodation for coal miners and munitions workers. The greatest anxiety concerned what would happen when the conflict ended—when the developments which had led to the short-lived glut of empty flats in 1914 and 1915 would suddenly be reversed while the cumulative effects of the wartime cessation of housing construction would be felt acutely and millions of returning soldiers and newly-wed couples would demand flats of their own. During 1917 and 1918 public authorities with responsibility for housing began to examine closely and with mounting panic the prospects for the forthcoming demobilization.[28] In October 1917 the Prussian Minister of Public Works reported to regional administrators throughout Prussia that 'the results of statistical investigations and assessments undertaken in the larger cities and industrial areas demonstrate that the fear of a worrying shortage of medium-sized and especially of small flats at the conclusion of peace can no longer be dismissed'— a fear which was given an added dash of paranoia by memories of the events

---

[24] Statistisches Amt der Stadt Mannheim (ed.), *Verwaltungsbericht der badischen Hauptstadt Mannheim für 1919/20* (Mannheim, n. d.), 7.

[25] StdALu, no. 3542: Bürgermeisteramt to Regierung der Pfalz, Kammer des Innern, in Speyer, 'Wohnungsverhältnisse in Ludwigshafen a. Rhein', Ludwigshafen/Rhein, 19 June 1920.

[26] G. See Bieber, 'Der Wohnungsmarkt', 22–4. For similar figures for Nürnberg, see ibid. 31.

[27] See e.g. BBA, Bestand 32/4327: Kgl. Berginspektion 4 to Kgl. Bergwerksdirektion in Recklinghausen, Waltrop, 24 Jan. 1917.

[28] Niethammer, 'Ein langer Marsch durch die Institutionen', 381. See also Dieter Rebentisch, *Ludwig Landmann: Frankfurter Oberbürgermeister der Weimarer Republik* (Wiesbaden, 1975), 76.

after the Franco-Prussian War, when severe housing-shortages had led to urban unrest.[29] In March 1918 all municipalities in Prussia with more than 10,000 inhabitants were required to establish housing agencies (*Wohnungs-nachweise*), which were to form a reliable statistical picture of the local housing-markets.[30] Municipal housing bureaucracies were revivified.[31] Throughout Germany small towns as well as large surveyed the housing situation and outlined the problems looming on the post-war horizon. In Neubrandenburg, for example, the municipal council reported in June 1918 not only that this small provincial centre was already suffering a housing crisis but that the town would be short of 120 flats after the demobilization because of the number of returning veterans expected to set up independent households.[32] In February 1918, the Prussian Ministry of Public Works estimated a total shortfall of at least 700,000 flats.[33]

The wartime deterioration of the housing situation and the certainty of catastrophic shortages once the War was over led to increasingly insistent calls during the last two years of the conflict for state intervention. In Berlin the local branch of the Society for Social Reform (Gesellschaft für Sozial-reform) urged the city administration to take action to alleviate the shortages and prepare for the coming emergency; in November 1916 the Association for Housing Reform (Verein für Wohnungsreform) joined with a variety of interested organizations (socialist and Christian trade-unions among them) to form a German Housing Committee (Deutscher Wohnungsausschuß), which presented a comprehensive set of proposals for initiating and financing new housing construction and centralizing the state administration of the housing market.[34] By the late stages of the War a broad spectrum of public figures, including social reformers and Social Democrats with a special interest in housing (such as Paul Hirsch and Albert Südekum), and interest groups were demanding action on the housing front. The insistent public lobbying and fears of imminent catastrophe and of the damage housing shortages might cause to German family life, especially when the birth rate was declining steeply, spurred government to act. In July 1917 the 'rent settlement offices' created in 1914 were given power to review rent increases

[29] StdABr, 011/37/1, fos. 1–2: Minister der öffentlichen Arbeiten to sämtl. Regierungsprä-sidenten and the Oberpräsident in Potsdam, Berlin, 6 Oct. 1917.
[30] StdADu, no. 604/17, fo. 1: Staatskommissar für das Wohnungswesen to sämtl. Regierungs-präsidenten, Berlin, 25 June 1918.
[31] e.g. in Berlin the municipal housing office, which had been closed at the outbreak of the War, was reopened in Apr. 1918. See Frauke Bey-Heard, *Hauptstadt und Staatsumwälzung. Berlin 1919. Problematik und Scheitern der Rätebewegung in der Berliner Kommunalverwaltung* (Berlin, 1969), 121.
[32] MLHA, Mecklenburg-Strelitzer Ministerium, Abteilung des Innern, no. 5071, fo. 16: Magistrat to Großh. Ministerium, Abteilung des Innern, in Neustrelitz, Neubrandenburg, 20 June 1918.
[33] Witt, 'Inflation, Wohnungszwangswirtschaft und Hauszinssteuer', 392.
[34] Preller, *Sozialpolitik in der Weimarer Republik*, 69–70; Niethammer, 'Ein langer Marsch durch die Institutionen', 379–80; M. H. Geyer, 'Wohnungsnot und Wohnungszwangswirtschaft', 128.

and eviction notices when requested to do so by the tenant (with landlords denied the right of appeal).[35] In March 1918 a twenty-year 'long march through the institutions' culminated with the enactment of a comprehensive Prussian Housing Law, which (among other things) strengthened public planning prerogatives and expropriation rights, promoted zoning, set a framework for housing regulations to promote the health, morality, and privacy of families, and provided for state loans of 20 million Marks to encourage co-operative building associations.[36]

This was followed during the last weeks of the War by large strides down the road towards a controlled housing-economy. On 23 September the Reich government published new measures to 'protect tenants' and 'work against the housing shortage'.[37] This placed responsibility for administering the expected post-war housing-crisis with local housing offices, and gave them substantial new powers. According to the provisions of the new decrees, a landlord no longer had the final say about who would be his tenant. Local authorities were empowered to prevent buildings or parts of buildings from being torn down, order that additional people be housed in a dwelling, stop owners of dwellings from using them for commercial or industrial purposes, and compel the owners of empty properties to advertise their availability. Thus German local authorities were armed with wide-ranging powers to intervene in the housing market by the time the demobilization began. Not only did the state become the arbiter of landlord–tenant relations; it also took a growing interest in financing new construction, and on 31 October 1918 the Bundesrat passed regulations for providing subsidies to compensate for wartime increases in building costs.[38] Throughout Germany the individual states enacted laws and decrees regulating landlord–tenant relations, and by the time the War ended, municipal housing offices had assumed a tight control over the availability and price of dwellings in their areas and the German state possessed powers to intervene in the housing market as never before. Many Germans no doubt looked forward to the rapid dismantling of wartime controls and the re-establishment of a free-market economy, once peace arrived and 'normal' conditions returned. However, a chronic housing-shortage, the effects of the

---

[35] Anker, 'Die Wohnungszwangswirtschaft', 17.

[36] Niethammer, 'Ein langer Marsch durch die Institutionen', 363–4.

[37] *Reichsgesetzblatt*, 1918, 1140–3: 'Bekanntmachung zum Schutze der Mieter vom 23. September 1918'; ibid. 1143–6: 'Bekanntmachung über Maßnahmen gegen Wohnungsmangel vom 23. September 1918'. See also Anker, 'Die Wohnungszwangswirtschaft', 18; Preller, *Sozialpolitik in der Weimarer Republik*, 70; Richard Bessel, 'State and Society in Germany in the Aftermath of the First World War', in W. R. Lee and Eve Rosenhaft (eds.), *The State and Social Change in Germany, 1880–1980* (Oxford, Munich, and New York, 1990), 217–18.

[38] Preller, *Sozialpolitik in der Weimarer Republik*, 69. These subsidies may have made matters worse, by further fuelling price rises for building materials. See *Verhandlungen der Sozialisierungs-Kommission über die Neuregelung des Wohnungswesens* (2 vols.; Berlin, 1921), i. 17.

wartime cessation of building, the return of the soldiers, the post-war marriage-boom, continued inflation, and shortage of capital provided the basis for extensive state intervention, and rent controls, during the demobilization period.

The suddenness of the defeat and the scale of the immediate problems in November 1918 pushed many of the general worries about the supply of housing temporarily into the background. The immediate challenge in November was how to accommodate the hundreds of thousands of soldiers passing through Germany on their way to the military establishment from which they were to be demobilized. Failure to provide food and shelter for these travelling soldiers promised to have terrifying consequences. It was already difficult enough to prevent the soldiers from setting out for home on their own, and this problem greatly worried a government desperately concerned to re-establish order and keen that the revolution to which it owed its existence should not get out of control. If the soldiers could not be reasonably certain of a bed and a meal provided they stayed with their military units, nothing would stop them from leaving. Not surprisingly, Joseph Koeth registered government alarm, immediately after the Armistice, over whether enough was being done in Berlin and elsewhere to prepare for the coming invasion of Germany by German soldiers.[39] Fears were expressed that housing demobilized soldiers in mass quarters, as opposed to putting them up in private homes, might increase the danger of unrest,[40] and there was concern about the difficulties of heating large halls.[41] At the end of 1918 all that stood in the way of the complete disappearance of the Imperial German Army was the promise of food and somewhere to sleep.

Confronted by the need to house thousands upon thousands of soldiers suddenly descending upon them, local authorities found their hand considerably strengthened by the Bundesrat Decree of 23 September 1918 on 'Measures against the Housing Shortage', which authorized them to take control of unused premises such as factories, halls, and barracks.[42] To meet the emergency, any available buildings were used to house the soldiers,

---

[39] SHAD, Gesandtschaft Berlin, Nr. 690, fos. 25–6: Der stellv. Bevollmächtigte zum Bundesrate to Ministerium der Auswärtigen Angelegenheiten in Dresden, Berlin, 23 Nov. 1918. Koeth was particularly concerned that not enough attention was being paid to the necessary sanitary provisions, such as providing delousing facilities near railway stations.

[40] This fear was expressed by Berlin Oberbürgermeister Adolf Wermuth in early November. See SHAD, Ministerium der Auswärtigen Angelegenheiten, Nr. 2494, Band I, fo. 98: Gesandtschaft Berlin to Ministerium der Auswärtigen Angelegenheiten, Berlin, 9 Nov. 1918.

[41] See e.g. APW, Akta Miasta Wroclawia, Nr. 31021, fos. 324–5: Magistrat, Abteilung für Militärangelegenheiten, to Kommandantur, Breslau, 7 Mar. 1919.

[42] *Reichsgesetzblatt*, 1918, 1143–6. See also StdALu, Nr. 3542: Geschäftsführer, Deutscher Städtetag, to Mitgliedsstädte des Deutschen Städtetages, 'Rundschreiben Nr. XI 1336/18 D Betr. Unterbringung der Heeresangehörigen während der Demobilmachung', Berlin, 16 Nov. 1918. However, local authorities were not necessarily keen to use the powers granted them by

and despite the concerns expressed in November 1918, local authorities appear to have been surprisingly successful in providing emergency accommodation—perhaps because so many soldiers had set out for home on their own.

Nevertheless, in other respects the wartime fears proved justified. With the collapse of the German army and the sudden return of the soldiers, the full scale of the housing shortage which had been building up during the war years became painfully apparent. The main pressure on the housing market came from the rapid establishment of hundreds of thousands of new households. Beginning in February and peaking in October and November, there was a predictable surge in the number of marriages in Germany in 1919.[43] The establishment of new households in the wake of the First World War was not a consequence of a single orgy of marriages in the spring of 1919, however; rather the post-war wave of marriages appears to have been somewhat staggered, which meant a considerable and steadily increasing demand for housing through 1919 and 1920, as more and more couples married and sought dwellings of their own. Not surprisingly, many couples reunited after November 1918 or married in 1919 and 1920 found it necessary to live with parents or in-laws.[44] This increased tensions in many households, and the arrival of children frequently made already cramped living-quarters even more difficult to tolerate. Many cities experienced a rapid increase in their population in the years immediately after the War, as soldiers returned, couples had children, refugees sought new homes, and people searched for urban employment—thus putting added pressure on overstretched housing-markets.[45]

Another development which affected Germany's housing problem was a drop in the *size* of households after the War. This meant that growth of the *number* of households outstripped the growth of the population in general, which in turn meant that even where the population held fairly stable or actually fell, there could be additional pressure for housing during the demobilization period.[46] Between 1910 and 1925 the average size of German households diminished by roughly 10 per cent, from 4.53 persons to 4.07.[47]

the decree of 23 Sept., preferring persuasion and voluntary co-operation, and turning to compulsion only as a last resort. See e.g. StdADu, no. 604/29, fos. 3–4: Demobilmachungsausschuß to Oberbürgermeister in Duisburg, Dortmund, 7 May 1919.

[43] Statistisches Reichsamt (ed.), *Statistik des Deutschen Reichs*, vol. cclxxvi, p. xvii. See also Thüringisches Statistisches Landesamt (ed.), *Statistisches Handbuch für das Land Thüringen, 1922*, 44.

[44] See e.g. reports in StdALu, no. 6360.

[45] The population of Duisburg, for example, rose by 25,557 (11.1%) between Dec. 1910 and Apr. 1921; more than half of this increase, 13,275, came in the eighteen months between Oct. 1919 and Apr. 1921. See StdADu, no. 604/12, fo. 1: response to a questionnaire sent by the Deutscher Städtetag on 11 May 1921; *Statistisches Jahrbuch für das Deutsche Reich 1926* (Berlin, 1926), 8. In Apr. 1921 the number of people looking for a flat in Duisburg was recorded as 10,189.

[46] See *Verhandlungen der Sozialisierungs-Kommission*, i. 59.

[47] See Anker, 'Die Wohnungszwangswirtschaft', 35.

Much of this decline occurred after the War. (That is to say, it appears not to have been a statistical consequence of the loss of territories and their populations to France, Belgium, Denmark, and Poland.) War casualties affected figures for the total population more than the number of households, since the families of fallen soldiers often continued to require dwellings of their own. Furthermore, the couples who flocked to the altar after the War proved less inclined to establish large families than their pre-war counterparts. The number of children born to each married couple dropped markedly after the War, part of a longer-term demographic trend towards smaller families. Whereas during the period 1910–12, 49 per cent of married couples had three or more children, during 1919–21 this figure was only 37 per cent; at the same time the proportion with either no children or just one child rose from 29 per cent to 39 per cent.[48] Due to the decline in births during the War and to the tendency to have fewer children, the proportion of the population comprised by children under 10 years old was significantly lower during the post-war years than before 1914, and the proportion of young adults (i.e. of people who wanted to live independently) was higher.[49] Thus both the immediate demographic consequences of the War and longer-term demographic trends in Germany combined to exacerbate the problems of an already extremely tight housing-market.

The difficulties posed by the reduced size of households can be seen from the changes which occurred in specific cities after the War. In Heidelberg, for example, only a small increase in population was registered between 1910 and 1919, from 56,016 to 59,832 (an increase of 6.8 per cent); however, the number of households grew at more than double the rate of the city's population, from 12,278 to 14,194 (an increase of 15.6 per cent).[50] In nearby Mannheim, which experienced a greater growth in population during the second decade of the twentieth century, the same trend could be seen. While the city's population grew by 10.3 per cent, the number of households grew by 20.9 per cent, reflecting the reduction in the average size of a household from 4.58 to 4.18. According to the city's Statistical Office, these figures contained 'the key to answering the question, so often posed in amazement, why there should be a shortage of housing everywhere despite the loss of millions of people in the War'. 'The housing shortage,' it went on, 'prevails mainly because, while the average size of household is smaller, the number of households has become very much greater and in general every household needs a flat, even if the number of its members is small.'[51]

---

[48] Table in Peter Marschalck, *Bevölkerungsgeschichte Deutschlands im 19. und 20. Jahrhundert* (Frankfurt/Main, 1984), 158.

[49] For details of this change in Munich, see M. H. Geyer, 'Wohnungsnot und Wohnungs-zwangswirtschaft', 135–6.

[50] Hermann Mächtel, 'Wohnungsverhältnisse und Wohnungspolitik der Stadt Heidelberg' (Univ. of Heidelberg, Phil. diss., 1923), 57.

[51] *Verwaltungsbericht der badischen Hauptstadt Mannheim für 1919/1920*, 3.

The pressures upon the post-war German housing-market may be illustrated by looking at the specific case of Bochum. Bochum differed from many German cities in that a large proportion of its adult male population had remained there during the War to work in vital industries and, as a consequence, its total population actually grew between 1914 and 1918. However, it was affected by many of the same problems which shaped the housing market elsewhere, as may be seen from data tabulated by the city's Statistical Office (see Tables 20–3).

Table 20. *The Housing Market in Bochum, 1913–1923*

| Year | Residential Buildings | Flats | Households | Population | Household Size |
|------|------------|-------|-----------|-----------|------|
| 1913 | 7,448 | 29,957[a] | 29,434 | 145,076 | 4.93 |
| 1914 | 7,519 | | 29,578 | 143,176 | 4.84 |
| 1915 | 7,519 | | 29,531 | 144,472 | 4.89 |
| 1916 | 7,517 | 32,072 | 30,109 | 146,251 | 4.86 |
| 1917 | 7,517 | 31,132 | 30,107 | 143,790 | 4.78 |
| 1918 | 7,515 | 30,963 | 30,252 | 140,928 | 4.66 |
| 1919 | 7,538 | | 30,923 | 142,787 | 4.62 |
| 1920 | 7,632 | | 31,697 | 148,263 | 4.68 |
| 1921 | 7,983 | | 32,976 | 156,157 | 4.74 |
| 1922 | 8,280 | | 33,668 | 159,060 | 4.72 |
| 1923 | 8,638 | | 35,118 | 156,224 | 4.45 |

[a] Figure for 1912.
*Source*: Statistisches und Wahlamt der Stadt Bochum (ed.), *Wohnungszählung in der Stadt Bochum, am 10. Oktober 1935*, 7–8.

Table 21. *Increase in Dwelling-Units in Bochum, 1918–1924*

| Year | Newly Constructed Residential Buildings | New Flats |
|------|------------------------|-----------|
| 1918 | 1 | 1 |
| 1919 | 2 | 26 |
| 1920 | 82 | 750 |
| 1921 | 188 | 518 |
| 1922 | 289 | 721 |
| 1923 | 208 | 526 |
| 1924 | 93 | 301 |

*Source*: Statistisches und Wahlamt der Stadt Bochum (ed.), *Wohnungszählung in der Stadt Bochum, am 10. Oktober 1935*, 11.

From these tables, two general points arise. First, the figures for population turnover suggest an extraordinarily fluid post-war housing-market. Many more people were moving about—in 1919 nearly one-fifth of the city's population left and nearly one-fifth were new arrivals!—than would be the

Table 22. *Marriages in Bochum, 1918–1922*

| | |
|---|---|
| 1918 | 879 |
| 1919 | 1819 |
| 1920 | 2228 |
| 1921 | 2117 |
| 1922 | 19797 |

*Source*: Statistisches und Wahlamt der Stadt Bochum (ed.), *Wohnungszählung in der Stadt Bochum, am 10. Oktober 1935*, 12.

Table 23. *Population Turnover in Bochum, 1918–1927*

| Year | Arrivals | Departures |
|---|---|---|
| 1918 | 22,407 | 27,194 |
| 1919 | 27,980 | 28,998 |
| 1920 | 28,308 | 26,934 |
| 1921 | 28,026 | 24,674 |
| 1922 | 25,883 | 24,970 |
| 1923 | 13,680 | 19,370 |
| 1924 | 12,601 | 17,525 |
| 1925 | 15,670 | 17,037 |
| 1926 | 14,237 | 14,886 |
| 1927 | 19,902 | 19,599 |

*Source*: Statistisches und Wahlamt der Stadt Bochum (ed.), *Wohnungszählung in der Stadt Bochum, am 10. Oktober 1935*, 13.

case during the mid-1920s.[52] Second, during the years immediately after the War Bochum saw a substantial increase in the number of households, which was matched only partially and belatedly by an increase in the housing supply. During 1919, when the mass of the soldiers returned and the post-war marriage-boom began, almost no new dwellings were made available. This exacerbated the chronic shortage of housing, as the supply of dwellings continued to lag behind demand during the entire period of demobilization and inflation: while the number of households in the city increased by 4,866 between 1918 and 1923, the number of flats increased by only 2,843. Yet the growing gap between housing supply and demand formed only part of the problem. The fact that the number of marriages during 1919 and 1920 exceeded by a considerable margin the recorded increase in the number of households suggests that economic and housing pressures compelled a significant proportion of newly married

[52] These mobility figures were still not as high as comparable figures for the city around the turn of the century; in 1900 arrivals into Bochum were the equivalent of nearly 29% of the city's population, and departures more than 25%. See David F. Crew, *Town in the Ruhr: A Social History of Bochum, 1860–1914* (New York, 1979), 61.

couples to share dwellings with parents or relatives.[53] Furthermore, in March 1921 the Bochum Housing Office claimed that '1,533 [presumably couples, although this was not made explicit] are waiting for a flat so that they can *marry*'.[54]

Further pressure on the housing market (not reflected in the statistics from Bochum) came from refugees. After the War hundreds of thousands of German refugees flooded in from the former eastern Prussian provinces which became parts of newly independent Poland,[55] from Alsace-Lorraine, from those parts of Germany which had been placed under Allied occupation. The refugees tended to congregate in cities and in regions bordering those they had left, adding to the demand for scarce low-priced housing. The strain on the housing market created by the refugees was supplemented by further waves of people let loose on to German civil society and expecting somewhere to live: the reduction in the size of the German army, as demanded by the Allies, meant that men who would previously have been housed in military garrisons now had to be housed privately; and during late 1919 and 1920 hundreds of thousands of war prisoners were released from Allied captivity and did not expect that the 'thanks of the Fatherland' should involve sleeping rough.

Perhaps more than anything else, during the demobilization period the German housing-market was shaped by continuing inflation. Due to the imposition of rent controls, rises in the price of rented accommodation had fallen far behind rises in the prices of most other goods. This meant that, according to calculations of the Reich Statistical Office, in February 1920 the average nominal cost of housing was 1.67 times the 1913–14 figures; in contrast, the cost of food stood at 9.48 times and the general cost-of-living index stood at 8.47 times the 1913–14 figures.[56] According to calculations of the Factory Inspectorate in Lennep, the average rent for a two-room flat had increased by only 38.7 per cent, for a three-room flat by 31.7 per cent, for a four-room flat by 38.5 per cent, and for larger flats by 46.2 per cent between 1913 and the end of 1919[57]—at a time when the general cost of

---

[53] e.g. the administration of one small community near Bochum reported at the end of Dec. 1918 that 'many people married during the War are still living temporarily with their parents for reasons of economy'. See StdABo, KrA 707: Amtmann, Amt Hordel, to Demobilmachungs-ausschuß des Landkreises Bochum, Bochum, 28 Dec. 1918.

[54] StdABo, B 153: Wohnungsamt to Magistrat, Bochum, 14 Mar. 1921.

[55] e.g. from the Border Province of Posen and West Prussia it was reported that in 1920 the pressure of refugees meant that in the towns sometimes 6–8 people had to live together in a single small room, and in rural areas rail cars were used as emergency accommodation for refugees. See APP, Rejencja w Pile, no. 2477: 'Jahresgesundheitsbericht 1920'.

[56] Statistisches Reichsamt, *Zahlen zur Geldentwertung in Deutschland 1914 bis 1923* (*Wirtschaft und Statistik*, 5, Sonderheft 1; Berlin, 1925), 33. See also Carl-Ludwig Holtfrerich, *The German Inflation 1914–1923: Causes and Effects in International Perspective* (Berlin and New York, 1986), 28–44.

[57] HStAD, Reg. Düsseldorf, no. 34345: Gewerbeinspektor zu Lennep für die Kreise Lennep und Remscheid, 'Jahresbericht für 1919', Lennep, 9 Feb. 1920.

living was roughly eight times the pre-war level. In Munich, rents in early 1920 were, in real terms, less than one-fifth what they had been before the War; in early 1922 they were less than one-tenth, and by the beginning of 1923 they were only about one-fiftieth of 'peace time rents' in real terms.[58] By the end of 1922 the general cost of living, as compared to 1913–14, had risen more than forty times as fast as housing costs (essentially rent).

Rent controls at a time of rapid inflation transferred wealth from landlords to tenants. Although many no doubt profited by having their mortgage costs reduced, landlords often found themselves in a difficult position. Rents were held down but the costs of owning property—insurance, property tax, sewerage and rubbish-disposal fees, wages for building-superintendents, the cost of water, cleaning, chimney-sweeps, repair work—continued to rise.[59] This had a number of detrimental consequences. On the one hand, it clearly reduced the incentive for owners of flats to offer them for rent, and made state intervention or the threat of intervention necessary to force dwellings on to the rental market. On the other hand, the swiftly rising cost of repairs, set against controlled rents, led some landlords to allow their properties to fall into serious disrepair.[60]

For the lucky tenants in rent-controlled flats, the picture looked very different. As nominal wages and salaries rose far more rapidly than did rents, housing claimed a smaller and smaller proportion of the household budget. Whereas previously the monthly rent had often gobbled up a week's wages, by 1920 workers often needed to pay out only a day's wages per month for housing.[61] Surveying the post-war housing-market in 1921, Professor Pohle of the University of Leipzig observed that 'among large sections of the population, which were previously accustomed to spending 12 per cent, 15 per cent or an even greater percentage of their income on rent, the amount required for housing has now sunk to 5 per cent of income or even less'. He went on to accuse tenants, 'especially in the lower income brackets' of having 'used the saving for increased consumption'.[62] Robert Kuczynski, the head of the Statistical Office in Schöneberg, calculated the minimum weekly expenditure of a four-person family in Berlin during the early 1920s and concluded that, while this hypothetical family needed to spend 5.5 Marks on housing out of a weekly expenditure of 28.8 Marks in 1913–14, in February 1920 the comparable figures stood at 8 Marks out of 254, and in December 1921 at 10 Marks out of 557.[63] In a study of metal workers' wages in the Kiel docks during the inflation, Hildegard Heuer determined

[58] See the table in M. H. Geyer, 'Wohnungsnot und Wohnungszwangswirtschaft', 145.

[59] See *Verhandlungen der Sozialisierungs-Kommission*, i. 176–7, 195.

[60] Ibid. ii. 103, 113–16, 124.

[61] BLHA, Rep. 30 Berlin C, Polizeipräsidium Berlin, Tit. 47, no. 1959, fos. 173–4: 'Jahresbericht für das Jahr 1920. Aufsichtsbezirk Berlin'.

[62] Pohle, 'Die Wohnungsfrage', 234.

[63] Holtfrerich, *The German Inflation*, 40–1.

that whereas rent comprised 24 per cent of total expenditure in 1914, it swallowed only 5 per cent in April 1921, 3.1 per cent in January 1922, 2.4 per cent in April 1922, and 0.9 per cent in October 1922.[64] Middle-class families also saw their real housing-costs plummet (see Table 24).

Table 24. *Rent as a % of the Expenditure of a German Three- Person Household, 1913–1922* (middle-ranking salaried employee)

| | |
|---|---|
| 1913/14 | 27.1 |
| 1914/15 | 22.4 |
| 1915/16 | 21.4 |
| 1916/17 | 18.1 |
| 1917/18 | 17.7 |
| 1918/19 | 13.1 |
| 1919/20 | 6.8 |
| 1920/21 | 4.3 |
| 1921/22 | 2.3 |

*Source*: Carl-Ludwig Holtfrerich, *The German Inflation 1914–1923: Causes and Effects in International Perspective* (Berlin and New York, 1986), 261.

Not only did the inflation cause rent virtually to disappear as a major item of expenditure; for owner-occupiers it also meant a reduction and then the virtual elimination of mortgage payments. As a consequence, many Germans were left with a much higher proportion of income to spend on other items, particularly food.[65]

As returning soldiers were generally able to find work fairly quickly and real wages rose during the early phase of demobilization, the extremely low rents meant that housing did not pose a serious financial burden for most Germans after the War. The major challenge was gaining access to a dwelling, not paying for it. Housing was rationed by scarcity, not price, and this made the post-war housing-shortages, if anything, even worse than they would otherwise have been. Not only did it make property owners reluctant to offer dwellings for rent; since rents were so low, there was also little financial pressure upon tenants who (perhaps because of war losses in their households) no longer needed a large flat to move to a smaller one. Perhaps even more importantly, low rents and rent controls left little incentive for the private building of new rented accommodation.

The combination of extreme housing-shortages and extremely low housing-costs was a key factor in shaping the popular experience of the post-war transition. However, it affected different groups in different ways. The winners in

[64] Hildegard Heuer, 'Die Entwicklung der Metallarbeiterlöhne auf den Kieler Werften (Deutsche Werke A.-G., Germaniawerft A.-G. und Howaldswerke) in der Zeit vom 1.4.1920 bis 30.10.1923' (Univ. of Kiel, Phil. diss., 1929), 29.
[65] e.g. food gobbled up more than half the white-collar workers' income after the War, while before 1914 it had taken less than one-third. See Holtfrerich, *The German Inflation*, 261.

the post-war housing-market tended to be the established households, who generally had little difficulty on the housing front; those who had a place to live were usually able to remain in their dwellings and benefit from the steep real decline in rent. This in effect formed an indirect incomes policy, and left some people with a fair amount of money in their pockets. At the same time, rent controls gave great scope for profiteering, for subletting rent-controlled flats at high rents and pocketing the difference.[66] This practice often disadvantaged those who could least afford housing, while it gave some official tenants of rent-controlled flats extra income. The losers in the post-war housing-market tended to be those who, for whatever reason, had to find a new place to live—in particular recently married couples looking for a dwelling of their own.

The German housing-market during the demobilization period was affected profoundly by state intervention—intervention which unambiguously favoured the interests of consumers (tenants) rather than producers (landlords). During 1918 and 1919 it was clear that a precipitate return to a free market in housing would lead to huge increases in rent levels, and therefore was not politically acceptable. Consequently a broad consensus formed that rents had to be controlled and the prerogatives of landlords curtailed during the post-war transition.[67] Consequently, after the War not only did the state regulate rent increases; as outlined above, it also circumscribed the rights of landlords in how they could dispose of their property, intervening in a sphere which before 1914 had essentially been a matter of private contract between landlord and tenant, and met with the predictable hostility of property owners.

It was characteristic of this state intervention that measures intended to be of limited duration remained in place for years. One good example is the wartime protection given to soldiers against eviction and legal writs over accumulated debt, which was extended again and again through 1919, 1920, and 1921.[68] Rent controls too proved far easier to introduce than to remove. The various states introduced rent-control decrees during 1919. Bavaria was particularly quick off the mark, when at the end of April the government of Johannes Hoffmann (while in 'exile' in Bamberg during the period of the Munich 'Soviet' Republic) introduced decrees to combat 'unwarranted rent increases' and the 'housing shortage'.[69] Rent increases in Bavaria had to be approved by the local authorities; rental contracts already entered into could be dissolved if the rents were judged to be excessive; all new rental contracts

---

[66] *Verhandlungen der Sozialisierungs-Kommission*, ii. 124.

[67] See M. H. Geyer, 'Wohnungsnot und Wohnungszwangswirtschaft', 139–40.

[68] See GStAB, Rep. 84a, no. 1764; *Reichsgesetzblatt* 1918, 1427–8: 'Verordnung zum Schutze der Kriegsteilnehmer gegen Zwangsvollstreckungen vom 18. Dezember 1918'; ibid. 1919, 521–2: 'Verordnung zum Schutze der Kriegsteilnehmer gegen Zwangsvollstreckungen vom 17. Juni 1918'; ibid. 1920, 2162–3: 'Gesetz zum Schutze der Kriegsteilnehmer gegen Zwangsvollstreckungen vom 22. Dezember 1920'.

[69] See M. H. Geyer, 'Wohnungsnot und Wohnungszwangswirtschaft', 130–1.

had to be approved by the housing offices; and if necessary flats could be seized and subdivided. The Prussian government acted in December 1919, when the Minister for Welfare, Adam Stegerwald, introduced regulations (based upon the authority granted by the Reich legislation of September 1918) obligating local authorities in Prussia to limit rents and fix percentage rent increases.[70]

The legal framework for state involvement in housing was set throughout the Reich with three major pieces of legislation during the early 1920s.[71] The first was the 'Law on Measures against the Housing Shortage' (Gesetz zur Maßnahmen gegen den Wohnungsmangel) of 11 May 1920. This law, which was revised repeatedly between May 1920 and July 1923, prohibited the demolition of buildings or the conversion of residential property for commercial purposes, required landlords to advertise all vacancies, empowered local authorities to seize large or empty flats and fill them to 'capacity', and allowed local housing administrations to requisition flats and compel landlords to let them to homeless families. Although this in effect confirmed measures already being taken by local government, it fixed a nationwide framework for intervention in landlord–tenant relations. The second important piece of national post-war legislation on housing was the Reich Rent Law (Reichsmietengesetz) of 24 March 1922, which imposed rent control on all housing built before 1 July 1918. This too provided a nationwide framework for action already being taken regionally and locally, and in effect acted as a disincentive to efforts to increase the housing stock. With new housing exempted from rent controls, escalating building-costs and high interest rates (for extremely scarce credit) ensured that rents for any new dwellings would be high while those for the rest remained ridiculously low, which undermined the financial basis of any private investment in housing.[72] The third component of this legislative troika passed during the inflation period was the Reich Law on Tenant Protection and Rent Settlement Offices (Reichsgesetz über Mieterschutz und Mieteinigungsämter) of 15 May 1923, which effectively removed the right of landlords throughout Germany to evict tenants (and did little to make being a German landlord more attractive). Designed to prevent property owners from taking advantage of housing shortages rather than to increase the housing stock substantially, this legislation served to make the state, rather than the market, the final arbiter in landlord–tenant relations.[73]

---

[70] *Preußische Gesetzsammlung*, 1919, 187–94: 'Anordnung des Ministers für Volkswohlfahrt betreffend Einführung einer Höchstgrenze für Mietzinssteigerungen. Vom 9. Dezember 1919'. See also Pohle, 'Die Wohnungsfrage', 234.

[71] See Anker, 'Die Wohnungszwangswirtschaft', 18–19; Preller, *Sozialpolitik in der Weimarer Republik*, 286–8; Silverman, 'A Pledge Unredeemed', 117–19.

[72] In addition to the studies cited above, see also Pohle, 'Die Wohnungsfrage', 234.

[73] It should be noted that not all housing was covered by the legislation. One important category not covered was housing of agricultural workers (*Deputatleute* or *Deputatarbeiter*), which were classified as *Werkswohnungen*. This, of course, gave agricultural employers—particularly in eastern Germany—considerable leverage over their work-force. See e.g. PLA, Rep. 65c, no. 944, fos. 117–19: Landrat to Oberpräsident in Stettin, Franzburg, 7 Dec. 1921.

Another manifestation of state intervention was the attempt to restrict residential mobility. Although Germans' freedom of movement had been guaranteed in law in 1867 (and reiterated in the Weimar Constitution), the right of Germans to live where they chose was in fact curtailed after the War. Urban politicians and administrators displayed a sometimes hysterical but none the less understandable concern to prevent large numbers of people congregating in the large cities looking for work (and stirring up unrest) and putting intolerable pressure upon already tight housing-markets. Consequently, they made great efforts to ensure that ex-soldiers moved on to their home communities. In many cases local authorities banned immigration into their towns.[74] Restrictive regulations issued by local authorities and Demobilisation Committees, and discriminatory practices such as refusing to distribute food-ration cards to those without a local residence (reinforced by public warnings, including notices placed in newspapers in other cities, posters placed in railway stations), in effect suspended legal freedom of movement in large parts of Germany after the First World War.[75] It is doubtful, however, whether these measures really did much to hinder movement into towns or whether they helped at all to relieve urban housing problems. They were responses to local political pressure, not part of a considered housing-policy, and during the months after the military collapse and political revolution local authorities' control over the comings and goings of Germans was limited.

Nevertheless, armed with the new legislation, city housing offices greatly increased their importance, activity, and staff after the War. They not only inspected dwellings and compiled statistics which supply a basis for our knowledge of the post-war housing situation, but also provided housing agencies, were responsible for controlling migration into cities and for allotting newly completed flats (both public and private) to tenants, advised property-owners and tenants on matters concerning the rental contract, and secured furniture and bedding for the poor.[76] Furthermore, municipal

[74] This happened, e.g., in Nürnberg in Mar. 1919. See Eric. G. Reiche, *The Development of the SA in Nürnberg 1922–1934* (Cambridge, 1986), 11. It also occurred in small towns. See e.g. APS, Landratsamt Randow, no. 1716, fo. 85: Magistrat to Kreissiedlungsgesellschaft in Stettin, Pölitz in Pommern, 8 July 1919. Not all demands for such restrictions were granted, however. In Frankfurt/Main, Ludwig Landmann's repeated attempts during 1919 to secure a ban on immigration into the city were rejected by the city's housing commissar, who argued that to deny entry to the thousands of refugees expelled from Alsace-Lorraine would be politically unacceptable. See Dieter Rebentisch, *Ludwig Landmann*, 98; for details of the stream of refugees coming from Alsace-Lorraine to and through Frankfurt, see Hans Drüner, *Im Schatten des Weltkrieges: Zehn Jahre Frankfurter Geschichte von 1914–24* (Frankfurt/Main, 1934), 350.

[75] See Albert Gut, 'Die Entwicklung des Wohnungswesens in Deutschland nach dem Weltkriege', in Albert Gut (ed.), *Der Wohnungsbau in Deutschland nach dem Weltkriege: Seine Entwicklung unter der unmittelbaren und mittelbaren Förderung durch die deutschen Gemeindeverwaltungen* (Munich, 1928), 39.

[76] A good description of the tasks and accomplishments of a municipal housing office during 1919 and 1920 may be found in StdALu, no. 3542: Bürgermeisteramt to Regierung der Pfalz, Kammer des Innern, in Speyer, 'Wohnungsverhältnisse in Ludwigshafen a./Rhein', Ludwigs-

government made public land available for housing construction, helped to finance the infrastructure for new dwellings (i.e. connecting new buildings to gas, water, and electricity supply) and took on a central role in the financing of housing construction as escalating costs and an uncertain financial climate made building possible only with public subsidy. With the promise of considerable financial aid from the Reich and state governments, local authorities prompted building activity which, with construction costs rising and rents held down, would not otherwise have been initiated.[77] According to the provisions of the Bundesrat decree of 31 October 1918, the Reich government would pay one-half and the state governments one-third of the building costs of approved projects over and above what these would have been before the War, with local government paying the remaining one-sixth. For the first time central funds were channelled into locally administered building projects (the costs of which continually escalated), stimulating a construction industry which would otherwise have had few contracts.

Yet despite considerable state intervention, little could be done in the short term to dent the housing shortage. The state subsidies to compensate for increased construction costs often served more to enrich builders than to unleash a wave of new building activity, and in 1920 the basis for state aid was changed from grants to low-interest loans (at roughly half the commercial rates).[78] In order to finance aid for housing construction, in mid-1921 the Reichstag approved a rent tax (on housing built before 1 July 1918). This proved a failure, as galloping inflation made it impossible adequately to finance construction and rapidly eroded the funds available, although it did foreshadow the rent tax (*Hauszinssteuer*) introduced in February 1924, which helped to finance the impressive programme of housing construction of the later 1920s.

Not surprisingly, housing became a distinctly unrewarding area of local government. Housing offices had to carry out unpopular tasks such as forcing property owners to let flats and removing families from dwellings they were occupying illegally, while they had no real prospect of solving the underlying problem.[79] Property owners were angered by the limits imposed on the rents they could charge; employers criticized restrictions on mobility, which made attracting much-needed labour more difficult and, in effect, made labour

hafen/Rhein, 19 June 1920. An additional task before the Ludwigshafen housing office was making flats available for the families of officers and civil servants with the French forces occupying the city. As of June 1920, 91 flats had been provided for the French and an additional 40 were required. See also Albert Gut, *Bericht über die Maßnahmen der Stadtgemeinde München zur Bekämpfung der Wohnungsnot und über die Tätigkeit des Münchener Wohnungsamtes* (Munich, 1920) (copy in Stadtarchiv Ludwigshafen, no. 3542).

[77] See *Die Maßnahmen der Stadt Ludwigshafen*, 8–9.

[78] See M. H. Geyer, ' Wohnungsnot und Wohnungszwangswirtschaft', 153; Silverman, 'A Pledge Unredeemed', 120–3.

[79] See *Verhandlungen der Sozialisierungs-Kommission*, i. 10; Rebentisch, *Ludwig Landmann*, 98.

more expensive; workers disliked being prevented from moving house as they wished; and housing offices inevitably attracted criticism because the housing shortage remained acute no matter what they did.[80] Illustrative of the inability of public authorities to make significant inroads into the housing shortages were proposals by local communities to build municipal or co-operative housing estates (*Siedlungen*). Town administrations worked together with state governments and building co-operatives to provide capital for housing projects.[81] But these were essentially long-term measures, and the effect they had upon the post-war housing-crisis was limited.[82] The length of time necessary before such projects could be completed, the difficulties created by the inflation, particularly for housing co-operatives struggling to finance projects,[83] and the vastness of the housing shortages meant that such initiatives could not have any significant impact during the demobilization period.[84] Altogether, the attempts by state authorities to respond to the housing crisis were probably significant more for how they altered percep-tions of the German state's legitimate responsibilities than for their contribu-tion towards solving the underlying problem.

That underlying problem was enormous. Nationally the housing shortage was estimated to be as high as 1.5 million dwellings in 1919–20, and in late 1920 the Reich Statistical Office pegged it at 1.4 million; against this, the net gain in housing units (as a consequence of renovation and new building) was a mere 56,664 in 1919 and 103,092 in 1920 (see Table 25). The worst shortages were in the cities, although smaller towns were not immune. In the city of Hamburg, which had had 15,159 flats (5.6 per cent of the total stock) empty in 1914, only 1,794 (0.7 per cent) were empty in 1919 and a

[80] See M. H. Geyer, 'Wohnungsnot und Wohnungszwangswirtschaft', 137–8. In Munich the housing office achieved such unpopularity that during 1921 and 1922 the police repeatedly declined to protect it from vandalism.

[81] For Berlin, see Bey-Heard, *Hauptstadt und Staatsumwälzung*, 121–2.

[82] Because of their long-term character, these measures were criticized by the Workers' Councils, which in Berlin called for the take-over by the city of rental property and building co-operatives. See Bey-Heard, *Hauptstadt und Staatsumwälzung*, 121–2.

[83] For an example of the problems involved in raising the money to meet escalating building-costs, see the correspondence relating to the 'Gemeinnützige Baugenossenschaft für Volks- und Kriegerheimstätten, Heidelberg', in StdAHd, 281/53,1. This co-operative was founded in mid-1918, and was able to complete 174 flats by the end of 1920 (with another 42 flats under way), but only due to loans periodically made available by the Heidelberg city administration. See ibid., fos. 261–3: Badischer Verband gemeinnützige Bauvereinigung zu Gemeinnützige Baugenossenschaft für Volks- und Kriegerheimstätten Heidelberg G.m.b.H., 'Revisionsbericht', copy sent to the Stadtrat in Heidelberg, Heidelberg, 11 May 1921.

[84] e.g. the local administration of Langendreer, to the east of Bochum, reported in Dec. 1921 that the 70 dwellings built there by the Miners' Housing Association (*Bergmannssiedlung*) and the 16 flats built by the town had done little to improve matters. During 1921 there had been 380 marriages in the town and during 1921 to Dec. there had been 362. See StdABo, KrA 581: Amt Langendreer, Langendreer, 12 Dec. 1921. At that time Langendreer had 29,000 inhabitants, a figure which—according to the town government—was a considerable increase over the number recorded in Oct. 1919.

Table 25. *Housing Production in Germany, 1919–1925*

| Year | Increase in dwellings | | | Decrease | Net increase | Total housing units at end of year |
|---|---|---|---|---|---|---|
| | New Building | Renovation | Total | | | |
| 1919 | 35,596 | 25,265 | 60,861 | 4,197 | 56,664 | 13,945,000 |
| 1920 | 75,928 | 32,379 | 108,307 | 5,215 | 103,092 | 14,048,000 |
| 1921 | 108,596 | 32,902 | 141,498 | 7,275 | 134,223 | 14,187,000 |
| 1922 | 124,273 | 30,697 | 154,970 | 8,355 | 146,615 | 14,329,000 |
| 1923 | 100,401 | 25,239 | 125,640 | 7,607 | 118,033 | 14,447,000 |
| 1924 | 94,807 | 20,569 | 115,376 | 8,874 | 106,502 | 14,554,000 |
| 1925 | 164,383 | 27,429 | 191,812 | 12,882 | 178,930 | 14,733,000 |

*Source*: Peter-Christian Witt, 'Inflation, Wohnungszwangswirtschaft und Hauszinssteuer: Zur Regelung von Wohnungsbau und Wohnungsmarkt in der Weimaer Republik', in Lutz Niethammer (ed.), *Wohnen im Wandel: Beiträge zur Geschichte des Alltags in der bürgerlichen Gesellschaft* (Wuppertal, 1979), 400.

mere 468 (0.2 per cent) empty in 1920.[85] In Ludwigshafen the municipal Statistical Office calculated, on the basis of the census taken on 8 October 1919, that—even before the expected return of the prisoners of war—there were 1,379 fewer dwellings in the city than there were households, and in June 1920 the municipal administration calculated the shortage of dwellings in the city as 1,587.[86] In neighbouring Heidelberg the municipal housing office claimed in March 1919 that the supply of flats 'stands in no relation to the extraordinary demand at the present time';[87] and two months later the position was reported as worse still.[88] In the Ruhr the lack of available housing restricted attempts to attract people from elsewhere in order to provide labour desperately needed in the mines.[89] From Neubrandenburg the city administration complained in October 1919 that, despite all the measures it had taken in accordance with the legislation of September 1918, the housing shortage in the city had become 'even greater' in the interim.[90] In December 1919 the local surveyor's office in the small Baltic port of

[85] Karin Hagemann, *Frauenalltag und Männerpolitik: Alltagsleben und gesellschaftliches Handeln von Arbeiterfrauen in der Weimarer Republik* (Bonn, 1990), 61.

[86] The number of households stood at 21,365—up from 20,001 in 1917 and 17,803 in 1910—whereas the number of dwellings was 19,986. See StdALu, no. 1510: Statistisches Amt der Stadt Ludwigshafen am Rhein to Bürgermeisteramt, Ludwigshafen am Rhein, 3 Nov. 1919; ibid., no. 3542: Bürgermeisteramt to Regierung der Pfalz, Kammer des Innern, in Speyer, Ludwigshafen am Rhein, 19 June 1920.

[87] StdAHd, no. 278,8: Städtisches Wohnungsamt, Heidelberg, 12 Mar. 1919.

[88] Ibid. 2 May 1919.

[89] StdABo, KrA 707: Amt Harpen, Landkreis Bochum, to Demobilmachungsausschuß für den Landkreis Bochum, Gerthe, 24 Dec. 1918; Jürgen Tampke, *The Ruhr and Revolution: The Revolutionary Movement in the Rhenish-Westphalian Industrial Region 1912–1919* (London, 1979), 146.

[90] MLHA, Mecklenburg-Strelitzer Ministerium, Abteilung des Innern, no. 5071, fo. 48: Magistrat to Meckl.-Strelitzische Landesregierung, Abtlg. des Innern, Neubrandenburg, 25 Oct. 1919.

Wismar catalogued the factors—the need to provide housing for returning veterans who had married during the War, the post-war wave of marriages, the influx of refugees from territories lost to Germany—which meant that the housing problem had not been reduced 'despite all the measures we have taken'.[91] Small towns and large cities alike faced housing shortages which it was far beyond their ability to overcome, despite the impressive array of new powers at their disposal.

Not only did the housing problem defy all attempts at solution in the immediate aftermath of the War; it also persisted during the early 1920s and was no less serious in the countryside than in the cities. Building activity (both new building and the maintenance and repair of existing housing) remained depressed; houses often fell into disrepair; owners of vacant properties had little incentive to let them, since rent levels were held so low; better provision of food drew people to the countryside and exacerbated rural housing-shortages; refugees, particularly from the lost eastern territories, continued to put pressure on the housing market and sometimes had to be housed in former army and prisoner-of-war barracks, or even in railway carriages;[92] flats suitable for large families with small incomes remained in short supply; and the shortage of suitable housing was given as one reason why it proved so difficult to attract German workers on to the land after the First World War.[93] During the early 1920s newly married couples continued to have great difficulty in finding a dwelling of their own; over-crowding remained common, and poor housing continued to affect people's health adversely; lack of housing continued to prevent workers from moving to areas where they were desperately needed. And in 1923 and 1924 the ravages of hyperinflation and a harsh currency-stabilization made matters even worse, as building activity was depressed further and 'flats for people with tuberculosis, families with many children, and families known to be bad payers' became 'scarcely available'.[94]

For families with large numbers of children or with a reputation as 'bad payers'—usually proletarian households—and, obviously, refugees, gaining

---

[91] MLHA, Mecklenburg-Schweriner Landeswohnungsamt, no. 21, fo. 149: Stadtbauamt der Seestadt Wismar i.M. to Landeswohnungsamt, Wismar, 16 Dec. 1919. The Surveyor's Office had just approved rent increases in the city of up to 40% of 'peace prices', i.e. of rents charged in 1914.

[92] This happened in 1921 in Frankfurt/Oder, which had received a large number of refugees from the east. See *Verhandlungen der Sozialisierungs-Kommission*, ii. 102–3. A description of the dreadful conditions in which refugees had to live in nearby Senftenberg may be found ibid. 105–6.

[93] A good description of the housing market in both urban and rural areas may be found in the report about conditions in the Regierungsbezirk Stralsund during 1921, in PLA, Rep. 65c. no. 2312, fos. 164–5: 'Gesundheitsbericht für den Regierungsbezirk Stralsund. Jahr 1921'. For a description of the poor housing available to agricultural workers in the district of Calau (to the west of Cottbus), including mention of one family which had to share its living-quarters with its pig, see *Verhandlungen der Sozialisierungs-Kommission*, ii. 116–19.

[94] PLA, Rep. 65c, no. 2312, fo. 410: 'Jahresbericht des Regierungs- und Medizinalrates in Stralsund für die Jahre 1923 und 1924'.

decent housing often proved the most difficult aspect of the post-war transition. Germany's impoverishment due to the War could be seen clearly in the deterioration of her housing stock and the severe housing-shortages. However, the burdens were not spread evenly through German society. Despite the commitment of the new republican goverments to promote social welfare, it was those at the bottom of the economic ladder, those least settled, and those who wanted to set up new households after the War, who had to bear most painfully the social costs of German participation in the First World War.

After the War it was sometimes argued, for example by some members of the Socialization Commission which met during late 1920 and 1921, that the post-war housing-crisis was a transitional phenomenon, which would eventually sort itself out.[95] Proponents of this argument pointed to the long-term decline of the German birth-rate, noted that the numbers of couples marrying would inevitably decline after the post-war peak, and stressed that the post-war influx of refugees was a temporary problem. Therefore in time the housing problem would begin to solve itself. To some extent this was true. Certainly the post-war housing-problem was *also* a problem of transition, of the additional pressure placed on the housing market by the return of the soldiers, the post-war marriage and baby boom, and the influx of refugees from Alsace-Lorraine and Poland. However, it is impossible to determine the extent to which Germany's housing problem would have solved itself once 'normal' times returned, if only because 'normal' times did not return. Demobilization and the post-war transition were followed by hyperinflation and then a harsh stabilization, itself followed a few years later by a depression which saw drastic cuts in housing construction. The state did not withdraw from the housing market; standards for what was regarded as acceptable housing rose;[96] and a quarter of a century later a bombed and devastated Germany faced a new housing-crisis of proportions unimaginable in 1919.

The fact that the housing market was shaped in large measure by long-term factors—the changing age-structure of the population and changing size of household, as well as the consequences of the stalled building-activity during the First World War—ensured that severe shortages remained long after 1918. Unlike employment, housing formed a sphere in which returning soldiers were often relatively disadvantaged—where the veterans of the trenches were more likely to face obstacles to adjusting to life in

---

[95] See the arguments presented by Hermann Luppe and Theodor Vogelstein among others, in *Verhandlungen der Sozialisierungs-Kommission*, ii. 15–17, 26–8, 31–2, 72–3. See also Silverman, 'A Pledge Unredeemed', 118–19.

[96] This was already apparent after the First World War, when working-class families frequently sought after larger and better-appointed flats. See *Verhandlungen der Sozialisierungs-Kommission*, ii. 110, for a description of the demand for such housing in Magdeburg.

post-war Germany than those who had stayed home. Of course there were exceptions, and wives and dependants of the former soldiers were no less affected by the housing shortages than were the men. But the problem was greatest among people who were unsettled, on the move, without an easy re-entry into domestic households. What made this problem particularly nasty and politically charged were the tremendous inequalities involved. While those who had adequate housing could pay rents which, in real terms, grew steadily smaller, those without decent housing found gaining access to this post-war bargain extremely difficult.

It was therefore to be expected that veterans' organizations would regard housing as a major problem facing their members and would seek preferential treatment for ex-soldiers and war invalids. Indeed, in the immediate aftermath of the Armistice it was not unknown for Workers' and Soldiers' Councils to try to prevent the eviction of returning soldiers from their flats.[97] The vocal Communist International League of War Disabled, War Veterans, and War Dependants (Internationaler Bund der Kriegsbeschädigten, Kriegsteilnehmer und Kriegshinterbliebenen) placed housing problems high on its propaganda agenda: demands were levelled at local authorities for the 'elimination of housing misery through the expropriation of villas and large flats for the benefit of the war victims', for a 'ban on rent increases and evictions', and for the 'granting of rent support to all needy war-invalids and dependants'.[98] Moral arguments were mobilized as housing became a major public concern and political rallying cry, although essentially there was little that interest groups acting on behalf of war victims could do to rectify the inequalities which characterized the post-war housing-market.

The post-war housing-crisis also amplified worries about an alleged decline in moral values. Homelessness, overcrowding, and unsanitary conditions linked the concern about the housing crisis with concern about healthy family life, at a time when anxieties had grown about the demographic future of a German people which had just lost 2 million men on the battlefield and whose birth rate appeared set on long-term decline. Damp, overcrowded dwellings were seen to threaten the nation's moral as well as physical health; inadequate sleeping-quarters, in which teenage siblings of different sexes had to share beds, aroused alarm; overcrowding, according to one expert giving evidence in April 1921 to the Socialization Commission about housing problems in various eastern and central German towns, meant that 'immorality has taken root (*hat sich eingebürgert*) in . . . flats where previous generations with stricter moral views than those of today have lived

---

[97] GStAB, Rep. 84a, no. 1764, fos. 165–6: (Preußischer Justizminister) to Staatssekretär des Reichsjustizamts, Berlin, 4 Dec. 1918. While members of the armed forces had enjoyed legal protection against eviction since the outbreak of the War, this protection lapsed one month after their discharge.

[98] See PLA, Rep. 38 b Jarmen, no. 710, fo. 219: 'Kommunale Forderungen der Ortsgruppe Jarmen des Internationalen Bundes der Kriegsbeschädigten & Hinterbliebenen', Dec. 1919.

irreproachably'.[99] Of course unsanitary conditions, overcrowding, and the sharing of beds had existed before the War. However, apparent threats to healthy family life became especially worrying at a time when so many things had been turned upside down and so much energy was being directed towards re-establishing pre-war stability and 'normality'.

While housing shortages remained, in many respects the economics of the housing market finally did return to normal after the stabilization crisis of 1923–4. In particular, there was a rapid rise in rents from the ridiculously low levels they had reached during the inflation. This was done by legal compulsion with the Third Emergency Tax Decree of 14 February 1924 (which also introduced the *Hauszinssteuer*), which stipulated that controlled rents throughout Germany were to reach 100 per cent of their pre-war ('peacetime') levels (i.e. their levels on 1 July 1914) by 1 July 1926.[100] Rents rose rapidly during 1924, 1925, and 1926. In Prussia, for example, they rose from 30 per cent of 'peacetime rents' in February 1924 to 66 per cent in January 1925 and 84 per cent in February 1926; in Bavaria the comparable figures were 36, 75, and 95 per cent respectively. The rise in rents allowed a partial dismantling of the 'controlled economy' in housing, and in 1925 the power to requisition large flats was rescinded. However, the central component of state control remained: the fixing of rent levels. Once the state began to intervene in fixing the cost of housing, it found extricating itself difficult. Instead of a return to 'normal', to the free-market idyll of the Empire, the demobilization and inflation left Germany with a housing market in which the state fixed rent levels and played a central role in housing construction.[101] The free-market housing economy was dead.

The rapid rise in rents which followed currency stabilization also meant that housing began to figure in household budgets roughly as it had done before the War—as a major item of expenditure.[102] Once again housing was rationed by price. To that extent, at least, normal conditions returned to the German housing-market in the mid-1920s. Another major change

---

[99] These comments refer specifically to conditions in Magdeburg. This expert also reported that Magdeburg's municipal housing office was completely convinced 'that compulsory billeting meant the devastation of (healthy) housing culture' (*eine Verheerung der Wohnungskultur*). See *Verhandlungen der Sozialisierungs-Kommission*, ii. 111.

[100] See Anker, 'Die Wohnungszwangswirtschaft', 18–19; Preller, *Sozialpolitik in der Weimarer Republik*, 332–4; Silverman, 'A Pledge Unredeemed', 137–8.

[101] Between 1924 and 1931 half of all housing construction was at least partly financed with public funds; in 1929 the proportion was nearly four-fifths. See Silverman, 'A Pledge Unredeemed', 123.

[102] Average housing-costs in Dec. 1923 were calculated to be only 21.6% of the 1913–14 figures; for Jan. 1925 the figure was 71.0%; for Jan. 1926 the figure was 91.1%; and for Jan. 1927 the figure was 104.9%. In Jan. 1927 the overall cost of living was calculated to be 144.6% of that in 1913–14. See *Statistisches Jahrbuch für das Deutsche Reich 1926*, 259; *Statistisches Jahrbuch für das Deutsche Reich 1927*, 297. For a perceptive short discussion of the effects of rent controls in the mid-1920s, see Harold James, *The German Slump: Politics and Economics 1924–1936* (Oxford, 1986), 206–8.

which came in the wake of the 1923–4 stabilization was a marked increase in residential persistence: Germans changed residence much less during the 'golden years' of the mid-1920s than they had done during the demobilization period (despite the attempts to restrict movement immediately after the First World War). The stabilization, rather than the demobilization, seems to have marked the introduction of more modern patterns of residential persistence, alongside a rapid rise in housing expenditure to more normal levels. Nevertheless, Germany's housing shortage persisted. Despite the marked increase in the number of new dwellings built in the *Hauszinssteuer* era, many households—an estimated 950,000 at the end of 1926—remained without homes of their own.[103]

The problems of Germany's housing market remained substantial throughout the post-war transition, and state intervention was both long-lasting and essentially ineffective in alleviating the country's chronic housing-shortage. This intervention was also fundamentally contradictory in its aims. Public authorities were called upon repeatedly to involve themselves in the workings of the German housing-market—to prevent evictions, to subsidize construction, to control rents, to compel landlords to let properties. Yet the underlying goal of policy was a return to 'peacetime' conditions, to a world in which the state did not intervene directly in the housing market. Of all the elements of the wartime and post-war 'controlled economy', the controls placed on the housing market lasted longest—partly because of political pressure, and partly because they could be enforced more easily than other controls: dwellings, unlike agricultural produce, for example, could not be hoarded easily; evading controls was difficult when the goods involved could not be moved. Indeed, the 'housing controlled-economy' continued to be extended while the 'controlled economy' was being dismantled elsewhere. Until the inflation was brought to an end, the political will was lacking in Germany to allow rents to rise to levels which might have encouraged private capital again to take the lead in house-building, and by that time, capital in Germany was very depleted.[104] In many respects, state intervention was the easy way out, at least in the short term. The measures enacted to protect tenants and make more dwellings available were essentially political—attempts by insecure governments to demonstrate to an unruly and embittered population that they were doing something.[105] These measures failed, but it

[103] Ruck, 'Der Wohnungsbau', 98. See also Hagemann, *Frauenalltag und Männerpolitik*, 53–64.

[104] The fairly broad agreement among housing experts during the early 1920s that rents had to be raised substantially is reflected in the proceedings of the Socialization Commission. See *Verhandlungen der Sozialisierungs-Kommission*, i, esp. 1–89.

[105] This was made quite explicit in Dec. 1919 by Adam Stegerwald, the Prussian Minister for Welfare, when he wrote to the Reich Treasury Minister that 'it would be politically inflammatory to the highest degree' if the Reich, states and other public authorities were excused from handing over buildings to be used for housing while so many families were searching without success for somewhere to live. See StdADu, no. 604/8, fo. 1: Preußischer Minister für Volkswohlfahrt to Reichsschatzmeister, Berlin, 11 Dec. 1919.

is doubtful whether any combination of government measures could have solved Germany's housing shortage during a period of soaring inflation, after a lost world war which brought hundreds of thousands of homeless refugees and millions of newly-wed couples into the housing market, and against a background of chronic shortages which stretched back many decades.

Yet for all its stubborn persistence, the housing shortage did not present an insurmountable problem for most Germans after the First World War. Like unemployment, homelessness was unevenly distributed. Despite the widespread and severe shortages of decent housing in post-war Germany, only a small minority of Germans did not have homes. Most Germans had somewhere to live; most soldiers had a home to which to return; and most Germans were able to profit from the steep drop in real housing-costs during the inflation. In so far as housing difficulties posed a serious obstacle to rebuilding lives in German civil society after the First World War, they did so primarily among the poor. In this aspect of paying the costs of a lost world war it was, as always, the poor who paid the price.

# 7

## Demobilization in the Countryside

Generally there exists little enthusiasm for work in agriculture.[1]

WHEN the First World War ended, the German countryside was a store of contradictions. In some respects it comprised that part of Germany altered least by the upheavals of late 1918.[2] The unrest which toppled the old order occurred in Germany's ports and cities, while the countryside was largely spared revolutionary enthusiasms and excesses. On the land the machinery of government remained in place; the Landrat and the rural gendarme remained at their posts; established patterns of authority did not evaporate suddenly when the German army was defeated and the Kaiser opted for exile. The memoirs of the *Junker* Lieutenant Elard von Oldenburg-Januschau are often presented as evidence of the persistence of old habits of dominance and deference in the countryside despite the collapse of the old order in Berlin. When his hopes for a military counter-revolution in Berlin were disappointed, the retired soldier returned to his estate in mid-November 1918 intending 'to provide for order and discipline at least within the boundaries assigned to me'. There he heard that one of his farm hands 'had declared himself master of Januschau':

Realising that here on my land and soil this called for swift, personal, and vigorous action, I took a solid stick and ventured out into the field where the aforementioned hand was at work. I approached him, took him by the ear and asked him 'Who governs here in Januschau?' When he gave no answer I yelled at him, 'I'll smash your head so hard in the mouth you won't know what hit you.' This language he understood. His courage left him and he acknowledged me as his master. Our mutual relationship of trust had been restored.[3]

Social relations in rural Germany seem to have survived the upheaval of November 1918 relatively unscathed.

Yet the God-given order and the 'relationship of trust' which appeared to prevail in the countryside had been eroded severely by the War and its aftermath. The solvent was the economic plight of agriculture and

---

[1] BAP, RMwD, no. 18/1, fo. 63: Kriegsamtstelle Allenstein to Reichsamt für wirtschaftliche Demobilmachung, Allenstein, 28 Dec. 1918.

[2] Martin Schumacher, *Land und Politik: Eine Untersuchung über politische Parteien und agrarische Interessen 1914–1933* (Düsseldorf, 1978), 85–8.

[3] Elard von Oldenburg-Januschau, *Erinnerungen* (2nd edn., Leipzig, 1936), 208 fos. Cited in Alf Lüdtke, *Police and State in Prussia, 1815–1850* (Cambridge, 1989), p. xi.

agricultural producers. The First World War left German agriculture with enormous problems.[4] Shortages of labour, capital, machinery, and fertilizer during the war years had damaged German farming deeply: in 1919 German grain production was a mere 48 per cent of the 1913 total, and during the 1920s it never exceeded three-quarters of the 1913 figure.[5] Not only were large tracts of productive agricultural land lost to Germany after the War, but yields per hectare declined sharply as compared with the years before 1914.[6] Severe food-shortages and the regulation of the prices and distribution of agricultural produce fuelled antagonisms between town and country, between farmers and workers, between producers and consumers of food. Furthermore, the military defeat and revolution of 1918 diminished the relative weight of German agriculture both politically and economically. When it jettisoned the protective tariff regime for agriculture in August 1914 and adopted a consumer-oriented food policy involving price controls during the War, the German government had made a fundamental shift in policy. Whatever the wishes of the agrarian lobby, this would not have been easy to reverse during the post-war transition, even if Germany had not been prohibited from reintroducing protective tariffs on agricultural imports until August 1925.[7] The loss of predominantly agricultural territories in eastern Germany after the War shifted the economic balance further in favour of industry, and, with the establishment of political democracy, landed interests lost the privileged position they had enjoyed within the constitutional structure of the Empire.[8] No longer protected by the 'iron sword' of the Kaiser, agriculture now had to fight for protection against powerful inter-est-groups in a parliamentary democracy, during a period of accelerating inflation and against a background of fierce antagonism between producers and consumers of food.

In November 1918, however, the immediate task was not to correct deep structural problems left behind by the War but to deal with an emergency created by social and political unrest, food shortages, military collapse, and

---

[4] See esp. Friedrich Aereboe, *Der Einfluß des Krieges auf die landwirtschaftliche Produktion in Deutschland* (Stuttgart, Berlin, and Leipzig, 1927), 29–107; Willi A. Boelcke, 'Wandlungen der deutschen Agrarwirtschaft in der Folge des Ersten Weltkriegs', *Francia*, 3 (1975), esp. 503–5.

[5] See Carl-Ludwig Holtfrerich, *The German Inflation 1914–1923: Causes and Effects in International Perspective* (Berlin and New York, 1986), 182.

[6] In 1919 yields per hectare of rye were 87% of the 1910–14 average, of wheat 85%, of oats 85%, and of barley 60%. In 1919–20 yields per hectare of sugar-beet, which provided both sugar for humans and feed for cattle, were only 58% of the 1913–14 figure. See Aereboe, *Der Einfluß des Krieges*, 31, 86.

[7] Schumacher, *Land und Politik*, 271; Dieter Gessner, *Agrarverbände in der Weimarer Republik: Wirtschaftliche und soziale Voraussetzungen agrarkonservativer Politik vor 1933* (Düsseldorf, 1976), 68.

[8] Generally, on the position of German agriculture after the First World War, see Dieter Gessner, 'The Dilemma of German Agriculture during the Weimar Republic', in Richard Bessel and E. J. Feuchtwanger (eds.), *Social Change and Political Development in Weimar Germany* (London, 1981), esp. 134–41.

economic disintegration. On 25 November the newly appointed head of the Reich Food Office (which was the new designation of the War Food Office from 19 November), the Independent Socialist Emanuel Wurm, presented a dramatic analysis of Germany's food situation 'as it really is' to the more than 100 assembled participants (including members of the new provisional government) at the Reich Conference in the Reich Chancellor's Palace in Berlin.[9] He began by stating bluntly that 'not a single one of the hopes and promises' of his predecessor in the War Food Office (Wilhelm von Waldow) could be kept, because during the War, conditions had been deliberately painted in overly rosy hues and because now the military collapse had led to an economic collapse. The harvest of root crops was threatened because there were not enough workers, as prisoners of war had left and as the influenza had taken its toll among the rural population; food processing had come to a standstill because of the coal shortage; the transport crisis meant that what had been harvested could not be distributed; areas of agricultural surplus lost to the Reich—including Posen and West Prussia—no longer provided food; the delivery of millions of tonnes of potatoes and grain was threatened; and what reserves Germany possessed would be needed to feed the millions of soldiers expected to come streaming back to the Reich in the coming weeks. Wurm asserted that in such circumstances 'it was impossible to draw up a precise food-plan for the future'. The only hope lay in outside help: 'We find ourselves in a real emergency situation, and if foreign countries do not help immediately, then Germany may be faced with the most terrible catastrophe in the near future.' According to Wurm, only aid from America could save a 'Germany ruined by the mismanagement of recent years', and everyone—Germans and those outside the Reich—needed to be told in unmistakable terms how desperate the food situation really was. With hindsight we may judge that the fears were exaggerated.[10] However, the people into whose laps the problems fell in late 1918 did not possess the benefit of our hindsight, and they had never lost a world war before.

The two most urgent tasks of the demobilization—securing the food-supply and providing employment for the millions of men due to leave the armed forces—were linked together in the countryside. If Germany was to avoid total collapse, those responsible for managing the post-war transition were convinced, agricultural production had to be increased and the returning soldiers had to be found work. The obvious solution was to put the de-mobilized men to work on the land; the obvious problem was how to induce

---

[9] Susanne Miller and Heinrich Potthoff (eds.), *Die Regierung der Volksbeauftragten 1918/19* (2 vols.; Düsseldorf, 1969), i. 201–5. See also Schumacher, *Land und Politik*, 132–6.

[10] The tone of Wurm's successor as Food Minister, the Majority Socialist Robert Schmidt, was far less dramatic and probably a good deal more realistic. See Schumacher, *Land und Politik*, 137–40.

them to accept farm work and thus help to provide the food which a weakened Germany so desperately needed. A low-wage sector of the economy, agriculture had long been vulnerable to the loss of labourers to higher-paid employment in the cities, and compulsory military service had long formed a turning-point in the lives of young men from rural communities. It had been estimated that before the War roughly 45 per cent of recruits from farms did not return to their old homes after military service, and that was worrying enough.[11] In November 1918, however, reluctance by young men to return to the land appeared to pose a threat to Germany's survival. Between 3 and 4 million men from rural regions, including about 2 million of the roughly 3.4 million agricultural workers of military age, had been conscripted into the German armed forces during the War.[12] Many of these had been in uniform longer than the three years which had comprised the peacetime tour of duty, and in extremely disruptive circumstances. While soldiers from rural regions had periodically been granted leave during the War in order to help with farm work, particularly at harvest time,[13] the probability that large numbers would not return to the farm was considerable. Against the background of severe wartime food-shortages, which had been instrumental in undermining the morale of the home front, and with the imminent departure of the roughly 360,000 foreign workers and 800,000–900,000 prisoners of war employed in agriculture on the eve of the Armistice,[14] it was more important than ever that demobilized soldiers who had come from rural areas return to the land.

During the War repeated calls had been raised, not least by agrarian interest-groups, for the demobilization to be organized so as to minimize the temptation for returning soldiers to seek their fortune in the cities. For example, in early 1916 the German Agricultural Council urged the Reich government to alter military procedures so that soldiers be discharged only

[11] See GStAM, Rep. 77, tit. 332d, no. 1, Bd. 2, fos. 166–7: Kriegsministerium to Minister für Landwirtschaft, Domänen und Forsten, Berlin, 8 June 1918. Copies of this letter, which stressed the particular danger that the soldiers might not return to the eastern regions of Germany, may also be found in MLHA, Mecklenburg-Strelitzer Ministerium, Abt. des Innern, no. 4462, fos. 8–9, and APS, Oberpräsidium von Pommern, no. 3951.

[12] SHAD, Ministerium des Innern, no. 16074, fos. 211–12: Sekretär des Reichswirtschaftsamts, 'Niederschrift über die 6. Sitzung des Arbeitsausschusses der Kommission für Demobilmachung der Arbeiterschaft am 28. Oktober 1918, nachmittags 4 Uhr, unter Vorsitz des Unterstaatssekretärs Dr. Müller'; Boelcke, 'Wandlungen der deutschen Agrarwirtschaft', 504 f.; Jens Flemming, *Landwirtschaftliche Interessen und Demokratie: Ländliche Gesellschaft, Agrarverbände und Staat 1890–1925* (Bonn, 1978), 82.

[13] See e.g. reports in BHStA, MKr 2454, and SHAD, Ministerium des Innern, no. 16701.

[14] SHAD, Ministerium der Auswärtigen Angelegenheiten, no. 2494, Bd. I, fos. 46–9: Kgl. Gesandtschaft Berlin to Kgl. Ministerium der Auswärtigen Angelegenheiten, Berlin, 29 Oct. 1918; Aereboe, *Der Einfluß des Krieges*, 23; Flemming, *Landwirtschaftliche Interessen und Demokratie*, 82–3; Boelcke, 'Wandlungen der deutschen Agrarwirtschaft', 504; Ulrich Herbert, *Geschichte der Ausländerbeschäftigung in Deutschland 1880 bis 1980: Saisonarbeiter, Zwangsarbeiter, Gastarbeiter* (Berlin and Bonn, 1986), 82–113.

in their home region or former place of employment, 'in order to combat the danger that, with the demobilization after the end of the War, a large number of discharged soldiers who originate from the countryside or small towns will pour into the large cities in search of work'.[15] Employment registry offices responsible for rural regions, and chambers of agriculture, particularly in eastern Germany, where emigration had been the greatest during the decades before the War, lobbied energetically. Formidable problems loomed: German agriculture would face not only an inevitable post-war loss of foreign and prisoner-of-war labour but also the gaps left by the 'great casualties which the rural population in particular, with its large percentage of men liable for military service, has suffered'. Should a significant proportion of rural labour then run off to the cities after the War, then Germany's food supply, it was claimed, would necessarily be threatened.[16] In order to prevent demobilized soldiers from flooding into the towns when their energies were needed desperately on the land, the government was pressed 'to steer the discharging of the war veterans in good time along the proper paths'.[17]

To those worried about the prospect of mass unemployment in the cities during the coming demobilization, the task of steering 'the war veterans in good time along the proper paths' did not necessarily seem insurmountable. In March 1918 the Regierungspräsident in Merseburg, von Gersdorff, informed the heads of local administrations in his region that, with the inevitable loss of 'Russian-Polish workers', 'agriculture will be in a position to receive large numbers of workers'.[18] While recognizing 'that it will not be easy to win back to agriculture those German workers who have become alienated from life on the land', the lack of other employment opportunities and 'the advantages which the agricultural worker had over the worker in industry and in the large city'—i.e. especially the proximity of food supplies—gave grounds for some optimism: 'Therefore with the demobilization there is now perhaps the possibility of supplying large numbers of native workers to agriculture through skilful, well-planned action.' Similarly, in Münster the regional administration expressed the belief in late July 1918 that, while large numbers of workers would be needed on the land after the War, 'it will present no difficulties

[15] BAP, RMdI, no. 13081, fo. 2: Deutscher Landwirtschaftsrat to Stellvertreter des Reichskanzlers Herrn Staatssekretär Dr. Delbrück, Berlin, 12 Apr. 1916.

[16] APS, Oberpräsidium von Pommern, no. 3951: Landwirtschaftskammer für die Provinz Pommern to Oberpräsident, Stettin, 13 Feb. 1918. See also ibid., no. 3951: Pommerscher Arbeitsnachweisverband to Oberpräsident, Stettin, 30 Jan. 1918.

[17] BAP, RMdI, no. 13081, fo. 2.

[18] GStAB, Rep. 180, no. 14430, fos. 7–8; and StAM, Oberpräsidium, no. 4128: Regierungspräsident to Landräte und Magistrate der Städte mit mehr als 10,000 Einwohnern des Bezirks, Merseburg, 20 Mar. 1918.

to get them, since living-conditions on the land will be far more favourable than in the cities'.[19]

Buttressed by the widespread assumption that demobilization would herald a speedy return to a *status quo ante*, such relatively rosy prognoses continued to be formulated up to the eve of the military collapse. At the end of October 1918, just two weeks before the Armistice, a working committee of the Reich Economics Office's Commission for the Demobilization of the Labour Force gave a positive assessment of the prospects for channelling workers into agriculture:[20] 'Agriculture', it claimed, would absorb not only 'all the members of the military forces who were conscripted from the countryside' and had formerly worked on the land; it could also provide employment for all those who would find it necessary to move into the countryside from the armaments industries. 'In so far as workers and artisans have migrated from the land or small towns into armaments factories, they must be persuaded to make a speedy return to the land, possibly through the suitable arrangement of unemployment relief.' Thus it would be possible 'to compensate for losses due to casualties and to strengthen the stock of agricultural labour'. Of course, the acute need for rural labour did not cause the planners in the Reich Economics Office to forget about the ethnic composition in the German countryside: 'Agriculture basically takes the standpoint that the substitution of foreign seasonal labour by native (*bodenständig*) German workers is to be aimed for.' However, in a final flight into fantasy they determined that prisoners of war and foreign workers were to be released 'only if full replacements of German workers are available'. The main problem, they felt, was the provision of adequate housing,[21] and they also urged promoting agricultural settlement through the gradual extension of the ownership of land farmed on tenancy arrangements.

After the Armistice the assessments of a few weeks earlier appeared unrealistically sanguine. The collapse of the German military effort left no more time to plan carefully for the needs of agriculture than to plan carefully for anything else. Furthermore, the general breakdown of estab-

---

[19] StAM, Oberpräsidium, no. 4128: Regierungspräsident to Kriegsamtsstelle Abteilung D in Münster, Münster, 24 July 1918. It was also assumed that fertilizer, which was so scarce, 'will be in plentiful supply after the War' because the armaments industry would no longer require nitrogen in such huge amounts.

[20] SHAD, Ministerium des Innern, no. 16704, fos. 211–12.

[21] Immediately after the Armistice the Association of Prussian Rural Districts also pointed to the importance of providing adequate dwellings for farm labour and demobilized soldiers, in order to prevent a further depopulation of the countryside. See LHSA, Rep. C 50 Querfurt A/B, no. 2808, fos. 15–16: Verband der Preußischen Landkreise, (printed circular), Berlin, 21 Nov. 1918. On rural housing-problems, see also Generaldirektor Nadelny, 'Die besonderen Verhältnisse der Kleinstädte und der ländlichen Bezirke', in Albert Gut (ed.), *Der Wohnungsbau in Deutschland nach dem Weltkriege: Seine Entwicklung unter der unmittelbaren und mittelbaren Förderung durch die deutschen Gemeindeverwaltungen* (Munich, 1928), 148–57.

lished authority and order at the end of the War left Germans less inclined to be guided along 'proper paths'. Many soldiers who originated
in the countryside displayed no desire to return to the land, and the state
lacked the means to compel them to do so. A solution to the rural
housing-problem remained a long way off. The challenge appeared overwhelming. Virtually overnight it became necessary to make up for the loss
of prisoner-of-war and foreign labour, to ensure that millions of soldiers
return to the land, and to secure food-supplies for Germany's urban population with agricultural production at low levels and with a continuing Allied
blockade.

The problem of labour supply on the land was complicated by post-war
changes in the legal and contractual position of agricultural workers. One
of the new provisional government's first acts, in its proclamation to the
German people on 12 November 1918, was to repeal the *Gesindeordnungen*,
the restrictive statutes governing the conditions and duties of farm servants
which dated from 1854 and which had made the breaking of a labour
contract by an agricultural worker in Prussia a crime.[22] At a stroke the
leverage which agricultural employers had possessed over their labourers was
reduced substantially. Labourers on the large landed estates of eastern
Germany became employees rather than servants, and they now enjoyed
freedom of association and the right to strike. On 24 January 1919 the legal
vacuum created by the lifting of the *Gesindeordnungen* was filled by a Decree
on a Provisional Regulation of Rural Labour.[23] Among other things, this
established a new legal framework for employment contracts and the payment of overtime, and fixed a maximum working day: not the eight-hour
day granted to industrial workers, but a regime which recognized the special
nature of agricultural work by allowing farm labourers to be called upon to
work eight, ten, or eleven hours per day each for one-third of the year.
Thus agricultural labourers were put on a footing partly, but not wholly,
comparable to that enjoyed by workers in industry—a 'provisional' arrangement which was to remain in force for a half a century and a compromise
which in the immediate aftermath of the War left problems all round. For
hard-pressed rural employers, costs were increased and the authority they
could exercise over their labour force was reduced; for workers, employment
in agriculture still meant disadvantage relative to employment elsewhere.
Such a compromise may have reflected the political balance in early 1919,
but it did not make easier the task of getting workers back into the fields
after the First World War.

[22] *Reichsgesetzblatt*, 1918, 1303: 'Aufruf des Rates der Volksbeauftragten an das deutsche Volk'.
[23] Ibid., 1919, 111–14: 'Verordnung über eine vorläufige Landarbeitsordnung'. For discussion,
see esp. Schumacher, *Land und Politik*, 105–17; Heinrich Muth, 'Die Entstehung der Bauern-
und Landarbeiterräte im November 1918 und die Politik des Bundes der Landwirte', in
*Vierteljahreshefte für Zeitgeschichte*, 21:1 (1973), 1–38.

In the weeks after the Armistice, calls for soldiers who had come from rural regions to return to the land were raised with increasing frequency and mounting concern. Agricultural producers complained about the difficulty, with the loss of prisoner labour and the disinclination of Germans to work for the wages on offer, of getting sufficient numbers of workers to keep farms operating properly; state authorities worried about the large numbers of former soldiers who were gathering, especially in Berlin, and avoiding contact with labour exchanges.[24] Joseph Koeth urged repeatedly that labour be channelled on to the land, that returning soldiers go to the rural areas, that measures be taken to ensure continued agricultural production. Koeth's Demobilization Office, which had its own administrative section to deal with agriculture, insisted that farm production be 'stimulated in every conceivable way' and that 'no measure remains untried in order to fulfil the urgent requirements of securing agricultural production'.[25] Regional Demobilization Commissars were ordered to work closely with agricultural interests, including the chambers of agriculture (*Landwirtschaftskammer*), and to form special 'agricultural committees' (*landwirtschaftliche Ausschüsse*) with representatives named by the *Landwirtschaftskammer* and the farm employees. The regional Demobilization Commissars were instructed to approach local farmers' and agricultural workers' councils for help in getting labour on to the land (although in fact there was little the newly formed councils could or would do). Urgent appeals were made to farmers that they welcome returning soldiers to the land, and to the returning soldiers (and to workers in the armaments industries) that they should turn to agriculture for employment. While the crippling shortage of coal and the severe transport-problems threatened employment in industry, 'the countryside', German workers were told, 'calls you and needs you'.[26]

It was not only workers that were in critically short supply in the German countryside. Draught animals were as well. Germany's agricultural producers, in particular the owners of the larger estates in northern and eastern Germany, had had to deliver more than one million horses to the army during the War, and the draught animals left on the farms were often in weakened condition because of inadequate feeding.[27] Not only did this create

[24] GStAB, Rep. 180, no. 14430, fos. 101–2: Arbeitsvermittlungsamt des Ministeriums für Landwirtschaft, Domänen und Forsten to sämtl. Oberpräsidenten, sämtl. Regierungspräsidenten, etc., Berlin, 23 Dec. 1918.

[25] HStAD, Reg. Aachen, Präsidialbüro, no. 1621, fo. 166: Reichsamt für wirtschaftliche Demobilmachung to Demobilmachungskommissare, Berlin, 17 Dec. 1918. See also Schumacher, *Land und Politik*, 101.

[26] Koeth's appeal 'to the rural population' and to workers was distributed widely. Copies may be found in MLHA, Mecklenburg-Strelitzer Ministerium, Abt. des Innern, no. 4445, fo. 111; and NHStA, Hann. 122a/XXXIV, no. 368, fo. 397: Reichsamt für die wirtschaftliche Demobilmachung, 'Aufruf', Jan. 1919.

[27] Flemming, *Landwirtschaftliche Interessen und Demokratie*, 82–6. Aereboe, *Der Einfluß des Krieges*, 35–6.

enormous problems on Germany's farms; it also meant that in addition to millions of men, hundreds of thousands of horses had to be 'demobilized' at the War's end. This presented yet another set of tasks to the demobilization authorities in rural regions. Army horses were to be auctioned off and special consideration given to small-scale family farmers—particularly in cases where the farmer had been disabled by war injuries.[28] However, the numbers of horses actually made available often turned out to be disappointingly small.[29] One important reason for this was that many of the horses released from the army in late 1918 found their way not to farmers' fields but to slaughterhouses.[30] For many of the horses which had served in the German army, demobilization meant being turned into sausage.

Despite the feverish discussions which accompanied the demobilization in the countryside, efforts to address the acute labour-shortages on the land appeared to have little effect. During late 1918 and early 1919, reports from rural regions throughout Germany had a similarly depressed ring. The provincial administration in Silesia passed on the complaints of Silesian Landräte and landowners in December 1918 that 'although demobilization from military service has made large numbers of workers available for employment', there was nevertheless a 'continued serious shortage of labour on the land':

The prisoners of war, in so far as they may still be found at their places of employment, are reluctant to work. The foreign workers for the most part cannot be induced to accept new contracts; instead almost all of them are returning home. The discharged soldiers who have returned to rural areas have also steered clear of work for the time being.[31]

Similarly, from Münster it was reported that few returning soldiers were taking up the work available in agriculture; married people willing to work on the land did not come, because housing was unavailable, while the 'unmarried appear to have no great inclination to return to agriculture from industry'.[32]

In the chaotic conditions after the military collapse, enthusiasm for hard work seemed to have evaporated. According to the Silesian chamber of

[28] See e.g. PLA, Rep. 38b Jarmen, no. 23, fo. 6: Landrat to Gemeindevorsteher des Kreises, Demmin, 24 Nov. 1918.

[29] e.g. in Kreis Grimmen, to the south of Stralsund, the number of horses available was reckoned to be only about 20% of what was urgently required. See PLA, Rep. 38b, Loitz, no. 476, fo. 245: Landrat to Polizeiverwaltungen and Amtsvorsteher des Kreises, Grimmen, 23 Nov. 1918.

[30] Ibid., Jarmen, no. 23, fo. 9: Regierungspräsident to Landräte des Bezirks, Stettin, 11 Dec. 1918.

[31] BAP, RMwD, no. 20, fos. 157–8: Oberpräsident der Provinz Schlesien to Staatskommissar für Demobilmachung in Berlin, Breslau, 22 Dec. 1918.

[32] StAM, Oberpräsidium, 5983, fo. 202: Kriegsamtstelle Münster to Demobilmachungsamt Berlin, Münster, 14 Dec. 1918.

agriculture, the easy money which soldiers could earn by volunteering for continued military service posed a major problem:

Soldiers who originate from the countryside . . . do not even consider returning there but prefer instead to draw the high *per diem* allowances with the armed forces. They no longer need to work or drill; they spend their day playing cards etc. and patrolling on the streets, and then they receive 8 Marks daily, 10 Marks in the frontier defence formations. It is therefore no wonder that these people are unwilling to return to their former occupations on the land.[33]

In Pomerania the central information office of the province's employment exchanges reflected similar sentiments when its officials noted that among the men recently discharged from the armed forces, many of whom had been agricultural labourers, 'the disinclination to work (*Arbeitsunlust*) proved to be greater than the urge for regular, permanent work'.[34] The 'disinclination to work', which dragged down productivity in just about every sector of the German economy during the months after the Armistice, created acute problems for agriculture, where the attractions of employment were relatively meagre and where the tyranny of the weather meant that tasks could not easily be postponed. Despite determined efforts by labour exchanges, the unwillingness of rural employers to offer sufficiently attractive terms and conditions—during a period when the bargaining-power of labour had grown significantly—made it difficult to tempt workers to the muck-heaps of rural Germany. In late January 1919 the Reich Office for Economic Demobilization despaired that, 'according to the unanimous reports of all the agencies working on the demobilization', attempts to channel people on to the land foundered 'again and again because workers lack the willingness to work' and because of 'excessive wage demands'; 'further measures' were required, if necessary 'compulsion to accept suitable paid work'.[35]

However, effective means to compel people 'to accept suitable paid work' was something which the German government did not have in its arsenal in the immediate aftermath of the First World War.[36] With the weakening of state authority, neither government officials nor employers could do much to force men to accept poorly paid work on the land. A vivid reflection of

---

[33] BAP, RMwD, no. 20, fos. 160–1: Arbeitsnachweis der Landwirtschaftskammer für die Provinz Schlesien to Regierungsrat Jacques (Breslau, Oberpräsidium), Breslau, 18 Dec. 1918.

[34] Ibid., no. 5, fos. 270–2: Zentralauskunftstelle und Pommerscher Arbeitsnachweisverband, 'Bericht über die Lage des Arbeitsmarktes in der Provinz Pommern im Monat Februar 1919', Stettin, 12 Mar. 1919.

[35] Ibid., no. 2, fo. 30: Reichsamt für wirtschaftliche Demobilmachung to Ministerium für Landwirtschaft, Domänen und Forsten, Berlin, 22 Jan. 1919. See also *Die wirtschaftliche Demobilmachung*, 2:3 (4 Jan. 1919), 22; ibid., no. 19 (24 Jan. 1919), 155.

[36] For discussion of the weakness of the German state and the reduction in its authority in the wake of the First World War, see Richard Bessel, 'State and Society in Germany in the Aftermath of the First World War', in W. R. Lee and Eve Rosenhaft (eds.) *The State and Social Change in Germany, 1880–1980* (Oxford, Munich, and New York, 1990), 200–27.

the changes in the German countryside was the explosive growth of trade-union membership among farm workers after the War: after unrestricted freedom of association was extended to agricultural labourers in November 1918 the membership of the Social Democratic German Agricultural Workers' Union (Deutscher Landarbeiterverband = DLV) shot up, from a mere 16,349 at the end of 1918 to 624,935 one year later.[37] Agricultural workers did not just organize; they also engaged in strikes (albeit without much lasting success), particularly in east Elbian districts and in Saxony.[38] More serious for rural employers than occasional strikes, however, was the disinclination of labourers to stick with farm work and a decline in work discipline, which affected agriculture as it affected industry. Of course, complaints about insufficient work-discipline reflect the fears and prejudices of employers as well as the actual behaviour of employees, but there was genuine cause for concern. In February 1919 authorities in the district of Teltow (to the south of Berlin) outlined the reasons why local landowners had been unsuccessful in attracting enough workers to secure the spring cultivation:

1. Male and female farm-helps indeed allow themselves to be recruited, but they do not report for work. There is no compulsion, and resorting to legal action is pointless.

2. Farm helps who do report for work often leave again shortly thereafter, in order to join a military formation.

3. The numerous amusements in the inns curb the desire to work, whereby in turn the farm helps are induced to look for easier employment.

4. The frequent billeting of troops in the villages, with their comfortable 'duty' and good pay, is seducing all young men into signing up.[39]

This last point was particularly telling. It would appear that recruitment for military units during the months after the War, whether into the army or into security formations and paramilitary units, which offered relatively attractive *per diem* allowances, drew men from the labour market in rural areas. While the appeal of military formations may have been slight for city dwellers, for many young men in the countryside these formations offered an appealing alternative to working long hours for low wages on the farm.

---

[37] Aereboe, *Der Einfluß des Krieges*, 129–30; Jens Flemming, 'Großagrarische Interessen und Landarbeiterbewegung: Überlegungen zur Arbeiterpolitik des Bundes der Landwirte und des Reichslandbundes in der Anfangsphase der Weimarer Republik', in Hans Mommsen, Dietmar Petzina, and Bernd Weisbrod (eds.), *Industrielles System und politische Entwicklung in der Weimarer Republik* (Düsseldorf, 1974), 750. Flemming, *Landwirtschaftliche Interessen und Demokratie*, 163.

[38] See Eric D. Kohler, 'Revolutionary Pomerania 1919–20: A Study in Majority Socialist Agricultural Policy and Civil–Military Relations', *Central European History*, 9 (1976), 250–93; Wilhelm Matull, *Ostdeutschlands Arbeiterbewegung: Abriß ihrer Geschichte, Leistung und Opfer* (Würzburg, 1973), 273–4; Flemming, *Landwirtschaftliche Interessen und Demokratie*, 275–315; Schumacher, *Land und Politik*, 296–304; Robert G. Moeller, *German Peasants and Agrarian Politics, 1914–1924: The Rhineland and Westphalia* (Chapel Hill, NC, and London, 1986), 68–9.

[39] BLHA, Rep. 2A, Reg. Potsdam I SW, no. 793, fo. 142: Amtsbezirk Glienick b/Zossen und Jachsenbrück to Landrat des Kreises Teltow, Zossen, 23 Feb. 1919.

During late 1918 and early 1919 local authorities across Germany's rural hinterlands reported 'little desire to work in agriculture',[40] the failure of attempts to place workers on the land due to 'low wages' and a 'general reluctance of the unemployed to accept outdoor work',[41] and the 'strongest resistance to the acceptance of agricultural work . . . although the landowners are now paying two or three times the peacetime wage-rates'.[42] Working on the land was widely regarded as the least desirable option, to be avoided if at all possible. This made government officials and rural employers all the more concerned that the money which actual or potential agricultural workers might receive elsewhere—whether in militia or paramilitary units, in urban employment, or in the form of unemployment benefits—should be reduced. Allegedly generous unemployment benefits, it was claimed, had particularly damaging consequences. From Münster came the report in December 1918 that 'the wage demands of workers returning from industry are so high that the farmers cannot take on these people'; one reason given why 'the unemployed do not volunteer for work in agriculture' was 'the high level of unemployment benefit'.[43] A month later the Reich Demobilization Office was told that, although great efforts had been made to draw attention to the labour shortages on the land by means of 'extensive propaganda, posters, and notices in the press' in the industrial centres, the campaign had met with little success; the failure was attributed to 'the general aversion to work, the negligible inclination to return to agricultural labour, and the high rates of unemployment benefit'.[44] In Breslau the labour exchange of the Silesian agricultural chamber complained not only that 'soldiers who originate from rural areas prefer to lie about with their military units than to offer themselves for employment in agriculture' but also that 'the so-called unemployed of the city of Breslau prefer to draw unemployment benefit rather than accept work on the land'.[45] In the province of Brandenburg the labour exchanges reported in mid-February 1919 that 40 per cent of jobs offered on the land remained unfilled because the wages were too low to attract people from Berlin;[46] it apparently made no difference that the Reich capital contained a major share of the country's unemployed at the time.

[40] BAP, RMwD, no. 18/1, fo. 63: Kriegsamtstelle Allenstein to Reichsamt für wirtschaftliche Demobilmachung, Allenstein, 28 Dec. 1918.

[41] Ibid., fo. 324: Kriegsamtstelle Breslau, 'Wochenbericht', Breslau, 15 Feb. 1919.

[42] Ibid., fo. 208: Kriegsamtstelle Danzig to the Reichsamt für die wirtschaftliche Demobilmachung, Danzig, 25 Jan. 1919.

[43] StAM, Oberpräsidium, no. 5983, fo. 205: Kriegsamtstelle Münster to the Demobilmachungsamt Berlin, Münster, 21 Dec. 1918.

[44] BAP, RMwD, no. 18/1, fo. 195: Kriegsamtstelle Münster to the Demobilmachungsamt, 'Lage des Arbeitsmarktes', Münster, 18 Jan. 1919.

[45] Ibid., no. 2, fos. 371–2: Arbeitsnachweis der Landwirtschaftskammer für die Provinz Schlesien to the Kriegswirtschaftsamt Breslau, Breslau, 4 Jan. 1919.

[46] Ibid., no. 4, fos. 98–9: Zentralauskunftstelle der Arbeitsnachweise für die Provinz Brandenburg to Reichsamt für wirtschaftliche Demobilmachung, Berlin, 14 Feb. 1919.

Nor was this just a passing phenomenon in the winter of 1918–19. In the spring, government authorities continued to express concern that 'vacant positions in agriculture could not be filled from the numerous unemployed from other trades because they could not be induced to accept any employment opportunity on the land at all'.[47]

Not only 'high rates of unemployment benefit' but also the emergency works-projects which had been initiated throughout Germany were blamed for causing workers to avoid agricultural work. Anxieties surfaced even before the projects were authorized. In late January 1919 the Demobilization Committee in Neubrandenburg pleaded against planning road improvements as emergency works-projects in the spring, because this 'would result in many agricultural labourers signing up'; 'agriculture', it was claimed, 'which today already suffers from a marked shortage of labour, would be severely affected to the detriment of the general public, and it appears quite doubtful whether it then would be able to fulfil its task of guaranteeing that the population is fed'.[48] In late March, Koeth told Demobilization Commissars around the country that 'the main purpose, the employment of the unemployed, was frequently not achieved' by soil-improvement projects in rural areas: 'on the contrary, the high wages deprive agriculture of the few workers it still has'.[49] Any alternative source of income or employment, it would seem, inevitably undermined attempts to channel workers on to the land.

Part of the problem was of the employers' own making, and lay in their unwillingness or inability to pay decent wages and offer attractive working-conditions. This was especially true on the large estates (and therefore posed a particular problem in the eastern Prussian provinces), as smaller farms enjoyed a somewhat better reputation for providing a tolerable working environment.[50] Urban labour-exchanges, keen to disperse their unemployed, complained of the 'inadequate living-conditions' on the land and the 'insufficiently sympathetic treatment of the transferred workers by agricultural employers'.[51] According to authorities in the rural areas around Berlin in February 1919, 'the main obstacle to the supplying of agricultural labour still lies with the employers': they were 'for the most part unwilling to increase wages', and the living-quarters they offered were 'inadequate for

---

[47] APP, Landratsamt Lissa, no. 118, fo. 49: Magistrat to Landrat, Lissa, 8 May 1919.

[48] MLHA, Mecklenburg-Strelitzer Ministerium, Abteilung des Innern, no. 4447, fos. 30–1: Demobilmachungsausschuß für den Amtsbezirk Neubrandenburg, Neubrandenburg, 24 Jan. 1919.

[49] StAO, Rep. 450 Mep, no. 762: Reichsamt für wirtschaftliche Demobilmachung to the Demobilmachungskommissare, Berlin, 24 Mar. 1919.

[50] See BAP, RMwD, no. 5, fos. 270–2: Zentralauskunftstelle und Pommerscher Arbeitsnachweisverband, 'Bericht über die Lage des Arbeitsmarktes in der Provinz Pommern im Monat Februar 1919', Stettin, 12 Mar. 1919.

[51] Ibid., fo. 399: Zentralauskunftstelle der Groß-Berliner Arbeitsnachweise, 'Situationsbericht', Berlin, 29 Mar. 1919.

German workers'.[52] (Such comments raised the spectre that, if the conditions remained unacceptable to *German* workers, then foreign—Polish—workers, whose standards were considered to be not so high, might take their place.) As the Landrat in Neiße in Upper Silesia put it in May 1919, the urban unemployed rejected agricultural employment because they 'do not approve of the living-conditions which exist on the land'.[53] These judgements did not reflect luxurious circumstances enjoyed by Germany's unemployed urban proletariat; at a time when urban dwellers faced severe food-shortages and when the prospects for getting enough to eat were far better on a farm, they formed a damning indictment of the conditions offered by rural employers.

Although housing has usually been viewed as an urban problem, the housing available to Germany's rural population, particularly to agricultural labourers, remained quite poor.[54] As the regional health officer for the (largely rural) Regierungsbezirk Stralsund described it in his 'Health Report' for 1921, most workers' housing in the countryside consisted of one living-room, a storage room, and a kitchen, and could not be considered adequate for the large families which were the norm.[55] Not only was the lack of decent housing a great disincentive to workers who might have considered working on the land; the overcrowding and the generally poor living-quarters also created serious health problems, especially with the sharp rise in the incidence of tuberculosis during the War.[56] In part the problems stemmed from conditions which had already existed before 1914, but the changes brought about by the conflict had made the housing situation in the countryside even worse. Failure to make necessary repairs during the War had led to many dwellings being declared unfit for habitation, while the wartime cessation of building activity put greater pressure on the housing market; and the floods of refugees created by the post-war border-changes, particularly into the rural regions of eastern Germany, exacerbated already severe overcrowding.

The dilemma which confronted rural employers was at root a structural one. German agriculture remained a low-wage sector, dependent upon paying either minimal wages to farm labourers or no wages at all to family members, who could be relied upon to work from dawn to dusk.[57] With the

---

[52] BLHA, Rep. 2A Reg. Potsdam I SW, no. 793, fo. 119: Kriegsamtstelle in den Marken to Regierungspräsident als Demobilmachungskommissar Potsdam, Berlin, 20 Feb. 1919.

[53] APW, Rejencja Opolska I, no. 12410, fo. 812: Landrat to Regierungspräsident, Neiße, 5 May 1919.

[54] On housing for agricultural labourers generally, see Aereboe, *Der Einfluß des Krieges*, 140–53.

[55] PLA, Rep. 65c, no. 2312, fo. 165: 'Gesundheitsbericht für den Regierungsbezirk Stralsund. Jahr 1921'.

[56] Ibid., esp. fos. 164–5; APP, Rejencja w Pile, no. 2477: Regierungs- und Medizinalrat, Grenzmark Posen-Westpreußen, 'Jahresgesundheitsbericht 1920', esp. pp. 39–40 of the report.

[57] Friedrich Aereboe contrasted the pre-war development of agriculture in Germany with that in the United States, where farmers paid their 'very high wages in comparison to Germany' and, as a result, invested much sooner and more extensively in farm machinery. The price

end of the War, important props of the low-wage farm economy were removed when hundreds of thousands of prisoners of war and foreign labourers left Germany and so many men showed little enthusiasm for returning to the land after their military service. Farmers were not simply being disingenuous when they asserted, as some of their number did at a meeting of the Demobilization Committee in a rural district near Osnabrück in January 1919, that unskilled labourers from the cities were unsuitable for farm work 'since agriculture would not be productive (*produktionsfähig*) were high wages to be paid'.[58] Whereas in industry company profits were sacrificed in order in effect to finance the demobilization and the allegedly high wages demanded by workers,[59] in agriculture this was not really an option: too many farm producers lived too close to the margins and felt themselves hemmed in by price controls. With controlled prices for their products and rising costs, they could not afford to pay 'high wages'. In its weekly survey of the labour market, the Pomeranian labour-exchange network reported on 25 January that 'the need for agricultural labourers still cannot be met because at present the work is generally rejected at the rates of pay which are offered, while the majority of the employers cannot commit themselves to paying high wages' and instead were still trying to get prisoners to work the fields. Characteristically, German officials looked to restrictive administrative measures to solve structural problems. In order to 'curb the unemployment and supply agriculture with the labour it so urgently requires', the Pomeranian labour-exchange organization urged that 'the payment of unemployment benefit to young people under 20 years of age and their employment on emergency works-projects must be forbidden by Reich decree as long as they are offered the possibility of finding paid work on the land'.[60] However, for a Reich government desperately concerned to prevent urban unrest and a further radicalization of the urban working class, such a suggestion was unlikely to be attractive or practicable.

There was, of course, another possible solution to the dilemma: to continue to recruit foreign, especially Polish, labourers, who would be willing to work for wages which Germans rejected as too low. However, this posed other problems for officials anxious to fortify the 'German' countryside. With Germany's eastern frontier being redrawn against the background of Polish nationalist uprisings, they believed that more *Germans*, not Poles, were required to provide the proper ethnic mix in the countryside. It was therefore

controls placed on agricultural products during and after the War ensured that in Germany there could be no fundamental change in this regard in the short term. See Aereboe, *Der Einfluß des Krieges*, 114–15.

[58] StAO, Rep. 450 Lin, no. 800: Landrat, 'Sitzung des Demobilmachungsausschusses 21.1.19', Lingen, 21 Jan. 1919.

[59] See above, Ch. 4.

[60] APS, Oberpräsidium von Pommern, no. 3952: Zentralauskunftstelle Stettin, 'Wochenbericht über den Arbeitsmarkt der Provinz Pommern', Stettin, 25 Jan. 1919.

a revealing sign of the desperation of the Berlin government that it effectively abandoned hopes of constructing a solid German wall in rural eastern Prussia in order to dam the Slav flood. In mid-March 1919 the government admitted defeat and permitted Polish agricultural labourers recruited through the Deutsche Arbeiterzentrale to cross the frontier:

The orderly cultivation of the fields and the necessary maintenance of intensive production in the interest of feeding the nation is possible only if the required labour is made available to farms. The need for rural labour, in particular with regard to root crops, will not be able to be met completely by the unemployed, most of whom are accustomed to urban life and industrial work. However undesirable is the admission of foreign workers in and of itself in the present situation, it has nevertheless proved absolutely necessary in this economic year again to permit the employment of Polish workers, large numbers of whom are trying to regain their old jobs in Germany.[61]

Rural employers, particularly the large landowners, began once again to recruit Polish labour—although it was not long before complaints were raised that Poles too were demanding 'very high' wages.[62] There was, as the Landrat in the Upper Silesian district of Kreuzburg reported in early May 1919, a continued 'need to employ foreign Polish workers in agriculture'; indeed, 'this need has now become even greater than in peacetime'—that is, before the War—'since the labour movement has caught hold on the land and as a result the productivity of domestic workers has declined by a not inconsiderable amount'.[63] Like it or not, Germany's rural employers lived in an industrial society in which the bargaining-power of labour had suddenly increased, and they found themselves compelled once again to look across the eastern frontier for workers to bring in the harvest. Where foreign labour was not readily available, as in southern and western Germany, women members of the family had to bear much of the extra burden.[64]

Despite the desperate labour-shortages, agricultural employers were not prepared automatically to hire urban workers when they were available, and their reasons were revealing. Already during the early stages of the War, when unemployment among urban workers had shot up temporarily, farmers had been less than enthusiastic about employing jobless workers from the towns.[65] Now, with political upheaval emanating from Germany's cities,

---

[61] APW, Rejencja Opolska I, no. 12410, fos. 764–5: Reichsministerium des Innern to Regierungen der deutschen Freistaaten außer Preußen, Berlin, 19 Mar. 1919.

[62] Ibid., fos. 807–8: Landrat des Kreises Tost-Gleiwitz to Regierungspräsident, Gleiwitz, 4 May 1919.

[63] Ibid., fos. 819–21: Landrat to Regierungspräsident, Kreuzburg O-S., 7 May 1919.

[64] See Jonathan Osmond, 'Peasant Farming in South and West Germany during War and Inflation 1914 to 1924: Stability or Stagnation?', in Gerald D. Feldman, Carl-Ludwig Holtfrerich, Gerhard A. Ritter, and Peter-Christian Witt (eds.), *Die deutsche Inflation: Eine Zwischenbilanz*, (Berlin and New York, 1982), 304–5.

[65] Flemming, *Landwirtschaftliche Interessen und Demokratie*, 83.

many farmers were fearful of hiring the urban unemployed and former factory-workers, who might be infected with revolutionary sympathies.[66] This was particularly true of the unemployed from Berlin, against whom, as Koeth observed in late March 1919, 'there is unquestionably a special antipathy'.[67] Such attitudes did not soften during the late summer, although the harvest made the need for labour doubly critical. From Hanover it was reported in late August that, while poor working-conditions, and especially poor housing, continued to pose obstacles to finding people willing to accept farm work, employers nevertheless displayed a 'reluctance to hire unemployed urban workers'.[68] In Düsseldorf the district Workers' Council claimed that agricultural employers preferred to have Russian prisoners working on their farms than to take on German workers from the cities: although workers in Düsseldorf were allegedly prepared to take jobs on the land, 'the great majority of our farmers in the rural districts nevertheless refuse to employ former industrial workers because they fear their demands, which naturally are not of so primitive a nature as those of the Russians'.[69] At least the Russians, like the Poles, whom many eastern German landowners preferred to employ on their estates, came from rural backgrounds. The last thing that agricultural employers wanted was a labour force infected with subversive urban values, such as the belief that workers ought to be paid decent wages.

Although the problem of labour supply dominated the thoughts of those concerned with demobilization in the German countryside, certain elements of the post-war agricultural labour-force were not deemed to demand attention—which reveals much about the unspoken assumptions at work in official circles. Perhaps most striking is that discussion about labour supply in the countryside during the post-war transition almost exclusively concerned *men*. It was *men* who needed to be convinced to return to the land after their military service; it was unemployed *men* who needed to be coaxed from the cities and off the relief rolls to work in the fields; it was *men* who demanded 'high wages' which were beyond the ability of agricultural employers to pay; it was *men* who displayed the widely reported disinclination to engage in hard work after the War. Women surfaced in the discussion

[66] BAP, RMwD, no. 18/1, fos. 140–5: Kriegsamtstelle to Reichsamt für wirtschaftliche Demobilmachung, Hanover, 11 Jan. 1919. See also Richard Bessel, ' "Eine nicht allzu große Beunruhigung des Arbeitsmarktes": Frauenarbeit und Demobilmachung in Deutschland nach dem Ersten Weltkrieg', *Geschichte und Gesellschaft*, 9 (1983), 222.

[67] StAO, Rep. 450 Mep, no. 762: Reichsamt für wirtschaftliche Demobilmachung to Demobilmachungskommissare, Berlin, 24 Mar. 1919. It should be remembered that this comment was made soon after attempts to organize a general strike and subsequent street-fighting had left over one thousand people dead in the Reich capital.

[68] StAO, Rep. 451 Lin, no. 405: Zentralauskunftstelle für Arbeitsnachweise to Regierungspräsident in Osnabrück, Hanover, 22 Aug. 1919.

[69] GStAM, Rep. 120, BB VII 1, no. 30, Bd. 5, fo. 56: Kreisarbeiterrat to Arbeitsminister in Berlin, Düsseldorf, 8 Aug. 1919.

very little, and when they did their contribution was more or less taken for granted. No doubts were raised over whether the women, who had shouldered so many additional burdens during the War, would continue to work in agriculture. The silence about the role of female labour on the land is all the more remarkable when one considers that agriculture, unlike industry, was not primarily a male occupation; the numbers of men and women employed in German agriculture during the 1920s were roughly equal. What is more, female employment in agriculture—in contrast to employment in industry or the service sector—was not primarily the employment of one particular age-group (i.e. of young women before they were married); like men, women tended to work in agriculture through their entire working lives.[70]

That so little of public discussion about demobilization in the countryside concerned the experience of women reflects not only the blindness of German officials with regard to women's lives. It also underscores the extent to which this discussion focused upon conditions in northern and eastern Germany—in regions where agriculture was characterized more by large estates (where it was necessary to have a paid—male—labour force) than by small family farms (where women played a more prominent role). It was in eastern Germany that the question of the ethnic composition of the countryside aroused the greatest concern. It was in regions dominated by the *Junkers* that labour was so desperately needed and simultaneously posed an apparently deadly threat to the established order. In regions where smaller family farms predominated, such problems were less alarming. Small family farms, it was tacitly assumed, could more or less take care of themselves. On such farms the overriding concern was not about labour supply but about the prices for farm produce. There the subject of debate was not how to get someone to do the work, but how to remove the *Zwangswirtschaft*—the controls on prices and distribution which had been put into place during the War.

To agricultural producers, and especially to family farmers, the *Zwangswirtschaft* was a hated expression of the deterioration in the position of rural interests in Germany during the War. It was a reflection of the fact that German governments no longer saw it as their task to protect agriculture but now felt compelled to intervene on behalf of urban consumers of food; it posed a constant threat to the viability of farms and the living-standards of the farm population; and it provoked massive discontent among agricultural producers, who looked forward to its abolition once the War was over.[71] However, in an environment characterized by food shortages, inflation, a thriving black market, a continued Allied blockade, a poorly functioning

[70] See the perceptive discussion in Rosa Kempf, *Die deutsche Frau nach der Volks-, Berufs- und Betriebszählung von 1925* (Mannheim, Berlin, and Leipzig, 1931), 69–77.
[71] See Moeller, *German Peasants and Agrarian Politics*, 43–67.

distribution-system, and the loss of large tracts of agricultural land, and with German grain-production in 1919 less than half what it had been in 1913, some form of government controls over food pricing and distribution was unavoidable.

It was also inevitably a source of friction. Rural producers, who had problems of their own and were then prevented from taking full advantage of an otherwise strong position on the market, regarded the *Zwangswirtschaft* with some justification as an expression of the increased political weight of urban industrial workers at their expense. The potential for bitter disappointment was made greater by the expectation that the end of the War would somehow be followed immediately by the dismantling of economic controls and a return to free-market conditions.[72] In the difficult post-war conditions, no doubt even the best-laid plans to organize food distribution would have led to failure and recrimination, and few would argue that the German government put best of schemes into operation. Nevertheless, at the end of the War the German government had little choice but to maintain the 'controlled economy' in agricultural goods and thus to provoke bitter anger among farm producers. For a new government precariously dependent upon the support of an undernourished industrial proletariat, not to do so would have been impossible.

So the *Zwangswirtschaft* continued into the post-war period, with controls maintained over the prices and deliveries of most key products until 1920–1, and it was not lifted completely until the summer of 1923. The result was a predictable failure characterized by a thriving black market, attempts by local organizations of agricultural producers to set their own prices, refusal to meet delivery quotas, an erosion of the authority of the state, and anger on the part of both producers and consumers of food.[73] As Robert Moeller has put it, the continuing gap between food supply and demand, and the consequent extension of wartime controls meant that 'tensions between producers and consumers of agricultural products, a central dimension of social conflict during the war and an inevitable consequence of chronic food shortages, survived undiminished in the transition from war to peace'.[74] In addition, after the military collapse, whatever sense of solidarity may have existed because of the war effort evaporated. How sharp the antagonisms had become was illustrated by the fact that military expeditions continued to be necessary to secure the delivery of agricultural produce from recalcitrant farmers. In Upper Silesia the problem was of such dimensions that the

---

[72] Ibid. 69.

[73] See id., 'Winners as Losers in the German Inflation: Peasant Protest over the Controlled Economy, 1920–1923', in Gerald D. Feldman, Carl-Ludwig Holtfrerich, Gerhard A. Ritter, and Peter-Christian Witt (eds.), *Die deutsche Inflation: Eine Zwischenbilanz* (Berlin and New York, 1982), 255–88; Moeller, *German Peasants and Agrarian Politics*, 68–94.

[74] Moeller, 'Winners as Losers', 266.

Army Command concluded in March 1919 that 'the resistance of the population to the delivery of livestock' required the creation of special twenty-man units in each garrison to 'help' the district authorities procure the required livestock. What this meant is illustrated by events in Klein Steinisch (a village of fewer than 1,000 inhabitants in the district of Groß Strehlitz), where a commando group of two officers and forty-five men was dispatched in motor vehicles 'in order to enforce the procurement of livestock and if necessary to break the resistance of the population'.[75] This was the language of civil war, and it does not require much imagination to envisage the effects of such expeditions upon the attitudes of the rural population. In places, attempts at confiscation provoked open opposition by the rural population; inspection teams were greeted with threats to their lives, while worried officials claimed that among the rural population 'respect for the law no longer exists and fear of punishment has almost completely disappeared'.[76]

The *Zwangswirtschaft* may not have succeeded in controlling the marketing of agricultural products—indeed, Moeller argues convincingly that in many key areas it had virtually collapsed in practice before the controls were dismantled formally[77]—but it did succeed mightily in fuelling antagonisms, not only between government and people but also between town and country. When the army recruitment office in Baden drew attention to the antipathy of the rural population towards the military in July 1919, its spokesman pointed out that this was 'only a secondary aspect of the general animosity towards the government and authorities because of the *Zwangs-wirtschaft*'. He went on to explain that 'the rural inhabitant hates the city dwellers, because they only want to work eight hours per day yet mostly strike and nevertheless demand deliveries of food from the countryside, while the farmers must be at work from the early morning until late in the evening, especially during the harvest', and concluded: 'The farmer hates everything urban.' *(Alles was der Stadt ist, ist vom Bauern gehaßt.)*[78]

The attitudes prevailing in rural Germany during the post-war transition reflected a long-established and profound antipathy among rural inhabitants and agrarian interests towards urban Germany which had a long pedigree.[79] Berlin evoked especially strong feelings. It was the fount of alien urban culture and of the alleged decadence which challenged healthy rural values,

[75] APP, Rejencja Opolska Pr. B. no. 326, fos. 329–31: Landrat to Regierungspräsident, Groß Strehlitz, 11 Mar. 1919.

[76] Moeller, *German Peasants and Agrarian Politics*, 74.

[77] id., 'Winners as Losers', 266–7.

[78] GLAK, 456/E.V.6, 121, Ie: Werbezentrale des XIV A.K. Radolfzell to Gen.Kdo. des XIV A.K. in Durlach, Radolfzell, 9 July 1919. See also Boelcke, 'Wandlungen der deutschen Agrarwirtschaft', 522–3.

[79] See Klaus Bergmann, *Agrarromantik und Großstadtfeindschaft* (Meisenheim Glan, 1970); Schumacher, *Land und Politik*, 17; David Blackbourn, 'Peasants and Politics in Germany, 1871–1914', *European History Quarterly*, 14 no. 1 (1984), 47–75.

the place where wealth and power were concentrated, the centre of a revolutionary movement which appeared to threaten rural property, the seat of a government which ran the hated *Zwangswirtschaft*, and home to nearly 4 million hungry people. The attitude prevalent in the countryside was summed up in February 1919 by the labour-exchange organization in the province of Brandenburg, which attributed the reluctance of farmers to answer requests for information (about wage levels, housing, and so forth) 'in large measure to the antipathy towards everything that comes out of Berlin'.[80]

The hatred and fear felt by Germany's rural inhabitants towards their urban fellow citizens was given sharp focus by the physical threat posed by hungry city-dwellers. Thefts of farmers' crops by a hungry urban population provided country dwellers with all the proof they needed of the dangerous and depraved nature of the inhabitants of Germany's cities.[81] Such thefts reached epidemic proportions in the aftermath of the War. An undernourished urban population, which had suffered for years from inadequate food-rations and extortionate black-market prices for food, made self-service expeditions into farmers' fields, as the ability of the police, whose numbers did not always increase in the countryside as they did in the cities, to control lawbreaking plummeted.[82] Workers sometimes walked off the job *en masse* in order to scour the countryside for food, on occasion with violent consequences. Villagers sometimes met their hungry urban compatriots with clubs and guns, and the widespread fear of the urban population, that hordes of workers were threatening to come out of their lairs in the cities in order to plunder the countryside, was a prime reason for the creation of armed self-defence organizations in rural districts.[83] The prejudices of the rural

[80] BAP, RMwD, no. 4, fos. 98–9: Zentralauskunftstelle der Arbeitsnachweise für die Provinz Brandenburg to Reichsamt für wirtschaftliche Demobilmachung, Berlin, 14 Feb. 1919. This antipathy towards Berlin and Berliners extended even to children. In 1923 the Pomeranian authorities overseeing the provision of country visits for city children (which had involved 40,000 children in 1917, nearly collapsed in 1919—when fewer than 5,000 children participated—and then recovered to involve over 28,000 children in 1922), noted that children from Berlin were the hardest to place: 'One district after another has requested that they no longer be sent Berlin children—their entire attitude to life and behaviour do not sit well with our rural population.' See APS, Oberpräsidium von Pommern, no. 2735: Provinzialstelle Landaufenthalt für Stadtkinder, 'Jahresübersicht über den Landaufenthalt von Stadtkinder in der Provinz Pommern im Jahre 1922', Stettin, 13 Feb. 1923.

[81] For reports of thefts of food, see SHAD, Ministerium des Innern, no. 11237; APP, Polizeipräsidium Posen, no. 9101. See also Osmond, 'Peasant Farming', 305; Moeller, *German Peasants and Agrarian Politics*, 71.

[82] e.g. whereas between 1913 and 1919 the number of police more than doubled in the industrial cities of Dortmund and Hagen, the rural gendarmerie in the Regierungsbezirk Arnsberg only increased from 290 to 306. Rural communities essentially had to rely on their own volunteer organizations to prevent thefts. See StAM, Oberpräsidium, no. 6523: Regierungspräsident to Minister des Innern, 'Störung der Sicherheit und öffentlichen Ordnung', Berichterstatter: Regierungsrat Dr. Schwenke, Arnsberg, 14. Sept. 1919.

[83] e.g. in Mecklenburg. See reports in MLHA, Ministerium des Innern, no. 21266 and 21267. Robert Moeller gives details of similar reactions in Westphalia. See Moeller, *German Peasants and Agrarian Politics*, 72.

population were thus confirmed: about a dangerous and lawless urban proletariat, and about a government which appeared either to side with the city dwellers or to be powerless to uphold law and order.

Nevertheless, in many ways the demobilized soldiers (and their families) straddled the bitter antagonisms between rural and urban Germany. At a time when hostility between town and country was so great, many young men took advantage of the opportunity offered by demobilization to abandon life on the farm for the city. While agricultural interests were complaining bitterly about government interference in their lives in the shape of the *Zwangswirtschaft*, millions of ex-soldiers from the countryside came home expecting some form of help from the government in Berlin. Although discussion of the rural way of life inevitably focused on agriculture, in western Germany in particular many small-scale farmers could not live off the land exclusively and also worked as self-employed or wage-earning artisans.[84] Whatever the context, it is probably a mistake to conceive of urban and rural (or, for that matter, producer and consumer, or male and female) interests as somehow being distinct and discrete. With the waves of migration from country to town before, during, and after the First World War, few farm families could have lacked friends or relatives in the cities. This is not to assert that the antagonisms outlined above were therefore muted. What occurred may, in fact, have been just the opposite: that migration and, particularly, the threat of an abandonment by new waves of healthy young men of their rural *Heimat* at the War's end, may have exacerbated anxieties which fuelled the hostility of the countryside towards the town. Not only did townspeople work shorter hours, demand cheap food through the iniquitous *Zwangswirtschaft*, and periodically embark on thieving expeditions through farmers' fields; they also drew away the sons of rural Germany.

For a variety of reasons, those who remained in the countryside could feel under psychological threat. The widespread disinclination of soldiers to return to the land was a challenge to those who, for whatever reason, chose to remain; the sinful ways of the city appeared to be gaining the upper hand against the allegedly more healthy habits in the countryside; and the political revolution which Germany had experienced was essentially an urban phenomenon. Even the rural efforts to form 'councils' in the aftermath of the November revolution were defensive. The 'farmers' councils' were envisaged essentially as protecting agriculture from the threat stemming from the revolutionary upheaval: 'to maintain agricultural production' and 'to provide adequate protection for agriculture against violent encroachments on private

---

[84] See Gerhard Wilke, 'The Sins of the Fathers: Village Society and Social Control in the Weimar Republic', in Richard J. Evans and W. R. Lee (eds.), *The German Peasantry: Conflict and Community in Rural Society from the Eighteenth to the Twentieth Centuries* (London and Sydney, 1986), 175.

property'.[85] It is therefore hardly surprising that attempts to organize voluntary citizens' militias in the aftermath of the War—attempts which frequently
came to nothing in cities, where workers shunned them—tended to be more
successful in the countryside.[86] The success of 'farmers' militias' (*Bauern-
wehren*), which patrolled the countryside and kept a watch on outsiders
passing through, and of the 'auxiliary gendarmes' stationed in the countryside[87] was a reflection of both concern to preserve a certain order and a
deep-seated suspicion of, and antipathy towards, a (largely urban) world
which appeared to threaten the rural way of life. Germany's rural population
was on the defensive, and acted accordingly.

Despite the enormous problems facing German agriculture, and the bitter
antagonisms which arose from the War, inflation, and the *Zwangswirtschaft*,
in some respects a normalization of social and economic relationships came
fairly quickly to the countryside. One aspect of this was the speed with which
the *Zwangswirtschaft* was effectively dismantled even before it was removed
from the statute-books.[88] Another was the rapid reconstitution of employer
strength *vis-à-vis* labour, particularly on the landed estates of eastern Germany. Indeed, it was the sudden growth of trade unionism on the land, and
the insecurity caused by the revolution which gave the impulse for agricultural employers to organize effectively for the first time.[89] Their organizations
grew rapidly and consolidated—forming a Reich Federation of German
Agricultural and Forestry Employers' Associations (Reichsverband der
deutschen landwirtschaftlichen und forstwirtschaftlichen Arbeitgebervereini-
gungen) in September 1919—and were able to present an increasingly united
response to employees' demands.[90] Trade-union membership among agricultural workers ebbed almost as quickly as it had surged after the abolition
of the *Gesindeordnungen*.[91] Workers' associations dependent upon the *Junker*-
dominated provincial agrarian leagues grew in membership, and agricultural

[85] StAM, Oberpräsidium, no. 6350, fo. 20: Landwirtschaftskammer für die Provinz Westfalen
to landwirtschaftliche Kreis- und Ortsvereine der Provinz Westfalen, Münster, 15 Nov. 1918.

[86] See the contrast between the failure in 1919 to form militias in Hagen, Hörde, and Iserlohn
and the success in rural communities in the Regierungsbezirk Arnsberg, described in StAM,
Oberpräsidium, no. 6523: Regierungspräsident to Minister des Innern, 'Störungen der Sicherheit
und öffentlichen Ordnung', Berichterstatter: Regierungsrat Dr. Schwenke, Arnsberg, 14 Sept.
1919,

[87] Ibid.: Regierungspräsident to Minister des Innern, 'Störung der Sicherheit und öffentlichen
Ordnung in Stadt- und Landbezirken', Berichterstatter: Regierungsrat Steuer, Münster, 20 Sept.
1919.

[88] Moeller, 'Winners as Losers', 266–7.

[89] Schumacher, *Land und Politik*, 19.

[90] See Aereboe, *Der Einfluß des Krieges*, 130–1.

[91] The DLV, which had numbered nearly 700,000 members at the end of 1919, had only
101,503 members (26,723 of whom were women) at the end of 1923. See *Statistisches Jahrbuch
für das Deutsche Reich 1924/25* (Berlin, 1925), 403. Despite rising again to 179,656 at the end of
1924, during the later years of the Weimar Republic it never again reached even one-third of
the Dec. 1919 figure. See Flemming, *Landwirtschaftliche Interessen*, 289, n. 175.

employers proved successful in beating back the influence of organized labour on the land.[92] This process was particularly brutal in Pomerania, where landowners used Freikorps members on their estates and provoked a series of conflicts from mid-1919 onwards in order to break the power of organized labour: trade-union members and labourers elected to 'works councils' were sacked and found themselves evicted from tied cottages; and by reaching agreements with the dependent workers' associations (with the DLV excluded from negotiations), landowners were able to impose increases in the working day.[93] The extraordinary situation which had greeted soldiers returning in 1918 and 1919 did not last long. Within a few years, pre-war social and economic relationships on the land had been reconstituted, in some cases with a vengeance. What could not be reconstituted, however, was a rural society in which people lived in harmony, stability, and security. The search for such a society was a search for the world that never was. This search was doomed from the start, and was a recipe for disappointment. As such, it contributed mightily to the dissatisfaction and political instability which characterized the German countryside through the remaining troubled history of the Weimer Republic.

How then are we to assess the panic which accompanied the demobilization in the countryside? Despite the forecasts of doom and the dire prophecies about what might happen if the returning soldiers were not forced on to the land or if the *Zwangswirtschaft* were not lifted immediately after the Armistice, German agriculture did not collapse completely after the War. While some of the returning soldiers who had originally come from the countryside no doubt chose to seek their fortunes in the cities, many, if not most, did not; as we can now see in retrospect, the War in fact marked the end of Germany's classic period of urbanization,[94] and the Weimar years did not witness a repetition of the massive *Landflucht* (flight from the land) which had been a feature of life in the Empire. Although for some time after the War food continued to be scarce in Germany's cities, and undernourishment widespread, and although the Allied blockade was not lifted until 12 July 1919, Germany's urban population did not starve. Notwithstanding the panic and despair which enveloped those looking at the sorry state of German agriculture in late 1918 and early 1919, the German countryside made it through the demobilization—battered but more or less intact. The history of the demobilization and of the post-war transition is, in large measure, a history of fears.

---

[92] See Flemming, 'Großagrarische Interessen und Landarbeiterbewegung', 754–62.

[93] APP, Rejencja w Pile, no. 95: 'Lagebericht vom 14. April 1920'; Ibid., 'Lagebericht vom 15. April 1920'; PLA, Rep. 65c, 944, fos. 117–19: Landrat to Oberpräsident, Franzburg, 7 Dec. 1921; ibid., 179–81: Landrat to Oberpräsident, Franzburg, 21 Mar. 1923. See also Flemming, 'Großagrarische Interessen und Landarbeiterbewegung', 754–5; Schumacher, *Land und Politik*, 297–312.

[94] See Jürgen Reulecke, *Geschichte der Urbanisierung in Deutschland* (Frankfurt/Main, 1985).

Yet demobilization was not just a disaster which did not happen. It also left the German countryside with deep problems: with an agricultural sector which remained dependent upon low-paid labour and was insufficiently productive; and with a rural population embittered by the *Zwangswirtschaft*, envious of the living-standards of their urban cousins, and convinced that the regime in Berlin could not be trusted to give rural interests the priority they deserved. Together with the inevitable disappointments which flowed from a post-war transition in which the goal had been somehow to reconstitute a mythical *status quo ante*, this legacy formed a precondition for the bitter political harvest in the later Weimar years, when Germany's rural population formed a vanguard of the popular crusade to undermine democracy.

# 8

## *The Post-war Transition and the Moral Order*

> Our people are suffering badly from the effects of the moral ruin which
> the War has produced; a moral renewal is necessary, if there is no other
> way, through the purifying bath of extreme misery.[1]

ON Friday, 11 April 1919 a curious debate took place in the German
National Assembly. The subject was a government proposal that summer
time (i.e. putting the clocks forward one hour), which had been introduced
as a war measure in 1916, be continued in the post-war period (from 28
April to 15 September 1919). Introducing the first reading of the bill, the
government spokesman (a Professor Köbner) claimed that it possessed
'little conceivable political content' and that 'one might believe—and that
was our hope—that this whole question of summer time would, as it were,
be a peaceful idyll between the heated conflicts over convictions and
ideas which have occupied the National Assembly in this fateful period'.
However, he went on to admit (to cries of 'quite right' from the right-
ming members of the chamber) that 'this now unfortunately appears not
to be the case'. The government's case was a practical one: maintaining
summer time in 1919 would result in savings of coal, gas, and electricity
at a time when these energy sources were in desperately short supply.
The response in the Assembly was almost completely negative. Only one
deputy, Rudolf Hartmann (a medical doctor and a representative of the
German National People's Party from Königshütte in Upper Silesia), spoke
in support of the bill, and his position was disavowed by the leader of his
own parliamentary faction. One speaker after another rose to condemn the
proposal. According to a spokesman of the Bavarian government (which
had been supplanted in Munich by the Räterepublik a few days before),
the rural population regarded it as 'contrary to nature'; Gottlieb Kenngott,
an SPD deputy and trade-union official from Eßlingen in Württemberg,
claimed that 'the introduction of summer time is regarded in many circles
as nothing short of chicanery' and that workers felt particularly unhappy
about the change; Carl Diez, a farmer and Centre Party deputy from
Baden, claimed that 'not a single person in Germany, with the exception of
the Reich Coal Commissar and the German government' wanted summer
time, which he described to loud cheers as a 'monstrosity of unreason'.
However, the most hysterical condemnation of summer time came from

---

[1] Wilhelm Groener, *Der Weltkrieg und seine Probleme: Rückschau und Ausblick* (Berlin, 1920), 104.

Wilhelm Koch, a DDP member from Merseburg and a farmer, who painted a lurid picture of what might be in store if summer time were retained:

What then would happen if the working day really ended somewhat earlier? An increase in *pleasure-seeking* would set in, the workers would not go to bed any earlier and therefore would be less refreshed than if they had really made the most of the day with proper work. We are witnessing what has come to pass after this disastrous war. The pleasure-frenzy, the dancing-mania, the cinema attendance, is downright sinister, and I fear that if summer time really is reintroduced, there would be no check whatsoever on pleasure-seeking. On the contrary, people would have even more time with which to satisfy the desire for dancing and playing, in short, for enjoying life.[2]

After cataloguing the allegedly detrimental effects summer time would have on farmers, milk deliveries, children who had to go to school in the morning, and various categories of workers, Koch sat down to 'stormy applause'—not least from other DDP deputies. The bill was rejected.

The debate—especially Wilhelm Koch's rousing speech—may seem somewhat silly today, yet it reflected widespread fears in Germany after the First World War. These fears were not at all the exclusive property of the conservative Right but—as the debate over summer time demonstrated—extended across the political spectrum. Social Democrats were no less keen than their conservative opponents to re-establish order and morality: it was, for example, the SPD Reichswehr Minister Gustav Noske who, in November 1919, introduced the *Polizeistunde* (closing-time at midnight), and the SPD Reich President Friedrich Ebert personally took the initiative in promoting measures to curb 'excessive public and private entertainment' in the dark days of 1920.[3] Contemporary observers of varying shades and hues convinced themselves that Germany was witnessing an appalling decline in moral standards, in proper traditional values of thrift, hard work, respect for property and for one's elders. To many Germans, the social and moral fabric had been unravelled by war and revolution. Heinrich Brüning no doubt shared the reactions of many when in March 1919 he arrived in Berlin (with its 'filthy streets as a result of the continuing strike by dustmen') and described what he saw as a 'picture of complete moral chaos'.[4] Four years of war, deprivation, political unrest, black-market trading, inflation, and immense strains upon family life seemed to many to have dissolved much of the social cement which had held German

---

[2] See the debate in *Die Deutsche Nationalversammlung im Jahre 1919 in ihrer Arbeit für den Aufbau des neuen deutschen Volksstaates*, ed. E. Heilfron, (Berlin, n.d.), iv. 2371–93. Koch's comments may be found on 2388–92.

[3] Cornelie Usborne, *The Politics of the Body in Weimar Germany: Women's Reproductive Rights and Duties* (London, 1992), 77.

[4] Heinrich Brüning, *Memoiren 1918–1934* (Stuttgart, 1970), 44.

society together before 1914. To be sure, people had been concerned about alleged moral decline before 1914 as well.[5] However, the intensity of these concerns was something new after the First World War. Wherever people looked they saw detrimental social consequences of 'this disastrous war' and a 'pleasure-frenzy' which afflicted a society no longer committed to building for the future but dedicated instead to indulging the desires of the moment.

State officials in particular saw evidence all round them of a collapse of discipline and authority. The increase in political radicalism, together with pleasure-seeking and the precipitate decline in labour productivity were regarded as symptoms of the same disease. 'Economic' and 'moral' conditions were seen as intertwined. Officials viewed the introduction of the eight-hour day, for example, as one of the main reasons why workers loitered about the market-squares of industrial towns and around the cinemas, and why taverns and cafés were filled with customers.[6] The hardships of daily life, the inflation, food shortages, and black-market trading, it was alleged, had

brought about an overturning of legal concepts and impaired the strict order of former times. The bad elements have come out on top and have exercised the most evil influence. The pursuit of easy profit has gripped all sections of the population, and the former disposition for diligent and assiduous working, for orderly business with modest but nevertheless adequate profit has been lost. As a result of the uncertainty over the future and the fear of the heavy burdens which the lost war and the hard peace-treaty impose, everyone lives for the moment and unscrupulously grasps after whatever advantages present themselves.[7]

The world, it seemed, had been turned upside down. Authority no longer commanded respect; 'bad elements' dictated the tenor of public life; respect for hard work and thrift were collapsing with the currency; cavalier disregard for civilized rules of behaviour had replaced pre-war social stability; a get-rich-quick mentality prevailed and success came to the unscrupulous rather than the industrious; and the 'strict order of former times' had dissolved in an anarchy in which sound moral values appeared to count for nothing.

The widespread conviction that Germany was experiencing a catastrophic decline in moral standards and a breakdown of social order thus framed the broader agenda for the demobilization. The concern to return to a *status quo ante* not only affected post-war policies concerning the economy

---

[5] On this subject, see esp. the recent study by Lynn Abrams, *Workers' Culture in Imperial Germany: Leisure and Recreation in the Rhineland and Westphalia* (London, 1992).

[6] HStAD, Reg. Düsseldorf, no. 34345: Gewerbeinspektor für die Kreise Lennep und Remscheid, 'Jahresbericht 1919', Lennep, 29 Jan. 1920.

[7] NHStA, Hann. 122a/XI, no. 103 l, fos. 19–21: Regierungspräsident to Minister des Innern, Lüneburg, 20 Sept. 1919.

and the labour and housing markets; it also surfaced in an anxious desire to reconstitute public morality and 'normal' family life. Demobilizing German society meant not just getting the soldiers out of uniform and into civilian employment, dismantling wartime economic controls and putting 'peacetime' arrangements for the labour market into place. To many people it also meant somehow reconstituting conventional, patriarchal social and family relationships and reimposing conservative moral codes.

The wish to resurrect a world in which moral standards and family and social relationships were intact was nevertheless profoundly misplaced and doomed to disappointment. Whatever were the real possibilities of picking up the pieces after 1918—and, as we shall see below, these possibilities were tiny—the desire to return to a pre-war world in which authority was allegedly respected, family life secure, and moral codes upheld was based upon a set of fundamental misconceptions. In contrast to what Germans caught in the upheavals of 1918 and 1919 may have believed, it is doubtful whether for many of them 'normal' family or social relations had existed anywhere but in their minds. Certainly the fact that millions of fathers had been called away to war (many never to return), and the fact that hundreds of thousands of women had been compelled to take up factory work meant the upheaval of family and social relationships which, at least in retrospect, appeared stable and comfortable. Yet it is important not to idealize the pre-1914 world—as many Germans appear to have done. For most (and certainly for most working-class) Germans, 'normal' family life as we have become accustomed to think of it had not existed before the First World War. Instead, everyday life had been characterized by high physical mobility (whereby perhaps a third of a city's population moved every year), the widespread practice of taking in lodgers (which occurred in 10 to 20 per cent of all households, and a much higher proportion of working-class households, in Imperial Germany), and by children frequently having to leave home to work at a young age.[8] The picture of a happy and healthy family life, in which parents were able to supervise their children closely, in which the stern discipline of the father and the loving care of the mother were ever present, was for many—if not most—Germans a fiction.

---

[8] Erhard Lucas, *Zwei Formen von Radikalismus in der deutschen Arbeiterbewegung* (Frankfurt/Main, 1976), 46–83; Franz J. Brüggemeier and Lutz Niethammer, 'Schlafgänger, Schnapskasinos und schwerindustrielle Kolonie: Aspekte der Arbeiterwohnungsfrage im Ruhrgebiet vor dem Ersten Weltkrieg', in Jürgen Reulecke and Wolfhard Weber (eds.), *Fabrik, Familie, Feierabend: Beiträge zur Sozialgeschichte des Alltags im Industriezeitalter* (Wuppertal, 1978), 148–58. See also Franz-Josef Brüggemeier, *Leben vor Ort: Ruhrbergleute und Ruhrbergbau 1889–1919* (Munich, 1983), 52–68; Michael Grüttner, *Arbeitswelt an der Wasserkante: Sozialgeschichte von Hamburger Hafenarbeiter 1886–1914* (Göttingen, 1984), 102–6; Reinhard Sieder, *Sozialgeschichte der Familie* (Frankfurt/Main, 1987), esp. 146–211; Richard J. Evans, *Death in Hamburg: Society and Politics in the Cholera Years 1830–1910* (Harmondsworth, 1990), 62–8.

However, even if the pre-1914 world *had* been a moral paradise, it would probably have been impossible to resurrect it after 1918. The immediate demographic consequences of the War alone virtually ruled out a rapid reconstitution of pre-war social relations. The size and structure of Germany's population was altered considerably by the consequences of the War and the peace settlement: the deaths of roughly 2 million soldiers, the effects of widespread undernourishment and disease, the steep decline in births while millions of men were away in uniform, and post-war border-changes which meant that territories containing roughly 6.5 million inhabitants (about 3.5 million of whom were German-speaking and more than 700,000 of whom came to Germany as refugees after the War) were removed from the Reich.[9] During the War mortality among males from the ages of 20 to 24 was nearly twelve times what it had been in 1913, and for males from 25 to 29 nearly eight times; and not only combatants were affected, as all age groups—both male and female—registered higher levels of mortality during the War than immediately before.[10] What is more, in the last months of 1918 the military demobilization coincided with a sharp increase in mortality caused largely by the influenza epidemic:[11] German civilian deaths shot up in October 1918 (when they were nearly two and a half times as high as they had been during September), remained extremely high in November, and returned to average wartime levels only in March 1919. Indeed, the months of October and November 1918 registered the highest civilian mortality rates in Germany for the entire war![12] Thereafter, however, the high mortality of the war years and the early weeks of the demobilization was reversed quite quickly. By 1919 and 1920, despite the continued shortages of food and fuel, it had returned to pre-war levels; from 1921 onwards it fell well below pre-war rates, continuing the long-term improvement which has characterized German mortality during the past century.[13] Nevertheless, the millions of extra deaths which occurred during the years 1914–19 cast a shadow across German society for many years.

---

[9] *Statistisches Jahrbuch für das Deutsche Reich 1924/25* (Berlin, 1925), 14–15; Peter Marschalck, *Bevölkerungsgeschichte Deutschlands im 19. und 20. Jahrhundert* (Frankfurt/Main, 1984), 70.

[10] See Eberhard Heinel, 'Die Bevölkerungsbewegung im Deutschen Reich in der Kriegs- und Nachkriegszeit' (Univ. of Berlin, Phil. diss., 1927), 155–8, and table 50, 'Die Sterblichkeit im Deutschen Reich in den Jahren 1913–22 nach Geschlecht und Altersklassen'. See also Marschalck, *Bevölkerungsgeschichte*, 169.

[11] See e.g. the monthly death-statistics for the Thuringian States in Thüringisches Statistisches Landesamt (ed.), *Statistisches Handbuch für das Land Thüringen, 1922* (Weimar, 1922), 62; and for Leipzig in Statistisches Amt, *Statistisches Jahrbuch der Stadt Leipzig*, v, 1915–1918 (Leipzig, 1921), 50–1, 61.

[12] It is worth noting that those most severely affected by the influenza epidemic were not the old but those in their late teens, twenties, and thirties; e.g. in Leipzig in Oct. 1918 there were 1,761 civilian deaths (as against 622 during the previous month). Of these, 44% (775) were aged between 15 and 39, whereas only 27.3% of the civilian deaths in the city during 1918 as a whole were from this age group. See *Statistisches Jahrbuch der Stadt Leipzig, 1915–1918*, 61.

[13] See the table in Marschalck, *Bevölkerungsgeschichte*, 165.

The War therefore left Germany with a profoundly skewed population-structure. Women far outnumbered men, particularly among the cohorts of people born between the mid-1880s and the turn of the century. In Leipzig, for example, in October 1919 out of a total resident population of 604,397, there were 44,283 more females than males; there were 36 per cent more women between the ages of 20 and 30 than there were men, and the number of women of 26 (6,584) was more than half as much again as the number of men of that age (4,306).[14] Germany's population was skewed in other ways as well. The high numbers of births during the pre-war years, the low birth-rates between 1915 and 1919, and the fact that disease tended to take a higher toll of the older members of the community during the War[15] combined to leave behind a quite peculiar age-structure. To remain with Leipzig: in 1919 the Saxon metropolis contained nearly 2.5 times as many 12-year-olds (11,486) as 2-year-olds (4,624); altogether, there were nearly twice as many children between the ages of 10 and 15 (56,981) in Leipzig as there were children up to 5 years old (29,231).[16] In other words, with the sharp fall in births during the War, and relatively high mortality among the elderly as a consequence of the deprivations on the home front, adolescents comprised a disproportionately large section of the population at the War's end. Not only did teenagers make up an extremely large proportion of the population (perhaps larger than ever before in modern Germany), but at the same time mortality among those very groups which might be expected to look after German youth—fathers, elder brothers, or grandparents—had been extraordinarily high. This formed the demographic context of the widespread anxiety during and after the War about youth running wild and the perceived need to re-establish discipline and respect for authority.[17]

The wartime losses were felt most deeply by women who had been robbed of their husbands. Their number was substantial. As approximately 2 million German soldiers met their deaths in the First World War, and just over 30 per cent of them had been married, it follows that the conflict left behind roughly 600,000 war widows.[18] (In 1923 the Reich Labour Ministry estimated

---

[14] Statistisches Amt, *Statistisches Jahrbuch der Stadt Leipzig*, v: *1915–1918*, 14. In 1910 there had been 15,538 more females than males in Leipzig. Ibid. 12.

[15] For Leipzig, see the tables showing mortality from 1915 to 1918 broken down by age of the population: ibid. 60–1.

[16] Ibid. 14.

[17] For an excellent concise discussion of the peculiar demographic position of the 'superfluous generation' youth in Weimar Germany, see Detlev J. K. Peukert, *Jugend zwischen Krieg und Krise: Lebenswelten von Arbeiterjungen in der Weimarer Republik* (Cologne, 1987), 30–8.

[18] This is also the figure arrived at by Karin Hausen, 'The German Nation's Obligation to the Heroes' Widows of World War I', in Margaret Randolph Higonnet, Jane Jenson, Sonya Michel, and Margaret Collins Weitz (eds.), *Behind the Lines: Gender and the Two World Wars* (New Haven, Conn., and London, 1987), 128. See also Karl School, 'Die soziale Lage der Kriegs-witwen in Hamburg: Eine Darstellung aufgrund der Ergebnisse von 300 Monographien' (Univ. of Hamburg, Phil. diss., 1924), 45.

the number of widows which the War left in its wake at 533,000.)[19] About 200,000 had been able to remarry during the immediate post-war period; thereafter, however, war widows appear much less likely to have found new partners.[20] Those who were able to do so were the lucky ones. In his survey of war widows in Hamburg in 1923, Karl Scholl found that, for those who remarried, the second marriage provided, 'at least economically, a complete and often better substitute for the loss caused by the death of the former breadwinner'.[21] Others were not so fortunate. In 1925 there were 250,000 (or 60 per cent) more widows in the 25–40 age group than had been the case in 1910,[22] and the numbers of women receiving war widows' pensions remained stable, at about 360,000, from 1924 through to the end of the Weimar period.[23]

While they formed only a minority of the 2.8 million widows recorded in the 1925 census, and headed only a small proportion of German households, war widows who did not remarry and became dependent upon state pensions were generally those who lived in most difficult circumstances after the War.[24] Their pensions were modest, often sufficient to meet the cost of food and little else, and the post-war inflation created enormous difficulties for those dependent upon fixed state benefits.[25] These were women for whom it had been impossible to take the step which for hundreds of thousands of others formed the most important aspect of the post-war transition: giving up paid employment and returning to the relative comfort of home.[26] Special

[19] See Robert Weldon Whalen, *Bitter Wounds: German Victims of the Great War, 1914–1939* (Ithaca, NY, and London, 1984), 95.

[20] Scholl, 'Die soziale Lage der Kriegswitwen', 88; Hausen, 'The German Nation's Obligation', 128; Whalen, *Bitter Wounds*, 109. In 1919 12.5% of the women who married were widows, in 1920 10.5% and in 1921 9.4% which means that nearly 270,000 widows (not all of whom were necessarily war widows) remarried during this period. See *Statistisches Jahrbuch für das Deutsche Reich 1924/25*, 34.

[21] Scholl, 'Die soziale Lage der Kriegswitwen', 98. Not surprisingly, it appears that those who remarried 'chose their new husbands from the same social standing as that to which the deceased belonged'. Ibid. 102.

[22] See Adelheid zu Castell, 'Die demographischen Konsequenzen des Ersten und Zweiten Weltkrieges für das Deutsche Reich, die Deutsche Demokratische Republik und die Bundesrepublik Deutschland', in Waclaw Dlugoborski (ed.), *Zweiter Weltkrieg und sozialer Wandel: Achsenmächte und besetzte Länder* (Göttingen, 1981), 118.

[23] In 1924 364,950 widows were receiving pensions, in 1928 359,560, and in 1931 360,930. See Whalen, *Bitter Wounds*, 110. Of the 364,950 widows receiving pensions in 1924, 78,326 had no children under 18 years of age; the remaining 286,624 widows were responsible for the support of 594,843 children eligible for dependants' allowance (30.5 per cent had one child, 24.9 per cent had two children, 13.8 per cent had three, and 9.3 per cent had four or more to support); and 88.9 per cent were aged between 30 and 50. See Hausen, 'The German Nation's Obligation', 128.

[24] See Scholl, 'Die soziale Lage der Kriegswitwen', esp. 86–8.

[25] For wartime widows' pensions and the problems widows faced, see Whalen, *Bitter Wounds*, 75–6; for details of wartime and post-war widows' pensions see Hausen, 'The German Nation's Obligation', 132–4. See also Scholl, 'Die soziale Lage der Kriegswitwen', 100, 122–35 (for the amounts of widows' pensions from 1922–5).

[26] See Richard Bessel, ' "Eine nicht allzu große Beunruhigung des Arbeitsmarktes". Frauenarbeit und Demobilmachung in Deutschland nach dem Ersten Weltkrieg', *Geschichte und Gesellschaft*, 9 (1983), 226–8; Hausen, 'The German Nation's Obligation', 137–40.

consideration had been given to war widows when women were dismissed *en masse* as the soldiers returned, and chivalrous authorities urged that widows be allowed to keep their jobs during early 1919 since 'they need to do so in order to maintain themselves and to care for their children';[27] nevertheless, the living-standards of many widows and their families deteriorated sharply as they were compelled to survive on limited pensions and meagre earnings from low-paid work.[28]

Closely linked to the fate of the war widows was that of the estimated 1,192,000 'war orphans' whom the conflict left in its wake.[29] In many communities such children formed the largest single group of recipients of war-related state benefits during the early 1920s,[30] and even as late as 1930 war orphans remained a major category of state-welfare recipients.[31] Although the consequent claims on public funds were enormous, the problem posed by the 'war orphans' was not regarded as merely financial. To many observers the most important aspect of the problem was that as a result of the War over one million German children had been deprived of a father's involvement in their upbringing. The large numbers of young people who thus had to grow up without the supposed benefits of 'the stern hand of the father' fed the fears of people anxious about a decline in discipline and moral standards after the War.[32]

War widows and orphans were not the only people to have suffered irreplaceable loss and consequent deprivation. So had many elderly and invalid parents who had depended for support upon sons subsequently lost in the War. These people aroused relatively little public concern, however; poverty-stricken and disabled old people do not pose threats to established patterns of authority as do the young. The financial demands which the 'war parents' placed upon the public purse were also much smaller than those made by the widows and orphans. For example, in Breslau there were only about one-eighth as many cases of parents requesting war-related welfare payments (516) at the War's end as there were of widows doing so

---

[27] PLA, Rep. 38b Loitz, no. 1010, fo. 18: Zentralauskunftstelle an sämtl. Bezirksarbeitsnachweise, Stettin, 18 Feb. 1919.

[28] See Karl Nau, *Die wirtschaftliche und soziale Lage von Kriegshinterbliebenen: Eine Studie auf Grund von Erhebungen über die Auswirkungen der Versorgung von Kriegshinterbliebenen in Darmstadt* (Leipzig, 1930), 28–30. Nau found in Darmstadt in 1930 that 31.5% of working widows had a monthly income of less than RM 25, and 50.6% earned less than RM 50 monthly; only one in four earned more than RM 100 monthly.

[29] This was the estimate of the Reich Labour Ministry in 1923. See Whalen, *Bitter Wounds*, 95.

[30] See e.g. the breakdown of benefit recipients in the Regierungsbezirk Stralsund in 1922, in PLA, Rep. 65c, no. 2312, fo. 257: 'Jahresbericht des Reg.- und Medizinalrates in Stralsund für das Jahr 1922 für den Regierungsbezirk Stralsund'.

[31] e.g. see the details of welfare recipients in Darmstadt during 1930 in Nau, *Die wirtschaftliche und soziale Lage*, 10.

[32] See Ute Daniel, *Arbeiterfrauen in der Kriegsgesellschaft: Beruf, Familie und Politik im Ersten Weltkrieg* (Göttingen, 1989), 158–67; Whalen, *Bitter Wounds*, 80–1.

(3,933);[33] and in the Pomeranian Regierungsbezirk Stralsund in 1922 the number of such parents receiving benefits was about one-quarter the number of widows and one-eighth the number of children.[34] Nevertheless, the difficulties they faced could be extreme: without even the limited earning-possibilities available to many war widows, 'war parents' often became dependent upon state welfare payments—which during a period of rapid inflation made life very difficult indeed.

To point out that Germans faced enormous obstacles to reconstituting conventional social relationships and moral codes after the First World War is to assert neither that they failed to try nor that none succeeded. Despite the difficulties, large numbers of war veterans did manage to settle into expected social relationships. After years away from home, in uniform, threatened with injury and death, most soldiers who survived the War were keen to settle into conventional family life—'to return home at any price!'[35] Similarly, many women who had spent the war years doing heavy work in difficult and often unhealthy conditions, no doubt found the prospect of falling into the role of housewife and mother quite attractive—providing, of course, that these options were open to them.[36] After years of war and deprivation, people desperately wanted 'normality' to return to their private lives.

The most obvious, and most predictable, expression of the widespread desire to return to 'normal' family life after the War was the upsurge in marriages and births from 1919 through to 1923. During the immediate post-war years hundreds of thousands of marriages and births occurred which would otherwise have taken place during the War; a comparison of the total number of marriages in 1919 and 1920 with the numbers before and during the war years suggests that roughly half a million such postponed marriages of veterans took place in the immediate aftermath of the conflict (see Tables 26 and 27).

The immediate effects of the demobilization upon marriage and repro-ductive behaviour were striking. As noted above, the soldiers returned to Germany very quickly after the Armistice; by mid-January 1919 virtually the whole of the armies from the western front, which had accounted for the bulk of German forces, had been demobilized, and two months later so

---

[33] APW, Akta Miasta Wroclawia, no. 6999, fo. 188: Fürsorgestelle für Hinterbliebene von Kriegsteilnehmern, Breslau, 30 Oct. 1918.

[34] PLA, Rep. 65c, no. 2312, fo. 257.

[35] Thus the Reich War Ministry describing the overriding preoccupation of German soldiers after the War in an account, published in 1936, of their return from the eastern front. See Reichskriegsministerium, Forschungsamt für Kriegs- und Heeresgeschichte (ed.), *Die Rückführung des Ostheeres (Darstellung aus den Nachkriegskämpfen deutscher Truppen und Freikorps)* (Berlin, 1936), 22.

[36] See Bessel, ' "Eine nicht allzu große Beunruhigung des Arbeitsmarktes" ', 226–9; Helgard Kramer, 'Frankfurt's Working Women: Scapegoats or Winners of the Great Depression', in Richard J. Evans and Dick Geary (eds.), *The German Unemployed: Experiences and Consequences of Mass Unemployment from the Weimar Republic to the Third Reich* (London and Sydney, 1987), 115–16.

Table 26. *Marriages, Births, and Deaths in Germany, 1910–1924*
(within German borders at the time)

| Year | Marriages | Births | Deaths |
|------|-----------|--------|--------|
| 1910 | 496,396 | 1,982,836 | 1,103,723 |
| 1911 | 512,819 | 1,927,039 | 1,187,094 |
| 1912 | 523,491 | 1,925,883 | 1,085,996 |
| 1913 | 513,283 | 1,894,598 | 1,060,798 |
| 1914 | 460,608 | 1,874,389 | 1,347,103 |
| 1915 | 278,208 | 1,425,596 | 1,493,470 |
| 1916 | 279,076 | 1,062,287 | 1,330,857 |
| 1917[a] | 308,446 | 939,938 | 1,373,253 |
| 1918[a] | 352,543 | 956,251 | 1,635,913 |
| 1919 | 844,339 | 1,299,404 | 1,017,284 |
| 1920 | 894,978 | 1,651,593 | 985,235 |
| 1921 | 731,157 | 1,611,420 | 911,172 |
| 1922 | 681,891 | 1,450,893 | 927,304 |
| 1923 | 581,277 | 1,340,154 | 900,603 |
| 1924 | 440,071 | 1,311,044 | 802,166 |

[a] without Alsace-Lorraine
Source: *Statistisches Jahrbuch für das Deutsche Reich 1924/25*, 41.

Table 27. *Marriages, Births, and Deaths per 1,000 Inhabitants in Germany,*
*1910–1924*
(within German borders at the time)

| Year | Marriages | Births | Deaths |
|------|-----------|--------|--------|
| 1910 | 7.7 | 30.7 | 17.1 |
| 1911 | 7.8 | 29.5 | 18.2 |
| 1912 | 7.9 | 29.1 | 16.4 |
| 1913 | 7.7 | 28.3 | 15.8 |
| 1914 | 6.8 | 26.8 | 19.9 |
| 1915 | 4.1 | 21.0 | 22.0 |
| 1916 | 4.1 | 15.7 | 19.7 |
| 1917[a] | 4.7 | 14.4 | 21.0 |
| 1918[a] | 5.4 | 14.7 | 25.2 |
| 1919 | 13.4 | 20.7 | 16.2 |
| 1920 | 14.5 | 26.7 | 15.9 |
| 1921 | 11.8 | 26.1 | 14.8 |
| 1922 | 11.1 | 23.7 | 15.1 |
| 1923 | 9.4 | 21.7 | 14.6 |
| 1924 | 7.1 | 21.1 | 12.9 |

[a] without Alsace-Lorraine
Source: as Table 26.

had most of the soldiers from the east. In February 1919, when comparable
pre-war levels were matched the numbers of marriages had already begun

to rise from their low wartime monthly totals; from that point on, through 1919 and 1920, the numbers of marriages far outstripped pre-war monthly totals, often being double the 1913 levels.[37] The months favoured for marriages nevertheless remained more or less as they had been before 1914: April and May were the most popular (with the peak reached in May 1920), closely followed by October and December. However, there was one reveal-ing difference: an extra upsurge in marriages which set in towards the end of 1919—roughly nine months after the military demobilization had largely been completed—and which rather digressed from the patterns seen before the War.[38] Many of these post-war marriages no doubt were precipitated by unplanned pregnancies, the 'most frequent reason for a marriage also in the Weimar Republic'[39] and an inevitable consequence of the sudden return of millions of young men to their *Heimat.*

Like the wave of marriages, the upsurge in births reflected with noticeable accuracy the timing of the demobilization. The number of births began to rise appreciably above wartime levels in August 1919, and by September was higher than pre-war levels.[40] From the spring of 1920, however, monthly figures for births fell somewhat; they were still far higher than the wartime totals, but they barely equalled the pre-1914 figures. After the first few years following the soldiers' return home, there was a rapid resumption—indeed an acceleration—of the long-term trend towards lower fertility which had set in well before the First World War. Notwithstanding the return of the soldiers and the immediate upsurge in births, couples were controlling their fertility and planning their families—behaviour which looked forward to present-day habits more than backward to the 'child-rich' families which had been so common during the Imperial period.[41] For those to whom

---

[37] A good view is provided by monthly figures for the Thuringian States from 1913 through 1920, in Thüringisches Statistisches Landesamt (ed.), *Statistisches Handbuch für das Land Thüringen, 1922*, 44. For month-by-month marriage-statistics for the entire Reich from 1914–19, see Statistisches Reichsamt (ed.), *Statistik des Deutschen Reichs*, vol. cclxxvi: *Bewegung der Bevölkerung in den Jahren 1914 bis 1919* (Berlin, 1922), pp. xvii–xviii.

[38] In the case of the Thuringian states, the Nov. 1919 figure was 210% that of Nov. 1913, and the Dec. 1919 figure was 223% of the comparable 1913 figure, whereas the 1919 total was 172% of the 1913 total. The Jan. 1920 figure was 217% that of the Jan. 1914 figure, and this pattern continued to May 1920, when the figure was 233% of the comparable total 6 years earlier. See Thüringisches Statistisches Landesamt (ed.), *Statistisches Handbuch für das Land Thüringen, 1922*, 44.

[39] Karen Hagemann, *Frauenalltag und Männerpolitik: Alltagsleben und gesellschaftliches Handeln von Arbeiterfrauen in der Weimarer Republik* (Bonn, 1990), 174.

[40] Statistisches Reichsamt (ed.), *Statistik des Deutschen Reichs*, vol. cclxxvi, p. xxxiv; Thüringisches Statistisches Landesamt (ed.), *Statistisches Handbuch für das Land Thüringen, 1922*, 55.

[41] A comparison of the proportion of 1919–21 marriages which brought forth more than 2 children with the proportion of pre-war marriages which did so demonstrates these points quite clearly; e.g. between 1900 and 1904, 63% of marriages resulted in at least 3 children; for 1910–12 the figure was 49%; and for 1919–21 the figure was only 37%. See the table reproduced in Marschalck, *Bevölkerungsgeschichte Deutschlands*, 158. For qualitative as well as quantitative evidence of this trend during the Weimar period, see Hagemann, *Frauenalltag und Männerpolitik*, 197–204.

families with large numbers of children signalled moral and physical heal-
thiness of the nation, the acceleration of the trend towards declining fertility,
and towards the widespread acceptance of a 'two-child system' was extremely
worrying.[42]

Another sign of the alleged post-war decline in moral standards was an
increase in the number of divorces. The Weimar Constitution of 1919 paid
the ritual tribute to marriage as the foundation of family life and to its
importance for the nation.[43] Introducing her 1927 study of divorce in Saxony
between 1920 and 1924, Ida Rost echoed sentiments which no doubt were
shared by most of her fellow citizens: 'If marriage is disturbed, family life
is thereby endangered, and if marriage difficulties become particularly
numerous, the preservation and propagation of the nation will also be
impaired.'[44] Although divorce rates during the Weimar period appear quite
low when compared with present-day figures, they nevertheless alarmed
contemporaries, who were convinced that family life was being undermined.
Divorces in Germany, which had averaged 15,633 per annum between 1909
and 1913, peaked at 39,216 in 1921 and remained at levels more than
double the pre-war rates after the stabilization (see Table 28).

Table 28. *Divorces per 100,000 Inhabitants
in Germany, 1909–1925*

| | |
|---|---|
| 1909–1913 (average) | 24.6 |
| 1913 | 26.6 |
| 1914 | 26.2 |
| 1915 | 15.9 |
| 1916 | 15.5 |
| 1917 | 17.7 |
| 1918 | 20.6 |
| 1919 | 35.0 |
| 1920 | 59.1 |
| 1921 | 62.9 |
| 1922 | 59.7 |
| 1923 | 55.0 |
| 1924 | 57.8 |
| 1925 | 56.8 |

*Sources: Statistisches Jahrbuch für das Deutsche Reich 1921/22,
48; 1924/25, 51; 1927, 44. Also Statistik des Deutschen
Reiches, vol. cclxxvi, p: xxxiii; and Ida Rost, Die Ehescheidungen der Jahre 1920–1924 von in Sachsen geschlossenen Ehen,
unter besonderer Berücksichtigung der Dauer der Ehen und des
Heiratsalters der geschiedenen Ehegatten (Leipzig, 1927), 31.*

[42] See Usborne, *The Politics of the Body*, esp. 31–42.
[43] Verfassung des Deutschen Reiches vom 11.8.1919, Art. 119.
[44] Ida Rost, *Die Ehescheidungen der Jahre 1920–1924 von in Sachsen geschlossenen Ehen, unter besonderer
Berücksichtigung der Dauer der Ehen und des Heiratsalters der geschiedenen Ehegatten* (Leipzig, 1927), 1.

Initially the War had led to a decline in the divorce rate, in part because some of the more frequent grounds for divorce—maltreatment, drunkenness, prison sentences—arose less frequently when so many men were away in the armed forces (and many had been killed!).[45] However, the end of the conflict had the reverse effect, as some couples discovered that hasty wartime or post-war marriages had been a mistake once they actually began to live together, that one or the other partner had been unfaithful during the long separation, or that financial independence during wartime had given the woman a new perspective on married life. It is fairly clear that many of the additional divorces during the demobilization period were breakdowns of wartime and post-war marriages of soldiers or veterans; the proportion of divorced couples who had been married for less than five years rose markedly between 1920 and 1924 (in Saxony, for example, from 27.3 to 37.1 per cent), while the ages of people who divorced changed little.[46] Thus the post-war increase in the number of divorces may be viewed, at least in part, as 'the other side of the often over-hasty wartime weddings and the "marriage epidemic" of the post-war period'.[47] Yet this point was lost on those who viewed the rising divorce-rate, and the fact that it was far higher than in other European countries, as clear evidence of moral decline, and who saw their fears confirmed by the stabilization of the divorce rate at a new, higher level during the 1920s.[48]

Similar anxiety was aroused by illegitimate births, which accounted for a rising proportion of total births during the War, and in the early 1920s remained relatively higher than before the conflict (see Table 29). However, like so much evidence of alleged immoral behaviour during and after the War, these figures reveal less than first meets the eye. More than anything else, they probably reflect more the changed composition of Germany's female population. Whereas in 1913 the majority (54.1 per cent) of the 17.1 million German women between the ages of 15 and 50 were married (9,265,913 married women as against 7,877,132 who were unmarried), the deaths of hundreds of thousands of husbands on the battlefield and the decline in the numbers of marriages during the War meant that four years later the proportions of married and unmarried were roughly reversed: of the 17,722,663 German women between 15 and 50 in 1917, 8,600,876 were married and 9,121,757 (51.5 per cent) were unmarried.[49] When this is taken

---

[45] Rost, *Die Ehescheidungen der Jahre 1920–1924*, 20.

[46] For the breakdown by length of marriage, see ibid. 43–4, for the breakdown by age of the partners, 55–6. The 1920 breakdown by length of marriage was similar to that before the War.

[47] Heinel, 'Die Bevölkerungsbewegung im Deutschen Reich', 20 fo.

[48] In 1921 the divorce rate in Germany was roughly five times as high as in England and Wales. See Usborne, *The Politics of the Body*, 91.

[49] Statistisches Reichsamt (ed.), *Statistik des Deutschen Reichs*, vol. cclxxvi, pp. xxxv–xxxvi; Heinel, 'Die Bevölkerungsbewegung im Deutschen Reich', 84.

Table 29. *Legitimate and Illegitimate Births in Germany,*[a] *1913–1924*

| Year | Legitimate births | Illegitimate births | Illegitimate births as % of total births |
|------|------|------|------|
| 1913 | 1,668,416 | 180,568 | 9.77 |
| 1914 | 1,650,328 | 180,564 | 9.86 |
| 1915 | 1,239,525 | 156,384 | 11.20 |
| 1916 | 925,208 | 115,001 | 11.06 |
| 1917 | 831,605 | 108,333 | 11.53 |
| 1918 | 830,998 | 125,253 | 13.10 |
| 1919 | 1,154,101 | 145,303 | 11.18 |
| 1920 | 1,463,543 | 188,050 | 11.39 |
| 1921 | 1,438,251 | 173,169 | 10.75 |
| 1922 | 1,293,891 | 157,002 | 10.82 |
| 1923 | 1,199,738 | 140,416 | 10.48 |
| 1924 | 1,174,304 | 139,321 | 10.61 |

[a] Without Alsace-Lorraine.

*Sources*: Eberhard Heinel, 'Die Bevölkerungsbewegung in Deutschen Reich in der Kriegs- und Nachkriegszeit' (Univ. of Berlin, Phil. diss., 1927), 83, 86. Also *Statistisches Jahrbuch für das Deutsche Reich 1924/25* (Berlin, 1925), 30–1; *1926* (Berlin, 1926), 29.

into consideration, the changes in the child-bearing activity of married as opposed to unmarried women becomes insignificant; indeed, during 1916 and 1917 the numbers of *illegitimate* children per thousand unmarried women were lower relative to the 1913 figures than were the numbers of *legitimate* children per thousand married women. That is to say, unmarried women had not become more likely to give birth to illegitimate children. Eberhard Heinel, who discussed these figures in a thesis on German population-movement completed in 1927, concluded that 'this favourable outcome must come as a surprise if one brings to mind the so often deplored relaxation of discipline and morals that . . . the War brought with it'.[50] Those who looked to evidence of changing social habits to confirm bald assertions of a rising tide of immorality often read their own fears and prejudices into the statistics before them, statistics which hardly provide unambiguous evidence of moral decline.

Perhaps the most revealing reflection of the anxiety about an alleged upsurge in immoral behaviour was the tremendous public concern about venereal disease. Fear of what the soldiers might bring back from the front

---

[50] Heinel, 'Die Bevölkerungsbewegung im Deutschen Reich', 85. According to Karen Hagemann, the decline in both legitimate and illegitimate births during the Weimar period was due to increased use of birth control. She also notes that, in Hamburg, the proportion of women aged under 20 among those who gave birth to illegitimate children dropped steeply in 1919 as compared with 1913, while the proportion of those aged 25–35 rose fairly sharply; the proportion aged 20–5, which accounted for nearly half of all illegitimate births, remained roughly steady. See Hagemann, *Frauenalltag und Männerpolitik*, 179–85.

combined with fear about the breakdown in moral standards to fuel near-panic among civil authorities concerned with public health and fearful that an epidemic of venereal diseases would lead to widespread sterility in marriage, diseased infants, and a decline in the quality of a population already severely depleted by war. The prospect of a return of millions of infected, sex-starved men had stimulated much wartime discussion of the need to combat venereal diseases, and after the Armistice almost everyone involved in public health appeared convinced that venereal disease constituted a major problem. There were genuine grounds for concern. The speed of the demobilization and the chaotic circumstances surrounding it undermined the War Ministry's intention to release soldiers with venereal disease only after treatment.[51] The spectre of sex-starved servicemen visiting prostitutes in hospital, where the women were undergoing treatment for venereal disease, fuelled fears.[52] Within weeks of the Armistice, in mid-December 1918, the new Reich government issued decrees for 'combating venereal diseases' (authorizing compulsory treatment for those with veneral disease and prison sentences of up to three years for those who were aware of being infected and nevertheless had sexual relations) and 'care for members of the armed forces with venereal disease' (ensuring that the treatment of soldiers with venereal diseases continued after their demobilization).[53] Policing-powers were given to public-health officials; compulsory treatment for those suspected of being infected was extended to include men as well as women. Government officials were reminded repeatedly about the threat posed to public health by the hordes returning from the trenches, and about the need to ensure that infected men received medical treatment.[54]

Soldiers were not the only objects of concern. Worry about the welfare of German women was particularly revealing of the anxiety about morality which spread across post-war Germany. In mid-December 1918 the Reich Office for Economic Demobilization expressed concern about the 'large number of the women employed hitherto in factories on war work' who were 'at present temporarily homeless and jobless', and warned: 'The danger exists that, especially in all the places likely to be transit stations for the

---

[51] NHStA, Hann. 174 Springe, IV, no. 22: Kriegsministerium to sämtl. iche Gen. Kdos. bezw. Stellv. Gen.kdos., Berlin, 12 Dec. 1918.

[52] Thus sailors in Wilhelmshaven when the War ended. See NHStA, Hann. 122a/XI, no. 103 1, fos. 33–6: Regierungspräsident to (Preuß.) Minister des Innern in Berlin, Aurich, 18 Sept. 1919. According to the author of the report, 'not until iron bars were attached and a special guard was posted could an end be put to these shameless goings-on'.

[53] *Reichsgesetzblatt*, 1918, 1431: 'Verordnung zur Bekämpfung der Geschlechtskrankheiten', 11 Dec. 1918; ibid. 1433: 'Verordnung über Fürsorge für geschlechtskranke Heeresangehörige', 17 Dec. 1918. See also Paul Weindling, *Health, Race and German Politics between National Unification and Nazism 1870–1945* (Cambridge, 1989), 357.

[54] See e.g. SSAL, Amtshauptmannschaft Döbeln, no. 2267, fo. 11: Ministerium des Innern to Kreishauptmannschaften, Dresden, 3 Feb. 1919.

returning army, a large proportion of these women will come on to the streets and that the danger of infection and of moral decay will thereby be heightened.'[55] The return of the soldiers was accompanied by the strict surveillance and medical examination of both registered prostitutes and 'girls who fall into clandestine prostitution', as well as by heightened determination that those found to have venereal disease be hospitalized.[56] In public-health reports during the immediate post-war years regional medical officers invariably referred to rises in the incidence of venereal disease;[57] even where they had to admit that the statistical evidence was lacking, doctors were convinced 'that at any rate venereal diseases crop up far more frequently than in peacetime'—i.e. before 1914.[58]

The fear that the sudden release of millions of soldiers into civil society had led to an epidemic of sexually transmitted diseases was amplified by the German Society for the Combating of Venereal Diseases. In a leaflet distributed in early 1920, the Society asserted that while 'venereal disease was formerly limited mainly to the large cities', the War had changed all that: 'During the War, however, many were infected while in the areas behind the lines and in the large military garrisons at home, infected with diseases which after the precipitate demobilization were carried into the smaller towns and the countryside and even into families themselves.'[59] Introducing his analysis of statistics of venereal disease between 1910 and 1921 (published in the Society's journal) the socialist eugenicist and Secretary of the Society, Dr Georg Löwenstein, painted a lurid picture of the post-war epidemic. According to Löwenstein, after the 'devastating effect' of the War 'with its enormous shocks to all bourgeois standards'—a war which had led 'millions of unmarried and married men' into immoral lives in foreign lands and during which 'not infrequently the women back home failed to conduct themselves perfectly'—there then came the revolution, 'which led to a lack of restraint in many fields, bringing a degeneration (*Verwilderung*), especially of sexual morals, to an extent not seen even during the War'. The revolution, Löwenstein reported, was accompanied by 'the sudden emptying of almost all military infirmaries for venereal disease', with the consequence that 'many tens of thousands of the infected discontinued regular treatment and returned to the bosom of their families or were submerged into the maelstrom of the

---

[55] StdABr, 025/11/1, fo. 40: Reichsamt für die wirtschaftliche Demobilmachung to Demobilmachungsausschüsse des Bezirks Lehe, Berlin, 11 Dec. 1918.

[56] StAO, Rep. 430, Dez. 303, Zug no. 19/43, 21: Polizeidirektion to Regierungspräsident, Osnabrück, 14 Dec. 1918.

[57] e.g. PLA, Rep. 65c, no. 2312, fos. 96–9: Regierungsbezirk Stralsund, 'Jahresgesundheitsbericht umfassend das Jahr 1920'.

[58] APP, Rejencja w Pile, no. 2477: Grenzmark Posen-Westpreußen, 'Jahresgesundheitsbericht 1920', 25.

[59] NHStA, Hann. 174 Springe IV, no. 22: Deutsche Gesellschaft zur Bekämpfung der Geschlechtskrankheiten to Magistrat, Berlin, 31 Jan. 1920.

big city'. Germany faced the prospect of being overrun 'in an undreamt-of manner' by hordes of people with sexually transmitted diseases.[60]

Venereal disease, once regarded as confined to the big cities, appeared to be invading and contaminating small towns and the countryside—reaching 'even into families themselves'! The plague was no longer restricted to the urban areas, which many regarded as degenerate in any event; now it was invading the hitherto healthy rural heartlands upon which Germany's moral regeneration depended. And not just moral regeneration: fears abounded that the spread of venereal diseases would make large numbers of women infertile and thus incapable of helping to make good the enormous human losses suffered during the War.[61] German society was seen in biological terms; the allegedly healthy body of rural and small-town Germany, with its defences weakened by the overturning of established authority, was under attack from an advancing plague. Venereal disease was only the most alarming consequence of the alleged breakdown of moral standards, which had to be reversed if Germany was ever to become healthy again.[62]

Were the fears well-founded? The answer remains uncertain. An incomplete national survey on the extent of venereal disease, attempted by the Reich Health Office between 15 November and 14 December 1919, led authorities to believe that in cities venereal disease had increased substantially—which provided justification for strong measures against it.[63] Medical men such as Löwenstein were undoubtedly concerned to emphasize the seriousness of the problem, in order to arouse support for measures to deal with the perceived demographic crisis created by Germany's declining birth-rate and the huge losses occasioned by war. To all appearances the defeat and revolution coincided with a substantial rise in the incidence of venereal disease within Germany as compared with the war years, and advice centres for those with venereal disease were overwhelmed with visitors— largely soldiers—in the weeks after the Armistice.[64] However, this may essentially have been an inevitable consequence of the sudden return to Germany of millions of men in their sexually active years, and it is questionable whether levels of venereal disease after the War were significantly higher than before 1914. Contrary to widespread belief, the proportion of soldiers with venereal disease was no greater during the War than it had been before; the wartime precautions taken by the authorities appear

[60] BAK, R 86, no. 1063: Dr Georg Loewenstein, 'Kritische Betrachtungen und Beiträge zur Statistik der Geschlechtskrankheiten (1910–1921)', Sonderdruck aus der *Zeitschrift für Bekämpfung der Geschlechtskrankheiten*, 20: 8-12, p. 139. On Löwenstein more generally, see Weindling, *Health, Race and German Politics*, 353.

[61] Usborne, *The Politics of the Body*, 110.

[62] See Weindling, *Health, Race and German Politics*, 305–98.

[63] Ibid. 357.

[64] See e.g. NHStA, Hann. 174 Springe IV, no. 22: 'Jahresbericht der Beratungsstelle für Geschlechtskranke in Hannover für 1919'.

to have had some effect. Statistics for the navy between 1912 and 1918 show that the proportion of sailors with venereal disease during the War was actually lower than before 1914: in 1913, for example, 5.78 per cent of sailors were infected; by 1915 the proportion had sunk to 4.72 per cent, and in 1918 it stood at 4.84 per cent.[65] Figures for the army also show little difference in the frequency of venereal disease among soldiers before and during the War: the proportion of men behind the lines (in the Besatzungs-heer) who were infected was slightly higher, and the proportion at the front (in the Feldheer) who were infected was actually lower (roughly one-quarter lower during the first three years of the War, and roughly equal in 1918) than had been the case in peacetime.[66] Yet these observations did not surface in the public discussion. It was the large absolute numbers of infected soldiers, particularly behind the lines and in some military hospitals, which aroused concern and which caused Germans to overlook that the proportion of soldiers with venereal diseases was no higher, and was probably lower, than before the War.

Table 30. *Numbers of Cases Treated by Medical Specialists for Skin and Venereal Diseases*[a] *in Berlin, 1914–1919*[b]

| Year | 1st Quarter | 2nd Quarter | 3rd Quarter | 4th Quarter |
|------|-------------|-------------|-------------|-------------|
| 1914 | 19,673 (3.88) | 20,784 (3.90) | 16,962 (3.88) | 13,194 (3.35) |
| 1915 | 14,485 (3.28) | 14,356 (3.09) | 13,392 (3.00) | 13,226 (2.97) |
| 1916 | 13,924 (3.13) | 13,926 (3.12) | 13,947 (3.14) | 13,090 (2.96) |
| 1917 | 13,089 (2.98) | 12,789 (2.90) | 12,154 (2.79) | 12,588 (2.82) |
| 1918 | 13,500 (3.04) | 13,439 (3.11) | 12,455 (2.99) | 13,310 (3.18) |
| 1919 | 18,187 (3.75) | 20,980 (3.84) | 21,271 (4.03) | 20,754 (3.92) |

[a] In the Verein Berliner Kassenärzte = VBK.

[b] Figures in parentheses, as a percentage of total membership of the insurance schemes connected with the VBK.

*Source*: BAK, R 86, no. 1063: Dr Georg Loewenstein, 'Kritische Betrachtungen und Beiträge zur Statistik der Geschlechts krankheiten (1910–1921)', Sondersdruck aus der *Zeitschrift für Bekämpfung der Geschlechtskrankheiten*, 20, no. 8–12, 168.

It appears that the actual extent of venereal disease among the civilian population after the defeat also gave less real cause for alarm than appeared to many at first sight. For example, the numbers of people treated by doctors in Berlin for sexually transmitted diseases from 1914 to 1919 suggest that the picture of a post-war upsurge in venereal disease may have been

---

[65] Loewenstein, 'Kritische Betrachtungen und Beiträge zur Statistik der Geschlechtskrank-heiten', 178–9.

[66] Dr Merkel, 'Die Gesundheitsverhältnisse im Heer', in Franz Bumm (ed.), *Deutschlands Gesundheitsverhältnisse unter dem Einfluß des Weltkrieges* (Stuttgart, 1928), 182–3; Wilhelm Hoffmann, 'Die wichtigsten Kriegsseuchen', in Wilhelm Hoffmann (ed.), *Die deutschen Ärzte im Weltkriege: Ihre Leistungen und Erfahrungen* (Berlin, 1920), 173.

somewhat overdrawn (see Table 30). While the incidence of venereal disease did shoot up once the soldiers returned home—in Berlin the number of people treated for venereal disease during the second quarter of 1919 was 56 per cent higher than a year before, during the third quarter 70 per cent higher—the increases essentially reversed the decline during wartime. Here was one area where Germans really were successful in restoring the *status quo ante*!

What then was the fuss about? As Cornelie Usborne has pointed out, 'there was never any conclusive evidence that VD had increased as a result of the war'; yet that did not prevent 'the image of a "polluted" nation' from persisting.[67] The discrepancies between the fear of rampant venereal disease and the fact that post-war developments essentially only reversed wartime trends suggest that expressions of panic should not be taken at face value. Here Paul Weindling's observation that 'statistics and commentaries on health conditions were more ideological constructs than reflections of actual conditions' seems particularly apposite.[68] The anxiety about venereal disease during and after the First World War may have been less about the health of the population *per se* than about the authority of the medical profession and the state. According to one post-war observer commenting on the fact that levels of venereal disease among soldiers during the War had not been terribly high, 'venereal diseases assumed their grave importance later'; the problem was 'that the strict and accurately directed medical care for those with venereal disease . . . and thereby the protection of the general public, was frustrated by the licentiousness (*Zügellosigkeit*) of the revolution'.[69] The 'licentiousness of the revolution' and the post-war breakdown in authority and deference promised to undermine the authority of medical professionals and state bureaucrats—of those who knew best how to ensure the 'protection of the general public'. The real problem was not that morals had collapsed or that venereal disease was rampant, but that the authority of established political, social, economic, and professional élites was threatened.

More than that, the often hysterical reactions of male representatives of the German state and the medical profession to the problem of venereal disease during and after the War point to deep-seated unease about women generally. The problem was not that venereal disease had reached this or that particular level, but that social and sexual behaviour, particularly of

[67] Usborne, *The Politics of the Body*, 83.

[68] Paul Weindling, 'The Medical Profession, Social Hygiene and the Birth Rate in Germany, 1914–1918', in Richard Wall and Jay Winter (eds.), *The Upheaval of War: Family, Work and Welfare in Europe, 1914–1918* (Cambridge, 1988), 428.

[69] Merkel, 'Die Gesundheitsverhältnisse im Heer', 183. Paul Weindling's research points in a similar direction, placing the post-war anxieties and proposals within a broader perspective of the professionalization of medicine and the medicalization of politics. See Weindling, *Health, Race and German Politics*.

women, appeared out of control; fear of venereal disease was only one expression of a general fear of (male) control being swept away by the revolutionary currents of the time. Traditional male roles had been severely challenged by the War; hundreds of thousands of women had managed households independently while their men lost the First World War and male ideals of heroism were destroyed in the anonymity of industrial conflict and the degradation of the trenches. It is more than coincidental that at this time women were so often assumed both publicly and in government policy-discussions to be frivolous, pleasure-seeking, easily seduced, and to be potential or actual prostitutes.[70] The upheavals of war, revolution, and demobilization may have aroused deep fears of a loss of masculinity and, perhaps, unconscious hatred of women. In such a situation, it may have been psychologically more necessary than ever to reassert authority and control over the behaviour particularly of those people who are traditionally expected to accept submissive economic, social, and sexual roles.

The variance between lurid perceptions of moral and physical degeneration and the ambiguous realities of public health was not limited to the problem of venereal disease. As we have seen, shortages of food and fuel, and poor working-conditions during the War had led to sharp declines in the health of the German civilian population, and the military collapse and political revolution of October–November 1918 were accompanied by the highest civilian mortality in the entire war. Not surprisingly, the prospect of sudden military demobilization filled officials with dread 'that the flooding-back of the troops will undoubtedly bring with it contagious diseases on a scale never experienced before'.[71] Nevertheless, the worst fears about the health of the German population were not realized. Civilian death-rates quickly fell below their high wartime levels, and during the demobilization period they stood at levels roughly similar to those just before 1914; by the mid-1920s they had resumed the downward trend which had been in place before the War.[72] Altogether, it appears that diseases associated with poor living-conditions took less of a toll during the post-war years. Tuberculosis, which had declined only slightly in 1919, claimed one-third fewer victims annually between 1920 and 1923 than during 1917–19.[73] Deaths due to

[70] See esp. the necessarily speculative but very perceptive comments in Klaus Theweleit, *Männerphatasien*, i: *Frauen, Fluten, Körper, Geschichte* (Frankfurt/Main, 1977), and ii: *Männerkörper: Zur Psychoanalyse des weißen Terrors* (Frankfurt/Main, 1978); Elisabeth Domansky, 'Der Erste Weltkrieg', in Lutz Niethammer *et al.*, *Bürgerliche Gesellschaft in Deutschland: Historische Einblicke, Fragen, Perspektiven* (Frankfurt/Main, 1990), 312–19.

[71] StdABr, 025/11/1, fo. 29: Deutsche Desinfektionszentrale to Magistrat, Berlin-Weissensee, 27 Nov. 1918.

[72] See the tables above, showing marriages, births, and deaths in Germany 1910–24.

[73] For this and the following statistics, *Statistisches Jahrburch für das Deutsche Reich 1924/25*, 44–5. The fact that tuberculosis declined only slightly in 1919 may have been due to the cool, rainy weather in Germany during that summer. See PLA, Rep. 65c, no. 2312, fos. 79–80: 'Jahresgesundheitsbericht umfassend das Jahr 1919'.

scarlet fever dropped marginally in the first two post-war years, but by 1922 stood at less than half the 1918 figure (which itself was 35 per cent below 1917). Diphtheria and croup, which claimed roughly 10,000 victims per year during the War, caused the deaths of roughly half that number in 1919, about a third in 1921, and less than a quarter in 1923. And the great killer of the last year of the War, influenza, claimed only a fraction of the 1918 total during the post-war years. The measurable improvements in public health may have been due in part to the fact that many weaker members of the community had already been killed off by the privations and epidemics of the war years.[74] However, they probably also reflected improvements in living-standards after the War, the reduction of the working day, wage rises, and the achievement of full employment in the early 1920s—not least among the soldiers of the First World War who managed to return home in one piece and who were generally able to find work fairly easily and quickly.[75]

The rapid, if temporary, diminution of male unemployment not only helped bring about an improvement in public health; it also had significant, if contradictory, consequences for the effort to put the moral universe back in order. It eased the exit of hundreds of thousands of women from paid employment and, for a short time, made it possible for many families to survive on the man's income. Women could thus assume more easily the role of housewife; ex-soldiers could assume more easily the role of bread-winner and head of household. A peculiar and short-lived set of economic circumstances in late 1918 and early 1919 thus favoured a reconstitution of patriarchal family structures and facilitated a return of soldiers to economic and social roles similar to those they had left before their military service. Yet at the same time higher wages and a shorter working day left more time and money for leisure pursuits—for 'the pleasure-frenzy, the dancing-mania, the cinema attendance' which so alarmed Wilhelm Koch in the National Assembly debate of 11 April 1919, and other self-appointed guardians of Germany's moral health.[76]

The indignation at the sight of people enjoying themselves after the Armistice was accompanied by an upsurge of two standard concerns of upright citizens everywhere: youth running wild and crime. In the eyes of most Germans, the rot had clearly set in during the War. Convictions of

[74] e.g see the comments in the 'Annual Health Report' for the Regierungsbezirk Stralsund for 1921, PLA, Rep. 65c, no. 2312, fo. 182: 'Gesundheitsbericht für den Regierungsbezirk Stralsund. Jahr 1921'.

[75] Richard Bessel, 'Unemployment and Demobilisation in Germany after the First World War', in Richard J. Evans and Dick Geary (eds.), *The German Unemployed: Experiences and Consequences of Mass Unemployment from the Weimar Republic to the Third Reich* (London and Sydney, 1987), 23–43. See also above, Ch. 5.

[76] Lynn Abrams also stresses the importance of the commercial motives of dance-hall owners, who had been deprived of business during the War and who took advantage of the ending of wartime restrictions on public entertainment. See Abrams, *Workers' Culture in Imperial Germany*, 107–8.

juveniles for offences against Reich laws almost doubled during the War.[77] Police protection was required for food depots, and theft became so common that it threatened to undermine even the solidarity of tightly-knit mining-communities.[78] There was widespread concern about the behaviour of children lacking parental supervision. The mayor of Stralsund offered a typical description of the corrosive social consequences of the War when, in the summer of 1918, he attributed the high numbers of children in the city caught stealing or not attending school and then taken into state care during the previous two years 'to the fact that strong discipline is missing in families because the fathers have been conscripted into military service'.[79] The effects of wartime shortages and the black market upon public behaviour appeared all too evident, and many believed that the War had gravely undermined family life and, with it, the structures of control and deference which held society together.

It was not just young people lacking 'the firm hand of the father' who appeared to be out of control. The behaviour of many soldiers on leave had also left much to be desired during the War,[80] and in late 1918 the imminent demobilization aroused considerable anxiety about what might happen when millions of men, trained in the use of weapons and doubtlessly brutalized by their experiences in the trenches—men 'who had been socially, psychologically, and physically abused'[81]—suddenly descended on the home front. There seemed ample reason to worry that the violence of the trenches would be brought home to the Reich, a prospect made more frightening by the fact that hundreds of thousands of army weapons went missing at the end of the War. Already in October 1918 anxious concern had been expressed that weapons were being stolen by soldiers 'in order to be used during the

[77] Daniel, *Arbeiterfrauen in der Kriegsgesellschaft*, 158–9; Eve Rosenhaft, 'A World Upside Down: Working-Class Youth on the Urban Home Front in Germany' (paper delivered to the conference on 'The European Family and the Great War: Stability and Instability 1900–1930' at Pembroke College, Cambridge, 11–14 Sept. 1983).

[78] See Michael Zimmermann, ' "Alle sollen auf dem Altar des Vaterlandes ein Opfer bringen": Die Bergarbeiterschaft im Kreis Recklinghausen während des Ersten Weltkrieges', in *Vestische Zeitschrift: Zeitschrift der Vereine für Orts- und Heimatkunde im Vest Recklinghausen*, 81 (1982). 74.

[79] He went on to lament that 'often also the mothers are at work for almost the entire day and the children, mostly looked after only by older siblings, are left on their own'. See PLA, Rep 65c, no. 1186, fo. 37. Bürgermeister to Regierungspräsident, Stralsund, 26 Aug. 1918. For similar observations from the rural Pomeranian district of Grimmen, see ibid., fo. 40: Landrat to Regierungspräsident, Grimmen, 21 Aug. 1918. See also Daniel, *Arbeiterfrauen in der Kriegsgesellschaft*, 158–62, 269.

[80] SHAD, Ministerium des Innern, no. 9574, fos. 237–9: report to Ministerium des Innern in Dresden, Osschatz, 28 Jan. 1916; ibid. 17721, fo. 131: Amtshauptmannschaft Plauen to Ministerium des Innern in Dresden, Plauen, 21 Feb. 1916; GLAK, 456/E.V.8, Bund 86: stellv. Gen.kdo. XIV. Armeekorps to Ministerium des Innern in Karlsruhe, Karlsruhe, 1 Feb. 1918; ibid.: stellv. Gen.kdo. XIV. Armeekorps to Ministerium des Innern in Karlsruhe, Karlsruhe, 1 Oct. 1918.

[81] Eric J. Leed, *No Man's Land: Combat and Identity in World War I* (Cambridge, 1979), 196.

imminent unrest';[82] in March 1919 the civil authorities in Leipzig estimated that between 20,000 and 25,000 rifles taken from the military during the demobilization were being held illegally;[83] and according to the tallies of the Reich government in 1920, 1,895,052 rifles, 8,452 machine-guns, and 400 mine-throwers were held illegally in Germany at that time.[84] After the War ended, the behaviour of many returning soldiers confirmed the fears. Many became involved in violent incidents and, particularly, cases of theft,[85] and in the months immediately after the Armistice Germany was plagued with bands of heavily armed men in military uniform, said to be composed 'primarily of deserters and criminals', who carried out armed

Table 31. *Criminal Convictions in Germany, 1910–1926*

| Year | Total of people brought to trial | Total of people convicted | Of whom | |
|------|------|------|------|------|
| | | | Women | Adolescents |
| 1910 | 685,751 | 538,225 | 86,926 | 51,315 |
| 1911 | 693,346 | 544,861 | 89,192 | 50,874 |
| 1912 | 722,745 | 573,976 | 91,653 | 55,949 |
| 1913 | 690,403 | 555,527 | 88,462 | 54,155 |
| 1914 | 560,024 | 454,064 | 77,870 | 46,940 |
| 1915 | 349,308 | 287,535 | 75,400 | 63,126 |
| 1916 | 350,400 | 287,500 | 86,400 | 80,399 |
| 1917 | 357,146 | 294,584 | 102,806 | 95,651 |
| 1918 | 408,147 | 341,526 | 127,923 | 99,498 |
| 1919 | 418,064 | 348,247 | 85,454 | 64,619 |
| 1920 | 733,458 | 608,563 | 118,749 | 91,171 |
| 1921 | 797,552 | 651,148 | 130,550 | 76,932 |
| 1922 | 760,706 | 636,817 | 113,884 | 71,124 |
| 1923 | 968,883 | 823,902 | 134,943 | 86,040 |
| 1924 | 827,021 | 696,668 | 114,488 | 43,276 |
| 1925 | 682,092 | 575,745 | 93,367 | 24,771 |
| 1926 | 700,201 | 589,611 | 89,344 | 24,066 |

*Sources: Statistisches Jahrbuch für das Deutsche Reich 1930* (Berlin, 1930), 556. See also Moritz Liepmann, *Krieg und Kriminalität in Deutschland* (Stuttgart, Berlin, and Leipzig, 1930), 98; Ute Daniel, *Arbeiterfrauen in der Kriegsgesellschaft: Beruf, Familie und Politik im Ersten Weltkrieg* (Göttingen, 1989), 158–9.

[82] SHAD, Ministerium des Innern, no. 11074, fos. 51–5: minutes of a meeting in the Saxon Ministry of the Interior, Dresden, 14 Oct. 1918.

[83] Ibid., no. 11094/1, fos. 32–40: Kreishauptmann to Ministerium des Innern in Dresden, Leipzig, 27 Mar. 1919.

[84] Moritz Liepmann, *Krieg und Kriminalität in Deutschland* (Stuttgart, Berlin, and Leipzig, 1930), 38.

[85] See e.g. HStAD, Reg Düsseldorf, no. 15974, fos. 12–13: Landrat to Regierungspräsident, Moers, 12 Nov. 1918; GLAK, 233/12402: Abschnitt V der neutralen Zone to Wehrkreiskommando 5 in Stuttgart, Karlsruhe, 16 Dec. 1918.

robberies of farms, food depots, and large shops.[86] According to the Army Command in Dresden, in a description of developments in the Pirna district in July 1919, conditions were 'reminiscent of the period after the Thirty Years War'.[87]

The perception of widespread post-war lawlessness appears confirmed by aggregate statistics of criminal convictions after the War (see Table 31).Particularly worrying were the increases in the numbers of women and young people convicted of crimes. Their numbers had risen enormously during the War (when the numbers of men convicted, not surprisingly, had declined), and then remained at high levels in the post-war period. Here, it seemed, was clear evidence of a breakdown in the social and moral structures which had previously underpinned an orderly society.

This increase in crime and anxiety over law and order developed as German policing too was in great flux. During the War Germany's police had come under severe pressure, as many police-officers were conscripted into the armed forces.[88] Older men who had previously been in the police force were called back into service, and an aged and undermanned police was confronted with an increasingly disorderly population. With the end of the War and the outbreak of revolution in November 1918, the police temporarily disappeared from Germany's streets and offered little resistance to the Workers' and Soldiers' Councils.[89] Although most police-officers returned to their posts within a few days, it was some time before before it became clear who was responsible for public security. In some places security formations of Workers' and Soldiers' Councils played a prominent role; in others, including those which remained relatively untouched by the revolutionary upheaval (particularly in the countryside), citizens' militias (*Bürgerwehren* or *Einwohnerwehren*) took responsibility for maintaining order and protecting property; and in the aftermath of the disintegration of the old army, the new government looked to paramilitary Freikorps units to enforce

[86] See e.g. StAM, Oberpräsidium, no. 6523: Regierungspräsident to Ministerium des Innern, Arnsberg, 14 Sept. 1919. This report gives details of a number of such incidents in and around Dortmund. By the second half of 1919, however, these armed bands had largely disappeared.

[87] SHAD, Kriegsarchiv/Kriegsministerium, no. 25012, fo. 289: Gen.kdo. XII A.K. to Ministerium für Mil. Wesen, Dresden-N., 31 July 1919.

[88] e.g. the Prussian Kriminalpolizei lost more than half its senior officers to the army during the War, as so many were reserve officers who were called up; at the end of the War one-third of the posts in the Berlin Schutzmannschaft were unfilled. See Ministerial Dr. Klausener, 'Die Organisation der Preußischen Polizei: Ein Rückblick', in *Die Polizei*, 25: 7 (10 Apr. 1928), 190–7; Hsi-Huey Liang, *The Berlin Police Force in the Weimar Republic* (Berkeley Calif., Los Angeles, and London, 1970), 30–1; Johannes Buder, *Die Reorganisation der preußischen Polizei 1918–1933* (Frankfurt/Main, Berne, and New York, 1986), 20.

[89] See Liang, *The Berlin Police Force*, 31–3; Jürgen Siggemann, *Die kasernierte Polizei und das Problem der inneren Sicherheit in der Weimarer Republik: Eine Studie zum Auf- und Ausbau des innerstaatlichen Sicherheitssystems in Deutschland 1918/19–1933* (Frankfurt/Main, 1980), 19–20; Buder, *Die Reorganisation der preußischen Polizei*, 20–3; Peter Leßmann, *Die preußische Schutzpolizei in der Weimarer Republik: Streifendienst und Straßenkampf* (Düsseldorf, 1989), 11–13, 16–17.

its will.[90] However, these improvised and, in the case of the Freikorps, politically disastrous arrangements could be only temporary responses to the problem of re-establishing order. The state needed to reassert its control of the organs of internal security and to establish a new organizational framework for the police, a process which was not really complete until late 1920.[91] After the War, therefore, the police faced new and fundamental problems. The collapse of the old army had removed the back-up upon which the police had previously relied; the victorious Allies were determined to prevent the creation of a large and heavily armed police-force as a means to circumvent restrictions imposed on the German military; the police were confronted with numerous and serious disturbances, including violent political demonstrations and food riots; and the state's authority among the population had eroded, while the upsurge in crime during the post-war period presented major challenges to those responsible for maintaining law and order.

While the available statistics fail to provide unambiguous evidence that the return of the men from the trenches led to a massive wave of violent crime against the person,[92] crime against property was a different matter. Evidence from throughout Germany points unmistakably to a massive increase in theft after the War—an increase which, as Moritz Liepmann demonstrated fairly conclusively more than sixty years ago, was a function more of the inflation than of the return of the 'front generation' to the Reich.[93] Inhabitants of many urban areas experienced a doubling or trebling of cases of theft. In Osnabrück, for example, the numbers of robberies and thefts reported in 1918–19 were more than three times as high as they had been in 1913–14 (2,038 as opposed to 657).[94] In Harburg (to the south of Hamburg) property crime rose threefold in 1918 as against 1913; in September 1919 property crime in cities in the western Ruhr region (Regierungsbezirk Arnsberg) was reported to have risen by 400 per cent as compared with 1913; and in Lüneburg the amount of property crime reported in the first six months of 1919 was 50 per cent greater than it had

[90] StAM, Oberpräsidium, no. 6523: Regierungspräsident to Minister des Innern, Arnsberg, 14 Sept. 1919; Peter Bucher, 'Zur Geschichte der Einwohnerwehren in Preußen 1918–1921', *Militärgeschichtliche Mitteilungen*, no. 9 (1971), 15–59; Siggemann, *Die kasernierte Polizei*, pp. 31–78; Leßmann, *Die preußische Schutzpolizei*, 17–43.

[91] For a concise description of this process, see Richard Bessel, 'Policing, Professionalisation and Politics in Weimar Germany', in Clive Emsley and Barbara Weinberger (eds.), *Policing Western Europe: Politics, Professionalism and Public Order, 1850–1940* (New York, Westport, Conn., and London, 1991), esp. 189–91.

[92] See the tables of convictions annually for murder and manslaughter and for assault in Liepmann, *Krieg und Kriminalität in Deutschland*, 35, 39.

[93] Ibid. 72.

[94] The reported cases of fraud also rose, from 144 in 1913–14 to 293 in 1918–19, but the cases of assault fell (from 288 to 158) as did the numbers of reported sexual crimes (*Vergehen und Verbrechen gegen die Sittlichkeit*) (from 13 to 7). See NHStA, Hann. 122a/XI, no. 103 l, fos. 28–31: Regierungspräsident to Minister des Innern, Osnabrück, 6 Sept. 1919.

been during the whole of 1913.[95] A further worry was the spread of such crime into the countryside, where the theft of food, animals, and clothing became increasingly frequent as a hungry urban population roamed farmers' fields in search of something to eat.[96] To rural inhabitants it appeared that an urban plague (this time of proletarian locusts) was invading the country-side. Cases of theft reached their peak during the hyperinflation year of 1923; the 'flight into real property' (*Flucht in die Sachwerte*) which accompanied the inflation did not occur solely within the law.

Juvenile crime aroused special concern. Officials claimed that the most serious source of crime and violence was not the returning soldiers but the 'so-called young hooligans', the youth among whom 'the sense of authority has been widely undermined'.[97] Here were the fruits of the oft-alleged disintegration of family life during the War, the lack of discipline, the decline in moral standards and respect for authority. High levels of juvenile crime after the War reflected the problems of socializing youth in particularly difficult circumstances, and in this regard (as in many others) it was not the immediate post-war period but the 'stabilization' of 1923–4 which saw the reassertion of traditional values. It was not until 1923–4, when unemploy-ment rose rapidly and the German population was stripped of protection from the harsh realities of a depressed economy, that structures of authority were rebuilt and the rise in crime which had characterized the post-war period was put into reverse.

The nature of the post-war crime-wave shows how important the collapse of the currency was as a catalyst for the apparent decline in order and moral standards. With the inflation, stable price relationships were first eroded and then destroyed, and people felt that virtue and hard work were no longer rewarded. Prices reflect more than just economic relationships; they also reflect moral ones—about what the value of goods relative to one another *ought* to be. The inflation provoked countless distributional conflicts, in which cries about 'justice' and 'morality' were raised in the defence of sectional interests.[98] The constantly changing relations between incomes and prices caused by the inflation ensured that questions about allegedly proper and moral economic and social relationships were posed constantly and with considerable bitterness. Of course, proper economic relationships were

[95] Ibid., fos. 19–21; StAM, Oberpräsidium, no. 6523: Regierungspräsident to Minister des Innern, Arnsberg, 14 Sept. 1919.

[96] NHStA, Hann. 122a/XI, no. 103 1, fos. 28–31; reports in SHAD, Ministerium des Innern, no. 11237.

[97] NHStA, Hann. 122a/XI, no. 103 1, fos. 22–6: Regierungspräsident to Oberpräsident, Stade, 10 Sept. 1919.

[98] For a particularly good example of this, see the account of the politics of German war-victims in Whalen, *Bitter Wounds*, esp. 107–53. For another example, see the account of the interest-group politics of German civil servants during the inflation in Andreas Kunz, *Civil Servants and the Politics of Inflation in Germany, 1914–1924* (Berlin and New York, 1986).

defined in different ways by different people. Those at the top of the social scale—who felt they ought to be in authority—were often distressed by the collapse of the 'former disposition for diligent and assiduous working, for orderly business with modest but nevertheless adequate profit';[99] those at the bottom of the heap were often enraged at what they regarded as profiteering, reaping unfair advantage from shortages, and unwarranted price-rises. Both expressed anger and dismay at the collapse of a moral aspect to economic relationships, which price stability had seemed to underpin.

The inflation *itself* was also seen as a moral problem, caused by the irresponsible and immoral behaviour of Germans who abandoned the good habits they had maintained before the War. Bringing the inflation under control was frequently regarded as a matter of reviving good habits among the German population. In August 1920 the Reich Labour Ministry hosted a conference on 'questions of consumption and pay', in which the discussions revolved around how workers, and young workers in particular, could be educated not to spend their money improvidently. The senior civil servant chairing the conference opened by pointing to the urgent need 'to channel expenditure of people's incomes into the most efficient possible patterns', and outlined the scale of the problem:

The entertainment establishments and the cinemas are filled to overflowing and an extraordinarily large proportion of incomes are spent on cigars and cigarettes, at a time when one does not know how it will be possible to keep our people alive . . . to feed them, to clothe them and to house them. This aberrant behaviour can be observed primarily among the young, whose wages have increased considerably as compared with previously, without being put into savings. The spread of pleasure-seeking is seen not only among black-marketeers and usurers but also among those who earn honest incomes.[100]

Two groups aroused predictable concern: young women and young workers. These were now accused of spending money in a manner which was wasteful, harmful to the economy, and often harmful to themselves. There was widespread agreement about the need to instruct young women in managing a household properly and economically, in becoming 'competent house-wives'. Numerous local authorities set up courses in household skills (cooking, sewing, etc.) for women who were expected to care for families in the post-war world.[101] However, 'the most difficult task', as the Labour Ministry's expert Dr Tibertius reported to the assembled conference at the Labour

[99] NHStA, Hann. 122a/XI, no. 103 l, fos. 19–21: Regierungspräsident to Minister des Innern, Lüneburg, 20 Sept. 1919.

[100] GStAM, Rep. 120, BB, Abt. VII, Fach I, no. 30, Band 7, fos. 451–2: 'Aufzeichnung über die am 16. August 1920 im Reichsarbeitsministerium abgehaltene Besprechung über Verbrauchs- und Entlohnungsfragen'.

[101] See e.g. StdALu, no. 6770, fo. 37: Industrie-Wirtschaftsamt für die Rheinpfalz to Bürger- meisteramt Ludwigshafen, Ludwigshafen, 31 Dec. 1918.

Ministry in August 1920, was 'the influencing of young workers'. In order to tackle this, Tibertius proposed specifying to youths 'more useful goals for spending their income', such as buying books, visiting museums, saving up for a future household, and purchasing insurance policies. The notion that these suggestions might meet with success was judged to be 'rather hopeless' by the following speaker, who represented industry. He recommended more down-to- earth measures: a reduction in young workers' wages, which would be raised when they married and prepared to establish an independent household; and compulsory saving.[102] However, he went on to admit 'that in the current circumstances [introducing] such a compulsion would not be possible. Today one is not allowed to mention the words "compulsion" and "duty" if one wants to accomplish something.'[103]

Again and again young people were accused of having too much time on their hands and too much money in their pockets. It was feared that, in the disorder of post-war Germany, new-found financial independence allowed youths to turn their backs on authority. War and political revolution 'and their accompanying phenomena'—not least the lifting of censorship—had undermined the social and moral standards of the young, or so it seemed from the office of the Regierungspräsident in Arnsberg (whose district included the industrial cities of the eastern Ruhr region). Schoolchildren allegedly displayed 'unruliness and a certain mania for destruction (*Zerstörungssucht*)'; 'the reading of bad books' was contributing to the 'brutalization of the young'; and schoolchildren, who often received 'large amounts of pocket-money', 'supply themselves with trashy literature, smoke cigarettes, and visit the cinema, which in the absence of censorship contributes to the moral corruption of young people'. The consequences were plain for all to see 'in the licentious and impudent behaviour of young people on the streets, in the aversion to work, in the reckless intercourse of young girls with male persons, in the participation of young people in meetings, demonstrations, and riots'.[104] From nearby Münster came a similar condemnation of the dangers posed to Germany's moral health by the 'shameless' spread of 'trashy literature and immoral and provocative motion-pictures in the absence of adequate censorship'—of the presentation to an impressionable public of uncensored films containing 'derision of any morality, especially of family life', 'incitement to class hatred' and a 'glorification of criminality'.

---

[102] Compulsory saving for young workers (18 and under) in fact had been introduced during the War, in 1916, by the military authorities in a number of regions (including Berlin, Hanover, Kassel, and Alsace-Lorraine) in order to control allegedly excessive consumption by the young. See Daniel, *Arbeiterfrauen in der Kriegsgesellschaft*, 163–5. The measures created considerable administrative difficulties and much public disquiet.

[103] GStAM, Rep. 120, BB, Abt. VII, Fach I, no. 30, Band 7, fo. 453.

[104] StAM, Oberpräsidium, no. 6523: Regierungspräsident to Minister des Innern, Arnsberg, 14 Sept. 1919.

To allow such films to be seen by young people, 'like permitting the above-mentioned trashy literature', was to 'permit the systematic cultivation of a generation into criminality'.[105] The revolution and the lifting of censorship dealt what moral crusaders regarded as a serious set-back to the long righteous struggle against 'trashy literature' by having produced, in the words of one prominent campaigner, 'the foaming-up of a shameless sexualism'.[106] However, the post-war moral panic created a platform for a successful campaign for the introduction of restrictive legislation on censorship, which culminated in the passing by the Reichstag of the Law against Dirt and Trash in December 1926.[107]

Germany's moral guardians became particularly worried after the War by the liberating effects of 'high wages' and shorter working hours upon young women who, the Regierungspräsident in Hanover asserted, were thereby tempted 'into spending a large part of the day and night in places of entertainment and in the streets'.[108] The consequence of this loosening-up of public life was an alleged 'extraordinary' increase in 'the number of those who secretly engage in prostitution, and in those with venereal disease'. (However, the precise connections between material conditions and allegedly immoral habits were not spelled out). Similar concerns were expressed by the Factory Inspectorate in Opladen, in the occupied Rhineland, which lamented the damage done to the 'moral life of female workers' by war and its aftermath, and reported that in 'a large chemical factory' (presumably Bayer) 'artificially induced abortion is a frequent occurrence among the female workers, and there are people who induce the abortions and supply the necessary means for 50 Marks'.[109] At a time when the number of abortions appeared to be rising substantially, the idea of young working-class women taking control of their reproductive behaviour—and thus endangering the demographic future of a country which had just lost millions of men on the battlefield—touched a very raw nerve indeed.[110]

To those who regarded their task as preserving social order, the conduct of the younger generation offered evidence that the cement holding German society together was crumbling. The unwillingness of people normally

---

[105] StAM, Oberpräsidium, no. 6523: Regierungspräsident to Minister des Innern, Münster i. W., 20 Sept. 1919.

[106] Paul Samuleit, quoted in Detlev J. K. Peukert, *Grenzen der Sozialdisziplinierung: Aufstieg und Krise der deutschen Jugendfürsorge von 1878 bis 1932* (Cologne, 1986), 177. See also Abrams, *Workers' Culture in Imperial Germany*.

[107] See Peukert, *Grenzen der Sozialdisziplinierung*, 175–91; Usborne, *The Politics of the Body*, 76–9.

[108] NHStA, Hann. 122a/XI, no. 103 l, fos. 9–12: Regierungspräsident to Minister des Innern, Hanover, 22 Sept. 1919.

[109] HStAD, Reg. Düsseldorf, no. 34345: Gewerbeinspektor zu Opladen to Regierungs- und Gewerberat in Düsseldorf, 'Jahresbericht für das Jahr 1919', Opladen, 12 Jan. 1920.

[110] On the increase in, and debates about, abortion in Germany after the First World War. See James Woycke, *Birth Control in Germany 1871–1933* (London, 1988), 68–88; Usborne, *The Politics of the Body*, 156–201.

expected to accept subordinate roles, both at the work place and within the home, to submit to authority, seemed fundamentally to threaten social stability. Concern about the behaviour of teenage youths, voiced in most industrial societies at most times, therefore assumed an often desperate tone, as in the following description of youth in Aurich (Ostfriesland) in September 1919:

A very far-reaching demoralization and brutalization (*Verwahrlosung und Verrohung*) of young people is particularly apparent in the cities. Respect for parents, teachers, authorities, etc., has declined among young people to a quite terrifying degree; insolent, brutal, and presumptuous behaviour, accompanied by an unbridled pursuit of pleasure, has spread among wide circles of our youth. This is especially apparent among those young people who have now reached the age of military service and many of whom lived through the War without the educational influence of the father. Precisely in these circles respect for state power has disappeared completely. The riots among the labour movement are almost always attributable to these elements, whose brutality and debauchery also gives labour leaders a great deal of trouble.[111]

Similar cries arose from among those responsible for youth in state care. Making their annual report to the Prussian Minister for Welfare in October 1919 about conditions in homes for youth in care, the authorities in Pomerania looked back at developments during the previous year:

A large number of the older youths became rebellious, insolent and disobedient, and only reluctantly performed their work. Many were of the opinion that with the change in government all laws had been repealed at a stroke and that corrective education had ceased. Some fathers came into the homes, referring to the Workers' and Soldiers' Councils, and demanded the immediate release of their children. In order to avoid further trouble, in some instances the heads of the homes gave in to the demands of these people, and the youths were released.[112]

Only gradually was order re-established in the homes, but not before those charged with running them had been given a severe shock. To many people in positions of authority, what Germany urgently required after the War was the reimposition of discipline, of a sort which in an allegedly well-

---

[111] NHStA, Hann. 122a/XI, no. 103 I, fos. 33–6: Regierungspräsident to Minister des Innern, Aurich, 18 Sept. 1919. The civil servant writing this report also condemned 'the many so-called "dance classes", in which young people are shown how to do foreign dances of the most vulgar kind by a medley of wild dance-teachers who have moved in from elsewhere'.

[112] APS, Oberpräsidium von Pommern, no. 2915: Landeshauptmann to Oberpräsidenten, 'Bericht über die Ausführung der Fürsorgeerziehung Minderjähriger im Rechnungsjahre 1918', Stettin, 5 Oct. 1919. For further discussion, see Richard Bessel, 'State and Society in Germany in the Aftermath of the First World War', in W. R. Lee and Eve Rosenhaft (eds.), *The State and Social Change in Germany, 1880–1980* (Oxford, Munich, and New York, 1990), esp. 200–2. Concern over the behaviour of youth in care after the First World War also needs to be seen within the longer-term context of growing doubts about the educative and corrective potential of state youth-care. On this theme, see Peukert, *Grenzen der Sozialdisziplinierung*.

ordered society would have been provided by compulsory military service and 'the educational influence of the father'.

The increase in unruly behaviour and allegedly morally subversive activities such as going to the cinema, visiting cafés, and attending dances had a number of interconnected causes: the decline in the authority of the state which had accompanied the revolutionary upheavals; the end of military conscription due to the Versailles Treaty (allowing young men, who would otherwise have been performing military drill, loose in civil society); the relative ease with which people were able to find jobs during the demobilization period; a housing crisis which left many young people unable to find dwellings of their own (and thus compelled to live with parents or in-laws); the depreciation of the currency which induced people to spend on the pleasures of today rather than save for tomorrow; the increase in leisure time created by the introduction of the eight-hour day; and a desire, after the privations of wartime, to enjoy pleasures which had been denied during more than four years of war.[113] In the post-war transition, Germany became a consumer society with a vengeance. Fear of future price-rises led, for example, to 'an unprecedented volume' of retail sales before Christmas in 1919, when there was a 'steadily increasing mass consumption of all imported luxury articles' and 'chocolates, marzipan, cigars . . . were being purchased in massive quantities'.[114] The jobless were accused of frittering away their unemployment money on alcohol and cigarettes while earning illegally on the side;[115] youths receiving allegedly high wages were said to be interested only in satisfying their immediate desires; farmers were accused of laying on lavish weddings and spending their money on dancing, the races, fairs, and expensive cigars;[116] and the big cities (Berlin, Hamburg, Cologne, Munich) were said to be gripped by a 'mass psychosis' of pleasure-seeking, dance-frenzy, eroticism, and decadence.[117] Indeed, to some the end of the world seemed at hand: according to the author of a report from Bavaria at the beginning of January 1920, public behaviour

---

[113] This is how increases in theatre attendance, participation by youth in sports, and the like during 1919 were interpreted in an official history of Frankfurt/Main during the period 1914–24. See Hans Drüner, *Im Schatten des Weltkrieges: Zehn Jahre Frankfurter Geschichte von 1914–1924* (Frankfurt/Main, 1934), 382–3.

[114] APP, Rejencja w Pile, no. 92, fos. 1–4: 'N.-Bericht vom 8. Januar 1920' (quoting a report from Bavaria). To correct this state of affairs it was pointed out that 'a recovery, however, can come about only when our people no longer feel richer than previously but instead learn to appreciate that they have become much, very much poorer and need to make sacrifices'.

[115] See e.g. StdALu, no. 6770, fos. 65–65a: Rechtsrat to Oberregierungsrat Matheus, Ludwigshafen/Rhein, 26 June 1919.

[116] Jonathan Osmond, 'Peasant Farming in South and West Germany during War and Inflation 1914 to 1924: Stability or Stagnation?', in Gerald D. Feldman, Carl-Ludwig Holtfrerich, Gerhard A. Ritter, and Peter-Christian Witt (eds.), *Die deutsche Inflation: Eine Zwischenbilanz* (Berlin and New York, 1982), 304–5.

[117] Usborne, *The Politics of the Body*, 75.

'really seems almost like an orgy of recklessness under the motto: after us the deluge'.[118]

Of course, complaints about uncontrolled pleasure-seeking and fears about the coming 'deluge' were often as much expressions of the preoccupations of officials as accurate reflections of reality. The numerous complaints that Germans were wasting their money on alcohol in a shameful manner illustrate this well. Notwithstanding assertions that the drinking of alcoholic beverages had 'visibly increased' despite high prices,[119] statistics of post-war alcohol-consumption show sharp declines in the immediate post-war period. Beer consumption per capita in 1919 was only 47 per cent of the 1913 figure, and in 1920 it was a mere 37.2 per cent; and the consumption of spirits declined even more steeply.[120] No doubt a lot of people made their own spirits, as was suggested in the report cited above; and no doubt the changed sex-ratios among the adult population (as millions of men had been killed in the War and women tend to drink less than men) helped to reduce per capita alcohol consumption. However, that hardly explains a reduction by more than half, and the figures suggest that the problem posed by alcohol was not so great as is often claimed. It seems more likely that officials frequently read their own fears into their accounts of the behaviour of people around them.

The real problem was not whether drinking actually increased, any more than it was whether venereal disease actually was on the rise or whether Germans actually had abandoned themselves to a 'pleasure-frenzy' or an 'orgy of recklessness'. The problem was that the position of established political, social, economic, and professional élites was threatened on a variety of fronts. The political upheavals, the decline in productivity at work, the behaviour of wayward youth, the rising divorce-rate, the increase in leisure activities, the alleged spread of venereal disease, the fall in respect for state authority—all these were seen as expressions of a dissolution of social and moral standards which needed to be put right in the aftermath of the First World War. For many Germans the key to a successful transition from war to peace was a moral regeneration, to recover a world they thought they had lost; in fact, this comprised an often hysterical urge to construct a world they never had.

What was so often regarded as a collapse of moral standards after the War was essentially a reflection of acute economic and social upheaval,

[118] APP, Rejencja w Pile, no. 92, fos. 1–4: 'N.-Bericht vom 8. Januar 1920' (report from Bavaria).

[119] Thus the 1920 Annual Health Report for the Border Province of Posen and West Prussia, ibid., no. 2477: Regierungs- und Medizinalrat, Grenzmark Posen-Westpreußen, 'Jahresgesundheitsbericht 1920'.

[120] *Statistisches Jahrbuch für das Deutsche Reich 1921/22*, 312–13. The consumption of wine and sparkling wine rose considerably after the War, but this rise was not sufficient to compensate for the sharp drop in beer consumption.

which exposed the cracks in society as never before, and of a temporary disintegration of authority—of men, parents, teachers, employers, the churches, the army, and the state. The tribulations of war and then revolution had threatened and, in some cases, overturned established authority; in the place of an authoritarian Imperial system stood a shaky Republic apparently incapable of imposing order. For people who had grown up in the seemingly stable hierarchical society of the Empire and who had been accustomed to giving the orders and receiving respect and deference, the changes which accompanied the end of the First World War were threatening indeed. Quite naturally, many Germans with senior positions in government, schools, business, and industry—even trade-union leaders—recoiled in horror at what they viewed as a descent into chaos and a collapse of moral standards; a society which no longer respected them was a society which was going to the dogs. Everywhere they looked they saw confirmation of their deep fears of moral decline. However, they tended to focus upon phenomena which confirmed their own preconceptions and prejudices, and in fact neither the structure of German society nor the everyday behaviour of Germans probably changed as much as had been feared.

This should lead us neither to deride the misplaced paranoia of Germans after the First World War nor to dismiss it as unimportant. All human endeavour can probably be seen as a search for stability which is doomed to disappointment in a constantly changing world, and this is particularly true of the history of the demobilization after the First World War. While we can see that the desperate search for stability and normality after the War may have been based upon false premises and thus was predestined to failure, it would be foolish and arrogant to ridicule the attempt. Germans who had experienced the War, whether in the trenches or on the home front, had faced danger, heartbreak, disease, poverty, death. Perhaps their reactions and fears appear, with hindsight, to be rather silly. But we should not forget that they were fallible human beings who had just experienced a calamity such as the world had never seen before.

It is not just as a token of respect that the moral panic of Germans after the First World War needs to be taken seriously, however. Their fears are important also because they helped frame public debate in Germany during the first years of the Weimar Republic. It may be argued that there was nothing unique in the widespread concern about immorality in post-war Germany. Cries about alleged declines in moral standards are heard in just about every modern society, a decline rediscovered by each generation as though it were a new and unique problem. What made the concern about moral standards in Germany after the First World War different was that it involved a desperate set of anxieties arising from the strains of war, defeat, political revolution, economic upheaval, and inflation. Concern about sexual morality was particularly great at a time when millions of households had to be patched together. The question of a just, moral wage was asked particularly insistently when wages, prices, and the labour market were so profoundly unstable. The issue of who had a right to a job took on particular importance after the War, when millions of soldiers returned to Germany expecting to get 'their' jobs back. The upheavals of war, revolution, and inflation thus made 'moral' questions highly visible, and 'moral' problems forced their way on to the political and economic agenda at a time when the obstacles to their solution were overwhelming.

After the First World War, sectional interests in Germany were advanced and defended with a new and urgent language of justice and morality—by reference to absolute moral values—at a time when circumstances made morality and justice virtually impossible to obtain. Consequently, the concern about alleged immorality helped to shape a peculiarly damaging political agenda for the Weimar Republic, reflecting an illusory belief that, if only a return to 'normal' peacetime conditions could be brought about, a reversal of the alleged moral decline might be achieved. This postulated a mythical past, suggested an illusory and deceptive response to an insoluble problem, and confronted the new political order with a set of demands which it could never hope to meet. The juxtaposition of moral panic and political impotence—the fact that anxiety about 'immorality' developed in an inverse relationship to the state's ability to do anything about 'immoral' behaviour—suggests that a 'moral' agenda can be particularly destructive and dangerous for a political democracy. By their nature, questions of morality are more expressions of illusions than reflections of reality, and therefore form particularly dangerous terrain on which to practise democratic politics. As such, they constituted a damaging legacy of the First World War for Germany.

# 9

## The Legacy of The First World War and Weimar Politics

Most honoured Herr Minister! I have worked my way through all agencies, from the War Invalids Welfare Office to the Main Pensions Office, regarding the fulfilment of my requests. I cannot bear yet another negative reply to my present request. The consequence of that would be a reorientation of my person in a political direction. I would ask Dr Goebbels and Kube most cordially to present my pension file to the Reichstag and to help me to my rights.[1]

FROM its birth after the First World War to its collapse in the early 1930s, the Weimar Republic was confronted with popular expectations which could not be met. The revolution of 1918–19, and the accompanying upsurge in (and subsequent suppression of) the radicalism of a working population demanding immediate improvements in living-standards, left a legacy of failure and created bitter divisions which lasted for years.[2] Having emerged from the First World War, Germans could not recognize that the task before their new government was to discover not how to distribute the benefits of a new socialist or democratic order but, essentially, how to apportion poverty. The vast majority of Germans refused to accept the post-war settlement, in particular the imposition of the Versailles Treaty,[3] and con-

---

[1] APS, Oberpräsidium von Pommern, no. 3938: 'Bitte des Kriegsbeschädigten Walter Kosinsky um Zahnersatz und Nachzahlung von Militär-Versorgungsgebührnissen' to preuß. Minister für Volkswohlfahrt, Stettin, 18 Oct. 1931.

[2] The literature which was generated during the 1960s and 1970s on the revolutionary events of 1918 and afterwards is enormous, although this subject has rather run out of historiographical steam in recent years. See esp. Gerald D. Feldman, Eberhard Kolb, and Reinhard Rürup, 'Die Massenbewegungen der Arbeiterschaft in Deutschland am Ende des Ersten Weltkrieges 1917–1920', *Politische Vierteljahresheft*, 13 (1972), 84–105; Reinhard Rürup, (ed.) *Arbeiter- und Soldatenräte im rheinisch-westfälischen Industriegebiet: Studien zur Geschichte der Revolution 1918/19* (Wuppertal, 1975); Erhard Lucas, *Zwei Formen von Radikalismus in der deutschen Arbeiterbewegung* (Frankfurt/Main, 1976); Wolfgang J. Mommsen, 'The German Revolution 1918–1920: Political Revolution and Social Protest Movement', in Richard Bessel and E. J. Feuchtwanger (eds.), *Social Change and Political Development in Weimar Germany* (London, 1981), 21–54; Heinrich August Winkler, *Von der Revolution zur Stabilisierung: Arbeiter und Arbeiterbewegung in der Weimarer Republik 1918 bis 1924* (Berlin and Bonn, 1984); Ulrich Kluge, *Die deutsche Revolution 1918/1919: Staat, Politik und Gesellschaft zwischen Weltkrieg und Kapp-Putsch* (Frankfurt/Main, 1985).

[3] See Ulrich Heinemann, *Die verdrängte Niederlage: Politische Öffentlichkeit und Kriegsschuldfrage in der Weimarer Republik* (Göttingen, 1983); Hans Mommsen, *Die verspielte Freiheit: Der Weg der Republik von Weimar in den Untergang 1918 bis 1933* (Frankfurt/Main and Berlin, 1990), esp. 63–140.

sequently failed to assess realistically the room for manœuvre left open to their government. The electorate of the new democratic Germany did not appreciate the limitations upon politics in a defeated and impoverished country, and the Weimar Republic ultimately proved too weak and vulnerable to bear the burdens of unrealistic popular expectations and the demagogy which fed off them.[4]

Central both to the generation of unrealistic expectations and to circumscribing the possibilities for satisfying popular demands was the legacy of a lost world-war. The costs of war and defeat not only limited Germany's room for manœuvre economically; they also left a deep imprint on the lives, attitudes, and expectations of a population which, for the first time, was able to vote governments in and out of office. Only a small proportion of the German population had been involved actively in the revolutionary unrest which brought about the collapse of the monarchy and made possible the birth of the Republic; an even smaller proportion took an active role in erecting the institutional framework of the new political order. The War and the subsequent demobilization, however, directly altered the lives of millions of Germans: the millions of men who had seen military service during the First World War and survived; the millions of workers who had found employment in armaments or other war-related industries; the millions of wives and parents who had to reconstruct their family lives once the veterans returned home; the hundreds of thousands of women who had been compelled to vacate jobs which they had taken up during the conflict; the hundreds of thousands of widows and orphans whom the War had left in its wake; the tens of thousands of employers who had had to run their firms within the framework laid down by the demobilization authorities. For millions of Germans the questions which demanded urgent attention during the stormy months when the Weimar Republic was born were not those concerning parliamentary or council democracy, socialism or the preservation of private enterprise; they were about finding work after getting out of military uniform, reordering family life once the men returned from military service (or, in so many cases, rebuilding family life without a husband or father), making the transition from war to post-war society.

That this transition played a major role in shaping the politics of the Weimar Republic is obvious. Less obvious is what, exactly, that role was. Many widely held assumptions about the legacy of the War for Weimar politics are at least open to question. Much discussion about the effects of

---

[4] For development of this argument, see Richard Bessel, 'The Formation and Dissolution of a German National Electorate, from *Kaiserreich* to Third Reich', in James Retallack and Larry Eugene Jones (eds.), *Elections, Mass Politics and Social Change in Modern Germany: New Perspectives* (New York, 1992).

the war experience upon Weimar politics has centred in particular on the impact of the 'front generation' in preparing the way for the later triumph of National Socialism. The focus has often been upon men who, as a result of their experiences during the First World War, were allegedly unable to readjust to civil society and therefore provided a ready reservoir of support for militarism and radical right-wing challenges to the new democratic political system. Historians have frequently described the German soldiers who fought in the First World War as men who 'had found an emotional home in soldierly comradeship' and who therefore returned home 'disillusioned', in 1918 and 1919 'and could not adjust to daily life'.[5] After four years of fighting, in a hierarchical organization to which they had been subordinated and which had given meaning to their lives, millions of German soldiers were thrown back into a chaotic civilian society where they had to take decisions for themselves. These men, so the argument runs, proved unable to integrate into civilian life, flocked to the Freikorps immediately after the War, and ultimately emerged as the misguided fanatics who were to find a home in the Nazi movement.

Two recent examples of such reasoning may illustrate this. The first, which focuses upon residual militarism in post-war German society, comes from the study by Arden Bucholz of the military historian and political commentator Hans Delbrück:

German society took on ominous militaristic overtones. Dispirited and worn-out troops, retiring from the front with arms and equipment, found a homeland in which the old order seemed to have vanished. . . . Following the example of the left-wing Spartacists and the conservative Freikorps . . . each segment of the political spectrum created a party militia. . . . Members included returned soldiers searching for the Germany they had left behind, for something different and better, or perhaps for the comradeship and excitement of life at the front.[6]

The second can be found in Peter Merkl's examination of the membership of the National Socialist activists in the Nazi storm troopers' organization, the *Sturmabteilung* SA:

The most disastrous effect of World War I, finally, consisted in the miseducation of a whole generation toward solving its problems in a military, authoritarian manner. The war generation fought in military units (Freecorps) against Polish irregulars and domestic revolutionaries in the years right after the war. In the 1930s they flocked

---

[5] Thus Jürgen Reulecke, 'Männerbund versus the Family: Middle-Class Youth Movements and the Family in Germany in the Period of the First World War', in Richard Wall and Jay Winter (eds.), *The Upheaval of War: Family, Work and Welfare in Europe, 1914–1918* (Cambridge, 1988), 444.

[6] Arden Bucholz, *Hans Delbrück and the German Military Establishment: War Images in Conflict* (Iowa City, Ia., 1985), 131–2.

to the Nazi Party and other right-wing organisations, bringing along a whole ideology of what it meant to be a front-line soldier fighting in the trenches.[7]

Such interpretations contain a number of assumptions which merit critical attention. The first, as suggested by Merkl, is that the great mass of ex-soldiers who became politically active were active on the Right. A second is that a large proportion of the 'front generation' became politically active at all. And third, that this political involvement of the veterans of the trenches led to a 'wholesale entry of military ways into politics' in Weimar Germany.[8] Can one, in fact, really speak of 'the miseducation of a whole generation toward solving its problems in a military, authoritarian manner'? Indeed, can one speak coherently of a 'front generation' in Weimar Germany at all?

The idea of the 'front generation' was, to a considerable extent, a literary invention—a product of the shock felt by middle-class prophets of cultural renewal as they were plunged into industrial warfare side by side with working people in the trenches.[9] It was perhaps as much an expression of middle- and upper-class intellectuals' embarrassed discovery of their poorer brethren as of the creation of 'a new man' in the classless community of the trenches.[10] Certainly the literary output of men who regarded themselves as changed irrevocably by the War, and as set apart from the rest of humanity by what they had experienced in the trenches (both the horror of industrial warfare and the camaraderie of a 'front community'), has done much to frame the concept of the 'front generation' in the popular and historical imagination. As Robert Wohl has observed: 'When we think of the army of returning veterans during the 1920s, we see them through the eyes of Remarque and Hemingway as a generation of men crippled.'[11]

While many ex-soldiers did return crippled, and experienced great difficulties when attempting to re-enter civil society—and while some never re-entered civil society at all, preferring instead to remain in a succession of uniformed, paramilitary organizations—it appears that most succeeded in returning to civilian life. The vast majority were able to put their war experiences behind them, find employment, settle back into or establish their

---

[7] Peter H. Merkl, *The Making of a Stormtrooper* (Princeton, NJ, 1980), 15.

[8] Bucholz, *Hans Delbrück*, 132. For a tentative attempt to come to grips with the problem of militarism in Weimar politics, see Richard Bessel, 'Militarismus im innenpolitischen Leben der Weimarer Republik: Von den Freikorps zur SA', in Klaus-Jürgen Müller and Eckardt Opitz (eds.), *Militär und Militarismus in der Weimarer Republik* (Düsseldorf, 1978), 193–222.

[9] Robert Wohl pointedly writes of the experience of Walter Flex, author of *Der Wanderer zwischen beiden Welten*, in the trenches near Verdun: 'It was probably the first time this prophet of community had ever found himself face to face and shoulder to shoulder with members of the real *Volk*.' See Robert Wohl, *The Generation of 1914* (London, 1980), 49.

[10] See Ernst H. Posse, *Die politischen Kampfbünde Deutschlands* (Berlin, 1931), 24–5.

[11] Wohl, *The Generation of 1914*, 223.

families, and 'adjust to daily life'—which suggests that it is misleading to assert that the War made a 'whole generation' unfit for normal civilian life. Given, on the one hand, that over 11 million Germans served in the armed forces during the First World War and survived and, on the other, that at most 400,000 men (not all of whom had been in the wartime army) joined the Freikorps,[12] it is obvious that far more veterans managed subsequently to lead an unremarkable, humdrum existence than sought refuge in a life of violence in paramilitary uniform. The image of millions of veterans indelibly branded by militarism and determined to put a military stamp upon the political life of the Weimar Republic is also inconsistent with the fact that the largest interest-group formed *by veterans* specifically *as veterans* was not organized by a band of right-wing military misfits but had been founded by Social Democrats: the Reichsbund der Kriegsbeschädigten, Kriegsteilnehmer und Kriegshinterbliebenen (Reich Association of War Disabled, War Veterans, and War Dependants). Far from seeking to glorify war and military exploits, the Reichsbund did just the opposite; for example, in early 1918 it organized a public rally during which veterans collected military decorations to be sent in protest to the leader of the Fatherland Party, Admiral von Tirpitz, and in 1924 it explicitly counted itself 'among the opponents of new wars'.[13]

The success of the anti-war Reichsbund—whose membership at its peak of 830,000 in 1922 was double the number of men who had been organized in all the Freikorps combined—suggests the breadth of the aversion among veterans to right-wing militarism. Far from wanting to glorify violence and things military, many men came away from their wartime experiences with a profound antipathy towards war. Virtually all the evidence we have about morale in the German army during the latter stages of the War and about the conduct of soldiers during the demobilization points to a deep hostility towards, and distrust of, the military.[14] The military spirit, so often praised in right-wing political propaganda, was far removed from the attitudes of

---

[12] On the membership of the Freikorps, see Harold J. Gordon, jun., *The Reichswehr and the German Republic 1919–1926* (Princeton, NJ, 1957), 59, 431–8; Robert G. L. Waite, *Vanguard of Nazism: The Free Corps Movement in Postwar Germany 1918–1923* (Cambridge, Mass., 1952), 40–3; Hagen Schulze, *Freikorps und Republik 1918–1920* (Boppard/Rhein, 1969), 36–7; Bessel, 'Militarismus', 201–2.

[13] Robert Weldon Whalen, *Bitter Wounds: German Victims of the Great War, 1914–1939* (Ithaca (NY) and London, 1984), esp. 121–9, 150. The quote is from an invitation by the Reichsbund in Hanover to the SPD Oberpräsident (and former Reichswehr Minister) Gustav Noske to attend a peace demonstration on the tenth anniversary of the outbreak of the War. See NHStA, Hann. 122a/XXXIV, no. 152c, fo. 111: Reichsbund der Kriegsbeschädigten, Kriegsteilnehmer und Kriegshinterbliebenen to Oberpräsident Noske, Hanover, 17 July 1924.

[14] This point is underscored by contributions to the recent collection edited by Wolfram Wette, *Der Krieg des kleinen Mannes: Eine Militärgeschichte von unten* (Munich, 1992). See esp. the articles by Bernd Ulrich ('Die Desillusionierung der Kriegsfreiwilligen von 1914'), Wolfram Wette ('Die unheroischen Kriegserinnerungen des Elsässer Bauern Dominik Richert aus den Jahren 1914–1918'), and Wilhelm Deist ('Verdeckter Militärstreik im Kriegsjahr 1918?').

many German soldiers as the War came to its end. Far more typical of soldiers' attitudes—particularly among men stationed within the Reich at the time of the Armistice—were those expressed by roughly 600 men from the garrison in Neiße (in Upper Silesia), who in late January 1919 demonstrated behind a banner reading 'Down with the authority of the officers'.[15] Attempts to recruit men for paramilitary formations or citizens' militias (*Bürgerwehren* or *Einwohnerwehren*) after the War rarely met with enthusiasm— and sometimes encountered outright hostility—among war veterans.[16] Those recruiting for the Freikorps often had better luck among school-leavers than among older men who had just returned from the senseless slaughter of the trenches.[17] The German army, it should be remembered, had collapsed completely at the end of 1918. As Michael Geyer has pointed out, 'the military strike had won'; 'the old military was dead', and a German army had to be built anew.[18]

Nor should the success of right-wing militarist politics at the end of the Weimar period necessarily be taken as evidence that the War predisposed the millions who fought in it to violence and militarism. In fact, when the Nazi movement grew to mass proportions in the early 1930s most of its active members (particularly the activists in the SA) were too young to have seen the trenches of northern France or ever to have experienced military service.[19] The young men who flocked to the Nazi formations in the early 1930s had been children at the time of the War. For them the War had often brought upheaval and insecurity, but they had not experienced the horrors of combat at first hand. Their experience of war was more likely to have come from films, cheap children's novels, and playing soldier with their

[15] APW, Rejencja Opolska, Pr.B., no. 326, fo. 285: Polizeiverwaltung to Regierungspräsident, Oppeln, 31 Jan. 1919.

[16] For an example of hostility to the Freikorps, see the account of attempts in early 1919 to recruit for the Ostpreußische Freiwilligenkorps disrupted by ex-soldiers and sailors, in GStAB, Rep. 12/11a/2, fos. 189–90: Magistrat to Oberpräsident in Königsberg, Tilsit, 11 March 1919. For an example of lack of enthusiasm to join the *Einwohnerwehren*, see BLHA, Rep. 3B Reg. Frankfurt/Oder, I Pol, no. 457, fos. 36–8: Landrat to Regierungspräsident in Frankfurt/ Oder, Reppen, 11 Apr. 1919.

[17] See Waite, *Vanguard of Nazism*, 42–3; Schulze, *Freikorps und Republik*, 51. One revealing indication of attitudes was the disturbance which followed the festive welcome of a returning regiment in Minden in early Dec. 1918. After a welcoming speech by the mayor and thanks by the regiment's commander, a member of the Soldiers' Council took the platform and began speaking about the 'mass murders of the war unleashed by (Germany's) former rulers' and praising the aims of the revolution. However, his speech was interrupted by shouts both from within the regiment and 'especially from among schoolboys' in the crowd; the regiment then withdrew, and the scene degenerated into fighting between soldiers and school pupils. See StAM, Oberpräsidium, no. 5844, fo. 24: Regierungspräsident to Oberpräsident in Münster, Minden, 10 Dec. 1918.

[18] Michael Geyer, *Deutsche Rüstungspolitik 1860–1980* (Frankfurt/Main, 1984), 117–18.

[19] See Conan Fischer, *Stormtroopers: A Social, Economic and Ideological Analysis 1929–35* (London, 1983), 48–50; Richard Bessel, *Political Violence and the Rise of Nazism: The Storm Troopers in Eastern Germany 1925–1934* (New Haven, Conn., and London, 1984), 33–45; Peter Longerich, *Die Braunen Bataillone: Geschichte der SA* (Munich, 1989), 89–91.

school comrades. For their generation, war was youthful fantasy, not the dreadful reality of the trenches.

The ambivalence and antipathy towards the military and war felt by so many people who had suffered as a result of the 1914–18 conflict was not a mere passing phenomenon, expressed only in its immediate aftermath (when one might expect anti-war sentiment to have been at its height). The scars left by War remained sensitive for years, well into the 'Third Reich'. The lack of enthusiasm among the German population when war broke out again in September 1939, despite the best efforts of Goebbels' propaganda machine to whip up enthusiasm for war and in stark contrast to the public reactions of so many Germans in the summer of 1914, suggests that memories of the First World War generally aroused aversion and fear among the German population. Similar conclusions may be drawn from observations by Social Democratic informants which were gathered together in the exiled SPD's 'Germany Reports' after Hitler came to power, in particular, when the German government reintroduced conscription in March 1935. According to Social Democrat informants, different sectors of the population responded in differing ways. Reactions, especially amongst workers, were 'very divided'. In Munich for example, 'the enthusiasm . . . was fantastic', and according to an informant from southern Bavaria, 'young people appear to be very pleased that they are able to join up'. Others registered misgivings, however. This was the case 'especially among older people', who feared a new war and were far from keen to see a new militarization of daily life.[20] And from Saxony one informant wrote:

The former participants in the War whom we could ask about their opinion on the introduction of general conscription gave expression in a very veiled manner that they were not keen to relive the years 1914–18. War invalids and war widows spoke to the effect that it would be better if the Reich Government first met its previous commitments and recompensed all the victims of that last war before it created new victims and spent money on armaments.[21]

The people most keen 'to relive the years 1914–18' were those who had not been compelled to endure them the first time round.

Nevertheless, 'the years 1914–18' did not figure in the political debates of the Weimar Republic principally as an admonition against war and the military. While Germany after the First World War was a society without a large military presence—due to the ban on conscription and the limitations on the size of the armed forces imposed by the Versailles Treaty—Weimar politics were stamped to an extraordinary degree by respect for, and glorification of, things military. Despite the antipathy towards war and the

---

[20] *Deutschland-Berichte der Sozialdemokratischen Partei Deutschlands (Sopade) 1934–1940*, ii (1935) (Salzhausen and Frankfurt/Main, 1980), 276–282.

[21] Ibid. 412.

military which 'the years 1914–18' had generated, the most bloody and futile war which Germany had yet experienced was followed not by more conciliatory patterns of political life but by an upsurge in violence and military practices in civil politics: by militaristic ideologies, by military forms of political organization, by the activities of uniformed formations which sought to recreate an idealized military community in civil society. While the upsurge in political violence during the Weimar period should not be interpreted simply as the contribution of a 'front generation', allegedly unable to adjust to civil society, to domestic politics, it *was* part of the legacy of the First World War.

Of course, before 1914 industrial conflict had on occasion had bloody consequences, police had not infrequently made use of sabres when quelling what they regarded as unrest, and Social Democrats had not been treated with kid gloves by the repressive apparatus of the Imperial German state.[22] However, the violence in German politics after 1918 was both qualitatively and quantitatively different.[23] The brutal suppression of revolutionary unrest by the Freikorps in the immediate post-war years, and the campaigns of political assassination which claimed the lives of Hugo Haase, Matthias Erzberger, and Walther Rathenau among others, injected a new dimension of terror into German domestic political life. Internal unrest was quelled on occasion with what can only be described as military campaigns, such as in the 'Ruhr War' of 1920 and the Leuna uprising of 1921.[24] During the terminal years of the Weimar Republic, formations of 'political soldiers' in the Nazi Sturmabteilungen, Social Democratic Reichsbanner, and

---

[22] e.g. see Richard J. Evans, ' "Red Wednesday" in Hamburg: Social Democrats, Police and Lumpenproletariat in the Suffrage Disturbances of 17 January 1906', *Social History*, 4, no. 1 (1979), 1–30; Herbert Reinke, ' "Armed as if for a War": The State, the Military and the Professionalisation of the Prussian Police in Imperial Germany', in Clive Emsley and Barbara Weinberger (eds.) *Policing Western Europe: Politics, Professionalism and Public Order 1850–1940* (New York, Westport, Conn., and London, 1991), 55–73.

[23] The classic text which catalogues the hundreds of political murders during the immediate post-war years is Emil Julius Gumbel, *Vier Jahre politischer Mord* (Berlin-Fichtenau, 1922). See also James M. Diehl, *Paramilitary Politics in Weimar Germany* (Bloomington, Ind., and London, 1977); Bessel, 'Militarismus', 193–222; id., 'Politische Gewalt und die Krise der Weimarer Republik', in Lutz Niethammer *et al.*, *Bürgerliche Gesellschaft in Deutschland: Historische Einblicke, Fragen, Perspektiven* (Frankfurt/Main, 1990), 383–95; David Southern, 'Anti-Democratic Terror in the Weimar Republic: The Black Reichswehr and the Feme Murders', in Wolfgang J. Mommsen and Gerhard Hirschfeld (eds.), *Social Protest, Violence and Terror in Nineteenth- and Twentieth-century Europe* (London, 1982), 330–41; Peter H. Merkl, 'Approaches to Political Violence: The Stormtroopers, 1925–33', in Mommsen and Hirschfeld (eds.), *Social Protest, Violence and Terror*, 367–83; Eve Rosenhaft, *Beating the Fascists? The German Communists and Political Violence 1929–1933* (Cambridge, 1983).

[24] On the 'Ruhr War', see George Eliasberg, *Der Ruhrkrieg von 1920* (Bonn-Bad Godesberg, 1974); Erhard Lucas, *Märzrevolution 1920* (3 vols.; Frankfurt/Main, 1973, 1974, 1978). On the suppression of the Leuna uprising, see *Die Märzunruhen 1921 und die preußische Schutzpolizei: Amtliche Denkschrift des Ministeriums des Innern* (Berlin, 1921) (copy in GStAM, Rep. 169 D, no. IX, A, 1, Bd. 1, fos. 105–27); Polizei-Major Urban, 'Betrachtungen über den Einsatz von Artillerie beim Kampf der Schutzpolizei um Leuna 1921', in *Deutsches Polizei-Archiv*, 11: 8 (25 Apr. 1932), 106–7.

Communist Rotfrontkämpferbund and Kampfbund gegen den Faschismus brought violence to Germany's streets in a seemingly unending succession of confrontations which left dozens killed and hundreds wounded. The police, despite concern to cultivate a new modern identity as friend and servant of the public, resorted on occasion to violence quite out of proportion to the challenges they faced—most notably in the bloody campaigns in proletarian districts of Berlin at the beginning of May 1929, when police bullets left dozens of people dead and hundreds injured.[25] Political struggle, *Kampf*, took on a new meaning in the wake of the First World War, as violence left its mark on almost all aspects of civil society.[26] A line had been crossed: physical violence had become part of the political armoury which, increasingly, Germans habitually employed. Domestic politics could no longer be described as peacetime politics; German domestic politics after 1918 became an expression of a latent civil war, which culminated in the brutal suppression of the Left by the Nazis in 1933.

The obverse of the success of violent and military politics in Weimar Germany was the failure of pacifism. Certainly many Germans—like their French and British counterparts—emerged from the War with profoundly pacifist convictions. But many more did not, and pacifism found no appreciable echo in the politics of Weimar Germany.[27] 'Pacifist' generally remained a term of political abuse, not a badge of honour. It remains one of the most telling characteristics of the political culture of inter-war Germany that pacifism failed to make a significant impact after so awful and senseless an armed conflict. Even where the First World War was presented to the German public in all its gruesome horror—this was the first major European war in the age of amateur photography, and, consequently, the wretched conditions created by this conflict were recorded as no war had ever been recorded before—the contribution of those who fought in it was

---

[25] On attempts by the police in Weimar Germany to develop a 'modern' face, see Richard Bessel, 'Policing, Professionalisation and Politics in Weimar Germany', in Emsley and Weinberger (eds.) *Policing Western Europe*, 187–218. On the events in Berlin in 1929, see Eve Rosenhaft, 'Working-Class Life and Working-Class Politics: Communists, Nazis and the State in the Battle for the Streets, Berlin 1928–1932', in Richard Bessel and E. J. Feuchtwanger (eds.), *Social Change and Political Development in Weimar Germany* (London, 1981), 224–8; Chris Bowlby, ' "*Blutmai*" 1924: Police, Parties and Proletarians in a Berlin Confrontation', *Historical Journal*, 29: 1 (1986), 137–58; Thomas Kurz, "*Blutmai*": *Sozialdemokraten und Kommunisten im Brennpunkt der Berliner Ereignissen von 1929* (Bonn, 1989); Peter Leßmann, *Die preußische Schutzpolizei in der Weimarer Republik: Streifendienst und Straßenkampf* (Düsseldorf, 1989), 266–78.

[26] This could be seen in behaviour in pubs, where before the First World War heated political discussions rarely erupted in violence but where during the Weimar period such violence became commonplace. See the introductory comments by Richard J. Evans in his edition of *Kneipengespräche im Kaiserreich: Stimmungsberichte des Hamburger Politischen Polizei 1892–1914* (Reinbek bei Hamburg, 1989), 31–2.

[27] See Wolfram Wette, 'Einleitung: Probleme des Pazifismus in der Zwischenkriegszeit' and Reinhold Lütgemeier-Davin, 'Basismobilisierung gegen den Krieg: Die Nie-wieder-Krieg-Bewegung in der Weimarer Republik', both in Karl Holl and Wolfram Wette (eds.), *Pazifismus in der Weimarer Republik: Beiträge zur historischen Friedensforschung* (Paderborn, 1981).

described almost ritualistically as an example of 'unparalleled immortal German heroism'.[28] Whatever had actually taken place in the trenches or on the way back home in 1918 and 1919, it is clear that the image of the heroic soldier—who had experienced 'that pure and noble comradeship which is generated only in war' and then was allegedly stabbed in the back by an ungrateful home-front—remained intact for millions. This image was reflected in political discussion throughout the Weimar period, from the ill-judged but politically necessary welcome given by Friedrich Ebert to returning soldiers in Berlin in early December 1918, when he declared that they had been undefeated on the battlefield,[29] to the propaganda of the Nazi Party.

The question remains: Why should the experience of the most awful and bloody war which Germany had yet fought be remembered in this manner? One reason may have been that the ambivalent realities of combat and the subsequent demobilization were difficult, if not impossible, to reconcile with the dominant social values prevalent in Weimar Germany once the revolutionary wave had ebbed. As we have seen, at the end of the War hundreds of thousands of German soldiers had in effect engaged in a covert 'military strike' and, after the Armistice in November 1918, had abandoned their military units to set out on their own for home. The conduct of many of Germany's soldiers as the First World War ended not merely failed to match the later descriptions of 'unparalleled immortal German heroism'; in many cases it had been almost precisely the opposite. This was not something which would have been easy for many men to admit in public during the 1920s or 1930s.

The image of the demobilized hero of the trenches coming home to an unappreciative, disrespectful, scornful home-front formed an important element of the political vocabulary of the Weimar Republic, particularly on the Right. It fitted in neatly with the frequently repeated and profoundly misleading assertions that Germany's fighting men had not been defeated on the battlefield but were stabbed in the back at home; that it was not the front but the home front which had cracked; that the nation's heroes had acquitted themselves honourably, while the shameful behaviour of those back home—poisoned by unpatriotic political movements and lacking the necessary steadfastness—had led to Germany's defeat. However, evidence from throughout Germany about the efforts made by the civilian population to welcome home the troops reveals how inaccurate were such assertions.[30] It

---

[28] These phrases, and the one which follows, come from the introduction by George Soldan, 'Reichsarchivrat, Major a.D.', to a collection of war photographs showing the conditions in which men actually fought, published in 1928: *Der Weltkrieg im Bild: Originalaufnahmen des Kriegs-Bild- und Filmamtes aus der modernen Materialschlacht* (Berlin and Oldenburg, 1928).

[29] Winkler, *Von der Revolution zur Stabilisierung*, 100.

[30] This is discussed at some length in Richard Bessel, 'The Great War in German Memory: The Soldiers of the First World War, Demobilization and Weimar Political Culture', *German History*, 6:1 (1988), 20–34.

would appear that in fact it was not the home front which failed to do its duty to the heroes returning from the War, but the 'heroes' who behaved in ways often far removed from conventional ideas of the heroic.[31] People back home, probably aroused by a mixture of patriotism and guilt at having enjoyed the comparative safety of the Reich while the soldiers were being killed in their hundreds of thousands at the front, did publicly display their gratitude. The problem lay in the soldiers' responses: it is not so much that the civilians failed to give the returning soldiers a hero's welcome, but that a large proportion of the 'heroes' failed to show up.

Similar discrepancies between image and reality arise from examination of the fate of demobilized soldiers on the German job-market. Part and parcel of the picture of the front soldier returning to an ungrateful Fatherland are images of veterans, more often than not disabled, reduced to begging on the streets of post-war Germany. Perhaps more than anything else, images from the work of George Grosz and Otto Dix—of war veterans without arms or legs, begging on the streets, ignored by prosperous bourgeois passers-by—have shaped our picture of how the 'front generation' fared on the labour market in Germany after the First World War.[32] Even Robert Whalen, in his extremely perceptive study of German victims of the Great War, has accepted rather uncritically the picture of veterans unable to find work: 'Being free in a bankrupt economy was no treat. . . . Even healthy veterans had a hard time finding employment.'[33] However, far from having particular difficulties finding employment, it would appear that—because jobs were reserved for them after the War, because they returned to a buoyant labour-market in the early 1920s, and because men aged between 20 and 40 formed the section of the working population most likely to be employed in any event—the former soldiers were generally relatively fortunate when seeking work in Weimar Germany.[34] This holds true not only for

---

[31] For a perceptive discussion of the widely propagated idea of 'heroism' and its fate during the First World War, see Whalen, *Bitter Wounds*, 22–31.

[32] There seems little doubt that during the post-war years large numbers of bemedalled, uniformed men were begging on German streets. However, it would be a mistake to regard these as representative of the war veterans as a whole. The war victims organizations opposed this practice, as it undermined public sympathy for their members, and charges were levelled that some of the beggars were not war veterans at all. See BAP, RMdI, no. 13045, fo. 212: Kriegsministerium to Reichsministerium des Innern, Berlin, 5 May 1919; ibid., Reichsarbeitsministerium, no. 9054: Reichsarbeitsminister to Preuß. Ministerium des Innern, Berlin, 10 Sept. 1919; ibid., no. 9054: Bund Deutscher Kriegsbeschädigter to Reichsarbeitsminister Schlicke, Hamburg, 25 Oct. 1919. In this last letter, the Bund Deutscher Kriegsbeschädigter spoke of 'professional beggars', estimated that two-thirds of the beggars were not war victims at all, and noted that it co-operated with the Hamburg police in rounding them up.

[33] Whalen, *Bitter Wounds*, 113.

[34] See above, Ch. 5; Richard Bessel, 'Unemployment and Demobilisation in Germany after the First World War', in Richard J. Evans and Dick Geary (eds.), *The German Unemployed: Experiences and Consequences of Mass Unemployment from the Weimar Republic to the Third Reich* (London and Sydney, 1987), 23–43.

the immediate post-war period but also for the final years of the Republic. The mass unemployment of the early 1930s hit the young harder than those in their thirties and forties;[35] middle-aged men, i.e. members of the 'front generation', were more likely to have work than were members of a frustrated younger generation coming of age and looking for employment in the increasingly grim economic climate after 1929.

Nevertheless, the picture of German soldiers returning to a hostile and ungrateful civilian population does contain an element of truth. While this picture may not have reflected the experience of the vast majority of the front soldiers, as we have seen, some *officers* did have quite unpleasant experiences when they returned to the Reich.[36] The significant point here is that the officers' experiences, rather than the experiences of the great mass of the veterans of the Great War, tended to frame how the War figured in political discussion in Weimar Germany. The fact that the public memory of the First World War came to be structured not by the experiences of the vast majority of those who fought in it, but by the perspectives of much narrower (and politically more conservative) groups, is illustrative of the basis upon which Weimar politics were stabilized in the mid-1920s.

The discrepancies between actual experiences of war and the unambiguous, heroic language with which the War came to be referred to left veterans of the Great War with a dilemma: how to come to terms with their own often ambiguous behaviour within a framework which left little room for admitting that things had been other than black and white. This provided perhaps all the more reason to accept heroic myths rather than face uncomfortable reality. Rather than confront the terms in which public and political debate increasingly came to be framed—and thereby to admit, perhaps, to having been a 'coward'—it was better to accept them. Thus politics in effect could serve to suppress discomfort about one's own past and to avoid public acknowledgement of its ambivalent and contradictory nature. During the Weimar period war veterans had to come to terms with their own behaviour in a society where nationalism and military values were able to reassert themselves. During the immediate post-war period, the experiences of the Great War were still too close perhaps for heroic myths to become dominant. The 'traditional' values bound up with things military, the monarchy, and the authoritarian political system had been weakened by war, defeat, and revolution. From the the mid- to late 1920s, however, a more conservative and militarist set of values made a comeback and shaped public discussion of the War.

[35] See Detlev Peukert, 'The Lost Generation: Youth Unemployment at the End of the Weimar Republic', in Evans and Geary (eds.), *The German Unemployed*, 172–93; Peukert, *Jugend zwischen Krieg und Krise: Lebenswelten von Arbeiterjungen in der Weimarer Republik* (Cologne, 1987), esp. 97–188.

[36] e.g. see GLAK, 233/12401: XIV. Armeekorps to Badisches Ministerium des Innern, Durlach, 7 Feb. 1919; and above, Ch. 3.

To be sure, this process was not a smooth one. The often bitter disputes about how the War should be discussed reveal a good deal about its impact upon politics in Weimar Germany. At stake were the ways in which the War could be imagined, the myths which could frame how the immediate past affected a bitterly contested present. This can be seen in the public discussion of two 'legends' of the War: one the one hand, Bertolt Brecht's 'Legend of the Dead Soldier'; on the other, the legend of the (otherwise not particularly noteworthy) battle of Langemarck. Brecht's 'Legend' is a bitter, cynical, grotesque account of a soldier who, having already died a 'hero's death', is exhumed, declared 'fit for duty' and sent back to the front.[37] Brecht's poem is a brutal and carefully aimed attack on militaristic language and the glorification of war, and it provoked a predictable reaction: as author of the 'Legend' Brecht was included on the list of those whom the Nazis intended to arrest once they seized power, and plans during the mid-1920s to publish a paperback collection of Brecht's poetry (*Taschenpostille*) were abandoned when the publisher, Kiepenheuer Verlag, refused to include this poem. The legend of Langemarck was quite different. In fact a costly and unsuccessful attempt to capture some positions in the vicinity of Ypres in the autumn of 1914, the battle of Langemarck was presented to the younger generation of Weimar Germany as a shining example of patriotic heroism.[38] The unnecessary sacrifice of poorly trained and poorly armed young soldiers by officers lacking either the necessary knowledge of the terrain or instruction in modern military tactics was glorified during the Weimar period as a symbol of German honour and unity. The annual celebration of 'Langemarck Day' by nationalist students, supported by conservative political organizations and, from the end of the 1920s, in the presence of official representatives of the Reich government, served as a right-wing counterpoint to Armistice Day, which also fell in November. A legend was created which served to repress contradictory and unpleasant representations of the War. Both the sharp reaction provoked by Brecht's 'Dead Soldier' and the potency of the Langemarck legend point to the inability of many Germans during the Weimar period to acknowledge publicly and come to terms with the contradictory experiences and negative consequences of the First World War.

Similar conclusions may be drawn from the stormy reaction to Erich Maria Remarque's *All Quiet on the Western Front*. Immediately after the War, while its horrors were still fresh memories, such a brutal attack against the glorification of war might not have provoked such hostility; in any event, it

---

[37] Bertolt Brecht, 'Legende vom toten Soldaten', in *Gesammelte Werke*, viii: *Gedichte I*, 256–9. On the genesis and language of, and reactions to, this poem, see Jan Knopf, *Brecht-Handbuch. Lyrik, Prosa, Schriften. Eine Ästhetik der Widersprüche* (Stuttgart, 1986), 20–1.

[38] See Karl Unruh, *Langemarck: Legende und Wirklichkeit* (Koblenz, 1986); Bernd Hüppauf, 'Langemarck, Verdun and the Myth of a *New Man* in Germany after the First World War', *War and Society*, 6: 2 (Sept. 1988), 70–103; George L. Mosse, *Fallen Soldiers: Reshaping the Memory of the World Wars* (New York and Oxford, 1990), 70–4.

was not a theme about which Germans were yet quite so keen to read. Ten years later, however, the attempt to write about the 'purely human experience of war' and 'about the horrors, about the confused, often raw instinct of self-preservation, about the tenacious strength of life which contrasts with the death and annihilation'[39] of war became *the* sensation of German (and international) publishing and a domestic-political *casus belli*.[40] When the book was published by Ullstein Verlag in January 1929, it became a massive best-seller. Launched with an unprecedented advertising campaign, within three weeks it had sold 200,000 copies, and by the end of 1929 nearly one million copies had been bought in Germany alone. The book was quickly translated into roughly twenty languages and precipitated a wave of 'front literature' which flooded German bookshops in 1929–30.[41] The wave also swept over the film world, and when the German version of the American film based on Remarque's book was shown for the first time in Berlin in December 1930, the premier was disrupted systematically by supporters of the NSDAP (under the direction of the Berlin Nazi Party gauleiter Joseph Goebbels) and banned soon thereafter by the Board of Film Censors for 'endangering Germany's reputation'. (In fact the film was shown again in Germany in September 1931, but was banned once more after Hitler came to power.)

As Modris Eksteins has pointed out, the furore generated by *All Quiet on the Western Front* was not primarily about the War itself: 'The "real war" had ceased to exist in 1918. Thereafter it was swallowed by imagination in the guise of memory.'[42] The controversies triggered by *All Quiet* involved coming to terms with the War politically and psychologically—or perhaps better: they involved the inability of many Germans to come to terms with the War. The real theme of Remarque's best-seller was in fact not the War itself but the confused position of the author and his generation ten years after the conflict had ended. Introducing his book, Remarque claimed that 'it only makes an attempt to report about a generation that was destroyed by the War—even when it escaped its grenades'; and close to its end, in Paul's last comments, he wrote that 'if we now return' to Germany, 'we will no longer be able to find our way'. The bitter literary and political conflicts

---

[39] Thus Remarque's description of his book in an interview initially published in June 1929 in the *Literarische Welt*. Quoted in Erich Maria Remarque, *Im Westen nichts Neues* (with material and an afterword by Tilman Westphalen) (Cologne, 1987), 305.

[40] On the reactions to *All Quiet on the Western Front*, see Modris Eksteins, 'War, Memory and Politics: The Fate of the Film *All Quiet on the Western Front*', *Central European History*, 13, no. 1 (1980); id. *Rites of Spring: The Great War and the Birth of the Modern Age* (New York, 1990), 275–99. See also Bernd Hüppauf, ' "Der Tod ist verschlungen in den Sieg": Todesbilder aus dem Ersten Weltkrieg und der Nachkriegszeit', in id. (ed.), *Ansichten vom Krieg: Vergleichende Studien zum Ersten Weltkrieg in Literatur und Gesellschaft* (Königstein/Taunus, 1984), 83–7.

[41] See Michael Gollbach, *Die Wiederkehr des Weltkrieges in der Literatur: Zu den Frontromanen der späten Zwanziger Jahre* (Kronberg, 1978).

[42] Eksteins, *Rites of Spring*, 297.

over the 'truth' about the War were at heart not about the experience of combat in 1914–18 so much as about the integration of the 'front generation' into the social and political landscape of Germany ten years after the Armistice. The book, and the controversy surrounding it, were about *imagining* the War, not about describing it accurately.

Perhaps for this reason the successful examples of the 'front literature' which swamped Germany's bookshops in 1929 and 1930 were almost always written from the perspective of the individual. Imagining the War as a whole was a very different proposition from imagining it from the limited perspective of one pair of eyes gazing out from the trenches. In the face of the enormity of the horrors of the War and the extent to which it had destroyed the apparent certainties of the pre-war world, imagining the War as a whole could probably be accomplished only within the simplifying framework of party politics and political ideologies. Assuming the narrow perspective of the individual 'worker' of the new industrial war, who could barely see beyond the trench in which he was stuck, was the only other way to make such an exercise manageable. Only within a limited compass might one hope to make sense of the senselessness of the War—either to demythologize the conflict or to discover some deep aesthetic meaning in it.

It would be a mistake to regard the success of *All Quiet* as a sign that the German public, a decade after the Armistice, was ready to demythologize the War and replace heroic images of soldiers with the 'purely human experience of war'. Instead, Remarque's novel in effect provided a focus around which a reaction (in both senses of the word) could coalesce. There is much to be said for Bernd Hüppauf's thesis that the real consequence of the disputes was a 'rehabilitation of warlike violence' during the final years of the Weimar Republic. Hüppauf suggests that, 'it was precisely these attempts at a rational approach to the War which, in the specific conditions of the Weimar Republic, contributed to a radicalization of the trivialization of war'; 'resistance to the glorification of death in battle in public celebrations, remembrance ceremonies, and the unveiling of monuments, and a flood of publications in the final analysis provided the necessary opposite pole for a radical and politically powered upsurge in an irrational mythologizing of war'.[43]

One may question whether Remarque's literary efforts really did mark 'a rational approach to the War', and there may even have been a rational basis for the attractions of 'an irrational mythologizing of war'. In the later stages of the Weimar Republic, the very discrepancy between the myth and reality of life in the trenches and the post-war transition may have helped give the 'irrational mythologizing' its political potency. The Nazis' success

---

[43] Bernd Hüppauf, 'Über den Kampfgeist: Ein Kapitel aus der Vor- und Nachbereitung eines Weltkrieges', in Anton-Andreas Guha and Sven Papcke (eds.), *Der Feind den wir brauchen. Oder: Muß Krieg sein?* (Königstein/Taunus, 1985), 92–3.

in posturing as the political representatives of the 'front generation'—and the Nazis never ceased reminding the electorate that their leader had been a front soldier—might have come about not so much in spite of but rather *because of* the fact that the propaganda was at odds with reality. The strength of their political message was not that it was based upon what people believed but that it reflected what people, increasingly, *wanted to believe.*

Not only the memories of the living but also the remembrance of the dead revealed political sensibilities after the First World War. In contrast to what had happened as a consequence of previous conflicts, during and after the First World War an elaborate 'cult of the fallen' developed among the combatant powers.[44] This reflected not only the fact that more people had been killed in the First World War than in any previous conflict, but also a change in the way in which war figured in public discussion. Honouring the dead became solemn rather than celebratory. As a defeated country, still lacking full sovereignty and with most of her fallen soldiers buried in former enemy territory, it was more difficult for Germany to develop a language with which to commemorate her war dead than it was for the victorious Allies. One reflection of this is the fact that whereas Britain, France, and Italy unveiled their tombs for the unknown soldier in 1920, in Germany a tomb of the unknown soldier was not unveiled until 1931, in the *Neue Wache* on Berlin's Unter den Linden. In contrast to monuments from earlier wars, and even more so than in other former combatant countries, memorials to the dead of the First World War in Germany were to be simple, solemn, dignified affairs. Even the Tannenberg Monument, unveiled in East Prussia in 1927 to commemorate Germany's great victory at the outset of the War, centred on a tomb containing twenty unknown soldiers from the eastern front. The appropriate sombre note was expressed clearly, for example, in the advice of the Pomeranian Provincial Advisory Office for War Memorials in September 1920 to local communities proposing to erect monuments in honour of their war dead.[45] The Office advised against erecting elaborate monuments commemorating the dead in prominent positions on streets, in public squares, or along village roads 'with their agricultural and profane traffic'; they were not to serve as 'a piece of decoration'. More fitting 'as a memorial of deep grief and as a sign of remembrance to the combatants who sacrificed their lives in vain in a war of such disastrous consequences for the salvation of the Fatherland' were simple memorial tablets placed within churches or in church cemeteries. Dignified reflection was called for, not ostentatious celebration of the War.

---

[44] See esp. Mosse, *Fallen Soldiers*, 70–106.

[45] APS, Landratsamt Schivelbein, no. 161: Provinzialberatungsstelle für Kriegerehrungen, 'Gutachten', Stettin, 20 Sept. 1920. Generally, see Meinhold Lurz, *Kriegerdenkmäler in Deutschland*, iii: *Der 1. Weltkrieg* (Heidelberg, 1985). For a discussion of the meaning of war memorials in France after the First World War, see Antoine Prost, *Les anciens combattants et la société française, 1914–1939*, iii: *Mentalités et idéologies* (Paris, 1977), 35–52.

The First World War was not an easy war to remember. The mass slaughter of industrialized war did not lend itself to glorification. Nor did the day-by-day participation in the War of front soldiers who, Ernst Jünger claimed, had become 'workers' who were employed by the state and whose product was the violence of industrialized war. Yet the new collective identity as the working class of industrialized war provided a sense of belonging to a 'front community'.[46] The problem with this identity was that, as we have seen, the War had in fact been experienced in many different ways by the many men who fought in it.[47] The idea of a single experience of the front which somehow united a 'front generation' can therefore better be understood as a myth of the post-war world than as an accurate reflection of the experience of the First World War. Indeed, the speed of the demobilization meant that most former soldiers of the First World War soon came to regard themselves, and to be regarded by public authorities, not primarily as ex-soldiers but as workers, businessmen, farmers, husbands, fathers; in this real sense, the 'front community' quickly dissolved into its constituent parts. Consequently, it is difficult to speak of the 'front generation' except in so far as the term was employed in public discussion, where it represented an attempt to cover over divisions rather than to describe real unity of experience and perspective. In the words of George Mosse: 'The reality of the war experience came to be transformed into what one might call the Myth of the War Experience, which looked back upon the war as a meaningful and even sacred event. . . . The Myth of the War Experience was designed to mask war and legitimize the war experience; it was meant to displace the reality of war.'[48]

Nevertheless, a substantial proportion of the adult population of Weimar Germany had fought in the War and subsequently participated, at least as voters, in political life. Altogether, roughly 11 million German soldiers survived the First World War and returned to Germany. Even in 1932, after approximately 650,000 of the men in Germany born between 1880 and 1900 had died since 1919, the surviving members of what might be termed the 'front generation' still numbered nearly 10.5 million.[49] They comprised

---

[46] See Michael Geyer, *Deutsche Rüstungspolitik*, 100.

[47] This argument is developed in Richard Bessel, 'The "Front Generation" and the Politics of the Weimar Republic', in Mark Roseman (ed.), *Generation Formation and Conflict in Modern Germany* (forthcoming).

[48] Mosse, *Fallen Soldiers*, 7.

[49] Mortality of the 'Front Generation', 1919–1932 (deaths of males born between 1880 and 1900):

| Year | |
|------|--------|
| 1919 | 67,698 |
| 1920 | — |
| 1921 | — |
| 1922 | 46,636 |

more than one-quarter of the German electorate during the 1920s[50] and, given the generally lower participation of women in elections,[51] an even higher proportion of those who actually cast their votes. What is more, First World War veterans came to constitute the backbone of many party organizations in Weimar Germany—most notably of the NSDAP. It could hardly have been otherwise: in 1930 the men born between 1880 and 1900 were aged between 30 and 50; that is to say, they were of an age when people normally establish themselves in their communities. They naturally assumed positions of importance in local organizations, or attempted to wrest control from their elders—from those who had been adults during the Empire and were approaching retirement from public life by 1930. Thus inevitable generational political conflict during the last years of the Weimar Republic was conducted by a group which also saw itself as the 'front generation'.

Yet to make this observation is essentially to state the obvious, and the question remains whether the political divisions and radicalism of the Weimar Republic may be explained with reference to the 'front generation' and their experience of the First World War. The main cleavages which characterized the German electorate were religious, occupational, and geographical (i.e. town and country), not a public posture towards the generation which had fought the War. All political parties attempted to court the 'front generation', and all heaped praise on the veterans of the trenches. Since men who fought in the First World War constituted so large a part of the electorate in Weimar Germany, it would have been highly unlikely for them to be found largely in one political camp and not in another. However, one

| Year | |
|------|--------|
| 1923 | 46,195 |
| 1924 | 39,998 |
| 1925 | 39,346 |
| 1926 | 38,608 |
| 1927 | 40,495 |
| 1928 | 41,183 |
| 1929 | 45,831 |
| 1930 | 43,448 |
| 1931 | 44,128 |
| 1932 | 43,815 |

This table is compiled from figures in the *Statistische Jahrbücher des Deutschen Reichs* between 1921/22 and 1934: *1921/22*, p. 44; *1924/25*, pp. 37, 39; *1926*, p. 30; *1927*, p. 32; *1928*, p. 36; *1929*, p. 34; *1930*, p. 36; *1931*, p. 32; *1932*, p. 32; *1933*, p. 34; *1934*, p. 34.

[50] The numbers eligible to vote in the Reichstag elections from 1920 to 1932 were as follows: 6 June 1920, 35,949,774; 4 May 1924, 38,374,983; 7 Dec. 1924, 38,987,385; 20 May 1928, 41,224,678; 14 Sept. 1930, 42,957,675; 31 July 1932, 44,211,216; 6 Nov. 1932, 44,374,085. See Jürgen Falter, Thomas Lindenberger, and Siegfried Schumann, *Wahlen und Abstimmungen in der Weimarer Republik: Materialien zum Wahlverhalten 1919–1933* (Munich, 1986), 68–74.

[51] Helen L. Boak, 'Women in Weimar Germany: The "Frauenfrage" and the Female Vote', in Bessel and Feuchtwanger (eds.), *Social Change and Political Development*, 156–7.

cleavage which the 'front generation' did parallel was that between men and women. The 'front generation' may have been too large to be confined to any one particular political preference, but it was one way of describing the majority of middle-aged men in Weimar Germany.

Although the War profoundly affected the German women who lived through it, in the public imagination they were not counted in the ranks of the 'front generation'. During the Weimar years German women were confronted with an image of a 'front generation' which excluded them and their experiences. The 'front generation' consisted of *men*; it was a representation of *male* experiences. The potency of the 'front generation' in the political language of Weimar Germany—and particularly during the final years of the Republic—was both a reflection and an assertion of the fact that politics formed a male realm. To assert that politics should reflect the needs and perspectives of the 'front generation' was in effect to assert that women should have no substantial role in political life. Indeed, it is worth considering the extent to which the political culture of the Weimar Republic generally may have been coloured by an underlying hostility towards women, which had its roots in a reaction to the wartime undermining of patriarchial social and economic relations.[52] In this context it appears more than just coincidental that the political party which was able ultimately to exploit the myth of the 'front generation' most successfully—that is, the Nazi Party—was also most militantly anti-feminist.

The most visible intrusion of the 'front generation' into German politics after 1918 was the activities of those officers who found a home in paramilitary and right-wing groups after the War. Much has been written of the men who returned to a defeated Germany 'deeply marked by their war experiences and hostile toward the civilian population, by whom they felt betrayed and abandoned', men who returned 'confused, embittered, angry, hungry, and with no hope of pursuing military careers because of the limitations placed on the German army by the Treaty of Versailles' and who 'soon found opportunities to use the destructive skills they had learned at the front'.[53] (Actually, as we have seen, it was the civilian population which was hungry rather than the soldiers!) Although they comprised only a tiny minority of the men who had fought in the First World War, their contribution to Weimar politics was significant: they were the men who led the Freikorps and occupied leading positions in the numerous military-style organizations (the *Kampfbünde*) which proliferated in Weimar Germany,[54] and many subsequently occupied leading positions in the Nazi Party. Nor was

[52] See the speculative but perceptive comments by Klaus Theweleit, *Männerphantasien* (2 vols ; Frankfurt/Main, 1977, 1978); and Elisabeth Domansky, 'Der Erste Weltkrieg', in Lutz Niethammer *et al.*, *Bürgerliche Gesellschaft in Deutschland: Historische Einblicke, Fragen, Perspektiven* (Frankfurt/Main, 1990), 312–18.

[53] Wohl, *The Generation of 1914*, 54.

[54] See Diehl, *Paramilitary Politics*.

the self-conscious expression of 'front generation' politics during the 1920s limited to the militarist antics of the right-wing racialist fringe. The most obvious example is the Stahlhelm, whose members identified themselves as 'front soldiers' throughout the Weimar period, whose full title was 'Stahlhelm, League of Front Soldiers', and whose self-proclaimed purpose was to promote politicians 'who will depend on us front soldiers for support'.[55]

The 'myth of the war experience' probably had its greatest, and politically most damaging, resonance among those who had been too young to fight in the First World War—not the war generation itself but the extraordinarily large cohort born in the first decade of the twentieth century, who had experienced the War not at the front but inside Germany. This was what Günther Gründel described in 1932 as the 'war-youth generation' (in contrast to the 'young front generation' of those born between 1890 and 1900, and the 'post-war generation' born after 1910), who could only read about what their older brothers had experienced but for whom the wartime worries and hardships nevertheless formed 'a quite unusually strong and unique youth experience'.[56] It was this generation, of Germans too young to know the horrors of the War at first hand, which could imagine war as something positive and unambiguous (and which provided so many of the Nazi movement's political activists in the early 1930s). Perhaps this generation was also driven by feelings of guilt at not having shared the horrors of the trenches in a country where, increasingly, the exploits of the 'front generation' were praised as the model of selfless heroism. Whatever the reason, the 'myth of the war experience' appears to have been more potent among the 'war-youth generation' and the post-war generation than among those who actually experienced life in the trenches.

The myths and illusions which arose from war and defeat were dangerous because they helped fix the political agenda in such a way as to favour the Right and to privilege irresponsibility. In order to function well, a democratic political system needs wide public recognition of the limits within which policy decisions have to be taken. As long as the truth about the 1914–18 conflict, its causes and consequences, did not really figure in mainstream public discussion, it was both possible to accept—and indeed to glorify—war and impossible to face fully the harsh economic and political realities which

---

[55] This is a comment by Franz Seldte, the leader of the Stahlhelm, given in his official biography (Wilhelm Kleinau, *Franz Seldte: Ein Lebensbericht* (Berlin, 1933), 49.), quoted in Waite, *Vanguard of Nazism*, 267. On the Stahlhelm generally, see Volker R. Berghahn, *Der Stahlhelm: Bund der Frontsoldaten* (Düsseldorf, 1966).

[56] E. Günther Gründel, *Die Sendung der Jungen Generation: Versuch einer umfassenden revolutionären Sinndeutung der Krise* (Munich, 1932), quoted in Ulrich Herbert, ' "Generation der Sachlichkeit": Die völkische Studentenbewegung der frühen zwanziger Jahre in Deutschland', in Frank Bajohr, Werner Johe, and Uwe Lohalm (eds.), *Zivilisation und Barbarei. Die widersprüchlichen Potentiale der Moderne. Detler Peukert zum Gedenken* (Hamburg, 1991), 116.

confronted the Weimar Republic. The result was a flight from political responsibility. Responsible politics remained a hostage to myths about the First World War throughout the tortured life of the Weimar Republic.[57]

These points are illustrated well by examination of one of the most intractable war-related problems which plagued Weimar politicians: the unquenchable expectations of war victims. When the First World War came to an end, Germany possessed extremely fragmented and inadequate arrangements for satisfying the social and economic needs of those who had lost limbs, sight, earning capacity, husbands, fathers, and sons. The system for dealing with war victims inherited from the Empire was ill-equipped to cope with the quite unprecedented needs and demands generated by the War, in which the victims were numbered not in tens but in hundreds of thousands. Although the German state had pioneered the establishment of social-welfare legislation, it played a surprisingly modest direct role in caring for the war victims during the conflict.[58] Looking after war victims had generally been left to volunteer groups and private organizations, from the trade unions to bourgeois women's and church groups. The Reich government was reluctant to face the mounting problem posed by the war victims, the solution of which would obviously require massive financial resources, and resorted instead to stop-gap measures, *ad hoc* increases in various payments, and stress upon the need to transform war invalids into productive members of society once again. Even the main forum for formulating national policy, the Reich Committee for War Invalids' and War Dependants' Care (Reichsausschuß für Kriegsbeschädigten- und Kriegshinterbliebenen-Fürsorge), formed in 1915, was essentially a voluntary organization run by civil servants. Not surprisingly, after four years of massive casualties on the field and growing economic distress and inflation at home, the ramshackle arrangements provoked widespread condemnation from those who had come to depend on them.

The obvious inadequacies of the existing system, and the enormity of the problem posed by the war victims gave rise to almost universal agreement about the necessity of providing a unified, national, and efficient system of meeting war victims' needs. The problem was providing the money. In December 1918 Friedrich Ebert described caring for the war victims' welfare as the 'principal duty' of the new government; the need to care for the war victims was emphasized in the programmes of all the major parties of the

---

[57] On the ramifications of the myth of Germany's innocence with regard to the First World War, see Wolfram Wette, 'Ideologien, Propaganda und Innenpolitik als Voraussetzungen der Kriegspolitik des Dritten Reiches', in Wilhelm Deist (ed.), *Ursachen und Voraussetzungen der deutschen Kriegspolitik* (vol. 1 of Militärgeschichtliches Forschungsamt (ed.), *Das Deutsche Reich und der Zweite Weltkrieg*) (Stuttgart, 1979), 25–173; Heinemann, *Die verdrängte Niederlage*. More generally, see Richard Bessel, 'Why Did the Weimar Republic Collapse?' in Ian Kershaw (ed.), *Weimar: Why Did German Democracy Fail?* (London, 1990), esp. 123–8.

[58] See Whalen, *Bitter Wounds*, 83–105.

new republic; and the Weimar Constitution explicitly charged the government with legislating for 'the welfare of the combatants and their survivors'.[59]
The National Assembly finally accepted in specific terms this constitutional
responsibility when, on 28 April 1920 (shortly before its dissolution), it passed
a Law on the Care of Military Persons and their Dependants—the Reich
Pension Law (*Reichsversorgungsgesetz*), which took effect retroactively on 1 April
1920, the beginning of the financial year. In terms of its implications for
both the subsequent development of social-welfare law and the finances of
the Reich government, this was among the most important pieces of
legislation enacted during the Weimar Republic.[60]

The scale of the problem faced by the German state was enormous.
Roughly 2.7 million German soldiers returned from the First World War
with some permanent disability, and in 1923 the Reich Labour Ministry
estimated the number of war widows in Germany at 533,000 and the number
of war orphans at 1,192,000.[61] Already by 1920, before the Reich Pension
Law was passed, roughly 45,000 state employees were kept busy administering the war-pensions schemes.[62] During the early 1920s the state bureaucracy processed millions of applications for war-related pensions—3 million
between July 1921 and February 1923 alone—and at the high point, in
March 1922, more than 200,000 applications were processed during a single
month.[63] The numbers stabilized during the second half of the 1920s, but
the scale of the problem and of the financial burdens remained huge. In
May 1928, for example, 761,294 people were receiving invalidity pensions.[64]
The number of widows receiving war-related pensions stood at 359,560, of
children without a father at 731,781, of children without either parent at

---

[59] Alfred Dick, 'Die Kriegsbeschädigtenversorgung' (Univ. of Frankfurt/Main, phil. diss.,
1930), 84–5.

[60] Ibid. 86–112; Whalen, *Bitter Wounds*, 131–9; Michael Geyer, 'Ein Vorbote des Wohlfahrtsstaates: Die Kriegsopferversorgung in Frankreich, Deutschland und Großbritannien nach dem
Ersten Weltkrieg', *Geschichte und Gesellschaft*, 9: 2 (1983), esp. 245–58.

[61] Whalen, *Bitter Wounds*.    [62] Ibid. 132.    [63] Ibid. 142–3.

[64] In terms of their disability as a percentage of their lost earning-capacity, these 761,294
people were divided as follows:

| | |
|---|---|
| 30 | 305,213 |
| 40 | 121,354 |
| 50 | 132,915 |
| 60 | 67,050 |
| 70 | 56,839 |
| 80 | 28,758 |
| 90 | 5,840 |
| 100 | 42,761 |
| No data available | 564 |
| Total | 761,294 |

These and the following figures are given in Dick, 'Die Kriegsbeschädigtenversorgung', 113–15.
See also Whalen, *Bitter Wounds*, 156.

56,623, and of parents of fallen soldiers at 147,230. For the financial year 1929 this meant an expenditure of 630,000,000 RM for payments to people with disabilities, 661,500,000 RM for payments to dependants, 45,710,000 RM for medical treatment, 12,963,000 RM for special hardship payments, and 64,591,580 RM to cover the administrative costs of the bureaucracy required to distribute the money and police the system. The total, more than 1.35 thousand million RM, was more than double the total cost of unemployment relief and unemployment insurance, and comprised over 18 per cent of the entire Reich government expenditure.[65] Small wonder then that this expenditure came under severe pressure when the German economy went into a tail-spin after 1929.

From the beginning of the Weimar Republic to its end, the welfare arrangements for the war victims were felt to be unsatisfactory by almost everyone involved. Already in April 1919 dissatisfaction among the war victims was serious enough for Prussian War Minister Walther Reinhardt to inform the Reich Cabinet that in his opinion the money being given to the war invalids was 'totally insufficient' and that failing to increase payments would be 'ominous' for the maintenance of public order.[66] During the early years of the Republic the accelerating inflation quickly made any financial settlement inadequate and guaranteed that the authorities responsible for war victims' welfare were constantly bombarded with complaints and demands for the upward revision of pensions and benefits.[67] Every day welfare offices received applications for increases in payments, applications which could not remotely be met with the 'limited means' at their disposal.[68] The rapid deterioration (due to inflation) of the value of Reich government contributions to the costs of welfare for war victims from the summer of 1922—in real terms the Reich's contributions in August 1923 were worth less than 3 per cent of what they had been one year before[69]—made matters even worse. Municipal finances were threatened, as war victims saw their state pensions fail to keep pace with price rises and were forced to turn to

---

[65] See Reich budget figures in *Statistisches Jahrbuch für das Deutsche Reich 1930* (Berlin, 1930), 463–7. Whalen points out that, once financial transfers from the Reich to the Länder and reparations payments are taken out of the equation, war pensions gobbled up roughly 30% of the funds available to the Reich. See Whalen, *Bitter Wounds*, 157.

[66] Hagen Schulze (ed.), *Akten der Reichskanzlei. Weimarer Republik. Das Kabinett Scheidemann. 13. Februar bis 20. Juni 1919* (Boppard Rhein, 1971), 178: no. 43, 'Kabinettssitzung vom 16. April 1919, 17 Uhr'.

[67] See Whalen, *Bitter Wounds*, 148–9.

[68] StdALü, Neues Senatsarchiv XVII, Gruppe 3, no. 3: Beirat der Amtlichen Hauptfürsorgestelle Lübeck, Abteilung 'Kriegshinterbliebenefürsorge', to Hoher Senat, Lübeck, 28 Feb. 1920. Ibid. XVIII, Gruppe 5, no. 5 contains many letters from the Reichsbund to the Senate from Jan. 1920 onward urging increases in financial help for war invalids and dependants.

[69] NHStA, Hann. 122a, XXXIV, no. 152a, fos. 295–6: Landesdirektorium der Provinz Hannover to Oberpräsident, Hanover, 10 Aug. 1923.

the local welfare offices for assistance,[70] and the inflation undermined the ability of private foundations and employers to help.[71]

Nor did the problems disappear when the currency was stabilized. The sharp economic downturn in late 1923 and early 1924, and particularly the cutbacks in public-sector employment, meant that large numbers of war disabled lost their jobs.[72] Many war victims also had difficulties gaining and keeping decent employment even during the relatively prosperous years of the mid-to-late 1920s. The standard of living of the war invalid depended on many things: the degree of disability he was judged to have had; income from whatever employment could be maintained; the need for special medical attention; his debts and housing costs.[73] For those who depended largely or wholly upon state pensions and benefits, making ends meet could be difficult. For example, the maximum widow's pension (including special local supplements) as of October 1927 stood at 93.40 RM; most had to make do with less, with the result that most war-widows who had not been able to remarry suffered a marked drop in their living-standards.[74] Furthermore, when the Depression struck in the early 1930s, it certainly did not spare the war victims.[75]

The language employed in the public discussion of the war victims and their plight is illuminating. In their programmatic statements in November and December 1918 the various political parties displayed remarkable

[70] See e.g. StdAlü, Neues Senatsarchiv XVIII, Gruppe 5, Nr. 5, fo. 236: Wohlfahrtsamt to Hoher Senat, Lübeck, 23 June 1922.

[71] e.g. the Nationalstiftung für die Hinterbliebenen der im Kriege Gefallenen saw its assets shrink from a pre-war figure of roughly 140 million Marks to roughly 1.2 million once the inflation was over. See ibid. XVI, Gruppe 36, Nr. 5: 'Bemerkungen und Vorschläge des Berichterstatters (Ministerialdirektor Dr. Schütze) zur Vorlage des Reichsarbeitsministers... betreffend Vertretung des Reichsrats im Präsidium der Nationalstiftung (für die Hinterbliebenen der im Kriege Gefallenen)', Berlin, 10 Oct. 1933. In Feb. 1920 the Prussian-Hessian State Railways suspended its welfare activities on behalf of war invalids due to 'insufficient funds'. See PLA, Rep. 38b Jarmen, Nr. 710, fo. 224: Kriegsbeschädigtenfürsorge der Preuß.-Hess. Staatseisenbahnen und der Reichseisenbahnen, Bezirksausschuß Nr. 20, to Ausschuß für die Kriegsbeschädigtenfürsorge in Pommern, Stettin, 12 Feb. 1920.

[72] See NHStA, Hann. 122a, XXXIV, Nr. 152a, fos. 310–20: 'Niederschrift über die 7. Sitzung des Beirats der Hauptfürsorgestelle der Provinz Hannover der Kriegsbeschädigten- und Kriegs-hinterbliebenenfürsorge am 29. Februar 1924 in Hannover'. On the reduction of the German civil service generally in 1923–4, see Andreas Kunz, *Civil Servants and the Politics of Inflation in Germany, 1914–1924* (Berlin and New York, 1986), 53–8.

[73] An instructive example is the case of a blinded veteran from Jena, who in July 1928 had a monthly income of over 400 RM, which included a military pension, nursing supplement, an invalidity pension, a supplementary pension, and a pension from his former employer Carl Zeiss. See StAW, Thür. Staatsministerium—Präsidialabteilung, no. 275, fo. 292: Stadtvorstand der Universitätsstadt Jena, Wohlfahrtsamt, to Thüringisches Ministerium für Inneres und Wirtschaft, Landesfürsorgeverband, Jena, 24 July 1928.

[74] Dick, 'Die Kriegsbeschädigtenversorgung', 107; Whalen, *Bitter Wounds*, 161–2.

[75] See e.g. the correspondence concerning the disabled veterans among the employees of the Portland Cement works in Göschwitz (Thuringia) between 1925 and 1934 in StAW, Thüringisches Kreisamt Stadtroda, no. 733.

unanimity. On the left, the Independent Social Democrats demanded that war widows, war orphans, and war wounded be guaranteed 'a carefree existence'; according to the German Democratic Party, 'the just claims of the war invalids and survivors of those who fell in the war require special consideration' and the state had a responsibility to provide 'an existence worthy of a human being' to the war invalids, widows, and orphans; the Catholic Centre called for 'conscientious and broad-minded welfare' for the war victims; the German People's Party demanded that the Reich government provide the war victims 'warm-hearted welfare and worthy public assistance'; and the conservative German National People's Party asserted that providing for the welfare of the war victims, was 'an obligation of honour' for the Reich.[76] The language of the 'obligation' of the state to provide 'worthy' care and treatment for the war victims, of the absolute responsibility of the nation to honour its debts to those who had sacrificed so much, was also employed by war victims' organizations in their campaigns to defend their members' interests. A typical example of the vocabulary deployed is a resolution passed at an extraordinary meeting of the Ludwigshafen branch of the Reichsbund der Kriegsbeschädigten, Kriegsteilnehmer und Kriegshinterbliebenen in September 1919, to protest against the continued employment of young women when, it was argued, jobs were needed by war invalids, returning prisoners of war, and war widows. The Ludwigshafen Reichsbund claimed that 'many young men and women dissipate in an irresponsible manner the money which they steal from the war victims in so shameless a manner', demanded that 'all positions, wherever they are suitable for war invalids, prisoners, and widows, regardless of what kind they are, must be filled by such people', and closed with the call: 'Not Thanks but Justice!'.[77] Morality and natural justice, the veterans organizations stressed, demanded that the state and the nation give the war victims their due.

Such calls were made with renewed force during the early 1930s, as veterans' organizations responded to government attempts to cope with the mounting economic crisis by reducing (among other things) the enormous burden of war-related pensions upon state finances.[78] Benefits were cut; the way in which the pensions were calculated was changed to the detriment of the applicant (from the date an application was approved rather than from the date of application); advance payments were refused; and the bureaucracy became increasingly keen to root out alleged scroungers. With experience of the War no longer so fresh in public consciousness and with millions

[76] Excerpts from party programmes quoted in Dick, 'Die Kriegsbeschädigtenversorgung', 84–5.

[77] StdALu, no. 1118: Bayer. Landesverband des Reichsverbandes der Kriegsbeschädigten, Kriegsteilnehmer und Kriegshinterbliebenen, Gau Pfalz, Bezirksverein Ludwigshafen Rhein to Bürgermeisteramt, Ludwigshafen, 11 Oct. 1919.

[78] See Whalen, *Bitter Wounds*, 169–70.

of Germans in desperate straits for other reasons, a readiness to assign priority to war victims' claims could no longer be assumed. Against this background the veterans' organizations waged a defensive struggle against welfare cuts, in which references to the 'duty' of the German nation and state to treat the war victims in a 'worthy' manner and protests against 'morally and politically questionable measures'[79] were the only major propaganda weapons they had left.

The embittered protests of the war-victims lobby, whose most powerful voice remained an organization which drew its support largely from among the organized working class—from among supporters of the SPD and the socialist trade-union movement—revealed the ambivalence with which these most visible veterans of the Great War approached Weimar democracy. They simultaneously condemned the old élites which had led Germany into war, glorified the alleged heroism of the 'front generation', and attacked the Weimar political system, which was in no position fully to satisfy their demands.[80] In a resolution presented at a demonstration in Stettin in April 1931 against the government cuts, the Pomeranian district of the Reichsbund made a typical appeal to 'the conscience of the public':

Even considering the necessity of the elimination of the existing deficit in the Reich budget, a further attack on welfare must be regarded as a challenge to the German war-victims. . . . It is unworthy of the German people to treat the surviving dependants of their fallen sons, as well as the ill, the wounded, infirm, and mutilated war-invalids who gave the best thing they had—health—as an unwelcome burden. . . . Hands off the rights of the war victims! They have every right to an improvement of their situation![81]

This rhetoric was digested and echoed by the war victims themselves. In the following protest—against a decision by the war victims welfare-office in Stettin in 1931 to refuse financial help for dental treatment—an angry petitioner (with a recognized 40 per cent disability) combined phrases borrowed from Reichsbund propaganda with threats to seek redress with the support of Nazi deputies in the Reichstag. After cataloguing the years of suffering which had resulted from a grenade attack that had cost him his teeth, and from the aluminium dentures fitted by the military in 1918, Walter Kosinsky levelled his 'flaming protest' at the Prussian Minister for Welfare:

Is that the thanks of the Fatherland, when a 'Welfare Office for War Invalids' today wants to know nothing more about disabilities stemming from war service and would like to get rid of the victims of the war with remarks of the most insulting nature?

---

[79] Quoted by Whalen, ibid. 170, from an article in the newspaper of the nationalist Zentralverband deutscher Kriegsbeschädigter und Kriegshinterbliebener, the *Zentralblatt*, in Feb. 1931.

[80] See Michael Geyer, 'Ein Vorbote des Wohlfahrtstaates', 254–5.

[81] APS, Oberpräsidium von Pommern, no. 3938: Reichsbund der Kriegsbeschädigten, Kriegsteilnehmer und Kriegshinterbliebenen, Gau Pommern, to Oberpräsident, Stettin, 27 Apr. 1931.

We war victims really do not recognize the burden which our welfare signifies for the German economy; we feel ourselves free of guilt, for ultimately no one can reproach us about our willingness to make sacrifices. Also, an enrichment at the expense of the people is far from all our thoughts. . . . With glowing devotion I volunteered to help defend my Fatherland. With smashed limbs and a broken body I stand, thirteen years after the end of the War, with the question still on my lips: Will anyone help me, give back my health? Where are the homesteads we were promised? Where is employment, bread, fraternity? Emergency decrees and cuts have increased the misery of numerous families of war victims to a point where they are unbearable. Hands off the rights of the war victims! They have every right to an improvement of their situation! . . . Most honoured Herr Minister! I have worked my way through all agencies, from the War Invalids Welfare Office to the Main Pensions Office, regarding the fulfilment of my requests. I cannot bear yet another negative reply to my present request. The consequence of that would be a reorientation of my person in a political direction. I would ask Dr Goebbels and Kube[82] most cordially to present my pension file to the Reichstag and to help me to my rights.[83]

It would have been difficult to satisfy the demands of men such as Walter Kosinsky—who was receiving a monthly pension of 57.50 RM during the darkest days of the depression[84]—in the best of circumstances. In the midst of the worst depression Germany had ever experienced, it was impossible.

It was not simply the inability of the Reich treasury to cope satisfactorily with the social problems left behind by the War which undermined popular support for democratic politics. Underlying the discontent and angry protests of the war victims was a fundamental disagreement, namely that they refused to accept the German state's general approach in dealing with them. For the state, the aim of welfare for war victims was therapeutic; that is, its goal was the rehabilitation and reintegration of war victims into civil society, enabling them to stand on their own feet and care for themselves. The war victims, however, were interested not in therapy but in 'justice'.[85] War victims' organizations were not primarily concerned about the limited room for manœuvre within which governments had to frame politics; they demanded 'justice'—i.e. preferential treatment—for their members, regardless of the consequences. Naturally enough, the activities of these organizations centred around wresting benefits for those they represented; this was why their members had joined up. The result was a conflict-ridden, adversarial relationship with the Weimar welfare state; mobilization of the war victims

[82] Wilhelm Kube, NSDAP Gauleiter in Brandenburg.
[83] APS, Oberpräsidium von Pommern, no. 3938: 'Bitte des Kriegsbeschädigten Walter Kosinsky um Zahnersatz und Nachzahlung von Militär-Versorgungsgebührnissen' to Preuß. Minister für Volkswohlfahrt, Stettin, 18 Oct. 1931.
[84] APS, Oberpräsidium von Pommern, no. 3938: Landeshauptmann, Landeswohlfahrtsamt, to Oberpräsident, Stettin, 11 Jan. 1932.
[85] Michael Geyer, 'Ein Vorbote des Wohlfahrtsstaates', 248.

involved arousing expectations which could not be satisfied and thus served
to cultivate antagonism towards the Weimar political system. In the process,
a political identity was created for the war victims which could not but be
hostile to the Weimar state.[86] Ultimately it was neither socialist nor democratic organizations, neither anti-militarist crusades nor the Weimar welfare
state, which reaped political rewards from the demands that the 'front
generation' receive 'justice'; it was the Nazi Party.

The National Socialists, of course, were keen to present their movement
as the political embodiment of the 'front spirit' and representative of the
'front generation', with a mission to recreate the unity of 1914 and of the
trenches, which had allegedly transcended class and religious divisions. They
never tired of pointing out that Hitler had been a front soldier and pledged
that in the 'Third Reich' the pension machinery would be reformed and
that the war victims would receive justice as the 'first citizens of the state'.[87]
Once the Nazis took power, they moved quickly to destroy the Communist
and Social Democratic war-victims' organizations and to 'co-ordinate' the
remaining organizations into a single national association—first the National
Fighting Community of German War Victims' Associations (Nationale
Kampfgemeinschaft deutscher Kriegsopferverbände) and then, in the summer of 1933, the National Socialist War Victims' Welfare (Nationalsozialis-
tische Kriegsopferversorgung).[88] Although the fundamental reform of the
pension system promised by the Nazis never materialized, and the manner
in which the welfare bureaucracy dealt with applications from war victims
did not change greatly after January 1933,[89] the early years of the 'Third
Reich' were marked by much activity aimed to improve—and to be seen to
improve—the lot of the war victims. During the first months of the new
regime Nazi organizations demanded that state officials 'see that the will of
our Führer and Reich Chancellor, Adolf Hitler, that the victims of the World
War are *not forgotten*', was enforced—putting pressure on local authorities to
hire greater numbers of war disabled and children of men who had fallen
in combat and thus 'to make good the injustice which the former state
leadership had inflicted upon the war dependants'.[90] It became the duty
(*Ehrenpflicht*) of the state administration to give special preference in employment both to veterans of the Nazi movement and to war invalids and war

---

[86] Ibid. 256–7.
[87] See Whalen, *Bitter Wounds*, 174.
[88] For details of this process, see ibid. 175–6.
[89] Ibid. 177–8. For examples of the welfare administration's continued tough attitudes towards
war victims' claims, see the rejections of applications by war victims for loans during 1933, in
APS, Oberpräsidium von Pommern, no. 3938.
[90] APS, Oberpräsidium von Pommern, no. 3938: National-Sozialistischer Reichsbund deutscher Kriegsopfer, Gau Pommern, to Regierungspräsidenten in Stettin and Köslin, Stettin, 9
May 1933; ibid.: National-Sozialistischer Reichsbund deutscher Kriegsopfer, Gau Pommern, to
Oberpräsident, Stettin, 16 May 1933.

dependants, and progress in providing war invalids with work was monitored.[91] Although they may not have effected fundamental changes in the position of the war victims, the Nazis explicitly framed their policies within the terms of 'duty' and 'justice' towards the 'front generation' and its dependants. In the absence of open public debate about how well they achieved their aims, and with both demographic factors (which led to a reduction in the number of disabled veterans claiming pensions)[92] and economic recovery on their side, the Nazis could claim to have satisfied the demands which had been presented so stridently by the war victims during the Weimar Republic.

Dictatorship, and the suppression of open public discussion, provided what political pluralism had been unable to deliver: the surface unity of the 'front generation'. Despite their rhetoric and despite their common interests, the war victims had been unable to set aside political differences and build a united platform during the Weimar Republic.[93] The experience of war and demobilization did not unite Germans who had allegedly shared a common fate. It did, however, give almost all the disparate groups of a fragmented German society a common reference-point—in the 'myth of the war experience' and the 'front generation'. The 'front generation' was not a social construct; it was an ideological one. It was a propaganda image, at odds with attempts at political mobilization which were concerned with real social needs and economic priorities. Indeed, this was one reason why the terms in which the war experience was discussed in Weimar Germany tended to favour National Socialism. Nazi mobilization was not based upon realistic discussion of social needs and economic priorities; Nazi propaganda was a successful attempt to transcend such discussion, to 'elevate' politics to the level of myth and fiction. Reference to the 'front generation' as though it were real was indicative of the extent to which politics in Weimar Germany had become removed from questions of priorities and had adopted terms of reference which made Nazi 'fanaticism' seem to many an appropriate response to the difficulties facing Germany in the early 1930s.

The damaging legacy of the First World War for the Weimar Republic consisted not just in the fact that the political landscape was littered with intractable difficulties which the War had left behind. Ultimately the most damaging consequence was that Germans did not really care to take a sober look at the difficulties before them. Where the demobilization and post-war transition succeeded, success consisted essentially of postponing

---

[91] e.g. APS, Oberpräsidium von Pommern, no. 3938: Oberpräsident to Minister des Innern, Stettin, 20 Feb. 1934; ibid.: Oberpräsident, Allgemeine Verwaltung, Stettin, 28 July 1934. Another example can be seen in the correspondence between the welfare administration in the Thuringian town of Stadtroda and the local Portland Cement factory in Göschwitz during 1933 and 1934, in StAW, Thüringisches Kreisamt Stadtroda, no. 733.

[92] See Whalen, *Bitter Wounds*, 178–9.

[93] Ibid. 172.

having to confront the deep structural problems left behind by participation and defeat in the First World War. Instead of facing the uncomfortable fact that the War and its legacy had limited their options, Germans retreated into an illusory world in which their problems were invariably the fault of others and, by extension, would be eliminated if only the external burdens, imposed by the vengeful Allies, could be lifted. It only added to the tragedy of Weimar Germany that the widespread unwillingness to face the unpleasant post-war predicament and the urge instead to retreat into uncritical and militant rejection of the Versailles 'diktat' constituted probably the broadest integrative mechanism which the Republic possessed.[94] Instead of recognizing the narrow limits of practical democratic politics in the Weimar Republic, millions of Germans retreated into irresponsible political demagogy, into the anti-democratic politics of propaganda and illusion finally purveyed with such devastating effect by Hitler and Goebbels.[95]

The 'internal denial of peace' in post-war Germany involved more than a rejection of the Versailles Treaty and the foreign-policy constraints which followed from defeat in 1918.[96] It also involved a denial of peace in domestic political relations. After the First World War, Germany never really made the transition from a 'war society' (*Kriegsgesellschaft*) to a 'peace society' (*Friedensgesellschaft*). Instead, it remained a post-war society. In public discussion in Weimar Germany, 'peacetime' was the period before 1914, not that after 1918. The years after 1918 comprised something quite different: years of upheaval and disorder, of unnatural disruption which had been set in motion by the great calamity of the First World War. So many of the political, economic, and social hallmarks of the Weimar period were (and were seen to be) consequences of the War: the revolution of 1918 and the establishment of the Weimar Republic, the inflation, the violent politics of the Freikorps, the economic burdens left by the War, the post-war crime-wave and alleged increase in 'immorality', the skewed demographic structure which left Germany with roughly one-quarter fewer inhabitants from 6 to 13 years old in 1925 than in 1910.[97] Order had been left behind together with 'peace' in 1914. The Weimar Republic never escaped this crippling

---

[94] Years ago Gerhard Schulz observed that 'in the end public opinion in Germany—in spite of some differences of opinion about the enemy and his motives—was unanimous in rejecting the treaty. It is certainly no exaggeration to say that on no other political issue has there been a like degree of unanimity.' See Gerhard Schulz, *Revolutions and Peace Treaties 1917–1920* (London, 1972), 224.

[95] For further development of this argument, see Bessel, 'Why Did the Weimar Republic Collapse?', esp. 126–8.

[96] On this, see esp. the chapter on 'the internal denial of peace' in Hans Mommsen, *Die verspielte Freiheit*, 101–40; Heinemann, *Die verdrängte Niederlage*.

[97] In 1925 the Reich contained 7,664,238 people from the ages of 6 to 13; in 1910 the comparable figure had been 10,103,624. See the table in Peukert, *Jugend zwischen Krieg und Krise*, 35.

legacy: that (despite the best efforts of Friedrich Ebert and Gustav Noske) it was associated with disorder rather than order, with war rather than peace.

Conflict was the hallmark of the Weimar Republic. Yet, like most people in most places, Germans after the First World War desperately sought stability. A desire for stability may be natural and understandable, but it is fundamentally illusory; the human condition is not stable, and a measure of the success of a social, economic, or political system is its ability to accept and accommodate change. In this regard, Weimar Germany offers an extreme example of failure. The popular desire for stability after the most destructive war yet experienced was extreme, as were the problems facing the first German republic, while the means available for their solution were extremely limited. In a world in which war had left a stamp of violence upon civil society, the expectation of achieving or recapturing stability, which is impossible to achieve and never existed in the first place, was bound to be disappointed. The Weimar Republic enjoyed too brief an existence to have had a reasonable chance of escape from the shadow of the First World War; Weimar Germany remained stuck in the post-war rut—a society whose points of reference had been fixed by the War. Weimar Germany enjoyed neither the time nor the domestic and international conditions which might have allowed it to become a peacetime society. The consequence of this was a tragedy of colossal proportions, for it helped condemn the first German democracy to destruction, and Europe to another world war.

# Bibliography

## A. ARCHIVE MATERIALS

1 Bundesarchiv Koblenz
  R 43 Reichskanzlei
  R 86 Reichsgesundheitsamt

2 Bundesarchiv-Militärarchiv, Freiburg i.B.
  RW 1 Reichskriegsministerium
  RM 3 Reichs-Marine-Amt
  RM 20 Reichs-Marine-Amt
  RM 31 Reichs-Marine-Amt (Kaiserliches Kommando der
    Marinestation Ostsee)

3 Bundesarchiv Potsdam
  Reichsministerium des Innern (= RMdI)
  Reichswirtschaftsministerium (= RWM)
  Reichsministerium für wirtschaftliche Demobilmachung (= RMwD)
  Reichsarbeitsministerium

4 Geheimes Staatsarchiv preußischer Kulturbesitz, Berlin-Dahlem
  Rep. 84a Preußisches Justizministerium
  Rep. 12 Regierung Gumbinnen
  Rep. 30 Regierung Bromberg
  Rep. 180 Regierung Danzig

5 Geheimes Staatsarchiv preußischer Kulturbesitz, Merseburg
  Rep. 77 Preußisches Ministerium des Innern
  Rep. 120 Preußisches Ministerium für Handel und Gewerbe
  Rep. 169 D Preußischer Landtag

6 Bayerisches Hauptstaatsarchiv
  Abt. IV, Kriegsarchiv
  Kriegsministerium (MKr)

7 Staatsarchiv Bremen
  Senatsregistratur 3-M.2.h.2. Krieg 1914/18

8 Sächsisches Hauptstaatsarchiv Dresden
  Ministerium der Auswärtigen Angelegenheiten

Ministerium des Innern
Kriegsarchiv/Kriegsministerium
Gesandtschaft Berlin
Amtshauptmannschaft Annaberg
Amtshauptmannschaft Pirna

9 Hauptstaatsarchiv Düsseldorf
    Regierung Aachen, Präsidialbüro
    Regierung Aachen, Handel und Gewerbe
    Regierung Düsseldorf

10 Pommersches Landesarchiv Greifswald
    Rep. 60  Oberpräsident von Pommern
    Rep. 65c Regierung Stralsund
    Rep. 38b Jarmen
    Rep. 38b Loitz

11 Staatsarchiv Hamburg
    Demobilmachungskommissar
    Senat-Kriegsakten (1914-1918)

12 Niedersächsisches Hauptstaatsarchiv Hannover
    Hann. 122a Der Oberpräsident der Provinz Hannover
    Hannover 80 Hannover II Regierung Hannover
    Hannover 174 Springe
    Hannover 174 Neustadt/Rbg.

13 Generallandesarchiv Karlsruhe
    233. Staatsministerium
    236. Innenministerium
    456. XIV. Armeekorps

14 Sächsisches Staatsarchiv Leipzig
    Amtshauptmannschaft Döbeln
    Stadt Delitzsch
    Gewerbekammer Leipzig
    Braunkohlenabbau-Verein 'Zum Fortschritt' des Mitteldeutschen
        Braunkohlensyndikats, Meuselwitz
    Grube Rositz der Deutschen Erdöl AG (DEA), Berlin
    Meier und Weichelt Eisen- und Stahlwerke, Leipzig

15 Landeshauptarchiv Sachsen-Anhalt Magdeburg
    Rep. C 48 I.e. Regierung Merseburg, Polizei Registratur

Rep. C 30 Landratsamt Salzwedel, A
Rep. C 50 Landratsamt Querfurt, A/B

16 Staatsarchiv Münster
   Oberpräsidium
   Regierung Arnsberg
   Regierung Münster

17 Staatsarchiv Osnabrück
   Rep. 430 Regierung Osnabrück
   Rep. 450 Mep Landratsamt Meppen
   Rep. 451 Lin Kreisausschuß Lingen
   Dep. 3b   Stadt Osnabrück

18 Brandenburgisches Landeshauptarchiv Potsdam
   Rep. 2A Regierung Potsdam I SW
   Rep. 3B Regierung Frankfurt/Oder, I Pol
   Rep. 30 Berlin C Polizeipräsidium Berlin

19 Archiwum Panstwowe w Poznaniu
   Polizei-Präsidium Posen/Prezydium Policji w Poznaniu
   Regierung Grenzmark Posen-Westpreußen in Schneidemühl/
      Rejencja w Pile
   Landeshauptverwaltung der Provinz Posen/Starostwo Krajowe w
      Poznaniu
   Landratsamt Grätz
   Landratsamt Lissa

20 Mecklenburgisches Landeshauptsarchiv Schwerin
   Ministerium des Innern, Schwerin
   Mecklenburg-Strelitzer Ministerium, Abteilung des Innern

21 Archiwum Panstwowe w Szczecinie
   Oberpräsidium von Pommern/Naczelny Prezydent Prowincji
      Pomorskiej
   Regierung Stettin/Rejencja Szczecinska
   Landratsamt Randow
   Landratsamt Schivelbein

22 Staatsarchiv Weimar
   Thüringisches Staatsministerium—Präsidialabteilung
   Thüringisches Wirtschaftsministerium
   Thüringisches Kreisamt Stadtroda

23 Hessisches Hauptstaatsarchiv Wiesbaden
    Abt. 405 Preußische Regierung Wiesbaden
    Abt. 430/1 Landesheilanstalt Eberbach/Eichberg

24 Archiwum Panstwowe w Wroclawiu
    Rejencja Opolska, Biuro Prezydialne/Regierung Oppeln, Pr.B.
    Rejencja Opolska I/Regierung Oppeln, Allgemeine Abteilung
    Akta Miasta Wroclawia/Akten des Magistrats zu Breslau

25 Stadtarchiv Bochum
    Magistrat der Stadt Bochum (= B)
    Kreis-Ausschuß des Landkreises Bochum (= KrA)

26 Stadtarchiv Bremerhaven

27 Stadtarchiv Dortmund
    Bestand 3 Stadtverwaltung
    Bestand 5 Polizeiverwaltung

28 Stadtarchiv Duisburg
    Bestand 500 Wohlfahrtsamt
    Bestand 604 Wohnungsamt

29 Stadtarchiv Heidelberg

30 Stadtarchiv Lübeck
    Neues Senatsarchiv

31 Stadtarchiv Ludwigshafen
    Akten des Bürgermeisteramtes

32 Bergbau-Archiv Bochum
    Bestand 32 Bergwerksgesellschaft Hibernia AG, Herne

33 Westfälisches Wirtschaftsarchiv Dortmund
    Bestand K1 IHK Dortmund
    Bestand K2 IHK Bochum

# B. PUBLISHED SOURCES

## 1. PRIMARY SOURCES

### a. Statistical and Documentary Material

AUSWÄRTIGES AMT and REICHSMINISTERIUM DES INNERN (ed.), *Amtliche Urkunden zur Vorgeschichte des Waffenstillstandes 1918. Auf Grund der Akten der Reichskanzlei, des Auswärtigen Amtes und des Reichsarchivs* (2nd. edn., Berlin, 1924).

BAYERISCHES STATISTISCHES LANDESAMT (ed.), *Der Kriegs-Volkszählungen vom Jahre 1916 und 1917 in Bayern* (Beiträge zur Statistik Bayerns 89; Munich, 1919).

—— (ed.), *Die Frau in der bayerischen Kriegsindustrie nach einer amtlichen Erhebung aus dem Jahre 1917* (Beiträge zur Statistik Bayerns; 92 Munich, 1920).

*Correspondenzblatt der Generalkommission der Gewerkschaften Deutschlands* (Berlin), 1918–1923.

DEIST, WILHELM (ed.), *Militär und Innenpolitik im Weltkrieg 1914–1918* (2 vols; Düsseldorf, 1970).

*Demobilmachungsplan für das Deutsche Heer* (Berlin, 1918).

*Die Deutsche Nationalversammlung im Jahre 1919/1920 in ihrer Arbeit für den Aufbau des neuen deutschen Volksstaates*, ed. E. Heilfron (9 vols.; Berlin, 1919–20).

*Deutschland-Berichte der Sozialdemokratischen Partei Deutschlands (Sopade) 1934–1940* (Salzhausen and Frankfurt/Main, 1980).

FALTER, JÜRGEN, LINDENBERGER, THOMAS, and SCHUMANN, SIEGFRIED, *Wahlen und Abstimmungen in der Weimarer Republik: Materialien zum Wahlverhalten 1919–1933* (Munich, 1986).

GOLECKI, ANTON (ed.), *Akten der Reichskanzlei. Weimarer Republik. Das Kabinett Bauer. 21. Juni 1919 bis 27. März 1920* (Boppard/Rhein, 1980).

HOFFMANN, WALTHER G., *Das Wachstum der deutschen Wirtschaft seit der Mitte des 19. Jahrhunderts* (Berlin, Heidelberg, and New York, 1965).

HOHORST, GERD, KOCKA, JÜRGEN, and RITTER, GERHARD A., *Sozialgeschichtliches Arbeitsbuch: Materialien zur Statistik des Kaiserreichs 1870–1914* (Munich, 1975).

HÜRTEN, HEINZ (ed.), *Zwischen Revolution und Kapp-Putsch: Militär und Innenpolitik 1918–1920* (Düsseldorf, 1977).

KAISERLICHES STATISTISCHES AMT, Abteilung für Arbeiterstatistik (ed.), *Erhebung von Wirtschaftsrechnungen minderbemittelter Familien im Deutschen Reiche* (*Reichsarbeitsblatt*, Sonderheft 2; Berlin, 1909).

KOLB, EBERHARD, and RÜRUP, REINHARD (eds.), *Der Zentralrat der deutschen sozialistischen Republik, 19.12.1918–8.4.1919* (Leiden, 1968).

*Kriegsbericht der Handwerkskammer zu Gumbinnen für 1913–1919* (Insterburg, 1920).

LUDENDORFF, ERICH (ed.), *Urkunden der obersten Heeresleitung über ihrer Tätigkeit 1916–1918* (4th edn., Berlin, 1922).

*Die Maßnahmen der Stadt Ludwigshafen am Rhein auf dem Gebiet der Wohnungsfürsorge seit dem Jahre 1914* (Ludwigshafen/Rhein, n.d.) (copy in Stadtarchiv Ludwigshafen).

MILLER, SUSANNE, and POTTHOFF, HEINRICH (eds.), *Die Regierung der Volksbeauftragten 1918/19* (2 vols.; Düsseldorf, 1969).

*Nachrichtenblatt des Reichsamtes für wirtschaftliche Demobilmachung* (9–31 Dec. 1918.). (From 1.1.1919 *Die wirtschaftliche Demobilmachung.*)

PETZINA, DIETMAR, ABELSHAUSER, WERNER, and FAUST, ANSELM, *Sozialgeschichtliches Arbeitsbuch,* iii: *Materialien zur Statistik des Deutschen Reiches 1914–1945* (Munich, 1978).

*Die Polizei, 1917–24.*

*Preußische Gesetzsammlung, 1919.*

*Reichsarbeitsblatt* (Berlin), 1917–19.

*Reichsgesetzblatt* (Berlin), 1918–23.

REICHSKRIEGSMINISTERIUM, Forschungsamt für Kriegs- und Heeresgeschichte (ed.), *Die Rückführung des Ostheeres (Darstellung aus den Nachkriegskämpfen deutscher Truppen und Freikorps)* (Berlin, 1936).

REICHSWEHRMINISTERIUM, *Sanitätsbericht über das deutsche Heer (Deutsches Feld- und Besatzungsheer) im Weltkriege, 1914–1918,* iii, *Die Krankenbewegung bei dem Deutschen Feld- und Besatzungsheer* (Berlin, 1934).

RITTER, GERHARD A., and MILLER, SUSANNE, (eds.), *Die deutsche Revolution 1918–1919: Dokumente* (2nd. edn., Hamburg, 1981).

SCHÖNHOVEN, KLAUS (ed.), *Die Gewerkschaften in Weltkrieg und Revolution 1914–1919* (Cologne, 1985).

SCHULZE, HAGEN, (ed.) *Akten der Reichskanzlei. Weimarer Republik. Das Kabinett Scheidemann. 13. Februar bis 20. Juni 1919* (Boppard/Rhein, 1971).

STATISTISCHES AMT, *Statistisches Jahrbuch der Stadt Leipzig,* V: *1915–1918* (Leipzig, 1921).

STATISTISCHES AMT DER STADT MANNHEIM (ed.), *Verwaltungsbericht der badischen Hauptstadt Mannheim für 1919/20* (Mannheim, n.d.).

STATISTISCHES BUNDESAMT WIESBADEN (ed.), *Bevölkerung und Wirtschaft 1872–1972* (Stuttgart, 1972).

*Statistisches Jahrbuch für das Deutsche Reich* (Berlin), 1919–32

STATISTISCHES UND WAHLAMT DER STADT BOCHUM (ed.), *Wohnungszählung in der Stadt Bochum, am 10. Oktober 1935* (Bochum, n.d.).

STATISTISCHES REICHSAMT, *Das deutsche Volkseinkommen vor und nach dem Kriege* (Einzelschriften zur Statistik des Deutschen Reichs, 24) (Berlin, 1932).

—— *Deutschlands Wirtschaftslage unter den Nachwirkungen des Weltkrieges* (Berlin, 1923).

—— *Statistik des Deutschen Reichs,* cclxxvi: *Die Bewegung der Bevölkerung in den Jahren 1914 bis 1919* (Berlin, 1922).

—— *Statistik des Deutschen Reichs,* cccxvi: *Die Bewegung der Bevölkerung in den Jahren 1922 und 1923 und die Ursachen der Sterbefälle in den Jahren 1920 bis 1923* (Berlin, 1926).

—— *Zahlen zur Geldentwertung in Deutschland 1914 bis 1923* (*Wirtschaft und Statistik,* 5, Sonderheft 1 (Berlin, 1925).

THÜRINGISCHES STATISTISCHES LANDESAMT (ed.), *Statistisches Handbuch für das Land Thüringen, 1922* (Weimar, 1922).

*Verhandlungen der Sozialisierungs-Kommission über die Neuregelung des Wohnungswesens* (2 vols.; Berlin, 1921).

*Der Weltkrieg im Bild: Originalaufnahmen des Kriegs- Bild- und Filmamtes aus der modernen Materialschlacht* (Berlin and Oldenburg, 1928).

ZENTRALRAT DER SOZIALISTISCHEN REPUBLIK DEUTSCHLANDS (ed.), *Allgemeiner Kongress der Arbeiter- und Soldatenräte Deutschlands vom 16. bis 21. Dezember 1918 im Abgeordnetenhaus in Berlin. Stenographisches Bericht* (Berlin, 1919).

*b. Memoirs, Speeches, etc.*

ALTROCK, CONSTANTIN von (ed.), *Vom Sterben des Deutschen Offizierskorps* (Berlin, 1921).

BAUER, MAX, *Der große Krieg in Feld und Heimat: Erinnerungen und Betrachtungen* (Tübingen, 1921).

BAUMGÄRTNER, G. A., *Deutsches Kriegsbuch. Tagesberichte und Stimmungsbilder von Daheim und Draußen. Die ersten Monate des Weltkrieges. Erinnerungsgabe der Bayerischen Kriegsinvalidenfürsorge* (Munich, 1916).

BRÜNING, HEINRICH, *Memoiren 1918–1934* (Stuttgart, 1970).

DICKHUTH-HARRACH, GUSTAV VON (ed.), *Im Felde Unbesiegt: Der Weltkrieg in 28 Einzeldarstellungen* (Munich, 1920).

DÖBLIN, ALFRED, *November 1918* (Munich, 1978).

FÖRSTER, WOLFGANG (ed.), *Wir Kämpfer im Weltkrieg* (Berlin, 1929).

GALLWITZ, MAX VON, *Erleben im Westen 1916–1918* (Berlin, 1932).

GROENER, WILHELM, *Der Weltkrieg und seine Probleme: Rückschau und Ausblick* (Berlin, 1920).

—— *Lebenserinnerungen: Jugend, Generalstab, Weltkrieg,* ed. Friedrich Frhr. Hiller von Gärtringen (Göttingen, 1957).

HÜRTEN, HEINZ, and MEYER, GEORG (eds.), *Adjutant im preußischen Kriegsministerium Juni 1918 bis Oktober 1919: Aufzeichnungen des Hauptmanns Gustav Böhm* (Stuttgart, 1977).

HURWITZ-STRANZ, HELENE (ed.), *Kriegerwitwen gestalten ihr Schicksal: Lebenskämpfe deutscher Kriegerwitwen nach eigenen Darstellungen* (Berlin, 1931).

JÜNGER, ERNST, *Der Kampf als inneres Erlebnis* (Berlin, 1922).

KÖPPEN, EDLEF, *Heeresbericht* (Kronberg, 1976).

KOETH, JOSEPH, 'Die wirtschaftliche Demobilmachung: Ihre Aufgaben und ihre Organe', in *Handbuch der Politik* (3rd edn.), iv: *Der wirtschaftliche Wiederaufbau* (Berlin and Leipzig, 1921), 163–8.

LEHMANN, FRIEDRICH, *Wir von der Infanterie* (Munich, 1929).

LUDENDORFF, ERICH, *Meine Kriegserinnerungen 1914–1918* (Berlin, 1919).

LUDENDORFF, ERICH, *Kriegsführung und Politik* (Berlin, 1922).

MAERKER, GEORG, *Vom Kaiserreich zur Reichswehr. Geschichte des freiwilligen Landjägerkorps. Ein Beitrag zur Geschichte der deutschen Revolution* (Leipzig, 1921).

MOELLENDORF, WICHARD VON, 'Wirtschaftliche Selbstverwaltung', in *Handbuch der Politik* (3rd edn.), iv: *Der wirtschaftliche Wiederaufbau* (Berlin and Leipzig, 1921).

NOSKE, GUSTAV, *Von Kiel bis Kapp: Zur Geschichte der deutschen Revolution* (Berlin, 1920).

OEHLER, ADALBERT, *Düsseldorf im Weltkrieg: Schicksal und Arbeit einer deutschen Großstadt* (Düsseldorf, 1927).

REMARQUE, ERICH MARIA, *Im Westen nichts Neues* (Cologne, 1987).

THAER, ALBRECHT VON, *Generalstabsdienst an der Front und in der O.H.L: Aus Briefen und Tagebuchaufzeichnungen 1915–1919*, ed. Siegfried A. Kaehler (Göttingen, 1958).

WERMUTH, ADOLF, *Ein Beamtenleben: Erinnerungen* (Berlin, 1922).

WETTE, WOLFRAM (ed.), *Aus den Geburtsstunden der Weimarer Republik: Das Tagebuch des Obersten Ernst van den Bergh* (Düsseldorf, 1991).

WISSELL, RUDOLF, *Praktische Wirtschaftspolitik: Unterlagen zur Beurteilung einer fünfmonatigen Wirtschaftsführung* (Berlin, 1919).

—— 'Die Lebenshaltung der deutschen Arbeiterschaft seit dem Kriege', in W. Külz (ed.), *Deutschland: Jahrbuch für das deutsche Volk 1927* (Leipzig, 1927).

WRISBERG, ERNST VON, *Heer und Heimat 1914/1918* (Leipzig, 1921).

—— *Der Weg zur Revolution* (Leipzig, 1921).

—— *Wehr und Waffen 1914–1918* (Leipzig, 1922).


2. SECONDARY SOURCES

ABRAMS, Lynn, *Workers' Culture in Imperial Germany: Leisure and Recreation in the Rhineland and Westphalia* (London, 1992).

AEREBOE, FRIEDRICH, *Der Einfluß des Krieges auf die landwirtschaftliche Produktion in Deutschland* (Stuttgart, Berlin, and Leipzig, 1927).

AY, KARL-LUDWIG, *Die Entstehung einer Revolution: Die Volksstimmung in Bayern während des Ersten Weltkrieges* (Berlin, 1968).

BACH, OTTO, *Rudolf Wissell: Ein Leben für soziale Gerechtigkeit* (Berlin, 1959).

BAJOHR, STEPHAN, *Die Hälfte der Fabrik: Geschichte der Frauenarbeit in Deutschland 1914 bis 1945* (Marburg, 1979).

BARCLAY, DAVID E., *Rudolf Wissell als Sozialpolitiker 1890–1933* (Berlin, 1984).

BAUDIS, DIETER, and NUSSBAUM, HELGA, *Wirtschaft und Staat in Deutschland vom Ende des 19. Jahrhunderts bis 1918/19* (Berlin, 1978).

BAUMGARTEN, OTTO, FOERSTER, ERICH, RADEMACHER, ARNOLD and FLITNER, WILHELM, *Geistige und sittliche Wirkung des Krieges in Deutschland* (Stuttgart, 1927).

BECKER, JEAN-JACQUES, *The Great War and the French People* (Leamington Spa, 1985).

BELLON, BERNARD P., *Mercedes in Peace and War: German Automobile Workers, 1903–1945* (New York, 1990).

BERGHAHN, VOLKER R., *Der Stahlhelm: Bund der Frontsoldaten* (Düsseldorf, 1966).

BERGMANN, KLAUS, *Agrarromantik und Großstadtfeindschaft* (Meisenheim Glan, 1970).

BERTHOLD, LOTHAR, and NEEF, HELMUT, *Militarismus und Opportunismus gegen die Novemberrevolution. Das Bündnis der rechten SPD-Führung mit der obersten Heeresleitung November und Dezember 1918. Eine Dokumentation* (Berlin, 1958).

BESSEL, RICHARD, 'Militarismus im innenpolitischen Leben der Weimarer Republik: Von den Freikorps zur SA', in Klaus-Jürgen Müller and Eckardt Opitz (eds.), *Militär und Militarismus in der Weimarer Republik* (Düsseldorf, 1978).

—— ' "Eine nicht allzu große Beunruhigung des Arbeitsmarktes": Frauenarbeit und Demobilmachung in Deutschland nach dem Ersten Weltkrieg', *Geschichte und Gesellschaft*, 9 (1983).

—— *Political Violence and the Rise of Nazism: The Storm Troopers in Eastern Germany 1925–1934* (New Haven and London, 1984).

—— 'Unemployment and Demobilisation in Germany after the First World War', in Richard J. Evans and Dick Geary (eds.), *The German Unemployed: Experiences and Consequences of Mass Unemployment from the Weimar Republic to the Third Reich* (London and Sydney, 1987).

—— 'The Great War in German Memory: The Soldiers of the First World War, Demobilization, and Weimar Political Culture', *German History*, 6: 1 (1988).

—— 'State and Society in Germany in the Aftermath of the First World War', in W. R. Lee and Eve Rosenhaft (eds.), *The State and Social Change in Germany, 1880–1980* (Oxford, Munich, and New York, 1990).

—— 'Why Did the Weimar Republic Collapse?', in Ian Kershaw (ed.), *Weimar: Why Did German Democracy Fail?* (London, 1990).

—— 'Politische Gewalt und die Krise der Weimarer Republik', in Lutz Niethammer *et al.*, *Bürgerliche Gesellschaft in Deutschland: Historische Einblicke, Fragen, Perspektiven* (Frankfurt/Main, 1990).

—— 'Kriegserfahrungen und Kriegserinnerungen: Nachwirkungen des Ersten Weltkrieges auf das politische und soziale Leben der Weimarer Republik', in Marcel van der Linden, Herman de Lange, and Gottfried Mergner (eds.), *Kriegsbegeisterung und mentale Kriegsvorbereitung. Interdisziplinäre Studien* (Berlin, 1991).

BESSEL, RICHARD 'Policing, Professionalisation and Politics in Weimar Germany', in Clive Emsley and Barbara Weinberger (eds.), *Policing Western Europe: Politics, Professionalism and Public Order, 1850–1940* (New York, Westport, (Conn.), and London, 1991).

—— 'Die Krise der Weimarer Republik als Erblast des verlorenen Kriegs', in Frank Bajohr, Werner Johe, and Uwe Lohalm (eds.), *Zivilisation und Barbarei. Die widersprüchlichen Potentiale der Moderne. Detlev Peukert zum Gedenken* (Hamburg, 1991).

—— 'The Formation and Dissolution of a German National Electorate, from *Kaiserreich* to Third Reich', in James Retallack and Larry Eugene Jones (eds.), *Elections, Mass Politics and Social Change in Modern Germany: New Perspectives* (New York, 1992).

—— 'The "Front Generation" and the Politics of the Weimar Republic', in Mark Roseman (ed.), *Generation Formation and Conflict in Modern Germany* (forthcoming).

—— and Feuchtwanger, E. J., (eds.), *Social Change and Political Development in Weimar Germany* (London, 1981).

BEY-HEARD, FRAUKE, *Hauptstadt und Staatsumwälzung. Berlin 1919. Problematik und Scheitern der Rätebewegung in der Berliner Kommunalverwaltung* (Berlin, 1969).

BIEBER, HANS-JOACHIM, *Gewerkschaften in Krieg und Revolution: Arbeiterbewegung, Industrie, Staat und Militär in Deutschland 1914–1920* (2 vols.; Hamburg, 1981).

—— 'Die Entwicklung der Arbeitsbeziehungen auf den Hamburger Großwerften zwischen Hilfsdienstgesetz und Betriebsrätegesetz (1916–1920)', in Gunther Mai (ed.), *Arbeiterschaft in Deutschland 1914–1918: Studien zu Arbeitskampf und Arbeitsmarkt im Ersten Weltkrieg* (Düsseldorf, 1985).

BLACKBOURN, DAVID, 'Peasants and Politics in Germany, 1871–1914', *European History Quarterly*, 14: 1 (1984), 47–75.

BOAK, HELEN L., 'Women in Weimar Germany: The "Frauenfrage" and the Female Vote', in Richard Bessel and E. J. Feuchtwanger (eds.), *Social Change and Political Development in Weimar Germany* (London, 1981).

BOELCKE, WILLI A., 'Wandlungen der deutschen Agrarwirtschaft in der Folge des Ersten Weltkriegs', *Francia*, 3 (1975), 498–532.

BOLL, FRIEDHELM, *Massenbewegungen in Niedersachsen 1906–1920: Eine sozialgeschichtliche Untersuchung zu den unterschiedlichen Entwicklungstypen Braunschweig und Hannover* (Bonn-Bad Godesberg, 1981).

BORSCHEID, PETER, 'Vom Ersten zum Zweiten Weltkrieg (1914–1945)', in Wilhelm Kohl (ed.), *Westfälische Geschichte*, iii. *Das 19. und das 20. Jahrhundert: Wirtschaft und Gesellschaft* (Düsseldorf, 1984).

BRANDT, JÜRGEN, *Hamburgs Finanzen von 1914 bis 1924* (Hamburg, 1924).

—— and RÜRUP, REINHARD, *Volksbewegung und demokratische Neuordnung in Baden 1918/19: Zur Vorgeschichte und Geschichte der Revolution* (Sigmaringen, 1991).

BREUNIG, WILLI, *Soziale Verhältnisse der Arbeiterschaft und sozialistische Arbeiterbewegung in Ludwigshafen am Rhein 1869–1919* (Ludwigshafen/Rhein, 1976).

BRIDENTHAL, RENATE, 'Beyond Kinder, Küche, Kirche: Weimar Women at Work', *Central European History*, 6 (1973), 86–95.

BRÜGGEMEIER, FRANZ-JOSEF, *Leben vor Ort: Ruhrbergleute und Ruhrbergbau 1889–1919* (Munich, 1983).

—— and NIETHAMMER, Lutz, 'Schlafgänger, Schnapskasinos und schwerindustrielle Kolonie: Aspekte der Arbeiterwohnungsfrage im Ruhrgebiet vor dem Ersten Weltkrieg', in Jürgen Reulecke and Wolfhard Weber (eds.), *Fabrik, Familie, Feierabend: Beiträge zur Sozialgeschichte des Alltags im Industriezeitalter* (Wuppertal, 1978).

BRY, GERHARD, *Wages in Germany, 1871–1945* (Princeton, NJ, 1960).

BUCHER, PETER, 'Zur Geschichte der Einwohnerwehren in Preußen 1918–1921', *Militärgeschichtliche Mitteilungen*, 9 (1971), 15–59.

BUCHOLZ, ARDEN, *Hans Delbrück and the German Military Establishment: War Images in Conflict* (Iowa City, Ia., 1985).

BUDER, JOHANNES, *Die Reorganisation der preußischen Polizei 1918–1933* (Frankfurt/Main, Berne, and New York, 1986).

BUMM, FRANZ (ed.), *Deutschlands Gesundheitsverhältnisse unter dem Einfluß des Weltkrieges* (Stuttgart, 1928).

BUR, LUDWIG, *Die Umwälzung der deutschen Volkswirtschaft im Kriege: Eine kriegswirtschaftliche Studie* (Strasburg, 1918).

BURCHARDT, LOTHAR, 'Konstanz im Ersten Weltkrieg', *Politik und Unterricht*, 7: 3 (1981).

——'The Impact of the War Economy on the Civilian Population of Germany during the First and Second World Wars', in Wilhelm Deist (ed.), *The German Military in the Age of Total War* (Leamington Spa, 1985).

BÜSCH, OTTO, and FELDMAN, GERALD D. (eds.), *Historische Prozesse der deutschen Inflation 1914 bis 1924: Ein Tagungsbericht* (Berlin, 1978).

CASTELL, ADELHEID ZU, 'Die demographischen Konsequenzen des Ersten und Zweiten Weltkrieges für das Deutsche Reich, die Deutsche Demokratische Republik und die Bundesrepublik Deutschland', in Waclaw Dlugoborski (ed.), *Zweiter Weltkrieg und sozialer Wandel: Achsenmächte und besetzte Länder* (Göttingen, 1981).

COMFORT, RICHARD A., *Revolutionary Hamburg: Labor Politics in the Early Weimar Republic* (Stanford, Calif., 1966).

CREW, DAVID F. *Town in the Ruhr: A Social History of Bochum, 1860–1914* (New York, 1979).

CYSARZ, HERBERT, *Zur Geistesgeschichte des Weltkrieges: Die dichterischen Wandlungen des deutschen Kriegsbilds 1910–1930* (Halle/Saale, 1931).

DÄHNHARDT, DIRK, *Revolution in Kiel: Der Übergang vom Kaiserreich zur Weimarer Republik 1918/19* (Neumünster, 1978).

DANIEL, UTE, 'Fiktionen, Friktionen und Fakten: Frauenlohnarbeit im Ersten Weltkrieg', in Gunther Mai (ed.), *Arbeiterschaft in Deutschland 1914– 1918: Studien zu Arbeitskampf und Arbeitsmarkt im Ersten Weltkrieg* (Düsseldorf, 1985).

—— 'The Politics of Rationing versus the Politics of Subsistence: Working-Class Women in Germany, 1914–1918', in Roger Fletcher (ed.), *Bernstein to Brandt: A Short History of German Social Democracy* (London, 1987).

—— 'Women's Work in Industry and Family: Germany, 1914–1918', in Richard Wall and Jay Winter (eds.), *The Upheaval of War: Family, Work and Welfare in Europe, 1914–1918* (Cambridge, 1988).

—— *Arbeiterfrauen in der Kriegsgesellschaft: Beruf, Familie und Politik im Ersten Weltkrieg* (Göttingen, 1989).

DEIST, WILHELM, 'Die Politik der Seekriegsleitung und die Rebellion der Flotte Ende Oktober 1918', *Vierteljahreshefte für Zeitgeschichte*, 14 (1966), 341–68.

—— 'Armee und Arbeiterschaft 1905–1918', *Francia*, 2 (1974), 458–81.

—— (ed.), *The German Military in the Age of Total War* (Leamington Spa, 1985).

—— 'Der militärische Zusammenbruch des Kaiserreichs: Zur Realität der "Dolchstoßlegende" ', in Ursula Büttner (ed.), *Das Unrechtsregime: Internationale Forschung über den Nationalsozialismus*, i: *Ideologie, Herrschaftssystem, Wirkung in Europa* (Hamburg, 1986).

—— 'Verdeckter Militärstreik im Kriegsjahr 1918?', in Wolfram Wette (ed.), *Der Krieg des kleinen Mannes: Eine Militärgeschichte von unten* (Munich, 1992).

DESAI, ASHOK V., *Real Wages in Germany 1871–1913* (Oxford, 1968).

DEUTSCHE AKADEMIE DER WISSENSCHAFTEN ZU BERLIN, Zentralinstitut für Geschichte, *Deutschland im Ersten Weltkrieg* (2nd edn., 3 vols.; Berlin, 1970).

DIEHL, JAMES M., 'The Organisation of German Veterans, 1917–1919', *Archiv für Sozialgeschichte*, 11 (1971).

—— 'Germany: Veterans' Politics under three Flags', in Stephen R. Ward (ed.), *The War Generation: Veterans of the First World War* (Fort Washington, New York, and London, 1975).

—— *Paramilitary Politics in Weimar Germany* (Bloomington, Ind., and London, 1977).

DOMANSKY, ELISABETH, 'Der Erste Weltkrieg', in Lutz Niethammer *et al.*, *Bürgerliche Gesellschaft in Deutschland: Historische Einblicke, Fragen, Perspektiven* (Frankfurt/Main, 1990).

DREETZ, DIETER 'Rückführung des Westheeres und Novemberrevolution', *Zeitschrift für Militärgeschichte*, 7 (1968), 578–89.

—— 'Bestrebungen der OHL zur Rettung des Kerns der imperialistischen deutschen Armee in der Novemberrevolution', *Zeitschrift für Militärgeschichte*, 8 (1969), 50–66.

—— 'Zur Entwicklung der Soldatenräte des Heimatheeres (Nov. 1918 bis März 1919)', *Zeitschrift für Militärgeschichte*, 9 (1970), 429–38.

—— 'Methoden der Ersatzgewinnung für das deutsche Heer 1914 bis 1918', *Militärgeschichte*, 6 (1977), 700–7.

DRÜNER, HANS, *Im Schatten des Weltkrieges: Zehn Jahre Frankfurter Geschichte von 1914–1924* (Frankfurt/Main, 1934).

EHLERT, HANS GOTTHARD, *Die wirtschaftliche Zentralbehörde des Deutschen Reiches 1914 bis 1919* (Wiesbaden, 1982).

EKSTEINS, MODRIS, 'All Quiet on the Western Front and the Fate of a War', *Journal of Contemporary History*, 15 (1980), 345–66.

—— 'War, Memory, and Politics: The Fate of the Film *All Quiet on the Western Front*', *Central European History*, 13: 1 (1980), 60–82.

—— *Rites of Spring: The Great War and the Birth of the Modern Age* (New York, 1989).

ELBEN, WOLFGANG, *Das Problem der Kontinuität in der deutschen Revolution: Die Politik der Staatssekretäre und der militärischen Führung von November 1918 bis Februar 1919* (Düsseldorf, 1965).

ELIASBERG, GEORGE, *Der Ruhrkrieg von 1920* (Bonn-Bad Godesberg, 1974).

ELLIOTT, C. J., 'The Kriegervereine and the Weimar Republic', *Journal of Contemporary History*, 10 (1975), 109–29.

ENGLANDER, DAVID, 'Die Demobilmachung in Großbritannien nach dem Ersten Weltkrieg', *Geschichte und Gesellschaft*, 9 (1983), 195–210.

—— 'Military Intelligence and the Defence of the Realm: The Surveillance of Soldiers and Civilians in Britain during the First World War', *Bulletin of the Society for the Study of Labour History*, 52: 1 (April 1987), 24–32.

—— 'People at War: France, Britain and Germany, 1914–18 and 1939–45', *European History Quarterly*, 18 (1988), 229–38.

EVANS, RICHARD J., ' "Red Wednesday" in Hamburg: Social Democrats, Police and Lumpenproletariat in the Suffrage Disturbances of 17 January 1916', *Social History*, 4: 1 (1979), 1–31.

—— (ed.), *Kneipengespräche im Kaiserreich: Stimmungsberichte des Hamburger Politischen Polizei 1892–1914* (Reinbek bei Hamburg, 1989).

—— *Death in Hamburg: Society and Politics in the Cholera Years 1830–1910* (Harmondsworth, 1990).

FARR, IAN, 'Populism in the Countryside: The Peasant Leagues in Bavaria in the 1890s', in Richard J. Evans (ed.), *Society and Politics in Wilhelmine Germany* (London, 1978).

FAUST, ANSELM, 'Von der Fürsorge zur Arbeitsmarktpolitik: Die Errichtung der Arbeitslosenversicherung', in Werner Abelshauser (ed.), *Die Weimarer Republik als Wohlfahrtsstaat: Zum Verhältnis von Wirtschafts- und Sozialpolitik in der Industriegesellschaft* (Stuttgart, 1987).

FELDMAN, GERALD D., *Army, Industry and Labor in Germany, 1914–1918* (Princeton, NJ, 1966).

FELDMAN GERALD D., 'German Big Business between War and Revolution: The Origins of the Stinnes–Legien Agreement', in Gerhard A. Ritter (ed.), *Entstehung und Wandel der modernen Gesellschaft. Festschrift für Hans Rosenberg zum 65. Geburtstag* (Berlin, 1970).

—— 'The Origins of the Stinnes–Legien Agreement: A Documentation', *Internationale wissenschaftliche Korrespondenz zur Geschichte der deutschen Arbeiterbewegung*, 19/20 (Dec. 1972), 45–103.

—— 'Economic and Social Problems of the German Demobilization 1918–19', *Journal of Modern History*, 47 (1975), 1–23.

—— *Iron and Steel in the German Inflation 1916–1923* (Princeton, NJ, 1977).

—— 'Socio-Economic Structures in the Industrial Sector and Revolutionary Potentialities, 1917–1922', in Charles L. Bertrand (ed.), *Revolutionary Situations in Europe, 1917–1922: Germany, Italy, Austria-Hungary* (Montreal, 1977).

—— 'Arbeitskonflikte im Ruhrbergbau 1919–1922', *Vierteljahreshefte für Zeitgeschichte*, 27: 2 (1980), 168–223.

—— 'German Interest Group Alliances in War and Inflation, 1914–1933', in Susanne Berger, Albert Hirschmann, and Charles Maier (eds.), *Organizing Interests in Western Europe: Pluralism, Corporatism and the Transformation of Politics* (Cambridge, 1981).

—— 'Die Demobilmachung und die Sozialordnung der Zwischenkriegszeit in Europa', *Geschichte und Gesellschaft*, 9 (1983), 156–77.

—— 'Saxony, the Reich, and the Problem of Unemployment in the German Inflation', *Archiv für Sozialgeschichte*, 27 (1987), 103–44.

—— *The Great Disorder: Politics, Economics and Society in the German Inflation, 1914–1924* (Oxford, 1993).

—— (ed.), *Die Nachwirkungen der Inflation auf die deutsche Geschichte 1924–1933* (Munich, 1985).

—— and HOMBURG, HEIDRUN, *Industrie und Inflation: Studien und Dokumente zur Politik der deutschen Unternehmer 1916–1923* (Hamburg, 1977).

—— KOLB, EBERHARD, and RÜRUP, REINHARD, 'Die Massenbewegungen der Arbeiterschaft am Ende des Ersten Weltkrieges 1917–1920', *Politische Vierteljahreschrift*, 13 (1972), 85–105.

—— and STEINISCH, IRMGARD, 'Die Weimarer Republik zwischen Sozial- und Wirtschaftsstaat: Die Entscheidung gegen den Achtstundentag', *Archiv für Sozialgeschichte*, 18 (1978), 353–439.

—— and STEINISCH, IRMGARD, *Industrie und Gewerkschaften 1918–1924: Die überforderte Zentralarbeitsgemeinschaft* (Stuttgart, 1985).

—— HOLTFRERICH, CARL-LUDWIG, RITTER, GERHARD A., and WITT, PETER-CHRISTIAN (eds.), *Die deutsche Inflation: Eine Zwischenbilanz* (Berlin and New York, 1982).

—— HOLTFRERICH, CARL-LUDWIG, RITTER, GERHARD A., and WITT, PETER-CHRISTIAN (eds.), *Die Erfahrung der Inflation im internationalen Zusammenhang und Vergleich* (Berlin and New York, 1984).

—— HOLTFRERICH, CARL-LUDWIG, RITTER, GERHARD A., and
WITT, PETER-CHRISTIAN (eds.), *Die Anpassung an die Inflation* (Berlin
and New York, 1986).

FERRO, MARC, *The Great War 1914–1918* (London, 1973).

FISCHER, CONAN, *Stormtroopers: A Social, Economic and Ideological Analysis
1929–35* (London, 1983).

FLEMMING, JENS, 'Großagrarische Interessen und Landarbeiterbewegung: Überlegungen zur Arbeiterpolitik des Bundes der Landwirte und
des Reichslandbundes in der Anfangsphase der Weimarer Republik', in
Hans Mommsen, Dietmar Petzina, and Bernd Weisbrod (eds.), *Industrielles System und politische Entwicklung in der Weimarer Republik* (Düsseldorf,
1974).

—— *Landwirtschaftliche Interessen und Demokratie: Ländliche Gesellschaft, Agrarverbände und Staat 1890–1925* (Bonn, 1978).

—— 'Die Bewaffnung des "Landvolks": Ländliche Schutzwehren und agrari-
scher Konservatismus in der Anfangsphase der Weimarer Republik',
*Militärgeschichtliche Mitteilungen*, 2 (1979), 7–36.

FUSSELL, PAUL, *The Great War and Modern Memory* (Oxford, 1975).

GEARY, DICK, 'Radicalism and the Worker: Metalworkers and Revolution
1914–23', in Richard J. Evans (ed.), *Society and Politics in Wilhelmine Germany*
(London, 1978).

GERSDORFF, URSULA VON, *Frauen im Kriegsdienst 1914–1945* (Stuttgart,
1969).

GESSNER, DIETER, *Agrarverbände in der Weimarer Republik: Wirtschaftliche und
soziale Voraussetzungen agrarkonservativer Politik vor 1933* (Düsseldorf, 1976).

—— 'The Dilemma of German Agriculture during the Weimar Republic',
in Richard Bessel and E. J. Feuchtwanger (eds.), *Social Change and Political
Development in Weimar Germany* (London, 1981).

GEYER, MARTIN H., 'Wohnungsnot und Wohnungszwangswirtschaft in
München 1917 bis 1924', in Gerald D. Feldman, Carl-Ludwig Holtfrerich,
Gerhard A. Ritter, and Peter-Christian Witt (eds.), *Die Anpassung an die
Inflation* (Berlin and New York, 1986).

GEYER, MICHAEL, 'Professionals and Junkers: German Rearmament in
the Weimar Republic', in Richard Bessel and E. J. Feuchtwanger (eds.),
*Social Change and Political Development in Weimar Germany* (London, 1981).

—— 'Ein Vorbote des Wohlfahrtsstaates: Die Kriegsopferversorgung in
Frankreich, Deutschland und Großbritannien nach dem Ersten Weltkrieg',
*Geschichte und Gesellschaft*, 9: 2 (1983), 230–77.

—— *Deutsche Rüstungspolitik 1860–1980* (Frankfurt/Main, 1984).

GOLLBACH, MICHAEL, *Die Wiederkehr des Weltkrieges in der Literatur: Zu den
Frontromanen der späten Zwanziger Jahre* (Kronberg, 1978).

GORDON, HAROLD J., jun., *The Reichswehr and the German Republic 1919–
1926* (Princeton, NJ, 1957).

GRADNAUER, GEORG, and SCHMIDT, ROBERT, *Die deutsche Volkswirtschaft: Eine Einführung* (Berlin, 1921).

GREBLER, LEO, and WINKLER, WILHELM, *The Cost of the World War to Germany and to Austria-Hungary* (New Haven and London, 1940).

GRÜTTNER, MICHAEL, *Arbeitswelt an der Wasserkante: Sozialgeschichte von Hamburger Hafenarbeiter 1886–1914* (Göttingen, 1984).

GUMBEL, EMIL JULIUS, *Vier Jahre politischer Mord* (Berlin-Fichtenau, 1922).

GÜNTHER, ADOLF, *Die gesunkene Kaufkraft des Lohnes und ihre Wiederherstellung.* ii: *Kriegslöhne und -preise und ihr Einfluß auf Kaufkraft und Lebenskosten* (Jena, 1919).

GUT, ALBERT, 'Die Entwicklung des Wohnungswesens in Deutschland nach dem Weltkriege', in id. (ed.), *Der Wohnungsbau in Deutschland nach dem Weltkriege: Seine Entwicklung unter der unmittelbaren und mittelbaren Förderung durch die deutschen Gemeindevertretungen* (Munich, 1928).

GUTSCHE, WILLIBALD, KLEIN, FRITZ, and PETZOLD, JOACHIM, *Der Erste Weltkrieg. Ursachen und Verlauf. Herrschende Politik und Antikriegsbewegung in Deutschland* (Cologne, 1985).

HAGEMANN, KARIN, *Frauenalltag und Männerpolitik: Alltagsleben und gesellschaftliches Handeln von Arbeiterfrauen in der Weimarer Republik* (Bonn, 1990).

HALL, ALEX, *Scandal, Sensation and Social Democracy: The SPD Press and Wilhelmine Germany 1890–1914* (Cambridge, 1977).

HARDACH, GERD, *The First World War 1914–1918* (London, 1977).

HARTWICH, HANS-HERMANN, *Arbeitsmarkt, Verbände und Staat 1918–1933* (Berlin, 1967).

HAUSEN, KARIN, 'Unemployment also Hits Women: The New and the Old Woman on the Dark Side of the Golden Twenties in Germany', in Peter D. Stachura (ed.), *Unemployment and the Great Depression in Weimar Germany* (London, 1986).

—— 'The German Nation's Obligation to the Heroes' Widows of World War I', in Margaret Randolph Higonnet, Jane Jenson, Sonya Michel, Margaret Collins Weitz (eds.), *Behind the Lines: Gender and the Two World Wars* (New Haven and London, 1987).

HEINEMANN, ULRICH, *Die verdrängte Niederlage: Politische Öffentlichkeit und Kriegsschuldfrage in der Weimarer Republik* (Göttingen, 1983).

HELFFERICH, KARL, *Deutschlands Volkswohlstand 1888–1913* (Berlin, 1914).

HERBERT, ULRICH, 'Zwangsarbeit als Lernprozeß: Zur Beschäftigung ausländischer Arbeiter in der westdeutschen Industrie im Ersten Weltkrieg', *Archiv für Sozialgeschichte*, 24 (1984), 285–304.

—— *Geschichte der Ausländerbeschäftigung in Deutschland 1880 bis 1980: Saisonarbeiter, Zwangsarbeiter, Gastarbeiter* (Berlin and Bonn, 1986).

—— ' "Generation der Sachlichkeit": Die völkische Studentenbewegung der frühen zwanziger Jahre in Deutschland', in Frank Bajohr, Werner Johe, and Uwe Lohalm (eds.), *Zivilisation und Barbarei. Die wiedersprüchlichen Potentiale der Moderne. Detlev Peukert zum Gedenken* (Hamburg, 1991).

HERTZ-EICHENRODE, DIETER, *Wirtschaftkrise und Arbeitsbeschaffung: Konjunkturpolitik 1925/26 und die Grundlagen der Krisenpolitik Brünings* (Frankfurt/Main, 1982).

HESSE, FRIEDRICH, *Die deutsche Wirtschaftslage von 1914 bis 1923: Krieg, Geldblähe und Wechsellagen* (Jena, 1938).

HICKEY, S. H. F., *Workers in Imperial Germany: The Miners of the Ruhr* (Oxford, 1985).

HIRSCHFELD, MAGNUS, *Sittengeschichte des Weltkrieges* (2 vols.; Leipzig, 1930).

HOFFMANN, WILHELM, 'Die wichtigsten Kriegsseuchen', in id. (ed.), *Die deutschen Ärzte im Weltkriege: Ihre Leistungen und Erfahrungen* (Berlin, 1930).

HOLTFRERICH, CARL-LUDWIG, *The German Inflation 1914–1923: Causes and Effects in International Perspective* (Berlin and New York, 1986).

HÜPPAUF, BERND, ' "Der Tod ist verschlungen in den Sieg": Todesbilder aus dem Ersten Weltkrieg und der Nachkriegszeit', in id. (ed.), *Ansichten vom Krieg: Vergleichende Studien zum Ersten Weltkrieg in Literatur und Gesellschaft* (Königstein/Taunus, 1984).

—— 'Über den Kampfgeist: Ein Kapitel aus der Vor- und Nachbereitung eines Weltkriegs', in Anton-Andreas Guha and Sven Papcke (eds.), *Der Feind den wir brauchen. Oder: Muß Krieg sein?* (Königstein/Taunus, 1985).

—— 'War and Death: The Experience of the First World War', in Mira Crouch and Bernd Hüppauf (eds.), *Essays on Mortality* (Kensington, NSW, Australia, 1985).

—— 'Langemarck, Verdun and the Myth of a *New Man* in Germany after the First World War', *War and Society*, 6: 2 (1988), 70–103.

HÜRTEN, HEINZ, 'Soldatenräte in der deutschen Novemberrevolution 1918', *Historisches Jahrbuch*, 90 (1970), 299–328.

JAMES, HAROLD, *The German Slump: Politics and Economics 1924–1936* (Oxford, 1986).

KALLER, GERHARD, 'Die Revolution des Jahres 1918 in Baden und die Tätigkeit der Arbeiter- und Soldatenräte in Karlsruhe', *Zeitschrift für die Geschichte des Oberrheins*, 75 (1966), 301–50.

KEMPF, ROSA, *Die deutsche Frau nach der Volks-, Berufs- und Betriebszählung von 1925* (Mannheim, Berlin, and Leipzig, 1931).

KENT, BRUCE, *The Spoils of War: The Politics, Economics and Diplomacy of Reparations 1918–32* (Oxford, 1989).

KITCHEN, MARTIN, *The Silent Dictatorship: The Politics of the German High Command under Hindenburg and Ludendorff, 1916–1918* (London, 1976).

KLUGE, ULRICH, 'Das "württembergische Volksheer" 1918/1919: Zum Problem der bewaffneten Macht in der deutschen Revolution', in Günther

Döker and Winfried Stefani (eds.), *Klassenjustiz und Pluralismus. Festschrift für Ernst Fraenkel zum 75. Geburtstag* (Hamburg, 1973).

KLUGE, URICH, *Soldatenräte und Revolution: Studien zur Militärpolitik in Deutschland 1918/19* (Göttingen, 1975).

—— *Die deutsche Revolution 1918/1919: Staat, Politik und Gesellschaft zwischen Weltkrieg und Kapp-Putsch* (Frankfurt/Main, 1985).

KNODEL, JOHN E., *The Decline of Fertility in Germany, 1871–1939* (Princeton, NJ, 1974).

KOCH, HANSJOACHIM W., *Der deutsche Bürgerkrieg: Eine Geschichte der deutschen und österreichischen Freikorps 1918–1923* (Frankfurt/Main and Vienna, 1978).

KOCKA, JÜRGEN, *Facing Total War: German Society 1914–1918* (Leamington Spa, 1984).

KOETZLE, HERMANN, *Das Sanitätswesen im Weltkrieg, 1914–1918* (Stuttgart, 1924).

KOHLER, ERIC D., 'Revolutionary Pomerania 1919–20: A Study in Majority Socialist Agricultural Policy and Civil–Military Relations', *Central European History*, 9 (1976), 250–93.

KOHLHAAS, WILHELM, 'Macht und Grenzen der Soldatenräte in Württemberg 1918/19', *Zeitschrift für württembergische Landesgeschichte*, 32 (1973), 537–43.

KOLB, EBERHARD, *Die Arbeiterräte in der deutschen Innenpolitik 1918–1919* (Düsseldorf, 1962).

—— (ed.), *Vom Kaiserreich zur Weimarer Republik* (Cologne, 1972).

—— and SCHOENHOVEN, KLAUS (eds.), *Regionale und lokale Räteorganisationen in Württemberg 1918/19* (Düsseldorf, 1976).

KÖNIGSBERGER, KURT, 'Die wirtschaftliche Demobilmachung in Bayern während der Zeit vom November 1918 bis Mai 1919', *Zeitschrift des bayerischen statistischen Landesamts*, 52 (1920), 193–226.

KÖNNEMANN, ERWIN, 'Der Truppeneinmarsch am 10. Dezember 1918 in Berlin: Neue Dokumente zur Novemberrevolution', *Zeitschrift für Geschichtswissenschaft*, 16 (1968), 1592–1609.

—— 'Die Einschätzung der politischen Lage durch die OHL nach den Märzkämpfen 1919', *Militärgeschichte*, 11 (1972), 61–71.

—— *Einwohnerwehren und Zeitfreiwilligenverbände: Ihre Funktion beim Aufbau eines neuen imperialistischen Militärsystems, November 1918 bis 1920* (Berlin, 1971).

KRAMER, HELGARD, 'Frankfurt's Working Women: Scapegoats or Winners of the Great Depression', in Richard J. Evans and Dick Geary (eds.), *The German Unemployed: Experiences and Consequences of Mass Unemployment from the Weimarer Republic to the Third Reich* (London and Sydney, 1987).

KUNZ, ANDREAS, 'Verteilungskampf oder Interessenkonsens? Einkommensentwicklung und Sozialverhalten von Arbeitnehmergruppen in der Inflationszeit 1914 bis 1924', in Gerald D. Feldman, Carl-Ludwig Holtfrerich, Gerhard A. Ritter, and Peter-Christian Witt (eds.), *Die deutsche Inflation: Eine Zwischenbilanz* (Berlin and New York, 1982).

—— 'Arbeitsbeziehungen und Arbeitskonflikte im öffentlichen Sektor: Deutschland und Großbritanien im Vergleich', *Geschichte und Gesellschaft*, 12 (1986), 34–62.

—— *Civil Servants and the Politics of Inflation in Germany, 1914–1924* (Berlin and New York, 1986).

LEED, ERIC J., *No Man's Land: Combat and Identity in World War I* (Cambridge, 1979).

LEßMANN, PETER, *Die preußische Schutzpolizei in der Weimarer Republik: Streifendienst und Straßenkampf* (Düsseldorf, 1989).

LIANG, HSI-HUEY, *The Berlin Police Force in the Weimar Republic* (Berkeley, Calif., Los Angeles, and London, 1970).

LIEPMANN, MORITZ, *Krieg und Kriminalität in Deutschland* (Stuttgart, Berlin, and Leipzig, 1930).

LOEWENSTEIN, GEORG, 'Kritische Betrachtungen und Beiträge zur Statistik der Geschlechtskrankheiten (1910–1921)', Sonderdruck aus der *Zeitschrift für Bekämpfung der Geschlechtskrankheiten*, 20: 8–12.

LONGERICH, PETER, *Die Braunen Bataillone: Geschichte der SA* (Munich, 1989).

LORENZ, CHARLOTTE, 'Die gewerbliche Frauenarbeit während des Krieges', in Paul Umbreit und Charlotte Lorenz, *Der Krieg und die Arbeitsverhältnisse* (Stuttgart, 1928).

LUCAS, ERHARD, *Märzrevolution 1920*, i: *Vom Generalstreik gegen den Militärputsch zum bewaffneten Arbeiteraufstand* (2nd edn.; Frankfurt/Main, 1974); ii: *Der Arbeiteraufstand in seiner inneren Struktur und in seinem Verhältnis zu den Klassenkämpfen in zwei verschiedenen Regionen* (Frankfurt/Main, 1973); iii: *Die Niederlage. Verhandlungsversuche und deren Scheitern; Gegenstrategien von Regierung und Militär; die Niederlage der Aufstandsbewegung; der weiße Terror* (Frankfurt/Main, 1978).

—— *Zwei Formen von Radikalismus in der deutschen Arbeiterbewegung* (Frankfurt/Main, 1976).

LÜDERS, Marie-Elisabeth, *Die Entwicklung der gewerblichen Frauenarbeit im Kriege* (Munich and Leipzig, 1920).

LUDEWIG, HANS-ULRICH, *Das Herzogtum Braunschweig im Ersten Weltkrieg* (Braunschweig, 1984).

LÜTGEMEIER-DAVIN, REINHOLD, 'Basismobilisierung gegen den Krieg: Die Nie-wieder-Krieg-Bewegung in der Weimarer Republik', in Karl Holl and Wolfram Wette (eds.), *Pazifismus in der Weimarer Republik: Beiträge zur historischen Friedensforschung* (Paderborn, 1981), 47–76.

LURZ, MEINHOLD, *Kriegsdenkmäler in Deutschland*, iii: *Der 1. Weltkrieg* (Heidelberg, 1985).

LYTH, PETER J., *Inflation and the Merchant Economy: The Hamburg Mittelstand, 1914–1924* (New York, Oxford, and Munich, 1990).

MAI, GUNTHER, 'Die Sozialstruktur der Württembergischen Soldatenräte 1918/1919', *Internationale wissenschaftliche Korrespondenz zur Geschichte der Arbeiterbewegung*, 14 (1978), 3–28.

—— *Kriegswirtschaft und Arbeiterbewegung in Württemberg 1914–1918* (Stuttgart, 1983).

—— (ed.), *Arbeiterschaft 1914–1918 in Deutschland* (Düsseldorf, 1985).

—— 'Arbeitsmarktregulierung oder Sozialpolitik? Die personelle Demobilmachung in Deutschland 1918 bis 1920/24', in Gerald D. Feldman, Carl-Ludwig Holtfrerich, Gerhard A. Ritter, and Peter-Christian Witt (eds.), *Die Anpassung an die Inflation* (Berlin and New York, 1986).

MAIER, CHARLES S., *Recasting Bourgeois Europe: Stabilization in France, Germany and Italy in the Decade after World War I* (Princeton, NJ, 1975).

MARSCHALCK, PETER, *Bevölkerungsgeschichte Deutschlands im 19. und 20. Jahrhundert* (Frankfurt/Main, 1984).

MARWICK, ARTHUR, *The Deluge: British Society and the First World War* (London, 1965).

MATULL, WILHELM, *Ostdeutschlands Arbeiterbewegung: Abriß ihrer Geschichte, Leistung und Opfer* (Würzburg, 1973).

MEERWARTH, RUDOLF, GÜNTHER, ADOLF, and ZIMMERMANN, WALDEMAR, *Die Einwirkung des Krieges auf die Bevölkerungsbewegung, Einkommen und Lebenshaltung in Deutschland* (Stuttgart, 1932).

MERKEL, DR, 'Die Gesundheitsverhältnisse im Heer', in F. Bumm (ed.), *Deutschlands Gesundheitsverhältnisse unter dem Einfluß des Weltkrieges* (Stuttgart, 1928).

MERKL, PETER H., *The Making of a Stormtrooper* (Princeton, NJ, 1980).

—— 'Approaches to Political Violence: The Stormtroopers, 1925–33', in Wolfgang J. Mommsen and Gerhard Hirschfeld (eds.), *Social Protest, Violence and Terror in Nineteenth- and Twentieth-Century Europe* (London, 1982).

METZMACHER, HELMUT, 'Der Novemberumsturz 1918 in der Rheinprovinz', *Annalen des Historischen Vereins für den Niederrhein*, 168/9 (1967), 135–265.

MILLER, SUSANNE, *Die Bürde der Macht: Die deutsche Sozialdemokratie 1918–1920* (Düsseldorf, 1978).

MOELLER, ROBERT G., 'Dimensions of Social Conflict in the Great War: The View from the German Countryside', *Central European History*, 14: 2 (1981), 142–68.

—— 'Winners as Losers in the German Inflation: Peasant Protest over the Controlled Economy, 1920–1923', in Gerald D. Feldman, Carl-Ludwig Holtfrerich, Gerhard A. Ritter, and Peter-Christian Witt (eds.), *Die deutsche Inflation: Eine Zwischenbilanz* (Berlin and New York, 1982).

—— 'Economic Dimensions of Peasant Protest in the Transition from Kaiserreich to Weimar', in Robert G. Moeller (ed.), *Peasants and Lords in Modern Germany: Recent Studies in Agricultural History* (Boston and London, 1986).

—— *German Peasants and Agrarian Politics 1914–1924: The Rhineland and West-phalia* (Chapel Hill, NC, and London, 1986).

MOMMSEN, HANS, *Die verspielte Freiheit: Der Weg der Republik von Weimar in den Untergang 1918 bis 1933* (Frankfurt/Main and Berlin, 1990).

MOMMSEN, WOLFGANG J., 'The German Revolution 1918–1920: Political Revolution and Social Protest Movement', in Richard Bessel and E. J. Feuchwanger (eds.), *Social Change and Political Development in Weimar Germany* (London, 1981).

MOORE, BARRINGTON, jun., *Injustice: The Social Bases of Obedience and Revolt* (London, 1978).

MOSSE, GEORGE L. *Fallen Soldiers: Reshaping the Memory of the World Wars* (New York and Oxford, 1990).

MUTH, HEINRICH, 'Die Entstehung der Bauern- und Landarbeiterräte im November 1918 und die Politik des Bundes der Landwirte', *Vierteljahreshefte für Zeitgeschichte*, 21:1 (1973), 1–38.

NAU, KARL, *Die wirtschaftliche und soziale Lage von Kriegshinterbliebenen: Eine Studie auf Grund von Erhebungen über die Auswirkungen der Versorgung von Kriegshinterbliebenen in Darmstadt* (Leipzig, 1930).

NIEHUSS, MERITH, *Arbeiterschaft in Krieg und Revolution: Soziale Schichtung und Lage der Arbeiter in Augsburg und Linz 1910 bis 1924* (Berlin and New York, 1985).

—— 'From Welfare Provision to Social Insurance: The Unemployed in Augsburg 1918–27', in Richard J. Evans and Dick Geary (eds.), *The German Unemployed: Experiences and Consequences of Mass Unemployment from the Weimar Republic to the Third Reich* (London, 1987).

NIETHAMMER, LUTZ, 'Ein langer Marsch durch die Institutionen: Zur Vorgeschichte des preußischen Wohnungsgesetzes von 1918', in id. (ed.), *Wohnen im Wandel: Beiträge zur Geschichte des Alltags in der bürgerlichen Gesellschaft* (Wuppertal, 1979).

—— and BRÜGGEMEIER, FRANZ-JOSEF, 'Wie wohnten die Arbeiter im Kaiserreich?', *Archiv für Sozialgeschichte*, 16 (1976), 61–134.

NUSSBAUM, MANFRED, *Wirtschaft und Staat in Deutschland während der Weimarer Republik* (Berlin, 1978).

OECKEL, HEINZ, *Die revolutionäre Volkswehr 1918/19: Die deutsche Arbeiterklasse im Kampf um die revolutionäre Volkswehr (November 1918 bis Mai 1919)* (Berlin, 1968).

OERTZEN, PETER VON, *Betriebsräte in der Novemberrevolution: Eine politisch-wissenschaftliche Untersuchung über Ideengehalt und Struktur der betrieblichen und wirtschaftlichen Arbeiterräte in der deutschen Revolution 1918/19* (Düsseldorf, 1963).

OFFER, AVNER, *The First World War: An Agrarian Interpretation* (Oxford, 1989).

OPPENBORN, HARRY, *Die Tätigkeit der Frau in der deutschen Kriegswirtschaft* (Hamburg, 1928).

OPPENHEIMER, HILDE, and RADOMSKI, Hilde, *Die Probleme der Frauenarbeit in der Übergangswirtschaft* (Mannheim, Berlin, and Leipzig, 1918).

OSMOND, JONATHAN, 'Peasant Farming in South and West Germany during War and Inflation 1914 to 1924: Stability or Stagnation?', in Gerald D. Feldman, Carl-Ludwig Holtfrerich, Gerhard A. Ritter, and Peter-Christian Witt (eds.), *Die deutsche Inflation: Eine Zwischenbilanz* (Berlin and New York, 1982).

—— 'A Second Agrarian Mobilization? Peasant Associations in South and West Germany, 1918–1924', in Robert G. Moeller (ed.), *Peasants and Lords in Modern Germany: Recent Studies in Agricultural History* (Boston and London, 1986).

PATCH, WILLIAM L., *Christian Trade Unions in the Weimar Republic, 1918–1933: The Failure of 'Corporate Pluralism'* (New Haven and London, 1985).

PEUKERT, DETLEV J. K., *Grenzen der Sozialdisziplinierung: Aufstieg und Krise der deutschen Jugendfürsorge von 1878 bis 1932* (Cologne, 1986).

—— *Jugend zwischen Krieg und Krise: Lebenswelten von Arbeiterjungen in der Weimarer Republik* (Cologne, 1987).

—— 'The Lost Generation: Youth Unemployment at the End of the Weimar Republic', in Richard J. Evans and Dick Geary (eds.), *The German Unemployed: Experiences and Consequences of Mass Unemployment from the Weimar Republic to the Third Reich* (London, 1987).

—— *The Weimar Republic: The Crisis of Classical Modernity* (London, 1991).

PLUMPE, GOTTFRIED, 'Chemische Industrie und Hilfsdienstgesetz am Beispiel der Farbenfabriken vorm. Bayer & Co.', in Gunther Mai (ed.), *Arbeiterschaft in Deutschland 1914–1918: Studien zu Arbeitskampf und Arbeitsmarkt im Ersten Weltkrieg* (Düsseldorf, 1985).

POHLE, L., 'Die Wohnungsfrage: Mieterschutz', in *Handbuch der Politik* (3rd edn.), iv: *Der wirtschaftliche wiederaufbau* (Berlin and Leipzig, 1921).

POSSE, ERNST H., *Die politischen Kampfbünde Deutschlands* (Berlin, 1931).

POTTHOFF, HEINRICH, *Gewerkschaften und Politik zwischen Revolution und Inflation* (Düsseldorf, 1979).

—— 'Gewerkschaften in Weltkrieg und Revolution: Kontinuität und Wandel', in Erich Matthias and Klaus Schönhoven (eds.), *Solidarität und Menschenwürde: Etappen der deutschen Gewerkschaftsgeschichte von den Anfängen bis zur Gegenwart* (Bonn, 1984).

PRELLER, LUDWIG, *Sozialpolitik in der Weimarer Republik* (Stuttgart, 1949).

PROST, ANTOINE, *Les anciens combattants et la société française, 1914–1939* (3 vols.; Paris, 1977).

—— 'Die Demobilmachung, der Staat und die Kriegsteilnehmer in Frankreich', *Geschichte und Gesellschaft*, 9 (1983), 178–94.

RAKENIUS, GERHARD, *Wilhelm Groener als erster Generalquartiermeister: Die Politik der Obersten Heeresleitung 1918/19* (Boppard/Rhein, 1977).

REBENTISCH, DIETER, *Ludwig Landmann: Frankfurter Oberbürgermeister der Weimarer Republik* (Wiesbaden, 1975).

REICHE, ERIC G., *The Development of the SA in Nürnberg 1922–1934* (Cambridge, 1986).

REICHSARCHIV, *Der Weltkrieg 1914–1918* (Berlin, 1925–44).

REINKE, HERBERT, ' "Armed as if for a War": The State, the Military and the Professionalisation of the Prussian Police in Imperial Germany', in Clive Emsley and Barbara Weinberger (eds.), *Policing Western Europe: Politics, Professionalism and Public Order 1850–1940* (New York, Westport, Conn., and London, 1991).

REULECKE, JÜRGEN, *Die wirtschaftliche Entwicklung der Stadt Barmen von 1910 bis 1925* (Neustadt/Aisch, 1973).

—— 'Der Erste Weltkrieg und die Arbeiterbewegung im rheinisch-westfälischen Industriegebiet', in id. (ed.), *Arbeiterbewegung an Rhein und Ruhr: Beiträge zur Geschichte der Arbeiterbewegung im Rheinland-Westfalen* (Wuppertal, 1974).

—— 'Städtische Finanzprobleme und Kriegswohlfahrtspflege im Ersten Weltkrieg unter besonderer Berücksichtigung der Stadt Barmen', *Zeitschrift für Stadtgeschichte, Stadtsoziologie und Denkmalpflege*, 2 (1975), 48–79.

—— 'Phasen und Auswirkungen der Inflation 1914 bis 1923 am Beispiel der Barmer Wirtschaft', in Otto Büsch and Gerald D. Feldman (eds.), *Historische Prozesse der deutschen Inflation 1914 bis 1924: Ein Tagungsbericht* (Berlin, 1978).

—— *Geschichte der Urbanisierung in Deutschland* (Frankfurt/Main, 1985).

—— 'Männerbund versus the family: Middle-Class Youth Movements and the Family in Germany in the Period of the First World War', in Richard Wall and Jay Winter (eds.), *The Upheaval of War: Family, Work and Welfare in Europe, 1914–1918* (Cambridge, 1988).

RICHTER, WERNER, *Gewerkschaften, Monopolkapital und Staat im ersten Weltkrieg und in der Novemberrevolution, 1914–1919* (Berlin, 1959).

RITTER, GERHARD A., and TENFELDE, KLAUS, *Arbeiter im Deutschen Kaiserreich 1871 bis 1914* (Bonn, 1992).

ROERKOHL, ANNE, *Hungerblockade und Heimatfront: Die Kommunale Lebensmittelversorgung im Westfalen während des Ersten Weltkrieges* (Stuttgart, 1991).

ROHDE, HORST, 'Faktoren der deutschen Logistik im Ersten Weltkrieg' in Gerard Canini (ed.), *Les Fronts invisibles: Nourrir, fournir, soigner* (Nancy, 1984).

ROSENHAFT, EVE, *Beating the Fascists? The German Communists and Political Violence 1929–1933* (Cambridge, 1983).

ROST, IDA, *Die Ehescheidungen der Jahre 1920–1924 von in Sachsen geschlossenen Ehen, unter besonderer Berücksichtigung der Dauer der Ehen und des Heiratsalters der geschiedenen Ehegatten* (Leipzig, 1927).

ROTHSTEIN, ANDREW, *The Soldiers' Strikes of 1919* (London, 1980).

RUCK, MICHAEL, 'Von der Arbeitsgemeinschaft zum Zwangstarif: Die Freien Gewerkschaften im sozialen und politischen Kräftefeld der frühen

Weimarer Republik', in Erich Matthias and Klaus Schönhoven (eds.), *Solidarität und Menschenwürde: Etappen der deutschen Gewerkschaftsgeschichte von den Anfängen bis zur Gegenwart* (Bonn, 1984).

RUCK, MICHAEL, 'Der Wohnungsbau. Schnittpunkt von Sozial- und Wirtschaftspolitik. Probleme der öffentlichen Wohnungspolitik in der Hauszinssteuerära (1924/25–1930/31)', in Werner Abelshauser (ed.), *Die Weimarer Republik als Wohlfahrtsstaat: Zum Verhältnis von Wirtschafts- und Sozialpolitik in der Industriegesellschaft* (Stuttgart, 1987).

RÜRUP, REINHARD, *Probleme der Revolution in Deutschland 1918/1919* (Wiesbaden, 1968).

—— 'Der "Geist von 1914" in Deutschland: Kriegsbegeisterung und Ideologisierung des Krieges im Ersten Weltkrieg', in Bernd Hüppauf (ed.), *Ansichten vom Krieg: Vergleichende Studien zum Ersten Weltkrieg in Literatur und Gesellschaft* (Königstein/Taunus, 1984).

—— (ed.), *Arbeiter- und Soldatenräte im rheinisch-westfälischen Industriegebiet: Studien zur Geschichte der Revolution 1918/19* (Wuppertal, 1975).

SALDERN, ADELHEID VON, 'Kommunalpolitik und Arbeiterwohnungsbau im deutschen Kaiserreich', in Lutz Niethammer (ed.), *Wohnen im Wandel: Beiträge zur Geschichte des Alltags in der bürgerlichen Gesellschaft* (Wuppertal, 1979).

SALEWSKI, MICHAEL, *Entwaffnung und Militärkontrolle in Deutschland 1919–1927* (Munich, 1966).

SAUL, KLAUS, 'Jugend im Schatten des Krieges: Vormilitärische Ausbildung, Kriegswirtschaftlicher Einsatz, Schulalltag in Deutschland 1914–1918', *Militärgeschichtliche Mitteilungen* (1983), no. 2, 91–184.

SCHÄFER, HERMANN, *Regionale Wirtschaftspolitik in der Kriegswirtschaft: Staat, Industrie und Verbände während des Ersten Weltkrieges in Baden* (Stuttgart, 1983).

SCHIFFMANN, DIETER, *Von der Revolution zum Neunstundentag: Arbeit und Konflikt bei BASF 1918–1924* (Frankfurt/Main and New York, 1983).

SCHMIDT, ERNST-HEINRICH, *Heimatheer und Revolution 1918: Die militärischen Gewalten im Heimgebiet zwischen Oktoberreform und Novemberrevolution* (Stuttgart, 1981).

SCHNEIDER, MICHAEL, *Die Christlichen Gewerkschaften 1894–1933* (Bonn, 1982).

SCHOLZ, ROBERT, 'Lohn und Beschäftigung als Indikatoren für die soziale Lage der Arbeiterschaft in der Inflation', in Gerald D. Feldman, Carl-Ludwig Holtfrerich, Gerhard A. Ritter, and Peter-Christian Witt (eds.), *Die Anpassung an die Inflation* (Berlin and New York, 1986).

SCHÜDDEKOPF, OTTO-ERNST, *Das Heer und die Republik: Quellen zur Politik der Reichswehrführung 1918 bis 1933* (Hanover and Frankfurt/Main, 1955).

SCHULZ, GERHARD, *Revolutions and Peace Treaties 1917–1920* (London, 1972).

SCHULZE, HAGEN, *Freikorps und Republik 1918–1920* (Boppard/Rhein, 1969).

SCHUMACHER, MARTIN, *Land und Politik: Eine Untersuchung über politische Parteien und agrarische Interessen 1914–1923* (Düsseldorf, 1978).

SCHWARTE, MAX (ed.), *Der Weltkrieg in seiner Einwirkung auf das deutsche Volk* (Leipzig, 1918).

—— (ed.), *Der große Krieg 1914–1918* (Berlin, 1921–3).

SCHWARZ, KLAUS-DIETER, *Weltkrieg und Revolution in Nürnberg: Ein Beitrag zur Geschichte der deutschen Arbeiterbewegung* (Stuttgart, 1971).

SCHWEYER, FRANZ, 'Die Versorgung der Kriegsbeschädigten und Kriegs-hinterbliebenen', in *Handbuch der Politik* (3rd edn.), iv: *Der wirtschaftliche Wiederaufbau* (Berlin and Leipzig, 1921).

SEIDEL, ANNELIESE, *Frauenarbeit im Ersten Weltkrieg als Problem der staatlichen Sozialpolitik. Dargestellt am Beispiel Bayerns* (Frankfurt/Main, 1979).

SIEDER, REINHARD, *Sozialgeschichte der Familie* (Frankfurt/Main, 1987).

—— 'Behind the Lines: Working-Class Family Life in Wartime Vienna', in Richard Wall and Jay Winter (eds.), *The Upheaval of War: Family, Work and Welfare in Europe, 1914–1918* (Cambridge, 1988).

SIGGEMANN, JÜRGEN, *Die kasernierte Polizei und das Problem der inneren Sicherheit in der Weimarer Republik: Eine Studie zum Auf- und Ausbau des innerstaatlichen Sicherheitssystems in Deutschland 1918/19–1933* (Frank-furt/Main, 1980).

SILVERMAN, DAN P., 'A Pledge Unredeemed: The Housing Crisis in Weimar Germany', *Central European History*, 3:3 (1970), 112–39.

SOGEMEIER, MARTIN, *Die Entwicklung und Regelung des Arbeitsmarktes im rheinisch-westfälischen Industriegebiet im Kriege und in der Nachkriegszeit* (Jena, 1922).

SOUTHERN, DAVID, 'Anti-Democratic Terror in the Weimar Republic: The Black Reichswehr and the Feme Murders', in Wolfgang J. Mommsen and Gerhard Hirschfeld (eds.), *Social Protest, Violence and Terror in Nineteenth- and Twentieth-Century Europe* (London, 1982).

SPEIER, HANS, *German White-Collar Workers and the Rise of Hitler* (New Haven and London, 1986).

STOLLE, UTE, *Arbeiterpolitik im Betrieb: Frauen und Männer, Reformisten und Radikale, Fach- und Massenarbeiter bei Bayer, BASF, Bosch und in Solingen (1900–1933)* (Frankfurt/Main, 1980).

TAMPKE, JÜRGEN, *The Ruhr and Revolution: The Revolutionary Movement in the Rhenish-Westphalian Industrial Region 1912–1919* (London, 1979).

TEUTOBERG, HANS, and WIEGELMANN, GÜNTER, *Der Wandel der Nahrungsgewohnheiten unter dem Einfluß der Industrialisierung* (Göttingen, 1972).

THEWELEIT, KLAUS, *Männerphantasien*, i, *Frauen, Fluten, Körper, Geschichte* (Frankfurt/Main, 1977); ii, *Männerkörper: Zur Psychoanalyse des weißen Terrors* (Frankfurt/Main, 1978).

TORMIN, WALTER, *Zwischen Rätediktatur und sozialer Demokratie* (Düsseldorf, 1954).

TRIEBEL, ARMIN, 'Variations in Patterns of Consumption in Germany in the period of the First World War', in Richard Wall and Jay Winter (eds.), *The Upheaval of War: Family, Work and Welfare in Europe, 1914–1918* (Cambridge, 1988).

ULRICH, VOLKER, *Die Hamburger Arbeiterbewegung vom Vorabend des Ersten Weltkrieges bis zur Revolution 1918–19* (Hamburg, 1976).

—— *Kriegsalltag: Hamburg im Ersten Weltkrieg* (Cologne, 1982).

UMBRIET, PAUL, and LORENZ, CHARLOTTE, *Der Krieg und die Arbeitsverhältnisse* (Stuttgart, 1928).

UNRUH, KARL, *Langemarck: Legende und Wirklichkeit* (Koblenz, 1986).

USBORNE, CORNELIE, ' "Pregnancy is the Woman's Active Service": Pronatalism in Germany during the First World War', in Richard Wall and Jay Winter (eds.), *The Upheaval of War: Family, Work and Welfare in Europe, 1914–1918* (Cambridge, 1988).

—— *The Politics of the Body in Weimar Germany: Women's Reproductive Rights and Duties* (London, 1992).

VINCENT, C. PAUL, *The Politics of Hunger: The Allied Blockade of Germany, 1915–1919* (Athens, Oh., and London, 1985).

VOLKMANN, ERICH OTTO, *Der Marxismus und das deutsche Heer im Weltkriege* (Berlin, 1925).

VONDUNG, KLAUS (ed.), *Kriegserlebnis: Der Erste Weltkrieg in der literarischen Gestaltung und symbolischen Deutung der Nationen* (Göttingen, 1980).

WAGENFUHR, ROLF, *Die Industriewirtschaft: Entwicklungstendenzen der deutschen und internationalen Industrieproduktion 1860 bis 1932* (*Vierteljahreshefte zur Konjunkturforschung*, Sonderheft 31; Berlin, 1933).

WAITE, ROBERT G. L., *Vanguard of Nazism: The Free Corps Movement in Postwar Germany 1918–1923* (Cambridge, Mass., 1952).

WALL, RICHARD, and WINTER, JAY, (eds.), *The Upheaval of War: Family, Work and Welfare in Europe, 1914–1918* (Cambridge, 1988).

WARD, STEPHEN R. (ed.), *The War Generation: Veterans of the First World War* (Port Washington, NY, and London, 1975).

WEHLER, HANS-ULRICH, *Das Deutsche Kaiserreich 1871–1918* (Göttingen, 1973).

WEINDLING, PAUL, 'The Medical Profession, Social Hygiene and the Birth Rate in Germany, 1914–18', in Richard Wall and Jay Winter (eds.), *The Upheaval of War: Family, Work and Welfare in Europe, 1914–1918* (Cambridge, 1988).

—— *Health, Race and German Politics between National Unification and Nazism, 1870–1945* (Cambridge, 1989).

WETTE, WOLFRAM, 'Ideologien, Propaganda und Innenpolitik als Voraussetzungen der Kriegspolitik des Dritten Reiches', in Wilhelm Deist (ed.),

*Ursachen und Voraussetzungen der deutschen Kriegspolitik* (vol. i of Militärgeschicht-liches Forschungsamt (ed.), *Das Deutsche Reich und der Zweite Weltkrieg* (Stuttgart, 1979).

—— 'Einleitung: Probleme des Pazifismus in der Zwischenkriegszeit', in Karl Holl and Wolfram Wette (eds.), *Pazifismus in der Weimarer Republik: Beiträge zur historischen Friedensforschung* (Paderborn, 1981).

—— 'Die militärische Demobilmachung in Deutschland 1918/19 unter besonderer Berücksichtigung der revolutionären Ostseestadt Kiel', *Geschichte und Gesellschaft*, 12 (1986), 63–80.

—— *Gustav Noske: Eine politische Biographie* (Düsseldorf, 1987).

—— (ed.), *Der Krieg des kleinen Mannes: Eine Militärgeschichte von Unten* (Munich, 1992).

WEX, ELSE, *Die Entwicklung der sozialen Fürsorge in Deutschland (1914 bis 1927)* (Berlin, 1929).

WHALEN, ROBERT WELDON, *Bitter Wounds: German Victims of the Great War, 1914–1939* (Ithaca, NY, and London, 1984).

WILKE, GERHARD, 'The Sins of the Fathers: Village Society and Social Control in the Weimar Republic', in Richard J. Evans and W. R. Lee (eds.), *The German Peasantry: Conflict and Community in Rural Society from the Eighteenth to the Twentieth Centuries* (London and Sydney, 1986).

WILLIAMSON, JOHN G., *Karl Helfferich 1872–1924: Economist, Financier, Politician* (Princeton, NJ, 1971).

WINKLER, HEINRICH-AUGUST, *Von der Revolution zur Stabilisierung: Arbeiter und Arbeiterbewegung in der Weimarer Republik 1918 bis 1924* (Berlin and Bonn, 1984).

WINTER, J. M., *The Great War and the British People* (London, 1986).

WINTER, JAY, 'Some Paradoxes of the First World War', in Richard Wall and Jay Winter (eds.), *The Upheaval of War: Family, Work and Welfare in Europe, 1914–1918* (Cambridge, 1988).

WISCHERMANN, CLEMENS, 'Wohnquartier und Lebensverhältnisse in der Urbanisierung', in Arno Herzig, Dieter Langewiesche, and Arnold Sywot-tek (eds.), *Arbeiter in Hamburg: Unterschichten, Arbeiter und Arbeiterbewegung seit dem ausgehenden 18. Jahrhundert* (Hamburg, 1983).

—— ' "Familiengerechtes Wohnen": Anspruch und Wirklichkeit in Deutsch-land vor dem Ersten Weltkrieg', in Hans Jürgen Teuteberg (ed.), *Homo habitans: Zur Sozialgeschichte des ländlichen und städtischen Wohnens in der Neuzeit* (Münster, 1985).

WITT, PETER-CHRISTIAN, 'Finanzpolitik und sozialer Wandel in Krieg und Inflation 1918–1924', in Hans Mommsen, Dietmar Petzina, and Bernd Weisbrod (eds.), *Industrielles System und politische Entwicklung in der Weimarer Republik* (Düsseldorf, 1974).

—— 'Bemerkungen zur Wirtschaftspolitik in der "Übergangswirtschaft" 1918/19: Zur Entwicklung von Konjunkturbeobachtung und Konjunktursteuerung in Deutschland', in Dirk Stegmann, Bernd-Jürgen Wendt, and Peter-Christian Witt (eds.), *Industrielle Gesellschaft und politisches System: Beiträge zur politischen Sozialgeschichte* (Bonn-Bad Godesberg, 1978).

WITT PETER-CHRISTIAN 'Inflation, Wohnungszwangwirtschaft und Hauszinssteuer: Zur Regelung von Wohnungsban und Wohnungsmarkt in der Weimarer Republik', in Lutz Niethammer (ed.), *Wohnen im Wandel: Beiträge zur Geschichte des Alltags in der bürgerlichen Gesellschaft* (Wuppertal, 1979).

—— 'Staatliche Wirtschaftspolitik in Deutschland 1918 bis 1923: Entwicklung und Zerstörung einer modernen wirtschaftspolitischen Strategie', in Gerald D. Feldman, Carl-Ludwig Holtfrerich, Gerhard A. Ritter, and Peter-Christian Witt (eds.), *Die deutsche Inflation: Eine Zwischenbilanz* (Berlin and New York, 1982).

WOHL, ROBERT, *The Generation of 1914* (London, 1980).

WOYCKE, JAMES, *Birth Control in Germany 1871–1933* (London, 1988).

WOYTINSKY, WLADIMIR, *Der deutsche Arbeitsmarkt. Ergebnisse der gewerkschaftlichen Arbeitslosenstatistik 1919 bis 1929*, i: *Text und statistische Unterlagen*, ii: *Graphische Darstellungen* (Berlin, 1930).

WUNDERLICH, FRIEDA, *Die Bekämpfung der Arbeitslosigkeit in Deutschland seit Beendigung des Krieges* (Jena, 1925).

ZIMMERMANN, MICHAEL, ' "Alle sollen auf dem Altar des Vaterlandes ein Opfer bringen": Die Bergarbeiterschaft im Kreis Recklinghausen während des Ersten Weltkrieges', in *Vestische Zeitschrift: Zeitschrift der Vereine für Orts- und Heimatkunde im Vest Recklinghausen*, 81 (1982), 67–87.

ZIMMERMANN, WALDEMAR, *Die gesunkene Kaufkraft des Lohnes und ihre Wiederherstellung*, i: *Die Bedeutung der Frage für die deutsche Volkswirtschaft und Sozialpolitik* (Jena, 1919).

ZUNKEL, FRIEDRICH, 'Die ausländischen Arbeiter in der deutschen Kriegswirtschaftspolitik des 1. Welkrieges', in Gerhard A. Ritter (ed.), *Entstehung und Wandel der modernen Gesellschaft. Festschrift für Hans Rosenberg zum 65. Geburtstag* (Berlin, 1970).

—— *Industrie und Staatssozialismus: Der Kampf um die Wirtschaftsordnung in Deutschland 1914–1918* (Düsseldorf, 1974).

## C. THESES AND PAPERS

BIEBER, GEORG, 'Der Wohnungsmarkt und die Bekämpfung der Wohnungsnot' (Univ. of Erlangen, Phil. diss., 1925).

BIECHELE, ECKHARD, 'Der Kampf um die Gemeinwirtschaftskonzeption des Reichswirtschaftsministerium im Jahre 1919: Eine Studie zur Wirtschaftspolitik unter Reichswirtschaftsminister Rudolf Wissell in der Frühphase der Weimarer Republik' (Freie Universität Berlin, Phil. diss., 1972).

DICK, ALFRED, 'Die Kriegsbeschädigtenversorgung' (Univ. of Frankfurt/Main, Phil. diss., 1930).

GEßNER, MANFRED, 'Wehrfrage und freie Gewerkschaftsbewegung in den Jahren 1918 bis 1923 in Deutschland. Unter besonderer Berücksichtigung des ADGB als Dachorganisation, des Deutschen Metallarbeiterverbandes, Transportarbeiterverbandes sowie des Verbandes der Bergarbeiter Deutschlands' (Freie Universität Berlin, Phil. diss., 1962).

GUT, ALBERT, 'Bericht über die Maßnahme der Stadtgemeinde München zur Bekämpfung der Wohnungsnot und der Tätigkeit des Münchner Wohnungsamtes' (Munich, 1920). (Copy in Stadtarchiv Ludwigshafen, no. 3542.)

HEINEL, EBERHARD, 'Die Bevölkerungsbewegung im Deutschen Reich in der Kriegs- und Nachkriegszeit' (Univ. of Berlin, Phil. diss., 1927).

HEUER, HILDEGARD, 'Die Entwicklung der Metallarbeiterlöhne auf den Kieler Werften (Deutsche Werke A.-G., Germaniawerft A.-G. und Howaldswerke) in der Zeit vom 1.4.1920 bis 30.10.1923' (Univ. Kiel, Phil. diss., 1929).

KNOOP, ARNIM, 'Wirtschaftliche Demobilisierung nach dem Ersten Weltkrieg: Zur Tätigkeit des Demobilisierungskommissariats in Hamburg 1918–1920' (Univ. of Hamburg thesis, 1981; copy in Staatsarchiv Hamburg, Maschinenschriftsammlung 1134).

MÄCHTEL, HERMANN, 'Wohnungsverhältnisse und Wohnungspolitik der Stadt Heidelberg' (Univ. of Heidelberg, Phil. diss., 1923).

METZMACHER, HELMUT, 'Novemberumsturz und Arbeiter- und Soldatenräte, 1918/19 im Rheinland' (Univ. of Bonn, Phil. diss., 1966).

MÜLLER, JOSEF, 'Die Regelung des Arbeitsmarkts in der Zeit der wirtschaftlichen Demobilmachung', (Univ. of Erlangen, Phil. diss., 1922).

ROSENHAFT, EVE, 'A World Upside Down: Delinquency, Family and Work in the Lives of German Working-Class Youth 1914–1918' (paper delivered to the conference on 'The European Family and the Great War: Stability and Instability 1900–1930' at Pembroke College, Cambridge, 11–14 Sept. 1983).

ROUETTE, SUSANNE, 'Die Erwerbslosenfürsorge für Frauen in Berlin nach 1918' (unpubl. MS, Apr. 1985).

SCHIECK, HANS, 'Der Kampf um die deutsche Wirtschaftspolitik nach dem Novemberumsturz 1918' (Univ. of Heidelberg, Phil. diss., 1958).

SCHOLL, KARL, 'Die soziale Lage der Kriegerwitwen in Hamburg: Eine Darstellung aufgrund der Ergebnisse von 300 Monographien' (Univ. of Hamburg, Phil. diss., 1924).

# INDEX